CHILDHOOD

CHILDHOOD

LAURENCE STEINBERG
Temple University

ROBERTA MEYER

McGRAW-HILL, INC.

New York   St. Louis   San Francisco   Auckland   Bogotá   Caracas
Lisbon   London   Madrid   Mexico City   Milan   Montreal   New Delhi
San Juan   Singapore   Sydney   Tokyo   Toronto

This book was set in Veljovic by York Graphic Services, Inc.
The editors were Jane Vaicunas and Jean Akers;
the designer was Wanda Siedlecka;
cover photos by André Baranowski;
the production supervisor was Kathryn Porzio.
The photo editor was Inge King.
R. R. Donnelley & Sons Company was printer and binder.

Library of Congress Cataloging-in-Publication Data

Steinberg, Laurence D., (date).
    Childhood / Laurence Steinberg, Roberta Meyer.—1st ed.
      p.   cm.
    Includes bibliographical references and index.
    ISBN 0-07-061234-X
    1. Child development.   I. Meyer, Roberta.   II. Title.
RJ131.S683   1995
305.23'1—dc20   94-9418

ABOUT THE AUTHORS

Laurence Steinberg is Professor of Psychology at Temple University. He received his A.B. in Psychology from Vassar College and his Ph.D. in Human Development and Family Studies from Cornell University. Prior to joining the Temple University faculty, Dr. Steinberg taught at the University of Wisconsin— Madison and the University of California at Irvine. A Fellow of the American Psychological Association, Dr. Steinberg is the author of numerous scholarly articles on child and adolescent development and author or co-author of the books *Adolescence, When Teenagers Work: The Psychological and Social Costs of Adolescent Employment* (with Ellen Greenberger), *You and Your Adolescent: A Parent's Guide for Ages 10 to 20* (with Ann Levine), and *Crossing Paths: How Your Child's Adolescence Triggers Your Own Crisis* (with Wendy Steinberg).

Roberta Meyer is a developmental editor and writer of introductory college textbooks in child development, psychology, and sociology. A graduate of Cornell University, where she majored in Human Development and Family Studies, she also received an M.A. degree in English from Columbia University, Teachers College.

To Wendy and Benjamin
L.S.

and

To Eric and Kenny
R.M.

CONTENTS IN BRIEF

CONTENTS

BOXES

PREFACE

This book grew out of our firm belief that a change in the structure and content of the standard introductory child development text was long overdue.

Although in the past two decades, the field of child development has become increasingly more contextual in its focus, many of the best-selling textbooks continue to present the traditional, exclusively psychological view of the child. *We take a multidisciplinary approach that emphasizes the broader context in which children develop.*

Although the field has moved beyond the tired debate over whether nature or nurture is more important to a far more sensible appreciation of the need to look at how nature and nurture interact, most textbooks inadequately address the considerable evidence supporting biological and environmental interaction. *We stress the interaction of nature and nurture and integrate the latest knowledge about biological influences on development into our discussions of the importance of environmental influences.*

Although more and better research appears regularly on *normative* development among children from diverse ethnic and cultural backgrounds, this research either has not found its way into most textbooks or, worse yet, is segregated into separate boxes on cross-cultural psychology or social problems. *We highlight diversity in normal patterns of development not only in boxed inserts but throughout the entire text. Material especially relevant to discussions of ethnic or cultural diversity in development is marked by a special icon in the margin.*

And although the field of child development has become increasingly more well informed and scientifically based, most best-selling textbooks continue to pack their pages with filler material: boxed inserts, journalistic accounts of children, and anecdotes about fictional youngsters. Students complain about the cost of these lengthy volumes, and their instructors complain that it has become impossible to complete an entire textbook in one semester. *We have tried to create a book that covers only the most important material on child development in a length that students can reasonably be expected to complete in one semester.*

In writing *Childhood,* we have tried to create a lively, practical book that students will enjoy reading, but that is not overstuffed with unnecessary filler material. We have minimized the lists of labels, levels, and categories that are likely to be forgotten before the final exam is graded. Instead, we emphasize basic research findings—in other words, the essentials—and the ways they apply to children, parents, and adults who work with both.

Childhood is organized chronologically from conception and birth through infancy, early childhood, and middle childhood. Within each developmental period, we examine physical, cognitive, and socioemotional development, but do so in a way that clarifies the interconnections between these three domains of development. And in each developmental period, we include a separate chapter on the *context* of development, in which we highlight the links between the major settings of the child's life—family, school, and peers groups—and his or her development. Because we learned from our consultants that few instructors have the time to devote adequate coverage to development in adolescence in a one-semester course on child development, we have limited our coverage of this age period to one concluding chapter, in which we specifically emphasize the transition from childhood into adolescence.

THEMES

Five themes are interwoven across the fourteen chapters that comprise *Childhood.*

1. We stress the ongoing **interplay of biological and environmental forces** as influences on children's development.

2. We continually place **development in it broader context,** noting how children's lives are affected by the larger forces of class, culture, society, and history.

3. We write from a view of the **child as an active shaper of his or her own development**—as someone who is not only acted upon but who actively influences others.

4. We emphasize the remarkable **plasticity of children,** the flexibility of development and individuals' extraordinary capacity for change throughout the childhood years.

5. Finally, when appropriate, we draw students' attention to the **practical implications of scientific research** on child development—the implications for parents, practitioners, educators, and policymakers.

FEATURES

Three types of boxed essays appear throughout the text. In **MAKING A DIF-FERENCE,** we discuss an innovative intervention, social program, or child-rearing strategy that has the potential to improve the quality of children's lives. These essays describe such interventions as home visits for families of premature infants, Head Start, and social skills training programs for aggressive schoolchildren.

In **CONTROVERSY**, we highlight a contemporary controversy in research or practice and present the scientific evidence that has been used to inform the discussion. Among the controversies we discuss are whether parents should worry about permitting their children to play with toy guns and whether adolescents are inherently risky decision makers.

In **HIGHLIGHT ON DIVERSITY,** we take a special look at how ethnic or cultural factors influence children's development. Diversity in development is a theme that we emphasize throughout the text, but in these essays, we draw special attention to an interesting or provocative issue.

SUPPLEMENTAL MATERIALS

This text's value as a learning and teaching tool is enhanced by the availability of a variety of supplementary materials. The *Study Guide,* written by Wendy Dunn of Coe College, contains material on effective studying and test-taking, learning objectives, chapter outlines, and self-tests. The combined *Instructor's Manual/Test Bank,* written by Thomas Moye of Coe College, features information that will assist in course planning and instruction, a variety of test questions, and a complete answer key. Computerized versions of the test items will be available for IBM and Macintosh systems. In addition, McGraw-Hill offers a variety of four-color overhead transparency packages for developmental psychology courses.

REVIEWERS

This text benefited from the constructive suggestions offered by the following reviewers: Douglas Behrend, University of Arkansas; David Conner, Northeast Missouri State University; Eric DeVos, Saginaw Valley State University; Sheridan DeWolf, Grossmont College; Robert Englehart, Northeastern State University, Oklahoma; Juanita Field, Plymouth State College; Virginia Gunderson, University of Washington; Harry Hoemann, Bowling Green State University; Melissa Kaplan-Estrin, Wayne State University; Kevin Keating, Broward Community College; Judy Lindamood, Bunker Hill Community College; Bradford Pillow, University of Pittsburgh; Leslee Pollina, Southeast Missouri State University; Susan Rosner, Professor Emeritus, University of Iowa; Nicholas R. Santilli, John Carroll University; and Robert Shilkret, Mount Holyoke College.

ACKNOWLEDGMENTS

Publishing a textbook requires the assistance and guidance of many people. We wish to thank a group of very talented people at McGraw-Hill, starting with our editing supervisor, Jean Akers. In addition, Suzanne Thibodeau, Jane Vaicunas, Wanda Siedlecka, Kathy Porzio, and Beth Kaufman helped to shape this book and keep it on schedule. Matt Zimbelmann performed many administrative chores, and Anne Fletcher and Beth Cauffman were extremely competent research assistants. Inge King is a gifted photo researcher. Brad Pillow's and Jay Belsky's expert counsel improved the content of many of the chapters. Finally, we wish to acknowledge our families, Wendy and Benjamin Steinberg, and Eric and Kenny Meyer, whose understanding and affection make both parenting and writing much easier than they would otherwise be.

Laurence Steinberg
Roberta Meyer

CHILDHOOD

THE STUDY OF HUMAN DEVELOPMENT

Alex Kotlowitz met Lafeyette and Pharoah Rivers during the summer of 1985 when they were 10 and 7 years old. Kotlowitz was a journalist, writing the text for a photo essay on children in poverty. A photographer friend of his had been taking pictures of the boys and their mother, LaJoe, in Chicago's Henry Horner housing project, where they lived. Two years later, Kotlowitz returned to write a newspaper story on the effects of inner-city violence on the children who live there. When he talked to LaJoe Rivers about writing a book about her sons and the other children in the neighborhood, she liked the idea. Then she said, "But you know, there are no children here. They've seen too much to be children." Kotlowitz stayed for 2 years, and in 1991 he published a book about his observations titled There Are No Children Here. *The material for the introduction to this book comes from his detailed and disturbing chronicle.*

On June 13, 1987, Lafeyette Rivers celebrated his twelfth birthday and, with his cousin Dede, was on his way to buy a set of headphones with the $8 he had gotten as a present.

Suddenly gunfire erupted. The frightened children fell to the ground. "Hold your head down," Lafeyette snapped, as he covered Dede's head with her pink nylon jacket. If he hadn't physically restrained her, she might have sprinted for home, a dangerous action when the gangs started warring. "Stay down," he ordered the trembling girl.

The two lay pressed to the beaten grass for half a minute, until the shooting subsided. Lafeyette held Dede's hand as they cautiously crawled through the dirt toward home. When they finally made it inside, all but fifty cents of Lafeyette's birthday money had trickled from his pockets. (p. 9)

When Kotlowitz first met Lafeyette 2 years earlier, he had asked him what he wanted to be. "'If I grow up, I'd like to be a bus driver.' *If,* not *when.* At age ten, Lafeyette wasn't sure he'd make it to adulthood" (p. x). Now, at 12, he knew how to duck bullets, as drug wars became part of daily life in the Henry Horner projects. Nine-year-old Pharoah called his neighborhood "the graveyard," and it seemed apt. Already that summer, 57 children had been killed in Chicago, 5 at Henry Horner. During the summer of 1987, LaJoe Rivers started paying $80 a month for burial insurance for her youngest children.

That same year, the 11-year-old son of one of the authors of this book spent the summer at a camp in New Hampshire. Eric Meyer wrote that he'd been hiking in the White Mountains. He had joined the baseball team and was learning to sail a small boat alone. The only thing he had to duck was a bunkmate named Chris who spit when he was angry. Eric's younger brother, Kenny, about Pharoah's age, passed his deep water test that summer in a day camp pool and began riding his bike around the neighborhood on the weekends.

Like LaJoe Rivers, Eric and Kenny's mother put away money for her children that summer too, but buying burial insurance would never have occurred to her. Like most of the other parents she knew, she was investing for college tuition.

The Rivers brothers and the Meyer boys returned to school in September, but the similarities were few. Ridgeway Elementary, a racially and economically diverse school in White Plains, New York, was well-equipped, clean, and safe. On staff were a psychologist, a speech therapist, teachers for those who learned fast and for those who needed extra help. There were music and art teachers and specialists in string, brass, woodwind, and percussion instruments. Behind the

Lafayette (center), Pharoah (right), and their cousin James in 1987 at Henry Horner. During that summer, five children were killed in their Chicago neighborhood.

school was a parking lot, a two-acre grassy play area, a blacktop, and a baseball field, all kept clean, repaired, and mowed.

At the Suder School, next to the Horner projects, gang wars took place in the parking lot. "When the powerful sounds of .357 Magnums and sawed-off shotguns echoed off the school walls, the streetwise students slid off their chairs and huddled under their desks" (p. 66). Teachers "dreaded the walk each morning and afternoon from and to [their cars]" (p. 67).

Inside, classrooms were overpopulated and undersupplied. Most of the students read below grade level, but Pharoah was one of the exceptions. He was imaginative, diligent, a good writer, and a spelling ace.

Lafeyette did not do as well in school, but as a young teenager, he was determined to stay away from drugs.

> "You grow up 'round it," Lafeyette told a friend. "There are a lot of people in the projects who say they're not gonna drop out, that they won't be on the streets. But they're doing it now. Never say never." . . . "But I say never." (p. 29)

Despite his good intentions, Lafeyette was not doing so well when Kotlowitz ended his chronicle. At 14, although he maintained his innocence, he had been convicted of breaking into a truck and received a year's probation. At 15, he graduated from the eighth grade. "It was one of the few times he seemed truly happy and at ease," wrote Kotlowitz (p. 321).

At 15, Eric Meyer was a junior in high school. He had always done well in school, and no one who knew him was surprised that he was an "A" student, an editor of the school paper, and a member of the cross-country team. Kenny was academically successful too and was showing talent as a violinist as well.

Looking across environments, at inner-city poverty and violence and at comfortable suburbia, it is undeniable that the Rivers brothers and the Meyer brothers have grown up in different worlds. And since *There Are No Children Here* was published, those worlds have grown further apart. In 1993, six children died of violence every day in the United States, most caught in the drug wars on city streets. Speaking in November 1993, President Clinton told of 160,000 children who stay home from school every day because they are too scared to go (*The New York Times,* November 14, 1993).

Can developmental psychology help us understand this tragic fact of American life? To be sure, developmentalists cannot solve these problems. But a knowledge of child development can help us identify the things that *all* children need to grow up healthy and points us toward ways to intervene in the lives of children who need assistance.

When we compare the lives of children in different environments, it is obvious that where and when children grow up, what we call *context,* matters tremendously. Without question the Rivers brothers' lives would have been different growing up where the Meyer boys did. And, one might reasonably ask, how would Eric and Kenny have turned out in the Henry Horner project? One of the points we will stress throughout this book is that *context matters.*

At the same time, it is important to understand that our account of development cannot be that simple. Even growing up *within* the same context, individuals turn out differently. The fact that siblings growing up in the same environment are often very different from one another shows that this must be the case. What made Pharoah succeed in school while Lafeyette floundered? Why does Kenny love classical music while Eric listens only to rock? A second emphasis of this book is that there is tremendous *diversity in normal development.*

As you read this book, you will come to understand the many factors that contribute to the diversity that we see in children's development. Yet despite the various influences that make children different from each other, there are also many things that children all over the world, regardless of the circumstances in which they come of age, share in common. Despite their vastly different life circumstances, Lafeyette Rivers and Eric Meyer, two preadolescent boys, shared many interests and traits. Physically, cognitively, emotionally, and socially, children pass through the same general stages of growth at roughly the same time. The third emphasis of this book, then, is that along with the contextual and individual factors that make children different from one another are important *universals in patterns of development.*

THEMES IN THE STUDY OF HUMAN DEVELOPMENT

● Biology and Environment: Interacting Forces

To understand why the Rivers brothers, the Meyer brothers, or, for that matter, any of us developed as we did, we first go back to a time before the 1970s, when a hot debate divided the study of human development. Were we products of an innate *nature* (our own biology) or of *nurture* (our environment)? At one pole were those who argued that biology, or nature, governed development. Biological factors are all those traits that are genetically based. These include characteristics that all or most humans share (the ability to speak, to walk upright, to think abstractly, for example), as well as traits that make each of us unique—a long or a short nose, straight or wavy hair, a fiery or a placid temperament.

At the opposite pole were the environmentalists who argued that upbringing—the way we are nurtured—influences development more strongly than genes. Whether we would grow up emotionally healthy, do well in school, and lead a successful adult life was grounded in our social environment, in elements outside of ourselves. These include the people with whom we live, the things we see and use, and the social class, culture, and time in which we live.

We would have asked whether Pharoah was a high achiever because he inherited genes that made him smart *or* because he was encouraged to work hard in school. Today, developmentalists don't ask such either/or questions. Research has confirmed that biology and environment work *together,* that inevitably both nature and nurture influence the course of development.

A major theme of this book, *the constant interplay of biology and environment,* stands out in research findings regarding "resilient" children (like Pharoah Rivers), children who thrive in spite of excessively harsh experiences (Werner & Smith, 1982). As infants, resilient children shared several personality traits that are partly a product of their inborn temperaments. These traits, in turn, tended to encourage certain learning experiences that make them better able to deal with stress. This inborn trait is related to a later tendency to "take charge" of adversity and try to overcome it. Taking charge of adversity, in turn, teaches a valuable lesson about one's own ability to control negative events. In this way, then, temperament and learning repeatedly interact, enhancing resilient children's ability to cope with stress. Similarly, most resilient children are cheerful, outgoing, and sociable by nature, traits that make it easier for them to form close relationships with adults. Such relationships, in turn, provide the emotional support needed to help deal successfully with stress.

● Development Is Dynamic

All children influence their own development. Accordingly, the second major theme of this book is that *development is a dynamic process,* a two-way street. Far from being passive recipients of environmental influences, children actively shape their world and give meaning to their experiences. By so doing, they help to create the very conditions that affect their own development.

From childhood on, the way we interpret experiences shapes the way others respond to us and the way we feel about ourselves. A child may isolate herself yet feel rejected by others.

This dynamic process involves attitudes, perceptions, and behaviors. Even young children interpret their experiences in very personal ways. A 4-year-old girl, for example, invites a little boy to play, but he refuses. The girl interprets this as personal rejection and concludes that other children don't like her. She retreats to a corner and makes no further overtures of friendship. The other children respond by ignoring her. She then feels even more rejected and spends more time in the corner. Soon, other children don't even think of playing with her. Notice that this child has isolated herself, yet she *perceives* other children's behavior in a way that reinforces her feelings of rejection. Another child, also rejected at first, shrugs it off and asks other children to play until she finds a willing partner. In this way, she positively shapes the events that affect her life. Throughout this book, we'll point to the dynamic nature of development, that mix of responding to others, eliciting reactions from others, and interpreting our own experiences.

● Development Occurs in a Social Context

Not long ago, a group of developmental psychologists spoke to a congressional committee debating the funding of day care programs for poor children. The legislators wanted the experts' opinions: How does day care affect children? What makes a good program? Do preschool programs really give deprived children a head start? Are the benefits worth the costs? Other experts have also testified in Washington about other child-related issues: Does televised violence increase aggressiveness? How does advertising affect children? Can sex education prevent teenage pregnancies and the spread of AIDS?

Although the experts don't always agree, congressional interest in these issues underscores our third major theme: No matter how much interpersonal dynamics and individual traits shape development, another very powerful component is the **social context** in which we live. Social context includes all the elements in your environment: your family's income, social class, neighborhood; the schools you attended; your family's values and attitudes; and society's attitudes toward you, even the time in which you live. Since it is the backdrop for every stage of development, the influence of social context is enormous. Our chances in life—even whether we are born healthy or at risk, or die during infancy—are directly related to social context (see Chapter 7). So too are the ways we view ourselves, how we view the world, and how the world views us.

● **social context**
all the elements in one's immediate and distant environment

As researchers have increasingly turned their attention to studies of children from different cultural, ethnic, and socioeconomic backgrounds, they have discovered the importance of taking social context into account when building models of child development. One recent study of black children growing up in South Africa illustrates this nicely (Goduka, Poole, & Aotaki-Phenice, 1992). The researchers were interested in the relation between characteristics of the home environment (for example, parental education, residential crowding, marital status) and various aspects of child development (such as intelligence test performance and self-concept)—topics that have received a great deal of attention over the years. This sample of youngsters was divided among three very different contexts, however: Some lived in the homeland, others lived in the resettlement, and still others lived on white-owned farms. When the researchers divided the sample into these three groups and then looked at the connection between home characteristics and child outcomes, they found that some of the

When *children live—not just where and with whom— strongly influences development. At the turn of the century in the United States, before laws were passed that required schooling and prohibited working, most children from poor families spent their days laboring in factories or in mines.*

predictors of healthy child development were identical across the three groups, while others were quite different. In all three contexts, for example, parental education was correlated with positive child development. But another variable, family mobility, had different effects on children's development depending on the broader context in which the family lived. As you will see throughout this book, a specific influence can have different effects on children depending on the context in which it occurs.

● Development Is Flexible

If you were to conclude from the above discussion that social context and innate traits fix the course of every child's life, you would be wrong. The fourth theme of this book, and perhaps its most important lesson, is that *development is flexible.* Undernourished, underweight babies can "catch up" to well-fed babies if their diets are improved in time; overly aggressive children can learn new ways to get what they want; teenage mothers can improve their lives and learn parenting skills; would-be dropouts can become motivated to stay in school and believe in their futures. Throughout this book, you'll see that through many kinds of intervention, or simply through changes in circumstances, children and adolescents can overcome the obstacles that their environments often present.

Even in one country, the "right" way to raise a child changes from generation to generation, as new research leads us to revise old theories.

THEORIES: HOW WE THINK ABOUT DEVELOPMENT

Developmental psychologists, as well as parents everywhere, have theories about how children grow and change, the reasons for these transformations, and the implications for child rearing. What makes psychologists' theories different from those of ordinary parents is that psychologists base their theories on the accumulation of scientific information, and they revise them as information changes. Psychologists always try to verify their explanations with extensive scientific research, a process we'll describe later in this chapter.

The major theories of human development fall into four categories: psychoanalytic, behavioral/learning, cognitive, and biological. Each type of theory tends to focus on a different aspect of development. Psychoanalytic thinkers, who study human *emotions,* are particularly interested in the psychological conflicts that arise at different stages of development. Learning theorists, or behaviorists, in contrast, focus on *behavior* rather than feelings. They contend that outside stimuli in the environment, not internal feelings, mold and shape behavior. Cognitive theorists are concerned with processes of *thought,* with how people perceive, understand, and think about their world. This school argues that we can best understand development by looking closely at how individuals reason. Finally, biological theorists emphasize aspects of development that are driven by *biology,* including traits that are common to all individuals in the species, as well as those that are unique to individuals because of their genetic makeup. No one theory is complete, but together these different theoretical perspectives provide insights that help us understand the path of development from infancy through adolescence.

● Psychoanalytic Theories

Sigmund Freud (1856–1939) was a medical doctor who specialized in treating nervous disorders, such as sudden paralysis in some part of the body, extreme agitation and inability to sleep, or overwhelming fears. Most physicians of his time believed that these were physical problems, disorders of the brain or nervous system, but Freud suspected otherwise. He was intrigued by the fact that when he placed his patients under hypnosis and encouraged them to talk about their problems, their symptoms were often relieved. Gradually, he came to believe that many nervous disorders were psychological, not physical, in origin. These ailments, he contended, were caused by unconscious drives and conflicts, often related to early childhood experiences and often sexual in nature.

● ***Freud's theory of psychosexual stages.*** The part of the life instinct that fascinated Freud the most was the sexual. Freud proposed that as children grow older, their sexual feelings center around different parts of the body: first the mouth, then the anus, and finally the genitals. In suggesting this progression of *psychosexual* stages, Freud outlined one of the first developmental theories that charted the stages individuals move through as they mature. He also was one of the first theorists to suggest that there were systematic childhood precursors of adult behavior and personality. Specifically, Freud hypothesized that failure to gratify sexual urges appropriately during early psychosexual stages could lead to problems later on.

The oral stage. During a child's first year, erotic pleasure comes from sucking, chewing, and biting on things—the mother's breast, a rubber nipple, a thumb, a blanket, a rattle, or any other object that can fit into the mouth. Freud believed that if babies are denied enough oral gratification, or given too much,

During the oral stage, babies will chew on just about anything, regardless of taste.

some of their libido (their sexual energy) can become fixated at the oral stage. As adults, such people may continue striving for oral stimulation by overeating or smoking, for example.

The anal stage. Freud contended that between ages 1 and 3, a child's libido is centered in the anal region. Erotic pleasure comes from using the anal muscles to expel or retain feces. In many Western countries, the anal stage coincides with toilet training, and if this training is too lax *or* too severe, the resulting frustration can make people either too loose (messy and wasteful) or too controlled (holding back everything, including their feelings).

The phallic stage. Freud believed that between ages 3 and 5, children's libido shifts to the genital region. A boy develops sexual feelings toward his mother, casting his father as a rival for his mother's affections. The boy wants to replace his father but fears his father will punish him for his incestuous feelings. This is the famous **Oedipus complex,** a term Freud drew from the Greek myth of Oedipus, who unknowingly killed his father and married his mother. Paralleling a boy's development, a girl falls in love with her father and fears punishment from her mother. Freud called this the **Electra complex,** after Electra, the tragic Greek heroine who plotted to kill her mother. The fact that both the Oedipus and the Electra complexes are depicted in Greek mythology did not surprise Freud. He believed that our literature naturally reflects our deepest psychological struggles. These struggles are not usually waged on a conscious level, Freud argued. Much of the battle occurs in the unconscious, the deep recesses of the human psyche that are outside our awareness.

How are the Oedipus and Electra complexes resolved? For Freud, the healthiest resolution is for the child to realize that he or she cannot triumph over the same-sex parent and sexually possess the parent of the opposite sex. So instead the child tries to become like the same-sex parent who enjoys the longed-for physical union. He or she adopts the same-sex parent's attitudes, behaviors, and moral values, a process called **identification.** In turn, this internalization of moral values gives rise to the **superego,** the part of the personality that serves as a conscience.

The latency stage. Following the phallic stage is a period of sexual latency, during which sexual urges move to the background while children concentrate on learning how to control their impulses and find appropriate outlets for their drives. Children become increasingly able to share, wait their turn, refrain from physically striking out at others, and so forth. They also engage industriously in sports, hobbies, and projects of various kinds that teach them how to direct their psychic energy toward socially acceptable goals. This period of psychological development generally lasts until about age 12.

The genital stage. At puberty, genital sexuality reawakens, but in a more mature form. Youngsters now become interested in peers as sexual partners. If healthy development has occurred in the preceding stages, adolescents are ready to enter into intimate relations that involve a *mutual* give-and-take of physical pleasure. In contrast, if previous stages have been problematic, youngsters are less able to meet the demands of adult sexual relationships.

Oedipus complex
according to Freud, a psychological conflict for boys, arising from their sexual feelings toward their mothers

Electra complex
according to Freud, a psychological conflict for girls, arising from their sexual feelings toward their fathers

identification
a process in which children adopt the same-sex parent's attitudes, behaviors, and values

superego
according to Freud, the part of the personality that serves as a conscience

● *Freud's view of personality structure.* In Freud's theory of personality development, competing forces struggle to influence behavior. One powerful force is the pool of psychic energy that includes the libido. This energy exists in the part of the personality Freud called the **id.** At birth, personality is all id; it consists only of inborn drives. With the development of the **ego** comes that part of the personality that regulates emotion, thought, and behavior. The superego, which represents ethical values and conscience, develops primarily during the phallic stage. From then on, it is constantly at odds with the id, for the two have very different goals. Whereas the id seeks instant satisfaction, without regard for reason or morality, the superego is a highly moralistic watchdog, trying to restrict how instinctual drives are expressed.

Mediating this struggle between the id and the superego is the ego. The ego tries to satisfy the demands of the id in ways that are simultaneously pleasurable, realistic, and acceptable to the superego. Frequently the ego uses **defense mechanisms** to repress or redirect the id's demands, but these aren't always satisfactory. Too much repression of instinctual drives can lead to great anxiety and psychological problems.

Freudian theory has made an enormous contribution to our understanding of psychological and emotional development. Many concepts that we now take for granted—such as the existence of unconscious feelings and wishes, or the influence of early childhood experiences—originated with Freud. Over the years, other psychoanalytic theorists have extended Freud's ideas to include a wider range of developmental issues and challenges. One of the most influential of these theorists is Erik Erikson.

● *Erikson's theory of psychosocial development.* Erik Erikson's theory of human development does not so much contradict Freud's as go beyond it. Erikson, like many other psychoanalysts who followed Freud, felt that Freud placed too much emphasis on the impulsive, pleasure-seeking id and not enough on the ego, with its ability to reason and solve problems. Erikson argued that all of us face a series of psychological and social challenges as we develop, and that the ego's job is to meet these challenges and in so doing shape personality. Whereas Freud outlined psycho*sexual* stages of development, Erikson proposed psycho*social* stages. He contended that the challenges we face as we mature have more to do with our relationships with other people and society's demands than with our libido and instinctual drives. At each stage, the important people in our lives (parents, siblings, peers, spouses, children, coworkers) and the social institutions we encounter (family, work, school, community) help to frame the challenges we face and influence our solutions to them.

As outlined in Table 1.1, Erikson (1963) proposed eight developmental stages. (In later chapters we discuss the first five of these stages.) He believed that each characteristic psychosocial issue is important over the entire life span, but paramount for only a limited time. We cannot linger indefinitely over a developmental challenge, for new ones inevitably arise as we enter new phases of life. So if we haven't successfully met a challenge by the end of a given stage, we proceed to the next stage handicapped by a set of unresolved conflicts and psychosocial shortcomings. Children who fail to acquire basic trust during infancy, for example, are handicapped as toddlers when they strive to become more independent from their parents because their feelings of anxiety interfere with their desires to explore the world. Similarly, youngsters who do not acquire

● **id**
according to Freud, the part of the personality that includes all inborn human drives

● **ego**
according to Freud, the part of the personality that regulates emotion, thought, and behavior

● **defense mechanisms**
mechanisms used by the ego to repress the id

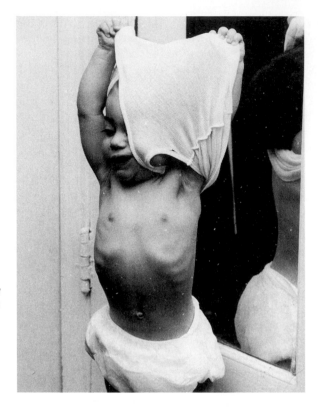

Struggling to dress themselves is one of the physical challenges toddlers face during the stage Erikson called "autonomy vs. shame and doubt." Freedom to keep trying until they succeed leads to self-confidence and feelings of control. Demands for perfection and criticism can elicit shame and self-doubt.

some independence as toddlers are plagued by self-doubts and find it hard to take initiative during the preschool years. Thus, how children resolve the developmental challenge at each stage affects their ability to cope with future developmental tasks.

● Learning Theories

While the theories of Freud and Erikson are different in many ways, they both hold that emotions and feelings are central to development. Other psychologists stress experience over emotions. They focus on the means by which we learn certain patterns of behavior from the experiences we have.

There are several different learning theories of human development. **Behaviorism** looks at how concrete stimuli in the environment can, through reinforcement and punishment, produce observable changes in people's behavior. Another, **social learning theory,** looks not just at the concrete circumstances that shape behavior but also at the way social rewards and punishments influence our behavior and our expectations. In the following sections we will examine both these learning perspectives.

● **behaviorism**
a learning theory that looks at how concrete stimuli can, through reinforcement and punishment, produce observable changes in people's behavior

● **social learning theory**
a learning theory that looks at the way social rewards and punishments influence behavior and expectations

● ***The behaviorist view.*** A little boy, age 2½, is being toilet trained. Every time he has an accident, his mother scolds him severely. Within a few months the accidents stop, but some unusual behavior begins. Unlike other boys his age, this child hates to get his hands or clothes dirty.

A Freudian would say that the child's id impulses were too severely punished, resulting in conflict and anxiety regarding bowel movements. The boy became

TABLE 1.1   ERIKSON'S PSYCHOSOCIAL DEVELOPMENTAL STAGES

Age*	Psychosocial Stage	Psychosocial Conflict	Favorable Outcome	Unfavorable Outcome
Birth to 18 months	Infancy	Basic trust vs. mistrust	Hope; tolerates frustration, can delay gratification	Suspicion, withdrawal
18 months to 3 years	Early childhood	Autonomy vs. shame, doubt	Will; self-control; self-esteem	Compulsion, impulsivity
3 to 6 years	Play age	Initiative vs. guilt	Purpose; enjoys accomplishments	Inhibition
6 to 11 years	Middle childhood	Industry vs. inferiority	Competence	Inadequacy, inferiority
Puberty to early twenties	Adolescence	Identity vs. role confusion	Fidelity	Diffidence, defiance, socially unacceptable identity
Early twenties to 40	Young adulthood	Intimacy vs. isolation	Love	Exclusivity, avoidance of commitment
40 to 60 years	Middle adulthood	Generativity vs. stagnation	Care; concern for future generations, for society	Rejection of others, self-indulgence
From 60 years	Old age	Integrity vs. despair	Wisdom	Disdain, disgust

*Ages approximate. Erikson (Erikson & Hall, 1987) recently has suggested that the period of generativity may last much longer today, now that adults remain healthy and active until an advanced age.

fixated at the anal stage of development and now expresses this fixation symbolically by being overly fastidious. But a behaviorist would argue that concepts like conflict, anxiety, and fixation are completely unnecessary in explaining the boy's responses. In fact, focusing on these internal thoughts and feelings diverts attention from the real cause of the problem—the *punishment* the boy has received. When a behavior is punished, we tend to avoid repeating it in the future, so this child, as expected, has stopped soiling his pants. What's more, he has generalized what he has learned to similar situations. He now avoids getting dirty in other ways as well.

Behaviorists have searched for universal laws of behavior, laws that specify how concrete, observable stimuli in the environment cause organisms to act in particular ways. In their search for these laws they have focused on several different kinds of learning. One, called classical conditioning, was first demonstrated by the famous Russian physiologist Ivan Pavlov. Another, called operant conditioning, is closely associated with the contemporary American psychologist B. F. Skinner.

Classical conditioning.   Fourteen-year-old Mark walks down the corridor of his high school heading for room 127. When the door is in sight, his stomach starts churning, his face becomes flushed, and his palms begin to sweat. Behind that door he must take a test in his worst subject, math.

● **classical conditioning**
learning through the repeated pairing of a stimulus and a response

Mark's response to the anticipation of taking a math test is an example of **classical conditioning.** Classical conditioning involves learning to make some reflex response upon encountering a stimulus that has previously been paired with another stimulus that evokes the reaction. In Mark's case, he sees a door (which would normally be a neutral stimulus) and he reacts with symptoms of anxiety because the door has been paired with taking math tests.

Pavlov discovered classical conditioning when working with dogs in his laboratory. He rang a bell just before feeding time when the dogs were given meat. After several pairings of the bell and the meat, the dogs began salivating at the sound of the bell alone, even when meat *wasn't* given. The bell (which had previously been a neutral stimulus) now elicited salivation because of its repeated association with food.

One of the first experiments applying classical conditioning to human beings involved an 11-month-old child named Albert and a harmless white laboratory rat. Albert showed no fear of the rat when he first saw it. In fact, he seemed to like watching it and even tried to play with it. But then behaviorist John B. Watson and his assistant Rosalie Raynor began pairing the rat with a stimulus that *did* arouse fear. Every time they presented the rat to Albert, they struck an iron bar with a hammer right behind the child's ear. This sudden loud noise made Albert jump, cry, and bury his face in the mattress. Soon the sight of the rat alone was enough to evoke the fear reaction. And Albert's fear generalized to similar-looking objects—a rabbit, a dog, a sealskin coat, even a bearded Santa Claus mask.

Children learn through classical conditioning outside the laboratory too. For instance, babies often begin reflexively sucking at the sight of the mother's breast, even before the nipple is in their mouth. The sight of the breast has been repeatedly paired with a stimulus that elicits sucking, until the sight alone is enough to evoke the sucking response.

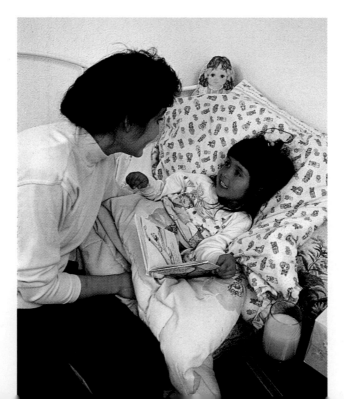

Behaviorists would encourage this mother to read a story or two, warmly say good night, and leave. Satisfying too many bedtime requests will only encourage children to stay up late.

TABLE 1.2 REINFORCEMENT VERSUS PUNISHMENT	
Positive Reinforcement Increases behavior through addition of a pleasant stimulus (e.g., giving a child a present)	**Negative Reinforcement** Increases behavior through withdrawal of an aversive stimulus (e.g., when a parent stops yelling)
Positive Punishment Decreases behavior through addition of an aversive stimulus (e.g., severely scolding a child)	**Negative Punishment** Decreases behavior through withdrawal of a pleasant stimulus (e.g., taking away a child's toy)

Operant conditioning. It is 7:30 and 3-year-old Joshua is being tucked into bed. "Now here's Teddy and here's Opus and here's Mickey Mouse," his mother tells him as she places the stuffed animals under the covers beside her son. "They're all tired and ready to sleep. You close your eyes and go to sleep too." Joshua smiles sweetly and closes his eyes, but 10 minutes later he is calling out: "Mom! Mom! Mommy!" His mother arrives. Joshua wants some water; she gets it. "Good night," she says again. Five minutes later, "Mom! Mom!" Mother returns. "You didn't kiss Teddy good-night." She complies, kissing Teddy's bedmates as well. Ten minutes later Joshua wants and gets a new bandage for the minor scratch on his hand. On it goes until finally, around 10:30, he falls asleep.

Joshua's parents describe their son as a real "night owl," but people who understand operant conditioning might reach a different conclusion. They know that the *consequences* of behavior influence future actions. Joshua's parents are inadvertently creating positive consequences for staying up late by giving their son lots of loving attention whenever he calls out. As a result, Joshua keeps calling and calling, and takes hours to fall asleep.

Operant conditioning is the process whereby an organism learns either to make or to withhold a voluntary response because of the consequences it brings. A consequence that produces *repetition* of the response is called **reinforcement,** or reward. Joshua's parents are providing **positive reinforcement**: They are introducing stimuli (hugs, kisses, words, attention) that their son finds pleasant. Behavior can also be rewarded with **negative reinforcement—** that is, the removal or avoidance of some *un*pleasant stimulus. If a child forces himself to stay awake to avoid a recurring nightmare, staying awake is being negatively reinforced. But whether negative or positive, reinforcement always has the same result: It *increases* the frequency of the response that precedes it.

Of course, some consequences *decrease* the frequency of the behaviors that precede them because those consequences are aversive. Such consequences are called **punishment.** If one of the stuffed dolls in Joshua's bed were removed every time he called out to his parents, this staying-awake tactic would be systematically punished and would probably decrease in frequency. Punishment, whether it involves the removal of some pleasant stimulus or the introduction of some unpleasant one (hitting, scolding, criticizing), always results in *suppression* of the response that precedes it. Table 1.2 summarizes the differences between reinforcement and punishment.

reinforcement
a consequence that produces repetition of behavior

positive reinforcement
reinforcement through the addition of pleasant stimuli

negative reinforcement
reinforcement through the removal of unpleasant stimuli

punishment
an aversive consequence that decreases the frequency of a behavior

Punishment works best under certain conditions. When a mother slaps her 2-year-old's hand as he reaches toward the stove and then says, "Don't touch that! It's very hot and will burn you!" her efforts to discourage this behavior are apt to be effective. The reason is that the punishment *immediately* follows the unwanted behavior and is accompanied by an *explanation* appropriate to the child's age (Aronfreed, 1968). Punishment tends to be effective also when it is given by someone with whom the child has a warm relationship, when it is meted out in a consistent fashion, and when the punisher suggests alternatives to the undesired behavior (Parke, 1977a; Sears, Maccoby, & Levin, 1957). Thus, a loving father who consistently scolds his daughter when she misses the school bus, but who also suggests that she get up earlier in order to have more time, is using punishment in a way that is likely to work.

Some psychologists believe that everything we do can be best understood by examining the rewards and punishments for the behavior. Chief among this group is B. F. Skinner. In Skinner's view, and in the view of others who are considered "radical" behaviorists, actions can be explained solely in terms of the environmental conditions that shape them (Skinner, 1938). We needn't talk about internal motives, feelings, or thoughts in order to understand the "why" of behavior, Skinner says. All we need to do is analyze the observable consequences that a certain action brings. A mouse, which lacks the higher reasoning powers of a human, is just as affected by rewards and punishments as a person, claims Skinner. According to him, all animals, including humans, learn from rewards and punishments in much the same way.

● *Social learning theory.* Andrew, age 5, catches a frog and picks it up by the legs. Dangling it, he approaches his 3-year-old sister Laura and waves it in front of her face. Laura is fascinated by the frog and gently strokes its body. Apparently disappointed by Laura's response, Andrew moves on to his older sister, Kim. Kim screams when she sees the frog and runs away from it, with Andrew in gleeful pursuit. Laura watches, and when Andrew approaches her again, she too screams and runs.

Laura has begun to acquire a new set of behaviors—screaming, running, and acting fearful at the sight of a frog. Yet there seems to be no reward shaping her response. How, then, can we explain the process by which Laura learned? **Social learning theorists,** psychologists who study the way people learn from one another, would say that Laura learned by watching her older sister and that concrete rewards or punishments are *not* needed for this kind of learning to occur. We all acquire a wide range of thoughts, feelings, and actions just by observing how other people behave. Such **observational learning** helps to explain how even very young children can acquire the habits, outlooks, and mannerisms of those close to them.

A classic study by psychologist Albert Bandura and his colleagues (Bandura, Ross, & Ross, 1961) demonstrated just how powerful observational learning is. Nursery school children watched one of two adults: either an adult who ignored a large inflated "Bobo" doll while playing quietly with another toy, or an adult who fiercely attacked the doll, pinning it to the floor and punching it in the nose, tossing it in the air, beating it with a hammer, and kicking it around the room. Later, the children were placed in a mildly frustrating situation and given access to the doll. Those who had observed the adult's "Bobo abuse" behaved more aggressively than the other children, and they tended to imitate what they had

● **social learning theorists**
psychologists who study how people learn from one another

● **observational learning**
learning through observation and imitation of others' behavior

In Bandura's experiment, preschool children who watched an adult attack an inflated doll later abused the doll themselves. Social learning theorists contend that much learning occurs through observation.

seen. They, too, punched, beat, kicked, and threw the doll, just as the adult model had done.

In a later study Bandura (1965) showed that watching a model being rewarded or punished can also influence an observer's behavior. Again nursery school children watched an adult attacking a Bobo doll, but this time some of the youngsters also saw consequences of the adult's behavior. One group saw the aggressive adult being praised and rewarded with candy; the other group saw the adult being punished with a scolding. Later, when mildly frustrated and given access to the doll, the children who had seen the aggressive adult rewarded were more likely to imitate abuse of the toy than those who had seen the adult punished. Apparently, the *expectation* of being rewarded or punished (even when we have not experienced that consequence ourselves) can influence whether we decide to imitate someone else's behavior.

For Bandura (1977) and other social learning theorists, the trouble with Skinner's behaviorism is that it ignores the qualities that set people apart from rats and pigeons. Unlike laboratory animals, Bandura argues, humans have expectations and motives. We do not just respond to rewards and punishments automatically; we analyze situations and think about how to behave. Sometimes we don't understand our own motives. Humans can be conflicted, impulsive, even self-destructive. Often we act without the promise of concrete rewards or punishments. Laura decided to imitate her sister Kim even though she did not see Kim praised for showing fear of frogs. Apparently, for Laura, being like her older sister is its own reward.

● Cognitive Theories

Much of modern social learning theory emphasizes cognition, or thought. Social learning theorists want to know how people interpret the stimuli around them, for these interpretations affect how the stimuli will shape their behavior.

Applied to the study of children, social learning theorists stress the perceptions that youngsters have of other people, themselves, and their prospects for rewards or punishments. For example, in deciding when, whether, or how much to study for a test, a child might weigh the costs and benefits: If she studies in the afternoon, she won't miss her favorite TV show at night; if she doesn't study at all or enough, she might fail or do poorly on the test. How much do those things matter to her?

Some cognitive psychologists focus less on perceptions and more on the development of thinking itself. Specifically, they study the way thought patterns change as children mature. For example, if you asked a 3-year-old and a 12-year-old why it gets dark at night, the 3-year-old might say that it gets dark "so I can sleep," whereas the 12-year-old can tell you about the rotating earth. The 3-year-old has noticed the setting sun, but at this age children interpret everything from their own perspective. It is natural for them to think of darkness in terms of its benefits for them.

Cognitive theorists try to understand changes in children's behavior and feelings in terms of such changes in thought. For example, young children who tend to see things only from their own perspective would understandably have trouble sharing toys or understanding that their actions can sometimes hurt others. One researcher who was highly insightful at identifying differences in how children think and the implications for behavior was the Swiss psychologist Jean Piaget (1896–1980). We will be discussing Piaget's research at many points in this book. Here we provide a broad outline of his theory of cognitive development.

● *Piaget's theory.* Piaget hypothesized that as children mature, they pass through stages of cognitive development; and in each stage, from birth to adolescence, their ways of thinking are qualitatively distinct (Piaget, 1959). Describing these progressive changes in thinking became Piaget's lifework (see Table 1.3). We will discuss each stage in more detail in later chapters.

Piaget believed that human thought is always organized, even in the youngest children. Youngsters automatically construct a view of reality, a way of mentally

TABLE 1.3   STAGES IN PIAGET'S COGNITIVE-DEVELOPMENTAL THEORY

Stage	Age*	Major Characteristic
Sensorimotor	Infancy (birth to age 2)	Thought confined to action schemes
Preoperational	Early childhood (ages 2 to 6)	Representational thought; thought intuitive, not logical
Concrete operational	Middle childhood (ages 6 to 12)	Systematic, logical thought, but only in regard to concrete objects
Formal operational	Adolescence and adulthood (from age 12)	Abstract, logical thought

*Ages approximate.

If his mother tells him often enough, this toddler will learn not to touch electrical cords. Piaget called the process of incorporating new information into one's behavior "assimilation."

representing the world and acting upon it. These mental representations and patterns of action that structure a person's knowledge are called **schemes** in Piaget's theory. For instance, a young baby's knowledge of the world is tied to sensing and doing. He or she does not "know" things in the abstract, as older children do. A ball is known only as something that can be squeezed and rolled; a teddy bear, only as something that can be hugged and chewed. Thus, a young baby's knowledge of the world is structured by simple actions that can be performed on objects—shaking, mouthing, smelling, sucking, biting, and so forth. These recurring patterns of action organize the infant's reality. They are schemes that give the world some order and structure. Piaget's aim was to identify the kinds of schemes that characterize each major stage of development. He did not see children at one level of development as "more intelligent" than children at another. As children mature, however, they do become capable of using increasingly complex and abstract schemes.

Important, too, in Piaget's theory was his belief that we actively participate in our own development: Children are constantly absorbing information and actively trying to make sense of it. Two important processes play a vital role in this task. One is **assimilation,** the process by which people incorporate new information into their current ways of thinking or acting—that is, into their existing schemes. The other is **accommodation,** by which people fundamentally alter their old ways of thinking or acting to adapt to new information that doesn't "fit" an existing scheme.

To understand the difference between assimilation and accommodation, consider a 15-month-old boy who has learned that radiators are hot and should not be touched. He toddles around the house, pointing at radiators, bringing his hand near them without actually touching, and saying "hot." Apparently, he has developed a scheme of certain things as both hot and not to be handled. Soon thereafter, he reaches for a pot of boiling water on the stove and again is told "Hot! Don't touch!" The same thing happens when he reaches for a lighted

● **schemes**
according to Piaget, mental representations and patterns of action that structure a person's knowledge

● **assimilation**
according to Piaget, the process by which people incorporate new information into their existing schemes

● **accommodation**
according to Piaget, the process by which people alter their existing schemes to adapt to new information that doesn't "fit" an existing scheme

candle and a burning electric bulb. The child *assimilates* all this new information into his scheme that a certain group of objects are forbidden and also hot.

But then one day he spots his father's briefcase, with papers sticking out. Hurrying over to it, he begins to touch and crumple the pages. "No!" shouts his father. "Don't touch!" The little boy points to the briefcase and solemnly proclaims it: "Hot." "No," says his father. "It's not hot. But you mustn't touch it anyway." Now the child looks puzzled. How could this be a "no touch" thing and not be hot? He is forced to *accommodate* his existing scheme of "no touch" objects to suit this new information. Gradually, he comes to realize that there are many reasons why certain things should not be touched. This new, more sophisticated view of reality constitutes a new scheme. Note how this change in thinking restores the child to a cognitive state of equilibrium, or balance, in which all the various pieces of his knowledge again fit together. Piaget called this process **equilibration.** It is through the processes of accommodation and equilibration, Piaget said, that children progress from one stage of cognitive development to another.

● *Contemporary cognitive views.* Piaget conducted much of his research from the 1930s through the 1950s. By the 1960s, his ideas had gained a prominent place in developmental psychology. But just as Freud's and Skinner's conclusions have been criticized, debated, and refined, Piaget's theory also has been tested and questioned. To it, the "neo-Piagetians" have added a number of important modifications. For instance, most neo-Piagetians believe that cognitive development is more gradual and more differentiated than Piaget proposed. Children do not move to a higher level of development in one giant step. Moreover, they seem to acquire a more advanced way of thinking in some areas before others. For instance, a 12-year-old might be able to reason quite abstractly about numbers and math, but not about moral issues. Why this unevenness in cognitive development? If the child has moved to a higher cognitive stage, as her math skills imply, why isn't this change reflected in all areas of her thinking? Some neo-Piagetians believe that explaining such inconsistencies should be a central part of any cognitive developmental theory.

Other cognitive psychologists are far more critical of Piaget's views. For instance, some argue that we indeed see improvements in cognitive abilities as children grow older. Especially prominent are the cognitive "leaps" that occur around ages 2, 6, and 12. But these, they say, are not due to fundamental changes in how children reason about the world, as Piaget maintained. Instead, they result from differences in how youngsters "process" information. According to this perspective, humans are information-processing systems, much like highly complex computers. As they develop, their processing skills improve because of both a gradual increase in their memory capacities and their acquisition of more sophisticated strategies for dealing with cognitive tasks. We will say more about information-processing theory later in this book. The point here is that it has become an important alternative to Piaget's theory.

● Biological Theories

Although psychoanalytic, learning, and cognitive theorists all assume that biological, as well as environmental, forces are important influences on develop-

equilibration
the process through which balance is restored to the cognitive structure

ment, there are some theorists who give special prominence to the role of biology in the growth of the child (MacDonald, 1988; Plomin, DeFries, & McClearn, 1990). Biological theorists don't ignore the environment, but they place a special emphasis on innate influences and how they are played out in development. There are two general categories of biological theories in the study of development: sociobiology and behavioral genetics. (They are compatible with each other but emphasize different levels of analysis.)

● *Sociobiology.*   The roots of **sociobiology** go back to Charles Darwin's theory of evolution. Darwin's investigations of the natural world led him to conclude that species developed and changed over exceedingly long periods of time through the process he called **natural selection.** Through this process, physical traits that enhanced a species' chances for surviving in its particular environment were passed on from generation to generation. Such a trait, said Darwin, was *adaptive* for the species: Having it increased the chances of reproducing, thereby continuing the species. Where competition for vegetation was fierce, for example, long-necked giraffes who could reach leaves on the higher limbs of trees would have a better chance of surviving and reproducing than their shorter-necked cousins. Over many generations, giraffes came to be distinguished by their adaptive, survival-enhancing long necks. Thus Darwin's theory of natural selection led to a belief in the *survival of the fittest.*

In the same way, say **sociobiologists,** certain *behaviors* endured during our species' evolution because of their adaptive significance. Sociobiologists always ask how a particular behavior could have helped a species to survive. Such behaviors, much like adaptive physical traits, would have been passed on from one generation to another through natural selection. In this regard, sociobiological theorists focus on what are called *ultimate* explanations of development. They seek to answer "the big whys" of behavior: for example, Why do infants become attached to their mothers? For sociobiologists, staying close evolved as a mechanism for protection and survival of helpless infants in a hostile environment. In contrast, "little why" explanations suggest that infants become attached because their mothers offer physical comfort.

Although the environment we live in today is quite different from that of our evolutionary ancestors, many of our behaviors may have originated in patterns of behavior established thousands of years ago. Reflexes easily fall into this category; for example, infants are born knowing how to suck and do so reflexively. More controversial is the sociobiologists' approach to sex differences, including why males are generally more aggressive than females. Again they seek answers in evolutionary history. How, for example, were sex differences adaptive in earlier times? Male aggression would have been highly adaptive for hunting animals; and female nurturance, equally adaptive for child rearing. We emphasize, though, that just because a certain behavior had some adaptive significance in human ancestral history, it does not mean that the behavior is still adaptive today. Simply put, just because something *is* doesn't mean that it *ought* to be. Today, for example, aggressive behavior seems to cause more problems for the human species than it solves. Although sociobiologists find the roots for behavior in the distant past, they do not believe that such behaviors are forever fixed. Rather, they recognize that we have the ability to adjust our behaviors to suit a changing environment.

● **sociobiology**
the comparative study of social organization in animals and humans, particularly concerning genetics and evolution

● **natural selection**
the process by which physical traits that enhance a species' chances for surviving in its particular environment are passed on from generation to generation

● **sociobiologists**
scientists who study social behavior in humans, particularly as it relates to genetics and evolution

Born friendly? Yes and no. While experience influences personality, children do inherit tendencies toward sociability or shyness.

While sociobiologists try to understand the adaptive role of human behaviors, another group of behavioral theorists seeks to understand the way particular traits or behavior patterns are actually passed on from generation to generation.

● **Behavioral genetics.** Some inherited traits make us like all other humans (two legs rather than four, for example), but others make us different from one another. (We are brown-eyed, blue-eyed, or green-eyed; long-legged, short-legged, or something in between.) Some traits are determined entirely by heredity (eye and hair color and most physical attributes), others are more subject to environmental influence (many personality traits, such as a need for achievement and sociability; talents such as musical ability), and still others fall somewhere in between (like intelligence). *Behavioral geneticists* try to determine the relative contributions of inheritance and experience and, more important, the interplay between biological and environmental influences. How much, for example, can the environment in which we grow up encourage us to be shy or sociable, anxious or easygoing, serious students or underachievers? They remind us that although experience, relationships, and learning all play important roles in influencing development, it would be foolish to forget that each of us comes into the world with some characteristics already inborn and others highly predisposed.

RESEARCH METHODS: HOW WE STUDY DEVELOPMENT

How do psychologists know that their theories of human development have validity? They cannot just assume that what "seems right" is valid, for sometimes what seems right turns out to be wrong. Consider, for example, pediatricians' changing attitudes on "spoiling" young infants. An earlier generation's argument against picking up a crying baby in the middle of the night stemmed from a strict behaviorist perspective. Rewarding an unwanted behavior would only increase its frequency. On the surface, this argument seems reasonable enough, but is it accurate? To find out, psychologists would need to apply the scientific method.

● Using the Scientific Method

The **scientific method** is a procedure to collect reliable, objective information that can be used to support or refute a theory. The first step in the scientific method is to define the question to be studied. In our example, the question is, Do babies cry more or less often when they are picked up promptly and comforted right after they start to cry? Next comes a review of the scientific literature on the topic to see what conclusions others have reached. This knowledge may help in formulating a hypothesis, which is the third step in the scientific method. A **hypothesis** is an educated proposition about how the factors being studied are related to each other. In this case, the hypothesis might be: If a crying baby is picked up promptly and comforted, it will cry more often. The fourth step is to choose a research design and a method for gathering data that can be used to test the hypothesis. Finally, researchers analyze their data and draw objective conclusions as to whether their hypothesis is correct.

When developmental psychologists tested the hypothesis used in our example, they found it to be wrong. Young babies generally cry *less* often when parents pick them up promptly after crying begins. Apparently, a behavioral explanation is wrong in this situation. The probable reason is that babies have little control over their crying; they cry *automatically* whenever they are distressed. So a better approach to reducing the frequency of crying is to eliminate the discomfort that causes infants' distress. This can be done by promptly picking up the baby whenever he cries. Over the long run, the child will feel less distressed; more secure in his relationship with the caregiver, he'll have less reason to cry.

Psychologists could never have discovered this link between comforting and crying without the scientific method. Through the use of this procedure, they have gathered a wealth of information about human development. The scientific method enables us to examine how development unfolds, what factors cause it to proceed as it does, and what interventions will be most effective when development goes awry.

● Choosing a Research Design

Our brief summary of the scientific method made step four sound easy: Investigators simply choose a research design and a method for gathering data that can be used to test their hypotheses. In practice, though, this step is far more complicated, and researchers often choose from among several designs, each appropriate in its own way.

● *The experiment.* The **experiment** is a scientific tool specifically designed to investigate causes. An experimenter systematically manipulates some factor suspected of causing a certain result and then objectively measures the actual consequences. She or he tries to ensure that all subjects in the experimental group experience exactly the same conditions so that no unintended influences bias the results. Experiments also have a control group to provide a source of

● **scientific method**
a procedure to collect reliable, objective information that can be used to support or refute a theory

● **hypothesis**
an educated proposition about how factors being studied relate to each other

● **experiment**
a scientific tool designed to investigate causes

comparison. The control group experiences all the conditions that the experimental group does *except* the key factor that the researcher is studying. This procedure enables the researcher to conclude that any significant difference in how experimental and control groups respond is due to the factor that has been manipulated.

For example, an experimental study was designed to test the hypothesis that young children who frequently witness angry confrontations between adults will become both distressed and more aggressive toward their own peers (Cummings, Iannotti, & Zahn-Waxler, 1985). In their experiment, a team of researchers brought pairs of 2-year-olds to play together in the living room of a small apartment. The control subjects played without interruptions, but while the experimental subjects played, two adults interacted in a room nearby. At first the adults talked to each other in a warm, friendly way, but then one got annoyed with the other, and an angry exchange followed. Finally, the two reconciled and were friendly once again.

The researchers watched the children's reactions through a one-way mirror. They found that the youngsters typically reacted to the angry exchange with signs of emotional distress. Some became more aggressive toward their playmate, just as the researchers had predicted. These responses intensified a month later when the experimental subjects were exposed to the same situation again. In contrast, control subjects, who merely played together with no adults interacting in the background, showed none of these negative effects. Apparently, hearing the arguing adults caused the experimental subjects to behave as they did.

Experiments like this one help us test whether the factor being manipulated *causes* a change in behavior. By standardizing the conditions to which subjects are exposed, the researcher makes it very unlikely that some extraneous factor

Do infants understand the concept of number? In experiments such as this one, performed by Dr. Karen Wynn, researchers explore infants' cognitive abilities by measuring the amount of time they stare at a changing configuration of dolls.

produced the results. An experiment has one important drawback, however. Sometimes the situation created is so artificial that one wonders whether the results can be generalized to behavior in the real world.

One way around this problem is to conduct a **natural experiment.** Here, the investigator takes advantage of an "experiment" that occurs naturally outside the laboratory. For instance, a developmental psychologist might hear that a local factory will be laying off workers after the first of the year, a situation that is bound to cause tension and conflict within families. So the psychologist might contact people at the plant who have kindergarten children and ask them if they and their families would participate in a study. Those who agreed would be asked to monitor the number and intensity of arguments between husband and wife that occurred in front of their children during a given period. The youngsters could then be observed in their kindergarten classrooms and assessed for their emotional adjustment and levels of aggression toward peers. This would give the researchers valuable baseline data. Later, when the layoffs at the factory occurred, those who were out of work would form the experimental group, while those who kept their jobs would be the control group. Again the number and intensity of family quarrels would be measured, and again the children would be evaluated. Suppose that parents in the experimental group (but not in the control group) experienced a significant increase in marital conflict, coupled with poorer emotional adjustment and more peer aggression among their children. In this case, the researchers would have evidence to suggest that the worsening marital quarrels were a *cause* of the children's negative behavior.

Natural experiments are clearly less artificial than experiments conducted in a laboratory, but they have one big disadvantage. In minimizing artificiality, investigators lose some of the control that they have in their own research settings. How do we know, for instance, that the children in the experimental group weren't experiencing other factors that made their behavior deteriorate? If so, their problem behavior could be causing their parents' increased conflict, rather than the other way around. Of course, the researcher could try to rule out such other influences by thoroughly investigating the subjects' lives. This process would be very time-consuming, however, and there is always the chance that something important would be overlooked. With natural experiments, in other words, you cannot be so certain that your cause-and-effect hypotheses are correct.

● *The correlational study.* **Correlational studies** yield even less certainty about causes. Here, a researcher assesses the extent to which two or more factors tend to be related—that is, to occur together. Such related factors are said to be *correlated* with each other. A correlational study can suggest *possible* causes, but it does not demonstrate them. Correlational studies merely tell us that certain factors go together, not that one necessarily causes another.

The relationships found in correlational studies are nevertheless intriguing. In one such study, researchers examined the relationship between high school students' grades and the parenting styles they experienced (Dornbusch et al., 1987). Researchers found that the children of parents with an "authoritative" style (expecting mature behavior and clearly setting rules, but also recognizing youngsters' rights and encouraging communication) received much better grades than children whose parents displayed either a "permissive" (anything

● **natural experiment**
an experiment that takes advantage of a naturally occurring event

● **correlational studies**
an assessment of the extent to which two or more factors tend to be related

goes) style or an "authoritarian" (domineering) one. This is an interesting finding, for it suggests that parenting style might be one factor causing academic success. This study, however, does not allow us to say that this hypothesis is correct. It shows only that good grades among teenagers *are related* to certain behaviors in their parents. It says nothing about the reason for this relationship. Perhaps youngsters who work hard in school and get good grades encourage the respectful style of parenting labeled *authoritative.* Other types of studies would have to be done to determine cause and effect.

Correlational studies are very common in the field of child development, where researchers want to know what behaviors are related to increases in age. Language skills, abstract thinking, intimacy in peer relations, and the ability to exert self-control are just a few of the things that tend to "go with" children growing up. But just knowing that these correlations exist does not explain them. Correlational studies are simply starting points for further investigations into causes.

● *The case study.* One benefit of a correlational study is that researchers can examine many different people. For instance, the study of parenting styles and high school grades that we just described solicited information from nearly 8,000 U.S. teenagers. With such a large number of subjects, researchers are more likely to find that the correlations they discover are reliable. Sometimes, however, investigators are willing to forgo the benefits of studying large numbers in order to obtain in-depth, detailed information about one person, or at most a few people. Such an in-depth investigation is called a **case study.**

● **case study**
a study that amasses detailed information about one person or, at most, a few people

In one interesting case study, a developmental psychologist explored dominance relationships among six boys who shared a cabin at a summer camp (Savin-Williams, 1976). The psychologist served as the cabin counselor and so had a chance to observe the boys closely for many hours each day. During certain times of the day he kept written records of all the dominance interactions that occurred (one boy ordering, threatening, ridiculing, or shoving another, and so forth). He found that a stable dominance hierarchy had emerged by the third day of camp. Each boy had a "place" in the pecking order, which rarely changed much. The higher-status boys organized and led activities; the lower-status boys followed orders and carried out tasks. Interestingly, the number of dominance interactions between high- and low-status youngsters dropped significantly after the first 2 weeks of camp. It was as though the hierarchy was now accepted, and the boys no longer had to vie for position.

Because case studies focus on a relatively small number of people, they usually yield more detailed information than we can get from studies with a large number of subjects. And when a particularly insightful researcher is involved, a case study may also suggest some important principles of human behavior and development. But a case study by itself, no matter how brilliantly conducted, cannot *prove* that certain principles operate. There is also a risk that case study results are specific to the people examined. The findings, in short, may not generalize to others.

● *Approaches to studying change over time.* Methods for studying how people change over time are essential to developmentalists, for such change is the very core of their subject matter. One approach to studying developmental change is the longitudinal study. In a **longitudinal study,** researchers follow the same group of people over a period and gather information about them at various points along the way. They then compare data collected at one time with data collected at another in order to draw conclusions about the nature and extent of change.

Consider, for example, a correlational study that also employed a longitudinal design (Vandell, Hendersen, & Wilson, 1988; Vandell & Powers, 1983). In this study, the researchers twice observed middle-class children who as preschoolers attended day care centers of different qualities. The first observations were made in the day care setting when the youngsters were 4 years old. The second observations were made when the children played together in groups of three at the age of 8. The researchers found that at age 4 the youngsters in poorer-quality day care spent more time in solitary play, while their peers in better-quality day care had more positive interactions with teachers. Would these patterns have any long-term effects? The follow-up study suggested they did. At age 8, the children who had previously experienced poor-quality day care had more developmental problems than their peers who had experienced high-quality care. In play groups they were relatively unfriendly, shy, and poor at social give-and-take. Of course, since this is a correlational study, we cannot be certain that poor-quality day care caused these negative effects. Perhaps there was something about the mothers and fathers of these children that caused them to select poor-quality day care. Perhaps the parents' own behaviors encouraged developmental problems. The results of the study, however, are suggestive enough to warrant further research.

A longitudinal design like this one is the most straightforward way to study change over time, for it follows the same group of people from one age to another. But longitudinal studies may take years to complete and are costly. There is also the danger that when people are repeatedly observed, interviewed, and assessed, they may respond differently than they would under normal circumstances.

An alternative to the longitudinal study is the cross-sectional design. In a **cross-sectional study,** researchers select subjects of different ages and assess them simultaneously in terms of the key factors under investigation. For instance, researchers interested in studying the long-term effects of day care could select a group of 4-year-olds and a group of 8-year-olds. Each group would have a similar profile regarding socioeconomic background, age of the parents, parents' child-rearing methods, and so forth. But in each group, some of the children would have attended poor-quality day care centers, while others would have gone to good-quality ones. The researchers would then evaluate all the children's social and emotional adjustment. If they found more social and emotional problems among the 4- and 8-year-old children with a history of inadequate day care, they would have evidence suggesting that a negative day care experience could have long-term ill effects on social and emotional development.

Cross-sectional studies are faster and less expensive than longitudinal ones, and since the subjects are examined only once, there is less chance that the observations themselves will affect behavior. The disadvantage of cross-sectional designs, however, is that they do not really study change over time; they merely estimate it. So the results of a cross-sectional study must be viewed cautiously. Subjects in the various age groups might differ in some significant way that

● **longitudinal study**
a study following the same group of people over an extended period of time

● **cross-sectional study**
a study using subjects of different ages and assessing them simultaneously

biases the results. This problem is magnified the farther apart the different age groups are, for people born in different eras—during the Depression or the 1950s, for example—will have had different experiences that shape their development in ways that researchers can't control for.

A compromise between the long and costly longitudinal study and the more risky cross-sectional design is the cross-sequential approach. In a **cross-sequential study,** researchers start with groups of different ages but also study them over a period of time. Because they have a range of ages to begin with, they usually don't have to study their subjects for as long as they would with a longitudinal design. Psychologists interested in the long-term effects of day care, for example, might select some 4-year-olds, some 6-year-olds, and some 8-year-olds with different day care histories and assess their social and emotional development. Two years later they could assess the same children again, thus obtaining data on youngsters between the ages of 4 and 10. This is one-third of the time required for a comparable longitudinal study.

● **Gathering Data**

The research designs you've just read about are frameworks for studying questions about human development, but they don't explain how developmentalists actually gather their data. Collecting information about how people think, feel, act, and change over time can be done in a number of ways.

● *Structured observation.* **Structured observations** are observations of people in structured or controlled environments. The experimenters discussed earlier, who deliberately exposed children to a fight between adults, used structured observation to collect their data. The children's reactions to the quarrel were videotaped from behind one-way mirrors. Later, trained observers viewed the tapes and used predetermined scoring procedures to rate each youngster for the emotions he or she displayed as well as for the amount and intensity of the child's aggression. Such structured observations are useful because they permit researchers to standardize the conditions under which data are gathered. But a highly structured setting can also be artificial and so might prompt people to behave in ways they otherwise would not.

● *Naturalistic observation.* Artificiality can be largely eliminated by conducting **naturalistic observations.** Here subjects are observed in their own "natural" environments. In the study of how a dominance hierarchy emerged among a group of campers, for example, the researcher did not interfere with the boys in any way. He simply kept a careful record of what they said and did as they interacted with each other. Naturalistic observations are clearly less contrived than structured ones, but by allowing the situation to be completely uncontrolled, researchers can leave key questions unanswered. How, for instance, might the dominance hierarchy among these young campers be affected if they were asked to perform tasks at which different boys excelled? Would the same children continue to dominate the activities, or would new leaders emerge? Would increased conflict be created, or would adjustments be made smoothly? The researcher involved had no chance to address these issues because he recorded only what was happening naturally.

---

cross-sequential study
a study using subjects of different ages studied over a period of time

structured observations
observations of people in controlled environments

naturalistic observations
observations of people in their own environments

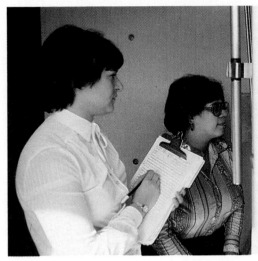
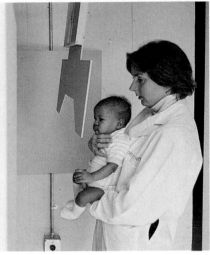

In experiments that recorded infants' reactions, researchers discovered that babies prefer striped patterns to solid gray.

● *Questionnaires.* In the correlational study we described earlier, where researchers looked for a relationship between parenting style and high school grades, the main tool for gathering data was the **questionnaire,** a written set of carefully prepared questions that subjects answer. The questions may have a set of possible responses to choose from (a multiple-choice format), or they may be open-ended, allowing people to answer however they wish. Questionnaires are often used when studying a large number of people. One important drawback to the questionnaire is its impersonality and superficiality. Respondents simply fill in their answers and return the survey. Researchers don't get an in-depth look at their subjects, and they never know if respondents have answered the questionnaire honestly. Also, it is important to make sure that questionnaire items are interpreted similarly by respondents from different backgrounds. One team of researchers using a parenting inventory to study child rearing in Hispanic and Anglo-American families needed to make sure that the questionnaire measured the same phenomena in the two cultural groups (Knight, Tein, Shell, & Roosa, 1992).

● **questionnaire**
a written set of carefully prepared questions given to subjects to answer

● *Interviews.* The **interview** overcomes the superficiality of the questionnaire by allowing researchers to personally ask people how they think, feel, or act. Some interviews are very tightly structured; subjects are asked specific questions in a specific order. Other interviews are loosely structured; the conversation takes many twists and turns depending on the respondent's answers. Piaget made excellent use of loosely structured interviews to find out exactly how children think at different ages. This topic lends itself nicely to the interview technique, for it is often hard to probe cognitive processes without asking people to explain their thinking. Interviews are also useful when observing behavior might cause people to act unnaturally. For instance, a mother who is a severe disciplinarian might treat her children less harshly than she normally does when she knows a researcher is watching. Yet in an interview, if the researcher is not critical, the same woman might discuss her usual child-rearing tactics. Of course, there is no guarantee that an interviewee will be completely truthful. This is one drawback to all self-report methods of gathering information. It is

● **interview**
a research technique in which researchers personally question people

especially problematical, however, in the face-to-face interview, where people are often reluctant to divulge attitudes, actions, or feelings that they think others might disapprove of.

● ***Standardized tests.*** Sometimes the best way to collect information about human development is to administer a **standardized test.** There are standardized tests for measuring many facets of human life, from intelligence quotient (or IQ) to self-esteem. Most standardized tests have been carefully developed, tried out on a great many people, and proved both reliable and valid. These tests have the benefit of allowing subjects' scores to be compared with previously established norms. But there might not always be a standardized test suited to a particular researcher's needs. In such cases, researchers must develop their own test questions.

● **standardized test**
a carefully developed test that allows individual scores to be compared with previously established norms

● Ethics and Research

Over 30 years ago, in the film *The Conscience of a Child,* kindergarteners confessed their misdeeds to a psychologist. While the researchers gained insight into their consciences, the children showed obvious distress. Conflicts between researchers' goals and subjects' rights have a long history. Ever since John Watson conditioned little Albert to fear furry white creatures, psychologists have been criticized for putting their own interests ahead of their subjects' feelings. Today, in the ethics code of the Society for Research in Child Development (SRCD), subjects come first. The code's principal guidelines are as follows:

1. *The child's interest always comes first, not the researcher's.* No matter how important the study seems to be, it should not be conducted if the children involved will be harmed in any way, either physically or psychologically. For instance, it would be useful to know the effects on growth and development of depriving children of certain nutrients. But we cannot deliberately withhold these nutrients from youngsters to find out. Doing so would clearly endanger their welfare.

2. *Children (if old enough) and usually their parents, too, must give informed consent before participating in a study.* This means that youngsters and their parents must be told in advance what the study is about and what the subjects will be asked to do. They then must be given the chance to refuse participation without coercion of any kind. And even when they agree to be involved in a study, subjects must be told that they still have a right to say no and withdraw from the study at any time. This is an especially important consideration in research on younger children, who may not know how to withdraw from a study once it has begun (Abramovitch, Freedman, Thoden, & Nikolich, 1991).

3. *Researchers should not deliberately deceive the subjects in their studies unless that deception causes no psychological harm and there is no other way to collect the information wanted.* Suppose, for instance, that researchers want to identify successful and unsuccessful ways of coping with failure. They could wait for each child in a group of selected students to experience failure in the classroom and then try to assess each child's reactions to it. This approach would be time-consuming as well as hard to carry out.

PART ONE

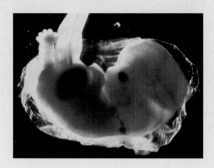
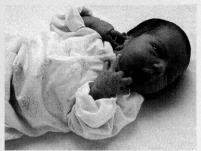

A NEW LIFE BEGINS

CHAPTER 2

CONCEPTION, HEREDITY, AND PRENATAL DEVELOPMENT

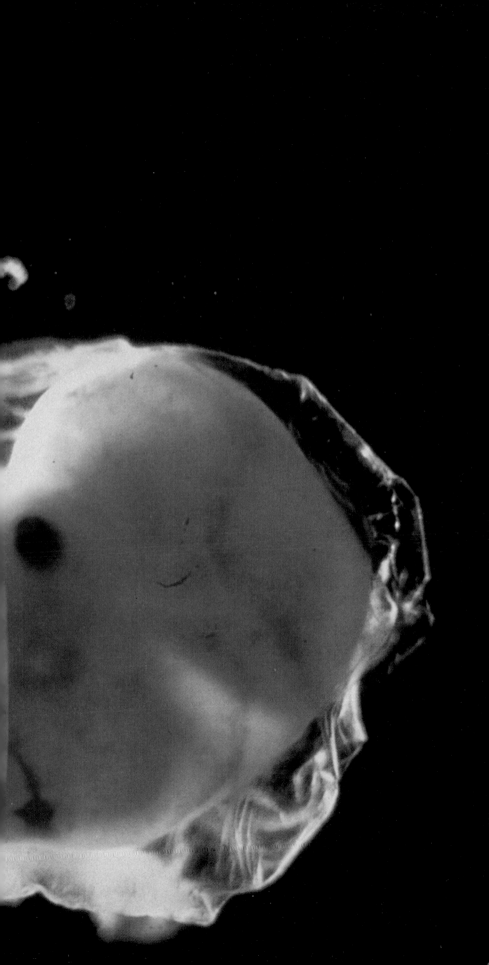

All normal, healthy babies are born with the capacity to develop skills: to walk upright, to speak, to smile and laugh, to use their hands to make tools and their heads to imagine a better world. In these and countless other ways, we are all alike. Moreover, many aspects of the basic story of human development are much the same, whether the plot unfolds in rural Minnesota, inner-city Chicago, a village in Guatemala, or on Manhattan's Park Avenue. We all babble before we talk and stand before we run; we take our first steps and speak our first words at about the same ages. The similarities among human beings are the result of a genetic "program" that is thousands, perhaps millions, of years old. This program is what makes each of us human: It is what makes each of us like other members of our species.

At the same time, each human being is unique. No one else looks, acts, or thinks exactly as you do; no one else has your voice or your smile. Individuality also has its roots in heredity. With the exception of identical twins, each person inherits a unique combination of genes. Even brothers and sisters are set apart by heredity, and the environment compounds genetic differences. Siblings grow up in the same family, live in the same community, and often attend the same schools, but each experiences and responds to these shared environments in his or her own way. Indeed, even in the same family, brothers and sisters can experience very different environments.

Chapter 2 first focuses on heredity: how genes establish both similarities and differences among people. We begin with conception, a more complicated process than most people imagine. Then we'll look at genes and how these basic units of heredity shape the development of each new life. We will also consider genetic abnormalities, and we'll discuss how counseling and medical technology can help would-be parents learn whether their children will be at risk for developing these abnormalities.

Next, we'll turn to prenatal development, the stages every human fetus passes through during its 9 months in the uterus. We will also pay particular attention to the environmental influences that can cause normal development to go awry.

HUMAN CONCEPTION

During sexual intercourse, a man may ejaculate hundreds of millions of sperm into a woman's body. To reach a mature egg, or ovum, the sperm must travel about 12 inches through the mucousy secretions of the vaginal canal—a distance thousands of times its own length. Only a few hundred sperm make this journey, and only *one* of these can fertilize the ovum. And the odds that a sperm will even find a mature ovum at the end of its journey are very low. That is because an ovum is available for fertilization only for a limited number of hours each month. The odds of a *particular* sperm fertilizing a *particular* ovum are infinitesimal, but conception itself generally occurs within 3 to 6 months for most women who have intercourse regularly without using birth control.

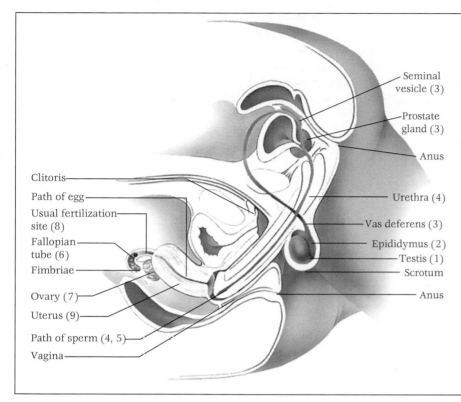

Sperm
1. Produced in the testes
2. Stored in the epididymis
3. During sexual arousal, travel through the vas and mix with seminal fluid from seminal vesicles and prostate
4. Released through urethra of penis during ejaculation
5. Deposited in the seminal pool of vagina, near cervix
6. Pass through cervix into uterus and fallopian tubes

Egg
7. Produced by one of the ovaries
8. Fertilization site in upper third of fallopian tube
9. Site of implantation for developing zygote around 6th day

Seminal vesicle (3)
Prostate gland (3)
Anus
Urethra (4)
Vas deferens (3)
Epididymus (2)
Testis (1)
Scrotum
Anus

Clitoris
Path of egg
Usual fertilization site (8)
Fallopian tube (6)
Fimbriae
Ovary (7)
Uterus (9)
Path of sperm (4, 5)
Vagina

● Fertilization

In generations of textbooks, fertilization is described as the first great contest of life: Millions of sperm compete for a lone egg, waiting to be united with the swiftest, hardiest of the lot. After ejaculation, 300 to 400 million sperm race up the vaginal canal, passing through the cervix, into the uterus, and up to the fallopian tubes where, it was believed, the winning sperm would fertilize the waiting, passive egg. (See Figure 2.1.) Although this description of the sperm's *route* is essentially correct, recent research suggests that its role is a bit different. The egg, it now appears, is an active player in fertilization, guiding the sperm with a series of well-timed molecular signals (Freedman, 1992).

During most of the month, a thick, opaque mucus plug blocks the opening to the cervix. (This plug helps to prevent infections in the uterus and fallopian tubes, a major cause of sterility in women.) At ovulation, the mucus is clear and thin, no longer a barrier to sperm traveling through the cervix. We have long known about this aspect of the chemistry and timing of fertilization. The environment in the woman's body must be ready for the sperm.

Once through the cervix, the sperm enter the uterus and move up toward the fallopian tubes. The rhythmic uterine contractions that occur during female orgasm help to carry the sperm toward the fallopian tubes. Mechanically, then, the female reproductive system assists the sperm on its journey toward conception.

But the female also creates *obstacles* to conception. The woman's immune system reacts to sperm in her uterus as foreign matter, coating them with anti-

Figure 2.1
Conception
Recent research suggests that the egg plays a more active role in fertilization by guiding the sperm with a series of molecular signals.
(SOURCE: After Allgeier & Allgeier, 1991.)

bodies. Many sperm are now disabled, so only some of the original millions will continue on toward the egg. (In some cases a couple cannot conceive because her antibodies kill his sperm.)

The next stage presents another challenge. The cilia in the woman's fallopian tubes gently push the ovum toward the uterus, creating a downstream current. Thus to reach the ovum, sperm must travel upstream. Why would the female body actively fight sperm, reducing the chances of conception? One possibility is that the female reproductive system "selects" or "chooses" the hardiest sperm among the contenders. How that selection process occurs has been studied, and debated, by biologists over the past 20 years. The role of the egg as anything but a sleeping beauty waiting for her sperm prince is, in fact, a revolutionary concept. Until about 20 years ago, biologists believed that the egg waited and the sperm swam; victory went to the swiftest and fittest. But recent studies have revealed a more active egg, one that may even choose her sperm, guiding it to her with a series of chemical signals.

Researching fertilization in many species, biologists found that the egg typically releases molecules that guide or "activate" the sperm, priming it to release proteins that help it adhere to the egg (Freedman, 1992, p. 62). In one model, the sperm behaves like a fly caught in a spider's web, struggling to escape, but the egg, like a spider, is biologically prepared to keep it. Molecules on the egg's surface link up with those on the sperm's surface, grabbing this sperm until the egg absorbs it. Other biologists claim that the egg is indeed active, but less aggressive, and the sperm is not really a foiled escape artist. Instead, these biologists posit a molecular dialogue, a chemical duet for sperm and egg (Freedman, p. 64). During the dialogue process, one sperm releases a digestive enzyme and "eats" its way into the ovum. The surface of the ovum then hardens, so that other sperm cannot enter. This is the moment of conception, the instant at which the development of the fetus begins.

One interesting footnote to this story concerns the sex of the baby. Sperm genetically coded to create male offspring are more likely to penetrate the ovum than sperm coded to produce females: Approximately 160 males are conceived for every 100 females. Yet at birth, only 105 boys are born for every 100 girls, suggesting that females are hardier than males.

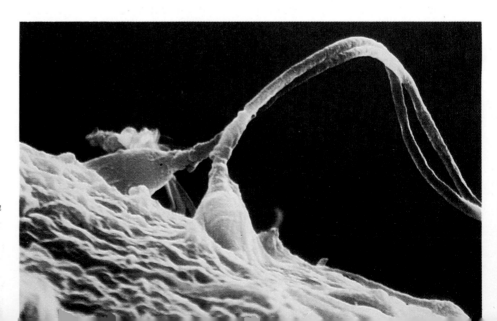

Of the 300 to 400 million sperm that approach the ovum, only one will penetrate and fertilize it.

HEREDITY: THE GENETICS OF LIFE

Within the single cell of a fertilized egg are complete instructions for creating a new human being. This extraordinary transformation is directed by genes and chromosomes, the molecular materials of life whose secrets scientists are only beginning to pierce.

● Genes and Chromosomes

Until a nineteenth-century monk named Gregor Mendel became curious about pea plants, heredity via body fluids was the theory of the day. Mendel's contemporaries believed that during conception, male and female body fluids went through a kind of body blender. The resulting mix, they thought, contained a blend of characteristics from each parent that were passed on to their offspring. This theory stood until Gregor Mendel noticed something in his monastery garden.

Mendel observed that some of the pea plants were wrinkled, some were smooth, some were green, and some were yellow. He wondered why. He found that when he crossed plants bearing smooth green peas with plants bearing wrinkled yellow peas, he did not get semismooth yellow-green peas, as one might expect. The different traits (smooth and wrinkled, green and yellow) did not blend but maintained their integrity across many generations. Mendel did not know why this happened, but after many breeding experiments he concluded that some mechanism within the plants carried instructions for specific traits to each new generation. Today we know that the messages of heredity are carried not by body fluids but by the discrete particles we call **genes.**

Mendel published his theory of heredity in 1865, and chromosomes were first observed under the microscope in the 1870s. But it was not until almost a century later that the chemistry of genetic inheritance was explained. For their work, James Watson and Francis Crick shared the Nobel prize in 1958.

Watson and Crick demonstrated that chromosomes are long strands of a chemical substance called **deoxyribonucleic acid (DNA),** shaped in a double helix. If you took a ladder and twisted it into a spiral staircase, you would have a double helix. In the case of DNA, the two sides or railings of the ladder are formed by sugar and phosphate molecules; the rungs are four amino acids: adenine, thymine, cytosine, and guanine, or "A," "T," "C," and "G." These four letters are the alphabet of heredity; the way they are arranged makes human traits, not words. Indeed, all the instructions needed for the making and maintenance of a human being are written in this four-chemical code. What distinguishes one gene from another is the *order* in which these chemicals are arranged on the chromosomes. This is where the analogy between the genetic code and the alphabet comes in. The letters of the Roman alphabet have created many languages (English, Spanish, Swahili), but the *order* in which those letters have been used makes each language different (*hello, buenos dias, jambo*). The order of letters also determines the meaning of words within a language (end, den, Ned). And words can be strung together in infinite ways, communicating different messages ("Jonah ate the whale," or "The whale ate Jonah"). So it is with the genetic code. A four-letter alphabet provides the instructions for creating

Gregor Mendel's experiments with pea plants revealed that genetic traits were transmitted across generations.

● **genes**
the basic units of heredity, each gene consisting of a segment of a chromosome that controls some aspect of development

● **deoxyribonucleic acid (DNA)**
a chemical substance that is the carrier of genetic information in chromosomes

As this model shows, the DNA molecule is shaped like a double helix with amino acid "rungs" connecting sugar and phosphate sides.

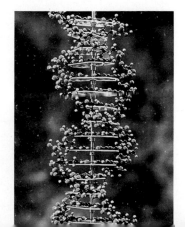

and maintaining life. The way those letters are arranged on the chromosomes will distinguish one person's genes—and one person—from all others.

Every human body cell contains approximately 20,000 genes, each one occupying a specific site, or locus, along a **chromosome.** Humans have 46 chromosomes, or 23 pairs in each cell nucleus. *Within the genes on these strands is all the information necessary for human development.*

The genetic codes for *Homo sapiens* evolved over millions of years, and today, the genetic instructions which make us all look and function like humans are essentially alike in each of us. We all display the trademark traits of our species, the things that make us people, not apes, birds, or snakes. Yet each of us carries an individual chemical stamp, a personal DNA identification that makes us like every other human yet like no one else at all. Many of these variations stem from both genetic and environmental factors—an interaction we will examine throughout this book.

● The Genetics of Conception

When a sperm fertilizes an ovum, the child-to-be inherits one set of chromosomes from the mother and another from the father. Our cells contain not 46 individual chromosomes but 23 *pairs* of chromosomes. These pairs of chromosomes are like different editions of the same encyclopedia. Each contains a volume on body build, with chapters on height, weight, and proportions; each includes a volume on building a nervous system, with chapters on sense organs, muscle connections, memory, emotional reactions; and so on through 23 volumes. But although the outlines of each volume are the same, the details within sections often differ. The chapter on eye color from the mother's chromosome may contain directions for brown eyes; and the chapter on height, instructions for making a short person. The chapters from the father may contain alternative sets of directions; for example, they may contain directions for blue eyes and a tall person.

Alternative genes for the same trait (such as eye color) are known as **alleles.** A child who inherits the same alleles for a trait (alleles for brown eyes, for ex-

● **chromosome**
a twisted strand of DNA that carries genetic instructions from generation to generation

● **alleles**
alternative genes for the same trait

Dark-haired parents may have a blond child if they carry recessive genes for light hair.

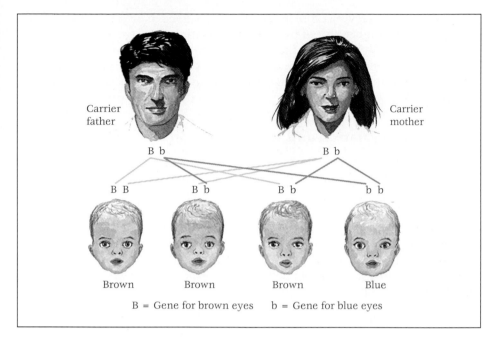

Brown | Brown | Brown | Blue

B = Gene for brown eyes   b = Gene for blue eyes

Figure 2.2
Recessive Inheritance for Blue Eyes
Both parents have brown eyes, but each carries a recessive gene for blue eyes. The odds for eye color for each child are (1) 25 percent chance of receiving two dominant genes, thus having brown eyes; (2) 50 percent chance of receiving one dominant and one recessive gene, thus being brown-eyed but carrying the recessive gene for blue eyes; and (3) 25 percent chance of receiving two recessive genes, thus having blue eyes. This same principle applies to the risks of inheriting a recessive genetic defect from parents who are both carriers.

ample) from both parents is **homozygous** (from the Greek *homo*, meaning "same"). A child who inherits different alleles for a single trait is **heterozygous** for that trait (from the Greek *hetero*, for "different").

What happens when a child inherits contradictory genetic directions for a trait depends on the genes in question. In some cases, the allele from one parent overrides the gene from the other parent. A child who inherits a gene for brown eyes from her mother and a gene for blue eyes from her father will have brown eyes, not brownish-blue eyes. This happens because the gene for brown eyes overrides the gene for blue eyes. The brown-eyes gene is called a **dominant gene.** The gene that is not expressed—the blue-eyes gene—is a **recessive gene.** To have blue eyes, then, a child must inherit two recessive genes—one gene for blue eyes from *each* parent. When that happens, a dominant brown-eyes gene does not mask the blue-eyes gene. Anyone who has blue eyes, then, is homozygous for eye color; both genes for that trait carry instructions to make blue eyes.

When the gene for a recessive trait, such as blue eyes, is masked by a dominant gene, such as that for brown eyes, the blue-eyes gene doesn't necessarily disappear from the family. If a brown-eyed woman with a recessive gene for blue eyes marries a man who also has a recessive gene for blue eyes (another blue/brown heterozygote), the chances are 1 in 4 that a child of theirs will have blue eyes. (See Figure 2.2.) Some of the traits controlled by recessive genes include gray, green, blue, and hazel eyes; baldness; blonde hair; thin lips; and color blindness. Traits governed by dominant genes include brown eyes, brunette hair, curly hair, thick lips, normal color vision, and farsightedness.

Many diseases and defects are carried on recessive genes, including sickle-cell anemia, Tay-Sachs disease, hemophilia, congenital deafness, and some 700 others. A child who inherits a recessive gene for a particular disorder from *each* parent will develop the disorder. That is why the taboo in most cultures

homozygous
inheriting the same alleles for a given trait from both parents

heterozygous
inheriting different alleles for a given trait from each parent

dominant gene
a gene that is expressed whether paired with an identical or a recessive allele

recessive gene
a gene that is not expressed if paired with its dominant allele

against people marrying close relatives makes good biological sense: Their children have a higher risk of inheriting a harmful recessive gene for a single trait from each parent than do the children of unrelated parents.

While the dominant-recessive mechanism is a very powerful means of inheritance, most inherited traits are determined by the combined effects of *many* genes. Height, skin color, and intelligence, for example, are **polygenic.**

● **polygenic**
caused by the interaction of a number of genes

● Sex Determination and Differentiation

In every baby, sex is determined by the twenty-third pair of chromosomes, the pair we call the **sex chromosomes.** Humans have two types of sex chromosomes: X-shaped and Y-shaped. Females have two X chromosomes in each of their body cells, and males have an X and a Y.

● **sex chromosomes**
the twenty-third pair of chromosomes, which determine the sex of the child; there are two types, X-shaped and Y-shaped

When the ovum and sperm are produced, a process called *meiosis,* each cell contains only half of the full set of chromosomes and genes. Each ovum carries one X chromosome, and each sperm carries *either* an X or a Y chromosome, half of the twenty-third pair. At conception, if an X-bearing sperm fertilizes the ovum, the twenty-third pair of chromosomes in the fetus becomes XX, female. If the ovum absorbs a Y-bearing sperm, an XY combination produces a male. It is the sperm, then, that determines the child's sex. However, until the thirteenth week of gestation, male and female fetuses have the *same* sexual structure (Diamond, 1992). If a Y chromosome is not present, during the thirteenth week this "basic" sex structure develops into ovaries. If a Y chromosome is present, then testes form instead of ovaries. (See Figure 2.3.)

**Figure 2.3
Normal Gender
Development**
In normal gender development, an all-purpose gonad develops as either an ovary or a testis depending on the combination of chromosomes present. With an X chromosome from both the male and female, it develops as an ovary; with an X from the female and a Y from the male, it develops as a testis. In males, the testes produce hormones, or androgens, that convert certain embryonic structures into the appropriate male parts. Without the influence of these androgens, the same structures normally develop into the female counterparts.
(SOURCE: After *Discover,* June 1992.)

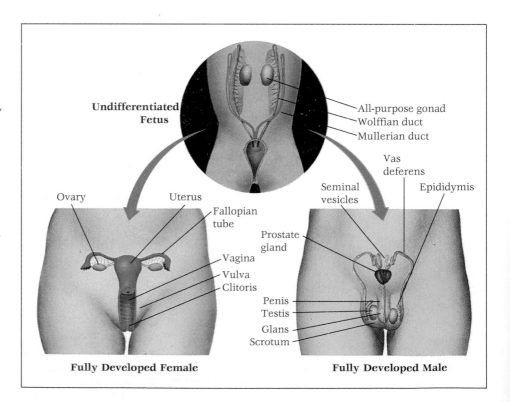

Sex differentiation is not limited to the differential development of sex organs, however. The process of becoming male or female also affects regions of the nervous system that regulate sexual behavior. Because male and female fetuses have different gonads, they produce and are therefore exposed to a different mix of sex hormones. Sex hormones, we know, affect the development of the brain; and as a result, the developing brains of males and females may end up organized, or "hardwired," in different ways. That is, just as some of the behavioral differences between adult males and females result from the different hormonal exposures they encounter at puberty, so too are some sex differences due to different hormonal exposures in the womb (Hines, 1982).

From Genotype to Phenotype

While biologists study the molecular structure and behavior of genes, developmental scientists want to identify the aspects of human traits and behaviors that are influenced by genes. We say *influence* because the environment plays an active role from the beginning. For this reason, scientists distinguish between a person's **genotype**—the set of genes the person inherits—and her or his **phenotype**—those observable physical and behavioral traits that emerge during development. A phenotype is not a direct reflection of a person's genotype but rather the expression of genetic *appearance* in a particular *environmental context.*

Some aspects of development are under such tight genetic control that the environment has little if any influence on their expression. The term **canalization** describes a trait's susceptibility to modification by the environment or by experience (Waddington, 1966). Highly canalized traits are difficult to modify, and individual differences for these traits are slight. For example, the major motor developments of the first year (turning over, sitting up, crawling) are highly canalized. Babies sit up when they are biologically ready to sit, despite parents' efforts to speed things up. Moreover, unless their environments are extremely depriving, virtually all normal babies follow similar timetables for motor development.

But most aspects of development are not highly canalized, leaving considerable room for variation in phenotype. Each child's genotype establishes a *potential*; what actually happens during development depends on the interaction of that potential with the environment. Height is a good example. Generally, tall parents have tall children, and short parents have short children. But nutrition and health clearly affect how tall a person will grow. A boy with "tall genes" who grows up in a poor rural village, or who is sickly as a child, may be only 5 feet 7 inches as an adult. If he is healthy and well-fed as a child, he might grow to be 6 feet.

Height is one of many instances in which genes do not determine a trait but establish a **reaction range,** or upper and lower limits on development. Intelligence is another. Like height, intelligence runs in families. Children tend to be about as intelligent as their parents. Suppose, though, that a child's parents both have IQs in the below-average range of 80 to 90. (An IQ of 100 is average.) The parents were not very good students, but they are able to hold jobs and function adequately. If the child grows up with his parents, his IQ will probably be about the same as theirs. But if he is adopted by parents with above-average IQs (about 130), parents who read to him, answer his questions, take him on trips to mu-

genotype
an individual's genetic makeup, consisting of all inherited genes

phenotype
an individual's observable physical and behavioral traits, the result of the interaction of genetic potential and environment

canalization
the extent to which a trait is susceptible to modification by the environment or by experience

reaction range
the genetically established upper and lower limits to development of a given trait; a trait's potential for expression

seums, and otherwise provide a stimulating environment, there is a very good chance that he will develop an average or even above-average IQ, say 110. However, if he is placed in an institution at an early age and given only minimal care, he may develop an IQ of only 70, which is in the mildly retarded range. For IQ, this child's reaction range is 70 to 110. He will never be a genius, but he should always be capable of learning basic skills. Where he falls within this range—his phenotype—depends on his environment.

● *Genes and the environment.* Until relatively recently, scientists thought that heredity and the environment were opposing forces: Either one or the other prevailed. Today, however, most recognize that genetic and environmental factors usually work in the same direction (see Chapter 1). In technical language, genotype and environment are often correlated (they co-relate, or go together). Robert Plomin, an expert in the area of behavioral genetics (the inheritance of behavior), and his colleagues have identified three types of gene-environment correlations (Plomin, DeFries, & Loehlin, 1977). Each can be illustrated by considering the development of intelligence and sociability. A child who inherits a high genetic potential for intelligence usually has highly intelligent parents. Intelligent parents are likely to do things with the child that stimulate her intellectual growth. Similarly, a child who inherits a predisposition to sociability is likely to have outgoing parents who chat with people they meet on the street, invite guests to their house, and generally provide their child with many opportunities to interact with others, thus encouraging her to be outgoing. These are called *passive* gene-environment correlations. The child is the passive recipient of genetic and environmental influences that work in the same direction—in these examples, to make the child more intelligent or more sociable.

Children who have the genetic potential for high intelligence are also likely to act in ways that evoke intellectual stimulation from the people around them. For example, they ask questions, beg to be taken to the library, and volunteer answers in school more often than children with less intellectual potential. Responding to their intellectual curiosity, adults and older children treat them differently. Similarly, inherently sociable children are more likely to smile and seek attention than shy children; as a result, others are more likely to respond to them, thereby reinforcing their tendency to be friendly. These are *evocative*

A child's environment includes experiences as well as things. When adults stimulate a child's curiosity they enhance intellectual development as well as emotional ties.

gene-environment correlations: Because of their genetic predispositions, the children evoke certain types of reactions from their environment.

Children who inherit high intellectual potential also actively seek environments that encourage or reward intelligent behavior. The intelligent child selects playthings that are cognitively challenging, chooses books that are a little beyond her current reading level, picks friends who are as advanced as she is. The child who is genetically sociable chooses play activities involving other children rather than solitary pastimes. Making these choices—which psychologists refer to as "niche-picking" (Scarr & McCartney, 1983)—tends to strengthen the phenotypic display of genotypic predispositions. The choices are called *active* gene-environment correlations: The child actively seeks and shapes an environment that fits his or her genetic predisposition.

● *Separating genetic and environmental contributions.* Given the overlap between genetic and environmental influences, how do psychologists know how much any one characteristic in any person is shaped by heredity? One approach is to study children who were adopted at an early age. Similarities in a given trait between these children and their adoptive parents (with whom they live but with whom they share no genetic history) reflect environmental influences; similarities between children and their biological parents (with whom they share a genetic background but no experience) reflect genetic influences. A second widely used approach is to compare identical and fraternal twins. **Identical twins** develop when a single fertilized ovum divides in two, leading to the birth of children with completely identical genes. They are the same sex, look strikingly alike, and have similar personalities as well. **Fraternal twins** (literally, "brotherly") are born when two ova are fertilized at the same time by two different sperm. Like identical twins, fraternal twins share the same prenatal and postnatal environment. But genetically, fraternal twins are no more alike than brothers and sisters. The degree of similarity for a given trait in identical versus fraternal twins is a clue to the strength of genetic influence on that trait. Twin studies are often difficult to interpret, however, because identical twins usually experience more similar environments (as well as have more similar genes) than fraternal twins.

Interestingly, the prevalence of twinning varies across cultural and racial groups. For example, the frequency of fraternal twins among Chinese couples is only 1 in every 300 births, whereas among African-American couples twins are more than three times more likely (twins account for about 1 in every 70 births). Differences in the rate of twinning probably reflect hormonal differences among women from different ethnic groups (Vaughan, McKay, & Behrman, 1979).

Much of what we know about the interplay of genes, experience, and intelligence comes from studies using twins and adopted children as subjects. The correlation in IQ scores for identical twins is .85 (on a scale where 0 indicates no relationship and 1.00 signifies total similarity); the correlation for fraternal twins, about .55 (Plomin & DeFries, 1983). As these correlations show, heredity is a major factor in intelligence. A study of adoption and IQ (Scarr & Weinberg, 1983) confirmed this conclusion. The researchers found that the correlation in IQ scores between children and their biological parents (who had given them up for adoption) was higher than that between children and their adoptive parents (who raised them). But the same study showed that the environment also

● **identical twins**
twins born from a single fertilized ovum that divides in two

● **fraternal twins**
twins born from two different ova fertilized at the same time by two different sperm

has a significant impact. The adopted children in this study were born to poor parents with below-average IQs but raised in middle-class homes by parents with above-average IQs. Apparently as a result of this stimulating environment, the children's IQ scores were significantly higher than those of their biological parents (an average of 110 compared to an average of 80). But the adopted children's IQs were not as high as those of their adoptive siblings, who had the double advantage of their parents' genes *and* a stimulating environment.

A study of transracial adoption reached similar conclusions about the importance of looking at the environment, and not simply at genetic factors, in the development of intelligence. This study found that African-American children who had been adopted into middle-class white families scored higher on IQ and achievement tests than their counterparts who had not been raised within the white majority culture (Scarr & Weinberg, 1976). Given the fact that IQ and achievement tests were developed to reflect intelligence as it is defined by the dominant culture, it is of little surprise to see that youngsters' scores on such tests reflect their degree of exposure to that culture.

What conclusions can we draw from these studies of genes and environment? Children inherit from their parents a set of genetic potentials. Within their genetic program, some traits are strongly canalized, and others have a wide reaction range. How children actually develop depends on the interplay between what they bring to the environment and the sorts of experiences they have in that environment. The question is not *how much* of intelligence, sociability, and so forth is hereditary and how much results from experience. Rather, the question is *how*? How do genes and the environment *work together* to influence development? And ultimately, how can we shape environments so that all children come closer to reaching their full potential? In the next section, we examine several genetically based abnormalities, and even here, the environment still plays an important role.

● Genetic Abnormalities

Normally, during fetal development, cells multiply and migrate to their appropriate destinations so that organs and limbs form where they should. But genetic instructions can go awry even at the earliest stages of pregnancy. Half of all conceptions are never implanted, and 25 percent of implanted embryos are spontaneously aborted in the first month or two of pregnancy. Genetic defects cause a high percentage of these miscarriages. After birth, many genetic defects are correctable by surgery, such as a cleft palate or a club foot, but others cause more serious, even life-threatening, conditions. Below we discuss some of the most common serious genetic disorders: Down syndrome, PKU, sickle-cell anemia, and Tay-Sachs disease.

● *Down syndrome.* Probably the best-known genetic disorder is **Down syndrome,** named for the physician who first described its symptoms. Down syndrome children have a distinctive appearance coupled with a range of mental and physical handicaps. Typically, their eyes are almond-shaped, with a downward-sloping skin fold at the inner corners. Their heads tend to be small and rounder than those of other children, and their noses flatter. Limbs are short, and these children walk with a distinctive flat-footed gait. Mental development is slower than normal, never reaching average adult levels. Down children suf-

● **Down syndrome**
a hereditary disorder caused by an extra twenty-first chromosome

Home life can foster the development of Down syndrome children in ways that institutional living rarely does. This girl enjoys a game of Scrabble with her siblings at home.

fer from higher than average rates of heart defects, and they are also more susceptible to a variety of physical diseases and disorders, including leukemia, respiratory infection, and eye and ear problems. They run a high risk of early death, but the risk decreases after the first few years of life.

The cause of Down syndrome has been traced to a defect in the twenty-first pair of chromosomes. The Down child has an extra twenty-first chromosome, or a piece of one. (The technical term for this is *trisomy 21,* or three chromosomes in the twenty-first pair.) In rarer cases, the extra chromosome, or part of it, is attached to another chromosome.

What causes this defect isn't completely understood, but we do know that the risk of bearing a child with Down syndrome has been linked to the age of the mother. In Table 2.1, notice that the risk increases greatly over age 35 and especially after age 40: Almost 10 times as much risk exists among 35- to 39-year-olds as among 20- to 24-year-olds. Between ages 40 and 44, the risk is 30 times greater than for 20- to 24-year-olds. Why should the incidence of Down syndrome increase so sharply with maternal age? Because a female is born with all

TABLE 2.1 INCIDENCE OF DOWN SYNDROME ACCORDING TO MATERNAL AGE

Maternal Age	Incidence of Down Syndrome
Under 30 years	1 in 1,500 live births
30	1 in 885
35	1 in 365
40	1 in 109
45	1 in 32
50	1 in 12

Source: B. Baird & A. Sadovnick, 1988.

the ova she will ever have, the ova of a woman who bears a child at age 45 are nearly twice as old as those of a woman who conceives at age 25. The older ova have been exposed to more diseases and environmental pollutants, so classifying Down syndrome as a genetic disorder identifies only part of the cause. Recent studies show that environmental influences are involved as well. Men whose jobs regularly expose them to lead, oil-based pesticides, and solvents are at higher risk of fathering a Down syndrome child (Olshan, Baird, & Teschke, 1989). An earlier study found that men over 40 also have an increased risk of fathering a Down syndrome child (Hook, 1980).

Highlighting the theme we'll note many times in this text, environmental factors can also powerfully improve the lives of Down children. Only a generation ago, most were placed in institutions, but today parents are advised to care for Down children at home for as long as they can. When encouraged by responsive parents to play and explore actively as infants, Down children do become more competent (Crawley & Spiker, 1983). Special education programs have shown, too, that these children have more learning potential than anyone suspected 15 or 20 years ago (Cicchetti & Beeghly, 1990).

Clearly, the environment strongly affects the expression of this genetic disorder: Its reaction range is much larger than was once thought. Perhaps as a result of the gains Down children have made, plastic surgeons are experimenting with techniques to alter the distinguishing features of the syndrome. Evoking more positive responses from others might enhance these children's development even further.

phenylketonuria (PKU)
a hereditary metabolic disorder caused by a double dose of a recessive gene that blocks amino acid breakdown

PKU. **Phenylketonuria (PKU)** is a metabolic disorder caused by a double dose of a recessive gene. If a child inherits this gene from *both* parents, his or her body will not produce the enzyme that breaks down the amino acid phenylalanine. High levels of this amino acid circulating through the bloodstream kill nerve cells, causing irreversible brain damage. However, if the disorder is diagnosed shortly after birth and the child is put on a phenylalanine-free diet (eliminating milk and other high-protein foods), little or no damage occurs. The genes are still there, but their effects are barely noticeable. PKU, then, is another case of gene-environment interaction: Only under certain environmental conditions—that is, when there are no dietary restrictions—does the potential of the gene express itself phenotypically.

Sickle-cell anemia. Some genetic disorders affect certain populations more than others. Sickle-cell anemia is an example. (Sickle cells are red blood cells bent in the shape of a sickle.) About 1 in every 100 Americans carries the

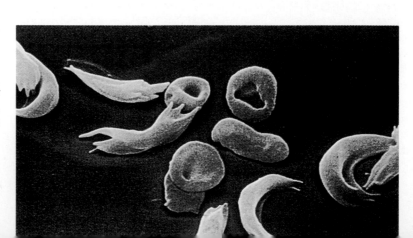

The crescent-shaped red blood cell signaling sickle-cell anemia appears in a high proportion of Hispanic and black Americans. In tropical regions, where those populations once lived, the sickle-cell gene confers immunity to malaria.

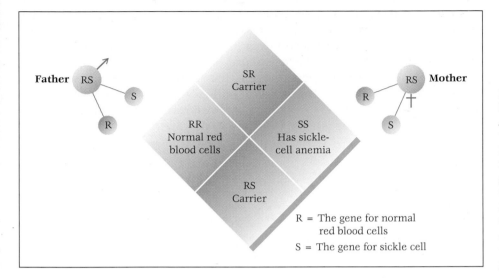

Father RS   S

R

SR
Carrier

RR
Normal red
blood cells

SS
Has sickle-
cell anemia

RS
Carrier

R = The gene for normal
     red blood cells

S = The gene for sickle cell

RS   **Mother**
R

S

**Figure 2.4
Inheritance of Sickle-Cell
Anemia**
*This chart indicates the proba-
bility that a man and woman
who both carry the sickle-cell
gene will have a child who has
the disease, carries the trait, or
has normal red blood cells. But
it is only a probability chart. In
actuality, their children's geno-
types depend on which sperm
fertilizes which egg.*

recessive sickle-cell gene; but among Hispanic-Americans, the ratio is 1 in 20,
and among black Americans, it is 1 in 10. Why does this disorder affect these
groups more than others? An allele that is carried on the same chromosome as
the sickle-cell allele provides protection from malaria; so in the tropical regions
of Africa, Central America, and the Caribbean, where malaria is common, the
trait is adaptive. People who inherited the sickle-cell gene from only one parent
stood a better than average chance of avoiding malaria, surviving childhood,
and bearing children. Some of their children inherited the trait, passed it on to
their children, and so on down many generations. As a result, the sickle-cell gene
is more common in groups that live or once lived in the tropics.

Heterozygotes, who have inherited the sickle-cell gene from only one parent,
have some normal and some sickled red blood cells. Inheriting the gene for
sickled cells provides protection from malaria, and the normal cells ensure that
sufficient oxygen is carried through the system to various organs. But for ho-
mozygotes, who have inherited the gene from both parents, the gene is not adaptive at all. (See Figure 2.4.) A double dose causes painful disabilities. All the red
blood cells are bent in the sickle shape, move slowly, and carry very little oxygen. The effects of a double dose of sickle-cell genes vary from individual to individual. In severe cases, sickle cells cause frequent crises, during which the individual's joints are painfully swollen, heart and kidneys fail, and early death
results. In milder cases, the person experiences frequent shortness of breath and
fatigue. Those afflicted can lead relatively normal lives, although certain situations (especially pregnancy and surgery) create special complications for them.

● *Tay-Sachs disease.* **Tay-Sachs disease** is another selective genetic disorder found mostly among Jewish people of Eastern European descent. Tay-Sachs
resulted from a mutation that remained within a small segment of that population, because for many generations Jews and Gentiles rarely intermarried.
Now, because many Jewish communities have encouraged screening for this genetic disorder, the prevalence of Tay-Sachs disease is declining rapidly among
Jews.

● **Tay-Sachs disease**
a hereditary disorder that
destroys nerve cells, leading to
mental retardation, loss of
muscle control, and death

A child who inherits the Tay-Sachs gene from both parents seems normal and healthy at birth. Then, gradually, development slows. The baby who was initially happy and responsive becomes lethargic; the child who was active becomes helpless, unable to move or even eat. A normally harmless chemical in the brain has built up to poisonous levels, destroying nerve cells. There is no known cure for this disease, and afflicted children rarely survive beyond their third birthday. Fortunately, a simple test can determine whether a man and a woman carry the Tay-Sachs gene, before they conceive.

PREVENTING ABNORMALITIES: GENETIC COUNSELING AND PRENATAL DIAGNOSIS

For Tay-Sachs, and for several other genetic disorders, tests can determine whether one or both prospective parents carry a defective gene *before* they conceive a child. (If only one carries the sickle-cell gene, for example, their child will not develop the disease because it is a recessive trait.) If there is a risk, they can learn through prenatal testing whether a particular fetus is afflicted and either choose to have an abortion or prepare to care for a handicapped child. Help in assessing such risks is provided through both genetic counseling and prenatal diagnosis.

● Genetic Counseling

Genetic counselors are physicians (usually obstetrician/gynecologists) who advise couples on the likelihood that they will conceive a child with a genetic defect. Couples who already have a child with a genetic disorder, whose relatives have a genetic disorder, who belong to an ethnic group known to be at risk, or who have suffered spontaneous abortions should seek genetic counseling.

The counselor begins by taking the couple's family histories, including causes of death of close family members. If there is reason to suspect that a genetic defect runs in one or both families, the counselor will recommend tests to determine whether these individuals are carriers. Tissue samples from the would-be parents are used to produce a profile of each spouse's chromosomes, called a **karyotype.** (Recall that all body cells contain a full set of chromosomes.) Carriers of sickle-cell anemia, Tay-Sachs, hemophilia, and other disorders can be identified this way.

Genetic counselors can inform a couple of their risk of bearing a child with a genetic disorder, but they *cannot* tell the couple whether a particular conception will produce a disabled child. If both parents carry a harmful recessive gene, the risk is 1 in 4, just as the "risk" of having a child with blue eyes is 1 in 4 if both parents carry the recessive blue-eyes gene. Most important, genetic counselors cannot tell the couple whether to take the risk. If the couple does conceive, prenatal testing can reveal the presence of certain (not all) genetic defects in the fetus. However, these tests are not foolproof, and they have raised controversial issues.

● **karyotype**
a profile of an individual's chromosomes created from a tissue sample

For example, amniocentesis is used as a means of detecting Down syndrome, a genetic disorder discussed on pages 50–52. For most women over 35 the results are negative, but what if tests show that the fetus *has* Down syndrome? The question of abortion presents a very difficult choice for many couples. Down syndrome children are mentally and physically handicapped, to be sure, but many can lead reasonably content (if not entirely normal) lives. Children with hemophilia or sickle-cell anemia are not retarded but usually experience bouts of intense pain and require frequent, expensive medical treatment. Can the couple afford to care for a severely handicapped child, emotionally as well as financially? Is it fair to their other children? Fair to the child? Some argue that it is morally wrong to deny a child life because he or she is not perfect. Others maintain that it is wrong for a couple to burden society with a child who will require lifelong support when they might have a healthy child from another pregnancy. These questions are being debated by scientists, clergy, and philosophers—and by anyone interested in the ethical dilemmas posed by the advances of technology.

A good example of this comes from looking at the impact of diagnostic technology in different cultures. In certain Asian countries, for example, where male infants are preferred over female infants for economic reasons, prenatal diagnosis has been used simply to identify the sex of the fetus, and such information has been used by parents in deciding whether to abort a pregnancy. In fact, outrage among Indian women about using the procedure in this fashion has led to bans on some diagnostic tests for any purposes other than diagnosing suspected genetic disorders (Weisman, 1988).

Another unanticipated consequence of the new technology is the illusion that physicians can guarantee parents a healthy child. They cannot. Prenatal tests identify only a small number of disorders, and no test is perfect. Couples of Eastern European descent can be screened for the Tay-Sachs gene, but the test isn't foolproof. If the test is negative, but the baby is born with Tay-Sachs, does the couple have the right to sue the doctor and the laboratory involved in the testing? Should doctors be held responsible for the birth of an imperfect child? Even those who believe they should be recognize that the costs of medical insurance for obstetricians, and hence the costs of prenatal care, have risen sharply because of the rise in malpractice suits.

● Prenatal Diagnosis

A generation ago, there was no way of knowing whether a baby would be genetically normal until the child was born (or in some cases, as with Tay-Sachs disease, until even later). Today there are a number of tests for identifying genetic disorders while the child is still unborn, or *in utero.* Couples who are known to carry genetic defects and women who are over 35 (and thus have a higher risk of bearing a child with Down syndrome or other disorders) are advised to take these tests.

The most widely used procedure for prenatal diagnosis is **amniocentesis.** A doctor inserts a syringe into the pregnant woman's uterus, drawing out some of the amniotic fluid that surrounds the fetus. This fluid contains some of the fetus's own cells, which are then analyzed in the laboratory for genetic defects. Because a complete set of chromosomes is analyzed, this test also tells parents the sex of the fetus.

● **amniocentesis**
a medical technique for diagnosing genetic abnormalities *in utero* by analysis of the amniotic fluid

● **ultrasonography**
a technique that produces a picture from sound waves bounced off the fetus; used for diagnosing development problems *in utero*

● **chorionic villus biopsy**
a prenatal diagnostic technique that analyzes cells taken from hairlike villi on the embryonic sac for genetic problems

Amniocentesis is usually accompanied by **ultrasonography** (ultrasound), in which sound waves bounce off the fetus, producing a picture, or *sonogram,* on a screen. Ultrasound by itself has become a very common prenatal diagnostic technique. The sonogram enables physicians to look for visible defects, which may or may not be genetic in origin. These procedures are highly accurate, relatively painless, and almost risk-free. Complications develop in fewer than 1 in 1,000 cases (Globus et al., 1979). The main drawback is that amniocentesis cannot be performed until the fourth month of pregnancy, and results take 3 to 4 weeks. By this time the fetus is nearly 20 weeks old; deciding whether to have an abortion that far into a pregnancy can be an exceedingly painful choice.

A newer test for detecting serious genetic defects is **chorionic villus biopsy.** CVB can be performed 6 to 8 weeks after conception, and results are available immediately. In this procedure, a physician extracts cells from the hairlike projections, or villi, attached to the sac surrounding the fetus. Results, available within a few days, can detect Down syndrome, Tay-Sachs disease, and other disorders; but neural tube defects cannot be detected this early. The risk of failure and of spontaneous abortion is slightly higher for CVB than for amniocentesis, (0.8 percent) (Rhoads et al., 1989). A very small number of CVB babies have been born with limb defects, but the evidence suggests that in those cases the test was not performed correctly.

When the fetus is believed to be at risk for developing spinal or brain abnormalities, a maternal blood test can be performed between the fourteenth and twentieth weeks of pregnancy. The fetus's liver produces a protein known as alpha feto-protein (AFP), some of which leaks into the mother's bloodstream. Normally, at this point in pregnancy, AFP levels in the mother's blood are low; high levels indicate that something *may* be wrong. We emphasize "may" because this test is not highly reliable. The mother's blood levels of AFP may be elevated for a number of reasons. According to the American College of Obstetricians and Gynecologists, if 1,000 women are tested, about 50 will have abnormal AFP levels. Further testing will reveal that only 1 or 2 carry a fetus with a neural tube defect.

In the near future, techniques similar to those now used for diagnosis may be used to actually correct defects before the fetus is born. Physicians have already used ultrasonography to aid in performing life-saving surgery on a fetus. Researchers are working on techniques to correct enzyme and vitamin deficiencies *in utero.* Someday it may even be possible to correct the genetic defects that cause Down syndrome and other disorders.

PRENATAL DEVELOPMENT

● **prenatal development**
development during the period before birth

From a single fertilized cell a human being develops in just 9 months. In every normal fetus a head forms, limbs take shape, organs develop, nerve cells connect, blood begins to circulate, movement begins—all in sequence, according to a common human pattern. This period before birth, the time of **prenatal development,** was carved by millions of years of evolution.

Students often assume that genes govern prenatally, but that after birth, environment rules. This is wrong. *Genetic and environmental factors interact from the beginning.* The mother's diet during pregnancy, whether she drinks alcohol, smokes, uses drugs, or takes medication—all play a major role in determining her baby's health and alertness at birth, and often for a long time after. Her physical surroundings, even the time in which she lives, strongly affect development as well. Wars, famines, and environmental pollution can hurt the fetus even more than they harm the living. We turn first to the universal path of prenatal development. Then we examine environmental factors that can disrupt that path.

Like most other large mammals, humans have a long **gestation** (the period before birth), small "litters," large brains, long life spans, and complex social behavior. Yet, unlike other large mammals, we are relatively helpless and undeveloped at birth. Baby zebras kick attackers and run with the herd after birth, but a human newborn is virtually helpless. In fact, compared to other animals, human babies are embryos at birth and for much of the first year of life (Gould, 1976). Developments that occur *in utero* in many other species happen after birth in humans, a fact that can have serious consequences for the child.

Unlike other species who mature in the relative quiet and calm of the uterus, we are exposed to all kinds of physical, social, and cultural influences while maturing. No other animal is as good at learning or as dependent on learning—throughout the life span—as we are. Moreover, because of our long period of immaturity outside the uterus, it is possible for each individual (even members of the same family) to be exposed to somewhat different environmental influences during maturation, contributing to variations among individuals.

Although we are still immature at birth, human anatomy, physiology, and behavior begin to take shape much earlier than you would probably predict. The human heart begins beating 3 to 4 weeks after conception, and thumb sucking begins long before birth. We turn now to the three major stages of prenatal development: the germinal period, the embryonic period, and the fetal period.

● The Germinal Period

The **germinal period** includes the first 2 weeks of fetal development. The 4 days immediately following conception are the fastest period of growth in the entire human life span. Within hours after their contact in a fallopian tube, the ovum and sperm fuse to become a unique new cell, the **zygote.** The zygote travels down the fallopian tube to the uterus. As it moves along, cell division by mitosis (when a cell divides and the chromosomes are copied identically) occurs, beginning sometime during the first day after conception. The single fertilized

● **gestation**
the period of prenatal development

● **germinal period**
the first 2 weeks of prenatal development

● **zygote**
the fertilized cell resulting from the fusion of the ovum and sperm

Four days after fertilization, the human zygote has grown to a blastula, 60 to 70 cells shaped in a hollow ball. Now it is ready to begin implantation into the uterine wall.

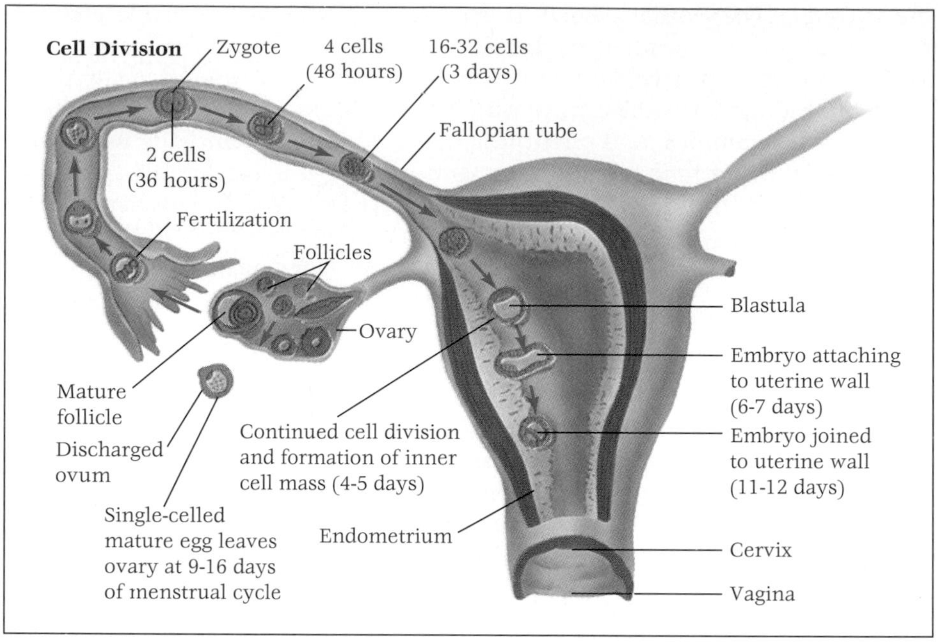

**Figure 2.5
Early Human
Development: The
Germinal Period**

*The drawing depicts the female
reproductive system, the fertilization of the ovum, and the
early growth of the embryo.*

● **blastula**
the hollow-ball form the new
organism takes from about 4
days to 2 weeks following
conception

● **embryonic disk**
the cells on the outer edge of
the blastula, which will develop
into the embryo

● **villi**
hairlike projections from the
blastula that burrow into the
uterine lining

● **implantation**
the process by which the
blastula attaches to the uterus

cell divides into two, these cells divide to produce four, those four divide into
eight, and so on—each with an identical set of chromosomes. By day 4 the new
organism consists of 60 to 70 cells, arranged in the form of a hollow ball called
a **blastula.**

Even before the blastula reaches the uterus, development has begun; cells on
the outer edge of the blastula join on one side and become the **embryonic disk,**
out of which the baby will develop. The other cells will develop into the structures that will protect and nourish the baby (the placenta, the umbilical cord,
and the amniotic sac, described below).

When it reaches the uterus, the blastula floats freely for a day or two. Then it
begins to develop microscopic, threadlike **villi,** whose job is to burrow into the
blood-rich lining of the uterus. (These are the villi that are sampled in the prenatal diagnostic technique chorionic villus biopsy, discussed earlier.) When the
villi make contact, blood vessels in the uterine lining burst, providing the zygote with its first nourishment. It is the villi that attach the blastula to the
mother, a process known as **implantation.** Full implantation occurs by the
twelfth day after fertilization. Even though the mother probably does not yet
know she is pregnant, the new organism is already "seeking" contact and nourishment. Figure 2.5 illustrates the events that take place during the germinal period, from conception through implantation. Implantation initiates the second
phase of prenatal development, the embryonic period.

● *Twins.* A normal exception to this process leads to the development of
twins. As you read earlier, identical twins form when a single zygote (a single
ovum, fertilized by a single sperm) divides into identical halves, each then developing independently but identically. These twins are called *monozygotic* because of their one-cell origin. It is not known why a zygote divides in this way.
When two ova are fertilized by two sperm, two genetically different zygotes form,
resulting in fraternal, or *dizygotic,* twins. These twins are no more alike genetically than any siblings.

● The Embryonic Period

During the **embryonic period** (weeks 2 through 8), a cluster of cells grows to resemble a tiny baby. This is the period of structural development, when all the parts of the body are formed.

● *Support systems.* Throughout gestation, the embryo and later the fetus are kept alive by three organs that form a vital support system: the placenta, umbilical cord, and amniotic sac. Present in rudimentary form at implantation, these structures mature during the embryonic period.

Almost as remarkable as the embryo itself is the **placenta.** This disk-shaped organ that forms along the wall of the uterus between the mother and the baby is a highly sophisticated organ of exchange. In the mature placenta, blood vessels from the mother and baby meet but do not actually merge. The placenta membranes form a barrier, sometimes preventing the mother's blood cells, which may carry harmful substances, from entering the fetus's bloodstream. The embryo is attached to the placenta through its **umbilical cord**—the lifeline that brings the embryo oxygen, water, and nutrients gathered from the mother's bloodstream in the placenta. Through the umbilical cord, too, carbon monoxide and other wastes from the embryo's bloodstream are carried back to the placenta and then pass into the mother's system for disposal (see Figure 2.6). Nourishment is not all the placenta provides. It maintains sufficient hormone levels so that menstruation does not occur during pregnancy. It also helps

● **embryonic period**
the second stage of prenatal development, from 2 to 8 weeks after conception

● **placenta**
the organ along the uterine wall where nutrients and oxygen from the mother and wastes from the baby are exchanged

● **umbilical cord**
the lifeline attaching the embryo (and fetus) to the placenta; it transports maternal nutrients from, and wastes to, the placenta

Figure 2.6
The Placenta at Work
The chorionic villi attached to the amniotic sac each house a blood vessel. Maternal blood fills the spaces around the villi, and exchange of materials takes place across the layer separating the maternal and fetal blood supplies. Thus the bloods never merge.
(SOURCE: After Postlethwait & Hopson, 1989.)

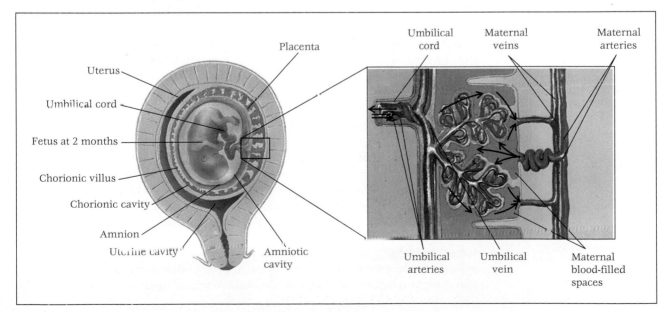

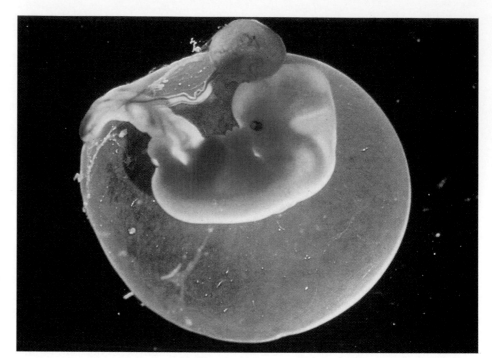

A 6-week-old human embryo floating in amniotic fluid. The dark spot is the retina of the eye; the arms and legs have budded; the heart is beating. The brain has three parts, with a large space at the base that will be filled by later growth. The placenta appears above the embryo, attached by the umbilical cord.

● **amniotic sac**
the protective, fluid-filled membrane surrounding the embryo and fetus

● **endoderm**
the innermost layer of the embryo, which will become the internal organs

● **mesoderm**
the middle layer of the embryo, which will become the skeleton and muscles

● **ectoderm**
the outer layer of the embryo, which will eventually become the skin and nervous system

● **differentiation**
the process by which groups of cells descended from the same zygote become specialized for the various tissues and organs

protect the embryo from the risk of infection. As the pregnancy continues, hormones released by the placenta prepare the mother's breasts to produce milk. Hormones from the placenta also trigger the uterine contractions that will deliver the baby.

The **amniotic sac** is a protective membrane that surrounds the embryo and grows with it. Filled with fluid, the amniotic sac cushions the baby from shocks caused by the mother's movements. Suspension in fluid also facilitates the fetus's own movements at a later stage of prenatal development.

In the first weeks of the embryonic period, the implanted blastula develops three distinct layers of cells. The innermost layer, the **endoderm,** will develop into the gut and related organs; the middle layer, the **mesoderm,** will become the skeleton and muscles; and the outer layer, the **ectoderm,** will give rise to the nervous system and the skin. At first the cells in each layer are indistinguishable from each other, yet invisible chemical changes are already taking place. Although all the embryo's cells are descended from the same fertilized egg and contain the same genes, some will develop into kidney cells and others into heart cells; some become blood cells and others branching nerve cells. This process, called **differentiation,** seems to be regulated by the chemical environment in and around the cells. As the embryo matures, some genes are activated by chemical messages to switch "on" while others remain "off."

The development of the blastula's three layers of cells into specialized tissues and organs follows a universal timetable. During the third week of gestation (the first week of the embryonic period), the heart takes shape, and the neural tube starts to develop. (The neural tube is the beginning of the nervous system; it develops into the spinal column.) By the end of week 4, the neural tube has closed and the brain is forming. If the neural tube remains open, the embryo has the defect called spina bifida. In week 5, limb buds are putting out dimpled shoots that will become hands and feet, and stalked eye cups have grown from the brain. The ears and teeth appear in week 6. In the seventh and eighth weeks, the embryo's face looks human, its limbs are hinged on joints, rudimentary hands and feet have appeared, and a primitive genital bud has formed. By the end of week 8, the internal organs are in place, and some have begun to function. Although the embryo *is barely an inch long,* it has all (or most) of the makings of a human being.

If a serious error occurs during the embryonic period—say, the basic structure of the heart or lungs is impaired—development usually stops. Spontaneous abortions are nature's way of reducing the frequency of birth defects. Examination of miscarried embryos suggests that most would have had an extremely small chance of survival if they had endured long enough to be born.

● The Fetal Period

Once the basic structure of a human being has been established in the embryonic period, prenatal development moves into its final and longest stage, the **fetal period** (8 weeks on, or the third through the ninth months). Whereas the major theme of the embryonic period was differentiation, the major themes of the fetal period are growth and maturation.

● **fetal period**
the third and final stage of prenatal development, from 8 weeks to birth

At the end of the third month, the fetus is about 3 inches long and weighs about ¾ of an ounce. The fourth and fifth months are times of rapid change. The fetus's weight increases tenfold. Eyelids, fingernails, taste buds, sweat glands, and hair form. By the fourth month, the mother has probably felt the "fluttering" or "quickening" of fetal movement. In the fifth month, activity is even more pronounced.

The seventh month is transitional for the fetus. It is about 16 inches long (nearly 80 percent of its final length) and weighs about 4 pounds (roughly 50 percent of its final weight). If it is born in the seventh month, it can survive with medical intervention. During the eighth and ninth months the fetus gains another 3 to 4 pounds, partly in the form of an insulating layer of fat under the skin. Its respiratory system matures, so that it will be able to breathe without help after birth. During the ninth month, the fetus is cramped for space, and

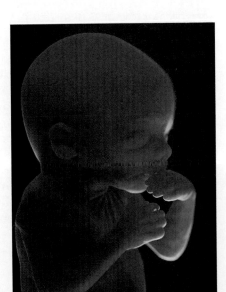

During the fourth and fifth month, the fetus's weight increases tenfold. Eyelids and fingernails have formed.

TABLE 2.2   THE SEQUENCE OF PRENATAL DEVELOPMENT

Period	Time	Developments
		First Trimester
Germinal	0–4 days	Cell division; zygote travels to uterus.
	4–8 days	Beginning of implantation.
	12–13 days	Implantation is completed.
Embryonic	14 days	Placenta begins to develop.
	15–20 days	Rapid development of placenta.
	21–28 days	Eyes start to develop; heart begins to beat; system of blood vessels develops.
	5 weeks	Arm and leg buds form.
	7 weeks	Facial structures connect.
	8 weeks	Major organ development completed.
Fetal	8–12 weeks	Arm and leg movement; emergence of startle and sucking reflex; appearance of genitals; facial expressions occur.
		Second Trimester
	13–16 weeks	Development of skin and hair; skeleton hardens.
	17–20 weeks	Quickening—noticeable movement; heartbeat can be heard.
		Third Trimester
	25–28 weeks	Fat is laid down; can survive (28 weeks) if born prematurely.
	38 weeks	Fetus is plump; testes descend in males.

the mother can feel it squirming to get into a comfortable position. Toward the end of this month, the fetus usually settles in a head down position. The top of its head moves down toward the mother's cervix, and its face turns toward her back. When this happens, the fetus is said to be *engaged*. Birth is imminent. Table 2.2 summarizes the principal stages of prenatal development.

ENVIRONMENTAL INFLUENCES ON PRENATAL DEVELOPMENT

In 1979, when the governor of Pennsylvania learned that something had gone wrong at the Three Mile Island nuclear power plant, he immediately ordered the evacuation of all pregnant women and preschool children within a 5-mile radius. He did not yet know what had happened at the plant, but he was not taking any chances. Unborn children are exceptionally vulnerable, and they may suffer irreversible damage from exposure to substances that cause little or no damage to older children and adults.

● **teratogen**
any substance, influence, or agent that causes birth defects

Any substance, agent, or influence that causes malformation in the developing fetus is a **teratogen** (from the Greek for "monster-creating"). Included are many prescription drugs, viruses, chemical pollutants, and radiation. Teratogens can cause physical or behavioral problems later in life. The most commonly ingested teratogen is alcohol.

Generally, the effect of any harmful substance depends on timing—when the embryo or fetus is exposed. The most vulnerable times occur during **critical periods,** when physical structures and organs are being formed. Parts of the body that are already established are least likely to be harmed. Consequently, teratogens are usually most dangerous during the embryonic period, when the basic structure of the baby is developing. Then, teratogens often lead to spontaneous abortions. Later, effects may vary.

Even when babies appear to be normal at birth, serious side effects of exposure to teratogens can emerge later on. For example, fetuses who were between 8 and 15 weeks old when the atomic bomb was dropped on Hiroshima became mentally retarded. For those children, the time of exposure coincided with a critical period for brain development. Older fetuses who had passed that critical period were at a much lower risk for retardation (Otake & Schull, 1984). (Figure 2.7 shows the critical periods during fetal development.)

● critical periods
periods during gestation when particular developing organs and structures are most vulnerable to environmental influences

Figure 2.7
Critical Periods in Fetal Development
Each organ, system, and body part has its own critical timetable, the period when it is most susceptible to disruption.
(SOURCE: After Moore, 1982.)

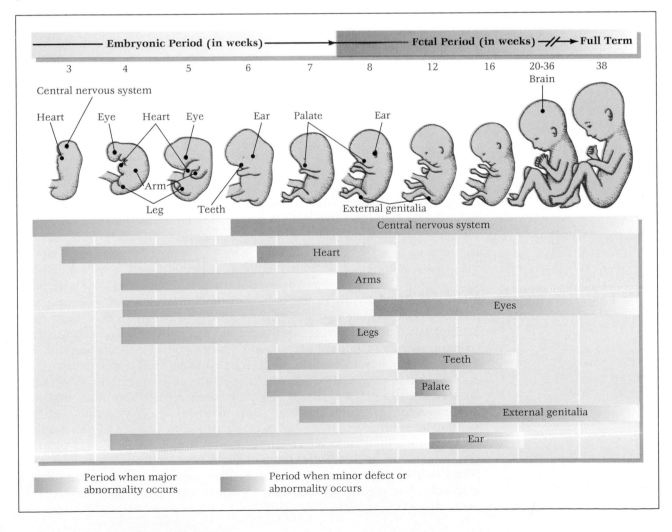

We turn now to the mother's environment—how her health, diet, use of drugs and alcohol, and body chemistry profoundly influence her baby's development. Because the environment that surrounds her affects the fetus as well, we will also discuss pollutants in the larger environment.

● Nutrition and Development

Studies of European women who gave birth during World War II made the effects of nutrition on prenatal development painfully clear. In Holland, where the Nazis severely restricted food supplies, most babies were born smaller than average, especially if the mother had gone hungry during the last trimester of pregnancy (Antonov, 1947).

A woman's diet during pregnancy affects both prenatal and *postnatal* development. In addition, women whose diets have been poor *before* pregnancy also run a greater risk of delivering low-birth-weight babies. Both early births and low birth weights are associated with a host of medical and behavioral problems (see Chapters 3 and 4). In short, a lifetime of nutritional experience shapes the environment of the developing child.

● *Malnutrition and the brain.*
Both anatomical and behavioral evidence indicate that nutrition affects brain development. During the first 6 months of pregnancy, the most important aspect of brain development is cell *division*—the multiplication of brain cells. We are born with all the brain cells we'll ever have, and the mature human brain has about 100 *billion* cells. During the last 3 months of pregnancy (and the first 2 years of life) brain development consists of cell *growth* (Winick, 1970). In several studies, autopsies of malnourished children revealed that their brain cells were both small in number and small in size (R. Brown, 1966; Naerye, Diener, & Dellinger, 1969). In addition, fetal malnutrition may disrupt **myelinization,** the process by which nerves become insulated by a layer of myelin, which forms a fatty sheath. Myelinization increases the speed and efficiency of neural transmission, the passage of nerve impulses from nerve to nerve throughout the body. Lack of such insulation is one reason that fetal malnutrition is associated with subsequent mental retardation (Davison & Dobbing, 1966). (Nutrition after birth is also important to the continuing myelinization process, as we'll see in Chapter 4.)

● **myelinization**
the process by which nerves become insulated with myelin, which forms a fatty sheath

To learn more about the consequences of malnutrition, researchers have compared the babies of poor women in third world countries who have been given food supplements to the babies of other poor women who were not (Habicht et al., 1974; Read et al., 1973). In one study in Bogotá, Colombia, mothers in the experimental group were given medical care plus food supplements (cooking oil, dry skim milk, and protein-enriched bread). Mothers in the control group were given the same medical care but no food supplements. At 15 days, the babies of mothers in the experimental group were more alert visually and responded to visual stimuli in a more sophisticated way than babies of mothers in the control group (Vuori et al., 1979).

A related study found that early nutrition can have long-term consequences for social development as well (Barrett, Radke-Yarrow, & Klein, 1982). In this research, prenatal supplements for the mothers were followed by supplements for the babies from birth to age 2. At ages 6 to 8, these children were interested in their environment, able to express anger and happiness, and actively involved with their age-mates. In contrast, children from similar villages where supplements were not available tended to be passive, dependent on adults, and anxious with their peers. The researchers hypothesized that babies who are alert, energetic, and responsive elicit more attention from their mothers than apathetic babies. As a result, they have more opportunities to learn basic skills for relating to other people, skills that carry over into friendships with peers when they begin to move beyond their family. Malnourished babies are less energetic, less demanding, and generally less emotionally rewarding to parents. As a result, they receive less attention and have fewer opportunities to learn basic social skills. In addition, malnourished babies often have malnourished mothers who simply lack the energy to offer stimulating care. News reports and pictures from Somalia and Ethiopia vividly tell us how widespread and tragic this problem has become.

A recent study of Guatemalan children shows the fascinating interplay between social context, nutrition, and infant development (Engle, 1991). This study found that infants' nutrition and growth varied as a function of whether their mother worked (and if so, what her wages were), how much of the family income was provided by the mother, and whether the infants were cared for by adults or by preadolescent siblings. The effects of maternal employment were complicated by factors such as poverty and child care. Thus, if maternal employment increased family income (and, in particular, the proportion of family income provided by the mother), the infant benefited, in part because the higher income allowed for better nutrition. But if maternal employment meant that the infant's primary caregiver was another child, the infant's growth suffered, presumably because of the lower-quality stimulation. We can see from this study that even something as basic as nutrition must be studied within a social context.

Infant malnutrition is not just a problem in faraway places. In the United States, 17 percent of children live in poverty, which (with Australia) equals the highest percentage in 11 industrialized countries (U.S. Government report, cited

Meals supplied by agencies such as CARE and other relief groups can help to offset the developmental consequences of poor nutrition.

in *The New York Times,* March 19, 1990). One of the most important correlates of malnutrition is low birth weight (see pp. 103–104). One in fourteen babies is born with low birth weight each year (Southern Regional Project on Infant Mortality, 1993), many to mothers who abused drugs or alcohol, and many others to women who simply did not have enough to eat or ate poorly. More distressingly, the prevalence of low-birth-weight youngsters *increased* between 1985 and 1990, particularly in regions with a high proportion of African-American families (Southern Regional Project on Infant Mortality, 1993). African-American mothers are almost twice as likely as European-Americans to give birth to low-birth-weight infants (Southern Regional Project on Infant Mortality, 1993; Taffel, 1989). On average, African-American infants weigh almost 338 grams less than European-American infants.

While the numbers are clear, the reasons for them are not. These differences are not all attributable to differences in income and physical health (Abell et al., 1991). Some researchers have speculated that the psychological and social stressors experienced disproportionately among African-Americans—for instance, living in crowded, dangerous environments—may contribute to the higher rate of infant mortality and of low-birth-weight deliveries in this group (Southern Regional Project on Infant Mortality, 1993). Interestingly, the rate of low birth weight among Hispanic infants, especially those of Mexican or Cuban ancestry, is comparable to that of white infants, although it does appear that the prevalence of low birth weight is higher among Puerto Rican infants than white infants (Garcia Coll, 1990).

Fortunately, many children can recover from the effects of early malnutrition. In one observational study, Korean children who were early victims of malnutrition were adopted by American families, who provided three nutritious meals a day. Most of these children performed about as well on intelligence tests as their age-mates in this country, whose families had never experienced hunger. However, those Korean children who had been severely deprived did not do as well on these tests as their Korean age-mates whose poverty had been less severe (Winick, Meyers, & Harris, 1975).

Most children who suffer from prenatal malnutrition are not magically transported to a life of plenty after they are born. As we will see in Chapter 4, for all too many children, here and abroad, the effects of prenatal malnutrition are compounded by the effects of postnatal poverty.

● Drugs

● *Prescription drugs and aspirin.* During the 1950s, 8,000 babies in 28 countries were born with severely deformed arms and legs. The environmental catastrophe was an internal one. These babies' mothers had taken the drug thalidomide. Physicians had prescribed it to combat sleeplessness and nausea during the early stages of pregnancy, the time when arms and legs are forming.

Babies whose mothers had taken thalidomide between the thirty-eighth and forty-sixth days of pregnancy were born with deformed arms or no arms, those exposed to the drug between the fortieth and forty-sixth days of pregnancy had deformed legs or no legs, and those whose mothers had taken thalidomide after the fiftieth day were born with normal limbs. Most of the severely deformed thalidomide babies did not survive. Animal testing of thalidomide had shown no harmful side effects (Schardein, 1976).

Even after the thalidomide tragedy, many prescription drugs still do not carry a warning to women who think they may be pregnant. Any drug the mother takes may pass through the placenta into the fetus's bloodstream. And even drugs that may help the mother—such as the antibiotics streptomycin and tetracycline, or megadoses of certain vitamins—can harm the fetus.

The best policy for any woman who thinks she may be pregnant is to be cautious. Avoid all drugs, unless the drug is essential to health. Always let a physician know about a possible pregnancy before taking any prescription or undergoing any medical procedures, particularly X rays.

Even aspirin can harm a fetus. Frequent use during pregnancy can lower birth weight and increase the risk of fetal or infant death both before and shortly after birth (Corby, 1978; Turner & Collins, 1975). Children whose mothers used aspirin frequently during pregnancy have also shown lowered IQs and poorer small and large muscle coordination at age 4 (Barr et al., 1990). Women who used the aspirin substitute acetaminophen did not put their children at risk (Barr et al., 1990; Streissguth et al., 1987).

● *Marijuana, heroin, and cocaine.* Even stronger cautions apply to illegal drugs, such as marijuana, heroin, and cocaine. Isolating the effects of a single drug is difficult, since women who use illegal drugs often use more than one, and drug use is correlated with a host of other factors known to be harmful to fetal development, including malnutrition, stress, and poverty. But scientists' best guess is that illegal drugs are indeed dangerous to the fetus, often causing problems far into childhood as well.

Marijuana use during pregnancy can impair the fetus's central nervous system (Osofsky, 1987), and even though the evidence is mixed (Day et al., 1991b), frequent use can lead to complications during pregnancy, retarded fetal growth, low birth weight, prematurity, and even death in the first days of life (Lester & Dreher, 1989; Zuckerman et al., 1989). Moreover, preschoolers whose mothers used marijuana during pregnancy continue to have sleep difficulties at age 3 (Dahl et al., 1989) and perform poorly on verbal and memory tests at age 4 (Fried & Watkinson, 1990).

Babies whose mothers used heroin during pregnancy are born addicted and are also at risk for dying within the first days or weeks of life (Ostrea & Chavez, 1979). Those who live suffer from withdrawal symptoms, such as sleeplessness, irritability, and tremors (Fricker & Segal, 1978; Strauss et al., 1975). Difficult to care for, these babies are often neglected or even abused. In turn, these children are likely to become more difficult.

Cocaine is the most commonly used illicit drug among American women of childbearing age (Hawley & Disney, 1992). Somewhere between 10 and 20 percent of youngsters are believed to be exposed to cocaine prenatally. Using cocaine—and its more concentrated smokable form, crack—during pregnancy puts babies at risk in almost every area of development. They are likely to be born premature; they weigh less and are smaller than average, all signs of retarded intrauterine growth (Hadeed & Siegel, 1989; Handler et al., 1991; Petitti & Coleman, 1990; Zuckerman et al., 1989). Typically, cocaine-addicted newborns have high blood pressure, putting them at risk for hemorrhaging and brain damage (van de Bor, Walther, & Ebrahimi, 1990; van de Bor, Walther, & Sims, 1990). They also show signs of neurological damage, becoming either overexcited or depressed. Highly excited babies cry excessively, making a distinctive high-pitched sound. Irritable and jittery, they are hard to feed and have problems sleeping. Depressed addicted babies withdraw from people and from other stimuli as well (Lester et al., 1991). Like heroin-addicted infants, cocaine babies are caught in a negative cycle: Their behavior makes them hard to care for; unresponsive, rejecting parents or caregivers increase their difficulties. And their problems do not end with infancy.

Infants exposed to cocaine during pregnancy develop specific language abilities later than other children, at least until they are 2½ years old (van Baar, 1990). (Additional research may reveal what happens as these children get older.) As toddlers, their attention to toys is less focused; they play for less time and in less sophisticated ways than children who had not been exposed to cocaine (Rodning, Beckwith, & Howard, 1989). Women who consider themselves merely "recreational" cocaine users may unknowingly risk their baby's health if they take cocaine before they know they are pregnant.

Emotionally, these children suffer as well. At 15 months, their ties to their mothers are less secure than those of other children, apparently because the care they received as infants was less emotionally supportive. Indeed, substance-abusing mothers who were observed with their infants at 3 months and again at 9 months were more rejecting and insensitive to their infants' distresses than mothers who did not use drugs (Rodning, Beckwith, & Howard, 1992).

Even the effects of prenatal exposure to cocaine are influenced by the environment, however. For drug-exposed babies, all too often it is an environment with inadequate access to both prenatal and postnatal health services (Mayes et al., 1992; Zuckerman & Frank, 1992). You can imagine, therefore, that it is extremely difficult to isolate the "pure" effects of cocaine on youngsters. Cocaine-exposed babies are more likely to come from poor families, from unstable home environments, and to have clinically depressed mothers (Hawley & Disney, 1992). But even among cocaine-exposed infants, there is considerable diversity in development. If environmental conditions can be modified, the negative effects of the drug may be reduced.

● *Alcohol.* When a pregnant women drinks, so does her fetus. Alcohol crosses the placental membrane almost immediately, enters the fetal bloodstream, and stays there for a long time, depressing central nervous system activity (Landesman-Dwyer, 1981). As with heroin and cocaine, prenatal exposure to alcohol affects physical, cognitive, and social development, often throughout life. It may also end the fetus's chance to be born. While adults can drink tonight and be fine tomorrow, drinking is always unsafe for fetuses. Pregnant women who drink even a little wine or an occasional cocktail still have a higher-than-average risk of spontaneous abortion (Harlap et al., 1979) or stillbirths (birth of a dead fetus) (Kaminski, Rumeau, & Schwartz, 1978). Their babies are also at risk for both major and minor birth defects (Oyellette et al., 1977).

Children with the severest problems are those whose mothers are alcoholics. From birth, they show a group of physical and behavioral symptoms, known together as **fetal alcohol syndrome (FAS).** These include:

● Mental retardation, poor motor development, hyperactivity, and limited attention span

● Retarded growth, both before birth and throughout childhood, even with an adequate appetite

● **fetal alcohol syndrome (FAS)**
a group of symptoms—including cognitive, motor, and growth retardation—suffered by some children of alcoholic mothers

- Distinctive facial characteristics, including short eye slits, low nasal bridge, short nose, indistinct ridges between nose and mouth, narrow upper lip, small chin, flat midface, and drooping eyelids (Streissguth, Landesman-Dwyer, Martin, & Smith, 1980).

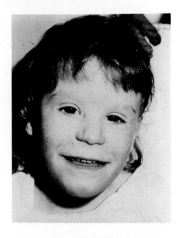

This child, with the facial features characteristic of fetal alcohol syndrome, was born to an alcoholic mother.

Estimates for babies born with FAS range from 1 per 1,000 live births in France, to 1 per 750 in the United States, to 1 per 600 in Sweden (Landesman-Dwyer, 1981). Higher still are the number of babies born to "social drinkers." Even moderate drinking has long-term effects, and they show up on the first day of life. In one study of newborns, the amount of alcohol consumed by the mother during pregnancy was related to increased body tremors, decreased alert periods, and less vigorous body movements in the infant (Landesman-Dwyer, Keller, & Streissguth, 1978).

From infancy at least through age 11, the effects of prenatal exposure to alcohol show up in every area of development: physical, behavioral, emotional, and cognitive. Smaller infants are smaller 3-year-olds (Day et al., 1990, 1991a). Four-year-olds have poorer small and large muscle coordination. Interestingly, mothers who drank *before* they knew they were pregnant were more likely to have children with motor problems, suggesting that it is not good enough for a woman to simply stop drinking after she learns that she is pregnant (Barr et al., 1990).

Emotionally, the children of women who drank moderately to heavily during pregnancy have much in common with cocaine babies. Like them, at 1 year old, they tend to be insecurely tied to their mothers, perhaps because of the effects of drinking on mothering behavior. Perhaps too, as with cocaine babies, alcohol-exposed babies are harder to care for and less likely to get the loving support that they need (O'Connor, Sigman, & Brill, 1987). These babies offer a clear, though sad, example of interaction in development. Physically compromised even before birth by toxins in their environment, they are born to mothers who may be unable to care for them properly. At the same time, the babies themselves are more irritable than most and hard to comfort. The emotional feedback between infant and mother can quickly become more negative than nurturing.

As you might predict, these babies also show cognitive and behavioral problems, linked, again, to the mother's consumption of alcohol. At 4 years old, children whose mothers had 1½ ounces of alcohol per day during pregnancy scored about 5 points lower on IQ tests than children who had not been exposed to alcohol prenatally (Streissguth et al., 1989). They also had poorer attention spans, appeared more fidgety, and were less likely to comply with parental demands than children of nondrinking mothers (Landesman-Dwyer, Ragozin, & Little, 1982; Streissguth et al., 1984). At 7 years of age these children still showed a shortened attention span (what psychologists call an *attention deficit*) that compromises their ability to concentrate on class work and succeed in school (Streissguth et al., 1986).

At 11 years old, children who had been exposed to varying levels of alcohol prenatally showed a range of problems that affected their success in school. Greater exposure was linked to more serious problems, but *all* of the children were affected to some degree. Teachers found them slower than other children to settle down and work; they did not persist in their work; and they were less interested in reading than children who had not been exposed to alcohol. These children also had difficulties with reading comprehension, arithmetic reasoning, word recognition, and spelling skills. In all cases, the greater the exposure to alcohol, the greater the problem (Olson et al., 1992). (In Chapter 3, we discuss the special risks experienced by low-birth-weight and alcohol-exposed babies.)

● *Nicotine.* Evidence that *smoking* is harmful to the embryo and fetus began to build in the 1940s and 1950s. Although it was largely ignored, today the evidence is overwhelming. Women who smoke increase their risk of spontaneous abortion or stillbirth by 30 to 50 percent, and even full-term babies of smokers typically have lower than average birth weights (Landesman-Dwyer & Emmanuel, 1979). These newborns also may be higher risks for **sudden infant death syndrome (SIDS)** (see Chapter 3).

● **sudden infant death syndrome (SIDS)**
death in early infancy for no apparent reason

Ectopic pregnancy (the fertilized egg starts to develop in the fallopian tube instead of implanting in the uterus) is also more likely among women who smoke (Coste, Job-Spira, & Fernandez, 1991; Stergachis, Scholes, Daling, Weiss, & Chu, 1991). These pregnancies must be surgically ended and can pose a serious threat to the mother's health.

The greatest threat to health among smokers is cancer, and women who smoke during pregnancy put their children at risk as well. In one recent study, children from infancy through age 14 who had cancer were matched with the same aged children who did not have cancer. After controlling for other factors, the results showed that "mother's smoking during the first trimester of pregnancy was associated with an increased risk *for all cancers combined*" (authors' italics) (John, Savitz & Sandler, 1991, p. 123). And passive smoking is just as harmful: When fathers smoked, the results were the same.

Maternal smoking during pregnancy also increases a child's chances for having febrile seizures from infancy through age 5. These seizures, for which no cause can be found, are rare, but the more a mother smokes during pregnancy, the greater the risk for her child (Cassano, Koepsell, & Farwell, 1990). Like alcohol, nicotine has long-term effects on children's behavior and intellectual development, findings backed up by two decades of research. During the 1970s, British and American teams studied 7-year-olds whose mothers had smoked during pregnancy. These children showed poor intellectual and social development, and the older they got, the greater the effects appeared (Butler & Goldstein, 1973; Davie et al., 1972; Nichols, 1977).

Recent studies show similar results. Children whose mothers smoked throughout pregnancy had lower IQs than children whose mothers had smoked 10 or more cigarettes per day but quit during pregnancy. These results appeared even though the researchers controlled for many factors that influence IQ (Sexton, Fox, & Hebel, 1990). In another study, again controlling for other variables, both language development and general intelligence were impaired among 3- and 4-year-olds who had been exposed to cigarettes prenatally (Fried & Watkinson, 1990).

● *Caffeine.* The cup of coffee or the can of cola that spikes an adult's energy can slow down growth in an embryo or a fetus. During pregnancy, heavy daily caffeine consumption (3 cups of coffee, 8 cans of cola) increases the risk of retarded growth and low birth weight. This was demonstrated in a study comparing women who frequently drank coffee, but drank less after conceiving, with women who continued to consume large amounts of coffee during pregnancy

Smoking during pregnancy increases the risk of spontaneous abortion and stillbirth. Low birth weight and long-term effects on behavior have also been observed. Posters like this one urge pregnant women not to smoke.

(Fenster et al., 1991). Although there is no evidence that caffeine causes birth defects, it seems to be related to clumsiness in 4-year-olds. Further research should tell us more about the long-term effects of caffeine (Barr, Streissguth, Darby, & Sampson, 1990). For now, the U.S. Food and Drug Administration simply recommends that pregnant women drink less coffee.

At this point some readers may balk. Perhaps you know women who smoke occasionally, drink socially, and never skipped their morning cup of coffee during pregnancy, yet gave birth to normal, healthy babies. Nevertheless, would you blow smoke into an infant's face or add a little alcohol or coffee to his formula? In effect, this is what a pregnant woman is doing to her fetus. Individual babies react differently to teratogens. By nature, some are heartier or more vulnerable than others. Perhaps the baby whose mother had wine every night with dinner, or just a few cigarettes each day, might have been less fussy, more cuddly, and more curious if the mother had abstained.

● Diseases

● *Rubella.* Most bacteria cannot pass through the placenta, but an embryo or fetus is vulnerable to viruses. Twenty-five years ago, the disease pregnant women feared most was **rubella,** or German measles. Mildly discomforting in adults, rubella has devastating effects on the fetus. Exposure during early development can cause retardation, heart defects, deafness, and blindness. Advances in immunology have all but eliminated this risk. If a woman has had rubella at any time before becoming pregnant, rubella antibodies will show up in a simple medical test. She cannot contract rubella again. Women who haven't had the disease can be vaccinated before becoming pregnant to stimulate the production of these antibodies.

● *Sexually transmitted diseases.* Some of the most serious risks to the fetus are posed by sexually transmitted diseases. The most common among these in the United States today is also the least well-known: **chlamydia.** Infecting between 3 million and 10 million Americans annually, this bacteria-caused disease can leave women sterile. If a pregnant woman contracts chlamydia, her fetus can become infected while moving through the birth canal. Conjunctivitis (an eye inflammation) or (more serious) pneumonia can result. Chlamydia also increases the risk of prematurity and stillbirths. All these consequences can be avoided by diagnosis followed by treatment of chlamydia with specific antibiotics (Wallis, 1985).

Gonorrhea and **syphilis** respond to antibiotics as well, but with syphilis in particular, early detection is crucial. Unlike other bacteria, syphilis bacteria can cross the placenta, infecting the fetus. But penicillin crosses the placenta too, killing the bacteria in the fetus. If left undetected or untreated, or if syphilis is contracted in the fourth month of pregnancy, the fetus may die. If it lives, the baby may suffer blindness, deafness, and/or other deformities. All these consequences are preventable if a man and woman are both tested for syphilis before conceiving a child. This is why most states require a syphilis test before issuing a marriage license.

Genital herpes, a sexually transmitted disease that infects up to 500,000 people each year, is caused by a virus and therefore cannot be treated with antibiotics. The disease may lie dormant for months and then suddenly erupt. Herpes does not affect a baby unless the infection is active at the time of delivery, when the baby may become infected as it passes through the birth canal. Exposure at delivery may cause a localized skin infection, or a more generalized infection, neurological damage, and even death (Nahmias et al., 1975; Peacock & Sorubbi, 1983). Delivering the baby by cesarean section can prevent herpes infection. A mother who knows or suspects she has herpes should inform her obstetrician.

● **rubella**
German measles

● **chlamydia**
a bacterial sexually transmitted disease that can harm the fetus during birth

● **gonorrhea**
a sexually transmitted disease caused by a bacterium

● **syphilis**
a bacterial sexually transmitted disease that can cross the placenta

● **genital herpes**
a sexually transmitted viral disease that can cause damage to the fetus during pregnancy and delivery

The gravest threat to unborn children is the lethal disease **acquired immune deficiency syndrome (AIDS).** When a woman who is infected with the HIV virus becomes pregnant, the virus can cross the placenta, infecting the fetus. It may be too that babies can ingest the HIV virus along with an infected mother's breast milk (Van de Perre et al., 1991). AIDS kills children by weakening their immune systems, making them susceptible to a host of serious diseases.

If current trends continue, by the late 1990s, AIDS may be among the top five causes of death for 1- to 4-year-olds in the United States alone. Already, it is the sixth leading cause of death among young African-American children (Chu et al., 1991).

● *Disease, poverty, and ethnicity.* The poorer health status of minority individuals in the United States translates into poorer health among their infants. Infant mortality is higher among African-Americans, Mexican-Americans, and Native Americans when compared with whites. There are also ethnic differences in the prevalences of specific diseases, owing to both genetic and environmental differences between the groups. African-American and Southeast Asian infants show higher rates of iron deficiency, for example, which is associated with a variety of behavioral and attentional problems (Garcia Coll, 1990).

● The Rh Factor

Here, in a tragic genetic twist, a mother's immune system attacks her own fetus. Most of us are born with a protein on the surface of our red blood cells, the **Rh factor.** If you have it, you are Rh positive; if you lack it, you are Rh negative. Rh makes no difference until a woman becomes pregnant for the first time. Then, if the father is Rh positive but the mother is Rh negative, something very interesting happens. If their first child inherits the dominant gene for Rh from the father, some of its Rh-positive blood cells cross the placenta into the mother's bloodstream just before or during birth, when the infant's blood normally mixes with the mother's. Detecting a foreign substance, her immune system makes antibodies to the Rh-positive cells. If a second child is also Rh positive, the mother's antibodies cross the placenta and attack the fetal blood cells. The baby may then be born deaf or with cerebral palsy, or may die.

None of this need happen. A blood test can identify a woman as Rh positive or negative. Then, shortly after giving birth to her first child, an Rh-negative woman is vaccinated to prevent Rh antibodies from forming in her blood. Tricked, her immune system cannot harm any future pregnancies.

● Environmental Hazards

After atomic bombs were dropped on Hiroshima and Nagasaki in 1945, not one of the pregnant survivors who had been within a mile of the blast gave birth to a live infant. Seventy-five percent of those within 4 miles of the explosion had miscarriages or stillborn babies, and many surviving infants suffered serious deformities and leukemia (Apgar & Beck, 1973). **Radiation** attacks the chromosomes of a fetus, distorting basic hereditary instructions carried by the genes. The greater the exposure, the greater the danger. We still do not know the extent of the damage caused by the Soviet nuclear accident at Chernobyl in 1986, but we can be certain that harm was done. Even low levels of radiation, absorbed through dental X rays, should be avoided during pregnancy. Ultrasound, now used to screen the developing fetus, is not harmful.

● **acquired immune deficiency syndrome (AIDS)**
a deadly viral disease, transmitted through body fluids, that attacks the immune system

● **Rh factor**
a protein found on red blood cells

● **radiation**
an environmental hazard resulting from the emission of radiant energy, such as from an atomic bomb

industrial pollutants
environmental hazards
resulting from the emission
of contaminants in the
atmosphere

PCBs
polychlorinated biphenyls; a
common industrial pollutant

Harder to avoid are the environmental teratogens that come from **industrial pollutants.** Among the most common are **PCBs** (polychlorinated biphenyls). Once widely used in a variety of products, these poisons have been banned since the 1970s. Nevertheless, they are still among the most widespread and persistent environmental contaminants.

The reason lies in the way they are transmitted—through the food chain. When factories spill their wastes into bodies of water, such as lakes or bays, pollutants begin moving into an environment that is first botanical, then animal, and on up the food chain to humans. PCBs dumped into Lake Michigan, for example, were absorbed by aquatic plants which, in turn, were eaten by small fish. Those fish, now contaminated, were food for larger fish, and the PCB trail moved along until it reached the fish that humans eat. Pregnant women who ate salmon and trout from Lake Michigan were exposing their fetuses to dangerous levels of PCBs, even if they ate only two or three fish dinners each month.

When tested at birth, their babies showed poor muscle control and depressed responsiveness; at 7 months they scored below their age level on tests of visual recognition and interest in new stimuli (Jacobson, Jacobson, Fein, & Schwartz, 1984). They also showed higher than normal amounts of PCBs in blood taken from their umbilical cords.

Tested at age 4, these children had several cognitive difficulties that could affect their reading ability (Jacobson et al., 1992). And as with children exposed to a host of other teratogens, they were more active and had less focused attention (Jacobson, Jacobson, & Humphrey, 1990).

Lead, long known as toxic to children and adults, damages fetuses as well. Infants with higher than normal levels of lead in their umbilical cord blood showed some slowing of mental development through age 2 (Bellinger et al., 1987). This finding is particularly disturbing because these children had been exposed to levels of lead previously considered safe. Fetuses may be highly vulnerable to this teratogen, whether exposed by their mothers or their fathers.

Industrial pollutants can affect fetal development in ways that are still being discovered.

Fathers and Fetuses

Even if a woman avoids all known teratogens during her pregnancy, her fetus can still be damaged—by the father's sperm. Toxins in the workplace can put a man's future children at risk for very serious illnesses. Men who work around lead have children who are three times more likely than other children to develop kidney tumors. Jobs with high exposure to paints, solvents, automobile exhausts, and machinery can cause children to have higher rates of brain cancer and leukemia. Working with benzene and other solvents can increase the risk for low birth weight, and "fathers who work in the glass, clay, stone, textile and mining industries sire twice as many premature babies" (The U.S. National Natality and Fetal Mortality Survey, cited in Davis, 1991).

Finally, as we noted earlier, when fathers smoke near their pregnant wives, the nicotine absorbed through the placenta increased the risk of low birth weight (Rubin et al., 1986). And children of fathers who smoked were twice as likely as others to develop cancer as adults (Sandler, Everson, Wilcox, & Browder, 1985).

The Mother's Emotions

Pregnancy evokes mixed emotions. Joyful anticipation alternates with worry and doubt, and even dread is not unusual. In one survey, 87 percent of pregnant women worried about the health of their unborn child, 74 percent were scared about childbirth, and 52 percent feared losing their physical attractiveness (Light & Fenster, 1974).

Anxious women are more likely to have pregnancies marked by pronounced vomiting, toxemia (a condition that can threaten the fetus's life and the mother if left untreated), and other problems. Their babies are more likely to be born prematurely, to have low birth weight, and to suffer from respiratory and stomach problems. Their newborns may be fidgety, irritable, and difficult to soothe (Carlson & Labarba, 1979; Norbeck & Tilden, 1983; Omer & Everly, 1988).

How can maternal emotions influence prenatal development and postnatal behavior? And how is the mother's anxiety transmitted to the fetus? Recent research points again to the impact of chemicals. Stress causes the mother to produce the hormones epinephrine and norepinephrine, which affect her vascular system. High levels of these hormones can reduce the flow of blood to the uterus and/or raise maternal blood pressure. At extremes, these conditions can cause severe risk to the fetus (Abell, 1992).

The best antidotes to maternal anxiety are support and information. A caring mate, relatives and friends, and an empathic obstetrician or nurse-midwife can all ease anxiety. Additionally, information about pregnancy, birth, and babies can allay many fears, especially for first-time mothers. We begin with these topics in the next chapter.

SUMMARY

1. Human conception begins with the process of fertilization. Although it had been believed previously that the process involved an active sperm and a passive ovum, recent research now indicates that the ovum plays a much more active role in orchestrating the event. (See pages 41–43.)

2. When a sperm fertilizes an ovum, the child-to-be inherits one set of chromosomes from the mother and another from the father. Our cells contain not 46 individual chromosomes but 23 pairs of chromosomes. Most inherited traits are determined by the combined effects of many genes. The fact that so many traits are determined by multiple genes has made it quite difficult to map one-to-one correspondences between genes and traits. (See pages 44–46.)

3. Scientists distinguish between a person's genotype—the set of genes the person inherits—and her or his phenotype—those observable physical and behavioral traits that emerge during development. A phenotype is not a direct reflection of a person's genotype but rather the expression of genetic appearance in a particular environmental context. (See pages 47–48.)

4. Children inherit from their parents a set of genetic potentials. Within their genetic program, some traits are strongly canalized, and others have a wide reaction range. How children actually develop depends on the interplay between what they bring to the environment and the sorts of experiences they have in that environment. (See pages 48–50.)

5. After a long period of gestation, humans are relatively immature at birth. Dependent on the care of others for many years after birth, we learn from and are influenced by our environment as we develop. (See pages 56–57.)

6. Prenatal development is divided into three stages or periods: germinal, embryonic, and fetal. In the germinal period (conception to 2 weeks), the zygote divides, becoming a hollow ball called a blastula in a matter of days. In the embryonic period (2 to 8 weeks), the life-supporting placenta, umbilical cord, and protective amniotic sac mature. Growth and maturation are the major tasks of the fetal period (8 weeks to birth). (See pages 57–62.)

7. The prenatal environment strongly affects fetal development. Maternal nutrition, for example, affects birth weight, prematurity, the development of the nervous system, and even social development. (See pages 62–66.)

8. Teratogens are substances that can cause malformation during fetal development or physical or behavioral problems later in life. Teratogens include certain prescription and over-the-counter drugs, addictive drugs, and social drugs; viruses and bacteria; and environmental toxins. A teratogen's effects depend mainly on when the fetus is exposed to it. (See pages 66–74.)

9. Pregnant women should avoid all unnecessary drugs—whether legal or illegal. Heroin-addicted mothers can pass on their addiction to their babies, and maternal use of cocaine has been connected with miscarriages and neurological problems. Social drinking and smoking also pose risks to the fetus, and pregnant alcoholics expose their babies to the risk of fetal alcohol syndrome. (See pages 66–72.)

10. A woman's emotional state may affect her pregnancy and her child. Highly anxious women can suffer from difficult pregnancies, and babies born to these women may be highly irritable. Body chemistry, genes, and the environment may all be contributing factors. (See pages 74–75.)

KEY TERMS

acquired immune deficiency syndrome (AIDS)
alleles
amniocentesis
amniotic sac
blastula
canalization
chlamydia
chorionic villus biopsy
chromosome
critical periods
deoxyribonuclcic acid (DNA)
differentiation
dominant gene
Down syndrome
ectoderm
embryonic disk
embryonic period

endoderm
fetal alcohol syndrome (FAS)
fetal period
fraternal twins
genes
genital herpes
genotype
germinal period
gestation
gonorrhea
heterozygous
homozygous
identical twins
implantation
industrial pollutants
karyotype
mesoderm
myelinization
PCBs

phenotype
phenylketonuria (PKU)
placenta
polygenic
prenatal development
radiation
reaction range
recessive gene
Rh factor
rubella
sex chromosomes
sudden infant death syndrome (SIDS)
syphilis
Tay-Sachs disease
teratogen
ultrasonography
umbilical cord
villi
zygote

SUGGESTED READINGS

Eisenberg, A., Murkoff, H., & Hathaway, S. (1991). *What to expect when you're expecting.* New York: Workman. An excellent book on prenatal development for prospective parents.

Kitzinger, S. (1985). *Birth over thirty.* New York: Penguin. With more and more women bearing a child, even their first child, well into their thirties, this book fills a void by addressing the unique needs and concerns of older mothers. Risks associated with such pregnancies are discussed and related conditions that lighten or reduce these risks are considered.

Nilsson, L., Ingelman-Sundberg, A., & Wiiersen, C. (1990). *A child is born* (2nd ed). New York: Delacorte Press. An outstanding photographer shares remarkable pictures of life in the making and life in the womb, along with clear descriptions of the genetics and biology of life.

Plomin, R., De Fries, J., & McClearn, G. (1990). *Behavioral genetics: A primer* (2nd ed.) New York: W. H. Freeman. A good introduction to the field of human genetics.

BIRTH AND
THE NEWBORN

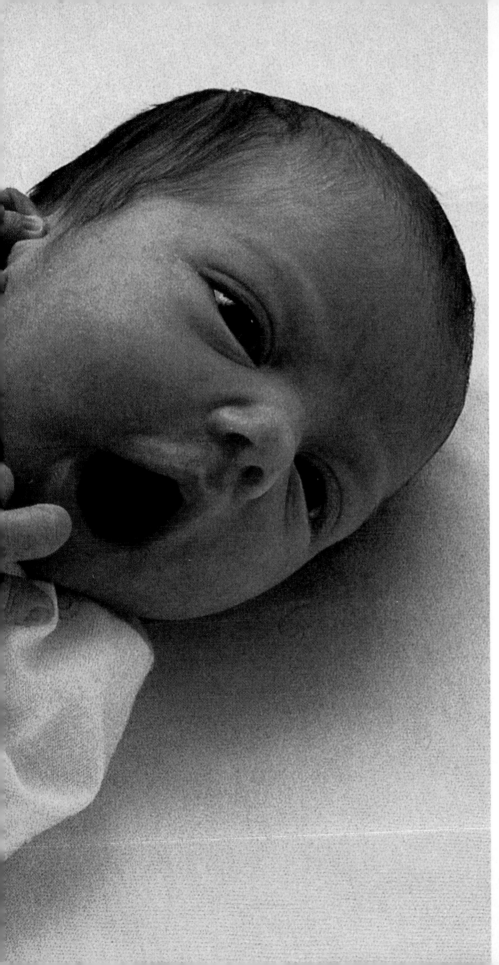

From the blank anonymity of all those sterile sheets, there now appeared a whole head. It was bloody, it was blue, its eyes were still closed, and the doctor was still wiping it with sponges, but it was our baby's head and it was wondrous.

MARZOLLO, 1976

Elated, amazed, exhausted, and relieved, parents finally see the baby they could only imagine for 9 months. We can only guess what the experience is like for infants, as they leave the protection of the uterus for the outside world. The subject of this chapter is that journey, the beginning of a new life for infants and for parents.

All babies adjust to the early months of life in ways that are at once universal and unique, and each infant's style marks the beginning of the "fit" between child and parents, as parents learn to read and react to their infant's personal signals. High-risk babies, born before their bodies are ready to support life, have special needs. We'll discuss some of the causes of premature births as well as support programs that can reduce the risks for many preterm infants.

PREPARING FOR CHILDBIRTH

For most of your grandmothers, hospital childbirth was typically a blur of pain and fear. Women were either left alone in a featureless room or grouped with other laboring women whose anxieties and pain intensified their own. Most likely, attendants and doctors were brusque and impersonal. If given general anesthesia to relieve their pain, many women awoke with a feeling not of joy but of loss (Kitzinger, 1972).

prepared (natural) childbirth
childbirth without medication or anesthetics, based on relaxation techniques and psychological and physical preparation

That was before the revolutionary changes of **prepared** (or **natural**) **childbirth,** which altered the whole experience of pregnancy and delivery for mothers, fathers, and babies, as well as for hospitals and doctors. For many parents, information, preparation, and confidence have replaced fear and ignorance. Being prepared for childbirth means making knowledgeable choices that influence the pregnancy, the delivery, and even the relationship between mother and father.

● Childbirth Classes

In the early 1950s, a French obstetrician observed a Russian childbirth technique based on conditioned learning (see Chapter 1). Women were taught to relax instead of tensing up when they had a contraction. Blood could then flow freely to the muscles, preventing and reducing pain. The doctor, Fernand Lamaze, added *effleurage* (a light abdominal massage) and called the method *accouchement sans douleur*—childbirth without pain. The **Lamaze method** does not discourage the use of pain-relieving drugs when needed, but women who have prepared childbirth tend to report less pain (Rosenblith & Sims-Knight, 1985).

Lamaze method
natural or prepared childbirth

During Lamaze childbirth classes, women learn relaxation techniques and men practice their roles as coaches.

Apparently, the classes foster positive feelings toward labor and delivery, lowering stress when birth occurs. These good feelings also enhance mothers' sensitivity to their infants (Lindell, 1988), and marriages benefit as well. Couples who have attended classes together feel less dissatisfied with their marriages after their infant is born (Cowan & Cowan, 1992; Markman & Kadushin, 1986).

● Obstetricians and Nurse-Midwives

Although the overwhelming majority of babies in the United States are delivered by obstetricians, some women choose a nurse-midwife for prenatal care and delivery. These specially trained nurses are usually affiliated with doctors, birthing centers, or hospitals, providing access to an obstetrician. Some expectant parents find nurse-midwives more caring and supportive than obstetricians, because a midwife is often more available throughout the pregnancy and for all of labor and delivery. Obstetricians may not have as much time to spend with each woman, but they are trained to deliver babies through all types of medical emergencies.

● Cultural Differences in Childbirth Practices

Practices surrounding pregnancy and childbirth vary around the world. The Cuna Indians of Panama treat pregnancy as a medical condition warranting treatment, and expectant mothers are medicated throughout pregnancy. For the Jarara of South America, pregnancy is a normal condition, and childbirth occurs without a great deal of fanfare or medical attention. Many cultures, including our own, fall between these two extremes.

Even within our culture there are important ethnic differences in practices surrounding childbirth and pregnancy, also related to the extent to which pregnancy is seen as a "condition" warranting treatment. Some groups use a variety of home remedies (for example, different sorts of herb teas) to ease morning sickness and "ensure" a safe delivery of the child. In many such groups—among them, immigrants from Hispanic or Asian cultures—women do not routinely seek medical care throughout pregnancy unless they feel that something is going wrong. Other groups—for example, middle-class Americans from the mainstream—tend to rely less on home remedies and more on "official" written information and frequent visits to health care professionals. In general, health care providers should be aware that different groups hold different cultural beliefs about pregnancy and that these beliefs will affect the pregnant mother's behavior. It is important to respect these cultural differences and support them as long as the health of the mother and child is not jeopardized (Jordan, 1980; Mead & Newton, 1967).

● Obstetrical Medication: Uses and Effects

On January 19, 1847, a Scottish obstetrician, James Young Simpson, used ether to relieve a woman's pain during childbirth. Within 5 months, ether was being widely used (Brackbill, 1979). Today, ether is rarely used in vaginal deliveries because of its potentially harmful effects on babies.

Many safer forms of anesthesia are available, but even these have potentially harmful effects on the unborn, just delivered, and developing child. The problem is twofold. First, drugs rapidly cross the placenta, entering the baby's system. They remain for a prolonged time because the baby's liver and kidneys are still too immature to break down the drugs easily and eliminate them. Several kinds of problems have shown up in babies whose mothers received heavy and prolonged doses of a variety of anesthetics. These babies need more stimulation to nurse; motor abilities can be affected during their first year; and they show less social interaction (Brackbill, 1979; J. V. Brown et al., 1975; Conway & Brackbill, 1970; Parke, O'Leary, & West, 1972; Richards & Bernal, 1972; Standley et al., 1974).

Harmful effects of medication are related to the kind used, the size of the dose, and how long the baby is exposed. When drugs are administered in small doses close to the time of delivery, risks to the infant are minimized.

Discussing medication with an obstetrician before labor begins is a good idea. Generally, the smallest effective dose, or no anesthesia at all, is best for both the baby and the mother *when circumstances permit* (Yarrow, 1984). But all births are different. If labor becomes lengthy, intensely painful, or unexpectedly complicated, medication can be very helpful. No woman needs to be a martyr.

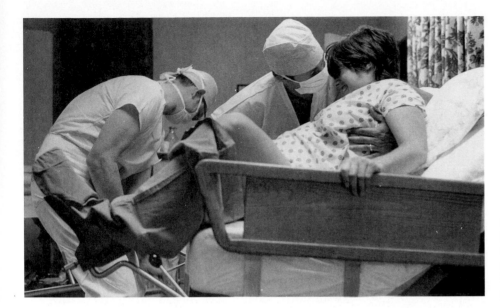

Giving birth takes time and work. This woman, in the final stage of labor, has been moved to the delivery room. While her husband offers support, she pushes the baby out.

LABOR AND DELIVERY

Few women give birth Hollywood-style—a sudden onset of intense labor pains, a reckless drive to the hospital, a just-in-time delivery. Usually, especially for first-time mothers, the term *labor* is all too apt. Giving birth is slow and proceeds in definite stages. During each stage, a woman feels specific sensations and emotions.

Before the earliest signs of labor, the cervix, the muscle controlling the opening from the uterus to the vagina, is closed. During labor the cervix *dilates*—that is, expands—until it is about 10 centimeters (4 inches) wide, large enough for a 6- to 8-pound baby to pass through. This slow, at times painful, process allows the baby to move through the cervix, into the vagina, and out.

● The Signs of Labor

One of the surest signs that labor is near is **engagement,** or **lightening:** The fetus moves into position for birth, low in the abdomen with its head very close to the mother's cervix. Some women experience engagement as long as 4 weeks before their baby's birth; others, especially those who have given birth before, may not feel it until labor actually begins. And for some, it doesn't happen at all. Not all fetuses get into position for a "classic" birth, but we turn first to the way labor most often begins.

After engagement, increased discharges of vaginal mucus may occur, and pressure builds in the woman's pelvic region. Often the earliest sure sign of impending labor is the **bloody show,** the appearance of blood-tinged mucus on underwear or in the toilet. This mucus, which formed a seal at the opening of the cervix, is dislodged as the cervix begins to *efface* (grow thinner) and dilate.

● **engagement (lightening)**
the movement of the fetus into position for birth

● **bloody show**
the blood-tinged mucus in a pregnant woman's urine or discharge, which is a sign of impending labor

When the cervix expels the mucus plug, small blood vessels around it break, adding a red tinge to the mucus.

A few days before labor begins, a woman's weight may drop a few pounds and she may feel pains similar to menstrual cramps. These early contractions, also called *false labor,* may occur on and off until true labor begins. About this same time, now cramped in a too-small space, the baby becomes less active. But the woman may become more so; many experience a spurt of energy 1 to 2 days before labor begins.

Another sign of labor is the *breaking of the amniotic membranes.* Inside the uterus, the fetus floats in amniotic fluid, encased by the membranes of the amniotic sac. This fluid, which serves as a shock absorber for the baby throughout pregnancy, is commonly called *the water.* As labor begins, the membranes may rupture, releasing the amniotic fluid. After this "breaking of the water," the protective seal of the amniotic membranes is gone. Any common virus or bacteria entering the vagina can now infect the unprotected fetus. To prevent illness, the baby is generally delivered within 24 hours after the membranes break. (Occasionally, the amniotic membranes do not rupture spontaneously, even though labor is under way. The obstetrician or nurse-midwife will then rupture them mechanically.)

The clearest sign that labor is beginning—one that may occur *before* either the bloody show or the breaking of the amniotic membranes—is the onset of rhythmic contractions. **Contractions** are movements of the muscular walls of the uterus that push the baby down through the birth canal and ultimately out of the mother's body. They are stimulated by the hormone oxytocin, produced by the mother's pituitary gland. We still do not know what leads to the release of this hormone (Mittendorf et al., 1990). The first contractions may feel like menstrual cramps, gas pains, backache, or pelvic pressures. When these pains begin to recur in a regular rhythm, and then become more and more frequent, the baby is definitely on the way. Figure 3.1 illustrates the stages of birth.

● **contractions**
movements of the muscular walls of the uterus that push the baby out of the mother's body

● Labor: First Stage

The first stage of labor is the longest, averaging 10 to 14 hours for first pregnancies. This period can be divided into several substages. In *early first-stage labor,* contractions occur at regular intervals. The cervix dilates to about 4 centimeters (approximately 1½ inches), and the amniotic membranes usually rupture. Although contractions may cause some pain in the back or abdomen, between contractions women may be quite alert and eager to sit up, walk, talk, or read.

During the middle of first-stage labor, contractions become stronger, longer, and closer together. The pain is more severe, and some women are given pain-killing medication. At the end of this substage, the cervix has opened to about 8 centimeters (over 3 inches).

The last part of the first stage of labor is **transition.** It is the shortest, most intense phase of the entire process, usually lasting for no more than an hour or two. Transition is the most painful part of labor; it does not seem short to the woman experiencing it. During this phase the cervix opens to about 10 centimeters; contractions are frequent and strong. The urge to push the baby out begins, but if this urge comes too soon—before the cervix is fully dilated—push-

● **transition**
the end of the first stage of labor, with the cervix fully dilated

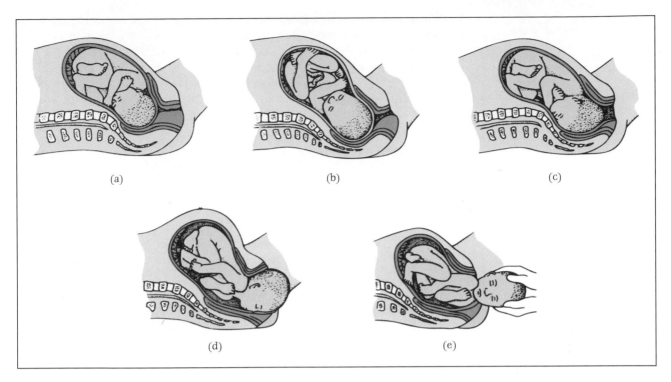

FIGURE 3.1
The Stages of a Normal Birth
(a) Engagement: The fetus's head is very close to the mother's cervix before labor begins; not all babies assume this position.
(b) Labor, first stage: Contractions increase, and the cervix dilates.
(c) Transition: Contractions intensify, and the cervix becomes fully dilated. The baby is positioned to enter the birth canal.
(d) Labor, second stage: The mother pushes, and the baby moves through the birth canal, until the head emerges through the vagina.
(e) The baby is turned, easing the shoulders and the rest of the body out.

ing must be delayed. Premature pushing only swells the cervix, narrowing the opening and delaying birth.

Because of the pain and the need to counteract the natural urge to push, a woman in the transition stage is usually very uncomfortable. The ordeal her body is going through may show itself in several ways: Some women feel nauseated and need to vomit. Other discomforts include hiccuping, sweating or shivering, and leg cramps. A woman in transition can easily become exhausted and irritable.

● Labor: Second Stage

The second stage of labor begins when the cervix is fully dilated. Contractions are less frequent, or even stop temporarily. Now the mother is told to push, and as she does, the baby moves through the birth canal. Soon the baby's head "crowns"—appears at the vaginal opening. Most obstetricians will now perform

● **episiotomy**
an incision made below the
vaginal opening during
childbirth

an **episiotomy.** This is a surgical incision made below the vaginal opening (in the perineum) that allows the baby to emerge without tearing the mother's vaginal tissues. (The incision is stitched up following delivery.) Once the baby's head has passed through the birth canal, the baby is turned to ease out the shoulders. The rest of the body usually slips out easily. With the cutting of the umbilical cord, birth is complete. In many hospitals, the baby is placed on the mother's abdomen for a few moments.

● Labor: Third Stage

The final stage of labor is the delivery of the placenta. Uterine contractions force the placenta out through the vagina. Then the uterus, which has expanded greatly to accommodate the growing fetus, begins shrinking back to its normal size. If an episiotomy was performed, the doctor now stitches it up. Parents can hold their baby and mothers can nurse.

● Problems and Interventions

The labor and delivery we have described is an ideal. Headfirst, the fetus moved down the birth canal and through the vagina, emerging as a healthy newborn. Often, labor does not go so smoothly, and birth can be more complicated. Sometimes the fetus's own position causes the problem. In about 4 percent of vaginal deliveries the fetus is in the *breech* position, with the feet or buttocks pointing toward the cervix. Because **breech births** can be difficult for the mother, many obstetricians elect to deliver the baby by cesarean section, as discussed below (Kitzinger, 1985). Breech births have also been linked to an increased risk of

● **breech births**
births in which the baby
emerges feet or buttocks first

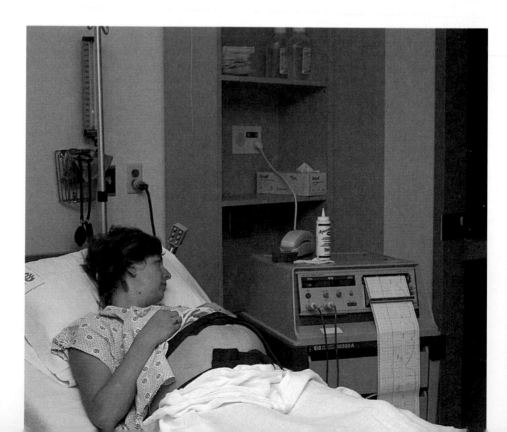

The fetal monitor tracks the rate of the baby's heartbeat and the strength of uterine contractions during labor.

sudden infant death (Buck et al., 1991). In a **transverse presentation,** the fetus lies horizontally or across the uterus, blocking the cervical opening. The obstetrician will try to move the fetus into the head-down position, but if this fails, a cesarean section is done.

Even when the baby is in the best position for birth, complications can occur. Labor may be delayed, what people mean when they say the baby is "overdue." It may also begin at the right time but progress too slowly. Prolonged labor occurs if the cervix doesn't dilate properly, or if contractions are too weak or too far apart. In either case, to prevent damage to the mother and/or the baby, the physician may induce or attempt to speed up labor.

Inducing labor involves rupturing the mother's amniotic membranes, giving her medication, or both. To rupture the membranes, the doctor places a long, thin plastic instrument up the birth canal and gently pricks the membranes, a procedure that is quick and usually painless. Often **pitocin** (a synthetic form of the natural labor-inducing hormone oxytocin) is used to speed a prolonged or delayed labor. This hormone produces uterine contractions or strengthens them if they are too weak or far apart.

A major source of concern during all deliveries is the prevention of **anoxia,** or lack of oxygen in the fetus, a condition that can cause brain damage. Damaging anoxia may occur during an overly long or stressful labor if contractions repeatedly reduce the flow of blood to the fetus. With the help of a **fetal monitor,** doctors can anticipate the likelihood of anoxia and can act to prevent it. The fetal monitor is an electronic device that tracks both the fetal heartbeat and the pressure of the uterus during contractions. Fitted around the mother's abdomen, the monitor's belt is hooked up to a screen. It produces continuous data that sometimes signals trouble. If the heartbeat is weak, or if labor is progressing too slowly, doctors frequently decide to intervene.

One method of intervention, rarely performed today, is the **forceps delivery.** Forceps are shaped like two large interlocking spoons, which the doctor fits around the baby's head. Then, as the obstetrician pulls, the mother pushes, and the baby moves down the birth canal. Forceps deliveries are risky: They may cause head injuries, resulting in permanent brain damage to the baby. Consequently, physicians are more likely to use a **vacuum extraction** tube, which pulls or "sucks" the baby out. A doctor may use this procedure when the monitor indicates true fetal distress or when the fetus's head is too large to pass through the mother's pelvis. The most frequent type of intervention, and lately the most controversial one, is the cesarean section.

In the **cesarean section,** a surgeon cuts the mother's abdomen through to the uterus, suctions out the amniotic fluid, and lifts out the baby. Known since ancient times, cesareans traditionally were a last resort to save the life of the baby, the mother, or both. Infection-fighting antibiotics and safer anesthesias made C-sections safer, but women who have cesarean deliveries experience a much higher rate of physical and emotional complications than women who deliver vaginally, and their babies are more likely to have early, albeit temporary, difficulties in respiration and responsivity (Trevarthan, 1987). Nevertheless, in some hospitals this method of delivery is so common now as to be almost routine. Growing too is the controversy surrounding cesarean deliveries. Why is the rate so high? We discuss this controversy in the accompanying Controversy box.

transverse presentation
a condition in which the fetus lies horizontally in the uterus

pitocin
a synthetic form of the natural labor-inducing hormone oxytocin

anoxia
lack of oxygen in the fetus

fetal monitor
an electronic device that keeps track of the fetal heartbeat and uterine pressure during childbirth

forceps delivery
a method of delivery using an instrument shaped like two large interlocking spoons, which the doctor fits around the baby's head

vacuum extraction
a method of delivery using a tube that pulls or "sucks" the baby out

cesarean section
surgery in which the uterus is opened and the baby is lifted out

CONTROVERSY

THE CESAREAN BOOM: WHO BENEFITS?

Barely 5 percent in 1965, the rate of cesarean sections in the United States had risen to 15 percent in 1980. In that year a government panel suggested the trend could be safely stopped and perhaps reversed. But by 1990 it had climbed to nearly 25 percent.

No one questions the need for cesareans in some circumstances: If the placenta separates prematurely from the uterine wall or if it covers the cervix, surgical delivery is necessary. It is indicated too if the baby is oversized or clearly in danger of being strangled by the umbilical cord. Cesarean deliveries can also prevent herpes in a baby whose mother has an active infection. But in the majority of cases, the signs for a C-section are less clear. How and why are doctors in the United States deciding to perform almost 1 million cesareans each year? What has changed?

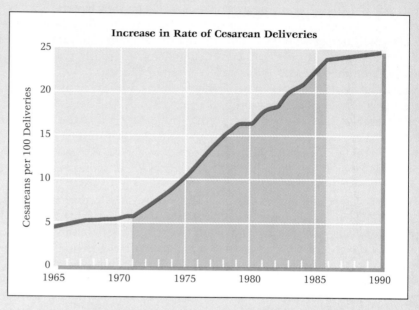

Cesarean rates turned sharply upward in the early 1970s, climbing by about a percentage point a year until recently.

Interestingly, part of the answer can be traced to a technological advance, the electronic fetal monitor. This device, which tracks contractions and the baby's heart rate during labor, alerts doctors to problems that can cause oxygen deprivation and possible brain damage. But while they do signal trouble, "only 10 percent of cesareans arise from a diagnosis of fetal distress" (*Consumer Reports*, Feb. 1991). More typically, the reason given is *dystocia*. Once used to denote a poor fit between the size of the baby and the mother's pelvis, today this term usually describes a labor that isn't progressing as ex-

THE FIRST HOURS

● **vernix**
a slippery substance that coats the newborn

The adorable babies on diaper boxes are surely not newborns. The baby emerging from its mother has had her head flattened and elongated and her nose, cheeks, and eyes bruised and distorted by pressure in a narrow birth canal. The **vernix,** which protected the skin from becoming waterlogged in the uterus, now appears as a sticky-whitish coating. Some babies have hair on their body as well as on their head, and many are completely bald. After a few days, the baby's head becomes more rounded and the marks of passage begin to fade. Without vernix, the skin is smooth, and the hair, or lack of it, begins to seem more nat-

pected. The incidence of dystocia on hospital charts rose 40 percent from 1980 to 1990. And for 40 percent of all first-time cesareans, this is the reason given.

Often the problem is simply time. Certain kinds of painkillers can slow contractions, and for many first-time mothers, labor just takes a long time. "Failure to progress," say critics, too often means "failure to wait" (quoted in *Consumer Reports,* Feb. 1991). "It's easy to go ahead and do a cesarean," says Dr. Stephen A. Myers, director of maternal-fetal medicine at the Mount Sinai Hospital Medical Center in Chicago. "Knowing when you don't have to takes more judgment, skill, and experience."

The question many ask then is, Why are so many doctors in the "best" hospitals doing so many cesareans each year? Are decisions being made for reasons other than the mother's or the baby's benefit? Indeed, one explanation is that doctors are primarily protecting themselves. With good reason, some would add. Malpractice suits against obstetricians have touched 75 percent of the profession, and most are dismissed at trial. The reason is not that more babies are being born imperfect, but that more parents expect perfection. And if they don't get it, they sue. So, say doctors, to protect themselves against the possibility of a lawsuit, they operate rather than intervene in other ways. For the unethical, fees may be a factor as well. Doctors charge an average of $500 more for a cesarean than for a vaginal delivery, and hospital costs increase by over $2,000 (Health Insurance Association of America, reported in *Consumer Reports,* Feb. 1991).

Lending credibility to these claims is the profile of women who are most likely to deliver their babies by cesarean section. As a group, they are the patients of private physicians, over 35, married and living in the Northeast. They have relatively high incomes, deliver in large private hospitals, and have adequate medical insurance. Perhaps, in their doctors' eyes, they are also the most likely to sue, more likely at any rate than the clinic patients who actually run a higher risk of complications but have a far lower rate of cesarean deliveries.

For women and babies, the controversy around high cesarean rates has more to do with health issues than with fees and lawsuits. Almost 40 percent of women who deliver by C-section develop infections of the uterus, urinary tract, or surgical wound. These are effectively treated with antibiotics but may add days to the hospital stay and may also interfere with breastfeeding. And, as with any major surgery, other unexpected complications can occur.

Even when all goes well, cesarean mothers must stay in the hospital for twice as long as mothers who deliver vaginally. They also feel more pain and fatigue, typical side effects of surgery, making it harder for them to care for their babies. Unexpected cesareans may have an emotional cost as well. Women often feel like failures for not delivering vaginally, and after all their preparation and expectations, couples feel cheated out of one of life's greatest experiences.

ural. While parents are quick to examine their babies' features, doctors are checking for signs of health or distress.

● Survival: The First Challenge

Birth sparks a series of radical physiological changes. Deprived of the placenta, its source of oxygen and nutrients, the newborn's lungs and circulatory system must function independently. The mother's 98.6-degree body temperature is abruptly replaced by an environment of about 72 degrees, another change to which the infant must adapt. Space changes too: Suddenly freed from the cramped uterus, the baby can move freely.

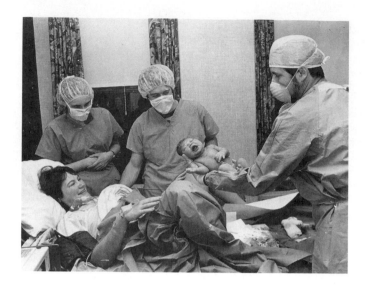

Immediately after birth, parents get a quick look at their baby before he or she is evaluated in five crucial areas of adjustment to life outside the uterus.

● **Apgar test**
a test that measures a baby's heart rate, breathing, muscle tone, reflexes, and color immediately after birth

● ***The Apgar score.*** The baby's transition to life is evaluated almost immediately after birth by the **Apgar test,** a series of observations typically made by delivery room nurses. Named for Dr. Virginia Apgar, who developed it, this test evaluates the baby's transition to a biologically separate existence in five crucial areas: heart rate, breathing, muscle tone, reflex irritability, and color. Each of these functions is rated (0, 1, or 2), and the five-figure total gives the *Apgar score* (see Table 3.1). An Apgar of 10 denotes excellent condition in all five areas. The test is performed twice: first when the baby is 1 minute old, and again 5 minutes after birth.

The Apgar score was designated to identify newborns who need special help, either immediately or during the first few days of life. A total score in the 7- to 10-point range is considered normal, the 4- to 6-point range is poor, and the 0- to 3-point range is considered dangerous. Because the newborn's condition is evaluated at both 1 and 5 minutes after birth, the *change* in score may also be very meaningful. Two low Apgars, or a dramatic decline in Apgar score, generally call for prompt intervention.

TABLE 3.1   CRITERIA AND SCORING OF THE APGAR TEST

Score	A Appearance (Color)	P Pulse (Heart Rate)	G Grimace (Reflex Irritability)	A Activity (Muscle Tone)	R Respiration (Respiratory Effort)
0	Blue, pale	Absent	No response	Limp	Absent
1	Body pink, extremities blue	Slow (below 100)	Grimace	Some flexion of extremities	Slow, irregular
2	Completely pink	Rapid (over 100)	Cry	Active motion	Good, strong cry

SOURCE: V. Apgar, 1953.

While the Apgar is a good index of immediate postnatal risk, this test is much less useful in predicting development in later infancy or childhood. Many babies come through difficult deliveries, have poor Apgar scores, seem dangerously feeble in their first days, and then develop into normal babies and children. Recent work suggests, however, that as the Apgar score increases, risk of sudden infant death declines (Buck et al., 1991).

● First Contacts with Parents

In some species the mother and her offspring *must* be together immediately after birth or a bond ensuring proper maternal care does not form. Do humans have the same need? Is early contact between human mothers and their babies essential for forming a strong mother-infant bond? This question seemed particularly important in the days when many hospitals were separating mother and baby minutes after birth, keeping them apart for most of their hospital stay.

To gain insight into the effects of this practice, Kennell and Klaus (1976) identified two groups of mothers. The control group followed the usual routine—"a glance at their baby shortly after birth; a short visit six to twelve hours after birth for identification purposes, and then 20- to 30-minute visits for feeding every four hours during the day" (Kennell et al., 1974). The other group had their babies with them for approximately an hour shortly after delivery and for several hours each day thereafter. When the researchers observed the two groups, both in the hospital and in several follow-up sessions, they concluded that the mothers who had more contact with their babies seemed more "motherly" as long as a year later. These mothers looked at, fondled, and picked up their babies more often than those in the control group (Klaus et al., 1972).

These initial findings have been disputed. Several researchers tried to reproduce the results of Klaus and Kennell's early experiment and failed (Gewirtz,

Whether or not babies need to bond with their parents right after birth is controversial, but spending time with their newborn is undeniably a joyous time for families.

1979; Grossman, Grossman, Huber, & Wartner, 1981; Svejda, Campos, & Emde, 1980). And critics have noted that many people studying bonding are strongly biased in favor of immediate and sustained contact between mother and newborn, perhaps making their research unreliable (Belsky & Benn, 1982; Lamb & Hwang, 1982). Probably the best way to sum up the conflicting research is to say that early contact between *some* mothers and infants may *sometimes* enhance the bond between them (Lamb & Hwang, 1982).

Whatever the evidence, the *debate* over bonding has had several consequences. On the positive side, hospitals and medical staff have become more sensitive to the needs of mothers—and fathers—to spend time with their newborns. Many mothers now opt for rooming-in arrangements, and fathers now participate in the birth process.

On the negative side, the emphasis on early mother-infant contact has made many mothers and fathers of high-risk babies (those with medical problems, who must be taken to the intensive care nursery) wonder whether their baby's emotional health may be damaged without immediate loving physical contact. What's most important is going home to a loving family, but premature infants in incubators do get a developmental boost from extra stimulation and physical contact. For normal full-term babies, close early contact with the mother does not seem to be crucial to the child's normal development or to the establishment of a maternal bond (Eyer, 1993).

● *Fathers and birth.* Fathers' active role in childbirth is so accepted now that we forget how isolated men were from the process just a generation ago. New fathers report that they enjoy just looking at and holding their babies. Many say that they can recognize their own babies in the nursery, and others talk of being drawn to the baby as to a magnet (Greenberg & Morris, 1974).

Fathers' involvement with their newborns is sometimes called **engrossment,** a term denoting absorption, preoccupation, and interest in the infant (Greenberg & Morris, 1974). Engrossment may exist as an innate potential among all fathers, but it can be blocked by reservations about what it is manly to feel, by hospital procedures that close fathers out, by mothers who may feel threatened by the father's interest, and by the father's fear of his new responsibilities.

● **engrossment**
parental absorption, preoccupation, and interest in the infant

BEHAVIOR PATTERNS IN NEWBORNS

One word best describes the newborn's first few days: instability. Random changes in skin color and body temperature, spurts of hiccuping and vomiting, and intervals of irregular breathing are all normal adjustments to life that disappear as the infant's nervous system matures. Crying, however, continues.

● **Crying**

The average newborn sleeps about two-thirds of every day and cries from 4 to 15 minutes of every hour (Korner et al., 1985). Like a built-in buzzer wired into the human repertoire over the course of evolution, a baby's cry is a distress call, signaling the need to be held, turned over, changed, or soothed. For some newborns, characteristics of the cry itself signal trouble. The duration, pitch, and other features of cries help to identify infants with major central nervous system disorders (Zeskind & Lester, 1978) as well as those with more subtle difficulties that might go unnoticed in the early weeks of life (Lester & Zeskind, 1982; Zeskind, 1983).

Besides medical attention, babies with unusual cries often need special care from their parents to promote normal development. As we saw in Chapter 2, low-birth-weight babies and Down syndrome babies benefit from extra calming attention. But some parents may find their baby's cry so unpleasant that they avoid, or even abuse, the infant. Ultimately, the effect of an unusual cry depends on the way parents respond. Indeed, cries are part of the first communications system between parent and child, and when a parent learns to read an infant's cry, both benefit.

● *The course of crying.* In most normal babies, crying follows a predictable pattern, increasing through the first 6 weeks to a peak of about 2¼ hours a day and then slowly decreasing (Barr, 1990b; St. James-Roberts & Halil, 1991). But even though the amount of time spent crying drops, the number of crying episodes during each 24-hour day stays the same (Barr, 1990a; Hubbard & van Izendoorn, 1991) (see Figure 3.2). And as every parent knows, evening hours are prime time for crying episodes (Barr, 1990b; St. James-Roberts & Halil, 1991). A baby's sex and birth order in the family don't affect the frequency of crying episodes, but parents of firstborns are more likely to talk to their doctors if they

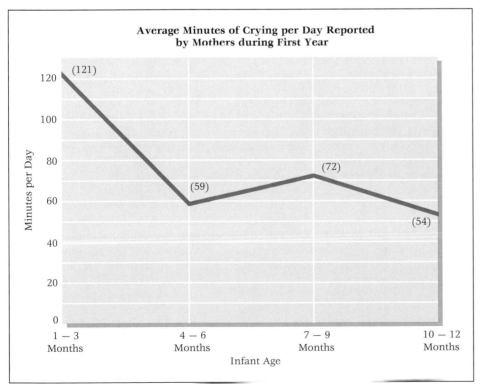

Average Minutes of Crying per Day Reported by Mothers during First Year

FIGURE 3.2
Crying during the First Year
During the first 6 weeks, most infants cry over 2 hours each day, for about 15 minutes every hour. Gradually, crying decreases to under 1 hour per day by the end of the first year.
(SOURCE: St. James-Roberts & Halil, 1991.)

● **colic**
a condition in newborns involving acute abdominal pains, high-pitched crying, and facial grimacing at the same time, babies will flex their elbows, clench their fists, and either pull up their knees or keep them stifflt extended

● **reflex**
a motor behavior not under conscious control

think their babies are crying excessively (St. James-Roberts & Halil, 1991). Not all pediatricians give parents the same advice, but some recent research suggests what methods work best. (For more information about this research, including a discussion of **colic,** see Making a Difference: When Babies Cry.)

● Reflexes

A **reflex** is a motor behavior that is not under voluntary control. Stroke a newborn's cheek with your finger or a nipple, and she will turn her head toward the stroke, open her mouth, and begin sucking. This is the *rooting* reflex. Put your finger on her palm, and the baby will clutch your finger tightly, a reflex called the *Palmar grasp.* These responses are two of the reflexes with which all healthy babies are born. (See Table 3.2.)

MAKING A DIFFERENCE

WHEN BABIES CRY

What should be done about crying? Will promptly picking up a crying baby cause "spoiling"? Will letting the baby cry cause emotional harm?

Families in traditional societies don't ask these questions. They carry their babies most of the time, nurse them when they cry, and often share their own bed with their infant. In southwest Africa's Kalahari Desert, hunter-gatherer mothers of the !Kung tribe carry their babies almost always, sleeping with them through the first years of life and nursing them when they whimper—as much as 100 times a day (Howell, 1979)!

But contemporary women in industrialized societies lead very different lives than hunter-gatherer mothers. They also carry their babies a lot less. In the United States, it seems that as carrying has gone down, crying has gone up. To explore the relationship between caregiving and infant crying, Dr. Ronald Barr, a pediatrician, ran two experiments (1990). In one, mothers in the experimental

group were encouraged to hold and carry their babies more than they might otherwise, whether the babies were crying or not. Mothers in the second experimental group were told to nurse their babies at shorter intervals and to quickly soothe their crying babies. In both studies, control group mothers were told to care for their babies in their usual way. Results showed dramatic differences. In the carrying study, when infants were 4 to 12 weeks old, experimental mothers held their babies over 4 hours a day, while control mothers did so for slightly less than 3 hours each day. At the peak crying period of 6 weeks, experimental babies cried 43 percent less than control babies. The babies who had been held more had as many crying episodes as the other babies, but each bout lasted for less time. In the debate over holding infants, these studies offer some answers.

The answer is not so simple for babies with colic, however. In the United States alone, over 700,000 infants, and their families, suffer from this condition, often described by the "rule of 3": crying for

more than 3 hours a day, 3 days a week, for 3 weeks in otherwise healthy infants during the first 3 to 4 months of life. A colic attack typically begins with a sudden fit of high-pitched crying coupled with facial grimacing that suggests severe pain. At the same time, babies will flex their elbows, clench their fists, pull up their knees or keep them stiffly extended. The abdomen bulges, the back arches, eyes open wide or tightly close. Red-faced, some babies hold their breath for short periods, and most emit considerable gas. Comforting a colicky baby is almost impossible. Many resist all attempts to soothe them, and the extra holding that shortens crying episodes in other babies does not work for colic.

Still poorly understood, explanations of colic have ranged from immature gastrointestinal tracts in babies to anxiety in mothers (Adams & Davidson, 1987; Lester et al., 1992; Pinyerd & Zipf, 1989). But whatever the cause, some of the best advice for parents of colicky infants is to get some relief for themselves by spending some time away from their baby.

TABLE 3.2   NEWBORN REFLEXES

Reflex Name	Stimulus	Description of Reflex	Age of Disappearance
Rooting	Stroke cheek with nipple or finger	Head turns toward stroke; mouth opens; sucking begins	2 to 3 months
Moro	Sudden loud noise; head is dropped a few inches	Arms extend outward from body; then brought toward each other; back arches	6 to 7 months
Palmar	Rod or finger pressed against infant's palm	Infant's fingers close around and grasp object	3 to 4 months
Babinski	Sole of foot, on the side, is gently stroked from heel to toe	Toes fan outward and foot twists inward	By end of first year
Sucking	Finger inserted into mouth	Sucking	(Persists)
Stepping	Baby held under arms to support in upright position; bare feet flatly touch surface	Rhythmical stepping movements	3 to 4 months
Placing	Top of foot rubbed	Foot withdrawn	3 to 4 months

Some reflexes, such as blinking and sneezing, remain throughout life, but others are present only during infancy and disappear at predictable times. (Many of these reflex actions reappear later, under conscious higher-brain control.) Physicians look for reflexes at birth and during routine office visits to assess neurological development. If reflexes are missing at birth, or present for longer than they should be, a neurological problem may exist.

Most surprising to new parents are the *stepping* and *placing* reflexes that make the infant appear to walk. Although these reflexes seem to disappear at 3 months, dipping the lower part of the infant's body in water elicits them again (Thelen, 1984). The legs, though heavier by 3 months, are light enough in water to "walk" reflexively once more.

Many reflexes seem to be protective: A blinking eye is less easily hit or poked, gagging prevents choking, and sneezing clears the nose and throat. And both

The Palmer, or grasping, reflex allows a newborn to hold on tightly. Toes fan out in the Babinski reflex when an infant's foot is stroked, and a 9-day-old baby demonstrates the walking reflex.

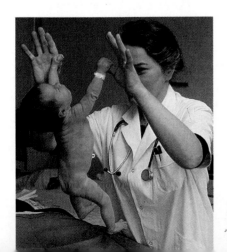
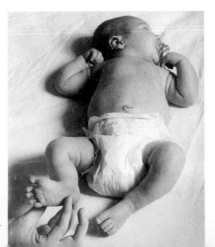

the *sucking* and *rooting* reflexes may be built-in survival tools, enabling infants to nurse soon after birth.

The Palmar grasp and the *Moro,* or startle, reflex permit infants to cling for support. These behaviors may have originated in our primate ancestors, and they still exist among young monkeys and apes, who cling tightly to their mothers.

● States of Arousal

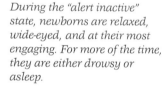

states of arousal
varying levels of energy, attention, and activity

Although they may seem to be either "on" or "off"—asleep or awake, crying or quiet—newborns experience a range of activity levels and moods. These shifts among states of sleep, drowsiness, alertness, and activity are known as **states of arousal.** Some newborns sleep through much of the night, take long naps, and doze off while nursing. Others sleep less and cry for much of the time they are awake.

Expanding on knowledge gained since the 1950s and 1960s (Wolff, 1966), Eve-lyn Thoman (1990) has identified ten states of arousal. These ten states can be further combined into six states: alert; nonalert waking; fuss/cry; drowse/daze/sleep-wake transition; active sleep; and quiet/active-quiet sleep (baby moves while sleeping, but is quiet) (see Table 3.3).

An infant's pattern of arousal signals his individuality and shapes his early relationship with his parents. The "alert state" seems to invite attention and interaction. During the first few days of life, though, infants spend very little time in this state. Sleeping occupies almost two-thirds of their time. The alert state is usually only a brief transitional zone between sleep, fussing, and feeding (Hofer, 1981). Parents who pay close attention to their infant's level of arousal eventually learn what kinds of stimulation cause distress, what kinds are welcome, and when.

Parents like regularity; it affects how they feel about and care for their baby and how competent they feel as parents. For some newborns, establishing a pre-

During the "alert inactive" state, newborns are relaxed, wide-eyed, and at their most engaging. For more of the time, they are either drowsy or asleep.

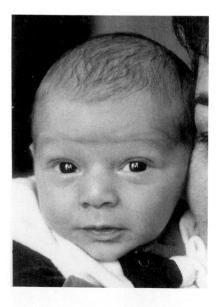

TABLE 3.3   INFANT STATES OF AROUSAL

State	Description
Regular sleep	Eyes remain closed and the body shows no movement. Breathing tends to be slow and regular, and the face remains relaxed (no grimaces or eyelid movements).
Irregular sleep	Eyes remain closed, yet rapid eye movements can be noted periodically. Respiration tends to be irregular, grimaces and other facial expressions can be seen, and gentle limb movements are observed.
Drowsiness	Relatively inactive state, with eyes opening and closing intermittently. Breathing is faster than during sleep, but regular. Eyes are dull or glazed when they do open.
Alert inactivity	This is the state for testing newborns. Eyes are open, bright, and shiny. Activity is limited, face relaxed.
Waking activity	Movements are uncoordinated and usually involve the whole body. Breathing is highly irregular. Eyes are open, though not alert.
Crying (distress)	Vigorous activity and grimacing occur along with crying.

SOURCE: Wolff, 1966.

dictable pattern can take months (Parmalee & Sigman, 1983). Generally, the amount of time an infant spends in any one state is about the same for a month-long period. A baby who spends lots of time alert at age 2 weeks will be likely to do so 4 weeks later. When infants *lack* this kind of stability of states over time, when they remain unpredictable, medical and behavioral problems often appear later in infancy (Thoman, 1990; Thoman, Davis, & Denenberg, 1987; Thoman & Whitney, 1990). Regularity of states in very young babies, then, offers some clues to the maturity and integrity of the nervous system (Bornstein & Lamb, 1992).

Recent research indicates that there are cultural or racial differences in the display of distress in early infancy. In one study, for example, the researchers examined Japanese and American infants' facial responses to a distressing experience (having their arms restrained) (Camras, Oster, Campos, Miyake, & Bradshaw, 1992). The study suggested an interesting mixture of similarities and differences. Whereas Japanese babies were less likely than American babies to display overt distress quickly, once they did feel distress, the two groups' facial reactions were similar. Other studies suggest that Asian babies (especially Japanese and Chinese babies) and Native American babies display distress less frequently than Caucasian infants (Freedman, 1979). Most likely, this difference is due to environmental as well as genetic factors. Japanese mothers, for example, are more inclined to try to minimize their infants' distress, which may make their infants more placid (Camras et al., 1992).

How parents respond to their baby's dominant state of arousal is influenced not only by their culture but by their own needs and temperaments. A quiet, sleepy baby may be ideal for the mother tired from a long labor, but a disappointment to an energetic, eager mother who wants a more active infant. And the parent who considers noise a form of healthy self-assertion may take pride in a baby who frequently fusses and screams. When the "fit" between baby and parents is right, both will thrive. In Chapter 6 we'll look closely at the mother-infant fit, what influences it, how it can change, and how important it is for the growing baby.

● The Brazelton Scale: Assessing Individual Differences

● Newborn Behavioral Assessment Scale
Brazelton's test evaluating a newborn's state of control, sensory capacities, reflexes, and motor abilities

Created by the prominent pediatrician T. Berry Brazelton, the **Newborn Behavioral Assessment Scale** (often referred to simply as "the Brazelton") assesses the baby's states of arousal and responsivity, as well as reflexes. Administered to babies 1 week to 10 days after birth, test results can help a physician, psychologist, or nurse assess the baby in two important areas of development: (1) capacity for interaction and (2) motor abilities (Brazelton, 1978).

● state control
the ability of newborns to shift from one state of arousal to another in response to either internal or external stimulation

These insights can help parents respond appropriately to their infant's individual needs. One aspect of behavior evaluated by the scale is **state control,** a newborn's ability to shift from one state of arousal to another in response to either internal or external stimulation. Some newborns can make the transition on their own: They can soothe themselves if they start crying. Others require intervention through touching, talking, or rocking. Some babies are visually responsive—they attend to a brightly colored ball moved across their line of vision—while others are more attentive to a voice. Some babies are prone to startle, while others simply pay attention to a bell rung near their ear.

The Brazelton examination identifies differences among infants and helps parents understand their own baby's unique needs. The test does *not* predict future development, partly because an infant's behavior changes dramatically during the early days of life. Researchers are now trying to understand if the pattern of change can itself predict later development.

● Postpartum Depression

For women, the period following birth is a time of change as well. What used to be brushed aside as the "new baby blues" is now recognized as depression for 25 to 40 percent of mothers. Weepiness and emotional ups and downs peak at about 3 months after their baby's birth (Bettes, 1988; Condon & Watson, 1987). During this period, postpartum hormonal changes make a woman susceptible to all emotions, both happy and sad (Hapgood, Elkind, & Wright, 1988).

Women worry about coping with the new baby and managing work and family obligations. They wonder how the baby will affect their marriage and focus on a host of other potential problems. Coupled with hormonal changes, the almost constant demands of caring for an infant, and too little sleep, conditions are ripe for feeling down. For most women, these feelings last for a few days or weeks, but women who have a history of susceptibility to negativity may need clinical help. (One of the best predictors of whether a woman will experience postpartum depression is whether she has had any symptoms of depression prior to becoming pregnant.) A husband who shares in the daily work of caring for an infant, as well as friends and relatives who can offer emotional support and some time off, can be a good buffer against depression (J. Hopkins, Marcus, & Campbell, 1984).

Predictably, depression affects the way mothers care for their infants. Compared with nondepressed mothers, depressed mothers respond less to their infants, provide less stimulation, and are emotionally flat. Their babies respond in kind: They show less attentiveness to their mothers, fewer contented expressions, more fussiness, and lower activity levels (J. Cohn et al., 1990; T. Field et al., 1990; Rutter, 1990). They are also less likely to develop secure attachments, or emotional bonds, to their mothers (L. Murray, 1992).

THE COMPETENT INFANT

Human infants are born small and immature, with a still-pliable skull. Apparently, this is an evolutionary adaptation to female anatomy: A hard-headed, better-developed baby simply could not fit through the human birth canal. "Early" birth also has turned out to be intellectually advantageous for the human species.

During the early years of life, while their bodies are developing, babies are being stimulated by other people; by objects; by interesting sights, sounds, and smells. Babies can benefit from this unique early exposure to the outside world, if they begin life with some capacity to sense, to perceive, and to act. How well developed are the newborn's senses? How does the newborn-adult interaction help ensure the infant's survival? And what kinds of learning are infants capable of?

● The Newborn's Senses

Newborns' senses function far better than we once thought. Indeed, research over the past two decades has led psychologists to speak of "the competent infant" (Stone, Smith, & Murphy, 1973).

● *Vision.* A newborn baby looks out at the world through a blur. With eyes that test 20/600, a baby's vision is about 30 times worse than that of most adults. But by the age of 6 to 12 months, **visual acuity,** or clarity, has improved to 20/20 (Cohen, DeLoache, & Strauss, 1979), but it will still take another 3 years before children's vision is as accurate as that of adults (Maurer & Maurer, 1988).

Even with only 20/600 vision, a newborn sees a good deal, especially at about 1 foot away from the face. When a newborn looks at you, one eye may seem aimed at you while the other seems to stare fixedly at the baby's own nose. At times the eyes will rove in different directions, only to roll back into a cross-eyed gaze. The capacity to focus both eyes on the same object, known as **binocular convergence,** will emerge later, but even from birth, infants can distinguish light from dark and respond to brightness and movement. They can follow a slowly moving object that is between 6 and 13 inches away, although their tracking is jerky and they often lose the object. By about 2 months their eyes can

● **visual acuity**
clarity of vision

● **binocular convergence**
the ability to focus both eyes on the same object

smoothly follow moving objects (Aslin, 1981). Infants' visual behavior is so predictable that scientists detailed the "rules" that guide the way infants look at the world (Haith, 1978):

1. Awake and alert, infants will open their eyes.

2. Even in the dark, infants seek something to focus on.

3. When they find something light enough to see, infants will look for outlines distinguishing that shape from its background.

4. Once infants see an outline, they will focus on it but also look around it, thus "holding their place" while exploring new sights.

These behaviors suggest that infants are motivated to learn about their world and that they have inborn strategies for seeking out information. We also know that they like some kinds of information more than others: They seem to prefer objects with fairly complex shapes, contours, and details to objects that are flat and plain; and patterns attract them more than solid colors (Fantz, 1963; Milewski, 1976). Parents can enrich a baby's environment with colorful shapes and interesting patterns, but they need not overdo it. No one wants to be stimulated all the time; in fact, too much stimulation can upset an infant.

● ***Hearing.*** Hearing begins even before birth. By 32 weeks, fetuses respond differently to a variety of sounds. A loud crash, for example, can startle. Immediately after birth, fluid in their ears impairs infants' hearing, but within hours they can react to all major aspects of sound, including pitch, loudness, and rhythm (R. Eisenberg, 1970).

As with vision, hearing improves during the first months of life, particularly the ability to hear high-frequency sounds (Weiner & Gillenwater, 1990). Under the right conditions, a newborn can orient—turn and look—toward a sound. What turns a newborn's head is a prolonged sound: a *voice,* not a tone. The baby's position is also important: If, at the same time the voice can be heard, the infant is held upright, she'll turn toward the sound (Chun, Pawsat, & Forster, 1960; Muir, Abraham, Forbes, & Harris, 1979). Interestingly, babies often seem to lose this skill of **sound localization** during their first 2 or 3 months, but regain it at 4 months. Why this ability declines and recovers later remains a mystery (Aslin, Pisoni, & Jusczyk, 1983), although it may have to do with neurological reorganization and a shift in control from lower to higher brain areas.

Infants prefer soft to loud sounds (R. Eisenberg, 1970), and they especially like sounds pitched within the range of the human voice (Webster, Steinhardt, & Senter, 1972). Newborns will turn toward a voice, suggesting that we may be born with the ability to pay attention to the human voice and human speech. With such sensitivity, babies soon learn to tell one voice from another. Even 3-day-old infants who listened to recordings of two voices discerned and preferred their own mother's (DeCasper & Fifer, 1980). And 3-day-olds whose mothers had read a particular story during the last few weeks of pregnancy preferred to listen to a tape recording of their mother reading that story over one she had not read aloud while pregnant (DeCasper & Spence, 1986). Even before birth, then, senses help babies learn.

● **sound localization**
the ability to locate the source of a sound

Whether babies actually benefit when their mothers read to them before birth is debatable, but studies have shown that babies can hear during the last few weeks of pregnancy.

Recent research also indicates that infants respond differently to different patterns of adult speech. What is especially fascinating about this research is that it has been conducted on youngsters from different ethnic groups and with exposure to different languages (for example, Masataka, 1992). For example, infants respond differently to emotional variations in adult speech patterns, even if the speech they are listening to is in an unfamiliar language (Fernald, 1993).

● **_Smell and taste._** The newborn's sense of smell is sharp. During the first 3 days of life, infants begin to distinguish odors (Self, Horowitz, & Paden, 1972). Once fully functional, the sense of smell remains relatively constant throughout life, unlike vision and hearing, which tend to decline more markedly in old age (Rovee, Cohen, & Schlapack, 1975).

Like vision and hearing, smell is a built-in tool for learning, and even newborns can use it effectively. In experiments, 6- to 10-day-old infants were exposed to breast pads worn by their own mothers and to pads worn by other mothers. These newborns spent more time turned toward the pads of their own mothers, suggesting that they recognized, and preferred, her smell (MacFarlane, 1975). Breast-fed babies have an acute sense of their mother's smell, probably because of the extra time spent close to their mother's breast while nursing (Cernoch & Porter, 1985; Porter et al., 1992).

If a sense of smell helps newborns find their mothers, taste too seems adapted for survival. A baby's first food, breast milk, is a very sweet liquid. Babies seem to prefer sweet liquids; generally, the sweeter, the better (Desor, Maller, & Greene, 1977). In one study, infants actually smiled after tasting sweet liquids but pursed their lips in response to sour tastes (J. Steiner, 1977). More recent research reveals that infants' sensitivity to sweetness actually affects their moods (Blass, 1992). When crying newborns and 2-week-old babies were given very small amounts of sucrose to taste, they cried less or stopped and opened their eyes. By 4 weeks, crying only slows and begins again unless the baby establishes eye contact with another person, the kind of contact they make, in fact, when they breast-feed or nurse from a bottle.

● Newborns and Adults: A Natural Match

Although newborns are "competent"—their senses function, and they have the capacity to develop and learn—without a dedicated adult to meet their needs, they would never survive. Parents and babies are interlocking pieces of a puzzle. A baby's hunger cry, for example, is a genetically programmed call for food— a built-in signal for survival (Wolff, 1969). Like an alarm, it goes off every few hours, and only food will stop it. When babies cry and parents feed them, the pieces fit. When hunger or fatigue is not causing the cry, an adult's built-in response to lift the infant to a shoulder tends to quiet the baby and bring it to a state of eye-open alertness, heightening its ability to be stimulated (Korner & Grobstein, 1967; Korner & Thoman, 1972). Again, infant and adult have formed a complementary pair, a natural match enhancing the baby's ability to survive. Similarly, just as infants can recognize their mothers by smell, after only a few days, mothers can recognize the smell of their babies, whether breast- or bottle-feeding (Porter, Cernoch, & McLaughlin, 1983).

Now consider sight. With 20/600 vision, newborns focus most clearly on things that are 6 to 13 inches away. Interestingly, most adults tend to hold their faces from babies at this distance, probably because of clues they pick up from the infant. The distance between mothers' eyes and breasts is also about 12 inches; when the baby is nursing, eye-to-eye contact between mother and baby is natural. Adults also tend to move their heads and exaggerate their facial expressions (with big smiles or frowns, for example) when talking to babies, all movements that fit nicely with what infants can see.

We see some evidence of infant-adult compatibility with hearing too. Recall that newborns prefer some sounds over others. Most adults, whether males or females, tend to raise the pitch of their voice when they talk to babies. They also exaggerate articulation in the same way they articulate facial expression: Speech is slowed down, and words and sounds are frequently repeated (D. Stern, 1974). All these adjustments fit perfectly with the newborn's or older infant's own skills, capacities, and preferences (Cooper & Aslin, 1990; Fernald et al., 1989).

● Do Newborns Learn?

● **learning**
a more or less permanent change in behavior that occurs as a consequence of experience

Learning is a more or less permanent change in behavior that occurs as a consequence of experience. If babies only a few days old can distinguish their mother's voice from a stranger's—and, almost as quickly, can discern their mother's smell—it is fair to say that newborns can learn. How do they do it?

Psychologists have identified several ways in which we learn, including classical conditioning and operant conditioning (see Chapter 1). Although some researchers have questioned newborns' capacity to be classically conditioned (Sameroff & Cavanaugh, 1979), one set of investigators demonstrated that if the mouths of 2- to 48-hour-old newborns were gently stroked immediately before giving them a sweet-tasting substance, the babies would eventually suck in response to the stroking alone (Blass, Ganchrow, & Steiner, 1984). Other researchers have found that newborns could be conditioned to show the sucking response by applying pressure to the palms (Cantor, Fischel, & Kaye, 1983).

Newborns also seem capable of learning through operant conditioning. When offered a sweet substance to suck (the reward) each time they turned their heads in a specified direction (the behavior), head turns in the "right" direction increased (Siqueland, 1968). Even a newborn can learn that a specific behavior can bring a specific reward.

Learning in infants is linked to three factors (Bornstein & Lamb, 1992). First is the infant's behavioral state; alert babies are easier to condition than drowsy ones. Second, the infant must be physically capable of making the desired response. And third, the response required has to seem "worth it" to the baby. Tasting a sweet liquid may be fine, but turning her head or kicking may just not be worth the effort (Rovee-Collier, 1987).

Even without rewards, newborns can learn by observing and imitating the behavior of others, or **observational learning.** Babies as young as 12 to 24 days old can mimic several adult facial gestures—pushing out their lips, opening the mouth, and sticking out the tongue (Meltzoff & Moore, 1977). Later experiments have found that newborns as young as 0.7 to 71 *hours* could also imitate mouth opening and tongue protrusion (Meltzoff & Moore, 1983, 1989). In another study, infants averaging 1½ days old could imitate an examiner's happy, sad, and surprised expressions (Field, Woodson, Greenberg, & Cohen, 1982). Not all researchers view these findings in the same way. Isn't it possible that these behaviors are just reflexes, that infants aren't actually imitating these actions (Anisfeld, 1991)? At least with tongue protrusion, babies are imitating that specific behavior (Legerstee, 1991).

For many newborns born at risk, competence may be months away as they struggle simply to survive. We look now at the problems they face, what causes their condition, and how they can be helped.

● **observational learning**
learning through observation and imitation of others' behavior

● **high-risk infants**
infants whose physical and psychological well-being may be in jeopardy as a result of premature birth and/or low birth weight

HIGH-RISK INFANTS

High-risk infants are born with problems so severe that their lives are in danger. Two of the most common causes of high-risk conditions are prematurity and low birth weight. Either or both of these complications, which commonly occur together, can lead to developmental difficulties. A **premature** (or **preterm**) baby is born at least 3 weeks before the normal 38-week term of pregnancy. A **low-birth-weight** baby weighs less than 5½ pounds, sharply under the 7½-pound-average, and a **very-low-birth-weight (VLBW)** baby weighs less than 1,500 grams. The earlier the birth, and the lower the weight, the greater the risk of death at birth or of developing complications in infancy. There is also a greater risk of problems in intellectual or social functioning as the child grows up (Collin et al., 1991, Hack et al., 1991).

● **premature (preterm) baby**
a baby born before 35 weeks of gestation

● **low birth weight**
a weight of less than 5½ pounds at birth

● **very low birth weight (VLBW)**
a weight of less than 1,500 grams at birth

As we saw in Chapter 2, the causes of low birth weight are often predictable, and in many cases preventable. Known environmental causes of high-risk infants include:

1. Insufficient prenatal care

2. Poor maternal nutrition

3. The mother's age (over 35 or under 19)

4. The mother's reproductive condition (too many pregnancies too close together)

5. The mother's drinking and smoking habits

6. The father's frequent exposure to teratogens

These characteristics have a cumulative effect. One alone may not cause serious problems, but babies of mothers with several of these conditions are likely to be born at risk. And for any one factor, extreme exposure, even if no others are present, increases the risk for the infant.

Before 1967, not a single infant who weighed less than 1,000 grams (about 2¼ pounds) and needed help breathing survived. By the early 1980s, over 73 percent were surviving, with the great majority free of major handicaps (Cohen et al., 1982). In the 1990s, the picture is even better. This dramatic change reflects great advances in **neonatology,** the branch of medicine that focuses on newborns (Lee et al., 1980).

> **neonatology**
> a branch of medicine focusing on newborns

● Physical Characteristics of High-Risk Infants

Probably the greatest threat to the health of the high-risk infant stems from an immature respiratory system. Such babies are prone to **respiratory distress syndrome (RDS),** also known as hyaline membrane disease. The leading killer of premature infants, RDS is usually treated by giving the baby oxygen through a tube placed in the nose. But even this may not save the very premature baby, since RDS infants lack an essential chemical, **pulmonary surfactant,** in their lungs. Before birth, pulmonary surfactant is found in the amniotic sac; after birth, it lubricates the lungs, helping them to inflate on inhalation and preventing surfaces from sticking together on exhalation. Surfactant does not develop until the fetus is about 35 weeks old, so infants born before this time are especially prone to RDS. A promising treatment for RDS involves dripping surfactant into the lungs of premature infants. Evidence suggests that this procedure may cut the rate of death among preterm infants by more than 50 percent (Merritt et al., 1986).

In addition to their respiratory problems, high-risk infants have trouble maintaining normal body temperature and are usually placed in an incubator, or isolette, a glass or plexiglass box in which temperature and air flow can be controlled. The incubator also protects the baby from germs, which might lead to life-threatening infection in so vulnerable an infant.

Weak reflexes, especially the sucking reflex, put the high-risk infant in danger as well (Bakeman & Brown, 1980). Low-birth-weight babies who have trouble sucking are at special risk, because they may not be able to take in enough

> **respiratory distress syndrome (RDS)**
> a breathing disorder in premature babies, caused by immaturity of the lungs and lack of pulmonary surfactant

> **pulmonary surfactant**
> an essential lubricating substance in the lungs

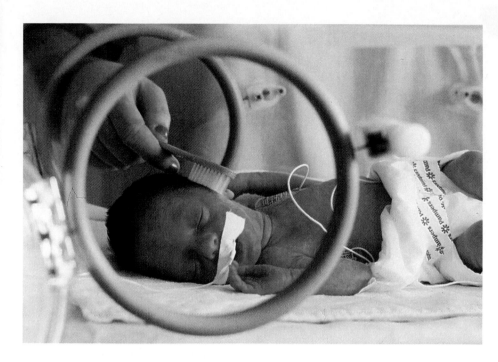

In the controlled environment of the incubator, high-risk premature infants can continue to develop while protected from infection.

food to gain weight. Such infants are usually fed intravenously until they can suck on their own.

Finally, high-risk infants *look* different: Eyes are small; head is narrow, almost pointy; and the distance between the nose and mouth is longer than average. This is not life-threatening, but it can affect emotional development if parents withdraw from these babies because they feel ashamed, embarrassed, or in some way disturbed by their baby's appearance. High-risk infants' behavior, too, can lead to problems.

● Behavioral Characteristics of High-Risk Infants

Normal newborns usually fall into a fairly predictable wake-sleep pattern, but high-risk babies may sleep according to almost no pattern at all. Irregular waking and sleeping, which can last throughout the first year of life, often puts great stress on parents, who can rarely count on a few hours of uninterrupted sleep. High-risk infants also cry more, and their cries sound more distressed than those of full-term babies (Friedman, Zahn-Waxler, & Radke-Yarrow, 1982; Frodi et al., 1978). Quieting these babies is hard, and their prolonged, highly distressed crying may increase their chances of being neglected, even abused (Belsky, 1992; Friedman et al., 1982).

High-risk infants have a narrower band of arousal than normal babies (Field, 1982); they slip from an alert state to a fussy state more quickly or from a drowsy state to an alert state more slowly. They tend to smile less than other babies and are less responsive to their parents' efforts to play with them (Coll et al., 1992). Finding the right kind of playful stimulation can make a difference. In one experiment, when parents calmly imitated their baby's own behavior—gurgling or yawning when the baby did, for example—the baby quieted down and became more alert (Field, 1982). Still, premature babies in general are less responsive to their parents' efforts to play with them (Goldberg, 1978).

Just as with normal babies, there are individual differences among high-risk infants. Not all of them look so different from other babies, not all have extremely piercing cries, and some are more active and responsive than others. All these differences can have consequences, for the infants and for their parents. Researchers have been particularly interested in studying the care of babies with RDS. Ten to twenty percent of premature RDS babies develop chronic lung disease and need supplemental oxygen and breathing support for many months after birth. These babies evoke less sensitive and responsive care from their parents than normal babies do, in part, it seems, because the babies themselves may be less responsive to their parents (Jarvis et al., 1989; Myers et al., 1992). Here, then, is another example of the way an infant's own characteristics will influence development. For many of these babies, especially the ones who will not survive their first year, their environment plays an even bigger role.

● Inequalities in Infant Mortality

For the majority of infants in the United States, the 1980s were a good time to be born. Medical advances increased chances for survival, and in fact, mortality rates dropped slightly: By the end of the decade, 9.8 per 1,000 infants died in their first year compared with 12.8 per 1,000 in 1980. Yet the number of low-birth-weight infants in the United States rose from 6.8 percent in 1980 to 7 percent by 1989 (Southern Regional Project on Infant Mortality, 1993).

The Children's Defense Fund reports that one-quarter of a million low-birth-weight babies are born in the United States annually, and they have a 1 in 10 chance of dying during their first year (Children's Defense Fund, 1987). In all, in the United States, nearly 1 in every 100 infants born dies within the first year of life. The infant mortality rate in the United States is one of the highest in the industrialized world. (See Figure 3.3.) Why?

Their death certificates don't say so, but for all too many, the cause of death is surely poverty and poor prenatal care. As late as 1989, over 111,000 U.S. babies were born in counties that had no prenatal clinics or obstetrical and gynecological services (Southern Regional Project on Infant Mortality, 1993).

The highest infant mortality rates occur in the poorest neighborhoods of large cities: In some poor urban areas, *30 or more infants in 1,000* die during their first year (National Center for Clinical Infant Programs, 1987). For African-Americans, who tend to have low incomes and inner-city lives, the combination can be lethal for their infants. According to a recent report, the infant mortality rate among African-Americans was more than twice that among whites: 18 deaths per 1,000 live births versus 7.6 per 1,000, respectively (Southern Regional Project on Infant Mortality, 1993). Infant mortality rates among Hispanic-Americans and Native Americans, while considerably lower than among African-Americans, are still higher than those among whites (Garcia Coll, 1990).

Many of these babies' mothers are teenagers, single, poorly educated, unemployed, unable to afford prenatal care, or unaware of the need for it; they may not want the child they carry, and they may drink or smoke heavily through-

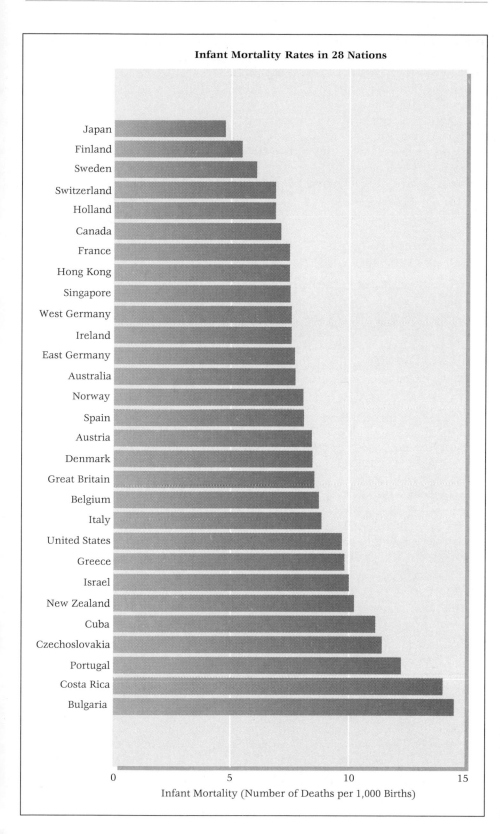

FIGURE 3.3
Despite its advanced health care technology, the United States ranks twenty-first in the world for infant mortality: 10 infants die per 1,000 births. (Source: After Wegman, 1991.)

MAKING A DIFFERENCE

PROMOTING DEVELOPMENT IN PRETERM INFANTS

Under optimal conditions, low-birth-weight babies can spend days or weeks or months in a hospital neonatal unit, depending on the severity of their health problems. There, they are electronically monitored and expertly checked by doctors and nurses. Typically, they go home when they weigh about 5 pounds and their respiratory and nervous systems are considered stable. But many of these babies will need other kinds of support throughout infancy and into childhood if they are to avoid serious developmental problems.

In Burlington, Vermont, a group of researchers wondered about the effectiveness of support programs for mothers and high-risk infants. In 1980, they began a long-term study of two groups of high-risk infants. For 1 week before taking their babies home, mothers in one group (the experimental group) were trained by an intensive care

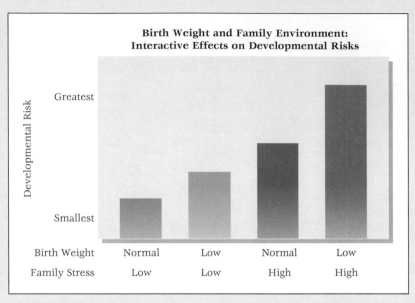

A low-birth-weight baby is usually considered to be at high risk at birth. But family stress, caused by factors including poverty and emotional problems, appears to be a more significant factor in predicting developmental risks than birth weight.

nurse. They were taught: (1) to appreciate that their babies were individuals, with their own temperaments and behaviors; (2) to be sensitive to their babies' cues, especially those that signaled too much stimulation, distress, and readiness for socializing; and (3) to learn how best to respond to their babies' signals, specifically,

out pregnancy. High infant mortality rates are also attributable to increasing numbers of pregnant women who are drug abusers (Johnson, 1989). Attempting to reduce the infant death rate, several cities offer outreach programs and free or low-cost prenatal care. Congress has also passed legislation to provide funding for such programs at a national level.

The bottom line is that affordable, high-quality prenatal care is far less available in the United States than in other industrialized countries, and disparities in prenatal care *within* the United States are especially dramatic. About 40 percent of African-American, Hispanic-American, and Native American mothers do not receive any prenatal care during the first trimester of pregnancy, as compared with "only" 20 percent of white mothers (Wegman, 1991). Hispanic women are three times more likely than other women to receive *no prenatal care at all.*

which responses would satisfy both their babies and themselves. Follow-up support and additional training were provided too. Mothers were visited in their own homes 3, 14, 30, and 90 days after leaving the hospital.

Mothers in the control group had no special training or visits. When the researchers tested both groups of children for intelligence at age 3, 4, and 7, the experimental group outperformed the control group by a substantial amount (Achenbach et al., 1990).

In another study, researchers focused on the atmosphere in the home. When that environment lacks intellectual and emotional support for both parents and infants, the opportunities for premature infants to catch up are very limited. In fact, premature babies born into highly stressed families are at greatest risk of developmental problems (McGauhey et al., 1991; Ross, Lipper, & Auld, 1990; Sameroff & Chandler, 1975). Par-

ents struggling with poverty, acute family problems, and perhaps drug and alcohol abuse are not likely to have the time, attention, and energy to care properly for a difficult, demanding baby. Of course, high-risk infants born into more comfortable families may not get the extra care they need either. Nevertheless, a child born prematurely into a well-functioning family and community is generally better off than a *healthy* child born into a high-risk environment.

With these realities in mind, pediatricians, psychologists, social workers, and early childhood educators developed the Infant Health and Development Program. Aiming to prevent the developmental deficits and problems often found in premature infants from impoverished families, the program combined weekly home visits by a child development specialist for the child's first year, visits every other week through the child's

third birthday, and high-quality 8-hour-per-day developmental day care during the child's second and third year of life.

When compared at age 3 with children from similar backgrounds, those who had been in the experimental program scored better on cognitive abilities tests and were less likely to function in the retarded range. They also showed fewer behavior problems at age 3 than the control children (Infant Health and Development Program, 1990). Another evaluation of this program found that the intervention, while successful across ethnic groups, may have been especially successful for ethnic minority families. Mothers in the experimental program showed more positive and responsive interaction with their babies, and infants in the experimental group scored higher on measures of competence (Spiker, Ferguson, & Brooks-Gunn, 1993).

● Prospects for Premature Infants

For high-risk newborns, intervention promotes life itself. The best programs will alleviate stresses, facilitate learning, and promote growth. Supported in the controlled environment of the incubator, high-risk infants continue to develop until their own bodies are mature enough to sustain life.

In most progressive hospitals, psychological health is promoted too. Preterm infants in incubators can hear recordings of a heartbeat or of their own mother's voice (Katz, 1971; Segall, 1972). They get extra chances to suck and are stroked and rocked, stimulation which helps to prevent developmental delays (Fajardo et al., 1990; Field et al., 1986; Ottenbacher et al., 1987; Scafidi et al., 1986). And premature infants who are massaged regularly gain weight faster even though they do not consume more calories (Scafidi et al., 1990).

One of the best ways to help high-risk babies is to offer their parents both support and training. In Making a Difference: Promoting Development for Preterm Infants, we describe such programs.

● Sudden Infant Death Syndrome

● **sudden infant death syndrome (SIDS)**
death in early infancy for no apparent reason

Each year, in the United States, 7,000 infants whose parents believed they were healthy go to sleep and never wake up again. Their parents find them suffocated. **Sudden infant death syndrome (SIDS),** or crib death, remains the leading cause of nonaccidental death for infants between 1 month and 1 year. Most SIDS victims are between 2 and 4 months old (McKenna, 1990a).

Recent research suggests that SIDS babies are not as healthy before death as both physicians and parents once thought, and several environmental factors seem to cluster around them: At greatest risk are infants from 1 to 5 months born to poor, single, teenaged mothers who smoked (Hoffman et al., 1988; Taylor & Emery, 1988). Most SIDS victims are low-birth-weight babies (less than 2,500 grams, or 5½ pounds) who continue to grow at a slower rate. Within 2 weeks before death, a significant number have colds and bouts with diarrhea and/or vomiting. During the 24 hours before death, SIDS babies appear to be both listless and more irritable; breathing difficulties and excessively rapid heartbeats are also common. These babies also tend to be bottle- rather than breast-fed. It is possible that they haven't gotten the immunity to infections which precede SIDS that breast-fed infants get (Hoffman et al., 1988).

One of the most interesting observations about SIDS concerns the way these babies sleep—alone. In traditional and aboriginal societies, as well as in modern Japan, infants sleep in the same bed or on the same mat as their parents. In these societies, SIDS rarely happens (McKenna, 1990c). What is the connection? Between 2 and 4 months, the period of greatest risk for SIDS, control of respiration shifts from the brain stem to the cortex (McKenna, 1990b). Most infants make this transition easily, but babies who sleep with their parents may have an advantage that protects them from SIDS. The theory is that sleeping with an adult may help infants to regulate their own breathing during this transitional time when breathing sometimes stops for brief periods. Regulation may happen in two ways: Infants may imitate the regular breathing pattern of adults, and the carbon dioxide parents expel may stimulate babies to breathe again if their own breathing stops (McKenna, 1990a).

Research done with premature babies in isolettes suggests that babies do learn to mimic breathing rhythms. When the infants slept next to a "breathing teddy bear" whose stomach was made to expand and contract in breathinglike fashion, their breathing became more regular and stable (Thoman & Graham, 1986). Finally, the baby's bedding itself may contribute to SIDS. Some infants are found face down on pillows or mattresses that are too soft. Not yet able to move their head to permit clear breathing, these infants may have suffocated (Kemp & Thach, 1991).

Over the next months, infants become less vulnerable, as their nervous system and motor abilities mature. We turn to these developments in the next chapter.

SUMMARY

1. Prepared childbirth has revolutionized labor and delivery in the last 20 years. Childbirth classes based on Lamaze techniques teach both parents-to-be how to minimize pain and maximize the experience of birth. Modern parents can make many choices about how they want their baby to be born. (See pages 80–83.)

2. Signs that birth is near include lightening (movement of the fetus into position for birth), the bloody show (appearance of blood-tinged mucus), rupture of the amniotic sac, and the beginning of uterine contractions. (See pages 83–84.)

3. The first stage of labor—the longest—has three substages: early first stage, during which contractions become regular; middle first stage, when contractions become stronger and the cervix begins to dilate; and transition, the shortest and most painful stage, in which the cervix dilates completely. Birth occurs during the second stage of labor, and the placenta is delivered during the third stage. (See pages 84–86.)

4. Most babies are born vaginally, emerging headfirst. Babies in the breech or transverse position are likely to be delivered by cesarean section, surgically removed from the uterus. Complications during labor may also lead to a cesarean delivery, especially if the fetal monitor shows a too-slow heartbeat. In such cases, doctors act to prevent anoxia, a lack of oxygen to the brain. (See pages 87–89.)

5. At birth, the baby's lungs and circulatory system must begin functioning independently. The 10-point Apgar test, given after 1 and 5 minutes of life, evaluates the baby's heart rate, breathing, muscle tone, reflexes, and color. Low scores signal the need for emergency medical intervention. (See pages 89–91.)

6. Reflexes are motor behaviors that are not under voluntary control. Most newborn reflexes, such as sucking or grasping, evolved because they were adaptive, increasing the infant's chances of survival. (See pages 94–96.)

7. Babies have six natural states of arousal: regular sleep, irregular sleep, drowsiness, alert activity, waking activity, and crying (or distress). States of arousal influence the way babies respond to stimulation as well as the way parents respond to babies. (See pages 96–98.)

8. The Brazelton Newborn Behavioral Assessment Scale is used to assess babies' reflexes, state control, vision and hearing, and motor abilities. The Brazelton examination identifies differences among infants and helps parents understand their own baby's unique needs. The test does *not* predict future development, partly because an infant's behavior changes dramatically during the early days of life. (See pages 97–98.)

9. The competent newborn has sensory capacities much greater than were once thought. Newborns have definite preferences for certain types of visual stimuli, sounds, smells, and tastes. Babies seem to begin learning shortly after birth. Recent research also shows that newborns probably learn in at least three ways: by classical conditioning, operant conditioning, and observation. (See pages 99–103.)

10. Premature and low-birth-weight babies are high-risk infants. Insufficient prenatal care, poor nutrition, exposure to teratogens such as nicotine and alcohol, and maternal age can all affect prematurity and birth weight. Premature babies raised in highly stressed families, especially poor ones, are at the greatest risk for developmental problems. (See pages 103–110.)

KEY TERMS

anoxia
Apgar test
binocular convergence
bloody show
breech birth
cesarean section
colic
contractions
engagement (lightening)
engrossment
episiotomy
fetal monitor
forceps delivery
high-risk infants

Lamaze method
learning
low birth weight
neonatology
Newborn Behavioral Assessment Scale
observational learning
pitocin
premature (preterm) baby
prepared (natural) childbirth
pulmonary surfactant
reflex

respiratory distress syndrome (RDS)
sound localization
state control
states of arousal
sudden infant death syndrome (SIDS)
transition
transverse presentation
vacuum extraction
vernix
very low birth weight (VLBW)
visual acuity

SUGGESTED READINGS

Hotchner, T. (1990). *Pregnancy and childbirth.* New York: Avon. A comprehensive guide to pregnancy and childbirth.

Lester, B., & Tronick, E. (Eds.) (1990). *Stimulation and the preterm infant: The limits of plasticity.* Philadelphia: Saunders. An edited collection based on a round-table discussion among experts on intervention with premature infants.

Leboyer, F. (1975). *Birth without violence.* New York: Knopf. In this volume a radical obstetrician shares his approach to delivery that has contributed to the revolution in childbirth that has occurred in America over the past two decades.

MacFarlane, A. (1977). *The psychology of childbirth.* Cambridge, MA: Harvard University Press. A classic book on emotional aspects of childbirth, including morning sickness, hospital versus home delivery, and mother-infant bonding.

INFANCY

PHYSICAL
DEVELOPMENT
IN INFANCY

The newborn we saw in the last chapter could neither turn her head nor lift her body. Unsupported, her head flops down, and her back slumps forward. In 6 months, she sits in a high chair feeding herself. Add a few months and she's crawling; by 15 months, she's walking. At 2, she's running.

As we look at this sequence of motor development, we will focus again on the universal and the individual, on the genetic timetable influencing all of physical development, on differences in individual infants, and on the environmental conditions that influence those differences.

GROWTH

An average newborn weighs about 7½ pounds, *3 billion* times more than the fertilized ovum from which he or she developed. While no longer at this rate, of course, growth during infancy is still rapid. In fact, if you had continued growing at the rate of your first year of life, by age 3 you would have weighed 200 pounds and measured over 5 feet tall! Not until puberty will we grow nearly so quickly again. In part, these physical changes are genetically determined: We all show the same patterns of growth, but some of us will grow taller and faster than others. But from infancy on, genetic instructions are influenced by the total environment—by a range of factors including nutrition, physical experiences, and emotional support.

● Changes in Weight, Height, and Shape

During the first year, a baby's weight triples to about 20 to 24 pounds. Until about 9 months, this gain is mostly fat; after that, it is mainly bone and muscle. Usually, fat disappears when walking begins, so even chubby babies tend to be lean toddlers. During the second year, weight gain slows to about half a pound per month: A 7-pound newborn quadruples in weight to about 30 pounds by age 2.

Along with pounds, come inches. By the end of the first year, the newborn, whose entire arm and hand fit in her parent's palm, has grown from 20 to 30 inches, a 50 percent increase. By the end of the second year, height has climbed another 25 percent—to about 35 inches. In just 2 years, infants grow to half, or even more, of their adult height. By tracking the growth of 31 infants, scientists discovered that babies grow in spurts; after a period of no change, they can grow up to a half inch in 24 hours. Before each spurt they become more irritable than usual (Lampl, Veldhuis, & Johnson, 1992). Growth slows from age 2 on, speeding up again at puberty. There are racial differences in physical growth, with African-American children in general growing somewhat faster and maturing earlier physically than their white counterparts (Garcia Coll, 1990).

Predicting adult height from length at birth is a bit tricky, because, like weight, a newborn's length is strongly influenced by the environment in the uterus. Teratogens or poor fetal nutrition (or both) can affect growth *in utero*. But by the second year, after the infant has had sufficient time to grow outside the uterine environment, predictions become more reliable. Tall 2-year-olds often do become tall adults.

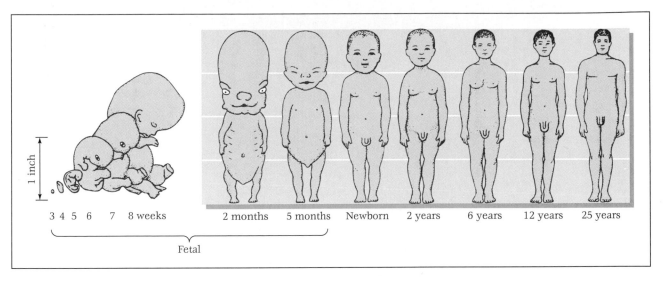

1 inch

3 4 5 6 7 8 weeks   2 months   5 months   Newborn   2 years   6 years   12 years   25 years

Fetal

FIGURE 4.1
Changes in the Form and Proportion of the Human Body
The drawing depicts the growth of a male's body during the embryonic, fetal, and postnatal stages. Note the developmental changes in the size of the head and limbs in relation to the size of the body.
(SOURCE: Rugh & Shettles, 1971.)

● Changes in Proportion

Growth involves more than a simple increase in height and weight. The parts of an infant's body grow at different rates, and their relative proportions change as well. This is called the **proportional phenomenon,** and it follows the same pattern we saw during fetal development, from the head down.

A newborn's head is unusually large relative to the rest of her body. At birth, the head accounts for about one-fourth of body length; by childhood, it equals only one-tenth of total height. The rate of head growth is tied to brain growth. The infant's skull must accommodate a growing brain. At birth, the brain already weighs one-quarter of its adult weight, and by age 2, the brain has reached three-quarters of its adult weight. But a 2-year-old's whole body is only about one-fourth of her full adult weight (Tanner, 1970).

In contrast to the head, which gradually decreases in its proportion to overall body length, the legs *increase* their relative proportion. At birth, they make up about one-third of an infant's length, but by adulthood, legs account for about half of height. Figure 4.1 illustrates these changes in proportional development from the prenatal period through adulthood.

As body proportions change, so does the baby's center of gravity. During infancy, a large head and short legs create a high center of gravity, so when babies walk, they keep their legs far apart to stay balanced. By age 4, longer legs shift the center of gravity downward, and posture straightens up (Sinclair, 1913).

● **proportional phenomenon**
the characteristic of an infant's growth in which different parts of the infant's body grow at different rates, resulting in alterations in their relative proportions

MOTOR DEVELOPMENT

Motor refers to motion, and **motor development** is the infant's growing ability to use his or her body for purposeful, voluntary motion. *Purposeful* is the key word here. Recall that newborns' movements are mostly reflexive, and even

● **motor development**
the increasing ability to control the body in purposeful motion

Short legs and a large head create a high center of gravity. To keep their balance, babies walk with legs apart.

though they can lift a foot or move a hand, they can't control their muscles. The newborn's reflexive kicks and squirms may seem random, but they fit into an overall sequence of development that is not random at all. As with all of human development, physical growth follows universal principles and sequences. Below we discuss the three basic principles of physical development during infancy.

● Developmental Trends and Principles

Notice in Figure 4.2 that motor skills develop from head to foot. Known as **cephalocaudal development** (head to tail), this sequence explains why infants can control their neck muscles before their chest muscles and why they sit before they stand. The cephalocaudal trend began during gestation, as the fetus developed from the head down.

The second trend concerns direction too: Growth and control proceed from the center of the body outward—**proximodistal development.** Infants can control their arms at the shoulders before they can direct their hands and fingers. At 3 months they may reach for and miss an object, but by 5 months their fingers can grab and hold things within reach.

A third growth trend is **mass-to-specific development**—large to small muscle control. At first, infants reach with both arms, but by 7 months, most can reach out with just one arm at a time. Actions become more specific and directed. A 6-month-old sees an object, wants it, reaches for and takes it in a smoothly controlled movement. The ability to make specific moves toward spe-

● **cephalocaudal development**
the pattern of growth proceeding from the head downward

● **proximodistal development**
the pattern of growth from the center of the body outward

● **mass-to-specific development**
the pattern of growth from large to small muscles

FIGURE 4.2
The Sequence of Motor Development
The ages at which the average infant achieves a given behavior.
(SOURCE: Shirley, 1933.)

● **differentiation**
the ability to make specific
moves toward specific goals

cific goals is the principle of **differentiation,** and it develops along with the infant's maturing nervous and muscular systems (also called the neuromuscular system).

● Gaining Body Control

Unless seriously impaired or uncoordinated, adults perform most simple motor acts skillfully and gracefully, whether drinking from a cup or putting on a glove. But what appear as simple, ordinary movements are actually complex motor behaviors, performed with exact temporal (time-related) and spatial coordination among limbs and other parts of the body. To drink from a glass, you straighten your arm at the elbow, extending your hand toward the glass; your fingers open on the way and close just as they connect with the glass. Then your elbow bends, bringing the glass to the edge of your lips, just as your mouth opens to take that drink.

By comparison, the young infant's movements seem jerky and uncoordinated. But a series of simple, yet elegant experiments revealed that even the limb movements of young infants are coordinated to a surprising degree. When 6-week-old babies lying on their backs had a weight attached to one leg, they kicked their unweighted leg faster, compensating for the drag on the other leg. This means that even by the second month of life, the two legs are not separate kicking instruments but are coordinated—in a way that resembles walking (Thelen, Skala, & Kelso, 1987).

With maturity such simple coordination is refined, and new motor skills emerge. For several days or even weeks before a new motor skill appears, many babies go through a kind of practice. Turning over may be preceded by rocking from side to side; crawling, by rocking back and forth on hands and knees. These

Because large muscle control precedes small muscle coordination, babies can reach for things before they can easily grasp them.

repetitive movements of the head, chest, and limbs are aptly named **rhythmi-cal stereotypies:** Both rhythmical and stereotyped, they are repeated almost exactly for a certain period and do not seem to be under voluntary control. They may represent a transition from random movements to deliberate, coordinated motor control (Thelen, 1981). When the stereotypy appears unusually early, so does the related voluntary activity. These relationships suggest that once the "wiring" in the nervous system is in place, the "circuits" are tested by the repeated practice of the stereotyped movement (Thelen, 1979). Later in this chapter, we'll discuss the way the maturing nervous system influences the appearance and efficiency of motor skills.

It is important to keep in mind that particular motor skills and abilities do not suddenly appear, fully formed, in a child's behavioral repertoire. Instead, they emerge according to a principle called **developmental gradualness** (Fischer & Bidell, 1992). Specific motor skills (such as reaching) appear initially in rudimentary forms (for example, extending the arm without moving the fingers) and specific contexts (for example, only when in the infant seat). Gradually, these skills become more complex and wide-ranging over time.

To sum up, all infants follow the same general sequence of motor development (see Figure 4.2), but skills may appear considerably earlier or later than charts predict. Some babies walk at 10 months or earlier and others not until 15 months. Similarly, some babies skip a step in the sequence—and some children develop their own adaptations: Instead of crawling, they may scoot along on their bottoms. Others may walk on their knees before getting up on their feet in the second year. Unless there is a series of delays or irregularities in motor development, there is no need to be concerned about somewhat advanced or delayed motor abilities. Variation is normal and does not predict future athletic skill.

Heredity and Environment

If motor skills develop in the same sequence at roughly the same age, in every normal infant, do genes determine motor development? Traditionally, the answer was yes (Gesell & Ames, 1937), until researchers began questioning the role of the environment. Much of what we know about the relationship between heredity, environment, and motor development comes from a series of classic studies carried out over 50 years ago by Wayne Dennis.

In his early research, Dennis compared two groups of Hopi Indians (Dennis, 1940). Because the groups were genetically similar, Dennis reasoned, any significant differences in development would have to be environmentally caused. One group cared for their infants in the tribe's customary way: Babies, tightly swaddled to "cradle boards," were carried on their mothers' backs. These infants could move only their heads. The second group used contemporary Western methods, allowing their babies free movement. In *both* groups, infants walked by 15 months. All showed the same degree of neuromuscular skills at the same time whether or not they had been attached to cradle boards. On the basis of these findings, Dennis concluded that genes, rather than specific child care practices, influence motor development most strongly.

But Dennis still wondered about environmental influences, and two decades later he published another report demonstrating that experience *does* influence the process of motor development (Dennis, 1960). Like the Hopi study, the later

rhythmical stereotypies apparently reflexive, repeated rhythmic movements that serve as transition from random to controlled movement

developmental gradualness the principle stating that specific motor skills appear initially in rudimentary forms and specific contexts; over time, these skills become more complex and wide-ranging

Although Hopi Indian babies can move only their head when laced onto a cradle board, their motor skills mature at the same rate as those of babies who are not confined.

research also involved infants who shared similar hereditary background but were cared for differently. This time, his subjects were Iranian orphans raised in three different institutions. In two of these, the babies were left lying in their cribs, fed by a bottle propped against pillows. Sheets covered the sides of their cribs, restricting their views. Except when they were picked up to be bathed, these babies neither touched nor saw other people. In the third orphanage, infants were encouraged to sit up, to play, and to interact with people.

Dennis found that in the first two orphanages, the major milestones of motor achievement were markedly delayed. Most of the children were not even sitting up by the age of 1 year, and many were still not sitting by 21 months. Even by 3 years, the majority of the children from these two institutions were still not walking. This study illustrates that genes alone do not direct motor development. Normal growth requires *both* physical and social stimulation.

But what if a child gets more than a normal amount of stimulation? Can some child-rearing practices speed up or enhance motor development? The answer is a cautious yes. In an experiment done in the United States, for example, walking was advanced by several months when parents stimulated the stepping reflex in infants during the first 2 months of life (Zelazo, 1983). An observational study in England comparing English, Jamaican, and Indian babies yielded similar results. Jamaican mothers expected their babies to sit and walk early, and from birth on, they massaged and gently stretched their babies' limbs. After 3 months, these babies practiced stepping movements with their mothers' help. As a group, the Jamaican babies did sit and walk earlier than the English and Indian babies living in the same city whose mothers did not offer such early stimulation (B. Hopkins & Westra, 1988a, 1988b, 1990).

Among the Kipsigi tribe of Kenya, different customs foster other motor skills. Here, where infants spend over 60 percent of their waking time sitting in someone's lap, they sit alone earlier than most other babies. In African tribes where babies are carried (unswaddled) on someone's back, infants do seem to develop stronger trunk, buttock, and thigh muscles. But African babies rarely crawl or creep early, apparently because they spend little time on the ground on their stomachs (Kilbride, 1977; Super, 1981).

Cross-cultural studies of infant development show quite clearly that differences in caregiving customs, reflecting differences in attitudes and beliefs, can create differences in infant motor development. In certain groups, such as the Baganda of Uganda, the Kipsigis of Kenya, or the West Indians of Jamaica, infants are handled in ways that speed the acquisition of certain motor achievements, such as sitting, stepping, or walking. Among the Baganda, for example, the ability to sit upright alone is seen as a highly desirable skill, in part because once infants can sit upright, their mothers do not have to carry them while tending to their gardens. As a consequence, Baganda mothers try to promote upright sitting in their infants by propping them up at a very early age with mats or cloths (Kilbride & Kilbride, 1975). American mothers are less likely to care if their babies sit up early, and they can use infant seats, high chairs, and the like to support their children if necessary. As a consequence of these environmental differences, Baganda children sit upright at a younger age than their American counterparts.

Evidence suggests that early locomotion, by crawling or by using an infant walker, may speed up development of certain emotional and cognitive abilities by about a month or so. In one series of experiments, infants who crawled sooner than others were found to be more afraid of falling off an edge (as on a bed), and noncrawlers who could move themselves around in an infant walker developed fear of heights before noncrawlers who had no experience with walkers (Bertenthal, Campos, & Barnett, 1984; Campos, Bertenthal, & Kermoian, 1992. The fear of falling and of heights seems to indicate some increased understanding of location in space.

The studies we've described above raise some interesting points. They tell us that motor development and related emotional and cognitive abilities *can* be accelerated at least in the short term, but *should* they be? No one really knows what the long-term effects are of speeding development (Bloch, 1989). We say this while acknowledging that the question itself may be an ethnocentric one. Are the Jamaican and African mothers described above "speeding" development, or are they simply doing what mothers in their cultures do? If we use only Western averages as the norm, then in other cultures with other customs, development may appear to be "speeded" up only relative to the timetables in our own culture. What all parents need to remember is that, in any culture, readiness comes first. When infants are not neurologically ready for further development, too much stimulation achieves nothing and may even be counterproductive.

We can conclude, again, that heredity sets the *sequence* of motor development, but its *expression* in each infant is influenced by experience. The culture infants live in, their families, and others in their lives will affect the outcome of every baby's genetic plan for growth and development. It can be delayed by emotional and sensory deprivation, or it can be speeded up—within limits—by extra physical stimulation. And whenever physical changes take place, they will always interact with and influence other areas of development.

● Consequences of Motor Development

A baby who can barely lift up his head sees very little, but each new motor skill expands his world, allowing him to see, reach, manipulate, and finally move toward anything he wants. Sitting enables babies to look around in any direction, gathering information. Upright, they can also manipulate objects with their hands, practicing and developing hand-eye coordination. And as we noted above, emotional and cognitive capacities develop along with motor skills. Newly walking toddlers are more independent than they were just a few days before. Besides showing a greater desire to separate from their mothers, they explore new territory and are more likely to play with things their mothers have prohibited (Biringen, Emde, & Campos, 1991; Jones, Liggon, & Biringen, 1991).

Clearly, relationships with adults and siblings are going to change, as people start protecting things from the baby and the baby from himself. In the above studies, after babies began walking, their mothers began saying "no" more than when their babies were crawling (Biringen et al., 1991).

When "childproofing," parents need to balance protection against the baby's need to use new skills and to satisfy curiosity. For every family this challenge is different, influenced in part by the baby herself. A not-too-active first child at home with relaxed adults may run up against very few restrictions. But suppose a relentlessly curious 10-month-old has tense parents and an active 3-year-old

With every new motor skill, toddlers can move a little further into the physical world. The simplest objects—a shell, a rock, a fist of sand—become fascinating playthings.

brother. After the baby begins crawling, her mother worries whenever the baby is out of sight. Soon the mother begins scolding ("Stop that"), and the playpen seems like the only way to keep the baby safe. A similarly active firstborn baby, or one with a more relaxed mother, could have a far different experience.

In short, motor skills affect relationships, which, in turn, affect development. This is a process we will observe again and again. The child's own development—whether it is motor, cognitive, or emotional—affects the way others respond to him, which in turn affects development. In Chapter 3, for example, we noted that the pitch of a cry can affect a newborn's relationship with his parents.

There is also evidence that motor development can enhance perceptual development (Bushnell & Boudreau, 1993). This has been nicely illustrated in research on the development of hand control and its relation to a fascinating phenomenon called **haptic perception.** Haptic perception refers to the ability to acquire information about objects by handling them, rather than simply by looking at them. (Imagine, for example, reaching into an enclosed container and differentiating among objects by feeling them.) As you would expect, the infant's knowledge about the world is enhanced significantly by gains in haptic perception. For example, by about 6 or 7 months, infants are able to distinguish through touch between objects that are rough versus smooth or hard versus soft.

● **haptic perception**
the ability to acquire information about objects by handling them, rather than simply by looking at them

The development of haptic perception shows how motor development and perceptual development are intricately interconnected. Advances in motor development permit the infant to gain control of his body and to sit upright and reasonably balanced. This achievement, in turn, frees the infant to use his hands to explore objects, rather than to support himself. It is no coincidence, then, that around 6 months, when most infants are first sitting upright without support, babies begin to engage in repetitive finger and hand motions while holding objects (scratching things, rubbing them, passing them from hand to hand) and examining them visually. Thus, the infant's perceptual development is facilitated by his ability to integrate information he has acquired through touch with information he has acquired through sight. And this perceptual advance is made possible by the development of motor abilities.

To sum up, then, we can make the following points about motor development:

1. Our common human heredity ensures a similar sequence of motor development for all infants.

2. At the same time, experience influences the expression of every infant's unique motor "timetable."

3. A serious lack of stimulation can retard motor development.

4. But most infants receive enough stimulation to ensure normal motor development.

5. Extra stimulation can speed development, but this is not necessarily good for infants, and too much stimulation offered at the wrong time can be stressful.

6. All infants influence their own development; new motor skills affect the way others respond to them as well as what they can learn about the physical world.

BRAIN AND NERVOUS SYSTEM DEVELOPMENT

neurons
nerve cells; the primary functional unit of the nervous system

cerebral cortex
the wrinkled outer layer of the brain, which is the most highly evolved part of the brain, responsible for perception, muscle control, thought, and memory

arborization
the proliferation of connections among neurons by branching

myelin
an insulating fatty sheath on nerve fibers

Every motor and cognitive skill that appears during infancy is influenced by the maturing *nervous system,* which includes the brain, the spinal cord, and the nerves. The nervous system controls the actions of all the bones, muscles, glands, and organs of the body. This control is exercised through electrochemical impulses which pass through bundles of long, thin cells called **neurons.** The brain is composed of at least 10 billion such cells. As an impulse passes from one neuron to another, it jumps across a tiny space called a *synapse.* To direct movement of your hand, for example, an impulse begins in the brain and jumps thousands of synapses in a fraction of a second.

The last part of the brain to develop and the least mature at birth is the outermost area, the **cerebral cortex.** Not fully developed until adolescence (Tanner, 1978), this part of the brain controls motor development, sensory skills, and higher-order cognitive skills. As you read this, for example, your cortex controls your ability to see and understand the words and to turn the page.

Between 6 months and 2 years, considerable development occurs in the areas of the cortex responsible for complex cognitive activities, such as anticipation and reasoning. From birth on, two kinds of changes are occurring: (1) The number of connections between neurons increases (*not* the number of neurons). This process, **arborization,** increases the brain's size and complexity (see Figure 4.3). (2) The neurons become insulated by a fatty sheath of **myelin,** which speeds up and improves the efficiency of message transfers (Morrell & Norton, 1980). These changes seem to come in periods of rapid growth and development, or growth spurts, and we can see their effects during the first 3 months of an infant's life.

Newborns' movements, inborn reflexes rather than controlled motions, reflect the immaturity of the cortex. But by 3 months, the cortex is at least partially controlling the movements of the upper body and arms. We know these changes have occurred because 3-month-olds have far more control over their movements than they had at birth. Voluntary actions have begun to replace reflexes. By this age, too, the cortex is more involved in the functioning of the senses, including hearing and vision. We focus now on the kinds of things that will influence the infant's developing brain.

FIGURE 4.3
Maturing Brain Tissue
In humans, the brain tissues mature rapidly after birth. These drawings of sections of brain tissue from the cerebral cortex illustrate the increasing complexity of the neutral networks in the maturing human brain.
(SOURCE: Conel, 1959.)

At birth   1 month   3 months   6 months   15 months   2 years

● Biology, Experience, and Brain Development

As with fetal and motor development, the interaction between biology and experience is a key principle in brain development. Genes determine the timing of changes within the brain, but normal development depends on adequate experience. Two types of experience that foster brain development are (1) sensory experience and (2) self-produced experience—experiences that infants actively produce on their own (Bornstein & Lamb, 1992).

Sensory experiences influence the size of neurons, the connectivity between them (arborization), and psychological and behavioral functioning (Black & Greenough, 1986). Because we cannot experimentally manipulate the environments of infants for prolonged periods, researchers use animals to study the effects of sensory deprivation and stimulation on the brain. In one now classic study, cats were reared so that they saw vertical lines but not horizontals. At a later age, their ability to respond to horizontal lines was impaired (Hirsch & Spinelli, 1970). And research with rats clearly shows the effects of sensory enrichment and deprivation. Rats who were reared with lots to look at had better-developed visual cortexes than rats who had little to see (Black & Greenough, 1986).

What is the evidence that self-produced experiences enhance brain development? One piece of evidence is that the right side of the brain develops faster than the left side, apparently because infants often perform large-scale motor acts (for example, flailing arms, rolling over, crawling) that are processed in and controlled by the brain's right side (Scheibel et al., 1985).

One especially fascinating feature of the young brain is its capacity to make up for modest damage that may have occurred at an earlier age. Early in devel-

After the fall of Romanian dictator Ceauşescu pictures confirmed reports of abandoned children housed in state-run institutions where both care and food had been inadequate for normal, healthy development.

opment, some cells can do the work of others, meaning that recovery of function after loss of neurons or damage is possible. This ability of some brain cells to substitute for others does not happen later in development, after some sensitive period has passed (Goldman-Rakic, 1987). Not only do early sensory experiences foster proper brain development, but enriching experiences also aid recovery from injury or insult. Such experiences allow the brain, through the branching and interconnecting of neurons, to "rewire" itself, compensating for the initial injury (Kolb, 1989). This kind of recovery, though, can happen only when the injury was not too severe.

For most infants, ordinary life offers all the stimulation needed for normal development of the sensory areas of the cerebral cortex (Greenough, Black, & Wallace, 1987). Parents do not have to give their infants any special "brain training." Although there is a trend among middle-class parents today to provide all kinds of special toys, games, and training in an attempt to produce a smarter, "better" baby, moderate stimulation, sensitive care, and balance are the things to keep in mind and in practice.

In Chapter 7 we shall see how intervention programs can alleviate the effects of deprivation during the early years. Now we turn to the most critical environmental influence of all for physical development: nutrition.

PHYSICAL DEVELOPMENT AND NUTRITION

One of the clearest examples of the interaction of genetic potential and the environment concerns infant nutrition. Even with all the other kinds of stimulation present, if an infant is not adequately nourished, the genetic plan for physical development will be compromised, sometimes so severely that serious disease or even death results.

Infant growth involves the creation of new cells at a very rapid rate. Recall that during the first year alone, infants triple their weight and increase their length by one-half. Like adults, they are also maintaining the cells and tissues that they already have. To meet these demands, each day an infant needs more than twice the calories and three times the protein per pound of body weight than an adult needs.

Starving children in Somalia and Ethiopia and malnourished children in our own poor communities are the most dramatic examples of the tragic consequences of inadequate diets. Even when children survive, malnutrition can still leave its mark. For example, nutrition can work toward either the upper or the lower level of potential for height. After World War II, children who had lived under near-famine conditions in Germany lagged 10 to 20 months behind their expected rates of growth (Sinclair, 1913). If proper nutrition begins, growth can speed up. If the period of malnutrition has been brief, *catch-up* growth can restore children to their genetically predicted height. But when serious malnutrition is prolonged, the lost potential for growth becomes permanent. Thus, though genes may predispose us toward a particular height, nutrition works toward either the upper or lower level of that potential.

Although breast-feeding offers some nutritional and immunological benefits to infants, there is no evidence that it enhances the mother-infant bond. What matters more—whether breast or bottle is used—are the feelings offered with the feedings.

● Breast- versus Bottle-Feeding

Probably the most passionately argued controversy surrounding the nutrition of infants has been the debate over the breast versus the bottle. For most of human history, mother's milk was all there was, but the advent of infant formula early in this century offered a choice. The first formulas were time-consuming to prepare and were used mainly as an occasional substitute for breast milk. But as they became more convenient, their use spread, and by 1971, 75 percent of U.S. babies were formula-fed (Martinez, 1984).

Despite this early enthusiasm for formula, American opinion and practice have swung back to favoring breast-feeding. During the late 1970s and the 1980s, the move toward natural childbirth among middle-class educated American women was accompanied by a rising interest in all things natural—including nursing.

Pediatricians urged the return to nursing too, as most consider breast milk the ideal first food. Why?

1. Breast milk is always sterile and at a comfortable temperature.

2. Breast milk is easier to digest than cow's milk, and far fewer babies develop allergies to breast milk than to formula.

3. The iron in breast milk is more readily absorbed, as are certain other nutrients.

4. Breast milk has a somewhat higher sugar content and also produces a softer curd, which helps to prevent constipation.

5. Breast milk contains antibodies that help babies resist minor infections. (Temporary resistance to major infections was conveyed in the uterus and is subsequently boosted by routine immunizations.)

6. Nutrients in breast milk are balanced to promote rapid brain growth and myelinization, whereas those in cow's milk are geared primarily for muscle growth.

Although nursing advocates frequently argue that infants and mothers form stronger emotional ties through nursing than they can through bottle-feeding, there is really no evidence suggesting that breast-fed babies as a group have better relationships with their mothers than bottle-fed babies. What matters are the feelings surrounding feeding. If either the breast or bottle is offered warmly, attentively, and with pleasure, the baby will thrive. Whether a woman continues to breast-feed, or even whether she chooses to nurse for just a few months, depends on her own needs and lifestyle. It is important to keep in mind that feeding an infant can be a close, rewarding experience for mother—or father—and baby regardless of the method.

Pediatricians today do encourage mothers to nurse their infants if it is possible, if only for the first few months, because of the nutritional and immunological benefits of breast milk. And, of course, bottle-feeding is far more expensive than breast-feeding. Ironically, however, breast-feeding is relatively less frequent among poor and minority mothers than in other groups, and mothers from minority groups are more likely to stop breast-feeding earlier than whites (Kurinij, Shiono, & Rhoads, 1988; MacGowan et al., 1991; Romero-Gwynn & Carias, 1989). Many observers believe that the manufacturers of infant formula have unfairly tried to promote its use among less affluent and less educated mothers, who are less likely to have access to pediatric advice and are therefore less likely to be informed of the benefits of breast-feeding. Recent studies show, however, that deliberate efforts to promote breast-feeding among poor minority mothers can be successful (Kistin et al., 1990).

● Malnutrition: Causes and Effects

Given the obvious importance of early nutrition to healthy infant development, it is especially disheartening to realize that the number of children living in poverty in the United States has increased over the past 20 years. Today, nearly one in every four children under the age of 6 lives in poverty. Poverty is espe-

FIGURE 4.4
Percentage and Number Distribution of All Children under Age 6 and of Poor Children under 6 by Race/Ethnicity, 1991
Of all children under age 6 in 1991, 32 percent were minorities. However, 60 percent of poor children under 6 were minorities.
(SOURCE: National Center for Children in Poverty, 1993.)

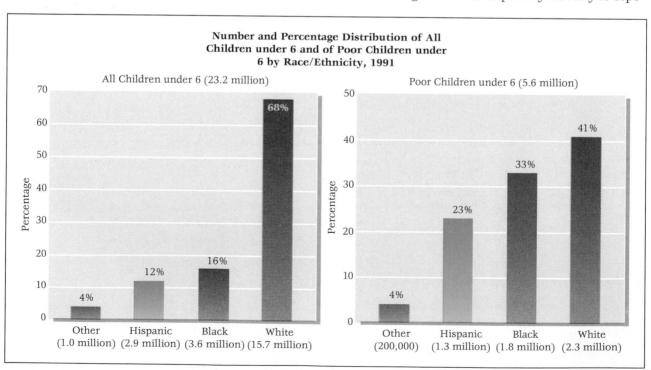

Number and Percentage Distribution of All Children under 6 and of Poor Children under 6 by Race/Ethnicity, 1991

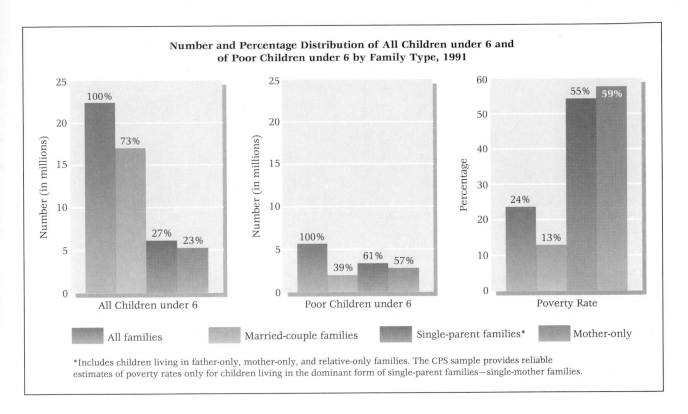

Number and Percentage Distribution of All Children under 6 and of Poor Children under 6 by Family Type, 1991

*Includes children living in father-only, mother-only, and relative-only families. The CPS sample provides reliable estimates of poverty rates only for children living in the dominant form of single-parent families—single-mother families.

cially prevalent among minority children, among children in single-parent households, and among children living in urban areas (see Figures 4.4, 4.5, 4.6). Indeed, more than half of all African-American youngsters grow up in poverty.

With poverty goes malnutrition, so poor babies are very likely to be small and underweight babies. For example, a recent study showed that among poor families in Chicago, nearly one-third of the children under age 2 fell below the tenth percentile for height and weight and were therefore likely to have been malnourished (National Center for Clinical Infant Programs, 1987).

Because normal physical growth demands protein, infants are particularly vulnerable to the consequences of malnutrition. In the brain, for example, neurons in the cortex grow rapidly during infancy, continuing to mature until adolescence. Too few calories toward the end of pregnancy and during infancy can slow the rate of brain cell growth and can actually lower the number of brain cells in malnourished infants (Winick & Rosso, 1969). Such children also show both reduced growth of individual cells and delayed neural maturation (Dobbing, 1964; Dyson & Jones, 1976).

Worldwide, the incidence of infant malnutrition is startling and is most widespread in sub-Saharan Africa. Malnutrition usually starts when infants are weaned from the breast to the bottle. Traditionally, infants in underdeveloped nations were breast-fed until age 2, but during the 1970s, mothers in these countries were encouraged to switch to formula during their infant's first year. Many of these mothers—inadequately instructed by distributors, unable to read manufacturers' instructions, and anxious to stretch food as far as possible because of poverty—diluted the formula (often with contaminated water), with tragic consequences. Many of their babies died. The contamination caused disease, and the dilution deprived infants of essential protein calories. Lack of proper

FIGURE 4.5
Number and Percentage Distribution of All Children under Age 6 and of Poor Children under 6 by Family Type, 1991
Children under age 6 living with single mothers are much more likely to be poor than those living with two parents. Even so, 39 percent of poor young children lived in married-couple families in 1991. (SOURCE: National Center for Children in Poverty, 1993.)

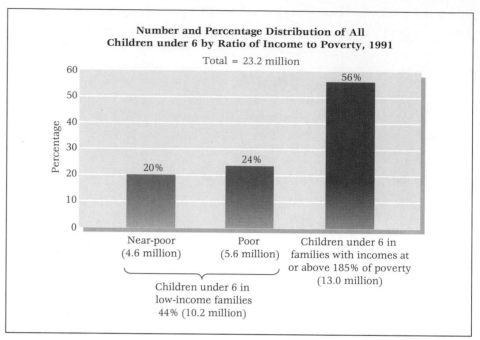

FIGURE 4.6
Percentage and Number Distribution of All Children under Age 6 by Ratio of Income to Poverty, 1991
More than 4 out of every 10 children under age 6 lived in low-income (poor and near-poor) families in 1991.
(SOURCE: National Center for Children in Poverty, 1993.)

refrigeration, another common problem among poorer populations, can also spoil formula and lead to illness.

A recent study of breast- and bottle-feeding among mothers in urban areas of Brazil, for example, found that infants who received powdered milk or cow's milk, in addition to breast milk, were more than 4 times more likely to die as a result of diarrhea compared to infants who did not receive artificial milk, while the risk of such death was more than 14 times as great for infants who did not receive any breast milk at all (Victora et al., 1989).

And among babies in a rural village off the coast of Indonesia, the less babies were breast-fed, the more days of respiratory illness they experienced and, as a result of such illness, the more weight they lost (Launer, Habicht, & Kardjati, 1990). One possible reason for the positive effect of breast-feeding in preventing illness is that nitrogen compounds in breast milk enhance immune-system functioning (Carver et al., 1991).

 Marasmus and kwashiorkor. The physical conditions most often associated with severe malnutrition in infancy are marasmus and kwashiorkor. **Marasmus,** linked with an overall insufficient amount of food, usually affects infants less than a year old. They stop gaining weight and eventually begin to lose weight. They appear more and more emaciated, with wasted muscles, wrinkled skin, wizened faces, and swollen bellies (Vaughn, McKay, & Nelson, 1975). These infants also suffer from diarrhea and anemia. Often, their food supply is contaminated, so intestinal infections worsen their condition (Galler, 1984). **Kwashiorkor** tends to affect children who are weaned at age 2 or 3 without being provided with a nutritionally adequate breast milk substitute. Stomachs swell, muscles waste, and growth is seriously retarded. Hair may discolor; skin grows pale and may develop irritations (Vaughn, McKay, & Nelson, 1975). Diarrhea, anemia, apathy, and irritability also mark this life-threatening condition (Galler, 1984).

marasmus
a disease affecting infants under 1 year of age, caused by an insufficient and often contaminated food supply

kwashiorkor
a disease affecting children ages 2 to 3, caused by a severe protein deficiency, usually after weaning

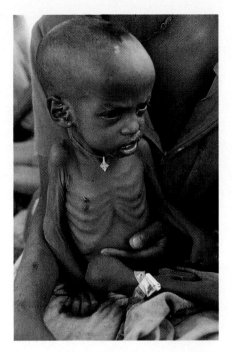

Infant malnutrition, a major world health problem, has been devastating in sub-Saharan Africa. This Ethiopian infant is suffering from marasmus. The disease, caused by severe malnutrition, affects physical, emotional, and social development. If not treated, it can lead to death.

As with infant mortality, the major cause of malnutrition among infants everywhere is poverty. In the accompanying Making a Difference box, you will see that combating malnutrition takes commitment, planning, and food.

● *Malnutrition and cognitive and social development.* Severe malnutrition affects both cognitive and social development. In a number of separate studies, malnourished infants have shown a range of difficulties, including lowered attention and responsiveness to other people (Brazelton, Tronick, Lechtig, Lasky, & Klein, 1977; Lester, 1975), heightened irritability, and lowered tolerance for frustration (Mora et al., 1979). Moreover, these effects continue. Guatemalan children who had been malnourished as infants were examined as 6- to 8-year-olds. Compared to children who had received food supplements during their first 2 years, the malnourished group was less socially involved, less active, more dependent on adults, and more anxious (Barrett, Radke-Yarrow, & Klein, 1982). By age 10, early food supplementation was associated with enhanced intellectual functioning (Pollitt & Martorell, 1992).

In another study, a group of 129 Barbadian children aged 5 through 11 who had suffered from marasmus as infants were compared to their properly nourished classmates. Predictably, the malnourished children were smaller and scored lower on intelligence tests. They also had more trouble with schoolwork and had more behavior problems as well: They were easily distracted, had poor attention spans, and were uncooperative. Malnourished boys also had more frequent temper tantrums and crying spells (Galler, Ramsey, & Solimanon, 1984).

Adequate nutrition in infancy is essential for later development; but malnourished children not only have inadequate food, they often have inadequate care as well (Chavez & Martinez, 1984; Salt, Galler, & Ramsey, 1988). They are

MAKING A DIFFERENCE

PREVENTING INFANT MALNUTRITION

The best way to treat malnutrition is to prevent it. With that as a goal, the U.S. Congress enacted the Women, Infants, and Children (WIC) program in 1972, authorizing $20 million to fund it. The program serves over 1 million children at a cost of over $1.5 billion annually (American Academy of Pediatrics, 1985). The funds provide supplemental nutritious foods to pregnant women, breast-feeding mothers, infants, and children up to age 5 who are considered at risk. Results have been promising. Improved prenatal care has helped to increase birth weights, possibly because the boost in nutrition has fostered longer pregnancies. To get these benefits, mothers must be enrolled in the program for at least 6 months of their pregnancy (General Accounting Office, 1984; Kotelchuck, Schwartz, Anderka, & Finison, 1984; Stockbauer, 1986). Infants who receive WIC benefits tend to be healthier children. It is believed that for every $1 spent on WIC benefits, $3 is saved in future

medical costs (National Public Radio, 1989).

Like all social programs, WIC's long-range success will depend on the quality of the service it delivers. Where quality is high, the number of low-birth-weight babies goes down (Rush et al., 1988). But it has been estimated that only about half of all eligible infants and children are receiving this benefit (National Public Radio, 1989).

Variations on the WIC program are also being tried in other parts of the world. In Colombia, food supplements in the early years of life increase physical growth (size and weight) by the time children are 3. And when food supplementation was coupled with a twice-weekly home visiting program to promote the child's cognitive development, severe growth retardation was dramatically curtailed at age 6, three years after the intervention ended. In the control group, 50 percent of the children showed extremely slow growth compared with 20 percent in the experimental group (Super, Herrera, & Mora, 1990). Data on possible differences in cognitive and social development are not yet available.

If the WIC program reached all the children who are eligible for its benefits, no American child would have to go hungry. Currently, though, only about half the infants and children who need its services are receiving food.

 undernourished emotionally, socially, and cognitively. A Mexican study, for example, found that malnourished boys and girls had received less social, emotional, and cognitive stimulation from their mothers *even before* they became malnourished (Cravioto & DeLicardie, 1976). And an Egyptian study found that poorly nourished children received less stimulation from their mothers (Wachs et al., 1992). These findings may help to explain why in Chile, malnourished 17- to 21-month-olds were found to be less secure in their emotional ties to their mothers than their better nourished counterparts (Valenzuela, 1990).

While poverty is the major cause of malnutrition, it is not the only cause. In studies done in Jamaica and Barbados, families with malnourished children were different from others—even when their social class was the same (Galler et al., 1984; Kerr et al., 1978). The Barbadian mothers arranged fewer social contacts for their children, told them fewer stories, and were more depressed than the mothers of adequately nourished children living in the same social and economic conditions (Galler et al., 1984; Salt et al., 1988).

Finally, malnourished infants may be treated differently by people who care for them because of the way they look. This can be a continuing cycle, with a mother who is malnourished herself responding poorly to her own malnourished child. The child, in turn, develops poor social skills, compromising his development still further (Lester, 1979; Rossetti-Ferreira, 1978). The point we want to stress is that, like the rest of development, even malnourishment occurs in a social context, and its effects on development can be determined only by looking at the infant's total environment.

● The Infant's Later Nutritional Needs

When infants weigh about 12 pounds, breast milk or formula alone doesn't supply enough calories or iron, so a small amount of solid food is usually added to the daily diet. Most American pediatricians recommend introducing solid foods by adding new categories one at a time. Cereal, which supplies iron and B vitamins, comes first, often accompanied by strained fruits. Yellow and green vegetables follow; and finally, meat, fish, and eggs are added.

Although all infants need an adequate number of calories and nutrients for healthy growth, the actual amount of food each needs will differ. Highly active and fast-growing infants will need more calories than more placid or slower-growing babies. Overfeeding an infant may satisfy some psychological need in a parent, but it may be at the baby's expense.

● *Infant obesity.* Bottle-feeding is more likely than breast-feeding to promote overeating. Whether overfeeding definitely leads to obesity either in infancy or in later life is currently being debated, as is the connection between infant obesity and obesity in adolescence or adulthood. Some studies have found that bottle-fed babies who eat solid foods at an early age are more likely to be obese than breast-fed infants who eat solids later (Kramer et al., 1985). But other studies have indicated that such feeding practices are unrelated to infant obesity (Wolman, 1984).

It was once widely believed that overfeeding in infancy increased the number of fat cells, which would remain throughout life. Therefore, it was argued that the number of fat cells developed during infancy would determine whether a baby would grow up to be an obese adult. Scientific evidence for this view is very weak (Edelman & Maller, 1982). About all that is certain is that genetic factors play a critical role in determining which *infants* will grow up to be overweight *children,* which may also indicate obesity later on (Stunkard et al., 1990). But even if an obese parent has an obese child, that does not necessarily mean that obesity in the two generations is genetically determined. Learned eating habits may be just as important, if not more so.

SUMMARY

1. Growth during infancy is very rapid, especially during the first year, when a baby's weight triples and length increases 50 percent. (See page 116.)

2. Parts of infants' bodies grow at different rates, and their relative proportions alter (the proportional phenomenon). Legs grow relatively longer, the head decreases in relative size, and the center of gravity shifts downward toward the center of the body. (See page 117.)

3. Motor development follows three trends. Cephalocaudal development refers to the fact that motor skills appear first in the head region and then proceed downward. Proximodistal development refers to the fact that motor skills appear first near the center of the body and proceed gradually to the extremities. Finally, mass-to-specific development refers to the fact that motor control proceeds from the larger muscles to the smaller. This is related to differentiation, the process by which movement becomes increasingly specific and goal-directed. (See pages 118–120.)

4. Although the general sequence of motor development is similar from infant to infant, there is a wide range of individual variations in timing and sometimes even in sequence. In all likelihood, heredity sets the sequence of motor development, but its expression in each infant is influenced by experience. Deprivation can cause developmental delays, and stimulation can accelerate the appearance of motor skills. (See pages 121–123.)

5. As new motor skills appear and become more coordinated and refined, the infant's relation with the environment and the family also changes. (See pages 124–125.)

6. Continuing maturation of the nervous system, especially the cerebral cortex, the most complex part of the brain, explains the infant's growing ability to control and coordinate movements. There are two very significant processes: the proliferation of connections among nerve cells and the insulation of some nerve fibers with myelin for efficient message transmission. (See page 126.)

7. As with fetal and motor development, the interaction between biology and experience is a key principle in brain development. Genes determine the timing of changes within the brain, but normal development depends on adequate experience. Two types of experience that foster brain development are (1) sensory experience and (2) self-produced experience, or experiences that infants actively produce on their own. (See pages 127–128.)

8. For most infants, ordinary life offers all of the stimulation needed for normal development of the sensory areas of the brain. Parents do not have to give their infants any special "brain training." Although there is a trend among middle-class parents today to provide all kinds of special toys, games, and training in an attempt to produce a smarter, "better" baby, moderate stimulation, sensitive care, and balance are the things to keep in mind. (See page 128.)

9. Nutrition plays a major role in infant development. Breast milk is the ideal food for infants, since it is sterile, easy to digest, and full of important nutrients. It also contains antibodies to guard against infection. Formula is still considered an acceptable substitute, if used properly. (See pages 129–130.)

10. Malnutrition, which often accompanies poverty in the United States and in underdeveloped nations, affects the infant's cognitive and social development. Effects include lowered attention and responsiveness, irritability, poor social skills, and difficulties with schoolwork. (See pages 130–135.)

KEY TERMS

arborization
cephalocaudal
   development
cerebral cortex
developmental
   gradualness
differentiation

haptic perception
kwashiorkor
marasmus
mass-to-specific
   development
motor development
myelin

neurons
proportional
   phenomenon
proximodistal
   development
rhythmical stereotypies

SUGGESTED READINGS

Caplan, F. (1993). *The first twelve months of life.* New York: Perigree Books. The twentieth anniversary edition of the classic summary of the major physical and cognitive milestones during the first year of development.

Leach, P. (1989). *Your baby and child: From birth to age five.* New York: Knopf. This sensitive and comprehensive book has become one of the best-selling reference guides for parents.

Sinclair, D. (1980). *Human growth after birth.* Oxford: Oxford University Press. The nature and course of physical growth and development are examined in detail by one of the world's experts.

Spock, B., with Rothenberg, M. (1993). *Dr. Spock's baby and child care* (6th ed.) New York: Pocket Books. America's most famous pediatrician provides important information about infant health in an easily accessible way that has proven handy to millions of parents in the United States and around the world.

Stern, D. (1990). *Diary of a baby.* New York: Basic Books. A prominent psychologist discusses what an infant sees, feels, and experiences during the first two years.

CHAPTER 5

COGNITIVE AND LANGUAGE DEVELOPMENT IN INFANCY

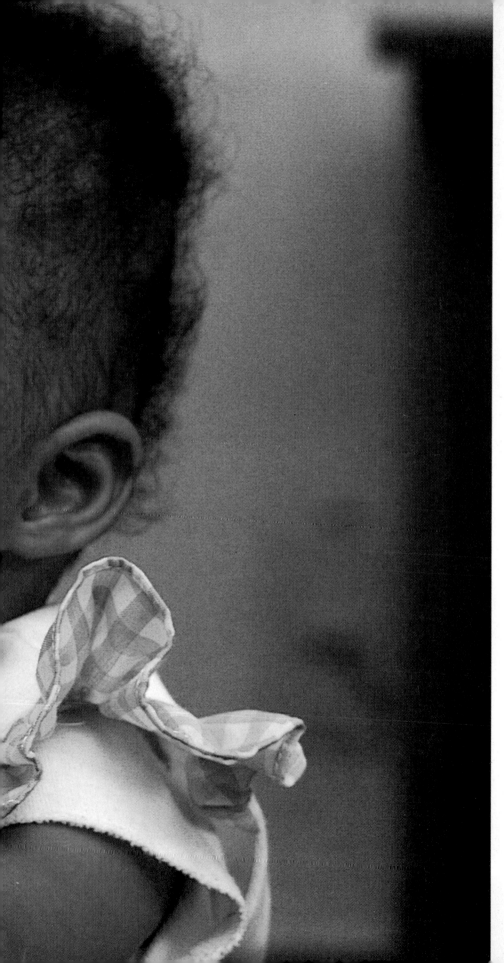

A little before his second birthday, Laurence Steinberg's son, Benjamin, became keenly interested in the story of *Snow White and the Seven Dwarfs*. He was especially fascinated by the witch (which he pronounced "vitch") and would plead with his parents to read and reread the story daily. One morning, he climbed into bed with his parents and pulled the blankets off his mother's feet. "This is Snow White," he said, grabbing one foot, "and this is the vitch," pointing to the other. "They are fighting." The next morning, he appeared again. His mother pointed to one of her feet and said, "Here's Snow White." "No!" Benjamin shouted. "That's the vitch!"

Benjamin's ability to substitute his mother's feet for Snow White and the "vitch" signals a cognitive milestone that marks the end of infancy: *representational thinking*. He was using one object (his mother's foot) to stand for, or *symbolize,* another (Snow White). Representational thinking, which develops along with the growth of language, is a major turning point in the development of cognitive abilities, for it allows children to use symbols to stand for things that they have experienced through sight, sound, touch, taste, or smell.

As a newborn, Benjamin couldn't understand what a foot was, no less pretend that it was Snow White. He knew the world only through his senses and reflexes. By the end of infancy, children can experience the world by *thinking* about it, in much the same way that adults do. Moreover, they are beginning to use the most important symbols available to humans—words—to communicate their experiences to others.

In this chapter, we trace the growth of cognitive and linguistic skills, highlighting several turning points, or transitions, along the way. These transitions—at about 3 months, 8 months, 12 months, and 18 months—correspond roughly to changes in the maturing brain and nervous system we noted in Chapter 4. Recently, scientists have begun to link specific biological changes to the emergence of specific cognitive skills. As yet, we can only speculate that major reorganizations in the way infants think originate from major developments in the brain and nervous system. We begin by looking at developments in three important cognitive processes: attention, perception, and memory.

ATTENTION, PERCEPTION, AND MEMORY

In Chapter 3, you learned that from birth, infants have the sensory capacities to receive information, permitting learning. How those capacities develop during the first years of life is particularly interesting to developmentalists. What captures infants' *attention?* What do infants *perceive?* How well do they *remember?*

● Attention

What an infant pays attention to determines what information enters the brain. The gateway to perception, attention is the infant's first step in learning about the world (Bornstein & Lamb, 1992). Bombarded by stimulation, infants seek out, select, and attend to certain kinds of stimulation more than others (Slater, 1990).

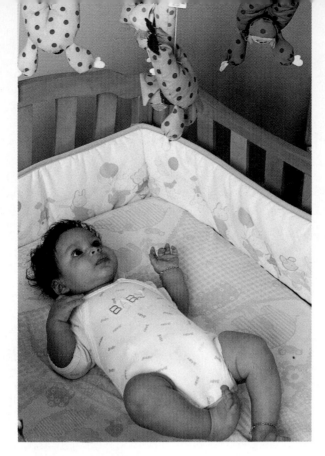

Pattern and movement attract this 3-month-old to the mobile overhead. At about 8 months, she will discover that she can make the mobile move just by kicking her leg.

How do we know what infants prefer to attend to? Researchers show infants designs and shapes that are more or less complex, and stimuli that move or are still. Then, the experimenters watch the babies: What do they *choose* to look at, and how long do they look? If, for example, infants see a complex geometric design (a hexagon) and a simple design (a triangle) at the same time, researchers record how long they look at each. More stares for the hexagon? Then infants prefer complex designs to simple ones.

During the first 2 months, newborns like familiarity; they want to see today what they saw yesterday (Hunt, 1970; Weizmann, Cohen, & Pratt, 1971). But by 2 months, infants can process more information, and novelty begins to interest them. As they grow older, infants look longer at pictures of unfamiliar toys than familiar ones. They also start to prefer real toys that look and sound different from the ones they've been used to (Eckerman & Whatley, 1975; McCall, 1974). But too much novelty may overwhelm immature nervous systems, and interest wanes. In short, infants seem to seek an optimal level of novelty—a balance between the familiar and the unfamiliar (McCall, 1974).

A moving stimulus attracts more attention than a still one. More complex images become interesting too, perhaps because they excite more neural activity in the brain (Cohen, 1991; Haith, 1981). (**Complexity** refers to characteristics such as number of colors and contrasts, pattern, organization, and intricacy of design.) A pentagon is more complex and captures more attention than a triangle, for example, simply because it has more sides. And infants look longer at a realistic drawing of a human face than at a circle with dots for the eyes and nose and a curved line for a mouth (Fantz, 1965; Greenberg, 1971). But as with novelty, complex figures or objects attract attention as long as they are not too complex; infants need to process information without being overwhelmed by it.

● **complexity**
the number and intricacy of traits like color or pattern in a stimulus

MAKING A DIFFERENCE

MORE IS NOT ALWAYS BETTER

Not long ago, a major newspaper reported that black and white were the "in" colors for infants. Researchers had learned that babies liked them. They were stimulating. Soon, trendy shops were stocking black-and-white patterned crib mobiles, outfits, sheets, and bumpers. And parents, eager to follow the experts' advice in the raise-your-baby's-IQ sweepstakes, were buying.

Black-and-white patterns *do* attract infants' attention, but babies don't need a special curriculum and special outfits for optimal cognitive development. What they do need is loving, playful attention. Simply stated, babies who receive a lot of attention from their parents function better intellectually as children than those who received less parental attention.

Russian theorist Lev Vygotsky (1962) has given this view a particular twist. According to Vygotsky, children's intellectual development is stimulated through interactions with people more capable than they. Children advance when adults encourage them to reach a little further intellectually than they can grab, to try out activities a bit more difficult, demanding, and challenging than those they can do on their own (Tudge & Rogoff, 1989). Vygotsky called this reach the **zone of proximal development.** Children naturally perform at a given level, but with adult guidance and support, they may go beyond their limits. For example, once a child learns how to drink from a cup, an adult might show him that a sea shell could be a cup too, expanding his ability to see the way things can function.

Physical contact between parent and child is also related to intellectual competence in infancy and beyond (Lewis & Goldberg, 1969; Tulkin & Covitz, 1975; Yarrow, 1961). Actually, it may not be the parents' attentiveness in itself but what they do while holding their infants that is the key factor. Parents who talk to their babies, for example, engage the infant's attention and encourage responses such as a smile or vocalization. Over time, infants who have received a lot of *verbal stimulation* become more skilled at using language themselves and show higher levels of general cognitive functioning (Beckwith, 1971; Clarke-Stewart, 1973; Engel & Keane, 1975; Nelson, 1973).

Parents also influence cognitive development by giving their infants toys and other objects to look at, touch, and manipulate. Such *material stimulation* is best when it is geared to the child's level of development and interest: A

● **zone of proximal development**
Vygotsky's notion that children's intellectual development is stimulated through interactions with people more capable than they; children advance when adults encourage them to reach a little further intellectually, to try activities a bit more difficult than those they can do on their own

● **perceive**
to interpret sensations

Infants' preferences can also be influenced by experience. For example, babies' interest in the things or the people around them can be shaped by others. When mothers encouraged their infants to attend more to the things around them than to the mothers themselves, their babies complied. In another group, where mothers directed their infants' attention more toward themselves, the babies paid more attention to their mothers (Bornstein & Tamis-LeMonda, 1990).

● Perception

Attention alone doesn't lead to understanding. A baby could look at a mobile all day and still not know that two of the figures are alike or that the clown's nose is the same color as a tomato. Interpreting what the senses can only transmit is a cognitive skill that develops along with the ability to **perceive,** to assign meaning to sensations. That ability, researchers say, takes a leap forward at 3 or 4 months, a time of significant changes in the brain and nervous system.

2-month-old is stimulated by mobiles hanging over her crib, for example, while an 8-month-old likes to explore a box full of soft blocks. Playthings need not be elaborate; often the best toys are ordinary household items. Pots and pans, wooden spoons, and plastic cups make excellent playthings; and toddlers love to "cook" beside their parents.

Whatever parents offer, Vygotsky's principle applies. Point out something interesting about the object that the child doesn't yet know. A glass of water on a sunny ledge can create a rainbow; cornmeal through a sifter can cover a plastic car with snow.

No matter what adults are doing with infants, they can always talk, and a certain kind of communication enhances development. When infants make noises, or vocalize, parents can talk back; when a baby shows an adult an object, the adult

can comment. Developmentalists call it *contingent responsiveness:* a way of showing the infant that she can be effective, that what she does matters. Watch a sensitive mother interacting with her 4-month-old baby: She talks, and he babbles back; she laughs and coos, and so does he. He drops a toy and fusses, and she picks it up. Children whose parents respond to them in this way are more competent intellectually—both in infancy and later on—than children the same age with less responsive parents (Bradley, Caldwell, & Rock, 1988; Tamis-LeMonda & Bornstein, 1989; Wachs, 1992). When parents are responsive, children may feel that they have some control over their world, and that feeling encourages them to seek out other activities from which they continue learning (Lewis & Goldberg, 1969).

As babies begin exploring, parents begin worrying about safety.

Balance is the key here. Too many gates, locks, and latches can foreclose opportunities to learn. Too frequent restrictions, whether verbal or physical, can undermine cognitive development (Clarke-Stewart, 1973; Engel & Keane, 1975; Tulkin & Kagan, 1972). Spending hours in a high chair or playpen—and frequently hearing "No. Don't. Stop that!"—sharply limits their natural information-gathering activities. (In a dangerous environment, of course, safety has to come first.)

In short, the most effective infant care provides intellectual stimulation that promotes cognitive development *and* protects the child from overstimulation and dangerous activities. No special outfits, colors, or equipment are required.

● ***Color perception.*** Infants like color almost at first glance. Newborns look longer at color pictures than at black-and-white images; and by 3 months, they favor red, yellow, blue, and green (Maurer et al., 1989; Teller & Lindsey, 1989). Finer distinctions occur after 3 months, when babies can tell blue from green (Adams, 1987; Bornstein, 1981; Bornstein & Lamb, 1992). When two colors are presented sequentially—say, a blue picture followed by a green picture of the same object—researchers measure the baby's heart rate and time spent looking at the pictures. When interest flags, eyes turn away and heart rate increases. This loss of interest to a constant stimulus is called **habituation.** Its opposite, **dishabituation,** occurs when a new image or color excites a baby's attention. Then she focuses on the new stimulus, and heart rate slows.

By 4 months, infants can perceive both similarities and differences between colors. They understand that colors can be slightly different yet still belong to the same category (Bornstein, 1981; Teller & Bornstein, 1986). In short, they know that shades of blue are still blue. This ability reflects one of the most im-

● **habituation**
the adaptation to (loss of interest in) an unchanging stimulus

● **dishabituation**
the reaction to (recovery of interest in) a novel stimulus

● **equivalence**
the recognition that similar stimuli, or the same stimuli under changed conditions, belong to the same basic category

portant concepts in the study of perception: **equivalence.** Like is grouped with like in spite of differences. Equivalence permits infants to make sense out of the welter of stimuli they face each day. As their cognitive skills develop, equivalence will be a basic tool for understanding the physical world. Even though two balls may be different colors and sizes, they are still balls. A spoon is still a spoon even when it has a slightly different shape or design; a pear and a peach are both "fruit." Without notions of equivalence, the world would remain a confusing, ever-multiplying mass of images.

● *Face perception.* When an infant stares at her mother's face, can she perceive all the features? Can she tell this face from a stranger's? From her father's or sister's? The answers depend on when you ask, because perceiving faces improves with age (Johnson et al., 1992; Sherrod, 1990). During their first 3 months, infants look mostly at the borders of a face (Maurer & Salapatek, 1976). At 3 months, eyes are the most interesting feature (Haith, Bergman, & Moore, 1977). This physical change has a social consequence: Now when parents look at their babies, their babies can look directly back.

At about 4 months, a major transition occurs, as infants begin to prefer pictures of whole faces over isolated features (Gibson, 1969). They know how a face is supposed to look, how the features should be arranged, that certain arrangements are more attractive than others. This shift illustrates a major principle in perceptual development: *Perception moves from the part to the whole* (Kagan,

This 1-month-old looks mostly at the borders of his father's face. By 3 months, he will be able to look eye-to-eye at whoever looks at him.

1967; Thomas, 1973). And when given the choice, infants prefer more attractive over less attractive faces (Langlois et al., 1990, 1991). Regardless of their culture, babies prefer what adults prefer: faces with "average" features, neither overly large nor small eyes, nose, and lips. Apparently, beauty is not simply "in the eye of the beholder." It seems to be in the genes as well (Langlois et al., 1991).

By 6 months, two more perceptual shifts occur. Infants like faces in which the eyes and mouth move (Johnson et al., 1992), a change that helps them to recognize facial expressions (Stucki et al., 1987). Now, they can also discriminate between different faces, and they'll recognize familiar faces even when they appear in unfamiliar expressions, angles, or contexts (Cohen, 1972; Fagan, 1976), another example of equivalence.

● *Perception and social and emotional growth.* Along with knowing who people are, infants begin to figure out what people feel, as they learn the language of facial expressions. Raised eyebrows are now part of a whole face that may be expressing delighted surprise or wariness. An upturned mouth signals happiness. Until babies can talk, perceiving and understanding facial expressions provides answers to unasked questions. Looking to someone else to find an emotional response for yourself is known as **social referencing,** such as when a child looks at a sibling's face to find out if her parents are angry.

● **social referencing**
looking to someone else for guidance in emotional response to new stimuli or situations

Our ability to read expressions of worry, danger, comfort, or happiness develops in infancy. In new situations, 7-month-olds will read a familiar person's facial expression before reacting themselves (Campos & Stenberg, 1981; Walden & Baxter, 1989). Babies look to their mothers when strangers approach; if mothers smile or look wary, so will the babies (Boccia & Campos, 1983). Babies will also take their cue from fathers (Dickstein & Parke, 1988; Hirshberg & Svejda, 1990) and from other familiar caregivers (Camras & Sachs, 1991). Generally, when they need emotional information, babies look most often to adults who are more emotionally expressive themselves. In uncertain situations, perhaps these are the people who are more reliable sources of emotional information (Camras & Sachs, 1991).

● Cross-Modal Transfer

In an experiment, a 6-month-old girl is given a paper towel tube to hold and manipulate for 30 seconds, but she is not permitted to see it. Then she looks at a picture of the tube. Does she recognize it? Does information gained by her sense of touch "cross over" to sight? Piaget, whose theory of cognitive development you read about in Chapter 1, said no. He held that each of our senses works independently at birth, and only after much experience does information from one sense transfer to another—from touch to sight, for example (Piaget, 1952; Piaget & Inhelder, 1956).

But newer research data suggest otherwise. It seems that the senses work *together* almost from birth. Information gained by one sense—by touch, taste, or smell, for example—can be processed by vision, without much experience at all (Walker-Andrews & Gibson, 1987). Proof of these early **cross-modal abilities** (abilities that cut across sensory modes) comes from laboratory studies.

● **cross-modal abilities**
abilities that cut across sensory modes

Researchers gave 6-month-olds two kinds of cylinders that they could hold but not see. One type was smooth-sided; the other had indentations. One group of babies had 30 seconds to manipulate the objects; the other had 1 full minute.

When shown *pictures* of the cylinders, the 1-minute group looked longer at the object they had held. The other group, with only 30 seconds of touching experience, did not seem to recognize a picture of their type of cylinder; but when given a full minute of holding and manipulation, they did as well as the other babies (Gottfried, Rose, & Bridger, 1977; Rose, Gottfried, & Bridger, 1981b). The researchers concluded that, after only 1 minute of experience, information was transferred from touch to sight.

In another experiment 4-month-olds watched a film of blocks hitting against each other and another film of water-filled sponges being squeezed. When the films were accompanied by sounds, the infants looked longer at the blocks when they *heard* the sounds of the blocks, and longer at the sponges while listening to squishing sounds (Bahrick, 1983). Even more surprising, 5-month-olds can match films of an approaching or retreating car with motor sounds that grow louder or softer (Walker-Andrews & Lennon, 1985).

Are infants making these connections between sight and sound because they have had enough experience to do so, even by 4 or 5 months? Perhaps, but other studies show that even 1-month-olds have cross-modal abilities (Gibson & Walker, 1984; Rose & Ruff, 1987). Even babies that young look longer at something they've held in their mouth than at something they haven't. So, while experience is needed, infants seem to begin life with some cross-modal abilities already in place. Apparently, some infants have more of these abilities than others, and although we don't yet know why, those who show better cross-modal skills at 1 year score better on tests of intelligence when they are 5 years old (Rose et al., 1991).

● Memory

While attention and perception enable infants to gather information, to store and retrieve it, they need memory. Developmentalists ask three basic questions about infant memory: When do infants begin to remember? How do our abilities to store and organize information change with age? How do long-term memory and forgetting change with age? (Bornstein & Lamb, 1992). Some of what we know about infant memory is gleaned from work on perception and attention. Recall that researchers look at how quickly infants become familiar with a stimulus and then lose interest, or habituate to it. They become newly interested when a different stimulus appears, signaling at least a rudimentary ability to remember. It's as if the infant says, "I've seen that before and I'm tired of it, but this is something new." During their first year, infants habituate faster and faster to a familiar stimulus, signaling faster and more efficient memory processes (Bornstein et al., 1988).

What about long-term memory, lasting months, or years, not just days and weeks? We return to babies and mobiles for some answers. Two-month-olds who learned they could move a mobile by kicking their legs forgot this after a couple of days, but it took 3-month-olds a couple of weeks to forget the same learned skill, and 6-month-olds even longer. Long-term memory seems to be functioning to some degree, then, even among *6-month-olds* (Rovee-Collier & Hayne, 1987).

These results have showed up in another study as well. Two groups of 3-year-olds were put in a dark room, where researchers wondered if they would reach toward the location of a sound. One group had been tested in the same

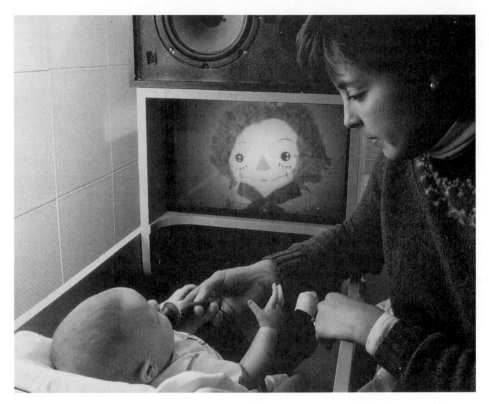

When this baby sees a new face, he will change the intensity with which he sucks on the rubber nipple. During their first year, infants habituate faster and faster to a familiar stimulus, indicating that their memories are becoming more efficient.

way at 6 months; the others were "first timers." The experienced children accepted the darkness more readily and were more likely to reach for the sound *even before researchers told them to* (Perris, Myers, & Clifton, 1990). In short, they behaved as if they remembered the experience.

This experiment is intriguing, but still, there is much to learn about the duration of infants' memories. Most of us can remember experiences we had at age 3 or so, but infancy generally draws a blank. Why do our memories seem to have vanished? One hypothesis is that memories are buried as a result of neural reorganization in the brain. That is, experiences in infancy may indeed be stored in memory, but they may be stored within an organizational system that has changed—and become less accessible—over the course of development. Early experiences may indeed be filed away, but it may be that the neurobiological "filing" system used during infancy is so markedly different from that used during childhood and adulthood that we have no idea how to retrieve the memories.

COGNITIVE DEVELOPMENT: PIAGET AND BEYOND

Jean Piaget, the Swiss psychologist who studied cognitive development, theorized that an infant's way of knowing the world is different from a child's, an adolescent's, or an adult's. He argued that cognitive development progresses through a series of stages, and at each succeeding stage we understand the world in more complex, more sophisticated ways. What we couldn't understand at 3, or what we "understood" incorrectly or partially, is easily grasped at 8, not just because we know more but because the *way* in which we understand and think about the world has advanced.

For developmentalists, changes bring questions. Do these stages unfold on their own, or do infants need some kind of special stimulation along the way? Piaget would have taken exception to the word *special*. He believed that biology and experience work together in cognitive development, and that the ordinary experiences of life ensure the unfolding of each stage at about the same time in every infant. Unless a child is severely deprived of contact with humans and objects, each cognitive stage emerges naturally. The first 2 years form the first phase in Piaget's scheme, the sensorimotor stage. And at its start, infants explore the world not with their minds but with their mouths.

● Sensorimotor Intelligence

To understand the kind of intelligence young infants have, first it helps to know what they lack. If you show a 1-month-old baby girl a picture of the mobile that hangs above her crib, it means little to her; she won't recognize it as the dangling object she looks at every day. If you give her the picture, she might try to suck it, because she explores the world with her mouth. Unlike an adult, or even a 2-year-old, she can't remember what the mobile does; she can't predict what will happen if someone shakes it; she can't connect the word *mobile* to the thing she looks at. Moreover, if the mobile were removed, she wouldn't know it still existed. For infants, the world is the present; there is no past and no future.

During the sensorimotor period of intelligence, infants learn about things through their senses and motor actions. For this 3-month-old, rattles are best explored by shaking and tasting.

There are no symbols either; one thing cannot stand for another. The word *mobile* or a picture of a mobile has nothing to do with the object hanging over the crib. Absent too is the understanding that actions have consequences, that one thing leads to another. If you drop a rattle on the floor, infants hear the noise, but they don't know what caused it, that *a* leads to *b*.

Piaget documented the emergence of the basic elements of intelligence during the first 2 years of life. First came the period he named **sensorimotor,** because it is based on the senses and on movements. A baby begins to understand an object by tasting, touching, seeing, hearing, and smelling it; by bumping into it, grasping it, lifting it, and dropping it.

As they move through the sensorimotor period, infants gain three basic cognitive abilities: First, they gradually understand that they are separate from the other things and people in their world. There is self, and there are others. Gradually, infants extend their activity and awareness beyond the boundaries of their own body. Piaget called this process **decentration**—literally, moving away from *centering,* or focusing, on their physical selves.

The second basic skill babies gain during the sensorimotor period is the ability to plan and coordinate their actions. Not until 8 months will most infants know that kicking their legs will make a mobile attached to the crib move. The new and very rudimentary skill is called **intentionality.**

Finally, the third cognitive skill emerges, **object permanence.** Infants begin to understand that even when they can't see, hear, or feel something, it still exists. Tracing the development of object permanence during the sensorimotor period was one of Piaget's greatest contributions toward our understanding of cognitive development.

Piaget initially proposed six substages within the sensorimotor period. Although he identified specific periods for the emergence of each stage of sensorimotor development, we now know that the timing varies from infant to infant: some babies will spend more time in some stages than others. The *sequence* of cognitive development, however, is always the same, and each accomplishment lays the foundation for the next (Flavell, 1985; Kuhn, 1992). In Piaget's view, the skills gained in one period lead to the unfolding of the next. The early skills do not disappear, however. Adults can still learn through sensorimotor experience if they need to, although they would probably find it cumbersome. As we grow, sensorimotor intelligence is simply incorporated into more sophisticated ways of knowing and learning.

● A New Look at Piaget

Sixty years have passed since Piaget first published his insights into the minds of infants. As with any theory, later research by others, as well as new discoveries by Piaget himself, led to modifications in Piaget's original framework. An important new proposal is that infants progress through four cognitive substages instead of Piaget's six, with important transition points at 3, 8, 12, and 18 months (Fischer, 1987; Fischer & Silvern, 1985). Figure 5.1 summarizes the traditional and new theories. At each transition a new aspect of sensorimotor intelligence begins to unfold. What is most interesting is that this new timetable coincides with changes occurring in the brain: New research shows

sensorimotor
describes Piaget's first stage of cognitive development, in which infants explore their world with their senses and motor actions

decentration
focusing on more than self; the extension of activity and awareness beyond one's own physical boundaries

intentionality
the purposeful coordination of activity toward a goal

object permanence
the slowly developing understanding that objects exist separate from one's perception of them

Substages (Piaget)	Transition Points (Fischer and Others)
0 to 1 month: Reflexes	
1 to 4 months: Adapting reflexes; primary circular reactions	
	3 months: Primary circular reactions
4 to 8 months: Secondary circular reactions	
	8 months: Beginnings of intentional behavior and decentration; secondary circular reactions; beginnings of object permanence (in moving objects)
8 to 12 months: Beginnings of object permanence and intentional behavior; anticipation of events	
12 to 18 months: "Little scientist" exploration (tertiary circular reactions)	12 months: Purposeful trial-and-error "little scientist" exploration; broadened object permanence
18 to 24 months: Representational thinking; deferred imitation; complete object permanence	18 months: Emergence of representational thinking; deferred imitation; complete object permanence

FIGURE 5.1
Achievements of the Sensorimotor Period: Overlapping Views
Organizing the sensorimotor period into four major transition points allows for individual variation in Piaget's timetable. In addition, the four transitions occur during times of major reorganizations in the brain during the first 2 years of life.

that brain waves, sleep cycles, and perceptual abilities are all changing *at the same time* that the new cognitive skills appear (Bornstein & Lamb, 1992; Fischer & Silvern, 1985). We turn now to these transitions, paying special attention to the major accomplishments in decentration, intentionality, and object permanence that occur at each point.

● **The 3-month transition: From reflex to accidental discovery.** A pacifier placed in a newborn's mouth will cause her to suck—not because she "wants" to suck but because the sensation in her mouth triggers a sucking reflex. Recall that for the first month, infants have very little voluntary control over their actions; they are mostly reflexive beings (see Chapter 4). Some of our inborn reflexes disappear, but others change, marking the beginning of cognitive development. For example, all newborns suck the same way whether on a breast or bottle nipple. Gradually, the nursing infant notices that the breast nipple differs from the bottle nipple, and both differ from the pacifier. She begins sucking one way on the breast nipple and another way on the bottle nipple. This kind of change—a shift in response keyed to differences between objects—marks the beginning of sensorimotor intelligence.

The next step occurs at about 3 months, when infants make another discovery. Picture a 3-month-old boy lying in his crib, staring at a mobile hanging above him. Excited, he waves his arms. He notices them, but then they disappear. Again he looks at the mobile; again he waves his arms, and again, he is intrigued. Now, he starts to move around, trying to see his arm again. Eventually, the arm reappears. He pauses and gurgles, then repeats the movements again and again. Piaget called the repetition of action and response a *circular reaction.* The early form of it is called **primary circular reaction,** because the infant's actions center around his own body. Remember that during this stage, the movements that lead to the infant's "discoveries" always happen first by *accident.* They are repeated as the baby tries to make the event happen again and again. As neuromuscular control increases, infants' skill at performing circular reactions improves. These primary circular reactions signal the earliest awareness of cause and effect. They also form the foundation for the development of intentionality, decentration, and object permanence, all of which begin to emerge during the next 5 months.

● *The 8-month transition: From accidental discovery to intentional behavior.* From 6 to 12 months, infants are still exploring their environment through circular reactions, but now the patterns of repetition include *objects* as well as parts of their own body. Piaget called these patterns **secondary circular reactions.** When an 8-month-old girl looks up at her mobile and moves her arms and legs with pleasure, the crib's vibrations shake the mobile. But now something new happens. She stops moving and stares at the mobile; she kicks her leg again, and the mobile moves again. Another kick, and the mobile quivers again. Now, she makes the connection, squealing as she purposely makes the mobile move. Her interest has shifted from her own movements to the mobile's; something in the "nonbaby" world has become more interesting than her own body. The emergence of secondary circular reactions marks the start of true decentration, one of the key achievements of sensorimotor development.

Whereas the 7-month-old discovers how to see his arm, the 8-month-old discovers what the arm can *do*: Shake a rattle, it makes a noise; bat a mobile, it moves. Infants' learning that their own actions cause *separate* results is the hallmark of this phase and signals the start of true **intentional behavior.**

● **primary circular reaction**
an infant's repetition of a chance action involving a part of the infant's body

● **secondary circular reactions**
repetitions of actions that trigger responses in the external environment (for example, squeeze a toy—it squeaks)

● **intentional behavior**
goal-directed activity, which begins to appear from 8 to 12 months

At about 8 months, infants are fascinated by the special properties of objects. Rolling out toilet paper or lifting the toilet seat over and over can be very intriguing.

Toward the end of the first year, infants make great strides in the development of intentional behavior. When his son Laurent was about 10 months old, Piaget placed a small pillow between the baby and a familiar toy. Laurent paused, batted the pillow out of the way, and reached for the toy. Laurent wanted something, and he got it. Sometime between 8 and 12 months, all infants can do what Laurent did: No longer are they merely responding to accidental events. Now they can deliberately act toward getting what they want. By this time, babies can also coordinate physical skills, as Laurent coordinated batting and reaching, to achieve a goal. In addition, they can recall the way that two actions can be coordinated, a sign of increased memory.

The development of object permanence.   During this phase, the baby also begins to perceive something new about the permanence of objects: What leaves may return. Until about 6 months, out of sight seems to be out of mind: If a ball rolls out of his crib, an infant won't look for it, even if he was just touching it. But by 8 months something changes. Now if any object drops out of sight, a baby will look toward the spot where it disappeared, as if expecting it to reappear. You can demonstrate this easily with a toy train and a tunnel. Show an 8-month-old a train moving into and out of the tunnel. Repeat this several times, and very soon the baby will look toward the end of the tunnel, waiting for the train to appear (Nelson, 1971). You can do the same thing with a ball that rolls behind a cushion and appears at the other side. Soon the baby looks for the emerging ball.

Although infants can now anticipate the reappearance of moving objects, at the beginning of this stage they are still uncertain about the permanence of stationary objects. If you cover a bottle with a towel so that an identifying part, such as the nipple, is still visible, the baby will reach for it. But if the bottle is entirely covered by the towel—even if you cover it while she is watching, *and even if she was already reaching for the bottle*—she will stop reaching when she can't see it anymore. For the 8-month-old, the object still seems to disappear, but within a few months, she'll pull the towel off the bottle.

Although babies of this age will search for an object that has been moved, they do not always look in the right place. If a ball on the left side of a table (location *A*) is covered by a cloth, and then uncovered and moved to the right side (location *B*) and covered with another cloth *while the infant is watching,* the baby will still search for it on the left side—where it was *first* hidden. This is known as the *A not B error.*

Why does a second move or second disappearance of an object confuse these babies—or does it confuse them at all? Piaget held that infants stop searching

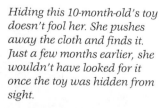

Hiding this 10-month-old's toy doesn't fool her. She pushes away the cloth and finds it. Just a few months earlier, she wouldn't have looked for it once the toy was hidden from sight.

During the "age of discovery," seeing what's inside a waste basket can be more interesting to a 12-month-old than an elaborate, expensive toy.

for an object because they think it no longer exists. But many psychologists today think otherwise. It may be that the child can focus on only one aspect of the object's existence, in this case, one location; they get "stuck" on the first place they discovered the object (Flavell, 1985). Or perhaps the infant's memory is not yet developed enough or adaptable enough to process and hold onto two locations in a sequence (Harris, 1983). It is also possible that infants simply do not know what to do when their initial attempts to find an object fail; they have no established routines for this sort of thing (Harris, 1983). But whether the problem is one of concept, memory, or learned routines, the main point is that the child cannot yet handle more than one dislocation or disappearance of an object. And psychologists agree that whatever the reasons, object permanence develops only gradually during the second half of an infant's first year.

● *The 12-month transition: From intentional behavior to systematic exploration.* At about the time of the first birthday, another cognitive transition begins: active, purposeful, trial-and-error exploration. The infant who at 6 months *accidentally* discovered that her mobile moved when she kicked now *searches* for discoveries with relentless abandon, moving from room to room emptying drawers, wastebaskets, and bookcases, and then examining her finds for their hidden potential. Pots can be drums, containers, or stools. A wooden spoon becomes a drumstick, a hammer, or a tool for exploring the toilet.

Selma Fraiberg, an astute observer of children, describes the "little scientist" this way:

> The study of a cup will occupy him for weeks, for countless mealtimes, while the function of the cup as perceived by his mother will hardly interest him at all. To drink milk from the cup will be the least absorbing activity in connection with the cup while he is conducting his research on the nature of a cup. He examines the outer surface of the cup, explores the inner surface, discovers its hollowness, bangs it on the tray for its sound effects. Rivers of milk, orange juice, and water cascade from cup to tray to kitchen floor, adding joy to the experiment. His mother, engaged in unceasing labor with sponges and mops, can hardly be blamed if she does not encourage these experiments, but she is never consulted. . . . Before he concludes these experiments he has discovered every property of a cup that can be extracted through his study and experimentation (including breakage) and then settles down to a utilitarian view of a cup which gratifies his mother. We can multiply such studies in the nature of objects to include nearly everything accessible to him. (Fraiberg, 1959, p. 53)

With a more mature understanding of object permanence, more things *are* accessible. Now, when a ball is hidden first under one cloth and then under another—if he *sees* the ball being moved—the child can find it. He picks up the second cloth and makes his discovery. Now children know that the ball is separate from the actions associated with it: It still exists, even in a new place (Flavell, 1985).

● *The 18-month transition: From sensorimotor functioning to symbolic thinking.* At around 18 months cognition shifts from the intelligence of infancy to the kind of thinking we use throughout life. Now begins the transition to true symbolic thinking, the ability to represent things mentally, to imag-

Wearing a bowl as a hat delights this 18-month-old girl who can now pretend that one thing can be another.

At about 1 year old, babies can imitate behavior they've seen before.

ine *what if.* Symbolic thinking (also called **representational thinking**) involves the mental manipulation of images or symbols; something can "stand for" something else (Bornstein & Lamb, 1992). Pretending is possible now: A block is a car or a building; a foot is Snow White (Fein, 1991; Tamis-LeMonda & Bornstein, 1990, 1991). A toddler puts a doll on a block and covers it with a newspaper blanket. At play, the question guiding the child shifts from "What is this and what can it do?" to "What can I do with this object?"

Symbolic thinking also makes mental experiments and **mental combinations** possible. That is, several actions can be coordinated and "acted out" mentally in a sequence. A 2-year-old goes to a cabinet, pulls out a pot, pauses, gets a spoon, throws a block into the pot, and stirs. He has performed a series of activities because he was able to imagine: "What do I want to do?" "What do I need?" "Where do I get it?" And then, "How do I do it?"

Finally, thinking symbolically allows children to apply their growing memory skills. The past becomes related to the present, and **deferred imitation** becomes possible. Because she can now duplicate behavior she has seen before, a child may take her toy dog for a walk, offer her teddy bear a drink, or imitate her mother reading a book.

No longer limited to the trial-and-error experiments of earlier periods, toddlers can solve problems mentally. Piaget's daughter Lucienne provided his classic illustration of this achievement. Lucienne wanted to get something that was inside of a matchbox, the kind that slides open and shut. Her father, the experimenter, refused to slide it open. She sat holding the box and, while looking at it, began to open and close her mouth, *representing to herself* the solution to the problem. Finally, having thought the problem through, she pushed open the box and claimed her prize.

● *Complete object permanence.* Children who can think symbolically can solve the most advanced object permanence problem, the one involving "invis-

● **representational thinking**
thinking that involves manipulation of mental images (symbols)

● **mental combinations**
mental coordinations of several actions in sequence

● **deferred imitation**
duplication of behavior seen or experienced earlier

ible displacement." Pick up a Ping-Pong ball, and then move your hand and the ball under a cloth. Then, remove your hand, leaving the ball under the cloth, where it makes an obvious lump. In earlier stages, infants would look for the ball under your hand, but by 24 months, children can find the ball even if you pass your hand under several cloths before or after actually placing the ball under one of them. If the child doesn't find it where she thinks it ought to be, she searches where she thinks it might be, and if she still cannot find it, she looks surprised. What has happened is that she now can represent the object mentally: She can imagine it, and she knows it exists *somewhere*. Only now, concluded Piaget, does the child fully possess the concept of object permanence.

LANGUAGE DEVELOPMENT

Like infants everywhere, Kenny began cooing "oo-oo-oo-oo," "ah-ah-ah-ah," at about 2 months. By 5 months, he moved on to "ba-ba-ba, na-na-na, da-da-da." At 10 months, "na-na" (for banana, naturally) became his first word, followed a few months later by some short commands: "Do it. Open it. Shut it. Do again." For his first full-length sentence, Kenny announced, "Want a piece of cake."

How did Kenny's cooing and babbling sounds change into one-syllable words, then two-word sentences, and finally more complex sentences? Because infants everywhere usually progress through the same stages at about the same time, biology is clearly at work. But while human genes allow us to create human speech, heredity is not enough. Without experiencing the speech of other humans, no child, despite genetic potential, would learn to talk. Again, it's not biology *or* environment, but both.

The process of language development begins long before words appear, as infants and adults communicate during the first year. In this period of prelinguistic communication, gestures, social games, and a lot of adult intuition prepare infants for the use of real language.

● **Prelinguistic Communication**

In every society, playing comes before talking. These first games—involving gestures, sounds, facial expression, and imitation—are forms of **prelinguistic communication.** Patty-cake and peek-a-boo, for example, resemble conversation because they require give-and-take, or **turn-taking.** The parents make a sound or movement, then pause for the baby's response, then make another sound or movement in response, and so on (Bloom L., Beckwith, R., & Capatides, J. B., 1988; Tronick, 1989).

This kind of interaction takes time to develop. In a primitive version of "catch," for example, a 5-month-old's mother may offer him a small toy. He doesn't actually catch the toy; rather, she places it in his hands or lap, from which it is likely to fall. She takes it back and repeats the action, with the same result. All this is very one-sided, but by about 10 months, the baby begins to play a more active role, actually grasping the toy and, still later, returning it to his mother. At some point, *he* initiates this "behavioral dialogue," waving the toy, later offering it to her, and subsequently tossing it to (or, more likely, *at*) her

● **prelinguistic communication**
literally, before-language communication; communication between parents and infants through games, gestures, sounds, facial expressions, and imitation

● **turn-taking**
conversational give-and-take

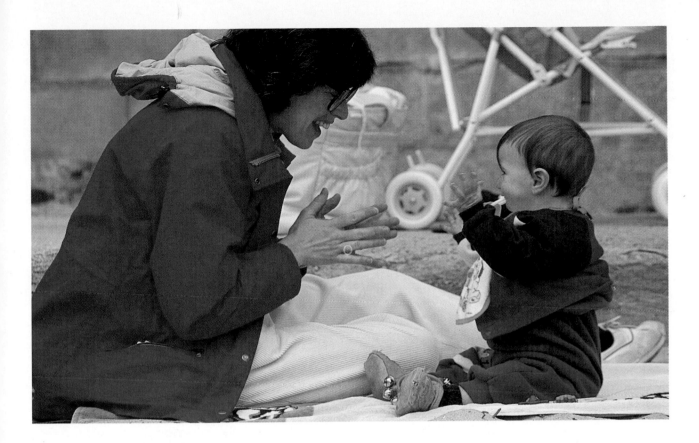

(Schaffer, 1979). By the baby's first birthday, he is skilled at this game. In a game like catch, a baby learns to take turns—a skill that will be essential for later conversations.

Essential too for effective communication is the capacity to use language *intentionally*, to say what you mean. Recall that one of the major milestones in cognitive development is the gradual emergence of goal-directed activity, or intentionality. Infants also grow in their ability to use language intentionally. This ability develops during the second year and is nurtured by adults who respond to infants' sounds *as if* they had meaning (Bates, Camaioni, & Volterra, 1975), as in the following "conversation" between a mother and her 3-month-old (Snow, 1977a):

Playfulness between adults and infants, besides being fun for both, is a kind of prelinguistic communication, which forms the basis for the give-and-take of conversation.

Mother	Baby
Oh, what a nice little smile!	[Smiles]
Yes, isn't that pretty?	
There now.	
There's a nice little smile.	
What a nice wind as well!	[Burps]
Yes, that's better, isn't it?	
Yes.	
Yes.	
Yes!	[Vocalizes]
There's a nice noise.	

Although the mother invents the meaning, early dialogues like this one lay the foundation for language development.

As they move toward real language, babies rely less on physical effort to get what they want (Baldwin & Markman, 1989). If a 5-month-old girl wants a teddy bear that is just out of reach, she will grab for it, fail, and cry. An adult or sibling may hand her the toy. By 9 or 10 months, the child, though physically more capable of getting the toy, may simply stretch an arm toward the teddy bear, at the same time looking toward mother. Again, the adult gets the message—but notice how the baby's communicative skills have improved. Soon, the child just points to the toy, and someone gets it. Typically, a parent talks while responding to the request, saying something like, "Oh, your teddy bear? Do you want your teddy bear? OK, here's the teddy bear." And one day, stretching, reaching, or even pointing won't be necessary. The baby will say "Teddy," and someone will get the bear. The more parents or caregivers and infants share such a joint focus on objects, while the adult names them, the more advanced the child's vocabulary will be (Dunham & Dunham, 1992).

By 12 months, many babies are communicating intentionally, beginning to use their first words. How do infants reach this next milestone in communication?

● Early Sounds

No matter what language their parents speak, all babies make many of the same sounds at about the same time. By 2 or 3 months, infants begin cooing: They repeat the same vowel sound, varying the pitch from high to low. By 5 months, they add consonants to the vowels and string the sounds together ("ba-ba-ba-ba," "do-do-do-do"). These sound combinations are called **babbling,** and the sequence of sounds that infants make when they babble appears to be universal, developing through a series of discrete stages (Rough et al., 1989). When medical problems of the throat prevent babies from babbling, their language is delayed. This suggests that babbling contributes to the development of speech (Locke & Pearson, 1990). Even deaf infants seem to do a kind of babbling. If they have been exposed to sign language, these infants go through a period of repeating particular motions with their hands, appearing to researchers to be silently babbling (Petitto & Marentette, 1991).

In general, the first sounds are the easiest for babies to say (Menyuk, 1985). For infants everywhere, sounds made with the lips ("p" or "b") precede sounds made with the tip of the tongue ("d" or "n"). Similarly, "stop sounds" (made with "b," for instance) appear after "nasal" sounds, such as those made with "m" (Irwin, 1947).

When they begin speaking, U.S. children will say "tut" before "cut"; Swedish children will say "tata" before "kata"; and Japanese children will say "ta" before "ka" (Lamb & Bornstein, 1987). In many languages the earliest sounds infants make are incorporated into terms used to refer to parents—in English, for example, "mama" or "papa."

Even children with deaf parents show the same babbling patterns (Lenneberg, 1967). This is further evidence for the universality and biological basis of early sound production. However, over time, this biological base interacts with the linguistic environment. For example, infants are more likely with development to experiment with and discriminate among speech sounds that

babbling
an infant's repetitive sound combinations, before first words are spoken

TABLE 5.1 UNIVERSAL MILESTONES IN LANGUAGE DEVELOPMENT	
Milestone	**Approximate Age**
Cooing	2 to 3 months
Babbling	5 months
First words	10 to 14 months
Ten words in usable vocabulary; comprehends about fifty	12 months
Two-word sentences	21 to 24 months
Two hundred words in vocabulary	24 months

are more common in the language to which they have been exposed (Boysson-Bardies, 1984). Thus, for example, Japanese newborns can tell the difference between the sounds "ra" and "la," but by the end of the first year they treat these sounds as if they are the same. This is because the Japanese language does not distinguish them (Werker, 1989).

Table 5.1 summarizes the universal stages of language development.

● The First Words

After babies begin speaking their first real words, at about 1 year, vocabulary grows slowly for the first 6 months but then increases rapidly over the next 6 months. It is as though children suddenly understand the purpose and meaning of speech, and that everything has a name (Huttenlocher et al., 1991; Lifter & Bloom, 1989; Reznick & Goldfield, 1992).

"More juice," says a toddler, long before she can say, "I want more apple juice, please."

At first most infants acquire words one at a time, mastering about 10 by 15 months, and about 200 by 2 years of age. Girls' vocabularies tend to grow more rapidly than boys' during the second year, but boys catch up later on. Interestingly, girls' early lead does not appear related to the fact that people speak to girls more than to boys (Huttenlocher et al., 1991).

For both sexes, first words tend to share the following characteristics:

1. The words babies say first are not necessarily those they hear most. They tend to name things that are important to them or that they have experienced often. "Mama," "dada," and "baba" (bottle) are apt to be early words, along with "baw" (ball), "bre" (bread), or whatever toys or foods may be most significant. All these are people or things they have frequently seen or heard in action or manipulated themselves (Dromi, 1987; Griffiths, 1987).

2. English-speaking babies usually say nouns, verbs, and pronouns before adjectives, adverbs, and other modifiers. They say the names of familiar things, along with "have" and "want," before "big," "fast," or "more" (Bowerman, 1976; Nelson, 1973).

3. At first, babies use words narrowly. Later, meanings become overly broad (Reich, 1986). In the following interchange (all too familiar to most parents), the child is after one very particular toy vehicle, which she has labeled "truck." The father attempts to give his daughter what he calls a "truck"—and they both end up frustrated:

   18-month-old: Truck.

   Father: Here's your truck.

   18-month-old: No. *Truck.*

   Father: Yes. Here's your truck.

   18-month-old (loudly): Truck!

● **underextension**
using words too restrictively

This is an example of **underextension,** too restrictive a use of words. Toddlers make this mistake when they use a word label to refer only to one type of thing actually included in the concept—*truck* means only red trucks, or real trucks, or dump trucks—or to one specific truck, as in the dialogue above. Later, just the opposite happens. A word may be used too broadly, so that *truck* may mean all vehicles or all things with wheels, even a wheelbarrow; any four-legged animal may be a *kitty.* This **overextension** shows that the baby is forming mental categories, an important cognitive advance.

● **overextension**
using words too broadly; using the same word to stand for a number of similar things

● **holophrase**
a single word that stands for whole thoughts

4. Single words often stand for whole sentences or phrases. The **holophrase** "dog" can mean "There's a dog." "I want my dog." "The dog is barking." "I'm afraid of this dog." "I like this dog."

As a rule, children understand many more words than they can say. Even during the second year, when both comprehension and speech spurt ahead, comprehension vocabulary may be 5 to 10 times greater than speaking vocabulary (Reznick & Goldfield, 1992). So, if a parent says, "Go get your blocks," the child may comply even if he can't say "blocks." Not surprisingly, toddlers who understand fewer words are less likely to do what their parents ask (Kaler & Kopp, 1990). Unfortunately, parents don't always realize that often toddlers aren't being willfully disobedient; they simply don't understand what their parents have told them.

As you might expect, toddlers who understand the most also tend to say the most (Bates, Bretherton, & Snyder, 1988; Tamis-LeMonda et al., 1992). Speaking and understanding influence each other and are probably fueled by the same developmental change. It is not coincidental that the complete acquisition of object permanence coincides with when infants begin to think symbolically, both of which are major cognitive advances. If you look back at Figure 5.1, you'll notice that a major transition in cognitive development occurs at 18 months. Knowing *when* different cognitive changes occur can lead us to understanding *why* they occur. In the case of symbolic thinking and object permanence, the answer probably lies in the maturing nervous system. Eighteen months is also a time when major reorganizations occur in the neural configurations of the brain (Goldman-Rakic, 1987).

● Two-Word Sentences

By 24 months, most children begin using two-word sentences: "More cookie." "Do again." "Ball fall." These brief sentences mark a big step. Language is now a **symbolic system,** where words not only name things but express the relations between them (Nelson, 1977). It is no accident that by this age, children have developed symbolic thinking. Words, after all, are symbols which express a child's wishes (Nelson, 1974). What was only implied by a single word, such as "car," now becomes explicit. "More car" can mean "Daddy, wind it up again" or, at other times, "I want to keep riding."

In these early sentences, again we see universal patterns, probably reflecting the level of cognitive development reached by most children toward the end of their second year (Slobin, 1970). Below are examples of the most common types of two-word sentences:

> *Recurrence:* More juice.
>
> Play again.
>
> *Attribution:* Big dog.
>
> Red ball.
>
> *Possessive:* Dada hat.
>
> Baby milk.
>
> *Agent action:* Barbara cry.
>
> Mama eat.
>
> *Action object:* Throw rattle.
>
> Hit dog.

Notice a few things about these early sentences: Some are requests, but most are observations about the world, maybe even attempts to understand it through language (Halliday, 1975). These sentences describe things that older children

● **symbolic system**
a system, like language, that represents and labels elements of the world and their interrelations

take for granted, and the order of the words mimics the patterns of adult syntax. Toddlers say "more milk," not "milk more"; "want that," not "that want."

● Individual Differences in Language Development

Most infants have a 50-word vocabulary by 24 months, but many reach that level earlier or later (Huttenlocher et al., 1991). And a small minority of children begin talking in phrases at 1 year or so, learning single words at a later time. These phrases, known as **compressed sentences,** are usually slurred, sounding more like one long complicated word ("I-no-know") than like a multiword phrase ("I don't know") (R. M. Brown, 1977; Nelson, 1973). How can we explain these individual differences?

● *The role of experience.*
Certainly, the environment plays a role. Both vocabulary growth and the way children use language appear to be influenced by the language environment to which they are exposed. In one study, researchers tracked the number of words mothers directed to their 16-month-olds. Babies whose mothers spoke to them the most also showed the fastest vocabulary growth during their second year (Huttenlocher et al., 1991). (Although this study looked at mothers and infants, we can assume that the same results would be true for any adult who regularly cared for an infant.)

In other research, Katherine Nelson found that early talkers, children with large vocabularies by age 2, had mothers who accepted their early speech as meaningful (1973). Later talkers had mothers who were more rejecting of their early attempts at talking. Nelson offered the following examples:

Accepting Mother

Mother: Jane. Here's a bottle. Where's the bottle? Here's a bottle.

Jane: Wah wah.

Mother: Bottle.

Jane: Bah bah.

Mother: Oh, bah bah. Here's a ball.

Jane: Baw.

Mother: Ball. Yes.

Jane: Uh. Uh boo?

Mother: Ball.

Rejecting Mother

Paul: Go.

Mother: What? Feel.

Paul: Fe.

Mother: What's that? A dog. What does the dog say? One page at a time. Oh, that one over there. What's that one there?

Paul: Boah.

Mother: What? You know that.

● **compressed sentences**
phrases made up of several words slurred into one long sound

Paul: Bah.

Mother: What?

Paul: Ah wah.

Mother: What?

Paul: Caw.

Mother: Car?

Paul: Caw, awh.

Mother: Little kitty, you know that.

It is not hard to imagine why the first child's acquisition of language is likely to be swifter than the second's.

Nelson and other researchers have also identified differences in the way children learn vocabulary and use language (Bates et al., 1988; Goldfield & Snow, 1989; Nelson, 1973, 1981). The early vocabulary of some children consisted mostly of nouns ("dog," "hat," "house"), proper nouns ("Steve"), and adjectives ("big," "red")—words all related to labels, objects, and descriptions. Other children used more words related to social routines and words indicating actions and feelings ("stop," "now," "want," "don't," "bye-bye") (Lamb & Bornstein, 1987). Nelson called the first group of children *referential,* because their words referred primarily to objects rather than people. She called the second group *expressive,* because their vocabularies expressed something about their involvement with people. The two types of vocabularies are not mutually exclusive; but they show, from a very early age, individual differences in the way we use language (Goldfield & Reznick, 1990).

Although both acquire their first 50 words by about the same age, expressive children build language at a slow and steady rate; referential children start slowly and then speed up. By 2½ years, referential children have larger vocabularies, but expressive children have more facility in forming two-word combinations (Nelson, 1973).

Where do these different language styles come from? Partly, says Nelson (1981), from the different language styles of mothers. Referential children have mothers who frequently label things and events, whereas expressive children have mothers who speak to them conversationally. Nelson also noticed family and social differences (1973). Referential children were most often firstborns in middle-class homes; expressive children were more likely to be later-born with less-educated parents. Why? Possibly because middle-class firstborns get their educated mothers' full attention, which often includes reading aloud and direct vocabulary teaching. Later-borns may get less direct teaching, either because the mother's time is more divided or because with more than one child, she becomes more focused on controlling their behavior than on their vocabulary. Less-educated parents, who may be under financial and other pressures, may tend to concentrate less on reading or building vocabulary.

Children's language development also seems affected by the quality of their emotional bond to their mothers. Children who were more linguistically advanced at age 3 also had a more secure emotional bond to their mothers at age 1 (Morisset et al., 1990). To sum up, a family's intellectual and emotional environment influences language learning.

Cultural differences even affect the way parents speak to infants. French mothers use language less to direct their babies than to establish emotional closeness.

● *Cultural and socioeconomic differences in parents' speech to infants.* There are both similarities and differences across cultural, ethnic, and socioeconomic groups in the ways in which parents interact with infants. One multinational team of researchers compared mother-infant interaction in the United States, France, and Japan (Bornstein et al., 1992b). Mothers in all three countries tended to respond to their babies' content vocalization (for example, babbling or cooing) with imitation, and to their babies' distressed vocalization (such as crying) with nurturance. Other studies have found that mothers in different cultures tended to adjust their speech patterns in similar ways in response to children of different ages (Bornstein et al., 1992a; Fernald & Morikawa, 1993). All over the world, parents use more simplified speech when they interact with younger infants than with older ones.

There are important differences in the content and degree of verbal stimulation parents provide their infants, however. For instance, American mothers are more likely than Japanese mothers to label objects when speaking to their children, which, in turn, leads American infants to have, on average, larger noun vocabularies than their Japanese counterparts (Fernald & Morikawa, 1993). American mothers also tend to use questions more when interacting with their infants than other mothers. And, whereas Argentinian mothers tend to use a lot of direct statements when talking with their babies, French mothers tend to be more egalitarian, using language not so much to direct the child as to establish emotional closeness (Bornstein et al., 1992b). These differences reflect cultural differences in parents' beliefs about how best to socialize, and speak to, infants.

Social class is also an important influence on the ways that parents interact with their infants. As a general rule, parents from higher social classes are more verbally responsive and more verbally stimulating with their infants. This social class difference has been found in several cultures, including the United States, Kenya, and Mexico, and no doubt reflects the influence of formal education on parents' beliefs and values (Richman, Miller, & Levine, 1992).

Despite these cultural and socioeconomic differences in patterns of parent-infant interaction, however, the *effects* of verbal stimulation on infant competence have been shown across a wide array of Western and non-Western cultures (for example, Tamis-LeMonda, Bornstein, Cyphers, & Toda, 1992; Wachs et al., 1993). Infants' cognitive and language development is facilitated by responsive, verbally stimulating interaction.

● *The role of health and genetics.* Because hearing and speaking are so intimately connected, impaired hearing during infancy can affect language development. Although relatively few infants are born with hearing problems, many suffer from frequent ear infections (*otitis media*). Fluid caused by the infection blocks the ear canal, and if the canal doesn't fully clear between infections, the infant's hearing and ability to perceive speech are affected, though catch-up growth may be possible later on (Fried-Patti & Finitzo, 1990). At least one researcher has found a consistent connection between ear infections during infancy and speech delays between ages 2 and 3 (Menyuk, 1993). Here, too, environmental factors interact with biology. Some children seem naturally more prone to ear infections than others, and those with high susceptibilities who also spend considerable time in group day care facilities suffer the most, because they are exposed to the infections of other babies (Howes et al., 1990). But regardless of where babies spend their days, ear infections need prompt medical attention.

Other researchers have looked specifically for links between language development, biology, and environment. Often such studies include adopted children and children living with their natural parents (see Chapter 1). In a study involving 1-year-olds, their biological mothers, and their adoptive parents, the adoptive mothers who responded frequently to their infants' vocalizations had the more linguistically skilled babies, again showing the influence of the environment. But the study also showed that genetic factors play a role as well (Hardy-Brown, Plomin, & DeFries, 1981). Children's language skills were more consistently related to the intellectual abilities of their biological mothers than to those of the adoptive mothers with whom they lived. In language development, as in every other aspect of human growth, biology and experience work together (Ho, 1987; Plomin & DeFries, 1983).

● ## Talking to Infants Effectively: Motherese and Expansion

"*See* the doggie!" "*Nice* doggie!" Whether in English, Japanese, Italian, German, French, or Mandarin Chinese, mothers speak it and infants like it (Fernald & Mazzie, 1991; Fernald et al., 1989; Grieser & Kuhl, 1988). This universal lingo, dubbed **motherese,** describes slow, high-pitched speech, with exaggerated intonation. Sentences are short, well-formed, and grammatically simple, usually referring to things that the baby can see (Cooper & Aslin, 1990; Fernald & Mazzie, 1991). Speech that has these characteristics is more likely to capture and hold babies' attention even in infants as young as 1 month old (Cooper & Aslin, 1990). And you don't have to be a mother to speak it. Fathers, other caregivers, and even other children use it often (Fernald & Mazzie, 1991).

One of the ways motherese reinforces language learning is by exaggerating the differences between sounds so that the child can clearly distinguish one sound from another (Karzon, 1985). In addition, parents and other sensitive adults tend to elaborate, or add details to a baby's speech, in a technique called *expansion:*

Baby: Doggie.

Parent: Yes, the doggie just went out the door.

Baby: Where blankie.

Parent: Where is your blanket? Let's look in your crib.

Parents' responses are typically a little more complex grammatically than their child's level of speaking, which gives the child a kind of linguistic foundation for further progress (Schaffer, 1979).

ASSESSING INFANT DEVELOPMENT

So far, we have focused mainly on universal aspects of infant cognitive development. But what about differences *between* individual babies? In the assessment of an infant's development, a particular baby's physical and cognitive skills are compared to established norms or averages. In later chapters, we will examine intelligence tests and their use in predicting school achievement. Here, we'll look briefly at the most commonly used infant tests.

● Gesell Development Schedules

Devised in the 1940s by a Yale University pediatrician, Arnold Gesell, the **Gesell Development Schedules** provided standardized procedures for observing and evaluating a child's development from 1 month through 6 years. These scales originated out of a need for "normative" information about "average" rates of growth and development in four different areas: *motor* (for example, balance, sitting, locomotion), *adaptation* (alertness, intelligence, exploration), *language* (vocalization, gestures, facial expression), and *personal-social behavior* (feeding, dressing, toilet training). Although no longer as widely used as they once were, the Gesell Development Schedules formed the foundation upon which many other infant tests were built. The best known and most widely used of these other tests are the *Bayley Scales of Mental and Motor Development.*

The Bayley Scales

The **Bayley Scales** focus on two areas of development. The mental scale assesses perceptions, senses, memory, learning, problem solving, and language. The motor scale assesses gross motor and fine motor capacities and coordination. On the basis of their performance, infants are given two scores: the *Mental Development Index (MDI)* and the *Psychomotor Development Index (PDI)*. Testers then compare these scores to those of most other children of the same age. A child who performs at about the same level as her age-mates receives a score called a **developmental quotient (DQ)** of 100. A child who performs at a level below what is expected for her age would score lower than 100, and a child who outscores her age norms would be rated higher than 100. The lower or higher the score, the more delayed or advanced the child is presumed to be, relative to babies of the same age. Table 5.2 lists several items from both the mental and the motor scales with their standard age of achievement.

Bayley Scales
tests for assessing an infant's mental and motor skills by comparison with age-related norms

developmental quotient (DQ)
a score on the Bayley Scales based on age-mates' scores

The Value of Infant Tests

We use infant tests such as the Bayley Scales for two general purposes: to assess development at the time of the test (is the baby developing normally?) and to predict the infant's future functioning (will a relatively slow 12-month-old be a relatively slow 3-year-old?). In general, the tests are far better at evaluating a child's present development than they are at predicting that child's future. In fact, neither the Bayley Scales nor the Gesell Schedules are a reliable predictor of later intelligence or school performance. The exception is in cases of severe retardation or other neurological or sensory difficulties, when the tests *are* useful for identifying children who will need special attention and intervention (DiLalla et al., 1990; Siegel, 1989; Uzgiris, 1989).

TABLE 5.2   SAMPLE ITEMS FROM THE BAYLEY SCALES OF INFANT DEVELOPMENT

Mental Scale		Motor Scale	
Age (in months)	Item	Age (in months)	Item
0.1	Responds to sound of rattle	0.1	Lifts head when held at shoulder
1.5	Social smile	1.8	Turns: side to back
2.0	Visually recognizes mother	2.3	Sits with support
3.8	Turns head to sound of cube	3.2	Turns: back to side
4.1	Reaches for cube	5.3	Pulls to sitting
4.8	Discriminates stranger	6.4	Rolls: back to stomach
6.0	Looks for fallen spoon	6.6	Sits alone steadily
7.0	Vocalizes four different syllables	8.1	Pulls to standing
9.1	Responds to verbal request	9.6	Walks with help
13.4	Removes pellet from bottle	11.7	Walks alone
14.2	Says two words	14.6	Walks backward
18.8	Uses words to make wants known	16.1	Walks upstairs with help
19.3	Names one picture (e.g., dog)	23.4	Jumps off floor

Sitting unaided by seven months is a sign of normal infant development.

● Infant Tests and Beyond: Predicting Later Development

During childhood most tests of intellectual development measure verbal skills and representational thinking. Testing these abilities in infancy is difficult, since first words appear only toward the end of the first year and representational thought doesn't emerge until about 18 months. Until recently, predicting young infants' future intellectual capacities during the sensorimotor stage seemed impossible.

However, developmentalists have recently discovered that some new sorts of tests, when given during the first year of life, *can* have predictive value. This discovery has altered developmentalists' views, not only about the value of infant testing but also around the issue of continuity from infancy through childhood (Bornstein, 1989b; Slater, 1989). Researchers found that tests of infants' **visual recognition memory** (how well they remember things they've already seen), given as early as 2 months, strongly predict intelligence test scores later in childhood, up to 8 years of age (McColl & Carriger, 1993).

Visual recognition tests assess an infant's ability to discriminate between two visual stimuli—one seen before and one never seen. How do these tests work? First, researchers show the infant two identical pictures, side by side. The presentation lasts long enough (for example, 30 seconds) for the infant to become

● **visual recognition memory** memory for stimuli seen before familiar with the image. After a brief interval, the infant is again presented with two pictures side by side—one of the previously shown image, and one of something new. By assessing whether and how long the infant looks at the new image, relative to how long the infant looks at the familiar one, the researcher can gauge whether the infant recognizes and remembers what was shown previously.

In a group of 3- to 9-month-olds, tests of visual recognition memory correctly identified 85 percent of infants who will be mentally retarded at age 3 (Fagan, 1992). Other infant tests that measure discrimination abilities—distinguishing strange from familiar people (Rose & Ruff, 1987) or familiar and unfamiliar sounds (O'Connor, Cohen, & Parmelee, 1984)—are also highly correlated with later intelligence (McColl & Carriger, 1993). Why is this so? Are discrimination abilities so important and so constant? They may well be. Discrimination tasks may tap very basic cognitive processing abilities, such as perceiving and remembering, that underlie intelligence at all ages (Bornstein, 1989b; Bornstein & Sigman, 1986; Fagan & Knevel, 1989).

The other key question to ask about these tests is, Why are they useful? Why does predicting intelligence matter? For developmentalists, the answer lies in intervention. To the extent that experience can enhance cognitive development, early identification and intervention can make a crucial difference (Fagan, 1992). The broad aim of evaluative testing, then, is to foster every child's intellectual abilities.

SUMMARY

1. Although newborns like familiarity, by about 2 months, they begin paying attention to more novel and complex images and objects. By 3 or 4 months, perception, assigning meaning to sensations, improves markedly. Information gained by one sense can be processed by another, an ability called cross-modal transfer. (See pages 140–146.)

2. Although infants demonstrate rudimentary memory abilities during the first months of life, most adults have difficulty recalling experiences prior to age 3. One hypothesis is that experiences in infancy may be stored in memory, but within an organizational system that has become less accessible over the course of development. (See pages 146–147.)

3. Piaget theorized that cognitive development progresses through a series of stages. In the sensorimotor stage, spanning the first 2 years of life, infants understand the world through their senses and physical actions. The major accomplishments of the sensorimotor period are decentration, intentionality, and object permanence. (See pages 147–149.)

4. Contemporary theorists describe four distinct substages in sensorimotor development, marked by transitions at 3, 8, 12, and 18 months. The 3-month transition signals the appearance of primary circular reactions, repetitive actions and responses centering around the infant's own body. (See pages 149–151.)

5. Intentional behavior begins to emerge during the 8-month transition. Now, infants begin to see that their own actions cause separate results. They can act purposefully to get what they want. Secondary circular reactions emerge now, as infants repeat actions involving objects. This interest in the non-baby world marks the appearance of decentration. Awareness of object permanence continues to develop, but it is not yet complete. (See pages 151–153.)

6. During the 12-month transition, active, purposeful, trial-and-error exploration begins. Babies become "little scientists," avidly studying everything around them. True symbolic thinking begins with the 18-month transition. This is the ability to represent things mentally, to imagine what if. It is the kind of thinking we use throughout life. Now, children can solve problems mentally without first performing trial-and-error experiments, and object permanence is now fully understood. Two-year-olds know that even when they can't see something, it still exists. (See pages 153–156.)

7. Universally, infants go through the same linguistic stages at around the same age. This tells us that language development is at least partly determined by genes. Language acquisition begins with prelinguistic communication between parents and infants, involving gestures, sounds, and facial expressions. (See pages 156–158.)

8. All babies begin to make the same sounds at about the same age, progressing from cooing to babbling. First words appear from 10 to 14 months, naming people or things infants most commonly experience. By 24 months, two-word sentences generally appear. By the end of infancy, then, language is a symbolic system, where words not only name things but express relations between them. (See pages 158–162.)

9. Both biology and experience influence individual differences in language development. Parents of early talkers generally encourage their infants' early language attempts. Some children tend to be referential: Their vocabularies have more labels and description. Others may be more expressive: Their vocabularies have more words associated with actions or social routines. (See pages 162–166.)

10. Infant tests like the Gesell Schedules and the Bayley Scales compare infants' motor and cognitive abilities to age-related norms. To predict later intellectual development, however, researchers have turned to tests of visual recognition memory and discrimination abilities. These tests, which can be given to infants as young as 5 months, have been found to correlate with later intelligence test scores. (See pages 166–169.)

KEY TERMS

babbling
Bayley Scales
complexity
compressed sentences
cross-modal abilities
decentration
deferred imitation
developmental quotient
    (DQ)
dishabituation
equivalence
Gesell Development
    Schedules

habituation
holophrases
intentional behavior
intentionality
mental combinations
motherese
object permanence
overextension
perceive
prelinguistic
    communication
primary circular
    reaction

representational thinking
secondary circular
    reactions
sensorimotor
social referencing
symbolic system
turn-taking
underextension
visual recognition
    memory
zone of proximal
    development

SUGGESTED READINGS

Bruner, J. (1983). *Child talk.* New York: Norton. An interesting discussion of language development by a prominent theorist and researcher of cognitive development.

Fowler, W. (1990). *Talking from infancy: How to nurture and cultivate early language development.* Cambridge, MA: Brookline Books. Suggestions for encouraging and facilitating children's early language development at home and in day care.

Ginsburg, H., and Opper, S. (1989). *Piaget's theory of intellectual development* (rev. ed.). New York: Prentice-Hall. One of the best summaries of infant cognitive development according to Piaget.

Gottfried, A., and Brown, C. (Eds.). (1986). *Play interactions.* Lexington, MA: Lexington Books. Leading experts in child development explain what play is, what it reveals about children's perceptions, and how it affects their development.

White, B. (1985). *The first three years of life* (rev. ed.). New York: Simon & Schuster. One of America's best-known parent educators outlines the major cognitive accomplishments in the early years and shows what parents can do to give their children a head start.

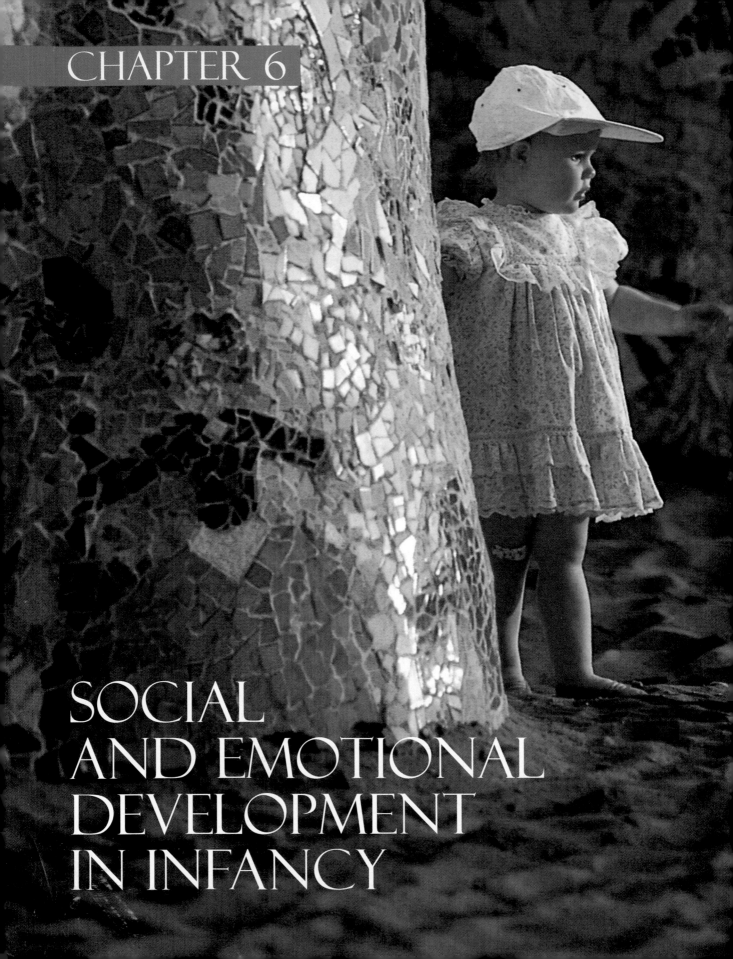

SOCIAL
AND EMOTIONAL
DEVELOPMENT
IN INFANCY

My mother had a good deal of trouble with me but I think she enjoyed it. She had none at all with my brother Henry, who was two years younger than I, and I think that the unbroken monotony of his goodness and truthfulness and obedience would have been a burden to her but for the relief and variety which I furnished in the other direction.

MARK TWAIN, *Autobiography*

We may not be able to say it with Twain's wit, but we've all seen it and probably lived it. Brothers and sisters can be as different as strangers—or as alike as twins. And many differences seem wired in. Far from being blank slates, every infant is born an individual, each with a trademark of body rhythms and a personal style of responding.

This unique set of inborn characteristics defines an infant's temperament and will shape her personality. In this chapter we focus on the landmarks that chart the social and emotional development of all infants. We examine temperament first and then consider mother-infant attachment. Outside the family, we look at infants' early relationships with their peers and with other adults. Finally, we discuss a period that irritates and confuses many parents, the time around 2 years when "me," "no," and temper tantrums mark the child's growing independence.

INFANT TEMPERAMENT

A friend of one of the authors of this book put it this way: "My older son was a model baby: He slept through the night at 6 weeks, took long naps, awoke predictably to be nursed, played, went back to sleep. Three years later, I had another baby. He cried more than he slept. No one had to tell me that my sons were born different."

Research has confirmed what every parent knows. Babies are born with a unique **temperament.** Temperament influences how susceptible babies are to emotional stimulation, how quickly and intensely they respond, their general mood and strength of mood, and how much their mood changes. While temperament is inborn, **personality** develops. It is a unique way of behaving and reacting that develops as we grow and learn. Personality is shaped and molded by experience and can continue to develop throughout life. Newborns, who have lived only a short time, cannot have much personality, but their inborn temperament is the raw material out of which personality is shaped.

● Dimensions of Temperament

In the 1960s, doctors Stella Chess and Alexander Thomas began studying patterns of infant temperament. In their early work, Chess and Thomas periodically observed 140 children from infancy through adolescence and described their findings in the now-classic **New York Longitudinal Study (NYLS)** (Thomas & Chess, 1977, 1980; Thomas, Chess, & Birch, 1968). Later research

● **temperament**
the unique, inborn pattern of responsiveness and mood

● **personality**
behaviors and response patterns developed through experience

● **New York Longitudinal Study (NYLS)**
a pioneering study of infant temperament

has focused on a few central dimensions of temperament: emotionality (positive and negative), sociability, and activity level.

Though all infants cry a lot during their first few months (see Chapter 3), some are highly irritable, crying often, strongly, and for long periods of time. These infants rate high on **negative emotionality.** Interestingly, the same baby who cries a lot may express a lot of joy as well. **Positive emotionality** exists separately from the negative side of temperament (Belsky, Fish, & Isabella, 1991; Goldsmith & Campos, 1990), so babies can show high or low emotionality in general, or express more of either positive or negative emotions. Physiologically, this makes perfect sense: Positive and negative emotions tend to be controlled by different hemispheres of the brain (left-positive; right-negative) (Davidson, 1992).

A baby's willingness to approach new people or situations, **sociability,** is another dimension of temperament that endures into childhood. At the extremes on this trait, *highly sociable* babies happily join new people and events, while *inhibited* and reserved babies hold back, even getting upset when they must meet a new person or enter a new situation (Kagan & Snidman, 1991).

The third main dimension of temperament involves **activity.** As infants, highly active babies flail and kick. And once they crawl, they're always on the go. Babies with lower activity levels look and listen more than they move (Buss & Plomin, 1984). We may write about these dimensions of temperament separately, but in actuality, every baby has a mixture of traits. Early in their research, Chess and Thomas found that they could identify three basic personal styles or temperaments in infancy, based on a variety of traits.

● ***Three types of babies.*** Negative emotionality is at the core of the **difficult child**'s temperament. Difficult babies cry a lot, are easily distracted, and tend to be fearful of new things and experiences. Like all babies, they set their own timetables for eating and sleeping, but unlike other babies, the difficult child's schedule is subject to frequent shifts: Irregularity is his benchmark. When this baby wakes from a nap, he lets you know it with cries, not gurgles. Difficult children may also have a high activity level and can show this trait very early in infancy (Buss & Plomin, 1984). Even in their cribs, they are the movers, and when they begin to crawl, action itself propels them on. Finally, sociability is relatively lower among difficult children. Perhaps because they are somewhat fearful of anything new, they react less positively to people than other babies do.

Parents of a difficult baby who later have an **easy child** are astounded at the differences between the two. Easy babies eat and sleep "on schedule." Usually calm and predictable, with little negative emotionality, they approach rather than shun new objects and experiences. Adaptability defines them. After napping, if they're not too hungry, they may amuse themselves until someone checks on them. Even when they crawl, these babies will sit for long periods. Easygoing babies also tend to be high in sociability.

In Chess and Thomas's original study, easygoing babies made up 40 percent of the sample, while only 10 percent were difficult. Between these two extremes is the **slow-to-warm-up child.** These infants are distressed by new things and experiences initially but, as the label implies, will "warm up" if given time. Their reactions and behaviors tend not to be intense or extreme. Fifteen percent of the

● negative emotionality
a dimension of temperament; negative emotional qualities in an infant include such things as a high degree of irritability

● positive emotionality
a dimension of temperament; positive emotional qualities in an infant include such things as the expression of joy

● sociability
a dimension of temperament concerning a child's reaction to new people and new situations

● activity
a dimension of temperament; highly active babies are always on the go, while those with lower activity levels look and listen more than they move

● difficult child
a baby with high negative emotionality and an undependable schedule

● easy child
an adaptable, calm baby with a predictable schedule

● slow-to-warm-up child
a child characterized by mild emotions and an initial fear of new experiences

Easy babies sleep well, have predictable moods, and can amuse themselves. Such babies can help even insecure parents feel competent, getting the parent-child relationship off to a good start.

babies in Chess and Thomas's sample were slow to warm up. The remaining infants in this study either did not fit neatly into one of these three categories or were classified as temperamentally "average."

The whole concept of infant temperament presents a challenge to parents and other caregivers. Learning to live compatibly with an infant whose nature is very different from your own can be trying, but it is also likely to be intriguing. An understanding of temperament can also be reassuring. Knowing that your infant is the way she is because she was born that way, that she cries or is irritable or fearful because of her own internal chemistry, can prevent a lot of guilt and insecurity. Rather than trying—and failing—to turn a difficult infant into an easy one, parents can learn to adapt to their baby. What sort of play suits an easily distracted infant best? How do you introduce a slow-to-warm-up baby to a new adult or situation? Children know early who they are; when parents respect those feelings, both can flourish.

● Temperament, Heredity, and Malleability

Thomas and Chess linked temperament to heredity, and more recent research has confirmed that link. The temperaments of identical twins (who are 100 percent alike genetically) are more alike than those of fraternal twins, who are not identical genetically (Emde et al., 1992; Plomin, 1987). Specifically, we seem to inherit the following traits, all of which affect temperament: activity level, sociability, attention span, fearfulness, and fussiness (Braungart et al., 1992; Emde et al., 1992; Saudino & Eaton, 1991).

Does this mean that temperament is fixed from birth, that a shy 3-year-old becomes a timid adult, that a difficult baby never loosens up? Not necessarily. See Making a Difference: Parents, Infants, and Temperaments.

Temperament and Development

Temperament affects development in two ways: It influences the responses babies *evoke* from others as well as the activities and experiences that infants *choose for themselves* (Scarr & McCartney, 1983).

The evocative effects of temperament, or how babies affect their own treatment.

Let's consider a highly negative and difficult infant. At 2 months old, Nancy still wakes several times every night, is difficult to comfort, and cries as soon as she's back in her crib. During the day, she fusses during feedings, baths, and diaper changes. Exhausted, Nancy's mother finds little pleasure in caring for her. During the brief periods when Nancy is quiet or calm, her mother avoids her, welcoming a few precious minutes of peace.

MAKING A DIFFERENCE

PARENTS, INFANTS, AND TEMPERAMENTS

When 3-month-old Terry first met the researchers, they did not get a warm greeting. She rejected their toys and attention, and while they observed her at home during the day with her mother, and in the evening with both parents, Terry cried often. She and nearly 20 other babies involved in the research project were rated high on negative emotionality. Babies who rarely cried and fussed, and who did so with very little intensity and for short periods, were considered low in negativity.

As they tracked these babies, the investigators noted an interesting change: Some of the babies who were among the most negative at 3 months, including Terry, were the *least* negative by 9 months of age. The reverse was true too: Some of the least negative 3-month-olds cried and fussed the *most* 6 months later. What had happened?

Babies whose negativity had fallen had mothers who showed high self-esteem, were happily married, and cared for their babies with sensitivity. Babies who became more negative had *fathers* who lacked empathy, were unhappy in their marriages, and were uninvolved in caring for their baby (Belsky, Fish, & Isabella, 1991). This study suggests that a happily married, well-adjusted, and sensitive mother can help a difficult baby become an easier one. But an insensitive, unhappy, and uninvolved father can turn an easy baby into a difficult one.

Other research with highly inhibited 1- to 2-year-olds also suggests that with skilled care, shyness can be reduced (Kagan, 1989). The key seems to be not pushing but encouraging. Saying, "Go over and play with that little boy," isn't going to make a shy child budge. Instead, the parent can hold the child's hand and, together, approach the new child. Then, the parent can start talking gently to the new child, perhaps asking about a toy he is playing with. Gradually, the parent can engage her own child in an activity near the new child, encouraging any overtures. Throughout, the parent needs to be available, letting the child know that he or she is safe.

You shouldn't conclude from the above that temperament can be shaped and molded as parents wish, however. Actually, much evidence shows that infants who are more negative, active, and/or inhibited tend to stay that way over time (Broberg, Lamb, & Hwang, 1990; Kagan & Snidman, 1991; Kochanska & Radke-Yarrow, 1992; Stifter & Fox, 1990; Wasserman et al., 1990). For example, infants who were most active at *4 days* were also among the most active children at age *8 years* (Korner et al., 1985).

In an earlier chapter, you read about the notion of "reaction range" in our discussion of genetic influences on intelligence: Individuals do not inherit a specific level of intelligence but, rather, a range or predisposition. A similar phenomenon exists with respect to temperament. While temperament tends to be stable, children can and do change, within limits. For the most part, these changes depend on the supportiveness of the environment in which they are reared.

This story is quite real for many mothers and babies. Not only is there evidence that mothers spend less time with and are less responsive to difficult infants, but mothers say they find it harder to cope with such babies and feel less satisfied as mothers (Campbell, 1979; Hagekull & Bohlin, 1990; Maccoby, Snow, & Jacklin, 1984; van den Boom & Hoeksma, 1993). Parents who do not react so negatively toward difficult babies are often getting support from others. Generally, the less able parents are to have breaks from a difficult baby, the more the baby is likely to evoke avoidance, another instance of environment interacting with heredity.

The larger culture plays a role too. Where extended families offer support, parents of a difficult baby will be less isolated (see Chapter 7). And since child care practices themselves differ across cultures, the larger culture will also affect how parents respond to difficult babies and, indeed, which traits are considered "difficult." In India, for example, difficult infants seem to cause less trouble for their mothers, in part because Indian mothers are more relaxed about when they feed their babies and put them to sleep. Feeding happens not by the clock but when babies seem hungry, sometimes 10 to 15 times a day. Mothers put their babies to sleep when they sense that their babies are tired, often sleeping with them (Malhotra, 1989).

● *Choosing their own activities.* The second way in which temperament affects development is through activities infants choose for themselves. At 1 year, Nancy, the difficult infant, quickly crawls from one activity to the next, first banging some blocks around, then rolling a ball across the floor, then pulling pillows off the sofa. Always moving around, she doesn't take the time to really explore and learn about the things in her path. She is likely to injure herself. Highly active and unpredictable babies do, in fact, suffer from more accidental injuries during their second and third year of life (Matheny, 1992). Even IQ scores can be affected by activity level. Highly active babies who score lower on IQ tests may be less focused and persistent, maybe even impeding their early cognitive development (Goldsmith, 1978).

The reverse seems true for less active types. At 1 year, an easy baby sits with a book and turns the pages; she fingers the dial of a play telephone trying to make the bell ring. Her attention span is longer, which may enhance cognitive development. On standardized tests of infant development, babies who have longer attention spans and are more persistent perform better than very active babies. Apparently, persistent babies with a high attention span can enhance their own development through the learning they generate for themselves (Campos et al., 1983; Goldsmith & Gottesman, 1981; Seegmiller & King, 1975).

To sum up, both the environment babies are born into and the temperaments they bring with them affect development. We look now at a third influence, the "fit" between babies and their parents.

● Goodness of Fit

Active Nancy and an anxious, relatively impatient parent would not have been too happy together. Her constant movement would have made the parent worry about accidents, and such a parent surely would have been frustrated by a baby who wouldn't sit still long enough to look at a book. But other parents, with different traits, would have loved Nancy's high energy.

Development is affected by the fit between parent and child. When parents' expectations are well-matched with children's temperaments, conflicts and disappointments will be minimized.

Neither easy nor difficult babies evoke the same response from all parents, and no one temperament is ideal for every set of parents. An easy baby whose needs are not met when she cries can become withdrawn and socially unresponsive. A slow-to-warm-up baby who is rarely offered a second chance may develop a resistance to anything new. The key is *interaction:* Both infant temperament and parental characteristics influence each baby's development. Psychologists use the term **goodness of fit** to stress that the outcome of these first social encounters depends on *both* sides, on how well the personalities and expectations of the parents mesh with the child's basic temperament (Buss & Plomin, 1984; Gunnar et al., 1989; Thomas & Chess, 1980).

● **goodness of fit**
the way the personalities and expectations of the parents mesh with their child's temperament

The baby boy who accepts new things easily, for example, is a perfect match for an anxious first-time mother. As they go through their first year together, his calm manner reassures her again and again. She enjoys spending time with him, reading and playing quietly. A highly active, assertive baby would probably be a poor fit for this mother but would mesh well with a parent who might admire her spunky, strong-willed spirit. This mother, eager to allow her baby to be herself, tries to stay a step ahead of her, responding to her needs before the baby loses control. This style of parenting is rewarding to this mother and extremely helpful to her baby.

Goodness of fit is not always determined by similar temperaments between parent and child. Sometimes, infants and parents can complement each other.

For example, low-activity toddlers who get lots of stimulation from their mothers explore more than low-activity toddlers who get little stimulation. With highly active toddlers, the reverse is true: When parents offer lots of stimulation, these babies explore *less* (Gandour, 1989). Because they naturally find stimulating experiences for themselves, too much stimulation coming from the environment can be overwhelming.

The important point is that temperament strongly *influences* development; it does not determine it. Development is a dynamic process in which the raw material of temperament is shaped by experience—experience that infants generate for themselves as well as the reactions they help to evoke from others. In Chapter 7 we will see how the social contexts of parents, family, class, community, and culture also influence individual development. Now, we turn from the ways infants differ to the patterns of social and emotional development that all babies share.

LANDMARKS IN SOCIAL AND EMOTIONAL DEVELOPMENT

An experimenter and a subject sit in a room; they can be anywhere in the world. The researcher holds up a picture and asks (sometimes with the help of an interpreter), "What is the person in this picture feeling?" When the face is smiling, everywhere, the answer is "happiness," "joy," "delight." Answers are uniform, too, when faces show sadness, surprise, fear, anger, and disgust. Americans and Aborigines, Germans and Nigerians, Filipinos, Peruvians, and Cambodians all find the same feelings in the same faces: Human emotions are universally recognizable (Ekman, 1972; Izard, 1971).

For some psychologists, this means that emotions, their expressions, and the ability to recognize them must be at least partially inborn. In this section, we'll look at the unfolding of several emotional landmarks: smiling and laughing; stranger wariness; separation protest. Toward the end of the chapter, after we've discussed the older infant's growing sense of herself as a separate person, we'll look at the development of pride and its painful opposites, shame and embarrassment.

● Changes in Emotional Expression

Even the faces of newborns show distress, disgust, and interest; and by 3 months, joy, sadness, and anger appear (Izard et al., 1987; Malatesta et al., 1989; Stenberg & Campos, 1990; Tronick, Cohn, & Shea, 1986). (See photos.) While even very young infants express specific emotions, we don't know if actual internal emotional states accompany these expressions. In other words, we do not know if infants *feel* what their faces *show* (Camras, 1992). But there is no mistaking the distress of a 2-month-old getting inoculated. Eyes tightly shut, he screams. At 19 months, anger joins distress (Izard, Hembree, & Huebner, 1987).

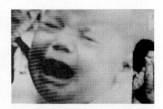

Joy: *Mouth forms smile, cheeks lifted, twinkle in eyes*

Surprise: *Brows raised, eyes widened, mouth rounded in oval shape*

Distress: *Eyes tightly closed, mouth, as in anger, squared and angular*

Interest: *Brows raised or knit, mouth may be softly rounded, lips may be pursed*

Sadness: *Inner corners of brows raised, mouth corners drawn down*

Fear: *Brows level, drawn in and up, eyelids lifted, mouth retracted*

As they get older, infants begin controlling the way they express emotions, particularly negative emotions (Thompson, 1990). Instead of flailing out whenever they are frustrated, for example, only their faces may redden. Rather than screaming every time they scrape a knee, they may try to hold back the tears. What's happening is that infants are learning social rules about when, and whether, to express certain emotions.

How does this happen? The way parents react to babies' distress sends a powerful signal. As their babies get older, many parents respond more to expressions of interest and less to pain. Gradually, infants express positive emotions more and negative emotions less (Malatesta et al., 1989). To some degree, then, parents begin shaping their children's emotional style. Some of the best evidence of this early "emotional socialization" comes from studies of depressed mothers and their babies. With their mothers and with strangers, these babies are more likely to be withdrawn, immobile, and unresponsive (Field et al., 1988).

● Smiling and Laughing

Every parent would say that babies smile almost from birth, yet the experts disagree. We do not know whether that wonderful, mysterious neonatal smile is a true **social smile.** Very young infants often smile when they are resting comfortably or even sleeping. [The stage of sleep accompanied by rapid eye movements is also the time when infants smile (Emde, Gaensbauer, & Harmon, 1976)].

Early smiles may look like smiles, but they don't seem to have anything to do with pleasure until about 6 to 9 weeks. Then, babies begin smiling in reac-

● **social smile**
an infant's smile for pleasure in response to familiar people

When a baby develops a social smile, adults begin to feel he is a "real person."

tion to pleasure, wonderfully rewarding to anyone taking care of an infant. Soon they will smile at anything that delights—not just people but things too, such as lights, bells, and toys (Lewis, Alessandri, & Sullivan, 1990; Malatesta et al., 1989). Many parents feel their infant is a real person once a reliable social smile sets in. By about 4 months babies smile more selectively and begin to laugh as well.

● **Where do smiling and laughter come from?** Social smiling begins so predictably that it must be biologically timed, keyed to the baby's developing central nervous system. Premature infants begin to smile socially at the same *gestational age* (see Chapter 3) as full-term babies, evidence that biological maturation, not the baby's experience in the world, governs the appearance of the smile (Dittrichova, 1969). Even babies blind since birth tend to start smiling around the same time as sighted infants, further evidence for the role of maturation (Fraiberg, 1977).

But even if smiling begins from within, its subsequent development is influenced from without. Social reinforcement—such as picking up the baby, vocalizing, and smiling back—can increase the frequency of smiling (Brackbill, 1958); and negative experience can disturb the timetable. Infants living in unstimulating institutional environments, for example, smile later than babies raised at home (Ambrose, 1961; Gewirtz & Gewirtz, 1965).

Psychologist Jerome Kagan believes that smiling is linked to cognitive maturation. Babies smile first at faces and things they have seen before, the *smile of recognition* (Kagan, Kearsley, & Zelazo, 1978). Cognition affects laughter too, as gradually infants understand that some things don't go together the way they are presented (Cicchetti & Sroufe, 1976). A hat on a head looks right, but put it on your foot, and an older baby laughs.

● Stranger Wariness

The 3-month-old who grinned at parent and stranger alike may be wary of her own grandmother 3 to 5 months later. At 7 months she often greets strangers with cries and grimaces, even if they are among her closest relatives. This fear of strangers, typically called **stranger wariness,** is so predictable that we consider it another major landmark of emotional development (Ainsworth, 1973; Dennis, 1940). Its emergence has been explained in several ways.

As with smiling, Kagan and his colleagues link the timing of stranger wariness to maturing cognitive processes (Kagan, Kearsley, & Zelazo, 1978). According to their hypothesis, between 6 and 9 months infants are slowly beginning to make sense out of their world. They have matured to the point where they know whom they know. And as they begin separating familiar from unfamiliar faces, most also become more wary of strangers. From then on, when they can't figure out why something is happening, they become afraid. Kagan argues that fear develops when a baby can raise questions about the unfamiliar person but is unable to answer them. How babies show stranger wariness seems related to temperament. Some babies cry and get very upset, while others retreat into quiet or clinging behavior.

Though wary, infants can also be *curious* about unfamiliar things and people. An infant may smile at and even approach a new person, if the conditions are right. The situation, the approach, and the behavior of the stranger all make a difference (Mangelsdorf, 1992; Thompson & Limber, 1991). Babies tend to be more fearful of a new person in a new setting (an observation room in a university, for example) than when they meet a stranger in a familiar setting, such as their own home (Sroufe, Waters, & Matas, 1974). Generally, babies are least fearful when a parent or special caregiver is holding them, or at least is nearby (Mizukami et al., 1990; Morgan & Ricciuti, 1969). As for the stranger's behavior, a friendly approach is best and may get a smile instead of a scream from the baby. Approach slowly, smile, talk to the baby, and offer a toy (Bretherton, 1978;

● **stranger wariness**
the fear of unfamiliar people, which sets in at about 6 to 8 months

Stranger wariness, which begins sometime after 6 months, signals children's ability to wonder about the people in their world. Adults in costume— even a baby's own father—can be very threatening, because they are so atypical.

Bretherton, Stolberg, & Kreye, 1981). Babies are most afraid of people who seem more controlling and less predictable (Mangelsdorf, 1992). Experience with strangers and strangers' behavior makes a difference too (Sroufe, 1977). Infants who are used to meeting strangers are less afraid than those who rarely meet new people.

The stranger's sex, age, and appearance also matter. Babies seem less afraid of females than males (Brooks & Lewis, 1976; Takahashi, 1990), probably because most infants have more experience with women, and they are more afraid of adults than children (Lenssen, 1973). Size is probably the key here; as infants become more aware of differences between themselves and others, the greater the difference, the greater the fear (Lewis & Brooks, 1974). Finally, babies are more afraid of unattractive than attractive strangers (Langlois, Roggman, & Rieser-Danner, 1990).

Even wariness of strangers differs across cultural and ethnic groups, however. One study, for example, found that Navajo infants were less fearful of strangers during the first year of life than Anglo infants. One explanation for this is that Navajo infants have more exposure to, and interaction with, unfamiliar adults early in life. In addition, there may be temperamental differences among children from different racial or ethnic groups that may affect their social behavior. Youngsters of Asian descent as well as Native American youngsters are generally less excitable than Caucasian youngsters. Ethnic differences in infant temperament may be due to genetic factors as well as differences in mothers' obstetrical histories (see Garcia Coll, 1990).

● Separation Protest

separation protest
an infant's reaction, based on fear, to separation from her mother or other caregiver

By 2 to 3 months, many infants cry when a stranger arrives and a parent leaves (Mizukami et al., 1990), but much more difficult separations are ahead. Almost everywhere, and at almost the same time, parents and infants struggle with that tearful, clinging, frantic leave-taking psychologists call **separation protest** (see Figure 6.1). Even when babies know the person who will substitute while a parent is gone, from about 10 to 12 months good-byes can be wrenching. Why?

Where are you going? Across the world, from about 9 to 12 months, babies hate to say goodbye.

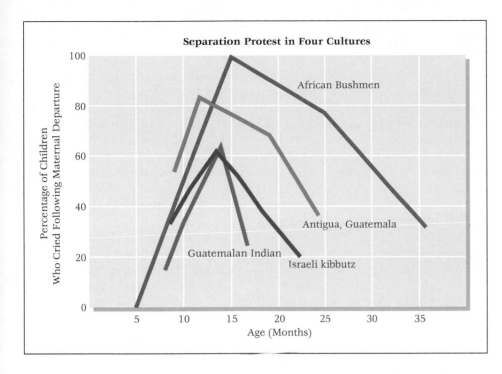

FIGURE 6.1
Separation Protest
Separation protest peaks at about the same age—10 to 12 months—in a variety of cultures.
(Source: Kagan, Kearsley, & Zelazo, 1978.)

Kagan's explanation echoes his view of stranger anxiety: The child is confronted with a situation he cannot explain—Why is Mommy leaving? Where is she going? When will she return? He responds with distress. To test this theory, Littenberg, Tulkin, and Kagan (1971) observed babies' reactions to their mothers leaving a room in their own homes. When the mothers simply went into another room in the house and closed the door behind them, the babies did not protest, presumably because this exit was familiar. But when mothers stepped into a closet and closed the door, the behavior was too unusual for the infants to process, and they became distressed.

If Kagan is right—that understanding is critical—providing children with information should relieve their uncertainty and reduce their distress. Weinraub and Lewis (1977) tested this notion with toddlers and observed less separation protest if mothers told their children when they would be back than if the mothers simply left without explanation. Separation protest dropped even further when mothers suggested an activity to fill the time until they returned. The worst way to handle separation protest is with an extended leave-taking. Parents who hesitate, double back, or delay their departure only prolong the anguish. A swift exit is far less upsetting to everyone.

Once a parent leaves, infants are much less distressed if their caregivers are warm and responsive throughout the separation (Gunnar et al., 1992). And predictably, temperament plays a role here too. As you would expect, more inhibited and negative infants tend to react more negatively to separation (Gunnar et al., 1989). For such babies, adult sensitivity to separation is especially important.

The themes we have touched on here reappear in the next section on attachment. Just as infants' fears about strangers and separation are balanced by their curiosity and their knowledge about the world, their needs for security, safety, and trust are offset by desires to explore and to be independent.

ATTACHMENT RELATIONSHIPS

In the beginning, there are *behaviors:* A baby cries, and a mother feeds her; a baby snuggles, and a mother hugs her. Day after day, night after night, mothers and fathers feed, burp, wash, change, dress, and hold their babies. Out of these interactions, feelings and expectations grow. The baby feels distressed and hungry, then satisfied; the mother feels tenderness, joy, annoyance, exhaustion, pleasure. Gradually, the baby begins to expect that her mother will care for her when she cries. Gradually, mothers respond to and even anticipate their baby's needs. These elements form the basis for a developing *relationship,* a combination of behaviors, interactions, feelings, and expectations that are unique to a particular parent and a particular baby.

The emergence of this first relationship marks a major milestone in the infant's social development. By the end of the first year, most babies who are cared for in families develop an *attachment relationship,* usually with their mother. (While infants also form attachments to other adults, especially fathers, most research has focused on mothers and infants.) This relationship is central to the child's developing sense of self, to how he relates to others, and to how he is likely to develop as he moves away from his mother to become an autonomous and curious toddler and preschooler.

Ties of love between mother and baby can grow from the simplest things they do together.

● Defining the Attachment Relationship

Mary Ainsworth (1973), a developmental psychologist who has studied infants around the world, explains **attachment** as "an affectional tie that one person forms to another specific person, binding them together in space and enduring over time." For Freud, the infant-mother relationship is, for the infant, "without parallel, laid down unalterably for a whole lifetime, as the first and strongest love-object and as the prototype for all later love relations" (1938, p. 66). Freud's work led him to conclude that an infant's tie to his mother influences all his future relationships—in childhood, in adolescence, and even in adulthood.

Freud may have been overstating the case for the lifelong effects of the infant's first attachment relationship. Most attachment theorists now believe that these relationships are important and influential because they *contribute* to, rather than determine, later emotional development. Later in this section we discuss research on the way the first attachment relationship influences the developing child.

● Theories of Attachment

Freud believed that the attachment relationship is intimately linked to the hunger drive. When a mother feeds an infant, at the breast or bottle, the baby's hunger is satisfied. Gradually, the baby comes to associate that pleasurable feeling with her mother's presence.

Learning theorists (see Chapter 1) have applied general principles of conditioning to explain why mothers acquire such positive value for their infants (Sears, Maccoby, & Levin, 1957). When hungry infants nurse, milk reduces their hunger. Milk, which satisfies the need, is a primary reinforcer. Because mother is present at the same time that a biological drive, such as hunger or cold, is being satisfied by milk or warmth, she takes on a value as a **secondary reinforcer.** She becomes associated with the milk and warmth. In time, the mere presence of the mother is pleasing, even when she is not satisfying a primary drive.

Over the years, researchers testing Freudian and learning theories of attachment found that it isn't actually the feeding of the infant that accounts for the strength of the mother-infant bond (Schaffer & Emerson, 1964a). A classic study of Rhesus monkeys, in fact, revealed that the monkeys would choose the "creature comfort" of a terry-cloth monkey-doll over the wire-mesh "mother" that provided milk (Harlow & Zimmermann, 1959).

Today, many social scientists believe that love between baby and mother exists not simply because the infant associates mother with food but to ensure the survival of the human species. This point of view, known as **ethological theory,** looks back to the early stages of human evolution (Bowlby, 1969, 1973). John Bowlby, who first applied this theory to the study of infant social development, argues that attachment behaviors such as smiling, clinging, crying, stranger wariness, and separation protest all increased infants' chances for survival. In the physically dangerous environment in which we think humans evolved—an environment filled with hungry and prowling animals—crying would have brought caregivers to the baby's side. Similarly, stranger wariness would have helped to keep a baby away from danger, and both separation protest and following made babies more likely to stay with their caregivers. In

● **attachment**
the close, significant emotional bond between the mother (or father) and the infant

● **secondary reinforcer**
anything (or anyone) associated with the satisfaction of a need, so chances of a given response recurring are increased by the presence of the reinforcer

● **ethological theory**
an analysis of human and animal behavior patterns in evolutionary terms

Harry Harlow discovered that baby monkeys will cling to a terry cloth doll for comfort even when a wire mesh "mother" provides food. Harlow's research supports the theory that emotional bonds between mothers and infants are not based on feeding only.

Bowlby's theory, then, infant-mother attachment is a biologically based relationship that evolved because it protected infants from the real dangers that once threatened our early ancestors.

● *Attachment and exploration: The "secure base."* One of the most interesting things about security is its link to separation. The 1-year-old has a conflict: He still needs to be near his "attachment object," usually his mother, but he also has a strong urge to see what else is around, to explore. For securely attached babies, these two needs are balanced. In a familiar setting, such as his home, or wherever the baby feels comfortable, the child leaves his mother, his **secure base,** to do some exploring. When he feels he's gone too far, or is frightened by something strange, the "attachment system" is activated, and the infant checks in with his mother. Refueled with emotional security, the child moves away from her secure base. As they travel around their environment, most 1-year-olds will meet both the need for attachment and the need to explore. Even if no threat arises, an infant will routinely check back with her mother. She stops exploring for a moment to make contact: either to touch, see, or hear her mother. Once reassured, she goes off again to explore. Bowlby believes that both *attachment and the exploring behaviors* were necessary for human survival.

● **Differences in Attachment**

With easy babies or difficult ones, with mothers who are relaxed or tense, warm or rejecting, no matter how good the fit, an attachment relationship develops. What differs is their quality. And for infants, the critical difference is in the strength of their security.

Security of attachment is the extent to which a child can count on his mother's availability to meet his needs, on her being there when he needs her. With its central role in developmental theory, researchers have been particularly interested in understanding individual differences in the quality of attachment. What makes these relationships different? How can we even determine that they

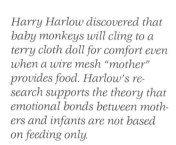

● **secure base**
an attachment object (usually the mother) who provides a foundation for curious exploration

are different? And perhaps most important, how do those differences matter for children? Over the last two decades, many researchers have searched for answers to those questions. Their conclusions have been both influential and controversial.

● *The strange situation.* Mary Ainsworth had studied with John Bowlby in England. When her husband took a job in Africa, she began doing research in Uganda, watching African babies as they grew up in rural villages. She saw that infants get wary around strangers, that they protest separation from their mothers, that unfamiliar settings can upset them—and she used these insights to devise an experimental procedure that would elicit attachment behavior. She called it the **strange situation** (Ainsworth & Wittig, 1969).

Ainsworth proposed that putting a child under stress would reveal the security of the attachment relationship. And, she knew, two things that stress babies a great deal are separation from their mothers and approaches by strangers. The strange situation allows psychologists to watch children under both kinds of stress. This is how it works: A mother and her child, a 1- to 2-year-old, are brought to an unfamiliar room. The room has only two chairs and a few toys. A stranger enters the room, and the mother exits after a few minutes, leaving the infant alone with the stranger. Soon, the mother returns and the stranger exits. The mother leaves again, and the infant is left alone briefly. The stranger then reenters, leaves, and finally the mother rejoins her child. During all the comings and goings, the infant's reactions are carefully observed and recorded. (When Ainsworth began her research, no filming was done, but now studies using the strange situation are routinely videotaped.)

Analyzing her data, Ainsworth discovered that some of the most telling moments about attachment occurred not when mothers left but when they returned. What mattered most was not how upset babies became when their mothers left but how they related to their mothers when they came back.

Children who use their mother as a secure base for exploration may or may not become distressed when their mother leaves, but they greet her in two distinctive ways: When distressed, they want to be picked up and find comfort in her arms; when content, they smile, talk to her, or show her a toy. When dis-

● **strange situation**
an experimental procedure for observing attachment patterns

The strange situation. A mother holds her infant in an unfamiliar room (left). *After leaving the baby with a stranger she will return* (right). *Babies' reactions during these separations and reunions reveal attachment patterns with their mothers that affect development in many ways.*

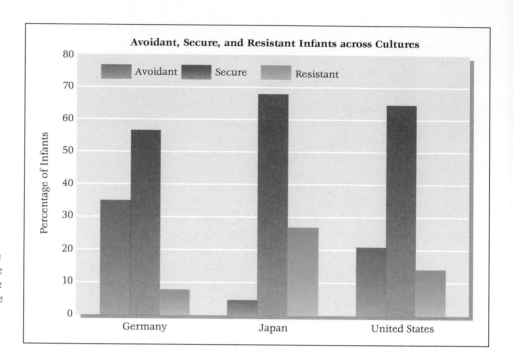

FIGURE 6.2
Avoidant, Secure, and Resistant Infants across Cultures
When observed in the strange situation, high percentages of Japanese babies appeared to be secure or resistant. German babies showed the highest rate of avoidant attachment. These differences reflect the influence of culture on child rearing. (SOURCE: After van IJzendoorn & Kroonenberg, 1988.)

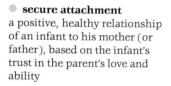

secure attachment
a positive, healthy relationship of an infant to his mother (or father), based on the infant's trust in the parent's love and ability

insecure attachment
a relation of an infant to her mother (or father) based on lack of trust

anxious-resistant attachment
an insecure attachment in which an infant shows much distress at separation from and anger at reunion with his mother or father

anxious-avoidant attachment
an insecure attachment in which an infant shows indifference to her or his mother or father and avoids interaction with her or him

tressed, they seek their mothers for comfort. For Ainsworth, these are children with a **secure attachment.**

Children with an **insecure attachment** show their distress in either of two ways. Unwilling to explore, they may want their mother close by and are very distressed when she leaves. When their mothers return, these children also want to be picked up, but they are not comforted; they kick or push away from their mothers. Ainsworth called their attachment **anxious-resistant.** A child who has formed an **anxious-avoidant attachment** seems indifferent to the mother's presence, tends to show little distress at her absence, and ignores or refuses to look at her when she returns (Ainsworth, 1979).

Over the years, many researchers from around the world have employed the strange situation in order to differentiate among secure, resistant, and avoidant babies. And although the procedure has been shown to be a valid means of distinguishing among infants in many cultures (Sagi, Van IJzendoorn, & Koren-Karie, 1991), studies also show that there are cross-cultural differences in the relative prevalence of the three types of babies. Especially pronounced are differences in the rates of different types of insecurity: In Germany, a relatively higher proportion of infants are classified as avoidant, whereas in Japan, a relatively higher proportion are classified as resistant (see Figure 6.2). Cross-cultural differences in attachment classifications undoubtedly reflect a combination of factors, including ethnic differences in infant temperament, cultural differences in the ways infants are reared, and cultural differences in the ways in which infants are perceived.

It is especially important to bear in mind that terms like *secure* and *insecure* partially reflect cultural differences in beliefs about healthy infant development. What may be seen as a sign of healthy social development in one culture may not be viewed this way in another. For example, Puerto Rican mothers are more likely when evaluating young children's behavior to focus on the child's ability to control himself, especially in public, whereas Anglo mothers are more likely to focus on the child's ability to behave independently (Harwood, 1992). As a consequence, to a Puerto Rican observer, an "insecure" child might be one who had difficulty playing nicely with other children, whereas to an Anglo observer, "insecurity" might be most clearly reflected in a child's inability to play by himself. Similarly, Japanese mothers are more likely to value and, hence, to try to promote patience and self-control in their children, whereas American mothers are more inclined to value independence and assertiveness (Bornstein, 1989a).

● Explaining Differences in Attachment

Ainsworth's observations of infants in natural environments and in the strange situation led to new questions, new theories, and new research. What was causing the differences among babies? Why do some infants form close, secure relationships with their mothers, while others do not? One account focuses on the way mothers behave toward their infants. Another emphasizes the behavior and temperament of the infants themselves.

For Ainsworth (1979), the attachment relationship grows out of infants' experiences with their mothers during the first year of life. And the key element in that experience is the mother's sensitivity in responding to her infant's signals. Does she go to the infant soon after he begins to cry? Does she understand the baby's different cries? Does she know when he is hungry or tired? Does she sense when he wants to play? Does the mother pick up her baby with pleasure and warmth, or is she tense and uncomfortable with physical contact? In Ainsworth's studies, secure infants did have mothers who sensitively read their infant's cues and responded appropriately to their needs. When mothers were sensitive to infants' hunger signals, when they responded to crying, when they offered a balanced amount of interaction, and when they comfortably held their babies when they needed holding, their infants were securely attached by 1 year (Ainsworth, 1979). In short, sensitivity does seem to promote security by fostering trust. That trust, then, forms the foundation for the baby's secure attachment to the mother.

Other researchers have lent considerable support to Ainsworth's ideas. In separate studies, sensitive mothering has also been linked to the security of German infants (Grossman & Grossman, 1982) and babies in the United States (Belsky, Rovine, & Taylor, 1984; Cox et al., 1992; Isabella & Belsky, 1991; Pederson et al., 1990). One of the most significant recent studies on attachment was carried out in the Netherlands and is described in the Making a Difference box on page 193.

Other research has also looked closely at the combination of temperament and care. Infants prone to distress who receive insensitive, often unresponsive care tend to develop insecure-*resistant* attachments, while those who are *not* prone to distress and receive insensitive, often intrusive, overstimulating care tend to develop insecure-*avoidant* attachments. Infants prone to distress who receive sensitive, responsive care are the secure babies who, while upset by the strange situation, express their security by seeking and finding comfort in their mothers' arms. Infants who are not prone to distress who receive sensitive, responsive care express their security by smiling at and vocalizing to their mothers across a distance (Belsky, Rovine, & Taylor, 1984; Isabella, Belsky, & von Eye, 1989). Figure 6.3 diagrams the interrelation of temperament, maternal care, and attachment security.

Experiences in the infant's social world also influence the developing attachment relationship. A study of recent immigrants to the United States from Japan illustrates this quite nicely. Recent immigrants reported more stress than Japanese mothers who had been living in the United States for at least 6 months, and this stress, in turn, was correlated with attachment insecurity in their infants. The recent immigrants who reported higher levels of support, however—especially from their husbands—reported less stress and had infants who were more likely to be securely attached (Nakagawa, Teti, & Lamb, 1992).

We might also ask how what takes place *outside the home* affects infant development. As more mothers work outside the home, other adults are sharing the care of their infants. Do such arrangements affect infants' attachments to their mothers? In Chapter 7 we will look thoroughly at this very important question.

● Consequences of Infant-Mother Attachment

Now the issue changes. We know that some infants are securely attached to their mothers, while others are not; but does it matter? Does attachment affect social and emotional development? Will a secure attachment ease the way in new situations, with new playmates and adults? Will independence be fostered? And will insecurely attached infants have more trouble relating to others and functioning independently? Considerable evidence suggests that the answer to all these questions is yes (Belsky & Cassidy, 1993). Before we discuss what researchers found, let's review what theory predicted.

FIGURE 6.3
Infant Temperament, Maternal Care, and Attachment Security
Negative emotionality refers to distress an infant may be prone to. Notice that maternal care influences a baby's security of attachment more than temperament. Even so, a baby not prone to distress (low negative emotionality) can develop an insecure attachment if maternal care is insensitive.

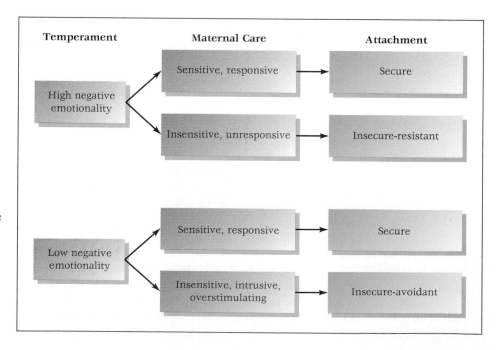

MAKING A DIFFERENCE

ATTACHMENT, NATURE, AND NURTURE

Not everyone agreed that Ainsworth's research proved that sensitive mothering *caused* babies to become securely attached. The two did seem to go together, but, said critics, Ainsworth's studies showed only a correlation between sensitive mothering and secure attachment; her results did not prove causation (see Chapter 1). What, they asked, was causing what? Perhaps sensitivity was linked to security because easy-tempered babies evoked sensitive care. How might a child's own nature influence her attachment to her mother? And how much of a difference does mothering make in the way babies respond? Can mothers learn the skills that foster close attachment, even with difficult babies? The Dutch psychologist Dymph van den Boom was curious about these questions.

Van den Boom was particularly interested in highly irritable newborns and their mothers. Would these difficult babies form distinctive attachments to their mothers because of their inborn traits? How much of a difference would the mothers themselves make? For her study, she selected babies who had been identified in the hospital as highly irritable newborns. Their mothers, with little education and low incomes, came from Holland's lower class.

In her study, van den Boom randomly assigned these negative infants and their mothers to an experimental or a control group. Observed at their homes, both groups of mothers showed the same kind of caregiving. Then, when their babies were 6 to 8 months old, intervention began. Mothers in the experimental group were taught how to recognize and respond to their infants' positive and negative emotional signals and other behaviors. Control group mothers, whose babies were just as negative, received no coaching. When the babies were 9 months old, researchers observed both groups again. This time, the coached mothers showed greater sensitivity to their babies than the control group mothers who had received no training.

At 12 months old, the babies were tested in the strange situation. Two dramatically different patterns appeared. As Ainsworth's theory would have predicted, more sensitive mothering was linked with more securely attached infants. In fact, 68 percent of the babies in the experimental group (whose mothers had had training) showed secure attachments to their mothers. In the control group, only 28 percent of the babies were securely attached. Clearly, the quality of a mother's care strongly affects the development of attachment security.

Does this mean that infant temperament doesn't affect attachment security? No. At the least, some infants are more difficult and more challenging to care for sensitively. This is especially true when their mothers lack the psychological resources to provide consistently sensitive care. And in fact, distress-prone infants who had mothers with rigid, inflexible personalities are most likely to form insecure attachments (Mangelsdorf et al., 1990; Mangelsdorf & McHale, 1992).

Recall that for Erik Erikson (see Chapter 1), the basic developmental task of infancy involves the establishment of a sense of **basic trust** (1963). Infants with a strong foundation of trust will have a developmental advantage as they become toddlers and preschoolers. During those stages, the basic psychosocial issues are the development of **autonomy and initiative,** or the ability to be independent, resourceful, and self-motivated. Preschoolers who, during infancy, have developed a strong sense of basic trust will see their world as dependable and safe. Free to relate to other people without too much anxiety or anger, they will learn how to give and take and to perceive the needs of others. These trusting children would probably welcome social experiences more than their less securely attached age-mates will. And, in fact, when researchers look at securely

● **basic trust**
an infant's strong sense that her needs will be met and the world is not a threatening place; according to Erikson, the establishment of trust is the major task of infancy

● **autonomy and initiative**
the ability to be independent, resourceful, and self-motivated

and insecurely attached children, the most striking differences concern relationships (Belsky & Cassidy, 1993).

With teachers, for example, preschoolers who were secure as infants are less emotionally dependent on their teachers, but they are more able to ask for help when they need it (Sroufe, Fox, & Pancake, 1983). As preschoolers and in elementary school, they get along better with classmates, show more empathy toward them, and are more popular (Sroufe, 1983; Sroufe, Fox, & Pancake, 1983). When they play, securely attached children are more likely to play make-believe games than to be involved in a conflict (Howes, 1991; Howes et al., 1990).

As children grow, secure attachment during infancy continues to affect the quality of their friendships. Predictably, secure histories and close friendships during the late preschool and elementary school years go together. These friendships also seem to have little conflict and to be less controlling (Park & Waters, 1989; Youngblade & Belsky, 1992). By age 10, children with secure attachment histories are more likely to have one or a few good friends who are trustworthy and reliable (Grossmann et al., 1989).

Some of the most convincing evidence of the effect of early security on later friendships comes from the follow-up of Dutch children in the study we described earlier (van den Boom, 1992; see box). The more secure experimental children were also more involved with and less hostile toward other children at age 3½.

With siblings too, security seems to smooth the way. Not only do preschoolers who were secure as infants offer more comfort to a baby sibling who is distressed, but when that sibling is older, they play together more happily and with less conflict (Teti & Abelard, 1989; Volling & Belsky, 1992).

● *A Foundation of security or insecurity.*   Overall, then, consistent with certain elements of Erikson's theory, infants with secure attachments to their mothers grow into secure, autonomous, industrious, interpersonally skilled, and achievement-striving preschoolers. And by the age of 4 or 5, peer relations for children with secure attachments in infancy are strikingly different from those formed by children with insecure early attachments. We will look more closely at these differences in Chapter 9.

What do we know about the way insecurely attached infants develop? We would expect that, without a strong sense of basic trust, they would be both more anxious and less socially skilled than more secure children. And that is exactly what some research studies have found: Insecurely attached infants do have more behavior problems as preschoolers (van den Boom, 1992). Some are more hostile and tend to be socially isolated. Others are more tense, helpless, and fearful (Erickson, Egeland, & Sroufe, 1985; Sroufe, 1983; Suess, Grossmann, & Sroufe, 1992). In one study, 40 percent of the boys who had been classified as insecurely attached at 1 year showed signs of psychopathology when they were 6 (Lewis et al., 1984). These boys were also more aggressive in first, second, and third grade than boys whose attachments had been secure (Renken et al., 1989).

● **A Long View: Attachment Relationships
over the Life Span**

It looks as though the quality of infant-mother attachment does indeed lay the foundation for the child's emotional future. In study after study, secure infant-mother attachment has been linked to many kinds of favorable outcomes in later years. The studies show, too, that insecure attachment not only undermines competence but also can point to actual problems in development.

These findings might tempt us to think that there is a direct, inevitable link between infant-mother attachment and later development. But in reality, that link is only as strong as the child's experience. In other words, *securely attached infants who continue to have good experiences continue to develop well. But insecurely attached infants whose experience improves can also improve emotionally.* How attachment develops depends on the quality of care the infant receives over time (Urban et al., 1992).

Given equal degrees of stress, the secure child is likely to manage better than the insecure child (Sroufe, Egeland, & Kreutzer, 1990). But infants whose first attachment was insecure may still develop competence if they have new experiences that foster security. Again, development is strongly linked to environment, or context. Experiences beyond infancy can either support the developmental patterns laid down in infancy or go in new directions—either positive or negative. None of us grows up with a direct, simple line from past to future.

In fact, recent research tells us that security does not *necessarily* prevent behavior problems in preschoolers, and insecurity is not *necessarily* related to later behavior problems. Some anxiously attached infants have developed into well-functioning preschoolers. How? The care they received after infancy became more responsive to their needs (Erickson et al., 1985; Sroufe et al., 1990). The reverse can happen too: Securely attached infants may show behavior problems as preschoolers. Again, conditions in the children's environment may have changed. Perhaps maternal care that had been high-quality during infancy changed at some point, and the children's needs were no longer met as effectively (Erickson et al., 1985). However, these children may be well-equipped to handle stress because of their early secure attachment. They can bounce back. An insecurely attached child, with fewer resources to begin with, might experience more lasting difficulties if conditions worsen or are not improved.

● The Infant-Father Relationship

We have spent a great deal of time thus far discussing infants and their mothers. What about fathers? Do infants become as attached to fathers as they do to their mothers? The earliest studies of infant-father attachment sought to answer that question. Reports by mothers in one English study revealed that by 18 months, 71 percent of the babies appeared to be attached to their fathers, which they showed by protesting separation from him (Schaffer & Emerson, 1964a).

Rather than relying on mothers' reports, other researchers observed babies and fathers in the strange situation, the experimental procedure used to learn about infant-mother attachment. This work also revealed that most infants who live with both their parents have developed close attachment relationships with their fathers by 18 months (Lamb, 1981). One-year-olds who become wary when a stranger approaches use their fathers as a secure base, especially if their mothers are absent. Research also reveals that infants who are securely attached to *both* parents appear more competent than those securely attached to only one, and infants securely attached only to their mother seem more competent than those securely attached only to their father (Belsky, Garduque, & Hrncir, 1984; Main & Weston, 1981; Suess, Grossmann, & Sroufe, 1992).

Fathers can be as "motherly" as mothers when they care for their children, but when they play, fathers are vigorous and active.

As with mothers, the quality of a father's care makes all the difference. When fathers are playful and affectionate to their children, their infants are likely to become securely attached to them (Cox et al., 1992). Actually, fathers can be just as involved and sensitive caregivers as mothers; they just do it less often (Lamb & Oppenheim, 1989). Mothers and fathers can be equally good at interpreting a newborn's subtle signals.

Fathers can talk like mothers, give bottles like mothers, and be sensitive like mothers. But when they play, fathers are fathers. In general, fathers' play is vigorous and physically stimulating (Lamb, 1981; Parke, 1978), while mothers' play is more likely to involve words, toys, and games (Clarke-Stewart, 1980; Power & Parke, 1983). Infants seem to prefer their fathers' play (Clarke-Stewart, 1977; Lamb, 1976), perhaps because it is usually more physically and emotionally stimulating.

But mothers—even those who work outside the home—spend more time with the baby overall than fathers (Belsky & Volling, 1989). Outside the laboratory, in their own homes, mothers are more involved than fathers in every type of behavior researchers have observed, including holding, talking, showing affection, and stimulating with a toy (Belsky & Volling, 1989; Greenbaum & Landau, 1982; Lamb & Oppenheim, 1989). But when men *do* become the primary parent for their infant, they adopt a more motherly style. The birth of a second baby also leads to more involvement among fathers, probably because there is more work to do (Stewart, 1990).

This gap between fathers' abilities and their performance raises a fundamental question: If fathers *can* become as sensitively and competently involved with their infants as mothers, why don't more fathers do it? The answer has to do with custom. In our society, men have been expected to support babies, while women take care of them. And even with both parents working, baby care is still defined primarily as woman's work. Fathers who become more involved in infant care usually are breaking some very strong social norms. They are behaving very differently from the way their fathers and grandfathers probably did. Such basic social change takes more than a generation to occur, no matter how reasonable and desirable it may be. And just as women vary in their ability to be sensitive and responsive to their infants, so do men.

RELATIONS WITH PEERS

Relationships with other children begin very early, and you can often guess a child's age just by watching her play. At about 3 months, babies will stare at each other, sometimes jerking their arms and legs excitedly and straining forward as if to get a better look (Fogel, 1979). At about 6 months, you'll notice a change: Babies begin to "say" things to each other and start communicating physically (Hay, Nash, & Pederson, 1983). They gesture, offer toys, and verbalize (Bakeman & Adamson, 1984; Bornstein & Lamb, 1992), but not for long; if the other child doesn't respond, then the first infant loses interest (Hay et al., 1983).

During the second year, socializing becomes more complex (Howes & Matheson, 1992). Children begin imitating each other and playing action games where they can have opposite roles: Hide and seek, along with run and chase, becomes very popular now (what is called *complementary-reciprocal play*) (Brownell, 1990; Howes et al., 1989). Toward the end of the second year, play changes again. Now they pretend and imagine together, trying on different roles (*cooperative-imaginative play*): "I'm the driver; you sit in the bus." "Let's play store. Do you want cookies?" (Howes et al., 1989)

Even just crawling toward another baby to get a better look is a way of making social contact. Simple give-and-take responses aid social development during infancy.

● Differences in Sociability with Peers

As in all other areas of development, in social development too we see individual differences within a universal pattern. Although all normal infants and toddlers show the same *sequence* of early social behaviors, the ability to begin and maintain social exchanges varies from baby to baby and is probably related to temperament. Some babies are outgoing and sociable, while others are less so. No doubt, this accounts for why Howes (1988) discovered that those young toddlers who were most engaged in complementary and reciprocal play with peers were, 1 year later, the most likely to be engaged in cooperative and imaginative play (Howes & Matheson, 1992). Beyond temperament, social ability is also influenced by security of attachment to parents and by children's experience with age-mates. More sociable children have both strong attachments and more experience with peers (Belsky & Cassidy, 1993; Howes, 1987).

LEARNING TO SAY "I": THE EMERGING SELF

If you dab red rouge on a 1-year-old's nose and show her a mirror, she probably won't touch her nose (Brooks-Gunn & Lewis, 1984). One out of three 18-month-olds will reach for the spot, and by age 2, nearly all will (Schneider-Rosen & Cicchetti, 1991). Why the change? Until her second year, a child doesn't know

Knowing oneself as a separate person is a concept that develops gradually during the first 3 years of life.

A favorite blanket can help a young child feel secure when he is tired or unhappy. As children become more independent, their transitional objects will be left behind.

that the reddened nose is hers. Until 18 months, she doesn't know that she exists as a person, separate from all others.

Psychologist Margaret Mahler, who has studied the infant-mother relationship in great depth, believes that a young infant feels completely merged with his mother. While nursing he doesn't know where he begins and his mother ends. In fact, the breast that he suckles during his first few months may seem to be a part of himself. Mahler called the young baby's inability to distinguish the self from another **symbiosis** (Mahler, Pine, & Bergman, 1975). She suggests that the baby is so completely helpless that fusion with the mother is essential for survival.

As babies begin to realize that they are separate people, they are also preparing emotionally to move away from near-total dependence toward greater independence. Mahler called this gradual process of discovering a separate sense of self **individuation and separation.** The process progresses from about halfway through the first year until age 3.

Mahler was particularly interested in the way mothers can affect this process. Some mothers are more comfortable with a passive, dependent baby; others take pleasure in their child's growing capacity for communication, because this enriches parent-child contact. Mothers who are strongly attached to the symbiotic relationship they share with their babies can feel a sharp loss when their children start testing their independence. Such mothers may have difficulty letting their children grow toward autonomy (Mahler et al., 1970).

The 2-year-old dragging a blanket around is trying to cope with the process of individuation. Young children often form attachments to **transitional objects** such as a blanket or a teddy bear, clutching these comforters when they are tired or upset, often insisting on taking them everywhere (Winnicott, 1971).

symbiosis
the merging of self with another, as an infant with his mother

individuation and separation
according to Mahler, the striving toward independence and a sense of separate self during infancy and toddlerhood

transitional objects
an object, like a blanket or teddy, to which an infant transfers attachment feeling as he or she moves toward independence

The child's feelings of attachment to another person, usually her mother, have been partly transferred to the "security blanket." Parents and other caregivers should accept a child's need for a transitional object, even when it is inconvenient. By the age of 4 or 5, even the most fervently attached child will have begun the journey toward independence, leaving transitional objects behind. Interestingly, there are cross-cultural differences in the extent to which children rely on transitional objects: While common in most industrialized societies, in which infants are expected to cope with frequent separations from their caregivers, transitional objects are rarely seen in nonindustrialized village and tribal groups in which infants have near-continuous access to a wide array of caregivers (Hong & Townes, 1976).

In this final section, we look at the older infant, struggling to separate and stay close. We'll see children beginning to defy their parents, and we'll consider the ways parents can navigate the "terrible twos" so as to encourage healthy autonomy and pride while minimizing the young child's feelings of embarrassment and shame.

● Growing toward Independence: Autonomy and the "Terrible Twos"

"Play in the sandbox," a toddler coaxes, but as you approach, he shouts "No come here!" "Do you want an ice cream cone?" "Yes," he nods, while saying "No!"

What's going on here? If the 2-year-old's message is mixed, so is his motive: He wants to break away while staying close, to be at once secure and independent. By saying "no," both when he is cooperating and when he isn't, a child signals to himself and to others his new sense of himself as a separate person, an "I." In short, the 2-year-old is doing what he must to become autonomous.

Erikson describes this conflict as the stage of **autonomy versus shame and doubt** (Erikson, 1963). The child who is moving away from dependency feels uncomfortable about severing the symbiotic relationship with his mother. He doubts his ability to go it alone, but he is nevertheless ready to say "I," "me," "mine"—and "no." If his need for independence is denied—if his "I behavior" is punished—guilt and doubt may plague him, keeping him from moving forward.

● *Embarrassment, pride, and shame.* "You look sooo beautiful today. I love your dress, and look at those adorable socks!" The visitor gushes; the child wants to flee. Once a child knows she is separate, a new set of emotions emerges, including embarrassment. Toddlers can be embarrassed by too many compliments or by being pushed to perform in front of a stranger (Lewis et al., 1990). Generally embarrassment emerges after 18 months, at about the time a child knows that the face in the mirror with the red nose is hers (Lewis et al., 1990).

A sense of self sets the stage for pride as well, but first the child needs another cognitive capacity: He needs to have a sense of standards, to know that some things are better than others. Now, when he builds a tower and his daddy claps, he claps too, as if to say, "I did it, and it's good" (Heckhausen, 1981; Lewis, Alessandri, & Sullivan, 1992). When he fails to live up to this standard, he feels ashamed (Lewis et al., 1992). Because these cognitive capacities typically don't emerge until after 18 months, pride and shame don't appear until the end of the second or during the third year. After that, a child's body language reveals a

● **autonomy versus shame and doubt**
according to Erikson, the toddler's major "crisis"—the conflict between the desire for independence and the desire for security—as the sense of self emerges

A child's pride in learning to use the potty can enhance feelings of self-esteem and self-control.

great deal. Feeling proud, children stand straight, shoulders back and head up. Shame slumps. Shoulders bend forward, eyes gaze down, and a frown seems to say, "I'm no good at this."

What can parents do to encourage their child's growing autonomy and pride? To minimize feelings of shame as he struggles to become his own person? The challenge, as two researchers discovered, is gaining the toddler's cooperation while giving him some choice in how he cooperates. We discuss their interesting and useful research in the Making a Difference box on the next page.

● *Autonomy and toilet training.* For 2-year-olds, the main event in the struggle to let go while holding on is toilet training. And for parents, the same principles of guidance and control can reduce conflict and increase cooperation. Again, Erikson argued that children who gain a sense of self-control without loss of self-esteem have a lasting sense of autonomy and pride. But children whose parents toilet train them too early and in an extremely controlling manner may experience feelings of impotence and a lasting sense of doubt and shame (Erikson, 1959/1980). What's needed is sensitivity to the child's still maturing physical and emotional systems. Patience and support, rather than rigid demands for quick control, will help children feel good about their success and about themselves.

MAKING A DIFFERENCE

GUIDING CHILDREN TOWARD AUTONOMY

"It's time to put these blocks away."

"No."

What comes next makes a crucial difference. For Erikson, the key to helping young children move toward autonomy was in gradual, "well-guided" free choice. Overcontrol, he believed, would lead to defiance and shame (Erikson, 1963, cited in Crockenberg & Litman, 1990). Seeking to discover if there was a link between mothers' behavior and childrens' autonomy, Susan Crockenberg and Cindy Litman observed and videotaped 95 mothers and children in the laboratory and at home, at dinnertime.

The researchers knew that if they were looking for autonomy, they had to be able to distinguish it from defiance. When is "no" a sign of autonomy, or self-assertion, rather than willful disobedience? *How* the child said no was the key. If, for example, she said, "No, play more," Crockenberg and Litman concluded she was asserting her wish to do something. If, instead, she took more blocks out of the basket or threw one across the room, it was assumed that her goal was not to play but to defy her mother. When a child responded to a mother's request, Crockenberg and Litman recorded it as either *compliant* (does what is asked), *self-assertive* (says "no"), or *defiant* (does the opposite of what is asked and gets angry).

In the laboratory, mothers were asked to have their child pick up all the toys in the playroom and put them in a large basket. They were allowed to help but were told that the task was to be the child's. Mother and child were then left alone while researchers videotaped them through a one-way mirror. If a child said "no" when asked to clean up, the researchers recorded the mother's response. For example:

1. "Well, see if you can do it. Do you need help? How about using this truck for the blocks. See?"

2. "I said put the blocks away now. Did you hear me? NOW." If the child still refuses, the parent threatens to punish her and may hit the child.

3. "Put the toy away or I won't read to you later." "If you put them away I'll give you a cookie. Come on now, do it."

4. "We really do have to clean the floor so the next child will have room to play. Oh, here's a truck. Do you think the truck can

SUMMARY

1. Babies are born with unique body rhythms and styles of responding to the environment. This set of characteristics is temperament. The three central dimensions of temperament are negative emotionality, activity level, and sociability. These traits combine to form several basic patterns of temperament: the difficult child, the easy child, and the slow-to-warm-up child. (See pages 174–176.)

2. An infant's temperament influences the responses babies evoke from others as well as the activities and experiences that infants choose for themselves. How the personalities of parents and infants mesh is called goodness of fit. The quality of this fit affects the infant's development. (See pages 177–180.)

3. Very young infants express specific emotions through different facial expressions, although we don't know if actual internal emotional states

help you to put the blocks away? Would you like some help, or do you want to do it yourself?"

Mothers' responses generally fell into one of four patterns:

(a) *Negative control:* Uses control that intrudes on the child, including anger, criticism, punishment, slapping

(b) *Control:* Tells the child what to do and/or offers a reward for compliance

(c) *Guidance:* Attempts to direct the child's behavior by offering help or persuading

(d) *Control plus guidance:* Makes it clear that something must be done, but invites the child to decide how to do it and offers help

Guessing how these responses would have been coded or which evoked the most defiance and the most cooperation shouldn't be hard: 1-c, 2-a, 3-b, 4-d.

The researchers found that children did best with "well-guided" free choice. When mothers offered both control and guidance, children who had at first refused were then likely to comply. Children were most defiant when their mothers asserted their power through negative control and most assertive when mothers used guidance alone.

What can parents and other adults learn from this study? Plainly put, even 2-year-olds don't like to be pushed around, to be forced to do things they don't want to do. Mothers and fathers need to convey another kind of message: "This is what I expect you to do, but we can find a way for you to do it that is agreeable to you. I will even

help you do it." This approach, control plus guidance, tells the child that the adult is in charge but also that the child is respected, that his or her feelings deserve to be acknowledged. It softens the power inequities between the adult and the child.

Parents who negotiate with their children rather than battle with them achieve several positive outcomes. They are gaining their children's cooperation, fostering their feelings of self-worth and autonomy, and also teaching them a valuable social lesson in getting along with others. As you will see in the chapters on development during early childhood, negotiating is an extremely useful social skill (Crockenberg, 1992). In later chapters we will also see that the use of control plus guidance helps children toward autonomy and high self-esteem.

accompany these expressions in newborns. One of the first clear emotional landmarks, smiling, appears between 6 and 9 weeks as a reaction to pleasure. (See pages 180–182.)

4. Two other landmarks in emotional development are stranger wariness, which emerges around 7 months, and separation protest, which is first seen between 9 and 12 months. Many theorists, like Jerome Kagan, believe that the emergence of emotional developments such as stranger wariness and separation protest is linked to the growing cognitive sophistication of the infant. (See pages 183–185.)

5. By the end of their first year, most infants have formed an attachment relationship, usually with their mother. This relationship strongly affects children's sense of self, how they relate to others, and how they are likely to develop as toddlers and preschoolers. Contemporary theorists, like Bowlby, believe that attachment behaviors such as smiling, clinging, crying, stranger wariness, and separation protest evolved in the human repertoire because they increased infants' chances for survival. (See pages 186–188.)

6. All infants form attachment relationships with their caregivers, but the attachments differ in security. Securely attached infants tend to become secure, autonomous, socially skilled preschoolers. Insecurely attached infants, with a weaker feeling of basic trust, are more anxious and less socially skilled preschoolers. Psychologists employ a procedure called the "strange situation" to assess infant attachment. (See pages 188–190.)

7. The attachment relationship reflects the infant's experience with his caregiver during the first year of life. Sensitive caregiving fosters trust and a secure attachment. Infants affect the relationship too: Whether or not they are temperamentally prone to distress affects how they express their security or insecurity. (See pages 190–192.)

8. Although the quality of an infant's attachment relationship strongly influences development, experience can sharply modify development. Insecurely attached infants whose emotional needs are met later can become well-functioning preschoolers. The reverse can happen as well. (See pages 192–195.)

9. Social relationships among children begin very early. During their first year, social exchanges progress from smiling, to offering toys, to playing social games such as peek-a-boo. Although all babies show the same sequence of social development, the degree of sociability varies from infant to infant. Sociability is related both to temperament and to the quality of the infant's attachment. (See pages 197–198.)

10. The growth of independence and autonomy is a central aspect of emotional development during the second year. Wanting to break away, yet at the same time remain secure, is a difficult issue for most 2-year-olds. Mahler called this the separation-individuation process. Erikson described it as a crisis of autonomy versus shame and doubt. Whatever the label, parents and other adults need to be sensitive to the child's needs for both independence and security. (See pages 198–203.)

KEY TERMS

activity
anxious-avoidant
  attachment
anxious-resistant
  attachment
attachment
autonomy and initiative
autonomy versus shame
  and doubt
basic trust
difficult child
easy child

ethological theory
goodness of fit
individuation and
  separation
insecure attachment
negative emotionality
New York Longitudinal
  Study (NYLS)
personality
positive emotionality
secondary reinforcer
secure attachment

secure base
separation protest
slow-to-warm-up child
sociability
social smile
strange situation
stranger wariness
symbiosis
temperament
transitional object

SUGGESTED READINGS

Brazelton, T., and Cramer, B., (1990). *The earliest relationship.* New York: Addison-Wesley. A world-renowned pediatrician discusses the nature of the parent-infant emotional relationship.

Greenspan, S., and Greenspan, N. (1985). *First feelings.* New York: Penguin. A clinically astute and sensitive child psychiatrist and his wife chart the stages of a child's emotional growth during infancy with an eye toward enabling parents to enhance early psychological development.

Lamb, M. (1987). *The fathers role: Cross-cultural perspectives.* Hillsdale, NJ: Erlbaum. Fascinating descriptions of fathers and their roles around the world

Thoman, E., and Browder, S. (1988). *Born dancing: How intuitive parents understand their baby's unspoken language and natural rhythms.* New York: Harper & Row. A developmental psychologist who has spent thousands of hours observing and recording the interactions that take place between mothers and their young infants shares her knowledge about the wisdom that parents and infants so often express in their communication with one another.

THE SOCIAL CONTEXT OF INFANCY

Think back to Lafeyette and Pharoah Rivers, the brothers chronicled in *There Are No Children Here* (Chapter 1). What if their mother had been happily married and better educated? What if they had lived in a house in Chicago's north lake suburbs instead of an inner-city project? What if their father were a lawyer? What if they were white instead of black? Would anyone say that these boys' lives would have been the same? Would your life have been the same if you had traded places with these children at birth?

Now consider three other infants, born today. One, the son of two teachers, will live in a middle-class neighborhood; his mother will be home by 3:30 in the afternoon. His father is eager to share experiences with his wife and child. Another baby born that day is the daughter of an unmarried, poor teenage mother. This baby will live with her grandmother and her mother's younger brothers and sisters in a small inner-city apartment. Her mother will return to school. Our third baby is born in a rural Chinese village to parents who work in the fields for much of the day. We know nothing about the inborn temperaments and abilities of these infants and nothing about the quality of care they will receive from their parents and other adults. Nor do we know anything about the attachment relationship each will form. But we do know that the social context of their lives will be dramatically different.

Social context is the total environment in which we live. It includes all the interpersonal, community, and cultural influences that surround each person, beginning at home: Every infant is born into some kind of family—whether an extended family of several generations living together, a nuclear family of parents and children, or a single-parent family. Whatever its size and makeup, every family influences children in complex and powerful ways. And that influence flows in many directions, with each family member affecting all others.

The social context surrounding each child extends far beyond the family, however, as human ecologist Urie Bronfenbrenner has pointed out (1979). Bronfenbrenner has compared the structure of the social context to a set of Russian dolls in which each doll is contained within another, somewhat larger one. Every family lives in a neighborhood, every neighborhood is contained in a society, and every society is part of a larger culture.

● **social context**
the total environment in which we live

Children growing up in San Francisco's Chinatown and in Lake Worth, Florida, will be shaped by the values and norms of two different subcultures, but they will also share the larger context of American culture.

A baby in the United States will be brought up differently from a baby born into every other society. And the suburb, inner city, and village that the infants we described above will call home represent only a fraction of the places in which babies live: an ethnic neighborhood of a larger city, a farm miles away from the nearest neighbor, an apartment house in a wealthy urban neighborhood, a poor rural town. In each of these settings children enter a way of life influenced by culture, class, geography, and ethnicity. All these elements of social context will forcefully shape children's lives, often even before birth. The prenatal care of a middle-class or wealthy woman differs significantly from that of an inner-city teenager, and this difference affects each of their babies' health and chances for survival. Significant too is *when* children live: Theories of child rearing and education, political movements, war, peace, a booming or depressed economy are all shifting social conditions that strongly influence our lives.

As we look at the ways in which family, community, and culture influence development during infancy, we will see that this influence moves in two directions: The social context both influences and is influenced by the child. This reciprocal process is most obvious when we consider the most intimate level of social context, the level closest to the baby: the family.

THE FAMILY AS A SYSTEM

Despite all their dependency, infants have enormous power. When they enter, every relationship in a family changes because the family is a **system,** an interacting and interdependent group that functions as a whole. Even the smallest traditional family includes several people (man, woman, child) and a variety of roles (wife, mother, husband, father). Additional children add one more role (sibling) but considerably more complexity to the family system, as each member influences and is influenced by all the others. We look first at infants, husbands, and wives.

system
an organized, interacting, interdependent group, functioning as a whole

● How Infants Affect Marriages

A couple's first baby changes everything—how they spend their time, which friends they see, what seems important, and the way they relate to each other (Cowan & Cowan, 1992).

Couples confront four kinds of problems in adjusting to parenthood (Sollie & Miller, 1980). The first involves the physical demands of caring for an infant who needs to be fed and changed at least every 3 to 4 hours. New parents report feeling stressed and fatigued by lack of sleep. Mothers seem to be more susceptible, as they are more likely to feel the strain associated with adding primary caregiver to the role of wife, homemaker, and often employee as well.

Strains in the husband-wife relationship create the second problem. New parents complain that they have no time together as a couple anymore and no time for or interest in their sexual relationship (Cowan & Cowan, 1992). Fathers often feel that their wives pay more attention to their infants' needs than to their

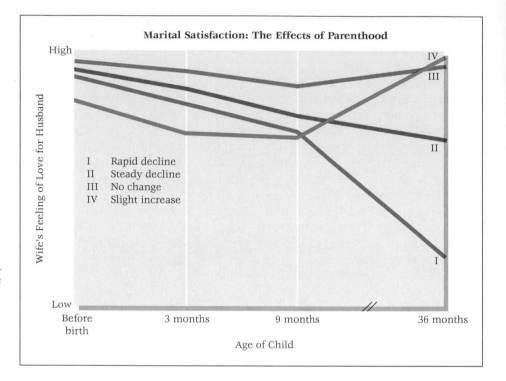

FIGURE 7.1
Marital Satisfaction: The Effects of Parenthood
How couples react to the birth of their first child varies. For some, feelings of love decline sharply; for others, only a little. In some cases, a brief decline is followed by a slight increase, and for still others, feelings of love remain relatively unchanged even 3 years after the child's birth.
(SOURCE: Belsky et al., 1991.)

own (Glenn & McLanahan, 1981). But for their wives, waking several times each night can easily create a need for sleep stronger than any need for sex or conversation.

Becoming parents has direct emotional costs, the third class of problems in the transition to parenthood. The responsibility of caring for an infant can seem overwhelming, and as parents come to realize that being a parent is a lifetime job, doubts about competence can also cause stress.

The fourth problem area involves loss of freedom and opportunities. New parents' social lives are constricted, freedom to travel is limited, and doing anything on very short notice is almost impossible. Most new parents discover that life with an infant is far more complicated than they had imagined. They want to go to a movie, but they can't find a babysitter; they take the baby to a restaurant, and he cries through dinner. Some new parents give up and just stay home. In addition to restrictions on mobility, having a child is expensive, and not just in money spent. If one parent stops working, income drops as expenses climb.

With all these strains on new parents, marriages can suffer. In fact, overall satisfaction with marriage tends to drop after parenthood begins (Belsky & Rovine, 1990; Cowan & Cowan, 1992; Wallace & Gotlib, 1990). Wives become more dissatisfied than husbands, no doubt because women are mainly responsible for child care in most families (Belsky et al., 1989; Cowan & Cowan, 1992). But keep in mind that rarely does having a baby ruin a good marriage or improve a bad one. (See Figure 7.1.) Couples that were happiest before their baby was born tend to continue that way, and those who are least content remain that way as well (Belsky, 1990a; Ruble et al., 1988).

Why does having a baby lead to more unhappiness in some couples than in others? Often, the main answer is housework: Who does it, and, more important, who does more of it? Generally, it's the wife who cleans the house, cooks, does the laundry (considerably more than before), and now, additionally, cares for the baby (Cowan & Cowan, 1992; MacDermid et al., 1990). The more unequally these chores are divided, the more dissatisfied wives become. Women who become most unhappy are those who are more independent and career-oriented (Belsky, Lang, & Huston, 1986; Ruble et al., 1988). Their lives have become inconsistent with their views of themselves, breeding conflict and dissatisfaction.

Another difference among couples affecting their transition to parenthood is how realistic their expectations about the baby have been. Couples often romanticize parenthood, imagining a blissful family unit instead of the combination of joy and stress that being a parent really is. When stresses such as reduced sleep, less frequent sex, and more housework for women are not anticipated, their impact can be quite strong. Unsettling, too, is advice from well-meaning parents, in-laws, friends, and neighbors. When the advice differs from the couple's own views or becomes a source of disagreement, it can increase stress (Belsky, Ward, & Rovine, 1986; Garrett, 1983; Kach & McGhee, 1982).

A couple's age and how long they've been married also affect their adjustment. Older couples and those who have been married longer report fewer problems that newly married and very young couples (Dyer, 1963; Russell, 1974). And finally, how a baby affects a marriage also depends on the baby. Infants with difficult temperaments, who are fussier, or who are often sick generate more stress for their parents, and this stress can harm a marriage (Belsky & Rovine, 1990; Engfer, 1988; Wright, Henggeler, & Craig, 1986).

Before you decide that babies bring nothing but stress to their parents, we will add that they also bring great pleasure. Babies add work, but they also add fun. The love, joy, and happiness that commonly accompany parenthood can be deeply enriching. For many couples, children tighten the bond, both to their own families of origin and to each other (Miller & Sollie, 1980). These pleasures,

Taking care of an infant can be exhausting, especially if middle-of-the-night feedings persist for months.

most strongly associated with the first child, balance the stress felt by many husbands and wives. Parenthood can also lead to emotional growth for mothers and fathers (Antonucci & Mikus, 1988). It can bring greater maturity, as caring for an infant can enhance feelings of accomplishment and self-enrichment. Parents often report that they feel more like adults, less self-centered, less selfish, and more thoughtful about the future (Gutmann, 1975).

● *Adoption.* The transition to parenthood can become even more complicated when couples adopt (Brodzinsky, 1990). Infertility, the main reason for adopting, can itself cause problems for both individuals and couples (Levy-Shiff, Goldschmidt, & Har-Even, 1991), including decreased self-esteem, anxiety, depression, and disruptions in both marital communication and sexual relations. If left unresolved, all these problems can undermine family relations that foster trust, security, and unity (Brodzinsky & Huffman, 1988).

Stress comes, too, from an uncertain timetable (Levy-Shiff et al., 1991). Biological parents know when to expect their baby's birth, but adopting couples live in limbo, waiting a few months or several years to become parents. Waiting is bad for babies, too. Attachment theorists favor adoption during an infant's first 4 to 6 months, before the child has formed a secure attachment to a caregiver, an attachment that will then be broken (Bowlby, 1980). And in fact, children who are adopted within the first few months of life are as likely to form secure attachments with their mothers as nonadopted infants (Singer et al., 1985); the emotional difficulties associated with adoption are more likely when placement occurs after 6 to 7 months of age (Yarrow et al., 1973).

Even with these special challenges, adoptive parents report more marital satisfaction than biological parents (Humphrey & Kirkwood, 1982; Levy-Shiff et al., 1991). They also appear to be less intrusive, less controlling, and less authoritarian as parents than nonadoptive parents (Hoopes, 1982). Such differences could result from the careful screening of prospective adoptive parents by adoption agencies or from the fact that adoptive parents are often older and thus more psychologically mature than other parents (Levy-Shiff, Bar, & Har-Even, 1990). Adoptive parents are also likely to have been married longer and may have had other stressful experiences that help prepare them for parenthood (Brodzinsky & Huffman, 1988).

● *Husbands and wives with handicapped infants.* Over time, the joy of loving their babies and watching them develop balances the stress of parenthood, but parents of physically handicapped infants have special burdens. Because a handicapped infant violates parents' expectations and can be extremely demanding, caring for such an infant can stress the entire family (Easterbrooks, 1988).

Many parents feel guilty and ashamed about "causing" the handicap. This may partly explain why some fathers of handicapped children are less involved with their disabled children than fathers with normal children (Bristol, Gallagher, & Schopler, 1988). Mother-infant relations can be affected as well. In one study, not only did handicapped infants smile and vocalize less than healthy infants, but their mothers were less responsive, smiling and talking to them less than mothers of normal infants (Brooks-Gunn & Lewis, 1982). And the more severely handicapped infants are, the less responsive mothers tend to be toward them.

The stresses of coping with a handicapped infant also affect a couple's relationship (Belsky, 1990a). Marriages that are already troubled can deteriorate further (Howard, 1978), but the opposite can happen as well. If a marriage is very strong, the birth of a handicapped child can actually bring a couple closer together (Gath, 1978). Ultimately, the effect of a child's handicap on the family depends on the severity of the handicap and on the family and community context (Bristol, 1987; Bristol et al., 1988). Are there other children to care for? Can the family afford extra medical expenses? Do relatives and friends provide relief? Can parents cope with their complex feelings toward the child? Availability of services within the community can make a big difference (Duncan & Markman, 1988). When home-visiting programs offer support to parents, or when relatives offer aid in a sensitive way, rearing a handicapped infant becomes less stressful (Parke & Beitel, 1988).

A family with a handicapped child can be as loving and close as any other. Some families are drawn even closer together by caring for a disabled son or daughter.

● How Marriages Affect Infants

Consider the workday of an at-home mother of a 1-year-old. By 4:30 in the afternoon she has changed six diapers, prepared and helped her child eat two meals and three snacks, mopped up innumerable spills, spoken thousands of words to him, praised his own efforts to talk, read three stories, piled blocks into towers, bruised her foot on a block, washed the teddy bear her son spit up on

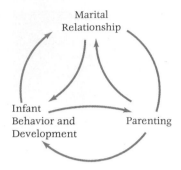

**FIGURE 7.2
Interaction in the
Family System**
*The interaction of marriage,
parenting, and infant develop-
ment in the family system.*
(SOURCE: Belsky, 1981.)

● **reciprocal feedback**
a pattern of mutual,
interdependent influences in
which each member of a
system affects and is affected
by the others

the night before, scolded, endured struggles, pushed the baby on the swing at the park, and tried to get him to take a nap. Now she is facing what is often the most terrible hour of her day. Mother and baby are both exhausted, and father won't arrive until 6:00.

When her husband comes home, she hands him the baby and heads for the bedroom, where she relishes a few minutes of privacy and relaxation. How does her husband respond? He has just come home from his own difficult day. Before the baby was born, he could relax after work. Now there is another job waiting for him at home.

In another household, both parents arrive home from work tired and eager to spend time alone together and with their baby. The sitter leaves. While they're eating dinner, the baby begins to cry. She needs to be comforted, diapered, and changed. It is the husband's turn to take charge, but soon he is complaining that he isn't as good at comforting the baby as his wife is. She stops eating and goes to the baby. He returns to the dining table and eats alone.

The unfolding of these family dramas can have strong implications for the child's development, because the quality of a couples' marriage affects the quality of their parenting (Belsky & Vondra, 1989; Hann, 1989; Levy-Shiff & Israelashvili, 1988). A close husband-wife relationship seems to encourage a father's interest in his infant's development (Cox et al., 1989); fathers who communicate well with their wives also show high involvement with their infants (Belsky et al., 1989; Nugent, 1991). For mothers, satisfaction with their marriage during the transition to parenthood influences the security of the infant-mother attachment (Belsky et al., 1989; Howes & Markman, 1989, 1991). It appears that marital stress can interfere with a mother's ability to respond sensitively to her infant, which, in turn, affects the child's emotional tie to his mother. Since insecurely attached infants often do not develop as competently as securely attached infants, the quality of the mother's marriage can influence both her parenting and her infant's development.

The key point here is **reciprocal feedback:** Babies and parents form a system of mutually affecting relationships. Parenting affects and is affected by the child, who both influences and is influenced by the marriage—which both affects and is affected by parenting. Figure 7.2 illustrates this network of marriage, parenting, and infant development.

● Infants and Siblings

Siblings make the family system even more complex; a new person means a new temperament to deal with. For parents, another child adds emotional and financial responsibilities. For older siblings, a new infant brings less attention from parents, a new playmate, and for some, new responsibilities. In many nonindustrialized societies, an older sibling plays a major role in caring for an infant or toddler. Often, a child not much older than a preschooler assumes the primary care for a newly weaned baby brother or sister (Harkness & Super, 1992; Nsamenang, 1992).

Infants like to watch their older siblings, and once they become mobile, they are likely to follow them around, imitating and trying to learn from them (Bornstein & Lamb, 1992). When distressed, infants often seek their siblings for comfort (Dunn & Kendrick, 1982; Stewart, 1983).

Young children who have had a close relationship with their mothers can enjoy the arrival of a new sibling.

Because the family is a complex system, what happens between members often depends on their relationships with others. Babies who have secure attachments to their mothers are more tolerant of the attention mothers give to their older siblings (Teti & Abelard, 1989). And if another baby arrives, these securely attached children have less conflict with a younger sibling by the time they are 5 to 7 years old (Volling & Belsky, 1992). Preschoolers also tend to adapt better to infant siblings if they have had a close relationship with their mothers before the baby's birth (Gottlieb & Mendelson, 1990). When children feel competitive and jealous of a new baby, parents can help them deal with those feelings, a topic we'll discuss in Chapter 10.

● Extended Families and Infant Development

Even the way we think about families depends on the broader social context in which we live. In some contexts, the strongest image is a nuclear family, with the infant's central attachment expected to be with his or her mother. Our beliefs about what is "normal" social development follow, in part, from this stereotype: We view healthy social development as proceeding from the one fundamental relationship outward, in a sort of hierarchy or sequence. We are tempted to view problems in infant social development as inherently linked to problems in the mother-infant relationship.

In other contexts, however, it is more common for children to be raised in **extended families,** that is, by relatives in addition to their parents. For example, in many African cultures, such as the Efe of Zaire, infants experience simultaneous relationships with several caregivers from birth on. Rather than viewing healthy social development as grounded in the "all-important" mother-

● **extended families**
relatives in addition to the child's parents

infant relationship, the Efe are more likely to view healthy development as having its roots in multiple emotional relationships early on (Tronick, Morelli, & Ivey, 1992).

Keeping this in mind, think back to our discussion in the previous chapter of infant attachment. Some psychologists have argued that our models of infant attachment may be too grounded in Western stereotypes of the "normal" mother-infant relationship. Jacquelyn Jackson (1993), for example, has suggested that models of infant development that do not take into account the potential role of extended family members may not be entirely applicable to understanding the development of African-American infants, who are more likely than their white counterparts to experience multiple caregivers drawn from an extended kin network early in life (Wilson, 1986). Research has shown that African-American youngsters who have frequent contact with extended family members (grandparents, aunts, uncles, and so on) fare better emotionally and socially (Wilson & Tolson, 1985) and are more likely to grow up in environments that stress moral and religious values (Tolson & Wilson, 1990). Thus, examining the impact of "the family" on infant development may necessitate using different definitions of what the family is in different cultures.

BEYOND THE FAMILY

We move beyond the infant's family now to the world in which they live. We'll see how the immediate community of neighbors and friends affects the way parents care for their children, both by offering support and by creating stress. We will also consider how infants are affected by day care.

● Parents and Infants in Social Networks

A couple walking down a street may go unnoticed, but add a baby in a carriage, and even strangers stop to talk. Babies are social magnets, especially attractive to other couples with babies. Infants affect their family's social relationships by bringing their parents into contact with other young families (Belsky & Tolan, 1981; Gottlieb & Pancer, 1988). Such contact, and the support it can bring, generally enhance both psychological and physical health (Gottlieb & Pancer, 1988). In fact, the quality of support parents receive, whether from friends or relatives, can influence the way they care for their infant (Belsky, 1990b; Feiring et al., 1987).

social networks
people who provide parents with emotional support, instrumental assistance (help with routine tasks), and social expectations (guidelines for child rearing)

Social networks support parents in three ways: They provide *emotional support;* they provide *instrumental assistance,* including information, advice, and help with routine tasks; and they provide *social expectations,* or guidelines for child rearing (Caplan, 1974; Cochran & Brassard, 1979).

Not all networks provide support, however. For some families, socializing with neighbors can do more harm than good, especially if their values are very different. Suppose a woman who has put a career on hold to have a baby and plans to return to work in 6 months is criticized by more traditional mothers. She may begin to feel less satisfied with herself as a parent. But if most of her

friends also plan to combine a career and motherhood, she'll probably feel better about her own decision to do the same (Power & Parke, 1983).

Mothers who receive the most support in caring for their babies report the fewest symptoms of depression (Colletta, 1983), a finding that has been replicated in several cultures (Thorpe, Dragonas, & Golding, 1992). They are also the most effective parents, the most responsive verbally and emotionally to their infants (Crockenberg, 1987; Roopnarine et al., 1992; Teti & Gelfand, 1991).

Infants bring their parents into contact with other parents, socializing that benefits adults and children.

● Infant Day Care

Margaret Hoffmann lives in Austria. After giving birth to her first baby she stayed at home for 4 months, at full pay from the company she worked for. So did her husband. Danielle and Jean Rosteau of France did the same for 16 weeks, and Anne and William Warren of England spent 6 weeks with their baby at full salary. When William returned to work, Anne stayed at home for 3 months more at a reduced salary. These couples' experiences are common for Europeans but unheard of for Americans. Under the 1993 plan passed by Congress, mothers are guaranteed only 12 weeks of leave, unpaid. Table 7.1 shows parental leave policies in other Western countries.

TABLE 7.1 MATERNITY LEAVE POLICIES IN OTHER WESTERN COUNTRIES

Country	Date	Duration of Paid Leave	Available to Fathers (Y = Yes)	Supplementary Unpaid or Paid Parental Leave
Benefit Level at 100% of Earnings[a]				
Norway	1984	4 months	Y	Y
Austria	1987	16 weeks		10 more months, at lower level[b]
F.R. Germany	1987	14 weeks[c]	Y	1 year at flat rate[d]
Portugal	1984	3 months		Y
Netherlands	1984	12 weeks[c]		
Benefit Level at 90% of Earnings				
Sweden	1987	9 months plus 3 months at flat rate	Y	Up to 18 months; 6-hour work day, up to 8 years
Denmark	1987	24 weeks	Y	Y
France	1987	16 weeks[c]		Up to 2 years
United Kingdom	1987	6 weeks + 12 weeks at flat rate		Maternity leave
Benefit Level at 80% of Earnings				
Finland	1987	11 months	Y	Y
Italy	1984	5 months[e]		Y
Belgium	1984	14 weeks		
Ireland	1982	14 weeks		
Benefit Level at 75% of Earnings				
Spain	1982	14 weeks		
Israel	1984	12 weeks		
Canada	1984	17 weeks, 15 paid		
Benefit Level at 50% of Earnings				
Greece	1982	12 weeks		

[a]Up to a maximum covered under Social Security.
[b]Plus 2 years for low-income single mothers if they cannot find child care.
[c]6 weeks must be taken before expected birth; in other countries this time is voluntary.
[d]Last 6 months available only on an income tested basis.
[e]100% paid for first 4 weeks; 2 months' leave before birth mandated.
SOURCE: S. B. Kamerman, *Caring for Children: Challenge to America.* Copyright © 1989.

In the United States, staying at home with an infant demands a financial sacrifice. Half of all American mothers with babies under a year old work either full- or part-time (Phillips, 1991; U.S. Department of Commerce, 1992), leaving their infants in some kind of alternative child care arrangement. For children under 2, as of 1990, 57 percent were cared for by a father or other relative; 20 percent were in a family day care home; and only 14 percent were in child care centers (Hofferth, 1992) (see Figure 7.3).

If ever there were a case of psychological theory hitting against social reality, the day care issue is it. If theorists are right about the importance of infant-mother attachment, and if separations are stressful, then how are thousands of infants being affected by their mothers' absences? Is infant-mother attachment affected? Are babies in day care more anxious than babies whose mothers are at home? The best way to answer these questions would be to compare children who are in day care with those who are not, but this is more complicated than it seems.

Until 1980, the research about the consequences of infant day care generally showed *no* differences between children cared for at home by their mothers and children reared in a variety of other settings during their first year of life (Belsky & Steinberg, 1978). But these were mostly studies of children cared for in centers set up by universities for research purposes, which provided care of the highest quality.

In studies appearing after 1980, results were less positive. Those studies used the strange situation (see Chapter 6) and examined children cared for in more typical community child care arrangements. Results suggested that the quality of infant-mother relationships among day care–reared infants may indeed differ from that of infants who spend most of their day at home with their mothers. In those studies, infants who spent 20 or more hours of each week in day care were more likely to appear insecurely attached to their mothers (Barglow, Vaughn, & Molitor, 1987; Belsky, 1988; Clarke-Stewart, 1989; Jacobsen & Willie, 1984; Vaughn et al., 1980; Weinraub & Jaeger, 1990). Boys in day care for 35 or

FIGURE 7.3
The Increasing Need for Child Care
While the proportion of women in the workforce has risen only 6 percent since 1975 (a), the percentage of working women with children under 3 years old has climbed by 20 percent (b). Figure (c) shows how people have responded to the need for child care.
(Source: Bureau of Labor Statistics, 1992; Hofferth, 1992.)

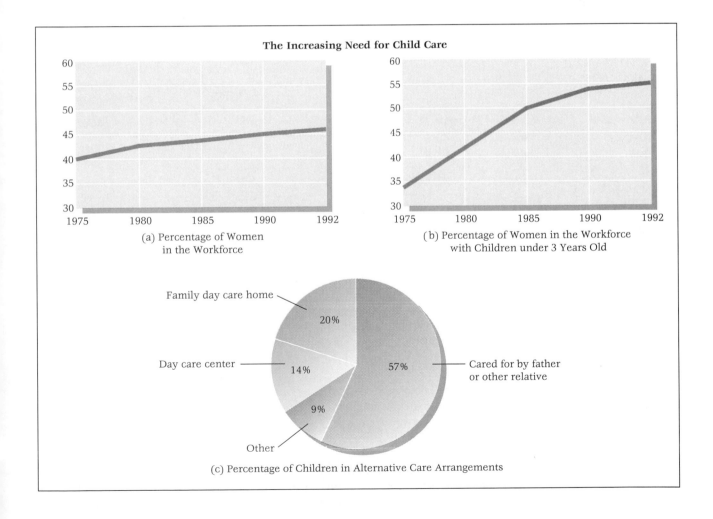

The Increasing Need for Child Care

(a) Percentage of Women in the Workforce

(b) Percentage of Women in the Workforce with Children under 3 Years Old

Family day care home — 20%
Day care center — 14%
Other — 9%
Cared for by father or other relative — 57%

(c) Percentage of Children in Alternative Care Arrangements

more hours each week are more likely to show insecure attachments to their fathers as well (Belsky & Rovine, 1988; Chase-Lansdale & Owen, 1987).

But these results are not *always* found (Howes, 1991). Indeed, most day care children do *not* feel insecure. What the research does mean is that children reared in some kind of nonparental care for an extensive period during their first year of life *may* be more likely to show this pattern of development. Their *risk* of insecurity is greater—at least in the kind of day care arrangements typically available to American families.

As we saw in Chapter 6, insecure attachments during infancy are linked to a greater risk of difficulties in future development. Recent research indicates that in some cases, preschool and school-age children who experience extensive nonparental care in their first year of life are more aggressive and disobedient and have more difficulty coping with frustration than children whose mothers were home with them during their first year (Baydar & Brooks-Gunn, 1991; Belsky & Eggebeen, 1991; Howes, 1990; Vandell & Corasaniti, 1990). These "consequences" of infant day care are not found in every study, nor do they apply to every child in nonparental care. They suggest, though, that full-time day care during the first year, at least as currently available and routinely used in the United States, *may* promote aggression, disobedience, and low tolerance for frustration (Belsky, 1990b).

Not all psychologists agree (Lamb & Sternberg, 1989; Melhuish & Moss, 1991; Thompson, 1991). First, the critics of studies of day care and attachment ask whether the children's responses are being interpreted correctly. When infants who spend 20 hours or more each week away from their mothers are reunited with them at the end of the day, they may not greet their mothers as warmly as children who rarely experience long separations. But are they showing "avoidance," a behavior to be concerned about, or "independence," a healthy adaptation to separation (Clarke-Stewart & Fein, 1983)? Different researchers observing the *same* behaviors have reached very different conclusions (Belsky & Braungart, 1991; Clarke-Stewart, 1989).

A second problem concerns the real source of the behaviors we are observing in infants with extensive day care experience. Is the amount, quality, and kind of day care itself *causing* trouble for these children, or is the problem in the families that use extended day care for their infant? If you think back to our discussion of the difference between causation and correlation (Chapter 1), you will get a sense of the kind of problem we face in day care research. Because we are observing children after separations from their mothers, we *assume* that the separation and the experience of day care cause the behaviors we see. But perhaps the root of these behaviors lies not in day care but within the child's family. Perhaps the stresses caused by money worries, cramped housing, and raising children alone create more problems for infants than their day care experience.

In short, the causes of the behaviors we see in day care children may be far more complex than the day care experience itself. Whenever we search for relationships between infants and day care, then, we must carefully separate correlations from causation.

If it seems complicated to figure out why some infants in early long-term day care show insecure attachments and are more aggressive and disobedient than others, think back to the start of this section on infant day care and development. We began by noting that in the United States, parents have only 3 weeks of guaranteed leave from their jobs. Nor is it easy to find skilled parent substitutes who are likely to stay with an infant for very long, establishing an enduring security-promoting relationship with the baby. When parents *do* find such people, not only do their children thrive during their first year but they also may have developmental advantages that appear as late as age 3. These results showed up in studies both in the United States and in Sweden (Andersson, 1989, 1992; Field, 1991; Field et al., 1988).

Not surprisingly, the kind of involved, sensitive, and responsive caregiving that promotes secure attachments between infants and parents does the same when provided by substitute caregivers (Goosens & van IJzendoorn, 1990; Howes & Hamilton, 1992; Howes et al., 1988). Sensitive, high-quality care is usually found in centers where the ratio of adults to children is 1:3 rather than 1:4 or 1:6. The poorer the ratio, the less likely the child is to develop a secure attachment to his or her caregiver (Allhusen, 1992). Unfortunately, the quality of center day care available to most infants is quite limited (Whitebrook, Howes, & Phillips, 1990).

To sum up then, the question about day care and infants is not simply, How does day care affect infants? We need to know, Which infants? Which day care? Recent studies have some answers. Infants from impoverished families, or whose mothers are both poor and young, can benefit from high-quality day care (Vandell & Ramanan, 1992; Wasik et al., 1990), as can babies whose mothers are depressed (Cohn et al., 1991). No one factor is critical, but several factors are strongly influential: How good is the care children receive? What are they giving up at home? When that care begins and how long it lasts will all shape a child's development.

Corporate day care centers offer mothers the convenience of on-site child care and the opportunity to visit with their infants during the day.

For too many infants and families, the equation is far from optimal, largely because of the limited child care options and lack of formal policies to support children and families in the United States.

What, then, should working parents do to meet their infants' needs as well as their own? If possible, one parent might decide to work part-time during the baby's first year. But not every parent can or wants to stay at home. If, for whatever reason, parents choose day care for their infant, what should they look for?

- *A nurturant caregiver is the top priority.* The single most important factor for infant development at home or away from home is the quality of the caregiver. Someone warm, responsive, and affectionate—a person who has experience with infants and genuinely likes them—is best.

- *A caregiver should be trustworthy, easy to talk to, and generous with time and information.* Parents need a full report at the end of the day, not just a few mumbled words. Information they get from the caregiver can help parents themselves provide more sensitive care. Feeling comfortable with the person who is caring for their infant can do a lot to relieve anxieties. By interviewing sitters before the baby is born, parents can avoid having to settle for someone who doesn't feel right.

- *Stability and consistency are important.* Frequent changes in day care arrangements are stressful for infants and make it difficult for them to form secure attachments. Such changes also can wreak havoc in parents' lives. Parents should choose a day care arrangement with a reputation for constancy.

- *The number of children per adult should be small.* Infants demand a lot of attention and need a lot of care. No more than three infants to one adult is best. Since day care centers typically enroll larger numbers of children and tend to turn over staff more often, a babysitter or family day care may prove to be a better arrangement for the baby's first year.

- *The setting is the least important consideration.* Don't be too influenced by fancy physical facilities. Infants don't need designer interiors or elaborate toys, but they do need a safe, sanitary setting. A warm, responsive caregiver and a limited number of other children are much more important than expensive toys.

- *Good-byes shouldn't be too long or drawn out.* To make the separation as easy as possible each morning, parents should say good-bye and *then leave*. Lingering in the doorway only makes the separation harder, as separation-protest studies (discussed in Chapter 6) have shown.

- *Infants need time for adjustment.* At both drop-off and pickup, a baby or toddler needs time to make the transition to a new setting, time to say good-bye and hello. Don't cut good-byes off *too* abruptly. And at the end of the day, parents should give their babies time to warm up and should stay alert to their cues. This sensitivity to the baby, as we saw in our discussion of attachment, is central to the development of trust, confidence, and well-being.

● *Infants can thrive in the care of others.* Parents need not despair. Finding the right situation for parent and infant can take a lot of effort but can add immeasurably to the well-being of both.

CLASS AND CULTURE

● Social Class, Parenting, and Infant Development

In Chapter 3, we noted that rates of infant mortality vary across socioeconomic boundaries. Nowhere is this more startlingly evident than in studies of impoverished families in the United States. In Greene County, Alabama, the sixty-sixth poorest of Alabama's 67 counties, a baby is seven times more likely to die during the first year of life than a Japanese baby (Children's Defense Fund, 1987; Wilkerson, 1987). American infants born to lower-income parents have up to a two to three times greater chance of dying before their first birthday than middle-class infants (National Center for Clinical Infant Programs, 1987). These figures reflect a high rate of teenage pregnancies, insufficient diets, and almost no prenatal care among the poor. In underdeveloped countries—where poverty, malnutrition, and often famine are widespread and the middle class is tiny—infant death rates are even higher.

Social class has important effects in infant development beyond survival, though. A family's level of affluence affects how well its children are fed, clothed, housed, educated, and otherwise provided for. And beyond the material things that social class determines, it affects parents' values and the way they treat their children (McLoyd, 1990).

Middle-class mothers tend to talk to and stimulate their infants more than lower-class mothers; middle-class mothers are more likely to be responsive and

Probably because they have had more education, middle-class mothers tend to stimulate their infants more than less advantaged mothers do. This difference appears across a variety of cultures.

MAKING A DIFFERENCE

SUPPORT PROGRAMS FOR HIGH-RISK FAMILIES

Aware that middle-class children seem to get a head start in cognitive development, psychologists wondered whether the same boost could be given to lower-class children. Would middle-class-style support and encouragement enhance lower-class children's development? The answer appears to be yes. Support programs designed to help lower-class mothers have enhanced their relationships with their children and their children's development as well. (We'll discuss programs for older children, such as Head Start, in Chapter 10.)

In a New Haven, Connecticut, study, a group of poor families (most headed by single mothers) received a variety of services from the time of a child's birth up to the age of 30 months. Services included a home-visitor program, pediatric care, developmental evaluations, and day care. Ten years after the mothers had been enrolled in this program, they

seemed more involved with and sensitive to their children than mothers in similar circumstances who had not been enrolled. The women in the program had gotten more education during the 10-year period; they had had fewer children, at more widely spaced intervals; and their families were more likely to be self-supporting. The children of these mothers were rated as better-adjusted by their teachers; the children missed fewer days of school and were less likely to have been enrolled in remedial programs. The effects of this experimental program were broad: Mothers as well as children were helped, and the benefits were lasting (Rescorla, Provence, & Naylor, 1982; Seitz, Rosenbaum, & Apfel, 1985).

In San Antonio, Texas, another enrichment program, called Avance, enrolled a large group of low-income Mexican-American parents (Johnson, Walker, & Rodriguez, 1993). This intervention program served children for 2 years, from the first year of life until almost age 3. A control group of

other families with similar incomes and background did not receive any special services. In the first year, the mother and child participated weekly in a parent-child education class at one of the program's facilities, and a home educator visited each family once each month as well. To promote interaction between mothers and their babies, the visitor emphasized the mother's role as a teacher and the value of being sensitive to her infant's emotional states and newly developing abilities. During the second year, children continued in the program while their mothers attended courses to study English as a second language, prepared for the high school general equivalency degree, or developed further educational or vocational skills. The results? At the end of the intervention, as well as 1 year later, mothers who had been in the program were more affectionate and positive, encouraged their children's speech more, and provided a more stimulating home environment.

These same researchers had re-

less likely to be negative (Hoff-Ginsberg, 1991; Ninio, 1980; Seifer, 1992; Tulkin & Kagan, 1972). These social class differences are observed across cultures: Among Mexican parents who had no more than 9 years of schooling, those who had the most years of education were more responsive to their 5- and 10-month-olds (Richman, Miller, & Levine, 1992). Middle-class mothers are also more likely to give babies freedom to explore their environments, childproofing an entire house, for example, rather than confining the baby to a crib or playpen (Gottfried, 1984). Most experts believe that social class differences in maternal behaviors are due mainly to differences in exposure to formal schooling, rather than to economic differences (Garcia Coll, 1990).

Lower-class parents as a group may be less likely than others to encourage independent, curious, achieving behavior in their infants. Controlling and disciplining infants often matters more than letting them explore and learn from

ported similar findings in an evaluation of a comparable program aimed at low-income Hispanic mothers in Houston (Johnson & Walker, 1987). In that evaluation, the children whose families had participated scored higher than controls on IQ tests at ages 2 and 3. And between the ages of 4 and 7, boys who had not participated in the program were more destructive, overactive, and negative, as well as less emotionally sensitive, than boys who had participated (Johnson & Breckenridge, 1982). Moreover, the benefits lasted. When teachers evaluated the children's behavior in the second, third, and fourth grades, the same results appeared (Johnson & Walker, 1987). What was especially encouraging about the San Antonio program was that the amount of intervention needed to achieve the positive outcomes was far less (in both time and money) than had been shown to work in the Houston program.

Infant cognitive development was the focus of still another enrichment program, this one aimed

at low-income black teenage mothers (Field, Widmayer, Stringer, & Ignatoff, 1980). Again, when mothers learned specific techniques for stimulating their infants—even by playing peek-a-boo—and when they became more sensitive to their infants' emotional needs, the babies scored higher on a test of mental development than control group babies.

Programs have also been devised to assist mothers where development is at risk for another reason: maternal depression. Infants who are raised by mothers suffering from clinical depression are more likely to develop social and emotional problems as a result. One team of researchers designed an intervention for depressed mothers of newborns that included home visits from public health nurses who administered a parenting curriculum designed to build mothers' self-confidence, parenting skills, and knowledge of normal infant development. After the initial stage of the intervention was under way, the nurses also encouraged the depressed mothers,

many of whom were housebound, "to get out of the house more often and to interact with people in the community" (Gelsand & Teti, 1993). After approximately 1 year of participation in the program (which consisted of visits about every other week), the mothers who had received the intervention reported less depression than those in a matched control group. More interestingly, the *infants* of the mothers in the intervention group were more likely to have formed secure attachments.

What these and similar studies show is that helping mothers helps babies. And programs that include the whole family benefit babies the most. As in the first study described above, a multifaceted family support program not only encourages more sensitive and stimulating mother-infant interaction but also aids the mother's own development by supporting her efforts to get more schooling, for example. When a parent's life improves, so do the family's environment, the parent-child relationship, and the developing child.

their environments (Luster, Rhoades, & Haas, 1989). These attitudes may be linked to a fatalistic view of life (Kohn, 1987). If your experiences have shown you that outside social forces restrict and shape your future, then encouraging independence and initiative may seem futile. But if, having been raised middle-class, your experience taught that ability and hard work bring success, you will be more likely to encourage your baby's efforts with "You can do it!"

The message parents provide, then, tends to "fit the niche." The impoverished parent, like the middle-class parent, reflects on his or her own life and prepares the child for the same kind of future. Fatalism derives from having little control over your life; hope, from seeing that effort and expectations make a difference. In Making a Difference: Support Programs for High-Risk Families (see box above), we examine several programs that are helping children by breaking the cycle of family poverty.

These differences in parenting may be linked to later differences in children's cognitive development (Bornstein & Lamb, 1992). Social class differences in cognitive functioning start to show up around the end of the second year, when tests of intellectual development begin to rely heavily on language. It may be that the extra verbal stimulation that middle-class parents typically give to their children enhances their understanding and use of language. And in fact, children adopted by families with high social status score higher on IQ tests than children adopted by lower-class parents (Capron & Duyme, 1989).

Although studies consistently show that parents with more education and money provide more cognitively stimulating care, they do not love their children any more than lower-class parents do. Many lower-class families provide their children with sensitive, stimulating care. When caregiving is compromised, it is usually because the stress that accompanies poverty saps the emotional resources needed to provide quality care.

● Cultural Differences in the Context of Infancy

It's 3 A.M. in Tokyo, and 6-week-old Eriko begins to wail. Her mother, in bed beside her, comforts the infant until she falls back to sleep. In Minneapolis, Lynn Potter awakens to the same distressed cry. She lies in bed for a few minutes waiting to see if her baby, in a crib in a separate bedroom, will fall asleep. Like many American mothers, she does not believe in rushing to comfort her baby every time she cries. And like her own mother, who believed that infants could be spoiled, she wants to give her daughter an early lesson in self-reliance.

The differences between Japanese and American mothers have more to do with culture than with kindness (Bornstein & Tamis-LeMonda, 1991; Tamis-LeMonda et al., 1992). As Erik Erikson, Jerome Kagan, and others have argued, the way we treat our infants reflects the values of our culture (Erikson, 1963; Kagan, Kearsley, & Zelazo, 1978). As we close these chapters on infancy, we'll focus on a powerful force that influences just about everything in children's lives: the values, beliefs, and attitudes of their culture.

● *Asia and the West: Interdependence versus independence.* Why do Japanese babies enjoy the comfort of sleeping with their parents, while American infants are off on their own? Contrasting values are at least partly responsible. In Japan, cooperation and community life are strongly valued, so parents naturally want to bring their infants into the group. Babies are considered too independent, so *inter*dependency is fostered (Bornstein, Tal, & Tamis-LeMonda, 1991; Messinger & Freedman, 1992; Toda et al., 1990). Until their fifth birthday, children are indulged by parents and other family members, and making a child sleep alone is considered a punishment. Japanese mothers rarely leave their babies with babysitters (Miyake et al., 1985; Vogel, 1963). Besides breast-feeding and sleeping with their babies, Japanese mothers also bathe with them and tote them on their backs (Lebra, 1976).

If the ways of Japanese and American mothers seem so different, part of the reason, again, lies with culture. In both countries, child-rearing practices are supported by the culture's view of a mother's role.

In China, too, babies sleep cuddled against their mothers, who breast-feed

(a)

(b)

(c)

Cultural values strongly influence child rearing. (a) Japanese mothers foster interdependence by keeping their infants close and rarely using babysitters. (b) While all parents feel proud of their toddlers' first steps, for Americans, walking is a sign of growing independence, a trait highly valued in their culture. (c) In many traditional cultures, older siblings care for younger ones while their parents are working in the village.

on demand. Soon after the baby is a month old, mothers return to their work outside the home, leaving the baby with a grandmother or another older female relative or family friend. As in other traditional cultures, older siblings also attend to the baby (Morelli & Tronick, 1991; Rogoff et al., 1991). In fact, the entire extended family and the other villagers as well are concerned about the infant's upbringing. The government provides a village day care nursery, but most families think home care is best, at least until the child can talk (Chance, 1984).

The Rajput of northern India have their own philosophy and a parenting style to match. Middle-class U.S. parents, believing they can strongly influence their children's development, actively try to shape it. Rajput parents think the opposite: A child's fate is determined by forces beyond human control; even the infants' future careers are predetermined by their caste. Accordingly, Rajputs do not try to shape their children's early experiences (Kagan, Kearsley, & Zelazo, 1978). For the first 2 years of life, while many American babies are being stimulated and encouraged to explore, Rajput children are passive observers of their world (Minturn & Hitchcock, 1963).

In the United States, values are sharply different, and so is parenting. Here, the highest honor goes to individual effort, overcoming obstacles, achieving personal goals. In a culture where the self-made man is a hero the message is different and clear: Infants should not become too dependent on their parents. Relatives, pediatricians, and child care books promote early separation of infants and parents, especially at night. In *Baby and Child Care,* read by millions of parents, Dr. Benjamin Spock has written, "It is good . . . for babies to get used to falling asleep in their own bed, without company, at least by the time any 3-month colic is over" (1989, p. 199). During the day, American mothers promote their babies' interest in things and objects more than their interest in people. Japanese mothers, in contrast, focus more on the infants' social behavior, directing their babies' attention more toward themselves than to things (Bornstein et al., 1990, 1991). Not surprisingly, American toddlers are more

HIGHLIGHT ON DIVERSITY

VALUES IN PUERTO RICAN AND ANGLO-AMERICAN CHILD REARING

"You try it." "Good work." "Go for it." There's no mistaking a Caucasian American middle-class mother talking to her toddler. Typically, like fathers, they encourage independence, achievement, and a try-try-again spirit. In a study comparing mothers' attitudes toward attachment behavior, R. Harwood selected two groups: Anglo-American women and Puerto Rican mothers, born on the island but now living on the mainland. He asked them to think about the ideal toddler and his or her behaviors—desirable and not.

The Anglo-American mothers stressed self-confidence, independence, and development of individual abilities. They wanted the

child to "fend for herself," "feel essentially worthwhile," "make goals and reach for them." But while stressing independence, these mothers also value empathy and kindness. Toddlers were expected to curb negative feelings and greedy, aggressive, and egocentric behaviors. Mothers discouraged children from feeling disappointed "every time [she] can't have what [she] wants." They also disliked "cruelty toward other children" and hoped to see their toddlers "outgrow selfishness."

For Puerto Rican mothers, cooperation matters more than independence. "Go with it" is better than "Go for it." Consistent with their own values stressing obligations to *others,* Puerto Rican mothers hoped their toddlers would respect others and behave with personal dignity. Kindness, friendliness, getting along with others,

good manners, and cooperation were all highly desirable.

How do these differences show up? When Harwood watched these mothers and children in the "strange situation" (Chapter 6), he noticed something very interesting and predictable. Anglo-American mothers were happiest when their children did *not* need them, when they acknowledged them from a distance rather than needing lots of close contact. They were least comfortable with toddlers who were clingy and distressed. In contrast, Puerto Rican mothers felt most favorable toward children who sought close physical contact; standoffish and avoidant toddlers were the least favored.

Harwood's study shows what theory predicted: Cultural values influence child rearing and are passed from one generation to the next.

autonomous than Japanese children during their second year of life (Messinger & Freedman, 1992).

When we write about American culture and American parents and infants, we have to be careful, of course. Because this society is a diverse one, where ethnic groups share their own values, parenting is not as uniform as in many other cultures. We can describe dominant values and patterns of child rearing in the United States, but clear differences exist. For women born in Puerto Rico, but living in the continental United States, for example, the model toddler is a little different than the Anglo-American mother's ideal (Harwood, 1992). See Highlight on Diversity: Values in Puerto Rican and Anglo-American Child Rearing above.

This chapter has described just a small sampling of the immense diversity among human cultures. But even this slice of family, class, and cultural influences raises an intriguing question: Would any of us develop into the people we are had we been raised in another culture? Probably not. Genes and innate temperaments strongly influence development, but we are shaped as well by who our parents are, and where and when we are reared.

SUMMARY

1. Development is strongly influenced by social context: the family, community, culture, and historical period in which an infant lives. (See pages 208–209.)

2. The family, the most intimate level of the infant's social context, is a system, with parents and children influencing and being influenced by each other. Couples confront four kinds of problems in adjusting to parenthood: the physical demands of caring for an infant, strains on the relationship caused by decreased desire for sex and conversation, fears about the life-long commitment of parenthood, and loss of freedom and opportunities. (See pages 209–212.)

3. How a couple adjusts to being parents and the quality of their marriage affect the quality of their parenting, which in turn affects their child's development. Marital stress is associated with insecure infant attachment. (See pages 213–214.)

4. Some psychologists have argued that our models of infant development may be too grounded in Western stereotypes of the "normal" mother-infant relationship. Models of infant development that do not take into account the potential role of extended family members may not be entirely applicable to understanding the development of African-American infants, for example. African-American youngsters who have frequent contact with extended family members fare better emotionally and socially and are more likely to grow up in environments that stress moral and religious values. (See pages 215–216.)

5. Support from social networks—from extended family, friends, and community groups—can also affect new parents' psychological and physical health in a positive way. The social contacts can provide emotional support, help with ordinary tasks, and information about child rearing. Parents who feel supported by friends are the most effective at parenting. (See pages 216–217.)

6. Half of all American mothers with babies under a year old work either full- or part-time, leaving their infants in some kind of alternative child care arrangement for part of the day. Experts disagree about the lasting effects of day care on infant development. Some researchers maintain that infants reared in some kind of nonparental care for an extensive period during their first year of life may be more likely to develop insecure attachments to their mother. Others, however, have questioned the validity of this conclusion. (See pages 217–221.)

7. The single most important influence on infant development away from home is the quality of the caregiver. In selecting a day care provider, parents should keep in mind that someone warm, responsive, and affectionate—a person who has experience with infants and genuinely likes them—is best. In addition, parents should choose a day care arrangement with a reputation for constancy. (See pages 222–223.)

8. Children's development is strongly influenced by their family's social class. Infant mortality rates, for example, are much higher for poor than for middle-class families. Social class affects values and parenting styles, with middle-class parents tending to offer more cognitive stimulation and freedom to infants than lower-class parents. Often the stress in poor families that is related to poverty compromises the quality of care parents would otherwise provide. (See pages 223–224.)

9. Support programs for poor families, especially those headed by young unmarried mothers, have helped both parents and infants over an extended time. In several research studies, mothers learned to become more sensitive to their infants and improved their own lives as well. (See pages 224–225.)

10. Cultural values strongly influence how parents treat their infants. Cross-cultural comparisons of parents show that parents around the world value different traits in their children and, as a consequence, socialize them in different ways. (See pages 226–228.)

KEY TERMS

extended families   social context   system
reciprocal feedback   social networks

SUGGESTED READINGS

Belsky, J and Kelly, J. (1994). *The transition to parenthood.* New York: Delacorte. A fascinating report of a longitudinal study of how marriages change after the birth of a baby.

Fraiberg, S. (1977). *Every child's birthright.* New York: Basic Books. A sensitive child psychologist outlines her beliefs on why babies need their mothers' care—rather than someone else's—in their first years of life.

Lande, J., Scarr, S., & Gunzenhauser, N. (Eds.) (1989). *Caring for children.* Hillsdale, NJ: Erlbaum. A comprehensive volume on child care in the United States and abroad.

Michaels, G., & Goldberg, W. (Eds.) (1989). *The transition to parenthood: Current theory and research.* Cambridge, England: Cambridge University Press. In a series of excellent chapters, the state of research on the transition to parenthood is examined, including research on prematurity, marital relations, adult development, and intervention programs.

PART THREE

EARLY
CHILDHOOD

CHAPTER 8

PHYSICAL, COGNITIVE, AND LANGUAGE DEVELOPMENT IN EARLY CHILDHOOD

233

I t is Sunday in the park. Julia, three years old, her jacket spread like wings, runs down muddy paths, leaving her father and his friend far behind. When Julia stops, it is only to turn around and call, "Come on you guys." She doesn't wait.

In parks, playgrounds, and preschools, indoors or on the street, play reveals and advances children's strides. No longer shaky-legged 2-year-olds, they climb, run, jump, and leap like junior gymnasts. By age 4, most have gained enough motor coordination to hop in a circle, hit a baseball, and kick a soccer ball. Five-year-olds favor games requiring greater physical coordination as well as more complex communication and understanding.

Visit a playground and watch preschoolers in action. You can identify the characteristics of their play and ask critical questions about their development. The little girl determined to climb to the top jungle gym reveals her motivation to master a challenge. How can parents and other adults promote such motivation?

The 5-year-olds arguing about who won a game reveal how hard it is for young children to negotiate rules and social contracts. Why do they stubbornly stick to rigid rules? The 3-year-olds in the sandbox playing with toys chatter away but seem to be talking to no one in particular. Is this playful language or poor communication? You may see groups of 4- and 5-year-olds pretending to be superheroes or unicorns as they chase each other. Does role playing depend on cognitive development? How have preschoolers' cognitive skills progressed since infancy?

In this chapter we discuss children's physical, cognitive, and linguistic growth from ages 2 to 6 years—growth that sets the foundation for the rest of childhood. Again, you'll see universal patterns and individual differences and, of course, that biology and environment jointly influence development.

PHYSICAL DEVELOPMENT

Infancy's lightning growth slows down during the preschool years. In fact, between their second and third birthdays, children gain fewer pounds and grow fewer inches than at any other age until after they enter puberty.

The other most obvious change from infancy is in body shape and proportion. Two-year-olds still have the short-limbed, large-headed, pot-bellied look of infants; but over the next 3 to 4 years, arms, legs, and torso grow quickly, becoming longer in proportion to the head. By age 5 or 6, children's body proportions are nearly the same as those of young adults. Throughout the preschool years, boys are slightly taller and heavier than girls, a difference that continues until adolescence, when girls, who mature earlier physically, shoot ahead of boys.

● Size and Growth Rates

Among young children, size and rate of development vary greatly, but 2-year-olds generally weigh 20 to 25 pounds. Over the next 3 years, most children gain about 6 to 7 pounds per year, so by age 5 or 6, an average child in the United

States weighs approximately 40 pounds. Preschoolers also grow an average of 2 to 4 inches per year; the average 5-year-old is about 43 inches tall.

The factors influencing size and growth of children are the same two that influence all development—heredity and environment. In this case, heredity is so powerful that from the age of 2 on, parents' height can be used to predict children's height. This prediction is moderately accurate but increases as children get older. Linked to heredity is race. Children from North America, Africa, and northern Europe are among the tallest in the world, whereas those from southern Asia are among the smallest. Within the United States, the tallest preschoolers tend to be those of African descent (Eveleth, 1986; Garn & Clark, 1975). Caucasians are a bit shorter, and children of Hispanic and Asian descent shorter still. Among 4- and 5-year-olds entering kindergarten in the District of Columbia, for example, African-American girls and boys were taller than their white and Hispanic peers (Kumanyika et al., 1990). Racial differences reflect hereditary influences and will vary widely depending on the stature and growth of children's parents.

● **_Growth and nutrition._** The environmental factor that influences growth most strongly is nutrition. When children do not get enough calories to maintain growth, they become listless and apathetic; and when the calorie level drops further during temporary starvation, famine, or malnourishment, growth stops. Short periods of malnutrition can be overcome with catch up growth if children are returned to a normal diet (Acheson, 1960), but prolonged periods can have long-lasting consequences, even when children do eventually get treated for malnutrition (Lozoff, 1989).

As this playground line-up shows, preschoolers grow at different rates, but by age 5 (the age of the last boy in line), limbs are longer in proportion to the head, and the toddler's pot-bellied walk has disappeared (see p. 118).

As in infancy, the causes of malnutrition are social or environmental. Researchers in a number of countries have found that children in upper socioeconomic groups are taller and heavier than their peers in lower socioeconomic groups, who often have irregular sleep and exercise habits, inadequate diets, and irregular health care (Butler, Starfield, & Stenmark, 1984; Meredith, 1984; Tanner, 1978). Many other environmental factors can affect children's growth and development as well. For example, western European children grow faster in the spring and summer than in autumn and winter. In tropical countries, seasonal variations in rainy and dry periods influence the food supply and frequency of infections, thereby affecting children's growth. Children growing up in densely populated urban areas are usually larger than children from rural areas. The reasons may lie with the availability of food as well as health, sanitation, and recreational services.

In homes where malnutrition is not a problem, parents still worry and complain about the way their children eat. Fearing emaciation or obesity, parents offer bribes, threats, punishments, and rewards contingent on eating behavior, urging their children to take "one more bite," or to "save the candy for later." Not only don't these strategies work, but they are unnecessary as well (Birch, Zimmerman, & Hind, 1984; Birch, Marlin & Rotter, 1984).

Children are very able to regulate their own diets. Monitoring of the eating habits of 2- to 5-year-olds revealed that although children's intake at individual meals varies greatly, their total daily intake is relatively consistent. Generally, high energy intake at one meal is followed by low energy intake at the next, or vice versa. Thus, rather than fighting with preschoolers to eat, parents and other adults should ignore it when they don't.

● *Growth abnormalities.* Delayed growth can be associated with both environmental and biological factors. Recall from Chapter 4, for example, that in some cultures, particularly in Central America, infants are often swaddled on a board during the first year of life. Although restricted movement impedes physical and motor development during early childhood, considerable catch-up growth occurs by age 5 or 6 (Dennis, 1960). Recall, too, that specific dietary deficiencies can also disrupt physical growth. Kwashiorkor, for example, caused by prolonged protein deficiency, is a common ailment among infants in developing countries. When deprivation is severe, irreversible physical and mental retardation can result (Cravioto & DeLicardie, 1970). At the other end of the scale, obesity is *increasing* among children in the United States, partly because of increased availability of junk food, more television watching, and less physical exercise.

● **growth hormone deficiency**
an endocrine disorder causing short stature

● **thyroxine deficiency**
a thyroid disorder that may cause short stature, stunted growth, and mental retardation

Short stature can result from two types of endocrine disorders, **growth hormone deficiency** and **thyroxine deficiency.** Too little growth hormone slows growth from birth on. This is a rare condition occurring only in about 1 in 10,000 births, afflicting boys four times more often than girls. Growth hormone deficiency is sometimes linked to problems in the pituitary gland and, when diagnosed promptly, can be treated effectively, sometimes by injections of growth hormone during childhood and adolescence. Shortness can also result from an insufficient amount of thyroxine, a hormone produced by the thyroid gland. An underactive thyroid can cause cretinism, a condition characterized by stunted growth and mental retardation.

● Brain Growth

By age 2, the brain has grown to about 75 percent of its adult weight and size, ←
and by age 5, it totals 90 percent of its adult weight (Schuster & Ashburn, 1986).
In contrast, an infant's birth weight is only about 5 percent of her future adult
weight, and by age 10, a child weighs only half of what she'll weigh as a young
adult. Although the brain grows most quickly during infancy, it develops continuously throughout childhood. Myelin, the fatty sheath that surrounds neurons and promotes the rapid transmission of information, continues to grow
until puberty. **Cerebral lateralization** continues as well. This is the process by
which brain functions are located in one hemisphere or the other. For example,
lateralization of hand dominance and speech continues until early adolescence.

cerebral lateralization
the process by which certain
brain functions are located in
one hemisphere

Brain waves, too, develop throughout childhood, taking on an adult form at
adolescence. Throughout early childhood the speed of transmission improves.
Babies respond slowly to new sights and sounds, but by age 4 children respond
as quickly as adults (Parmalee & Sigman, 1983). Because the brain and nervous
system grow continuously during childhood, there is a **plasticity,** or flexibility,
in response to early damage caused by malnutrition, tumors, deprived environments, or closed head injuries. There is a strong possibility that the brain
can recover or show catch-up growth later on.

plasticity
flexibility

The brain develops fastest while children are beginning to speak, becoming
physically coordinated, and experiencing rapid cognitive and social development. Although it is tempting to see brain maturation as *causing* the other
changes, it is important to remember that these are reciprocal developments;
that is, one influences the other. The stimulation provided by physical activity,
language, and thinking promotes brain growth as much as neurological
changes influence the way young children respond to the environment. The key
point here is that environment strongly affects a child's cognitive and social development, a topic we focus on in Chapter 10, when we discuss early education
programs and the effects of poverty.

One feature of the environment that can severely affect brain maturation in
early childhood is exposure to high levels of lead. **Lead poisoning** is an especially prevalent problem among children living in old, run-down housing
(which may have chipped and peeling lead paint on its walls), who live near
lead processing plants, or whose parents work in jobs that expose them to lead.
Although lead poisoning is especially prevalent among poor children living in
the inner city, research shows that the *effects* of lead poisoning in childhood
are comparable across cultures, ethnic groups, and socioeconomic brackets.
Regardless of their background, children who are exposed to high levels of
lead in early childhood are more likely than their peers to perform poorly on
IQ tests and experience academic difficulties (Mahaffey, 1992).

lead poisoning
an illness that can severely
affect brain maturation in early
childhood; caused by exposure
to high levels of lead

● Motor Development

Gradually, preschoolers leave the clumsiness of toddlerhood behind as coordination and agility continue to increase. Maturing **gross motor skills** improve
children's ability to jump, climb, and pedal. By age 3, children can run in a
straight line and leap off the floor with both feet. Four-year-olds can throw objects and catch a large ball with both hands. They can skip, hop, and pedal a
tricycle on their own. Five-year-olds resemble adults more than toddlers be-

gross motor skills
physical abilities involving the
large-muscle groups

TABLE 8.1 GROSS AND FINE MOTOR SKILL ACCOMPLISHMENTS

2	2½	3	3½	4	4½	5
Gross Motor Skills by Age						
Walks up and down stairs alone, one step per tread	Can walk on tiptoe	Runs well but will stumble or fall occasionally	Runs smoothly with acceleration and deceleration	Balances on one foot for 4 to 8 seconds	Hops on non-dominant foot	Two-hand catch (often fails to catch ball)
Can walk backward	Balances for 1 second on one foot	Can use hands and feet simultaneously, e.g., stamping foot while clapping hands	Skillful in balancing on toes, can run on tip-toes	Skips "lame duck" on one foot	Leaps over objects 10 inches high	May bounce ball in place, catch each bounce
Can throw a ball overhand	Jumps with both feet "in place"	Can throw a ball without losing balance	Briefly hops on one foot	Descends stairway with alternating feet (may need some help)	Hops forward three hops, maintains balance (knees should flex slightly)	May be able to hit a swinging ball
Kicks large ball forward on request	Helps dress and undress self	Jumps from bottom step (12 inches)	Catches bounced ball (hands held in viselike position, elbows extended)		Can turn somersault	Skips rope
May pedal tricycle		Alternates forward foot going up stairs			Dresses self except for tying shoes	
		Rides tricycle with no difficulty				
		Handles most of dressing; puts on own shoes				
Fine Motor Skills by Age						
Can deal with some mechanical devices: screw-type toys, door knobs, faucets	Copies a crude circle	May be able to unbutton some front buttons; side buttons with difficulty	May be able to copy a crude square (square will be lopsided with rounded corners)	Copies square (vertical lines usually longer)	May copy a recognizable triangle (sides will not be equal, nor will base be parallel to edge of paper)	Can manipulate buttons well
	Can imitate vertical and horizontal strokes on paper	Can copy a circle reasonably well		May button front buttons		
		May be able to use scissors				
		Completes simple puzzles				

Source: After L. Skinner (1979).

cause their bodies have lengthened and become less top-heavy. A 5-year-old's balance has improved; her muscles have grown stronger; and she can ride a bicycle, swim, and do acrobatics. Many of these changes reflect stronger muscles, greater physical coordination, and improved balance stemming from better body proportions (Table 8.1).

Fine motor skills—which include smaller, more precise, and delicate movements—improve markedly as well. Three-year-olds struggle with buttons, zippers, and shoelaces; but by age 5, children can usually dress themselves and manipulate a variety of tools as well. For example, most 5-year-olds can cut out shapes with scissors, use rulers, play video games with joysticks, and easily copy letters and numbers with crayons and pencils. The increased coordination of small muscles and manual dexterity also allows children to play simple musical instruments, draw more precisely, and begin to write. (See Table 8.1.)

One clear developmental change for preschoolers is **hand dominance.** Most toddlers tend to use one hand more often than the other when throwing a ball, drawing, and so forth, but strong preference for handedness may not appear until age 5 (Goodall, 1980). Although some people believe that left-handed children are more awkward than right-handers, children who prefer *either* hand consistently are more coordinated than children with inconsistent hand preferences (Gottfried & Bathhurst, 1983; Tan, 1985).

Although there are gender differences in the development of motor skills, differences between boys and girls are not exclusively due to innate characteristics. Boys tend to have more muscle and better gross motor skills, and they are somewhat stronger than girls (Garai & Scheinfeld, 1968), but girls usually excel at fine motor skills. One explanation for these differences is environmental: From toddlerhood on, boys are encouraged to run, jump, and play in a rough-and-tumble way; whereas girls are encouraged to use their hands at drawing,

● **fine motor skills**
physical abilities involving the small-muscle groups

● **hand dominance**
a strong preference for using the left or right hand

What children do influences what they can do. Boy-girl differences in motor skills may have more to do with children's activities than with their gender.

sewing, or playing musical instruments. In Chapter 9, we'll consider how biology and society influence the ways that girls and boys choose to play. We turn now to cognitive development, to the stages of intellectual growth that mark the preschool years.

COGNITIVE DEVELOPMENT: PIAGET AND BEYOND

You are sitting across a table from Suzanne, a 4-year-old child. You have been having an interesting conversation about how she and her family spent the weekend, and you have been impressed with how bright this little girl seems. Now you are about to try a little experiment.

On the table are two identical piles of raisins, each with six raisins in it. You ask Suzanne if one pile has more than the other. She looks at them for a few seconds and says, "They both have the same." With Suzanne watching you, you spread one pile out but leave the other pile as it was. Now you ask her again, "Does one pile have more than the other?" "Oh yes," Suzanne says, pointing to the spread-out pile. "This one has more."

You wonder how this bright little girl could be so easily fooled. But Suzanne's failure to understand—that making a group of objects *look* larger by having them occupy more space does not actually increase their number—is a typical error seen among preschoolers. Although children of this age are leaps and bounds beyond infancy in the sorts of intellectual skills they have, their reasoning abilities are still limited in important ways, and there is much cognitive development yet to take place before the early childhood era comes to a close.

What are the similarities and differences between Suzanne's thinking and that of an adult? In the remainder of this chapter, we take a look at what young children *do* understand, at what they do not, and at the tremendous growth in thinking abilities that occurs between the ages of 2 and 5.

● **Piaget's Approach**

Recall from Chapter 1 that Piaget pioneered in charting the major stages of cognitive development. He wanted to understand how children solve problems and how our thinking changes as we mature. And as you read in Chapter 5, Piaget's research showed that the origins of intelligence lie in the coordination of sensory and motor responses during the first 2 years of life. But a dramatic shift to symbolic thinking occurs by age 2 and continues to develop until a rapid change in logical thinking occurs at around 7 and again around puberty. We will consider these more sophisticated forms of reasoning in Chapters 11 and 14.

It is important to place Piaget's theory and methods in historical perspective. Most of Piaget's observations were groundbreaking at the time they were published. He collected information from his own children and Swiss children in the community, developed a theoretical interpretation of his observations, and wrote his findings in a series of books that span more than 50 years. During those 50 years, Piaget changed his methods, his terms, and his interpretations.

As we noted in Chapter 5, new methods and theories have challenged many of Piaget's conclusions. Today, Piaget's theory is regarded as an extraordinary first step in charting cognitive development—a first step that, understandably, has been modified and tempered with new data. For example, in the following section we discuss some of Piaget's claims about the limitations in the reasoning of young children. Piaget believed that from ages 2 to 5 years, children had a very limited ability to understand concepts and relationships. However, recent research has shown that when tasks and instructions are simplified, young children show more sophisticated reasoning than Piaget thought possible. Still, it is important to keep in mind that young children cannot solve the same logical problems as older ones can.

Below, we describe some of Piaget's claims about the limits of young children's reasoning, as well as the recent research that shows them to be more sophisticated problem solvers than he thought possible. First, however, we need to take a closer look at the hallmark of cognitive development during the early childhood years: the development of symbolic, or representational, thought.

Symbolic thought is the ability to represent the world mentally. Symbolic thinking develops in two important ways in early childhood. First, children develop the ability to use internal symbols, or mental images, to solve problems. For example, Piaget saw that one of his children, Lucienne, was trying to get an object out of a matchbox, the kind that slides open and shut (Piaget, 1952, p. 338). At first, Lucienne did not understand how the matchbox worked. She would turn it over and over, but the object would not fall out. Piaget saw, though, that as Lucienne explored the matchbox, she opened and closed her mouth, wider and wider. Why? Piaget reasoned that Lucienne was using the image of opening and closing her mouth to represent the opening and closing of the box. In other words, she was using the mental image of opening and closing to solve the problem of the matchbox.

> **symbolic thought**
> mental representation of the world

Second, children begin to use external symbols—such as words, pictures, or maps—to stand for objects and events. We see this quite clearly in children's artwork (discussed later in this chapter). Ask a 2- or 3-year-old, "What are you drawing?" and the answer you're likely to get is "I'm just *drawing*!" That is because the youngest preschoolers are much more interested in the drawing *process* than in the finished product. By the time children are 4 or 5, however, drawing becomes *representational* (Kellogg, 1970). They draw people, settings, and objects. With the development of symbolic ability, children are able to use pictures to depict scenes or stories.

The development of symbolic thinking can also be seen in children's play. Pretend play begins at around 18 to 24 months, when children begin to use one object to stand for another. For example, in one observational study, a 2-year-old child was using a doll to symbolize a person and a set of blocks to symbolize a bathtub. The child relied on his own experience to "create" imaginary faucets in the pretend bathtub and "filled" the bathtub with water. He even went so far as to imagine the "water" being too hot at first: "Oh, no, sooooo hot, too hot. Ouch. Gotta put some cold in" (Wolf, Rygh, & Altshuler, 1984, p. 197).

The ability to use external symbols to stand for real objects develops gradually. For example, using a map to learn how to find something is a skill that develops over time, as children's symbolic thinking improves. By age 4 or 5, children can use maps to acquire information about spatial locations (Uttal & Wellman, 1989). Interestingly, children seem to be able to use two-dimensional

Symbolic thinking develops gradually. A 2-year-old can use blocks to represent buildings, but 4-year-olds can imagine that each block is one story high.

● **preoperational period**
according to Piaget, the period of transition from sensorimotor intelligence to rule-governed thought

maps to represent places before they can use three-dimensional models (DeLoache, 1991). This may be because three-dimensional models seem more like objects in their own right than symbolic representations of places, and are therefore more confusing than two-dimensional maps. It is not until a later age that children can understand that something can be *both* a symbol and an object simultaneously.

The earliest instances of symbolic thinking occur at about 2 years of age, marking the beginning of the **preoperational period** in Piaget's theory of cognitive development.

● Preoperational Thought

Piaget identified the time period from 2 to 7 years as a transition from the sensorimotor intelligence of infants to the rule-governed thought of school-age children. He named this time the *pre*operational period because preschoolers were thought to lack the sophisticated cognitive operations he saw in school-age children. According to Piaget, younger children thought intuitively and conceptually but not logically. Perhaps the best way to examine this is by considering some of the ways Piaget believed that preoperational thinking was limited.

● *Centration.* According to Piaget, preschoolers tend to believe "what you see is what you get." For example, when researchers place a mask of a dog's face on a cat's head, 3- and 4-year-olds thought that the cat had become a dog (DeVries, 1969). They thought the cat would bark and prefer dog food because the cat *looked* like a dog. These children were thinking as Piaget thought they would. That is, they were focusing, or centering, their attention on only one aspect of the stimulus (the mask). Piaget called this **centration.**

● **centration**
focusing on only one aspect of a stimulus

These young children would be amazed if Mickey Mouse removed his head and "became" a person. In the pre-operational period, children are still fooled by appearances.

Because preschoolers do not process all the available information, they are often fooled by appearances. Six-year-olds are not as easily fooled. They predicted that the cat would remain a cat, but when the mask was placed on the cat's head, they were not so sure. The same thing happens when preschoolers see people dressed up as Santa Claus or the Easter Bunny, or wearing Halloween costumes. Preschoolers often become afraid, reacting as though the costume changes the person within it. Why? Piaget believed that because thought is centered, children do not perceive that one person can be two different things simultaneously. At this stage, appearance overpowers any other possibilities.

Understanding centration helps to explain why children sometimes have difficulty solving logical problems that appear on the surface to be easy, such as the problem of the raisins described earlier. In that instance, Suzanne focused her attention (that is, "centered") on the amount of space taken up by each of the piles rather than the number of raisins in each.

● *Reversibility.* "Do you have a brother?" "Yes," says a 4-year-old boy who has a new baby brother. "Does your brother have a brother?" "No."

Typical for his age, this little boy doesn't perceive that the relationship of brother points two ways. As Piaget discovered, young children tend to think in one direction at a time. They have not yet acquired what Piaget called **reversibility,** the ability to understand how two opposite or complementary actions are related to each other. For example, if you pour some juice from a short, wide glass into a tall, thin one, the level of the juice will rise. Adults realize that the volume of the juice hasn't actually increased, but that one dimension of the glass (increased height) is offset, or "reversed," by another (decreased width).

● **reversibility**
the concept representing that an action can be done and undone

More, or the same? Without special training, preschoolers think that the shape of a container affects the amount of the water within it. Once they grasp the concept of conservation, children know that a quantity doesn't change just because its appearance does.

Preschool children, unable to understand how two opposite actions work together, are easily fooled into thinking that the actual volume of the liquid has changed.

● *States and transformations.* Part of the reason for this deficiency, Piaget believed, is that preschoolers are likely to pay attention to the state of something in its present form, a limitation in thinking about **states and transformations.** For example, when looking at a pile of raisins that was spread out, Suzanne tended to think of it only as a large pile (its present state) and not as a smaller group that had been distributed over a larger area (the process of transformation). In other words, while preschool children can understand that objects can be transformed, they don't think about the *process* of change. The acquisition of reversibility enables the child to understand how objects are transformed.

● *Conservation.* When children do understand that the number of raisins in the piles stays the same even if they are rearranged, Piaget would say that they had learned to *conserve* number. **Conservation** is the term that Piaget used to describe the understanding that basic physical dimensions—such as number, mass, distance, volume, and area—remain the same despite superficial changes in the appearance of objects. Conservation of quantity despite changing appearances is a fundamental accomplishment of the concrete operational period that Piaget thought appeared at about 7 years of age. Although conservation is an ability that can be applied to understand different sorts of transformations— conservation of number (for example, in the raisin problem) and conservation of liquid volume (in the juice problem) are two familiar examples—Piaget believed that it was a general logical principle that, once acquired, was applied across different sorts of problems at roughly the same age.

● **states and transformations**
the concepts involved in understanding that objects and states can be transformed and rearranged

● **conservation**
the knowledge that basic physical attributes remain the same despite superficial changes in appearance

● Current Research on Children's Cognitive Abilities

Although the limits in young children's reasoning that Piaget identified are often apparent during the preschool years, research during the past two decades suggests that Piaget probably underestimated the cognitive abilities of preschoolers. Let's take a look at some of the more interesting and exciting work in this area.

● *Appearance and reality.* We now know that children's ability to distinguish between appearance and reality is evident before the end of the preoperational period. Although 3-year-olds often confuse appearance and reality, 5-year-olds do not (Flavell, Green, & Flavell, 1986). When a 3-year-old is shown a glass of milk behind a green filter, the child says that the milk *looks* green and actually *is* green. When given a sponge that is gray and looks like a rock, a 3-year-old says that it *is* a rock and *looks* like a rock. When 3-year-olds watched a familiar woman put on a Miss Piggy costume, they insisted that she had turned into Miss Piggy. Because they have trouble distinguishing between the way things look and the way they really are, reasoning is difficult for young children. But this confusion may be briefer and more selective than Piaget had imagined. By age 5, children can often distinguish between appearance and reality.

Even 3-year-olds can make the distinction between appearance and reality if the issue is the way things *feel* rather than the way they look. In one experiment, a group of 3-year-olds was asked to touch an ice cube bare-handed and with a gloved finger. Even after they touched the cube with the covered finger, about 80 percent of the children confirmed that the ice cube was "really and truly" cold, even though it no longer felt icy (Flavell, Green, & Flavell, 1986). On the basis of such experiments, Flavell and other cognitive researchers suggest that between the ages of 3 and 6, preschoolers develop a theory of the mental world in which they begin to distinguish between appearance and reality.

In short, young children's thinking may not be as ruled by their perceptions as Piaget believed (Flavell, 1988; Wellman, 1988). For example, when taught information about a particular type of animal (such as, dogs use their lungs to breathe), preschool children will generalize this information to other animals (for instance, horses), even though their external appearance is quite different (Gelman, 1988).

● *States and transformations.* Other research has countered some of Piaget's conclusions about preschoolers' limited ability to understand states and transformations. Studies suggest that young children *can* attend to transformations and that reversibility can be taught to preschoolers (Gelman & Baillargeon, 1983). In one study, for example, children learned that given a certain number of dolls and the same number of doll beds, any rearrangement of either the dolls or the beds would maintain the one-to-one fit of dolls to beds (Wallach & Sprott, 1964). In another study, 3- and 4-year-olds looked at picture sequences where changes had been made. Children were then given a selection of possible answer cards that would complete the sequences and were quite able to put the cards in the proper order. Thus they understood that objects can be reordered into different sequences and were not always fooled by attending only to the present states (Gelman, Bullock, & Meck, 1980).

● *Conservation.* It also appears that children can employ conservation skills at an earlier age than Piaget had suggested. In one study, for example, even young children, 3- to 6½-year-olds, were consistently able to distinguish between rows of two and three toy animals, no matter how much space appeared between the animals (the experimenter changed the amount of space in various ways) (Gelman, 1982). Piaget would have expected children to explain their answers in terms of the density or length of the row, but that is not what happened. Of course, it is not clear from this experiment whether children solved the problem successfully because they understood conservation of number or because they were able to count accurately. As you will read in a moment, researchers have found that children are able to count at an earlier age than had previously been thought.

Researchers also have successfully taught conservation to preschoolers. Dorothy Field (1987) reviewed 25 of these conservation training studies and concluded that, with training, 4- and 5-year-olds can do better than Piaget originally proposed. Thus, although preschool children may not always spontaneously demonstrate conservation, this skill is within their reach given appropriate instruction.

● *Understanding of number.* Recent studies have shown that preschoolers can count spontaneously and *systematically* (in a consistent way). This has been revolutionary news for researchers studying cognitive development. One of the leaders in this area, Rochel Gelman, argues that, like the ability to learn language, number abilities may also be inborn and universal (Flavell, 1985; Gelman, 1982). Even the 3- and 4-year-olds in Gelman's study were counting (Gelman, 1982).

Gelman has suggested that young children can not only count but count according to five discoverable principles (Flavell, 1985; Gelman, 1979; Gelman & Gallistel, 1978). First, preschoolers tend to assign only one number to each item and count each item only once. Children don't always follow this rule, especially when confronted with large groups of items, which they find daunting. But they do tend to correct their own mistakes and notice others' mistakes of this type.

Second, preschoolers use names for numbers—though not necessarily the correct names—in a consistent way. For example, a 2½-year-old who counts "2, 6, 10" will consistently count items as 2, 6, 10 and will often say there are "10" items in the set (Gelman & Gallistel, 1978). Gelman compares the use of incorrect but consistent number names to the kind of consistent, rule-oriented language mistakes children make at a certain age (Gelman & Baillargeon, 1983). (We'll come back to this pattern when we look at preschoolers' language later in the chapter.) Again, the youngest preschoolers may not always follow the principle that the last number name in a counting list is the correct number of items. Nevertheless, they will often correct others' incorrect answers, and they can often answer correctly themselves if someone else does the actual counting for them and then asks them "How many?"

Third, preschoolers understand that a sequence of counting numbers refers to a sequence of amounts, and not just an order of numbers. That is, they understand that "two" is *more* than "one" (not simply the number that comes after "one"), and that "three" is *more* than "two."

Fourth, young children also seem to consider anything countable—people, animals, events, ideas, toys. Finally, children as young as 3 seem to understand that unlike number *names,* the counted items themselves can be rearranged without altering the amount: Count them backward or forward; it's all the same. (This could also be considered an aspect of number conservation.)

By age 3 or 4, many children have acquired the five principles of early number knowledge. They use this knowledge in many ways. For example, most 4-year-olds can answer questions such as "Which is bigger, 6 or 2?" Children this age usually can add and subtract numbers from 1 to 10 and may be able to count up to 100. These skills are refined by 5- and 6-year-olds when they enter school.

From research on children's early counting and number knowledge, we know that 3- and 4-year-olds can judge numerosity, compare quantities, and infer numerical correspondence to a greater extent than Piaget thought (Sophian, 1988). Preschoolers understand a great deal about numbers and quantities that helps prepare them for schooling and more complex problem solving. It is important, however, to keep in mind the difference between what children *can* do and what they actually do. Although Gelman's research indicates that children's competencies are probably greater than we had once believed, young children still make plenty of mistakes in counting objects.

What do all these updates on Piaget, children, and numbers tell us? First, no one is proposing that preschoolers are mathematical whizzes—only that they have some grasp of numbers from fairly early on and are generally much more competent and resourceful in using numbers than was once thought. According to Gelman, Piaget and others did not see this competence before for a simple reason: They were neither looking for it nor designing tests with it in mind (Gelman, 1979). Gelman has urged psychologists to concentrate less on what preschoolers can't do and more on what they can do. In the Controversy box on pages 248–249, we discuss the push toward early academics for preschoolers.

● *Causal reasoning.* Recent research on children's causal reasoning also has indicated that children may be more capable than previously thought. Although Piaget had asserted that young children may confuse cause and effect—that is, they could see one event as having caused something that *preceded* it (for example, "I fell off my bicycle because I skinned my knee")—newer studies indicate that this is generally not the case. Children may make causal errors when asked to explain things they have not had direct experience with (for instance, a child might say that the sun rises in the morning because it gets light outside, rather than the reverse). But when asked about things they have experienced directly, children *do* expect causes to precede effects, just as adults do (Bullock, Gelman, & Baillargeon, 1982).

Young children's causal reasoning is different from that of adults, however, in the *types* of causes they use for explanations. Children tend to give human reasons (such as wanting or needing something) for events that have mechanical causes. Preschoolers may do this even when discussing inanimate, or nonliving, phenomena. Piaget called this kind of thinking **animism,** giving nonliving things the capacities and qualities of living things—sometimes including the thoughts and feelings of humans. Children often assign animistic qualities to the sun, the moon, and the mountains. A 4-year-old might worry that a tree could get lonely or that a stone would feel pain if someone kicked it. It is im-

● **animism**
crediting nonliving things with human qualities

CONTROVERSY

SUPERBABY, SUPERKID: A HEAD START OR A MISSTART?

Give Your Child a Superior Mind reads the title of a parents' manual. Can you? Should you? Also on the shelves are *Supertot, Superkids, Smart Toys.* These books are being gobbled up by parents eager to spur their children's intellectual development by starting formal kinds of training earlier and earlier. But do children need to begin academic training at 3 or 4? Do French lessons at 5 and 6 do more for the parents or the child?

The 1980s saw the start of a "superkid boom," as a generation of educated, competitive parents began the "search for excellence" for their preschoolers. The children, however, are showing signs of wear. Just as infants can be overstimulated by overeager parents, so can preschoolers be overwhelmed with inappropriate cognitive and physical demands. Psychologists and counselors are

reporting increased incidence of stress symptoms such as stomachaches, headaches, and sleeping problems in preschoolers and depression in school-age children. Many think these are the results of what noted child psychologist David Elkind (1981) calls the "miseducation" of the young. Like many other child development experts, Elkind finds the whole trend to involve preschoolers in formal training disturbing and potentially quite dangerous.

Not only do they increase stress, but early academics also decrease the child's freedom to find her own fun, to learn through play. Young children learn by discovering, spurred along by their innate curiosity. And curiosity is reinforced by the very pleasure of gaining understanding. The 3-year-old who pulls all the pots and pans off the kitchen shelves may look like she's into mischief—but her mischief is often educational. Not only may she be learning about size and shape—which is bigger,

which fit inside which—but the fantasy play that she can engage in encourages intellectual growth. Practicing sums or drilling vocabulary drains pleasure from the experience of learning, which is one of young childhood's greatest gifts. When school starts, will that pleasure be recoverable? Very often it is not.

Paradoxically, educators and parents who stress early lessons are ignoring one of Piaget's most important ones: Children are not and do not think like little adults. The drive to find out how things work, the desire to know why things are the way they are, the hunger to explore—processes that come naturally to preschool children—are threatened by formal lessons and overly competitive experiences. Psychological research has also been misapplied. Look at Head Start programs, say some well-meaning legislators and parents. Don't they raise the intellectual capacities of children from impoverished homes? Yes, they do

portant, however, to understand that animistic thinking comes not from a lack of logic but from a lack of knowledge about the physical world.

● ***Theory of mind.*** In one of his best known experiments, Piaget showed children a scene of three mountains and a group of pictures showing the scene from different directions. He asked children to select pictures that showed what other children seated around the table would see from their position (Piaget & Inhelder, 1956). Most of the preoperational children chose pictures identical with their own perspective: They thought that other children saw what they saw. We know that preschoolers tend to focus their attention on the salient features of an object or a situation. They do not know that what you see depends on where you look (Shantz, 1983). Piaget regarded this inability to consider other people's perspectives as a self-centered outlook on the world, and he labeled it **egocentrism.** It doesn't mean egotistic or selfish; egocentrism means that people tend to see things from their own points of view.

● **egocentrism**
the inability to consider others' perspectives

(see Chapter 10), but this does *not* mean that more educational experiences will benefit preschoolers whose days are already filled with interesting things to play with and caring people to share discoveries with. And yes, it is also true that preschoolers are more competent than was once thought. Nevertheless, simply because 3- and 4-year-olds do have rudimentary concepts of number and numerical principles, it does not follow that these children should be *taught* addition and subtraction before they reach first grade.

Academic gains, warns Elkind, may lead to personal losses. Needing to know the right answers at too early an age can enhance conformity as it stifles curiosity. When demands for right answers are made too soon, fear of failure replaces the fun of discovery. Feelings of inadequacy, inferiority, and shame may grow, while lifelong potential may be undercut.

Many parents who feel pressed to enroll their preschoolers in aca-

For whose benefit are these girls performing? Formal lessons for young children can backfire later, causing stress and fear of failure.

demic lessons or structured physical activities need reassurance. There is so much for young children to learn and so much for them to do: Life itself, in these early years, provides more than enough of a curriculum. Sharing discoveries, reinforcing curiosity, and participating in the joy of knowledge are probably what count most.

Some researchers have contended that Piaget's three-mountain task is not a fair test of children's ability. Like many of his tasks, it is very complicated. It requires children to use mental imagery and to rotate objects in a spatial arrangement. Perhaps these tasks are too difficult. In order to see whether this were so, another researcher simplified the experiment by letting children turn the table to find the view that other children would see. In this form of the experiment, preschoolers were not egocentric as Piaget had claimed (Borke, 1975).

Whatever the methodology, the study of egocentrism provides a window on youngsters' development of a "theory of mind." By theory of mind, we mean the child's understanding of mental states, such as beliefs, emotions, desires, intentions, and dreams. Do young children distinguish between mental states, such as thoughts, and reality? Can children infer another person's beliefs and understand that the other person may believe things the child knows are false? How well can children infer others' emotional states? These are all questions that researchers interested in children's "theory of mind" study.

Although Piaget once asserted that "the child knows nothing about the nature of thought," recent research indicates that young children actually have a fairly sophisticated understanding of the mind, especially by age 4 or 5. For example, 3- to 5-year olds can distinguish between mental entities (for instance, a wish for a cookie) and physical entities (a real cookie). Preschoolers know that physical objects can be touched and seen by themselves and by others, but that mental representations of objects cannot (Wellman & Estes, 1986). By age 4, a child can understand that another person can hold a false belief and that this belief will influence the individual to behave in a certain way (Wimmer & Perner, 1983).

Despite these competencies, though, there are still many things absent from the preschooler's theory of mind. For example, although preschoolers can see how a given situation might make a person feel (for instance, being in a new class might make someone nervous), they have difficulty understanding that individuals with different past experiences may react differently to the same situation (that a child who is used to changing schools might feel less nervous in a new class than one who has never had to do it before) (Gnepp & Gould, 1985). Furthermore, young children appear to have difficulty learning the words that refer to mental states, such as *remember* and *forget*. For instance, if a child finds a hidden object, a preschooler describing the situation may say that the other child "remembered" where it was, even though this was the first time the child had found the object (Wellman & Johnson, 1979). Children's understanding of different terms to describe mental states (such as *guess, think, know*) improves steadily over the preoperational period (Moore, Bryant, & Furrow, 1989).

All in all, then, recent research on children's theory of mind—like that on causal reasoning, number, and conservation—indicates that children's thinking, while not as advanced as adult thinking, is a good deal more sophisticated than initially proposed by Piaget.

INFORMATION PROCESSING

● **information processing**
one of the theories concerning the development of thinking; it emphasizes the growth of basic cognitive processes over time

In recent years, a number of researchers have examined the development of young children's thinking from a different perspective than that suggested by Piaget. The most important of these theorists have taken an approach that is called **information processing,** one that emphasizes the growth of basic cognitive processes over time. Perhaps the one cognitive process that has received the most attention from this perspective is memory.

● Memory Development: Recognition and Recall

Show a group of preschoolers some toys, mix them up with some unfamiliar ones, and then ask them to identify the ones you showed them. Even the 2-year-olds will choose correctly almost all the time. But if you ask the same children to just *name* the toys you have shown them, without looking at them, accuracy drops to 20 percent for 3-year-olds and 40 percent for 4-year-olds (Myers &

Perlmutter, 1978). Why the difference? Because two types of memory are required, and preschoolers are much better at one than the other. The first task, such as a multiple-choice test where you are asked to pick the right answer, relies on **recognition memory.** The second task is more like an essay exam: You have to retrieve information at request (either yours or someone else's) *without strong cues.* This type of task relies on **recall memory.** Both kinds of memory improve as preschoolers gain more knowledge and experience, but recognition continues to be stronger than recall (Myers & Perlmutter, 1978).

Actually, recognition memory is stronger than recall throughout development. Sometimes children's recognition memory is astounding. Even preschoolers can remember whether they have seen long lists of pictures (Kail, 1984). For example, 4-year-olds can recognize which pictures they have seen before when given a long series of pictures that are not too different (Brown & Campione, 1972). Recognition memory is aided by parents' repetitive reading of books and stories. Even 2-year-olds will quickly fill in missing words from their favorite picture books.

Young children also remember sequences of day-to-day activities, sometimes referred to as **scripts,** quite well. Ask a typical 4- or 5-year-old what goes on at preschool each morning, and she will be happy to tell you: First there's a play period downstairs, then the group goes upstairs for circle time, then everyone works at the tables, and then they have a snack. Not surprisingly, studies show that preschoolers are much better at recalling events that occur within logical sequences than ones whose order is arbitrary (Fivush, Kuebli, & Clubb, 1992). Children this age know, too, when a script has been changed, and they respond to the humor of an illogical script. If you tell a preschooler that you woke up this morning, got out of bed, got dressed, took a bath, and ate your dinner, he will find this very funny because he knows that's not the way things are (Nelson, 1981b; Nelson & Gruendel, 1981).

Young children remember familiar events by incorporating them into scripts, or schemes, based on experience. Recurring events such as meals and errands or birthday parties may be collections of many specific episodes, which may make it difficult to remember what happened on a specific errand or who attended a particular birthday party. Novelty helps children distinguish specific episodes from these more general scripts (Nelson & Hudson, 1988). Even 1- and 2-year-olds have knowledge of simple event sequences and can use this knowledge to remember sequences they have witnessed previously (Bauer & Mandler, 1989, 1992). Even if young children are too young to recount a sequence of events verbally, they can act it out accurately with dolls and other props.

Some of the first and most salient memories of young children involve familiar routines established around eating, play, bedtime rituals, and other familiar activities. In one study, 2- and 3-year-olds easily recalled familiar household routines such as taking a bath, brushing teeth, and saying prayers at night (Wellman & Somerville, 1980); and for 3- and 4-year-olds, remembering advertising jingles, nursery rhymes, and TV characters is a simple task. In one study of intentional memory in 2- to 4-year-olds, children were asked to remind their parents to do something in the future; 4-year-olds were much better than 2-year-olds when reminding parents to do some dull tasks such as taking the laundry out, but both ages were equally good, correct about 80 percent of the time, at reminding their parents to buy them candy.

recognition memory
memory based on recognition of a previously seen object

recall memory
memory based on information retrieved without strong clues

scripts
sequences of day-to-day activities

Young children easily memorize their favorite books if they hear them often enough.

memory strategies
plans that aid recall

Memory strategies are tricks or plans that aid recall. For example, the simple statement "Every good boy does fine" helps music students remember the treble clef lines: E, G, B, D, F. Memory strategies organize information for us and repackage it economically. Even preschoolers can use memory strategies effectively. For example, 3- and 4-year-olds can remember which cup is covering a hidden object if they stare at it, point at it, and touch it (Wellman, Ritter, & Flavell, 1975).

When you look up a phone number and then walk to the phone repeating it to yourself over and over again, you are using the powerful memory strategy called **rehearsal.** By 4 to 5 years of age, many preschoolers spontaneously label and rehearse the names of objects they are asked to remember (Weissberg & Paris, 1986). Early efforts to remember are gradually reinforced with effective strategies as children learn to devote time and effort to the goal of remembering. Strategies such as rehearsal than become deliberate ways to repackage and practice items for later recall (Ornstein, Baker-Ward, & Naus, 1988).

rehearsal
the labeling and repeating of names or other information to aid memory

Again, however, it is important to differentiate between what children *can* do and what they *do* do. Children under 5 or 6 don't usually organize or rehearse information on their own, but if strategies are *specifically suggested* to them, they will use them. In one study, preschoolers were shown pictures of two normally unrelated objects (sheep, pillow) in some relation (sheep stands on pillow). The children who were instructed to "think back to the pictures" had much better recall later than children who did not receive the thinking back instruction (a strategy known as **interactive imagery** or **elaboration**) (Pressley, 1982).

interactive imagery (elaboration)
a stategy for recall

It may be that young children do not think of using strategies on their own because they don't feel the need to remember things. They don't say to themselves, "Ah, I should remember this," unless an adult asks them to try (Flavell, 1985; Pressley, 1982). Their increasing awareness of the usefulness of strategies and the need to apply them is part of the development of **metacognition,** that is, learning to understand and control one's own thinking skills (Flavell, 1985).

metacognition
the understanding and control of one's own thinking skills

Being aware of the usefulness of such strategies doesn't necessarily go hand in hand with their accurate use, however. In one study, researchers asked children to predict how many of 15 common nouns they would remember after having a chance to study the list: On average, the kindergartners recalled only about half as many nouns as they thought they would (Yussen & Berman, 1981). Obviously, in order to effectively use a memory strategy, a child has to have some idea of whether and to what degree the strategy is necessary. It may not be until the elementary school years that children have sufficiently accurate knowledge of their own memory strengths and weaknesses to know when to employ mnemonic strategies.

In research studies, preschoolers learn how to remember word pairs; and in their daily lives, without trying hard, they are remembering more, more, and still more words and how to combine them. Increasingly, their world is becoming a place made meaningful through language.

Thought and Language

The relation between thought and language is an old, old question, debated over centuries and still not answered. No one questions whether language and thought *are* related, but as to which "comes first," theories differ.

CONTROVERSY

CHILDREN AS EYEWITNESSES: HOW RELIABLE IS A CHILD'S MEMORY?

By now it is all too familiar: A dramatic courtroom trial unfolds, and one of the star witnesses is a young child. Jury members pay close attention to the youngster's testimony. But how reliable are children as eyewitnesses? How good are young children's memories, and how easily are young children's minds changed by adults' suggestions?

Researchers disagree about the answers to these questions. On the one hand, Stephen Ceci and his colleagues (Ceci, Ross, & Toglia, 1987) have found that children are highly susceptible to misleading information, especially if the information is provided by an adult authority figure. That is, although their memories may be reasonably good, they are easily shaped and altered by others' suggestions. For example, when children first hear a story (such as the tale of Little Red Riding Hood), then are asked questions about the story that imply false information ("What color was Little Red Riding Hood's dog?"), and are later asked to recall the story, some of the false information contained in the questions (the existence of a dog in the tale) will creep into their recall of the story. This is important in understanding children's courtroom testimony, because it suggests that lawyers can shape a child's memory by asking misleading questions that will lead the child to inadvertently modify his recollection of an event.

Not all researchers agree that children's memories are so malleable, however. One team of researchers, studying children's recall of real-life events, found that even preschool children will reject misleading suggestions (Rudy & Goodman, 1991). Much depends on the nature of the event, the child's actual experience, and the approach used by others to try to shape the child's recollection. Research in this area continues today, but it appears that the key question now is not whether children's testimony is accurate but rather "Under *what conditions* is their testimony accurate and under what conditions is it not?"

For Piaget, language develops as a form of representational or symbolic thought (Piaget, 1959). Others, particularly the Russian psychologist A. R. Luria (1961), have argued that language directs thinking and organizes what we do. In this view, children's thinking is shaped and directed by their increasing language abilities.

For another Russian psychologist, Lev Vygotsky, and for Jerome Bruner, a noted U.S. psychologist, language skills and cognitive growth interact and influence each other; according to these writers, separating thought from language is almost impossible. Language transforms experience, and development influences language. For example, preschoolers gradually internalize language and use "inner speech" to help them plan their actions or control their thinking. They literally talk to themselves, saying "don't touch" as they near a stove, for example. Older children automatically keep their hands off without having to say the words. The concept of inner speech describes how speech *becomes* thought. But under some circumstances, language and cognition may be more independent than Bruner and Vygotsky suggested. Studies of deaf children, for example, have shown that even without speech and, in some cases, without good language skills, deaf children's cognitive processes are not hampered (Furth, 1971).

"Hot. Don't touch." Language helps to guide behavior, as preschoolers begin using "inner speech," repeating to themselves the words they have heard others tell them over and over.

For most children, however, thought and language are interrelated. The relationship between cognitive and language development will become clearer as we discuss how children acquire vocabulary, grammar, and communication skills.

LANGUAGE DEVELOPMENT

In Chapter 5, we traced the development of language from prelinguistic parent-baby exchanges through babbling, first words, and finally, at the end of the second year, rudimentary two-word sentences. Now, in the preschool years, children's vocabularies are growing rapidly, they are learning and applying the rules of their language, and they are becoming increasingly skilled at using language to communicate. Just as infants repeat physical actions over and over, exercising new abilities, preschoolers flex their growing verbal skills. At night, for example, many children chatter away in bed, repeating the names of everyone they saw that day. As we'll see when we discuss language's role in "inner speech," language can also help children guide their own actions as they talk themselves through activities ("No, not that way, this way!") and even scold themselves ("No! Don't go near there!").

● **Building Vocabulary**

During the preschool years children learn as many as two to four new words daily (Pease & Gleason, 1985), and by age 6, vocabulary totals between 8,000 and 14,000 words (Carey, 1978). These words fill many grammatical categories—they are not just nouns—but the words children seem to use the most are the "five W's." As they search for causal explanations, what, where, who, when, and why loom large (Bloom, Merkin, & Wootten, 1982; R. Brown, 1968; Ervin-Tripp, 1970). "Why does the sun shine? Why is it raining? Why isn't *Sesame Street* on now?" And when children answer "when" questions themselves, we find that they are not as limited to one-directional thinking as Piaget thought. When an appropriate context is provided, 3- to 5-year-olds can reason about antecedents or consequences as they answer "when" questions (French, 1989).

One common error that young children frequently make in the early stages of vocabulary development is known as **overextension.** This occurs when a child uses a word to refer to things that are similar to, but not identical with, what the word actually refers to (Clark, 1983). We think children do this because they have gaps in their vocabularies. For example, a child who knows the word *ball* but does not know the word for an apple may call an apple *ball* because both items are round. The child is stretching her limited vocabulary to refer to things for which she does not yet have a name.

Several theorists have described the strategies that children use to fill gaps in their vocabularies. Two- and three-year-olds often fill gaps in their vocabulary by inventing compound words. A team of researchers tested young children's understanding of compound words by showing them four pictures (a hat, a mouse, a hat on a mouse, and a hat on a fish). When the researchers pointed to the hat on the mouse and said "Show me the mousehat," most 4-year-olds readily picked out the hat on the mouse. Two-year-olds were often wrong. In fact, 2-year-olds had difficulty generating compound words to describe the pictured objects, but 3- and 4-year-olds used compound words almost as often as adults (Clark, Gellman, & Lane, 1985).

A second way that children fill gaps in their vocabulary is through a strategy called **fast-mapping** (Carey, 1978; Dollaghan, 1985; Rice, 1989). This occurs when a child relates a new word to a general domain of meaning immediately after hearing it for the first time. For example, a child may hear the word *purple* and realize that it refers to an object's color before he actually knows what the word means exactly. Over time, the child will figure out just what color the word *purple* refers to.

Finally, children will follow what has been called the **mutual exclusivity** principle in acquiring new words (Markman & Wachtel, 1988). According to this principle, children assume that a word can refer to only one object. Thus, when children hear a new term, they are more likely to associate it with a novel object than with something they already are sure they know the word for. For instance, a child who knows the word *tiger,* and who is shown a picture of a tiger and a picture of an elephant, will point to the elephant (and not the tiger) if asked to do so, even if he had never heard the word *elephant* before. By using the principle of mutual exclusivity in this instance (*tiger* can only refer to the tiger), the child has acquired the new word, *elephant.*

As children begin to understand more complex relations among objects, people, situations, and time periods, they also learn to use the words that help express these relationships: prepositions such as *in, on, under, before, after;* and comparative adjectives such as *more, less, bigger, smaller, older, younger.* These words emerge in a predictable order, and even within each category, a sequence is followed. *In,* for example, usually appears before *on,* which appears before *under* (Halpern, Corrigan, & Aviezer, 1983). Earlier in the chapter, we noted that preschoolers use words such as *yesterday, tomorrow, next week, last year*—words that express time relations—but sometimes their grasp of the real meaning of the concept is fuzzy. *Tomorrow* may mean any time in the future, and *yesterday* may mean any time in the past, including the hour just gone by.

overextension
using the same word to stand for a number of similar things

fast-mapping
a strategy used by children to fill gaps in their vocabulary; a child relates a new word to a general domain of meaning immediately after hearing it for the first time

mutual exclusivity
a principle in acquiring new words whereby children assume that a word can refer to only one object

Even children's acquisition of prepositions and adjectives reveals the interplay between the development of cognition and language. Children's use of words such as *in front of, behind, next to, beneath,* and *over* suggests that they are beginning to understand spatial relations. Although some 3-year-olds confuse the dimensions "more-less," "big-small," and "tall-short," most 5-year-olds understand the differences between these related constructs.

● Grasping the Rules of Grammar

"We runned from the playground and seed the mouses in the cage," Ronnie tells the teacher. By the time he is 5 or 6 years old, Ronnie will be saying "ran," "saw," and "mice," applying the rules of English grammar.

Grammar is simply the set of rules that governs the use of words—how they are combined or altered—in a language. Formal schooling teaches us technical terms such as the parts of speech, participles, subjects, and objects; but young children figure out and apply many rules automatically simply by hearing other people speak.

For example, very young children catch on quickly to the basic structure of English sentences: subject-verb-object ("Dog chases ball"), and they learn to build on it. "*The big* dog chases *the red* ball" includes two articles and two modifiers. Soon, simple sentence structure gets expanded by joining two sentences with *and*: "The big dog chases the red ball, and he catches it," or "The big dog chases the red ball, and I chase the big dog."

Preschoolers also learn to modify statements in other ways—to negate, for example. At first they will simply add "no," as in "No dog chase ball"—which may mean anything from "The dog didn't chase the ball" to "I don't want the dog to chase the ball." Later they begin inserting negatives within a sentence: "Dog not chase ball." Still later, children start using the syntax that makes their meaning clear: "The dog didn't chase the ball," or "I don't want the dog to chase the ball."

Paradoxically, the kinds of errors children make reveal how much grammar they actually know. When Ronnie said, "We runned from the playground and seed the mouses in the cage," he used two rules of English grammar: He formed the past tense by adding *-ed* to the verb ("runned"), and he formed the plural by adding *-s* ("mouses"). But because the English language has many irregularities—"run/ran," "see/saw," "mouse/mice"—when children follow a rule too consistently, they make mistakes. Errors like these, applying the rules of grammar too regularly, are called **overregularization.**

Interestingly, 2- to 3-year-olds will use the correct past tense of irregular verbs, saying "ran" and "saw"; but later when they induce the *-ed* rule, they begin saying "ranned," "sawed," and even using a double past tense, saying "ated" and "wented" (Kuczja, 1978). Typically, preschoolers continue to overregularize, no matter how often others correct them:

> Child: My teacher holded the baby rabbits and we patted them.
> Mother: Did you say that your teacher held the baby rabbits?
> Child: Yes.
> Mother: What did you say she did?
> Child: She holded the baby rabbits and we patted them.
> Mother: Did you say she held them tightly?
> Child: No, she holded them loosely. (Cazden, 1968)

overregularization
applying grammatical rules too stringently

Preschoolers tend to be confused by complex sentences, especially when time relations are involved. Some of this confusion may stem from the child's still hazy sense of past, present, and future. If a parent says to a 4-year-old "Before you turn on the TV, you must finish your dinner," the child assumes that the first thing in the sentence is the first thing to be done, so she slides away from the table and turns on the television. It's as though she had heard "You turn on the TV, and then you finish your dinner"—two simple sentences joined together.

Finally, sentences that depart from the basic rule of simple sentence structure—subject-verb-object—may also confuse preschoolers. In a sentence such as "The dog was chased by the girl," the verb "was chased" is passive, and the grammatical subject of the sentence ("dog") is actually the object of the action described. But most children under 5 would interpret the sentence to mean that the dog chased the girl (Bever, 1970). Even so, preschoolers do understand passive constructions that make sense only in one direction: They would not hear "The food was eaten by the baby" as "The food ate the baby."

Although the rules of language can be acquired at any age, there is some evidence that language—whether a first language or a second language—is learned most easily and fluently in early or middle childhood (Newport, 1990). As you may know from your own experience, learning a new language after adolescence can be exceedingly difficult. Some researchers believe that there may be maturational changes in the brain that make certain periods of development more suitable to learning language quickly and efficiently than others (Johnson & Newport, 1989).

Language acquisition is also influenced by experience, especially in the family. Children whose parents regularly repeat back the child's ungrammatical statements and fill in missing words to make the statements grammatical (for example, Child: "Cat go Susie?" Parent: "Is the cat going to Susie?") display more complex grammar at an earlier age than children whose parents simply ignore their grammatical mistakes (Bohannon & Stanowicz, 1988; Nelson, Carskaddon, & Bonvillian, 1973). Although this sort of parental response is helpful, it is not necessary for children to learn language.

Several researchers have examined ethnic differences in early language development. In general, socioeconomic differences *within* ethnic groups (such as the differences in the speech of middle-class versus working-class African-American youngsters) are greater than ethnic differences between children from similar socioeconomic backgrounds (middle-class African-American youngsters versus middle-class white youngsters) (Brice-Heath, 1988; Feagans & Haskins, 1986). However, in assessing ethnic differences in language patterns, it is important to keep in mind the context in which the assessment is made: Black and white children may show similar patterns of speech when with their families and friends, but may show different patterns in school. In one study, for example, the researchers found that white children were more likely than black children to make requests of their teachers and teacher aides (Hall, Bartlett, & Hughes, 1988).

● **Communicating**

By ages 3 and 4, vocabulary is increasing rapidly, and most children have grasped basic grammar rules. But how skilled are they at communicating?

Communication preschool-style often resembles a monologue more than a conversation.

In many ways, children of 3 and 4 are quite accomplished: They can say what they want, they can bargain, they can hurl insults, they can lie, and they can manipulate. A 4-year-old can delay his bedtime for a long time with announcements and pleas. ("I want a drink of water." "I have to go pee-pee." "Sing me just one more song." "There's a tiger behind the door.") (Garvey & Hogan, 1973)

But still, communication is far from mature, especially when preschoolers are describing something for someone else to identify (Krauss & Glucksberg, 1977). (This is called **referential communication,** because it is communication that refers to something specific.) For example, a 3½-year-old tells her friend to go and get "Jenny doll" from her bedroom. The bed is covered with dolls. How will he know which one is Jenny? Typically, preschoolers fail to mention the relevant features of whatever it is they're describing. They also may describe something only in terms of their own experience—which may be meaningless to the listener.

If this reminds you of the egocentrism we discussed earlier, Piaget would have agreed. When children play, he noted, much of their talking resembles a monologue more than a conversation. They seem to talk to themselves without any regard for the listener. Thus Piaget considered the speech of preoperational children as egocentric. Consequently, he felt that the problems preschoolers have in communicating stem from their limited perspective-taking abilities and their egocentric cognitive viewpoint (Piaget, 1952). Communication does improve when we can see things from another's perspective. Preschoolers who are more advanced in perspective taking are also better at describing things—what we call referential communication (Roberts & Patterson, 1983). But Piaget seems to have overstated the relationship between egocentrism and preschoolers' speech. Newer research shows that preschoolers are better at communicating with language than Piaget assumed, and that it is not so much egocentrism that limits communication at this age but difficulty with processing information and coordinating communication skills (Shatz, 1983).

● **referential communication**
communication that refers to something specific

Preschoolers can take another's perspective and communicate effectively when speaking to younger children. Just as adults do (recall "motherese" from Chapter 5), 4-year-olds speak differently to 2-year-olds than to adults, altering their language to suit the younger child's cognitive level. For example, in one important study, 4-year-olds showed a new toy to adults and to toddlers (Shatz & Gelman, 1973). Speaking to the toddlers, they used simple short sentences and attention-grabbing language ("Watch this!" "Look here!"); but with adults, they were more polite, asked for more information, and referred to the adults' thoughts. Young children playing with mentally retarded peers will also simplify their language to be better understood (Guralnick & Paul-Brown, 1977).

Clearly, preschoolers' speech is more sensitive to others and less egocentric than Piaget thought. Preschoolers are also aware of what confuses them in a conversation, and at times, they know how to clear up their confusion (Schmidt & Paris, 1984). In one study, 3-, 4-, and 5-year-olds had to listen to a description of an object and then identify it (Lempers & Elrod, 1983). Some descriptions were clear; others were deliberately confusing. On the whole, the children *did* recognize the need for more, or more logical, information in two circumstances: when a red-haired doll was described but not shown, and when the description was not specific enough. When there were several red-haired dolls, the children didn't know which to pick.

Nevertheless, there are important limits on preschoolers' communication skills that are consistent with Piaget's characterization. In the study described in the preceding paragraph, the children did not realize that they needed more information, nor did they know how to ask for it when the description was interrupted by a fit of coughing or when the descriptions contained a mispronounced or nonsense word. Studies also show that preschool children do not recognize that someone cannot understand an ambiguous message (for example, someone points to a hat rack full of caps and says "Please get me my hat")

"Feather tickles." Explaining is only part of communicating. Even though a 3-year-old understands a young child's attempt to take turns, he may still go ahead and do as he likes.

without having the same knowledge as the speaker (that is, which hat belonged to the speaker) (Sodian, 1988).

We come now to the second major point about Piaget's claims of egocentrism and language. The preschoolers' problems with language may actually have more to do with information processing than with egocentrism (Menyuk, 1977). A speaker or a listener must figure out things such as: Is my partner (Am I) listening carefully? Does she (Do I) know what's really being talked about? Is she (Am I) familiar with the topic generally and/or specifically? Does she (Do I) care about it? As adults, we make these judgments almost automatically, but we didn't always. At 3 or 4 we could not have handled so much at once.

Preschoolers cannot easily *coordinate* all the skills we use in conversations—skills like gaining and keeping a listener's attention, paying attention to someone else, giving (or asking for) information, considering another person's point of view, and adjusting language accordingly. Preschoolers have these skills, but they don't use them automatically yet (Schmidt & Paris, 1984).

● Self-Communication: Inner Speech

"Put this piece here and this one here," says a 4-year-old doing a puzzle. When they think aloud, preschoolers are communicating with themselves, guiding their own actions (Vygotsky, 1962). Children frequently regulate their impulses by cautioning themselves the way a parent would. "Wait till company comes!" says a 4-year-old to herself, trying to stay away from a plate of cookies.

inner speech
verbal self-communication

Gradually this kind of self-communication, or **inner speech,** becomes silent, moving "inside" the head. Transitional steps include whispering or muttering to oneself and, later, silently mouthing the words.

The course of inner speech is well illustrated by recent studies (Berk & Garvin, 1984; Frauenglass & Diaz, 1985). Children aged 3½ to 6 solved complex problems like assembling puzzles and sorting pictures into categories (people, pets, furniture, foods—all things they were familiar with). As they worked, they talked aloud, whispered, muttered, or mouthed: "That piece won't fit here, it goes there"; "Cat goes with dog"; "That's ice cream, that's to eat." The youngest children spoke out loud far more than the older ones, who did much more whispering and muttering. The investigators concluded that inner speech does indeed go "underground" and helps direct children's thinking as the child matures.

Inner speech never disappears altogether. We've all heard ourselves and others say things like "1 cup of flour, 2 tablespoons of sugar" or "O.K., insert cassette, right . . . set input signal selector, right . . . push selector button." Psychologists and educators have found that teaching preschoolers as well as school-age children to "talk through" the steps of a troublesome process or repeat important instructions or reminders helps memory, increases patience, and improves schoolwork. Here, then, as at so many points, language, memory, and cognitive competence intersect.

● Bilingualism and Language Learning

Thousands of preschoolers whose parents recently emigrated to the United States are learning English and their parents' language simultaneously. Researchers who wondered about the effects of bilingualism found that young children tend to mix the two linguistic systems, thus developing an "interlanguage" system. In time, though, the two languages become distinct and develop independently (Garcia, Maez, & Gonzalez, 1981). Usually, at about age 3 or 4, children become aware of speaking two different languages (McLaughlin, 1984).

Problems are most likely to occur when children speak one language at home and learn a second through contacts with acquaintances and playmates. In many Mexican-American households in the Southwest, for example, parents and children speak Spanish to each other; but at school, children speak mostly in English (Garcia, 1983). This is a special problem for Spanish-speaking youngsters whose in-school English-language interactions are limited in either quantity or quality (Shannon, 1990). That is, simply because a Spanish-speaking child attends a school in which English is the primary language does not ensure that the child will have the high-quality interactions in English with teachers or other students that are necessary to become facile in the language. Conditions like these can upset the language-learning process as interference between the two languages increases. But even when learning a second language proceeds slowly among bilingual preschoolers, they usually catch up by the early elementary school years (McLaughlin, 1984).

Recent research shows that the development of English vocabulary, at least in the case of children from Hispanic backgrounds, is most advanced among first graders when *both* Spanish and English are spoken at home (Umbel et al., 1992). Moreover, learning a second language tends to be speediest for those most skilled with their primary language (Hakita & Garcia, 1989).

Beyond language development, researchers are also interested in knowing how bilingualism affects intellectual development overall. Among Spanish-speaking kindergartners and first graders who were learning English as a second language, studying English actually enhanced their general cognitive development (Diaz, 1985). For these children, researchers speculated that "the positive effects of bilingualism are probably related to the initial efforts required to understand and produce a second language" (Diaz, 1985, p. 1387). In fact, it

At the Metz School in Austin, Texas, a Hispanic kindergarten teacher reads to children in English and Spanish. Bilingualism has been shown to enhance the cognitive development of young children.

appears that the more bilingual a child is, the more intellectually flexible he is, and the more advanced is his concept formation and creativity. In short, bilingualism enhances cognitive development in young children (Hakita & Garcia, 1989).

CHILDREN'S ART: A SILENT LANGUAGE

Preschoolers happily cover sheets of paper with crayon, paint, and pencil marks, and their art reveals much about their development. First, progressive physical coordination allows children to move from scribbles to designs to representational art. Second, children learn to express their emotions through their art and symbolic play. Third, as children learn number sequences, the alphabet, and common words, they begin to draw and write to express their increasingly complex thoughts. Although 3-year-olds produce repetitive scribbles that may not have a theme or an apparent message, 4- and 5-year-olds invent elaborate stories for their art. Because drawing involves the manipulation of symbols, it can be a silent language, a nonverbal window on the young child's mind.

For example, in one research study, after children transferred to a new preschool program, some of them drew pictures with no mouths, distorted facial features, misplaced limbs, and dark colors, revealing the sadness and stress they were feeling after their move (Field, 1984). In another study, the drawings of 5-year-olds were related to the security of their attachments to their mothers (Assor, 1988). Researchers concluded that insecurely attached children were more likely to create drawings showing either too much or too little attention to their mothers. Sometimes the mother was much larger or much smaller than other figures; sometimes there were too many or too few details used to depict her (that is, with or without hair, ears, shoes, jewelry), and sometimes children drew themselves either very close or very far from their mothers.

By studying children's art, then, we can explore their thoughts and feelings about important people and events. Developing drawing skills, and possibly drawing styles as well, also reflect growing cognitive capacities. Just as in the development of language—where words come to stand for objects, people, and events—pictures also have a symbolic purpose: A picture of a horse is a symbol of the horse and proves that the child has some mental image of a horse. Being able to represent the world around us within our own minds, visually as well as verbally, and then to communicate these images in words or pictures is central to our intellectual growth; and like all development, these skills grow in stages.

● **From Scribbles to Pictures**

Until about age 3, drawing consists primarily of simple random marks—scribbles, basically. Rhoda Kellogg (1970), who has studied children's art extensively and identified four stages in its development, calls this scribbling phase the *placement stage.* In the next stage, the *shapes stage* (ages 3 to 3½), children combine marks to create crosses, squares, and closed curves. Recognizable geometric figures, such as rectangles and circles, combined and attached to one another—circles within circles or cross marks inside or radiating from a rectangle—emerge in the next stage, the *design stage* (from about 3½ to 4 or so). Finally, at about age 4 or 5, drawing becomes *representational:* Children begin

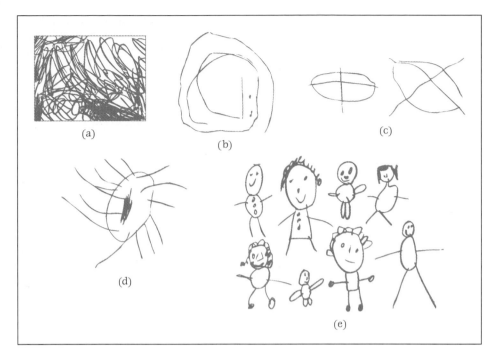

FIGURE 8.1
Children's Art: From Scribbles to Pictures
(a) Placement stage: scribbles (age 32 months); (b) basic shapes: circle (42 months); (c) design stage: combination designs (40 and 47 months); (d) pictorial stage: sun (45 months); (e) pictorial: humans (48 to 60 months). (SOURCE: Kellogg, 1970.)

to depict people, animals, buildings, flowers, and trees. This is called the *pictorial stage.* From this point on, children add increasing levels of detail to their drawing. Eventually, they will be able to combine images of single objects or people in one drawing or painting and so depict an entire scene or story: "Mommy on a business trip" or "Daddy and Mommy at home" (Fischer, 1983). Figure 8.1 provides some examples of the various stages in children's drawing.

Overall, children move logically from random marks to mastering simple components such as circles and rectangles, to more and more complex combinations of these things. This progression from simple to complex reflects the course of most development (Bruner, 1973; Fischer, 1983). Similarly too, there is considerable variation from child to child, as each pursues his own developmental way with pencil or crayon in hand. By 4 or 5, some children have even developed their own *style* of drawing, using favorite colors and shapes and even personal themes or subjects (Gardner, 1980).

Children's art creatively expresses their language, thoughts, and emotions. In the next chapter, you'll continue to see the interactive nature of development, as physical and cognitive development help to shape emotional and social development as well.

SUMMARY

1. During the preschool years, children gain less weight and grow fewer inches than at any other time until after puberty. By age 5 or 6, they have lost their baby look, as body proportions have become more adultlike. Both heredity and environment, especially nutrition, influence individual differences in children's growth rates. (See pages 234–236.)

2. Brain growth during early childhood promotes cognitive and social growth and is in turn promoted by those developments. Brain maturation is highly plastic in early childhood, and its rate and nature can therefore be affected by the child's experiences. (See page 237.)

3. Maturing gross motor skills and improved coordination and agility mean that preschoolers can ride bikes, throw and catch balls, swim, and do other athletic activities. Fine motor skills—which include smaller, more precise, and delicate movements—improve as well. A preference for one hand over the other appears by about age 5. (See pages 237–240.)

4. The ability to use symbols is the key feature of cognitive development at this age, according to Piaget's theory. Piaget described the thinking of 2- to 7-year-olds as preoperational, meaning that it was based on intuition, not on the rules of logic. According to Piaget, young preschoolers are often limited by their tendency to focus on one particular aspect of a problem at a time (centration), by a lack of understanding of how two processes can reverse each other (reversibility), and by a lack of understanding of states and transformations. One of the classic illustrations of these limitations is the failure of young preschoolers to understand conservation. (See pages 240–244.)

5. Although many of Piaget's conclusions about preschoolers' cognitive abilities have been supplanted by more modern research, his findings still have much to tell us about the limits of children's thinking. Nevertheless, recent studies indicate that children's abilities to "decenter," distinguish appearance from reality, understand cause and effect, work with numbers, and employ a naive "theory of mind" appear to be far more sophisticated than Piaget had proposed. (See pages 245–250.)

6. Information-processing theorists approach the study of cognitive development by studying the basic processes of thinking, such as memory. Studies show that throughout development, recognition memory is stronger than recall. Preschoolers use a variety of memory strategies, such as rehearsal, to aid their recall. (See pages 250–254.)

7. Language development during the preschool years includes an expanding vocabulary, acquiring the rules of grammar, and learning how to communicate with others. Typically, preschoolers apply grammatical rules too rigidly, making errors of overregularization. They also tend to be confused by complex sentences, especially when time relations are involved. Preschoolers have no trouble making their desires known, but when they are describing something for someone else to identify—referential communication—they are less accurate. (See pages 254–260.)

8. Inner speech describes a form of self-communication. When children speak aloud to themselves, they are guiding their own actions and regulating their impulses as a parent would. Gradually, their words become silent, what we call inner speech. We use inner speech even as adults, as an aid to memory and to assist us in solving problems. (See page 260.)

9. Children born to non-English-speaking parents tend to mix their parents' language and English until they are about 3 or 4. By that time they are aware

of speaking two different languages. Problems occur most often when children speak one language at home and another with friends. But even in such situations, bilingual children usually do well with their second language by the time they reach the early elementary school years. Furthermore, there is some evidence that bilingualism enhances cognitive development in young children. (See pages 260–262.)

10. Children's artwork reflects developing motor skills as well as cognitive abilities. It can also reveal a great deal about feelings and relationships. Technically, artwork moves from random marks to simple shapes (such as circles and rectangles) to complex combinations of figures. By age 4 or 5, many children have developed their own style of drawing, reflected in favorite shapes, colors, or subjects. (See pages 262–263.)

KEY TERMS

animism
centration
cerebral lateralization
conservation
egocentrism
fast-mapping
fine motor skills
gross motor skills
growth hormone
   deficiency
hand dominance
information processing

inner speech
interactive imagery
   (elaboration)
lead poisoning
memory strategies
metacognition
mutual exclusivity
overextension
overregularization
plasticity
preoperational period
recall memory

recognition memory
referential
   communication
rehearsal
reversibility
scripts
states and
   transformations
symbolic thought
thyroxine deficiency

SUGGESTED READINGS

de Villiers, P., and de Villiers, J. (1979). *Early language.* Cambridge, MA: Harvard University Press. A husband-wife team of researchers clearly present the process of language acquisition during the infancy, toddler, and preschool years. The many examples provided richly illuminate the phenomena under consideration.

Fraiberg, S. (1959). *The magic years.* New York: Scribner's. A classic by a renowned child psychologist who reveals the meaning of a child's behavior in terms of his or her own developing capabilities and limitations.

Gardner, H. (1980). *Artful scribbles.* New York: Basic Books. A developmental psychologist with expertise in neurological development provides an illuminating analysis of the drawings of children.

Rogoff, B. (1990). *Apprenticeship in thinking: Cognitive development in social context.* New York: Oxford University Press. An ecological perspective on the roles of culture and social relationships in children's cognitive development.

CHAPTER 9

SOCIAL AND EMOTIONAL DEVELOPMENT IN EARLY CHILDHOOD

Mollie, Stuart, and Margaret are absorbed in their latest version of "Are you my friend?" in which one child answers no, and then repeats the question to the next person.

"Are you my friend, Stuart?"

"No. Are you my friend, Mollie?"

"No. Are you my friend, Margaret? Now say yes. Now we all have to say yes, okay?"

Libby rushes into the doll corner, breathless. "Watch out, Mollie. Move! Samantha, hurry! Scream when you see John!"

"Can I do it?" Mollie asks.

"Hide, Amelia. Under there. Boys can't come in. No boys in here."

"No you don't, Libby," John shouts. "I'm Tri-Klops. Dump it out. I broke my leg."

"Well, I'm Trap Jaw," Erik says, "I'm eating this chair. Get off, Stuart."

"No, you don't," Libby warns. "No chair-eating in houses."

"Only girls live in houses," Maria calls from the crib. "Except if they're fathers."

"I'm a girl," Margaret says happily.

"Are you a girl, Erik?" Mollie asks.

"No, he ain't a girl, *girl*!" Maria screams.

"Can't you see he ain't a girl? Are you crazy?" (Paley, 1986, pp. 41–42)*

Mollie isn't at all crazy. She's a curious 3-year-old asking the questions all young children ask: Who are my friends? What sex am I? What can I do? Who will I become? Children puzzle over these questions throughout the preschool years, acting out their answers in fantasy after fantasy.

One of the most complicated puzzles preschoolers are piecing together concerns sex roles: How are boys and girls and men and women supposed to behave? Young children's thoughts on this subject will surprise many adults.

In this chapter, we'll explore *what* preschoolers think and *why*: Where do their ideas about sex roles come from? We'll focus too on the social skills with which preschoolers struggle—learning to share, to help, to wait, to make friends, to know when and how to be aggressive and when not to be. Why do these skills come more easily to some children than to others? We turn first to an aspect of development that we introduced in Chapter 6, one that we will follow throughout this book: the child's growing sense of self.

THE GROWING SELF

The toddlers of Chapter 6, taking their first shaky steps toward independence, struggled with remaining safe while moving away. Expressed in the temper tantrums and negativism of the "terrible twos," their conflict centered around becoming separate *from* one's mother (in Erikson's theory, the crisis of *autonomy versus shame and doubt*). Now the issue is on growing up in relation *to* mother, father, and the adult society. Secure enough to be independent from

*Several excerpts in this chapter are from V. G. Paley, *Mollie Is Three: Growing Up in School,* 1986. Reprinted by permission of the University of Chicago Press.

During the developmental period Erikson refers to as initiative versus guilt, *3-year-olds often try activities that are "off limits." When parents sensitively balance what is allowed and what is not, children are free to act with a minimum of anxiety about doing the wrong thing.*

parents for part of the day, preschoolers want to be *like* Mom and Dad. By age 3, most children would rather imitate adults than defy them.

Fantasies about adulthood fill their play. For example, when 3-year-old Alice gives herself a makeover with her mother's lipstick, eyeliner, powder, and blusher, she explains that she is trying to be a mommy and that when she is a grown-up, she will wear mommy's lipstick and live with daddy. Proud of their growing physical and mental skills, preschoolers like Alice don't always understand that they can't do everything adults can. But society's agents, parents and other adults, reveal the truth: Children may not do many of the things they think they can do or would like to do. From this conflict, says Erikson, comes the crisis of **initiative versus guilt,** a crisis balanced on one side by the wish to do and on the other side by prohibitions against doing.

Children who emerge from this developmental period with a sense of initiative feel confident that what they are inclined to do, as well as what they are inclined not to do, is consistent with the expectations of others. Not only does such a sense enable them to function free of worry—to take the initiative—but it also bolsters their positive feelings about growing up.

In contrast, children who emerge from this period with a strong sense of guilt are inhibited and remain unsure of the appropriateness of their actions. Rather than experiencing the pleasure of having done good, they often feel the anxiety of not doing right.

For parents and other caregivers, the challenge in fostering initiative rather than guilt involves striking a sensitive balance between the "mays" and the "may nots." Alice's mother, for example, can tell her that she may not wear mommy's makeup, but she can have some cosmetics of her own to play with. And when 4-year-old Mitchell drops eggs all over the floor while trying to imitate his father making pancakes, a sensitive parent can show him how to clean up the mess without belittling his attempt to cook like an adult.

initiative versus guilt
in Erikson's theory, the conflict for preschoolers between the wish to do and prohibitions against doing

Erikson subtitled this stage the "anticipation of roles." While pretending to be superheroes or mere adults, boys and girls are doing the emotional work of this stage: imagining themselves as competent adults, learning the rules of adult society. Among the most interesting and mysterious rules are those about gender—what it means to be male and female.

SEX-ROLE DEVELOPMENT

A 1950s picture book chronicles a Saturday afternoon in the lives of Bobby and Jane. Bobby helps his father build a bird house while Jane and her mother cheerfully clean house. When the children help their father hang a picture, Bobby wields the hammer while Jane holds the nails. In the kitchen, Mom is busy cooking.

> **sex roles**
> the tasks and traits that society assigns to females and males

> **sex-role development**
> how children learn to behave in the ways we call feminine and masculine

Between the lines of this innocent little book about middle-class family life is a powerful message about **sex roles,** the tasks and traits that society assigns to males and females: who does what work, who cares for the children, who can show which emotions. How children grow into these roles, how they come to behave in the ways we call masculine and feminine, is the process of **sex-role development.** How this process unfolds has been hotly debated by Freudians, Skinnerians, Piagetians, and sociobiologists. And fueling the debate today is the issue of the roles themselves. How did traditional sex roles affect children and the men and women they became? Are today's boys and girls getting a different message about masculinity and femininity than Jane and Bobby got? If they are, then why do preschool teachers still find more boys in the building corner than at the doll house (Paley, 1984)? The answers are multifaceted, as are the ways we think about masculinity and femininity in the 1990s.

● Masculinity and Femininity: A New View

Traditionally in Western society, masculinity and femininity were viewed as opposites. Independence, competitiveness, self-confidence, strength, and dominance were masculine traits. Gentleness, helpfulness, kindness, empathy, appreciativeness, and sentimentality were feminine traits. A person was *either* masculine or feminine. If you were strong, you could not also be sensitive: Real men didn't cry.

> **agency**
> active, assertive, and self-confident behavior

> **communion**
> supportive, helpful, and empathic behavior

Psychologists now emphasize that the qualities we call masculine and feminine exist to some extent in *both* sexes (Hall & Halberstadt, 1980; Harter et al., 1993; Huston, 1983). People who are helpful, gentle, and supportive, for example, can also be self-confident, independent, assertive, and competitive—whether they are men *or* women. To describe this new approach to masculinity and femininity, many social scientists use the terms *agency* and *communion*. **Agency** refers to active, assertive, and self-confident behavior that we do independently. **Communion** refers to supportive, helpful, empathic behavior that we do with or for others (Chodorow, 1978; Gilligan, 1982). People with many *communal* traits are considered strongly feminine, while those with strongly *agentic* traits are considered masculine. Men and women strong in both communal and agentic behaviors are *androgynous*.

While social scientists are coining new terms, children are busy trying to fig-ure out what it means to be male or female. And because of their cognitive lim-itations, most cling to more rigid views of what men and boys, women and girls, are really like. As we look at the way sex-role development unfolds, we'll try to answer three basic questions:

Sexism at a young age? Because of their cognitive limitations, preschoolers cling to sex-role stereotypes. Typically, boys shovel the dirt and girls pour the tea.

1. When do children know that they are either male or female?

2. Do boys and girls behave differently in early childhood?

3. Where do the differences come from, and do they have to exist at all?

Before we turn to these questions, we need to say a few words about the terms *sex* and *gender*. Some experts believe that the term *sex* should be reserved for dis-cussions of *biological* differences between males and females and the term *gen-der* for discussions of differences that are *socialized*, or learned. While we ap-preciate the spirit of this distinction, the problem with it, as you will read, is that we simply do not know whether many of the observed differences between males and females are due to biology, experience, or (most likely) a combina-tion of both. Gender and sex have been used more or less interchangeably in discussions of sex-role development (or is it "gender-role development"?), and that is how they are used in our discussion here.

● Gender Identity

Could you be a boy . . . if you wanted to be?

When you are grown up, will you be a woman or a man?

Have you ever been or can you ever be a boy?

Will you still be a girl if you wear boys' pants and cut your hair? If you play with trucks and soldiers?

When researchers asked preschoolers these questions, they got some sur-prising answers (DeVries, 1969; Marcus & Overton, 1978; Slaby & Frey, 1975). Three-year-old girls said they could become boys if they acted like them. And

A 3-year-old may really believe that he can become a she if he dresses for the part. By age 6, most children know that clothes can change, but gender is forever.

● **gender identity**
the knowledge that one is male or female

● **gender labeling**
differentiating between males and females

● **gender constancy**
the understanding that one's sex will never change

boys of this age report that a change of clothes or hairstyle can turn a George into a Georgia. The reason for this uncertainty about gender lies in the cognitive limitations of this age. As you read in the previous chapter, preschoolers often are easily fooled by appearances; they tend to focus on end states, not transformations. It is for this reason, too, that preschoolers believe that if a child's name is changed, so is his or her gender (Beal & Lockhart, 1989).

Children don't reliably know their **gender identity,** that they are boys or girls, until age 2 to 3. In fact, it is not until this age that children can reliably use the terms *boy* and *girl* to differentiate between males and females (**gender labeling**) (Etaugh, Grinnell, & Etaugh, 1989). And even after that, they aren't certain that gender is for life.

Not until age 6 or 7 do children understand that their sex will never change, that changing appearance cannot change gender (**gender constancy**) (Beal & Lockhart, 1989; Huston, 1983). This realization develops in stages. First, preschoolers begin to realize that wishing will not change their sex. Then, slowly, they comprehend that they *cannot* change their sex no matter what they do.

● Sex Stereotypes

By age 3, girls and boys "know" that blocks, hammers, trucks, and rough-and-tumble are for males; while pots and pans, dolls, and aprons are for females (Connor & Serbin, 1977; Huston, 1983). They "know" that pink is for girls and blue is for boys (Picariello, Greenberg, & Pillemer, 1990). Three-year-olds will actually avoid playing with toys associated with the other gender even when there are few alternatives (Hartup, Moore, & Sager, 1963). By age 5, boys often tell you that all the television commercials selling girls' toys are "yucky."

These social expectations about how boys and girls are to behave are **sex stereotypes** (or gender stereotypes). By age 4 or 5 children even have stereotypes for careers: When they play, nurses, teachers, and secretaries are girls; doctors, police officers, firefighters, truck drivers, and superheroes are boys (Huston, 1983).

sex stereotypes
social expectations about how males and females behave

Young children stereotype personalities as well as professions. Women are soft and gentle; men are brave and strong. In one study, when 5-year-olds from the United States, England, and Ireland listened to a story about a very gentle adult, nearly 80 percent of them said the person was a woman. Similarly, almost all the children identified a strong and robust character in another story as a man (Best et al., 1977).

Did the children of the 1980s, half of whose mothers worked outside the home, learn a different lesson? No. Sex stereotypes continue to thrive among preschool girls and boys (Liben & Bigler, 1987). They may even be a necessary step in the gender-identification process (Stangor & Ruble, 1987). That is, just as crawling usually precedes walking, stereotyped thinking may be the foundation for nonstereotyped thinking (Lobel & Menashin, 1993).

Recent research in this field suggests that boys are less likely to change their stereotyped views of gender differences than girls (Katz & Walsh, 1991). This may be because when it comes to sex-stereotyped behaviors, breaking the rules is riskier for boys than for girls. Boys who play with Barbie or princess dolls, for example, are more likely to be teased, or simply ignored, than girls who play with Ken or X-Men. And when adults try to encourage less stereotyped ideas and behaviors, men get better results than women, perhaps because male adults are seen as more powerful and reinforcing of stereotypes in the first place (Katz & Walsh, 1991). If a man indicates that it's all right to do some "girl things," then a boy can relax his guard a bit.

Differences in Boys' and Girls' Behavior

In her vividly detailed book, *Boys and Girls: Superheroes in the Doll Corner,* Vivian G. Paley records the behaviors of preschool boys and girls. In scene after scene, boys play more physically and aggressively than girls: While the boys chase Darth Vader to the "death star," the girls play mother and baby in the doll corner. In the "tumbling room" boys run and climb, resting only when they "fall down dead." The girls do somersaults and then "stretch out on the mats and watch the boys." But when the boys leave, the girls indulge, at least temporarily, in more characteristic "boy" behavior. "The change is dramatic," writes Paley. "With the boys gone, the girls run, climb, and tumble with a new vitality" (1984, p. 66). But soon they return to their doll play. Even in very recent research, "boys tend to think and behave in a more sex-stereotypical manner than do girls" (Lobel & Menashin, 1993).

Throughout this discussion, though, remember that statements about sex differences are statements about *averages.* Many boys and girls are more or less aggressive than the norm, an example of the overlapping distributions commonly found in scientific research. We are talking about consistent *patterns* of behavior. The main pattern Paley observed is the basic difference between young boys and girls everywhere: *Most* boys are more active and aggressive than *most* girls (Block, 1983; Parke & Slaby, 1983). Their play is rougher, they try more often to dominate their peers, and their behavior is more antisocial. Boys are far more likely than girls, even during the preschool years, to respond to a physical assault with physical force (Duvall & Cheyne, 1981). Even children themselves notice the difference.

> Karen: Girls are nicer than boys.
>
> Janie: Boys are bad. Some boys are.
>
> Paul: Not bad. Pretend bad, like bad guys.
>
> Karen: My brother is really bad.
>
> Teacher: Aren't girls ever bad?
>
> Paul: I don't think so. Not very much.
>
> Teacher: Why not?
>
> Paul: Because they like to color so much. That's one thing I know. Boys have to practice running.
>
> Karen: And they practice being silly. (Paley, 1984, pp. 25–26)

Boys also tend to do more exploring than girls. For example, they will work harder to get around barriers blocking them from things they want (Block, 1983). Preschool girls handle frustration and control their impulses better than boys do, but they are also anxious and timid more often than boys. Three- and four-year-old girls also tend to be both more nurturant and more compliant (Best et al., 1977).

These behavior differences show up once children are firmly aware of their gender identity. At 2 and 3, boys will still join the girls in the doll corner, but by age 4 or so, most boys keep out or enter only on brief forays. Superheroes have taken over. However, while they may not like to admit it, boys too are playing with dolls. Their "action figures"—cartoon characters, soldiers, robots—are just dolls in tough-guy clothes. The real difference is in the way they think about and use them. Again, the boys focus on action fighting and physical strength, while the girls play at mothering and dressing up.

By the time children reach kindergarten, the division between the sexes is firmly set, and as they play, children seek separate social distinctions for "boy" and "girl." In one kindergarten class, for example:

> You hop to get your milk if you are a boy and skip to the paper shelf if you are a girl. Boys clap out the rhythm of certain songs; girls sing louder. Boys draw furniture inside four-story haunted houses; girls put flowers in the doorways of cottages. Boys get tired of drawing pictures and begin to poke and shove; girls continue to draw. (Paley, 1984, p. xi)

There is no disputing the evidence that sex-typed behavior begins early and matches, in many ways, the adult sex stereotypes of our culture. Why?

● Nurture/Nature and Sex-Typed Differences

In the classic nature/nurture debate, the nature side claimed that inborn, biological differences shaped behavior as well as bodies, while the environmen-

Nature and *nurture predispose preschool girls to play more quietly than preschool boys.*

talists said boys and girls are *taught* to be different. Today, we would argue that both sides are right; as with all other aspects of development, biology and experience are both at work.

● *Biological explanations.* Animal behavior studies reveal that in every mammalian species, males are more aggressive than females, beginning early in life. Among our own species too, in preschools and on playgrounds, boys tend to hit, push, and shove more than girls do. Such universals always *suggest* (even if they do not prove) at least a partially biological basis for behavior. It may be that the hormone testosterone, at higher levels in boys' blood at birth, accounts for greater aggression in males (Maccoby, Doering, Jacklin, & Kraemer, 1979; Susman et al., 1987). In fact, girls who have been prenatally exposed to especially high levels of **androgens** (the class of hormones, including testosterone, that males have in higher levels) develop more traditionally masculine and fewer traditionally feminine interests. They are more likely than other girls to be described as tomboys, and they tend not to play with dolls (Berenbaum, 1990; Money & Ehrhardt, 1972). In one study, both girls and boys who had been exposed before birth to synthetic androgens scored higher in physical aggression than their unexposed siblings (Reinisch, 1981).

This kind of evidence underscores the influence of biological factors on aggression and other sex-typed behavior. But we must also point out that biochemistry and behavior affect one another. Not only do hormones influence behavior, but experience and behavior can affect hormone levels. Being aggressive, for example, can stimulate the production of androgens, leaving researchers wondering which comes first.

● **androgens**
the class of hormones, including testosterone, that occur in higher levels in males

● **Psychoanalytic explanations.** Recall from Chapter 1 that Freud saw infant and child development as a series of stages in which children gain control of basic biological urges. Emotionally healthy children can resolve the conflicts between their biological drives and the demands of society at each stage of development. For Freud, the conflict of the preschool years centers around the biological urges of genital sexuality. (See the discussion of the *phallic stage* in Chapter 1.) During this stage, children wish to "possess" the opposite-sex parent: "I'm going to marry daddy," says a little girl, while a little boy imagines himself as mommy's husband.

In these wishes, said Freud, are the seeds of conflict. A little boy needs his father but fears he will be punished for being his father's rival, a fear Freud labeled **castration anxiety.** Freud termed this struggle the Oedipus complex (Chapter 1) because of its similarity to the classic Greek story of Oedipus, who unknowingly killed his father and then married his mother. The Oedipal conflict is resolved when the boy *represses* (removes or rejects from consciousness) his desire for his mother and identifies with his father. In this process of **identification,** the boy works to become just like his father—to incorporate the father's behaviors, attitudes, beliefs, and values into himself. That is how he learns what it means to be a male.

In the same way, a girl, said Freud, wants her father for herself and fantasizes about her mother going away or dying. He called this internal struggle the Electra complex (see Chapter 1) after the Greek legend in which Electra plots to kill her mother. The little girl becomes aware of her father's love for his wife and feels jealous but also fears her mother. Gradually, she represses her desire for her father and identifies with her mother. Through this identification the little girl learns what it means to be female. Freud also believed that girls were

● **castration anxiety**
Freud's label for a little boy's fear that he will be punished for being his father's rival

● **identification**
a process in which children adopt the same-sex parent's attitudes, behaviors, and values

According to Freudian theory, learning to use tools like his father promotes this 4-year-old's identification as a male.

jealous of the male's penis and felt diminished by its absence, a condition he called "penis envy."

Many psychologists disagree, suggesting that what girls want is the independence and power that boys are raised to expect. Theories of identification differ too. Nancy Chodorow (1974) argues that girls have an easier path to their sexual identity because their mothers see them as similar to themselves. They view their sons as different and opposite. Boys, then, define themselves as being different from and separate from their mothers, while girls grow up feeling connected.

This theory also suggests that because girls do not have to distinguish themselves from their mothers in the way that boys do, they develop a capacity for closeness that is denied to boys. Some psychologists believe that boys' struggle to become separate and different from their mothers makes it harder for them to achieve intimacy as adults. And their different paths to selfhood may explain why males are more threatened by intimacy while females are more threatened by separateness (Gilligan, 1982).

Along with the attitudes and behaviors that come with gender identification, children also internalize their parents' moral standards. These standards form the *superego,* or conscience, and they mark the beginning of moral development (see Chapter 1). Freud believed that with the resolution of the Oedipal/Electra complex, children would become increasingly able to regulate their moral behavior from within, via the superego. But research suggests that much younger children experience guilt, undermining the validity of some psychoanalytic claims, or at least of Freud's timetable (Zahn-Waxler & Kochanska, 1991).

Several research studies do support Freud's view that sex-role development hinges on the child's identification with the same-sex parent. When same-sex parents are accepting, warm, and nurturing, children generally show "appropriate" sex typing and are apt to imitate that parent (Biller & Borstelmann, 1967; Mussen, 1969). "Appropriate" appears in quotes here because in Freud's world, late-nineteenth-century Viennese society, girls were expected to be submissive and sweet. Self-assertion, let alone aggression, was for males only.

Although Freud's ideas about the sexes reflected the thinking of his time, his understanding of the *process* of sex identification is important. When the opposite-sex parent encourages sex-typed behavior, a child is even more likely to behave in traditionally masculine or feminine ways. So a little girl with an affectionate, supportive mother and a father who gives her dolls and praise for acting like a "little lady" is most likely to behave in a typically feminine way (Hetherington, Cox, & Cox, 1978b).

What happens when the same-sex parent is absent? Some research on boys without fathers seems to support Freud's ideas. In a number of studies, boys with absent fathers did score lower on sex-role orientation scales and were less interested in masculine-typed activities than boys whose fathers lived at home (Beere, 1979; Drake & McDougall, 1977). Boys who showed the most lasting effects had been separated from their fathers before age 5—before gender identity was set. The point is not that boys must have fathers at home for healthy sex-role development, but that, according to Freudian theory, a boy needs to identify with some involved male figure: stepfather, uncle, older brother, or family friend (Chapman, 1977; Shinn, 1978). Even without a father or father substitute, however, mothers can encourage their sons (and their daughters) to be assertive and independent (Biller, 1970).

● *Cognitive explanations.* Biological explanations for sex-role development stress biochemical and genetic factors. Psychoanalytic explanations stress emotion and the process of identification with the same-sex parent. For cognitive theorists, the child's developing intellectual abilities and limitations are critical. According to cognitive developmental theorists, such as Lawrence Kohlberg (1966), sex-role development begins by age 3, when children first label themselves boys or girls. Recall that during the period Piaget called preoperational thinking, children slowly come to understand that gender never changes (Chapter 8). We can think of gender constancy, then, as conservation of gender, another conservation task to be mastered: Like liquids, number, and mass, gender stays the same despite changes in appearance. Research studies confirm that understanding conservation of gender happens only after children comprehend the conservation of physical quantities (Marcus & Overton, 1978). Indeed, the two go together: When children of the same age are tested on conservation tasks, those who perform best are also more aware that gender is fixed (DeLisi & Gallagher, 1991). Just as they need to decenter before they know that Miss Piggy is a costume, by the end of the preoperational stage, children understand that a boy is a boy is a boy even if he's wearing a dress, and a girl is a girl is a girl even if her hair is short and she climbs trees.

Cognitive theorists contend that once children have finally identified their sex, new information gets sorted by gender. Boys do this; girls do that. Children learn what *is* appropriate and what is *not* appropriate for their own sex by watching adults and processing the information they gather. Then they act according to the way they've divided the world. Such processes have been observed in children as young as 2 years of age! In one recent study, 24- to 26-month-olds watched as adults used children's toys to perform traditionally male and female activities, such as building a house, cooking, and shaving a teddy bear or changing its diaper. Then, the children were asked to imitate the adults' activities using the same play materials. While young boys were willing and able to imitate such traditionally male activities as building a house and shaving a teddy bear, they did not imitate traditionally female activities, such as pretending to cook or changing the teddy bear's diaper (Bauer, 1993).

Not only do children divide the world into male/female functions, but cognitive theorists stress that they actively process whatever behavior they see. If what they see doesn't match what they think they *should* see, they change it. If, for example, you show young children pictures or videotapes of girls playing with trucks and boys playing with dolls and then, several days later, you ask them what they saw, they are likely to tell you that boys were playing with the trucks and girls were playing with dolls. In effect, preschoolers transform what they saw into what they think they *should* have seen (Liben & Signorella, 1993; Martin & Halverson, 1981). In the study described above, for example, some of the boys who watched the teddy bear being diapered insisted on shaving the bear instead (Bauer, 1993).

Because of the way children process information, we can't count on them to abandon stereotypes from a few exposures to nontraditional situations: Seeing a female doctor on television or looking at a book about a father who stays home with the baby won't revamp their thinking. What parents and teachers think young children are seeing and learning may be far different from what they are actually comprehending (Liben & Bigler, 1987). In fact, efforts to modify sex-role stereotypes in the preschool years have not been very successful, in part because of young children's tendency to transform nonstereotyped roles (a male nurse, for example) into traditional sex-stereotyped images (a female nurse or a male doctor) (Bigler & Liben, 1990). Sex-stereotyped behavior becomes rewarding in its own right, say cognitive theorists, because it is consistent with the child's ideas about being male or female, and because imitating mom and dad reaffirms this belief.

Recent research carried out in Israel supports the role of cognition in sex-role development. When children are less stereotyped in their thinking about the way boys and girls should behave, they are more likely to play with nonstereotypical toys (boys-dolls, girls-cars) (Lobel & Menashin, 1993).

● *Social learning explanations.* "Can I have this doll, Daddy?" asks 3-year-old Michael in the toy store. "Wouldn't you like this truck instead?" says Dad. Over and over, boys and girls hear, see, and experience different messages about what it means to be male or female; and, say the social learning theorists, they learn these lessons well, through both *direct reinforcement* (rewards for specific behaviors) and *modeling* (imitation).

Sex-based messages begin even before babies leave the hospital. In a number of studies, parents perceived their own newborn girls as smaller, finer featured, softer, and less alert than boys. Adults who didn't know each baby's sex saw none of these differences, and indeed, they did not exist. Both men and women offer a doll more often to the baby dressed in pink and give a stereotypical masculine toy more often to the baby in blue (Frisch, 1977; Smith & Lloyd, 1978; Will, Self, & Datan, 1976). Fathers "see" greater sex differences than mothers, judging newborn sons as hardier and stronger than daughters (Rubin, Provenzano, & Luria, 1974). Even children assign different traits to babies, depending on what color the infants are wearing (Stern & Karraker, 1989).

As they grow up, boys and girls aren't just perceived differently, they are reinforced (rewarded) (Chapter 1) for *behaving* differently—according to sexual stereotypes (Block, 1983). Contrary to what many developmentalists have thought, parents *do not* play with boys more or encourage sons to be more achievement-oriented than daughters. And girls *are not* nurtured more or treated more warmly than boys. What parents do, though, is expect boys and girls to play with different things and to do different household chores. In fact, a survey of studies involving over 27,000 children and their parents found that the only reliable differences in the way parents treat sons and daughters center around sex-typed play and activities (Lytton & Romney, 1991). Parents expect and encourage boys to play with trucks and blocks and to help with snow shoveling and "fix-it" jobs. They offer their daughters dolls and dust cloths.

How, though, do we know that parents aren't simply reacting to differences they see in their children? Are they responding to what their sons and daughters seem to want, or are parents actively guiding their children toward traditional male and female behaviors? Although both are possible, a look at infants' (5-, 13-, and 25-month-olds) rooms, at least in white middle-class families, suggests an answer. Sports equipment, toy tools, cars, and trucks fill boys' rooms, while more dolls and fictional characters waited for the girls (Pomerleau, Bolduc, Malcuit, & Cossette, 1990).

Parents who hold the most traditional attitudes about sex roles are also those who most strongly encourage sex-typed behaviors in their children. As an offshoot, these children can label males and females as boys and girls earlier than

Showing children that most things in life can be done by either sex will help them avoid stereotypic thinking about sex roles.

other children do (Fagot, Leinbach, & O'Boyle, 1992). Apparently, parents' values affect their behavior, which then influences children's understanding of gender.

But the agents of social influence aren't only parents. Children themselves socialize each other toward traditional sex-typed behaviors (Langlois & Downs, 1980; Martin, 1989). The harshest treatment falls to boys who cross the line. A girl who prefers building to Barbies may be considered odd, but the boy who routinely opts for the doll corner courts teasing and worse (Fagot, 1977; Roopnarine, 1984). Perhaps because they are sensitive to what their peers think about them, preschoolers tend to follow the crowd when it comes to play. Boys tend to go where the boys are, and girls group with girls. In effect, then, peers socialize each other to play by the gender-typed rules (Shell & Eisenberg, 1990).

Theorists would argue that real change will come only when what children hear matches what they see. The second component of social learning, **modeling,** or imitation, is a powerful teacher. When only mothers do housework, for example, children can grow up thinking that vacuums and mops are for women only. Mother may indeed work outside the home, but she is still very likely to make dinner and clean the house. Dad may do some laundry now, but mom is more often the one who changes the diapers. Only when parents share these chores will children learn that housework and child care are gender-free activities.

Nevertheless, children's ideas are changing. Daughters whose mothers are employed show less traditional and stereotypical thinking about family roles (who does the laundry), careers (who can arrest bad guys), and even toy play (who can play with superheroes) (Baruk, Feldman, & Noy, 1991; Katz, 1987; Levy, 1989).

● *Television, books, and sex roles.* A major source of both sex-role models and reinforcement of traditional sex-role stereotypes is television (Calvert &

● **modeling**
a component of social learning that involves imitation

Huston, 1987; Huston et al., 1992). Despite her career as a lawyer, Claire Huxtable on *The Cosby Show* was always home and available to her children. And Carol Brady is there for her bunch on television reruns. Even newer programs with up-to-the-minute technology are often saturated with sex-role stereotypes. Most superhero cartoon shows include a token female warrior among the male characters, but in these cartoon series, guess which sex is most often captured or caged or tied up by the villain. It's the woman almost every time who plays the victim's role.

Women characters are greatly underrepresented in all television programming, and especially in programs for children, though the 1980s saw some improvement (Huston et al., 1992). Even during commercial breaks, sex stereotyping is the rule: Little boys play with building sets, robots, and cars, while little girls play with dolls, stuffed animals, and jewelry. In adult commercials, too, the message continues. For the most part, the men still clinch the deals, drive the cars, and have the fun, while the women do the laundry and shine the floors.

Exceptions to sex typing in the media certainly exist. On *Sesame Street, Mister Rogers, 3-2-1 Contact* and *Barney,* women can be leaders, men can talk about feelings, and both sexes perform nontraditional activities. And in many new children's books, girls and women are strong central characters. Nevertheless, the media are still more likely to reinforce traditional sex roles than to be a force for change.

We began this discussion by noting that no one theory can fully explain sex-role development. If you review the material you've just read, you can see the overlap among them. Freudians and social learning theorists both acknowledge the role of models, for example. Each theory represents a different emphasis—feeling, thinking, biology, and behaving—and so all four help to explain how children acquire sex-typed behavior. Unconscious emotional development (psychoanalytic theory) blends with cognitive development and is reinforced by social learning. And all these processes are influenced by the inborn, biologically based characteristics of every child.

Given the fact that, through a variety of processes, young girls and boys do show sex-typed behaviors, primarily around aggression, this raises another question: How do these differences matter?

● How Do Sex Differences Matter?

Until the women's movement gained momentum in the 1970s, few people cared very much about the different ways in which boys and girls were raised, about the different ways they were taught to think about their futures, or about the vastly different opportunities that were open to them just because of their sex. But the writings of feminists forced us to consider the implications of sex differences for boys and girls and for society as a whole.

If we lived in a nonindustrial culture, where men hunted for food and women tended to the children and did the agricultural tasks, it would make sense to encourage aggression in boys and nurturance in girls. But in industrial societies, where food is mass produced and distributed, what do we gain by fostering traditional sex-related differences? In the workplace and at home some assertiveness and nurturance are needed by *both* sexes. In modern societies, it would make more sense to deemphasize the differences between the sexes.

The women's movement has also made many of us aware of the potential both sexes have for the full range of human behavior and emotions. Not all men are good at sports; not all can be as assertive as others. Not all women are comfortable being full-time nurturers, and when girls are encouraged to be too passive, society loses as well. If, instead, all children are encouraged to be fully themselves, boys and girls may then grow up to be more complete men and women.

DEVELOPING SOCIAL SKILLS

"Use your words; don't hit!" "Wait your turn," "Share the crayons." "Don't throw the sand." "We don't spit." The timeless litany of parents and teachers encourages children to control aggression, to talk rather than fight, to cooperate, to share, and to wait one's turn. All are social skills that children struggle to learn for many years. Maturing as social beings can take a lifetime, but from 2 to 6, children begin to learn the patterns of social life and the way adults expect them to behave.

● The Development of Prosocial Behavior

Five-year-old Candace is trying to comfort Elihu, a younger friend:

> "Want some pizza?" Candace asks.
> "No, I don't want pizza," Elihu says through his tears.
> "Want to ride on my bicycle?" Candace offers.
> "No, I don't wanna ride on a bicycle," Elihu says, tears still streaming down.
> "Want to see a dragon?" Candace asks in a conspiratorial tone, putting her arm around him.
> "Yeah," Elihu replies, his expression shifting almost instantly from a sorrowful frown to an eager smile. (Rubin, 1980, p. 20)

empathize
to know what another person is feeling

Candace's ability to **empathize**—to know what another person is feeling—may have begun in the crib. Infants and 1-year-olds cry when they hear other babies crying, and while some claim that this is just emotional copying, sharing feelings may actually be the first step toward mature empathy (Radke-Yarrow et al., 1983; Sagi & Hoffman, 1976; Simner, 1971). One toddler will pat another who is crying, and 2-year-olds offer more elaborate help. They may bring a teddy bear to the distressed child, and if that doesn't help, they'll try something else. They sympathize, bring someone to help, and try to change the other's sad feelings (Radke-Yarrow et al., 1983; Zahn-Waxler & Radke-Yarrow, 1982).

Two- and three-year-olds will spontaneously give gifts and share their toys with other children and with unfamiliar adults. At these ages, gift giving is a way to begin and maintain social contact, and the gifts may be everyday objects such as pieces of wood or stone (Stanjek, 1978). Helping, too, begins early. Children will stop what they are doing to clear an obstacle from another's path. They'll also help each other clean up spilled puzzles and the like (Iannotti, 1985, p. 53).

Children who comfort others most often tend to be more sociable and happier than children who are less empathetic.

Empathy for other children in distress, cooperation with others to achieve common goals, and helping all increase during the preschool years (Bar-Tal et al., 1982; Hart et al., 1992; Marcus et al., 1979; Rheingold, 1982). Some children show more of these positive behaviors than others (Murphy, 1937, 1992), and the *tendency* for some children to be more benevolent than others seems to be stable over time: Four-year-olds who were generous, cooperative, empathic, considerate, and helpful were also generous at 5. And children who are socially responsible in nursery school are still behaving more responsibly than their peers 5 to 6 years later (Eisenberg, 1992; Mussen & Eisenberg-Berg, 1977).

Developmentalists call these positive, helping acts **prosocial behavior,** and they have studied it in several different ways. Researchers are curious about both *who* is likely to be prosocial and *why*? Which children are most likely to care for others? Which are most likely to be cared for? And where does caring behavior come from to begin with?

Whether a child is first- or later-born, from an economically advantaged or disadvantaged family, or a boy or a girl does not seem to affect prosocial behavior. Two qualities that do make a difference are sociability and how often children express happiness and other positive emotions. Children who are interested in being with others offer help more than shier children; and those who laugh and smile often help more than children who show positive emotions less often (Eisenberg, 1992).

Prosocial children also tend to be more assertive: Those who defend their own needs are more likely to help others defend theirs as well and to share spon-

● **prosocial behavior**
positive, helping acts

taneously. In contrast, timid children tend to help only when asked, perhaps because they want to avoid conflict. Finally, prosocial children are generally well adjusted and good at coping with stress. In sum, "children with strong prosocial dispositions tend to be emotionally expressive, socially skilled, assertive and well adjusted" (Eisenberg, 1992, p. 43).

But even among this group, help isn't offered equally and to all. Children are kindest and most helpful toward those they play with the most. Generally these are also the children who share with and help *them* the most (Eisenberg, 1992).

While the research we described above reveals many characteristics of prosocial children, it doesn't explain how children become prosocial. Three major explanations have been offered to explain why some children are more prosocial than others. They are derived from attachment, cognitive, and social learning theories.

● *Attachment explanations.* Recall from Chapter 6 that securely attached infants are also more secure as preschoolers, and that a sense of security fosters positive social skills. Research has shown that social skills are indeed better developed in children who had secure attachments. In one study, 3½-year-olds who had been securely attached were the ones other children wanted to play with. They were less withdrawn, more likely to be leaders, and more sympathetic to their peers' distress than preschoolers who had been judged insecure as infants (Kestenbaum, Farber, & Sroufe, 1989).

In effect, preschoolers who, as infants, had developed a strong sense of basic trust tend to see the world as dependable and safe. Free to relate to others without too much anxiety and anger, they learn more readily how to give and take, how to perceive the needs of others. These children will probably welcome social experiences, and by the time they are 4 to 5 years old, they'll have a well-developed set of social skills. Relating to their peers in a friendly, positive way will come naturally.

● *Cognitive explanations.* "Why were you nice to Scott?" "Why did you give him a cookie?" When researchers ask these kinds of questions, boys and girls explain their behavior by talking about the needs of the other ("He's hungry") or about their own needs ("I wanted to"). Other reasons include friendship ("He's my friend") and the wish for approval ("He'll like me") (Eisenberg, 1992; Eisenberg-Berg & Neal, 1979). Sometimes, simple pragmatism motivates helping behavior: Why did a 4-year-old wipe up a table after snack? "Because it was wet," he explained.

For cognitive theorists, empathy and prosocial behavior are linked to perspective taking (Eisenberg, 1992). Recall that Piaget thought that egocentrism limited preschoolers' abilities to take another's perspective. Indeed, sometimes children comfort one another in ways that suggest cognitive limitations: "Suck your thumb!" one child may say to a friend (or an adult) who is crying. A young child will even bring his own mother to comfort another child, even if the crying child's mother is already present. Such responses to another's distress can sound very much like the egocentrism Piaget identified in young children (Chapter 8). As their egocentrism lessens and perspective-taking capacities grow, young children's prosocial behaviors increase. "Doing the right thing" increases, too, as children learn to identify what others are actually feeling (Cassidy et al., 1992; Eisenberg, 1992). This kind of sensitivity is enhanced when parents speak to their children about feelings—sadness, anger, happiness, jealousy—during the preschool years (Dunn, Brown, & Bearsdall, 1991).

● ***Social learning explanations.*** For social learning theorists, kindness can result from imitation. In one study, preschoolers who had observed an adult model sharing, helping, and being sympathetic acted more like that themselves 2 weeks later than children who had not seen such a model (Yarrow et al., 1973). And the effects of more extensive modeling seem to endure beyond several days and sometimes even several months (Radke-Yarrow et al., 1983). Children also get reinforced for being sympathetic and for sharing, helping, and cooperating: "That's a good girl." "You're a nice boy." "Thank you for helping" (Fabes et al., 1989). Finally, the act of giving can itself make a child feel good, becoming rewarding in itself (Hay & Rheingold, 1979).

The results of research on prosocial behavior have had some direct practical benefits, shaping the creation of both classroom and parent-education programs to promote prosocial behavior (Doescher & Suganara, 1992; Honig & Pollock, 1990; Mize & Ladd, 1990). Typically these efforts focus upon making children aware of the feelings of others and how nice it feels to be helped, rewarding prosocial behavior, and modeling it as well.

● Controlling Aggression

Christopher pushes Barney down in the playground and then again in the hallway. I [teacher, Vivian Paley] stand between the boys, glaring down at Christopher.

"No, Christopher. You can't push people."

"I'm pushing Barney," he says without emotion.

"No, you must not do it. We won't let you."

"I'm pushing Barney."

"He saw someone doing it on the playground," Mrs. Alter explains. "Some boy in the other class. Now he keeps saying that he's pushing Barney."

Mollie screws up her face. "Don't push Barney!"

"Don't say it," Christopher tells her.

"Mollie can say it, Christopher. Everyone can tell you not to push Barney."

[author's italics] (Paley, 1986, p. 22)

Later that morning, Christopher pushes Barney off a step and Ms. Paley intervenes again. "Christopher, you'll have to stay next to me all morning. You can sit in my lap or in a chair or hold my hand." "Why?" "So I can be sure you won't push Barney. You have that idea in your mind and it keeps coming out" (p. 25). Sensitively, patiently, Vivian Paley helps Christopher control his aggression, but it is a lesson he will have to keep learning throughout the preschool years. Many preschoolers become physically aggressive until they gradually learn to use words instead of fists.

This change is possible because language skills and emotional control are both maturing. While children are getting better at saying what they want, they're also better at controlling what they do. At the same time, adults expect more control from them, so what's happening within the child is encouraged from without as well. Preschoolers begin to follow their teachers' instructions to "use words" to handle disputes, and they may be punished for fighting. The older a child is, the more likely that she or he will react to an insult with some

Until preschoolers gain emotional control, force often takes the place of words.

● **instrumental aggression**
aggression arising out of conflicts over ownership, territory, and perceived rights

● **hostile aggression**
physical and/or verbal aggression that is deliberately harmful

choice words rather than with a slap or a kick. Even though boys tend to be more aggressive than girls at all ages, both sexes show these developmental trends.

Boys and girls also show the same two types of aggression: **Instrumental aggression** arises out of conflicts over ownership, territory, and perceived rights. Mary, for instance, might slap Paul for playing with her stuffed dog. Annie's older brother may kick her if her foot gets too close to his sand castle. This type of aggression decreases first. The second type, hostile aggression, abates more slowly. **Hostile aggression** can be both physical and verbal and is directed against another person. In short, it is deliberately harmful.

A child's level of aggression tends to be stable, so a highly aggressive preschooler is likely to be a more aggressive school-age child as well (Olweus, 1979, 1982b; Parke & Slaby, 1983). But researchers have found that this tendency need not mean inevitability. If the forces that encourage a child to be highly aggressive change, we can expect the child's tendencies to change too. But if conditions remain the same, aggressive children are very likely to become troubled adolescents. In fact, after updating the New York Longitudinal Study, Alexander Thomas concluded that *aggression in childhood is the emotional trait that is the strongest predictor of later maladjustment.* Why some children have trouble controlling their aggression is a question with many answers. (See Controversy: Guns in the Toy Chest, page 288.) Cognitive and social learning theories offer explanations that may actually work together.

● *Cognitive explanations of aggression.* Two children standing in line waiting for a drink are each bumped from behind. One turns and pushes the child who bumped him, who then pushes back. Fighting begins. The other child casts a questioning look and says, "Be careful." The child who did the bumping then apologizes, explaining that another child pushed *him.*

Two bumps, two reactions. Why? For cognitive theorists, interpretation is extremely important. How you respond to people depends in large measure on how you *think* they treated you. In the bumping incident, the first child instantly assumes that the child who bumped him wanted to harm him, and he strikes back. The second child is either unsure why he got bumped or even assumes it was an accident (Dodge, 1982; Dodge, Pettit, McClaskey, & Brown, 1986). Besides misperceiving situations, overly aggressive children don't think of other possible ways to react. They push back, which ends up turning an accident into a fight. In view of such an explanation of aggression, efforts to lower children's aggressive tendencies need to focus not only on how children act but on how they *think* other people act toward them.

● *Social learning and aggression.* How does aggressiveness become a child's main way of dealing with others? A social learning theorist looks at the bumping incident and concludes that the aggressive child *learned* to behave that way through observation, modeling, and operant conditioning (being rewarded for one's behavior—see Chapter 1). If a child's models—her parents and older siblings—frequently hit and yell at each other, she'll learn those behaviors too. The reward for aggression is attention, along with getting your own way by overpowering others. Peers who make a fuss about overly aggressive children or laugh at the victims are actually reinforcing the behaviors they dislike. And the child who pushes ahead of another child in line, or who snatches a toy and gets away with it, is encouraged by success to try it again.

But while social learning processes can generate, maintain, and even increase behavior, they can also be used intentionally to change it. Preschool teachers can help to reduce inappropriate aggression by ignoring it, while attending to and rewarding cooperative and pleasant behavior instead (Brown & Elliot, 1965). This requires the teacher's self-control, as the worst behavior often gets the most attention, only reinforcing it. But sometimes ignoring a minor scuffle or incident is useful. Children can learn to resolve their own conflicts so long as no one is threatening to spill blood. When a child consistently abuses others, physically or verbally, the teacher should intervene. An adult must be able to judge the *degree* of aggressiveness, given the age of the child.

Social learning explanations, which emphasize the reinforcement and modeling of aggression, and cognitive explanations, which stress thought processes, are by no means mutually exclusive. The kind of experiences (especially in the family) that social learning theory emphasizes seems to foster the thinking processes that cognitive theorists stress (Pettit, Dodge, & Brown, 1988): Children who frequently witness aggression or whose parents treat them harshly grow to expect the world to be a nasty place. They begin treating others as they have been treated themselves.

Attachment theory adds to our understanding as well, because it stresses the link between children's experiences in the family and the way they expect others to treat them. Such expectations guide not only what they do but how they interpret what others do (Belsky & Nezworski, 1988). (In Chapter 13 we discuss intervention programs for overly aggressive school-age children.)

It is important to keep in mind, however, that adults' decisions about whether they *should* intervene to discourage aggression are themselves influenced by the broader context in which they live. One cross-cultural comparison of mothers from Japan and Israel, for example, found that Japanese mothers were far

CONTROVERSY

GUNS IN THE TOY CHEST

Not too many years ago, almost every American boy had a favorite toy gun for playing cowboys and Indians, cops and robbers, good guys and bad guys. No one worried about their influence on development. But times have changed. Many families' daily lives are touched by *real* violence, either in their neighborhoods or on their local newscasts. Even parents who live in relatively safe communities—especially parents who want their children to appreciate the more tender, nurturant aspects of life—are uneasy about buying toy guns. Do toy guns numb children to the effects of real violence, or is playing with them a normal part of growing up?

Opinions differ: In the latest edition of *Baby and Childcare,* Dr. Benjamin Spock writes, "If I had a three- or four-year-old son who asked me to buy him a gun, I'd tell him . . . that I don't want to give him a gun . . . because there is too much meanness and killing in the world, that we must all learn how to get along in a friendly way together."

But another adviser counsels: "The issue is really simple. There are things that make children angry, and playing battle games is one safe, healthy outlet for anger and aggression. Some people say that playing with guns teaches kids to be violent. That's nonsense. Children have violent fantasies with or without a toy gun or knife; they'll just use sticks instead. . . . If you try to stop them, their aggressive feelings will just be channeled elsewhere, probably into less acceptable behavior. But give them their arsenal of guns at age three or four, and they'll be bored with them by the time they're six or seven, and that will be the end of it" (Siegel, 1989).

Which advice should parents follow? Many refuse to buy toy guns, hoping to teach their children that weapons can hurt people and that aggression is bad. But they soon discover a rude fact of child development: Children often are so fascinated by guns and other implements of power that what they aren't given, their imaginations will create. Deny a child a gun, and his baseball bat becomes a rifle. On any street, sticks can double as swords and lasers, and even a cardboard tube can be a pretend weapon. Then what? Should parents try to tell their children not to pretend? That would be a foolish struggle.

A more productive approach is for parents to talk about weapons as instruments of destruction. Discussing what guns do and how they are used by police, hunters, soldiers, and criminals can help to educate children. And if children play with imaginary or store-bought toy weapons, parents and

Many toy stores have stopped selling toys like these, but when children do play war games, parents can set limits.

teachers can still limit their use. Adults can forbid real battles with baseball bats, and they can tell children not to touch others with their "swords." In the end, the toy weapons of childhood may be something that adults have to live with, but mastering the limits of their use can help children to express and control their aggression at the same time.

Unfortunately, the challenge facing far too many parents today is how to limit their children's exposure not to *toy* guns but to very real, and very dangerous, weapons. As Alex Kotlowitz described in *There Are No Children Here,* in many inner-city neighborhoods, young children may witness multiple shootings even before completing preschool. In Chapters 10 and 13, when we look at the social contexts of early and middle childhood, we'll examine some of the consequences of exposure to violence.

 less troubled by children's fighting than Israeli mothers (Osterwell & Nagano-Nakamura, 1992). The Japanese mothers were more likely to see aggression as natural and even potentially constructive, as long as it was not used to harm others (that is, as long as it was instrumental and not hostile). The Israeli mothers, in contrast, were more likely to see aggression as harmful and dangerous. Even within the United States, there likely are differences among parents in the extent to which they view aggression as a behavior to be discouraged. (See Controversy: Guns in the Toy Chest.)

● Peer Relations: Making Friends

Interviewer: Why is Caleb your friend?
Tony: Because I like him.
Interviewer: And why do you like him?
Tony: Because he's my friend.
Interviewer: And why is he your friend?
Tony: (With mild disgust) Because . . . I . . . choosed him . . . for my friend.
   (Rubin, 1980)

Preschoolers choose their friends because of physical qualities ("He is tall"; "She has a pretty face"), common activities ("We like trucks"), possession of interesting things ("He has lots of army men"), and physical closeness ("He sits near me") (Berndt, 1981; Hayes, 1978). By the end of the preschool years, they begin valuing social support (sharing, helping, giving, comforting) and affection (loving, liking, caring for) in their friends.

One of the strongest criteria for choosing friends is gender. From age 2 until about 11, children everywhere usually choose friends of their own sex (Edwards & Whiting, 1988; LaFreniere, Strayer, & Gauthier, 1984; Maccoby & Jacklin, 1987). By age 5, while both sexes prefer playing with their own kind, boys are determined to keep their friendships female-free (LaFreniere et al., 1984). Why this sex segregation? It may be because boys and girls play differently, and each sex finds its own style more comfortable (Maccoby, 1988). Regardless of gender, both sexes begin practicing the fine art of negotiating, a social skill that depends on understanding another's feelings:

"Margaret, this time I want to be the mother."
"No, I am."
"You were the other day."
"But Mollie, don't you know? I can't be the mother at home because my sister always is."
"Then when I get to your house I can be?"
"Yes. Tell my sister she could see your Pac-Man eyeglasses." (Paley, 1986, p. 84)

A year ago, at age 2, Margaret and Mollie's conversation would probably have gone like this: "I am the mother." "No. I am." "No. I am (louder)." Tears. Now, at 3 years, socially more mature, they can consider each other's feelings, as can Erik and John in the excerpt below:

"I'm a bad Superman."
"I'm a good Superman."
"But, John, I'm going to be a bad Superman. Aren't you?"
"Okay, I'm bad, too. No, I mean, I'm still good."
"Look, John, what if you say you want to be a good guy? Say you were still my friend and I say I want to be a bad guy Superman and you say, you can say, 'I want

to be a good guy Superman,' cause the other person could tell you when you're not your friend."

"Well, Erik, I'm going to be a good Superman but I'm still going to be your friend."

"But just be a bad Superman, can't you? Because I'm going to be one. C'mon, can't you, John? See, good really means bad. See, if I say good it really means *bad*."

"Okay, we're bad, but we still could kill the bad guys, okay? (Paley, 1986, pp. 77–78)

If *good* and *bad* are sometimes ambiguous, so is the meaning of *friend*. It is often used to exclude others, as in, "I'm not playing with Bill, *just* with you, because *you* are my friend." And while threats to end friendships occur almost minute to minute, they are quickly forgotten.

> "Margaret's not my friend, Mrs. Paley."
> "Why do you think that?"
> "She said she's not my friend. She even told me. . . ."
> Mollie informs Christopher the moment he arrives.
> "Margaret is not my friend."
> "Oh," he says, not asking for reasons. "Am I your friend?"
> "Yes, if you help me make a restaurant. Bring those big blocks before Margaret gets them."
> "Hi, Margaret. Are you going to be my friend today?"
> "Yes."
> "Then do you want Chinese noodles?"
> "Cheese regular."
> "Margaret, you're coming to my birthday." (Paley, 1986, p. 113)

● *Individual differences in peer relationships.* Not every child knows the intimacy of Mollie and Margaret. Some lack a special friend, while others have several. Why are some children better at making friends than others? What determines whether children are accepted, rejected, or ignored by their peers? Several factors come into play. Physically attractive children benefit from the social stereotype that beautiful is good: Attractive children are often rated as friendly and nonaggressive, while the physically handicapped and learning disabled are more likely to be avoided and rejected by their peers (Adams & Crane, 1980; Hartup, 1983; Vaughn & Langlois, 1983).

The most important factor determining how children are regarded by their age-mates is their own behavior. Popular preschoolers are more friendly and socially skilled than other children. Disliked and rejected children seem not to know the rules: Rather than waiting to be invited, they tend to intrude into others' play (Coie, Dodge, & Kupersmidt, 1989). They also share less and tend to be disruptive, often hitting, pushing, and taking things from others (Das & Berndt, 1992; Denham & McKinley, 1993; Hart et al., 1992).

Poor communication skills seem to influence everything disliked children do: They are less likely than well-liked children to verbally respond to peers; and they tend to make irrelevant comments when trying to join others, ignoring the topic of conversation or the activity that the other children are engaged in (Kemple, Speranza, & Hazen, 1992). They also tend to talk less to a specific child than to the general group (Black & Hazan, 1990). Naturally, these very

Attractive children benefit from the "beautiful is good" stereotype. Popular preschoolers also have better social skills than less sought after children.

ways of communicating and behaving lead others to stay away from them, so disliked children often lose the opportunity to refine their skills. As a result, they fall into self-perpetuating cycles of social behavior, maintaining their reputations as unpopular and disliked (Hartup, 1983; Kemple et al., 1992).

The process works something like this: Suppose that an unpopular and a popular child each want a toy phone that a third child has been playing with. The unpopular child grabs the phone. The popular child starts talking about how much fun the phone is and then asks to play with it. Usually, the friendly request is granted while the aggression of the child who grabs the toy meets with anger. Thus, the popular child's behavior is reinforced and the unpopular child's rejection is reaffirmed. In short, because popular children are socially skilled, they enjoy the acceptance of their peers, which further encourages friendly behavior and reinforces their popularity.

But what makes some children more socially skilled than others? One trait that seems to be important is emotional knowledge and emotional behavior (Cassidy et al., 1992). Young preschoolers who can relate specific emotional expressions—for example, a sad or happy face—to the feelings that go with them also show more prosocial behavior. For instance, they respond positively to others' expressions of joy and are more liked by their peers (Denham et al., 1990). Abilities like these may be influenced by family behaviors. For example, children who had secure attachments as infants often have better social skills as preschoolers (Waters, Wippman, & Sroufe, 1979), especially when closer relationships such as friendships are involved (Belsky & Cassidy, 1993; Youngblade & Belsky, 1992).

How parents play with their children during the preschool years also seems to influence social skills (Parke et al., 1988). Fathers of neglected or ignored preschoolers were least likely to engage their sons in emotionally arousing, physical play, while fathers of rejected boys—those whose classmates actively disliked them—tended to overstimulate their sons during physical play (MacDonald, 1987). This kind of interaction may explain why fathers of rejected boys and their sons are more likely to become angry with each other during physically arousing play than the nonrejected children and their fathers (Carson & Parke, 1993).

Disciplinary styles matter too. When parents control their toddlers and preschoolers with physical punishment and threats, rather than by explaining and offering suggestions, preschoolers tend to have more trouble with their peers at school. They are more antisocial and disruptive, less prosocial, and more disliked by their age-mates (Hart et al., 1992; Kochanska, 1992). Children whose parents use physical aggression also tend to misunderstand other children's behavior, which only increases miscommunication and disliking. In contrast, when parents are more emotionally supportive, preschoolers are less likely to think that peers want to take advantage of them and are more likely to get along well with classmates (Pettit, Dodge, & Brown, 1988). In short, family experiences shape the way children think about and behave toward peers and, in turn, how they are regarded by others.

● *Enhancing social skills.* We shouldn't conclude from this evidence, though, that socially inept children are doomed to have trouble with their peers. When concerted efforts are made in classrooms to improve children's behavior, friendly interpersonal relationships can be promoted (Mize & Ladd, 1990). Two things seem to be important: *decreasing* the frequency with which children engage in aversive behavior such as taking objects from others, calling them names, and hitting or pushing; and *increasing* the frequency with which children engage in sharing and other cooperative behaviors, such as asking questions of peers, making comments to them, and supporting them.

These goals can be achieved in several ways. A teacher can model the appropriate behavior for the child or show him another child's successful behavior. It helps, too, to explain why some interpersonal strategies, such as requesting or offering to trade when you want something, are more effective in the long run than taking. Finally, teachers can praise children whose behavior with peers improves (Bierman, Miller, & Stabb, 1987; Ladd & Asher, 1985).

THE WORK OF PLAY

Play is the work of childhood: When children play, they produce, whether it's a fantasy or a product. A pile of blocks becomes a fort one day, a road or a train the next. When children slather paint across a piece of paper, not only are they creating something but they are learning to complete a sequence of events—wait for a turn at the easel, get a smock, paint, wash hands, hang up smock.

Play is an arena for many kinds of social and emotional as well as cognitive growth. Children create new worlds, act out their fantasies, and cope with their fears. They learn to share and to take, to follow and to lead. When the fighting starts, they learn about bullies and self-protection. Also through play, they begin to learn about themselves: what they like to do and who they like to do it with; what's fun to do with another; when it's time to be alone. Play is a training ground for expressing emotions and building relationships.

What makes the more complex types of play possible are the cognitive changes of the preschool years. Symbolic thinking permits the fantasy play through which children can safely express their emotional needs and conflicts. And the complicated plans of superhero games require children to juggle and remember a great deal of information. Similarly, the cognitive skills that enable a 5-year-old to follow the instructions for building a Lego village were only rudimentary at age 3.

From Solitary to Social Play

When 12- to 18-month-olds "play together," each is really "doing her own thing" next to, rather than with, another child. During such **parallel play** (Parten, 1932), children may be coloring at the same table or digging in the same sandbox. In time, play becomes a little more social, as children begin to acknowledge each other by making eye contact, the stage of **parallel-aware play** (Howes & Matheson, 1992). Eventually, contact grows, and as they play near each other, children begin talking, smiling, and exchanging toys with one another. Now they are engaged in **simple-social play** (Howes & Matheson, 1992).

parallel play
play in which children are apparently playing together but are actually focused on their own activities

parallel-aware play
play in which children begin to acknowledge each other by making eye contact

simple-social play
play in which contact grows, as children play near each other and begin talking, smiling, and exchanging toys

For 4-year-olds, play becomes more complex, with each child having an assigned role in staging a fantasy. One child might build a bridge, another a tunnel, and another a building, while a fourth manages the job.

● **complementary and reciprocal play**
active, turn-taking play

● **cooperative social pretend play**
play in which two children act out complementary roles in a make-believe scenario

● **complex social pretend play**
play in which children get more involved in who plays what role and in how they are supposed to behave

When children are about 2 years old, **complementary and reciprocal play** emerges (Brownell, 1986; Howes, 1988). This is the kind of active, turn-taking play that young children love. "Run and chase" and "hide and seek" are two of the most popular games of this type. Closer to 3 years, play becomes a little more sophisticated. In **cooperative social pretend play,** two children act out complementary roles in a make-believe scenario (Howes & Matheson, 1992). Husband/wife, doctor/nurse/, parent/child are the most common pairs: At this age, though, children don't talk about the roles; they just play at them.

By about age 4, a change occurs. Now, in **complex social pretend play,** children are far more involved in who plays what role and in how they are supposed to behave (Griffen, 1984; Howes & Matheson, 1992). Here is an example of the kind of dialogue that can go on during complex social pretend play, as preschoolers share an imaginary train ride to New York City:

> Four-year-old Alfred . . . started to build what looked like a train. He set five blocks in a long row on the floor. At one end he put two blocks on top of each other and sat on them. Danny had just come in and walked over to Alfred:
> Danny: "Is that a bridge?"
> Alfred: "No, it's a train."
> "Where's it going?" Danny asked.
> "To New York," replied Alfred. "I'm the engineer. I build trains."
> "I'm conductor. I drive the train," boasted Danny.
> Alfred (impatiently): "No, no. I'm the engineer. I made it."
> Danny: "What can I do?"
> Alfred: "You collect the tickets."
> Danny: "What tickets?"
> Alfred: "The ones the passengers give you . . . (out loud): Who wants to ride on the train? . . . All ab-o-ard . . . All ab-o-ard. Train going. Woo . . . woo . . . It goes so fast."
> Harry came into the room and ran over to the train.
> Harry: "I want to get on." Using a small block as a telephone, he yelled, "Hello, hello. What's wrong with you? We're leaving and we gotta have food. Bring hundreds of boxes. . . . Right away, you hear?" He slammed the telephone down.
> Alfred: "We got a flat. I'll fix it. Got to fix it now."
> With swaggering pretentiousness he removed one of the blocks from the line and turned it upside down and replaced it. Then he got back on the two blocks. (Cohen, Stern, & Balaban, 1983, pp. 74–75)*

All three children have accepted the blocks as a train and with little conflict have accepted one another's roles in the whole scheme as well. They are sharing fantasies, rules, and materials, improvising incidents, accidents, and conversations as they go. Note again how the capacity for symbolic thought fuels their play and propels their train forward.

Dramatic play often involves standard plots that children learn from daily life—cooking in the kitchen, going to the doctor, grocery shopping, attending a birthday party. Preschoolers' scenarios also draw heavily on the TV shows and movies they see. Usually these scenarios are stereotyped as well, involving he-

*From Cohen, Dorothy; Stern, Virginia; Balaban, Nancy, *Observing and Recording the Behavior of Young Children* (New York: Teachers College Press, © 1958, 1978, 1983 by Teachers College, Columbia University pp. 74–75).

roes and villains, cars, trains, space stations, mommies and daddies and babies. Children take the parts of favorite characters, and they enact fights, rescues, chases, tracking down the bad guys, and rescuing the good.

From age 4 on, planning usually precedes the action, as parts and props are assigned and defined: "You be the prisoner and I'll be Superman." "This box is the space station" (Fein, 1979; Matthews, 1978; Rubin et al., 1983). Sometimes, as in the imaginary train ride, they perform as they plan, improvising their way through and changing plots and characters as the mood strikes them: "I'm the vampire. You're Batman. You're the monster. I'm the Green Slime. I'm the Hulk. Pretend I killed you. No, you be the Green Slime. Pretend you killed my brother" (Paley, 1984, pp. 80–81).

Adults sometimes miss the point of such a conversation, which can go on for some time. They can't understand why their kids take so long planning: It seems like "talking but not doing." But play planning is a very significant cognitive activity, a way of directing and monitoring oneself in relation to others. The talking and planning can be as important as the action itself.

Pretend play is not just an arena for safely acting out fantasies; it lets children express their developing sense of self as well. In the doll corner, it's all right to be the baby *and* the grown-up, cared for *and* autonomous. You can see how much such role playing can help a child work through conflicts between the need for protection and safety and the need for separation and independence.

Solidifying their identity is another very important function of dramatic play. As seen earlier, preschoolers' play is also typically gender-bound. Boys play the superheroes; girls are the nurturers at the home front. It may sound paradoxical, but it seems to be true that acting out male and female stereotypes helps young children know who they are, providing a firm basis for growth, not necessarily as carbon copies of Mom and Dad but as unique individuals.

The shift from playing alone to playing cooperatively with others happens gradually (Parten, 1932), and children continue to play in all the ways we've described throughout the preschool years (Barnes, 1971; Hartup, 1983; Smith, 1976). Four- and five-year-olds in a group, for example, may at different intervals pull out to play by themselves for a while alongside the rest of the children; then they rejoin the others, resuming group play again. Preschoolers may return to solitary or parallel kinds of play to get a break from the demands of true interaction, which they are only just learning to initiate and to maintain.

In a study of a large number of children over the course of their preschool years, researchers found that as children grew from age 2 to age 5, they spent less time in parallel and parallel-aware play and more time in cooperative and complex social pretend play (Howes & Matheson, 1992). And *when* children begin to engage in complex play also tells us something about their overall social development. In the Howes and Matheson study, children who participated in complex kinds of play at earlier ages were those whom their teachers considered more sociable, more friendly to other children, prosocial, and less aggressive. In short, play sophistication and social competence are clearly related to one another.

● *Individual differences in style.* In play, as in every other aspect of development, group patterns don't describe every child. At play, children cope with their fears and express their wishes, but they also seem to be expressing their

FIGURE 9.1

Patterners' and Dramatists' Solutions to the Classification Task: "Put things together that go together."
(SOURCE: Shotwell, Wolf, & Gardner, 1979.)

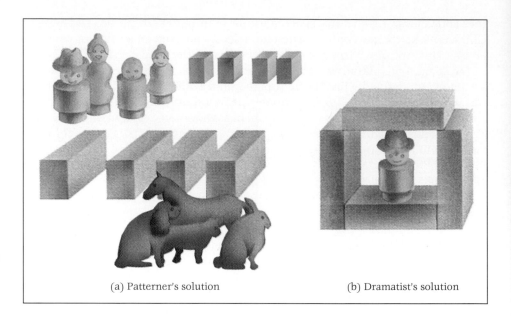

(a) Patterner's solution   (b) Dramatist's solution

own basic styles (Shotwell, Wolf, & Gardner, 1979; Wolf & Grollman, 1982). Some are *patterners:* Their play is tied to the properties of the materials they are using. In the sandbox, they dig and mound; at the clay table, they pound and shape. Other children prefer stories and social interaction, using play materials as props. These are the *dramatists.* In the sandbox, trucks can sprout wings and fly over roads; clay is shaped into cookies and fed to a doll. (See Figure 9.1.)

By age 2, children show their preference for one style or the other, and by 3 years, most will show both styles, although they continue to prefer one or the other. Neither style is better; they are just different. The distinction may even persist into adulthood, although we don't know this yet. Do children with different play styles have different personality styles as well? Future research may have some answers.

● *Playfulness.* Besides having different play styles, some children are also just more playful than others. Every day care center or preschool has its "live wires"—the children who are everywhere, do everything, and make everybody else feel happy because of their own positive outlook (Singer & Singer, 1976; Singer, Singer, & Sherrod, 1980). Playful children are more verbal than others and more likely to engage in social and imaginative play.

Parents, teachers, and others who care for children can foster playfulness by acknowledging its importance and providing enough time, space, and materials. *Materials* is not a code word for expensive toys. With empty boxes, paper bags, cartons, and paper, children can travel to the moon or to the supermarket; they can play office or build a skyscraper. Young children love to use unusual materials: litter and glue, food coloring and water or a plain dough made from flour and salt, wood scraps, an old dryer or vacuum cleaner hose can spark hours of inventive play. Add to any of these an adult who is interested in what the child wants to do, who will listen and watch and admire—helping when needed—and you've created an environment in which a playful spirit can flourish.

SUMMARY

1. Children now are concerned with growing up in relation to their parents and adult society. By age 3, most children have grown past the defiance of the terrible twos and would rather be like their parents and other adults. While children want to do what adults do, often their parents must tell them that they cannot. From this conflict comes the crisis of initiative versus guilt. (See pages 268–270.)

2. During these years, children are learning their society's rules for male and female behavior, a process we call sex-role development. Until age 2 or 3, children are uncertain of their gender identity, that they are boys or girls. At about 4 or 5, they accept gender constancy, the fact that their sex will never change. Preschoolers are very bound, in their play and in their attitudes, to traditional sex stereotypes, the social expectations about how boys and girls should behave. (See pages 270–274.)

3. In the development of gender differences, biology and experience are both at work. In biological theories, differences between males and females are believed to result from inborn biological differences between the sexes. In psychoanalytic theory, sex-role development is linked to the child's identification with the same-sex parent. For cognitive theorists, sex-role development unfolds once gender constancy has been established. Children then sort the world into male and female categories: This is appropriate for my sex; this is *in*appropriate for my sex. Social learning theorists connect sex-role development to rewards and punishments for what adults consider sex-appropriate and sex-inappropriate behaviors. (See pages 274–281.)

4. From 2 to 6, children begin to develop the prosocial skills that adults expect them to have. Both empathy and helping behaviors begin very early. Explanations for these prosocial behaviors come from attachment theory, which suggests that securely attached children are most likely to develop strong prosocial skills; cognitive theory, which links prosocial behavior to the decline of egocentrism during early childhood; and the social learning perspective, which emphasizes children's exposure to prosocial models and the reinforcement of prosocial behavior. (See pages 282–285.)

5. A child's level of aggression tends to be stable over time, and excessive aggression during childhood is the best predictor of emotional problems later in life. Cognitive theorists explain inappropriate aggression as a failure in interpretation: Children perceive hostility from someone when none was intended. Social learning theorists say that overly aggressive children model their behavior on overly aggressive adults, usually their parents. Attachment theory stresses the link between children's experiences in their families and the way they expect others to treat them. (See pages 285–289.)

6. Preschoolers choose their friends because of physical qualities, common activities, and physical closeness. By age 5, children generally choose only same-sex friends, probably because boys and girls at this age play very differently. (See pages 289–290.)

7. Popular children are more friendly and socially skilled than others, and disliked and rejected children engage in more disruptive, antisocial behaviors. Often, disliked children are caught in a vicious cycle: The ways they behave cause them to be disliked, but being disliked may further their inappropriate behavior. Sociability seems to develop from a combination of inborn traits, secureness of attachment, and the degree of warmth or hostility in the child's family. (See pages 290–291.)

8. When concerted efforts are made to improve disliked children's behavior, friendly interpersonal relationships can be promoted. Two things seem to be important: decreasing the frequency with which rejected children engage in aversive behavior, such as taking objects from others, calling them names, and hitting or pushing; and increasing the frequency with which rejected children engage in sharing and other cooperative behaviors, such as asking questions of peers, making comments to them, and supporting them. (See pages 291–292.)

9. Play is an arena for social, emotional, and cognitive growth. Cognitive advances, such as growth in symbolic thinking, permit the fantasy play through which children express their emotional needs and conflicts. Developmentalists have charted changes in play from play that is more solitary to play that is more social. (See pages 292–294.)

10. Among 4-year-olds, group or cooperative play emerges. Children can share both conversations and projects now, even though they will still play alone or next to one another from time to time. Their play is much more planned and often revolves around scripts and stories. (See pages 294–295.)

KEY TERMS

agency
androgens
castration anxiety
communion
complementary and
  reciprocal play
complex social pretend
  play
cooperative social
  pretend play

empathize
gender constancy
gender identity
gender labeling
hostile aggression
identification
initiative versus guilt
instrumental aggression
modeling
parallel play

parallel-aware play
prosocial behavior
sex-role development
sex roles
sex stereotypes
simple-social play

SUGGESTED READINGS

Bergen, D. (Ed.) (1988). *Play as a medium for learning and development.* Portsmouth, NH: Heinemann. A collection of articles on the developmental and educational significance of play.

Boehm, A., and Weinberg, R. (1987). *The classroom observer: Developing observation skills in early childhood settings* (2nd ed.). New York: Columbia University Press. Two keen observers of children's behavior provide insight into how to systematically observe the behavior of young children.

Elkind, D. (1987). *Miseducation: Preschoolers at risk.* New York: Knopf. Are we pushing our children too hard to excel during the preschool years? An insightful observer of American childhood argues that we have lost sight of the process of developing by focusing too much on the products of development.

Hopson, D., and Powell-Hopson, D. (1990). *Different and wonderful: Raising black children in a race-conscious society.* Englewood Cliffs, NJ: Prentice-Hall. Practical advice from two clinical psychologists and parents on the socialization and education of black children.

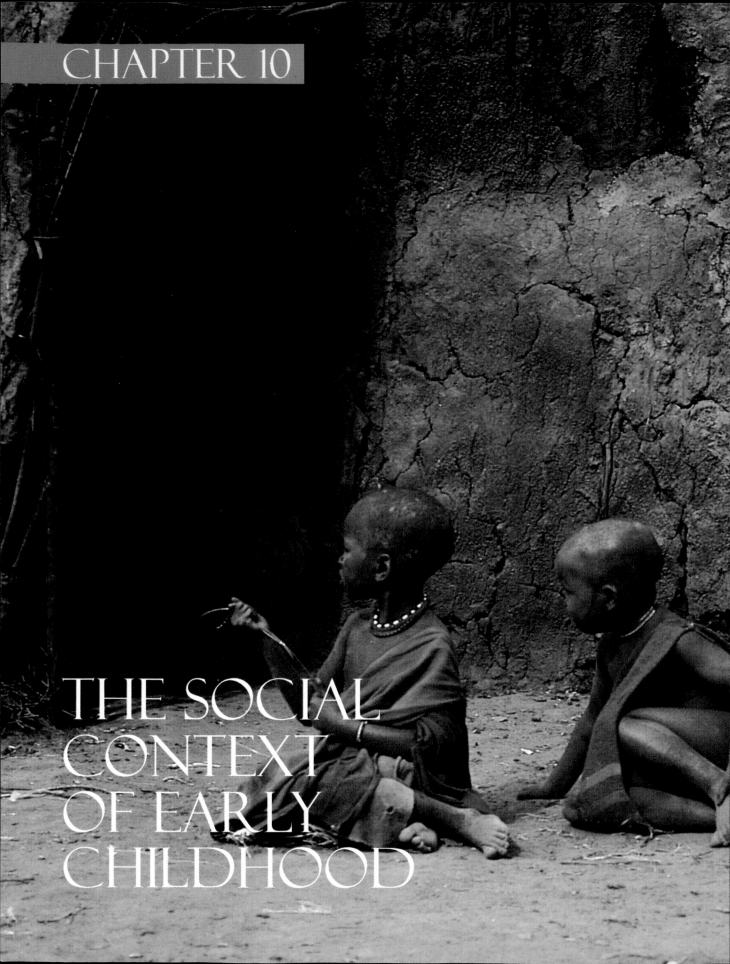

THE SOCIAL
CONTEXT
OF EARLY
CHILDHOOD

● MAKING A DIFFERENCE
PREVENTING AND TREATING
CHILD ABUSE

● MAKING A DIFFERENCE
HEAD START: PROGRESS,
PROBLEMS, AND POSSIBILITIES

In the doll corner of a preschool classroom, Rachel grabs a baby bottle and blanket and curls up on a mat. "I'm the baby taking my nap. You be the daddy," she tells Michael. At story time, Rachel sits next to the teacher, as she has for the past month. We notice Richard playing with wooden figures of a man and a woman. "This is the mommy. She lives over here. This is the daddy. He lives over there," he says, moving the figures to separate places on the table. At another table, children are cutting "C-word" pictures from magazines to add to their alphabet books.

The teachers in this ethnically mixed, middle-class preschool are trained and licensed, and the ratio of children to staff is 15 to 2. Lining the walls are shelves stocked with puzzles, books, magazines, pegboards, art supplies, wooden figures of animals, men, women, and children, cars, trucks, and traffic signs. In other corners are miniature furniture, store supplies, old clothes, dolls, blocks, boards, wooden trucks. Daily, children hear a story, sing a song, share experiences.

Across town, two untrained adults loosely supervise thirty 3-year-olds. The class seems to be run by the children themselves, and the feeling is chaotic. Toys, books, and magazines are scant.

We all know that the first setting is the better one for children's emotional and cognitive development. But any day care setting is only one of the contexts in a young child's life. Rachel is adjusting to a new baby in her family, and Richard's parents recently separated. Children in both classes go home to mothers and fathers with different parenting styles, with marriages, jobs, and lives that are more and less satisfying. Some of the children in each group will later watch 4 hours of television at home. Some will be greeted warmly by their mothers or another caring adult, and some will be rejected or even abused. Some are poor, some have college funds, and some have no homes.

How are children affected by day care? What sort of parenting brings out the best in young children? How are young children affected by parental divorce and remarriage? How do preschoolers react to the arrival of younger siblings? What causes child abuse, and how does it affect young children? What do children learn from television? These are some of the many questions we examine in this chapter as we look at the social context of early childhood.

We begin our study of the preschool child's social world with the most significant context in any child's life—the family.

THE FAMILY

What child hasn't watched *The Cosby Show* or *Family Ties,* or a host of other sitcoms dating back to *Leave It to Beaver* and *Father Knows Best,* and wished to live in such a family, where parents are always wise and understanding, where conflicts are easily solved, where good humor reigns?

In real families, life is complex. Are the parents well-off, poor, alcoholic, emotionally healthy, depressed, happily or unhappily married, divorced? How does the child's own temperament mesh with his or her parents and siblings? As we discuss the family's impact on young children, we'll consider a range of parenting styles, how children themselves influence the way they are treated, what can happen to the emotional lives of children when their parents divorce, and young children's relations with siblings.

● Parenting Styles

When Georgia finds her 3-year-old daughter trying to dress herself, but getting things a little bit backward, she praises Sarah's efforts and helps her finish dressing: "Let's see if we can make this fit a little better." Karen scolds her child for dressing slowly and for doing it "wrong": "What is taking you so long, Jimmy? I have been calling you for 5 minutes. What have you got on? You can't wear those clothes in October. Stop crying. We'll have to start all over and be late."

Developmentalists think of parenting styles in terms of two continuums, or pairs of opposite traits: responsive/nonresponsive and demanding/nondemanding (Maccoby & Martin, 1983) (see Figure 10.1). At the responsive end of the first continuum are the parents like Georgia who tend to be warm and accepting toward their children, enjoying them and trying to see things from their perspective. At the other end of the continuum are parents like Karen, who tend to be aloof, rejecting, or critical. They show little pleasure in their children and are often insensitive to their emotional needs.

At one end of the second continuum—demanding/nondemanding—are parents who have and maintain standards for their child's behavior. Such a parent might refuse her child's request for candy before dinner, explaining that "eating candy now will spoil your appetite for healthier food; maybe you may have a piece after dinner." At the other end of this continuum are the lenient parents who exercise little control, provide little guidance, and often yield to their child's demands.

On the basis of these two general dimensions, Diana Baumrind, one of the leading researchers in this field, has identified three main styles of parenting: *authoritarian, authoritative,* and *permissive* (Baumrind, 1967, 1971, 1980, 1989b). How children feel about themselves and how they relate to other people is linked to the way their parents treat them at home (Belsky, 1990b). In the following scenario three types of parents are reacting to the same situation: It is time for their child to turn off the television and come to the table for dinner.

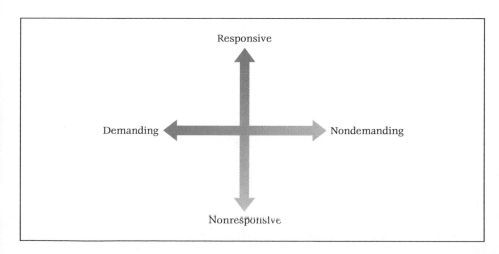

FIGURE 10.1

Parenting styles can be thought of on two continuums: demanding and nondemanding; responsive and nonresponsive. Responsive parents tend to be warm and accepting; nonresponsive parents are more rejecting and critical. Demanding parents tend to set rules for their children; nondemanding parents are more lenient, often giving in to their children's demands for control.

● *Authoritarian parents*

Mother: Come to the table, John.

John: (No response.)

Mother: (Walks into the television room, switches off the TV, and announces in a loud voice:) Get to that table and sit down!

John: (Whining.) Turn it back on!

Mother: (Glaring at her son.) Get to that table now!

● **authoritarian parent**
a parent who has an absolute set of standards and expects unquestioning obedience

John's mother is behaving like an **authoritarian parent.** She values unquestioned obedience to her authority and does not allow discussion of the specific issue or situation. She sees no need to explain why she does what she does. Authoritarian parents have an absolute set of standards in mind with which they try to shape, control, and assess their child's behavior and attitudes. They are demanding, but not responsive. The child is expected to obey a request instantly, and if he resists, punishment usually follows. Because authoritarian parents anger easily and often, their children tend to worry about when the next storm will strike.

Authoritarian parents tend to assert their power through discipline, which can include physical punishment, threats of punishment, and physical handling such as grabbing the child by the arm. These parents may also punish by temporarily withdrawing affection. They may walk away from the child or refuse to talk (Hoffman, 1970). One of the real difficulties with this type of discipline is that if a child feels rejected in the first place, any withdrawal of love will only reinforce that sense of rejection.

Children who are routinely treated in an authoritarian way tend to be moody, unhappy, fearful, withdrawn, unspontaneous, irritable, and indifferent to new experiences (Baumrind, 1967; Baumrind & Black, 1967). As they grow older, they show low self-esteem (Coopersmith, 1967). Not surprisingly, children who live with hostile and inconsistent parents think that unfriendly, assertive methods (threatening to hit, for example) will solve their own conflicts with peers (Hart, Ladd, & Burleson, 1990). Such attitudes often lead to antisocial acts, and then to rejection by other preschoolers (Hart et al., 1990; Pettit, Dodge, & Brown, 1988). In time, children of harsh and insensitive parents become *less* assertive, withdrawn, and ineffectual with their peers (Denham, Renwick, & Holt, 1991).

● *Permissive parents*

Mother: Dinner time, Laura. Turn off the TV.

Laura: (No response.)

Mother: (Pleading.) Come on, Laura; it's time to eat.

Laura: (No response.)

Mother: (Walks into the TV room.) Please, Laura; come sit down and have dinner.

Laura: I don't want to. I'm watching this show.

Mother: Oh, Laura! (Walks back to the table.)

Laura: (After 5 minutes, walks over to the dinner table, takes several bites of food.)

Mother: Sit down and eat with us.

Laura: Can't I take it into the other room?

Mother: (Sighing.) Oh, all right.

Permissive parents such as Laura's mother are generally nondemanding. They have few expectations of their children and impose little discipline. Instead, children in these households regulate their own behavior and make their own decisions, consulting with their parents only if they want to. Permissive parents are often responsive, but some are cool and uninvolved. Some writers have described these permissive parents as "disengaged" (Maccoby & Martin, 1983). Children of disengaged parents tend to interpret this behavior to mean that parents don't really care what they do.

Permissive rearing that is responsive and uncontrolling may sound attractive, but it poses some problems for preschoolers. How can young children regulate their own behavior in a world that demands some degree of self-control if limits are rarely set for them? Too much freedom is inappropriate at this developmental level, and in fact, Baumrind has found that permissively reared children tend to be impulsive and aggressive, lacking both self-reliance and self-control. In preschools, children of permissive parents are low in both social responsibility and independence. But they are usually more cheerful than the conflicted and irritable children of authoritarian parents.

● *Authoritative parents*

Father: Kenny, it's dinner time. Turn off the TV please and come and sit down.

Kenny: (No response.)

Father: (Enters TV room.) Kenny! What did I just ask you?

Kenny: To turn off the TV.

Father: That's right. Do it now, please. We all want to eat together. You can tell us what you've been watching. Come on now. If we wait any longer the food will be cold.

Kenny: (Turns off the TV and sits down at the table.)

Kenny's father is behaving like an **authoritative parent** (Baumrind, 1967). He sets clear standards for his child and expects cooperation, but he is also willing to explain the reasons for his actions and requests: It's dinner time; we want to eat together; the food will get cold. Authoritative parents are also willing to listen to their child's feelings and opinions, as long as they are expressed appropriately. For example, a child who becomes angry when he has to stop what he's doing might be told, "I'll listen, but first you have to calm down. You can do it. I'm here; I'll wait." Authoritative parents will usually listen to reasonable requests and are open to some degree of negotiation. Had Kenny explained that he was watching a special show, his father might have delayed dinner. The important distinction is that authorit*arian* parents expect complete obedience to their authority, whereas authorit*ative* parents have authority because they explain their demands and treat their children warmly.

● **permissive parents**
parents who are generally noncontrolling and nonthreatening, allowing children to regulate their own behavior

● **authoritative parent**
a parent who sets clear standards but legitimates authority through warmth and explanation

Cleaning up isn't fun, but it's necessary. That's the message an authoritative parent gives to his child. An authoritarian parent might be angered by the mess, and a permissive parent would do or say nothing about it.

● **induction**
discipline involving the use of reasoning to explain the expectations of the parent

To discipline their children, authoritative parents rely primarily on reasoning, trying to make the child understand *why* they expect one kind of behavior and reject another. This kind of discipline, called **induction** (it *induces,* or brings about, understanding in the child), is especially effective over the long term.

Authoritative parents are both demanding *and* responsive, and their children are socially competent, energetic, and friendly. Preschoolers with authoritative parents tend to be curious about new situations, even if they are stressful. They tend to be focused and skilled at play (Jennings & Connors, 1989), and self-reliant, self-controlled, and cheerful (Baumrind, 1967). They also get along well with age-mates: They are both assertive and prosocial (Denham et al., 1991; Hart et al., 1992; MacDonald & Parke, 1984; Pettit, Dodge, & Brown, 1988). Among older children, authoritative parenting fosters high self-esteem (Coopersmith, 1967).

Of course, even authoritative parents cannot always be at their best. Any parent can sometimes sound authoritarian or permissive, particularly when stressed. And there are times when an assertive, more authoritarian approach *is* called for—when children dart out into a busy street after a ball, for example, or in any way court danger (Kuczynski, 1984). These styles are *general types,* providing *guidelines* for both professionals and parents. These concepts can help psychologists in their work with children who are having emotional problems, and the guidelines can help parents understand the potential consequences of their own behavior.

Furthermore, the advantages of particular parenting styles may be linked to the larger community and cultural context in which the family lives. Authoritarian parenting, for example, may not be as harmful to families living in a dangerous and threatening environment (Baumrind, 1972; Grusec & Lytton, 1988). In inner cities, where drugs and violence are part of daily life, it is risky to encourage children to explore and expect that the world is a friendly place. Indeed, it seems that the more unstructured and precarious the world outside the family is, the more beneficial it is for parents to provide control and structure.

Having stressed the importance of parenting style as an influence on children's development, it is also necessary to interject a few words of caution. Some experts, like the behavior geneticist Sandra Scarr (1992), have argued that the effects parents have on their children actually may be rather modest, once other factors, such as the child's inborn temperament and influences *outside* the family, are taken into account. Scarr acknowledges that when parents' behavior is *extremely* abusive or negligent, children will certainly suffer the consequences. But she also makes the point that most children can develop normally with parenting that is "good enough." While Scarr does have a point—there is little evidence that children need "superparents" to develop normally—critics of Scarr's view, most notably Diana Baumrind (1993), have countered that given the apparently sizable prevalence of children in contemporary society who seem to be troubled psychologically or behaviorally, what many parents think is "good enough" may not really be good enough after all.

● Why Do Parents Behave as They Do?

If parenting were a multiple choice exam, most of us would gladly select "authoritative." But behavior is a complicated business, shaped by interacting forces as well as by deliberate choices. In fact, a similar pattern of forces shapes every parent's behavior (Belsky, 1984, 1990b) (see Figure 10.2). These forces include the parents' personalities and their satisfaction with marriage and work, the child's own temperament and behavior, and the social forces of class and culture.

● ***Personal traits of parents.*** Many parents don't treat their children in the best Cliff Huxtable–authoritative way because they can't. Their personalities simply don't fit the role. Parents who are irritable, anxious, depressed, or low in self-esteem tend to be authoritarian with their children, while authoritative

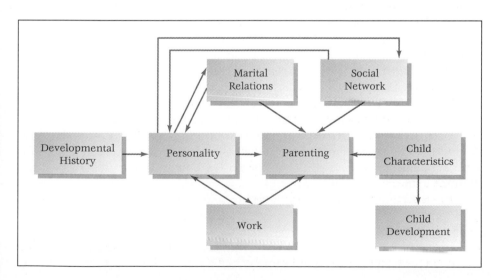

FIGURE 10.2
What Affects Parental Behavior?
Many interrelated factors influence parents' behavior toward their children, including their own developmental histories and the characteristics of the child.
(SOURCE: Belsky, 1984.)

Playfulness comes more naturally to some parents and children than to others. But in addition to personality traits, parents' satisfaction with marriage and work will strongly influence how much fun they have with their children.

parents tend to have more positive self-images (Belsky, 1990b; Conger et al., 1992; Downey & Coyne, 1990; Menaghan & Parcel, 1991; Stevens, 1988). This is true whether we look at Anglo or non-Anglo families. In a study of working- and middle-class African-American families, for example, men who were more emotionally expressive and open were also more involved with their young children than other African-American men who were less expressive (Hossain & Roopnarine, 1993).

How can we explain the link between personality and child rearing? One factor has to do with the capacity to manage emotions and cope with stress. People struggling with their own problems may have little patience for a young child's behavior. Other parents actually *misinterpret* what their children do. Parents who think their children are willfully "out to get them" react more hostilely to the same behavior than parents who can separate themselves from their children's actions (Dix & Grusec, 1983).

Of course, how parents were treated by their own parents influences their adult personalities and thus how they care for their own children (Simons et al., 1991; van IJzendoorn, 1992). But the past does not create a binding script. Those lucky adults who, as children, had secure, supportive relationships with their own parents are likely to repeat those behaviors with their own children (Crowell & Feldman, 1988, 1991). But the opposite is not necessarily true.

Interviews designed to assess parents' feelings about their childhood experiences suggest some encouraging conclusions. A childhood spent with neglecting, insensitive, hostile, or even abusing parents does not doom you to become your father or your mother (Rutter, 1989). What matters as an adult is not just what happened to you as a child but how you respond to it now. The riskiest situation occurs for adults who are still struggling with, making light of, or even denying the persistent disregard, hostility, and/or rejection they experienced while growing up (van IJzendoorn, 1992). When adults can confront a difficult childhood and resolve the anger they felt, they can free themselves to be sensitive, loving parents (Gossman et al., 1988; Main & Goldwyn, 1992).

● *The nature of the child.* As we saw in Chapter 7, from birth on, children themselves influence the way their parents treat them. Easygoing, compliant children generally evoke warmth and build a comfortable relationship with most parents. They learn quickly that negotiating for what they want gets them further than demanding. In contrast, difficult children make many demands and often resist their parents' wishes. If parents respond harshly, the child becomes even more difficult (Grusec & Kuczynski, 1980). With both types of children, self-perpetuating cycles of the child's behavior and the parent's reaction can develop (see Figure 10.2). The goodness of fit between parent and child (see Chapter 7) influences the child's behavior and developing personality, which continue to affect parental response, and so on.

● *Marriages, social relationships, and work.* We saw in Chapter 7 how the quality of a marriage, the birth of a baby, and the quality of parenting all affect one another. When marriages are emotionally supportive and harmonious, both mothers and fathers tend to be more nurturing and responsive toward their young children and to feel more competent as parents (Barber, 1987; Belsky et al., 1991; Engfer, 1988). Conversely, parents in conflict—with themselves and with each other—are more likely to nag and scold their children (Conger et al., 1992; Floyd & Zmich, 1991; Holden & Ritchie, 1991). Conflict between parents is especially troublesome for children when the children themselves are at the center of disagreements (Jouriles et al., 1991).

Just as in infancy, relationships that parents have outside the marriage affect parenting as well. Mothers who feel supported by friends and relatives use fewer authoritarian punishments, such as yelling and spanking (Belsky, 1990a; Cotterell, 1986). Mothers who are part of tightly knit social networks feel more competent and self-assured as parents and praise their preschoolers more (Jennings, Stagg, & Connors, 1991). Mothers who are more isolated and lack strong support networks are more apt to feel trapped and to become irritable (Pascoe et al., 1981; Stevens, 1988).

Social support from family members is especially valued and important among African-American parents, who often feel alienated from or rejected by the white majority culture (Allen & Majida-Ahi, 1990; Slaughter-Defoe et al., 1990; Wilson, 1989). Help from family members can enable teenage mothers, in particular, to stay in school, enhancing their ability to support their children. A recent study involving three generations of poor African-Americans found that new mothers did best as parents when their own mothers encouraged them to be independent and to mature as they needed to. In these families, the grandmothers helped care for the young children (Wakschlag, Chase-Lansdale, & Brooks-Gunn, 1993).

Finally, no matter how much help parents have, life at work affects life at home (Bronfenbrenner & Crouter, 1982; Menaghan & Parcel, 1991). For both mothers and fathers, satisfaction at work increases the possibility for harmony at home. But when tension and unhappiness build at work, perhaps due to fears about losing one's job, authoritarian discipline often increases at home (Conger et al., 1992; McLoyd, 1989). When mothers are satisfied with their work—and their husbands do not resent their working—mothers are more attentive to their children and, again, use more authoritative kinds of discipline than dissatisfied working mothers or those who work despite a husband's resentment (Hoffman, 1963; Stuckey, McGhee, & Bell, 1982). And if mothers' jobs are interesting and complex, they also provide a more intellectually stimulating and more emotionally supportive home environment for their young children (Menaghan & Parcel, 1991).

Where families live also shapes parents' behavior. In low crime neighborhoods, where neighbors tend to look out for each other's children, harsh control is not likely to be needed, and parents can encourage their children to explore and be relatively independent. But where the guns on the street aren't toys, strict discipline makes more sense. In such neighborhoods, encouraging exploration would put children at physical risk (Kelley et al., 1992).

 ● *The broader context of parenting.* In addition to the influence of forces in the family's immediate environment, how parents rear children is also affected by the broader context in which they live. Cross-cultural comparisons of parenting practices teach us that parents in different cultures rear their preschoolers differently. In general, in cultures that stress conformity as a desirable outcome, parents tend to be more controlling and lecture to their children more frequently. In cultures that stress independence, in contrast, parents tend to be somewhat less demanding and more likely to engage their children in dialogue (Ellis & Petersen, 1992). One contrast of Chinese- and Anglo-American parents found, for instance, that the Chinese parents were more restrictive and less responsive than Anglo parents with children of the same age (Kelley & Tseng, 1992), consistent with the greater emphasis placed in Asian cultures on the importance of obedience and in Anglo cultures on the importance of self-reliance. Other studies (for example, Okagaki & Sternberg, 1993) have found that immigrant parents (whether from Asia or Mexico) tend to stress conformity more than native American parents, who tend to stress independence. It is not that one type of child rearing is inherently better than another; rather, the point is that parents from different cultural groups have different socialization goals, and these goals affect how they raise their children.

Ultimately, what we want to stress is that parenting is shaped by many factors: the parent's developmental history and personality, the child's behavior, and the immediate and broader context of the parent's adult life. Positive factors, such as a satisfying marriage, can help to offset difficult ones, but the more weaknesses there are—a depressive personality, for example, a difficult child, little help from friends or relatives—the more likely it is that parenting will become authoritarian or even abusive (Belsky, 1984, 1990a).

● Child Abuse and Neglect

Every year in the United States, nearly 3 million children are reported to be abused (see Figure 10.3). Because they reflect only reported cases, it is difficult to know how accurate these estimates are. On the one hand, there is reason to think that the estimates are low, since like all family violence, abuse occurs behind locked doors, and many cases go unreported. On the other hand, many reported cases turn out to be unfounded, which may lead to an overestimate of the true prevalence.

Abused children have been beaten, burned, wounded, sexually assaulted, and emotionally maltreated. Others have been neglected or abandoned—starved for emotional and/or physical attention, nurturance, or protection. Many accidents

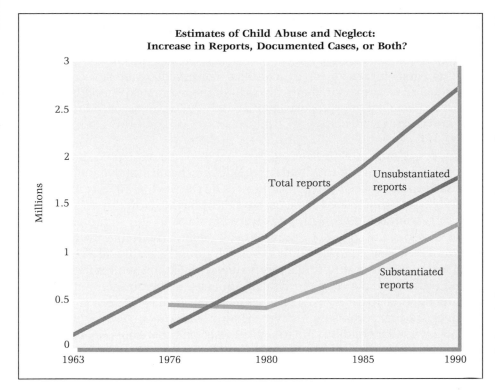

Estimates of Child Abuse and Neglect: Increase in Reports, Documented Cases, or Both?

FIGURE 10.3
The graph at left shows the widely cited increase in the number of child abuse reports over the past three decades. But note that the number of actual child abuse incidents may not be increasing as rapidly as the first curve would lead one to believe. Reports may have increased as a result of heightened consciousness in the general public as well as new laws that require certain professions (social workers, teachers, health care workers) to report suspected abuse. But the rate of unfounded reports (reports of abuse that could not be confirmed) has increased nearly as fast as the rate of total reports. Nevertheless, documented reports of abuse numbered approximately 1.75 million in 1990.
(SOURCE: Besharov, 1992.)

that injure or kill children stem from neglect, and parents can maltreat their children *whether or not they intend to*. In fact, most abusers have never intended any harm and are often shocked and frightened to realize what they have done.

Interestingly, there is some evidence that individuals from different cultural groups have different perceptions of what constitutes abuse. One study found that Chinese individuals were less likely than either Hispanic or Anglo individuals to rate the same parental behavior as abusive or negligent, and were less likely to recommend that the observed parent be referred to a social service agency for intervention (Hong & Hong, 1991). It is important to keep in mind, therefore, that definitions of child abuse—like definitions of optimal parenting—are influenced by the broader context in which parents live.

● ***Enduring effects of abuse.*** The effects of abuse and neglect are deep and enduring, with the potential to damage every aspect of a young child's social and emotional development (Cicchetti, 1990). Abuse compromises children's feelings about their own worth as well as their ability to trust others. Abused infants, toddlers and preschoolers often have very insecure attachments to their parents (Cicchetti & Barnett, 1991; Crittenden, 1988; Lyons-Ruth et al., 1987). As young preschoolers, they have trouble communicating, especially about their own activities and feelings (Coster et al., 1989). Other signs of abuse are overaggressiveness, impulsivity, frequent temper tantrums, self-destructive behavior, and low self-esteem (Alessandri, 1991; Kaufman & Cicchetti, 1989; Vondra, Barnett, & Cicchetti, 1990). As older children, they have trouble forming close ties with others, they tend to find new experiences threatening, and they are less curious and less ready to learn than other children (Aber & Allen,

1987; Hoffman-Plotkin & Twentyman, 1984). As teenagers and adults, they are more likely to commit delinquent acts and crimes (Widom, 1989).

Why do the victims of abuse lash out at others? Social learning theorists argue that not only do abused children learn antisocial behaviors but they *don't* learn nonviolent ways for solving conflicts. For psychodynamic theorists, expectations shape behavior. Maltreated children grow up expecting hostile responses; ultimately they provoke conflict and aggression because that is what they are used to (Dodge, Bates, & Petit, 1990).

● *Causes of abuse.* Child abuse grows out of a web of factors: the parent's history and personality, the child's influence on the destructive relationship, and the impact of social and cultural forces on the parents (Belsky, 1992)

A powerful force in an abusing parent's life is having grown up as an abused child (Egeland et al., 1987; Whipple & Webster-Stratton, 1991; Widom, 1991). Because abused children have insecure, fearful relations with their own parents, emotional and social growth suffers. Abusive parents have not learned how to form warm, secure relationships. Consequently, relations with other people—including friends, spouse, and eventually children—suffer. If their only models of parenting were their own abusive parents, abusers have little to go on when it comes to being parents themselves. They often have unreasonably high expectations of their children, and when the expectations are not met, frustration and a sense of their own failure may lead to abuse.

Years of berating and belittling can damage children as surely as physical abuse can. Parents who abuse their children emotionally are often scapegoating them for problems the parents would rather not face themselves.

A history of child abuse does not *inevitably* lead parents to abuse their own children, however (Egeland et al., 1987; Kaufman & Zigler, 1989). When parents who were poorly treated as children experience nurturing, caring relationships later on, they are much more likely to nurture rather than mistreat their own children (Belsky, Pensky, & Youngblade, 1990; Crockenberg, 1987; Rutter, 1989).

A child may, inadvertently, contribute to his or her own abuse or neglect. Many abused children were premature babies, or sick or handicapped—children who might have been difficult and needed more care or support than most (Hunter, Kilstrom, & Kraybill, 1978; Starr et al., 1982). In turn, when children receive poor quality parenting, they become even more demanding and negative, evoking more hostile or neglectful parenting (Trickett & Kuczynski, 1986; Wolfe, 1985). But children do not cause their own maltreatment (Dodge, Bates, & Petit, 1990). It is more likely that parents who are already vulnerable or stressed cannot cope with the added demands of caring for an especially difficult or needy child (Belsky, 1992).

Outside the family, the main stress on parents is poverty (Trickett et al., 1991; Whipple & Webster-Stratton, 1991; Zuravin, 1989). For people with little or no money saved, what often separates abusers from nonabusers is a job (Krugman et al., 1986; Steinberg et al., 1981). People with too little money usually have too little space as well, and cramped living conditions only add to stress. Data from a recent national study of child abuse and neglect reveal that children from families with incomes below $15,000 were much more likely to be maltreated than those above this level. Among these low-income children, the overall rate of maltreatment was more than five times greater than for those in households with incomes above $15,000 (Sedlack, 1989).

Poverty also increases the risk of drug and alcohol dependency, and substance abusers often become child abusers. Poverty is associated too with a low level of education and with teenage childbearing—two more elements in the abuser profile (Gelles, 1989; Whipple & Webster-Stratton, 1991; Zuravin & Grief, 1989). And recall from Chapter 3 that teenage mothers are also at high risk for bearing low-birth-weight babies, babies whose medical and behavioral difficulties may add stress to an already stressful situation.

Another pressure increasing the stress on potential abusers is social isolation. Raising a child is both physically and emotionally demanding, and when a parent who is already at risk for becoming an abuser lacks the support of friends or relatives, the danger increases (Garbarino & Sherman, 1980; Korbin, 1991; Zuravin & Grief, 1989). And if abuse begins, no one really knows what is going on in a "loner" family, and so intervention is unlikely.

Finally, some contend that U.S. culture itself tacitly contributes to child abuse (Kaufman & Zigler, 1989). Not only are we a violent society but we revere both privacy and personal freedom, regarding as sacred a family's right to rear their children as they wish. Child-rearing practices in the United States contrast sharply with those of other nations (Zigler & Hall, 1989). In China, for example, children are rarely punished physically (Kessen, 1979). And in Sweden, it is *illegal* to spank, hit, or otherwise physically punish children. But in this country, where disputes are often settled with violence, where children are regarded as solely their parents' responsibility or property, where many still believe that "sparing the rod spoils the child," where spanking is an accepted means of discipline, child abuse can grow in silence.

MAKING A DIFFERENCE

PREVENTING AND TREATING CHILD ABUSE

Preventing child abuse is the best kind of intervention (Dubowitz, 1989; Kelly, 1990). One successful program focused on the needs of parents at highest risk for abusing their children—poor, single, teenage mothers (Olds & Henderson, 1989). During visits to a group of teenage mothers both before and after pregnancy, a nurse taught the women about infant development, helped them to develop stronger ties to their friends and relatives, and provided a link between the family and social service agencies. Most important, the nurse emphasized the women's strengths, thus enhancing their self-esteem. After 2 years, only 4 percent of the mothers had maltreated their children, compared to almost 20 percent for a control group that had not received such help. Other research suggests that when parents can turn to other parents and counselors for support with child rearing and for their own emotional problems, abuse decreases (Belsky, 1993).

● Divorce and Preschoolers

Almost one-half of all children born in the last decade in the United States are likely to see their parents' marriage end (Cherlin et al., 1991; Hetherington, 1992). Many are younger than 5. The rate of divorce rose dramatically in the United States and many other Western countries between 1960 and 1980 and has remained relatively stable since the early 1980s (see Figure 10.4).

All children of divorce are affected in some way, but younger children show the greatest immediate signs of stress (Allison & Furstenberg, 1989; Zaslow, 1989). There are two reasons for this. First, young children have few relationships outside the family to which they can turn for emotional support (Hetherington, 1992). Second, grasping the reasons for divorce is particularly hard for young children because they are emotionally and cognitively immature. Still tending to view the world from their own perspective (Chapter 8) and limited in their ability to reason logically, they tend to blame themselves for their parents' breakup.

Young children often feel responsible for causing the separation, and at the same time they fantasize about a reconciliation, usually exaggerating the chances of this happening (Hetherington, 1979; Wallerstein & Kelley, 1980). Not only do preschool children believe they did something "bad" to make a parent go away but they also assume that the parent who moves away no longer likes or loves them (Neal, 1983). Having been told that "Mommy and Daddy have stopped loving each other," it's easy for young children to assume that their parents can stop loving them too.

Preschool boys and girls show different reactions to divorce. A boy's reaction tends to be both louder and more visible than a girl's, though both may feel equally angry, guilty, and rejected (Hetherington, 1992; Zaslow, 1989). Young boys tend to react in one of two extreme ways. They may act out their anger, becoming impulsive, rebellious, demanding, and generally less self-controlled (Hetherington, Cox, & Cox, 1982; Kline, Johnston, & Tschann, 1991; Zill, 1985). These angry boys often seem to be taking on the very emotions and behavior they have been witnessing at home around the time of a separation or divorce—hostility, rage, aggressiveness. Indeed, angry parents are more likely to fight openly before a son than before a daughter (Hetherington, Cox, & Cox, 1982).

At the other extreme, young boys whose parents divorce may become much more dependent and seem less masculine: the Mama's boy syndrome (Hetherington, Cox, & Cox, 1978a). The risk for this is greatest among boys younger than 5. After that age, sex-role identification with the father is usually established. But if a mother encourages independent behavior in her young son and expresses positive attitudes toward her ex-husband and toward males in general, her son will not be likely to show any major sex-role differences from his peers (Hetherington, Cox, & Cox, 1978b). Preschool girls seem to adjust better and more quickly to the changes and stresses following divorce, although among girls, negative developmental effects often show up much later, typically during adolescence (Hetherington, 1992; Zaslow, 1989). (One hypothesis is that many of the ill effects of divorce on females do not become apparent until they themselves begin to form intimate relationships with males.) Studies that have examined racial differences in familial adjustment to divorce have found few meaningful differences between racial groups once socioeconomic factors have been taken into account (McHenry & Fine, 1993).

Although divorce is associated with behavioral and emotional problems in children, children's problems often are evident *before* the divorce occurred (Block, Block, & Gjerde, 1988; Cherlin et al., 1991). In fact, the negative effects of divorce appear to result not simply from the parents' separation itself but from the breakdown in effective parenting that often accompanies the separation (Amato, 1993; Long & Forehand, 1987; Tschann et al., 1989). Generally, the greater the hostility involved in the breakup of a marriage, the poorer the par-

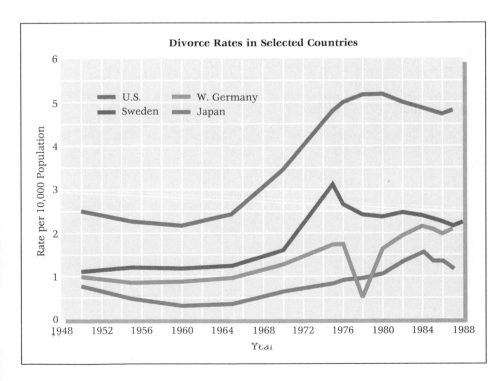

FIGURE 10.4
Rising divorce rates have leveled off since 1980, but still, nearly one-half of the children born in the United States since 1985 will probably live in a divorced family for some period of time. Note that the lower rates in other countries don't necessarily mean that children in those countries are growing up in happier families. Social and religious sanctions often make divorce more difficult to obtain.
(Source: Burns, 1992.)

enting (Camara & Resnick, 1988; Kline et al., 1991). If relations between parents improve after the divorce, children will benefit (Amato, 1993), and in time, many do adjust to their new family situation (Hetherington, 1989). Sadly, though, most divorced fathers gradually withdraw from their children, often creating further problems.

● Children in Single-Parent Families

After a divorce, nearly 90 percent of the children live with their mothers (Hetherington, 1992). And with the increase of never-married parents as well, the number of single-parent families has risen steadily over the past several decades. Today, in the United States, single parents head approximately one-fourth of all families: about one-third of Hispanic families, one-half of black families, and one-fifth of white families (Burns, 1992; Glick, 1989). These figures refer to the percentage of single-parent families living at any specific point in time. The proportion of children who will *ever* live in a single-parent household is much higher, of course: Current estimates are that more than one-half of all children born in the United States today will spend part of their childhood in a single-parent household (Garfinkel & McLanahan, 1989).

While divorce is the leading contributor to the high rate of single parenthood in contemporary America, single-parent families actually are a diverse group. Over the past decade the number of babies born to unmarried mothers has risen dramatically, both to teenagers and to women over 30 who decide that being unmarried need not deprive them of being mothers. The rate of increase in births outside of marriage has been especially dramatic in the United States and Sweden (see Figure 10.5).

Among divorced parents, the two characteristics that strongly affect children's well-being are the custodial parent's emotional satisfaction and financial

Finding time for crafts projects isn't easy for single mothers—or for most mothers—but even a few hours a week of warm attention can enhance a child's feeling of well-being.

Births Outside of Marriage in Selected Countries

FIGURE 10.5

In the United States and Sweden, the rate of increase in births to unmarried women has risen sharply since 1970. The former West Germany had a more modest increase, and in Japan, the rate has remained extremely low.
(SOURCE: Burns, 1992.)

security. Anger about the divorce and toward the ex-spouse affects parenting, as will depression, guilt, and a sense of being overwhelmed and overburdened. Financial pressures intensify these feelings. During the year following a divorce, the income of a woman and her children drops by nearly *75 percent,* while that of divorced men *rises* by over 40 percent (DeVillier & Forsyth, 1988). Among all families headed by women, 60 percent have incomes under the poverty line (Martin, 1989). These statistics reflect the fact that many fathers simply stop paying child support. The impact of child support on children's well-being goes beyond economics, however: Studies show that child support payments from noncustodial fathers may have positive effects on children's educational achievement, even after taking family income into account (Knox, 1993).

For the large number of single parents who were never married, low incomes are strongly related to poor job skills and limited education (Burns, 1992). Parents struggling to pay their bills and provide for the future may be too emotionally burdened to be supportive and sensitive to their children's needs.

The proportion of children raised in nonmarried households is influenced by other social trends as well. Gay men and lesbians, for example, are also choosing to be parents. In fact, between 6 and 14 million children are being raised in gay and lesbian households (Patterson, 1992). The controversy around this issue, as well as the desire to know what kind of home environments enhance *all* children's psychological growth, has led to some interesting research. These studies show that how children of gay and lesbian parents fare depends on many circumstances besides the sexual orientation of their parents. Researchers have found no significant differences in the development of these children when compared to the children of heterosexual parents (Patterson, 1992).

For all children, far less than their social address—whether they live in divorced or intact families, with single mothers, or with gay or lesbian parents—

what matters most is the extent and quality of their parents' involvement and the quality of their daily lives.

● *Gender and custody issues.* The sex of the child and single parent may also make a difference in children's adjustment following divorce. Some research indicates that boys may do better with fathers and girls with mothers (Santrock & Sitterle, 1987; Zill, 1988), although this is not always the case (Buchanan, Maccoby, & Dornbusch, 1992). In about 90 percent of all divorces, the mother is given **custody** (care or guardianship) of the child (Hetherington, 1992). Although some initial research suggested that **joint custody** (when both parents share equal responsibility) may be better for children than single-parent custody (Elmen, DeFrain, & Fricke, 1987), newer and better studies indicate that, to the extent that ex-spouses have difficulty resolving issues of how the child should be reared, joint custody may result in more costs than benefits. This is especially true when children feel caught in the midst of their parents' conflicts (Buchanan et al., 1992).

● Stepfamilies

Within 5 years after their parents' divorce, most children will be adjusting all over again, to a stepparent and perhaps to step-siblings as well (Glick & Lin, 1986). And since remarriages are even less stable than first marriages, 10 percent of the children will experience two divorces before they turn 16 (Furstenberg, 1988).

If you attend a self-help group for stepfamilies, no matter where it is, you will hear similar worries and complaints: Stepfamily members don't know how to treat each other (Cherlin, 1981; Hetherington et al., 1989). How, for example, should a stepparent behave toward a new spouse's child? Like a parent? An adult friend? How should stepsisters and brothers relate to each other? What about grandparents? Predictably, multiple, undefined roles in a single family can lead to hurt feelings, jealousy, and confusion.

Young children adjust to a stepparent best when the adult builds a warm relationship with them without trying to take over as the disciplining parent too soon (Hetherington, 1989, 1992). Even the most well-meaning authoritative parenting can be resented by young children still coping with their own anger, loss, and even guilt over their parents' divorce. Being a stepbrother or sister is not easy either, and often these relationships are more hostile than friendly as children compete with new arrivals for the attention and affection of their parents (Hetherington, 1989; MacKinnon, 1989). Managing family relations when two households are joined is quite a challenge.

● Sibling Relationships

Six-year-old Sally is talking about her sister Annie. "She's nice . . . sometimes nice. It's good to have a sister, because you can play with her. . . . I do have lots of friends but my best friend is Annie." Another child, Rachel, began her autobiography with a list of dislikes: "Violence, eggplant and my brother" (Dunn, 1985, p. 1).

Between these extremes lies the emotion that may best describe the way brothers and sisters feel toward each other: *ambivalence.* Siblings are rivals and opponents, pals and helpmates (Dunn, 1983). Older children, despite their complaints, often offer comfort and security to their younger siblings. Many even act as teachers (Dunn, 1985; Stewart, 1983). In fact, explaining things to younger brothers and sisters is a form of cognitive stimulation for older siblings that may advance the intellectual development of some firstborn children (Zajonc & Markus, 1975). Preschoolers who are close in age tend to spend a lot of time together in fantasy play, a stimulus for each child's social and cognitive development (Dale, 1982).

How siblings feel about each other, at first, has a lot to do with their parents, specifically with how the older sibling has been prepared for the younger one's arrival, and how he or she is treated after the baby's birth. A new baby usually means that an older preschooler gets less attention from mother (Stewart, 1990; Stewart et al., 1987). And typically, as attention drops, resentment grows. Many children begin to feel less secure and misbehave, like the little boy who, on finding his mother absorbed in his little sister, ran outside and pulled a full line of drying laundry into the mud (Dunn, 1985; Teti et al., 1991). Deliberate naughtiness often leads to confrontations between mother and child, increasing tension even more (Stewart, 1990). Given the circumstances, the older child's anger and resentment are natural, even logical, and do not mean that the child is "bad." Immature behavior is natural too, and preschool siblings are likely to cry more, want more help, cling to a parent or a security object, and seek greater closeness to mother and father (Stewart, 1990; Stewart et al., 1987).

As we saw in Chapter 6, parents can help older children (and ultimately themselves) by talking about and accepting the full range of the child's emotions.

A pinch for brother. What firstborn hasn't acted on at least some of his or her resentful feelings toward a new sibling? Sensitive parents let older children know they are still loved but that they may not hurt the baby.

Children need to know that they may not hurt the baby, but they also need reassurance that they are still loved and accepted. When older children are allowed to help take care of a baby, they see that the younger child has needs and feelings like their own. Communication and participation, then, encourage a positive sibling relationship, and family cohesiveness is likely to be strengthened as well (Dunn & Kendrick, 1982; Stilwell, 1983).

How siblings get along appears to depend upon a variety of factors. Older preschool siblings seem to do better with their younger siblings when the two children are more alike temperamentally (Munn & Dunn, 1989), when the preschooler is able to talk about feelings, and when the older sibling gets along well with friends—perhaps a training ground for dealing with a younger sibling (Howe, 1991; Kramer & Gottman, 1992). Preschool girls seem to fit into the role of older sibling more easily, too, than boys (Blakemore, 1990).

CHILDREN IN POVERTY

The figures are startling: During the 1980s, the number of young children living in poverty rose so steadily that by 1989, in the United States, *nearly one out of every four children under age 6 was poor.* In fact, children under 6 are more likely than any other age group including the elderly, to be poor, and the gap is growing. The child poverty rate increased from 20.6 percent in 1990 to 21.8 percent in 1991. "In 1991, 900,000 additional children became poor, bringing the total number of poor children to 14.3 million—the largest number of poor children in 25 years. Poverty was especially high among children under age six . . . one of every four young children in 1991" (Social Policy Report, Fall 1992, p. 1). (See Figure 10.6.) Hardest hit are minority preschoolers. In 1989, slightly less than one-third of all children under 6 were minorities, but *nearly 60 percent of poor children were minorities.*

Poverty is not just for single mothers and the unemployed. Almost 40 percent of poor young children live with married parents, and married or single, most poor parents work. In fact, more than one-third of all poor preschoolers live with single parents who work full-time, or with married parents who together work the equivalent of one full-time job or more.

Why were the 1980s, boom years for so many, so devastating for millions of children? The reasons have to do with economics, politics, and personal choices. During the 1980s, high-wage manufacturing jobs dwindled, families headed by single mothers rose, and child support payments from absent fathers dropped. At the same time, government payments to families with children were cut (Huston, 1992). By the start of the new decade, 5 million American children lived in poverty (National Center for Children in Poverty, 1991; Huston, 1992). Childhood poverty remains a persistent problem in most of the developing world as well, as you may recall from our earlier discussion of infant malnutrition (Chapter 4).

If the numbers of poor children surprise you, the consequences won't. As in infancy, when families live with severe economic stress, their children suffer (see Chapter 7). Poor children get sick more often, achieve less in school, and have more psychological problems than children who are not poor (Huston,

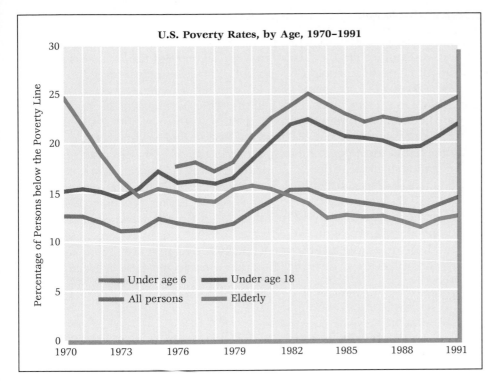

U.S. Poverty Rates, by Age, 1970–1991

Under age 6   Under age 18

All persons   Elderly

FIGURE 10.6

Poverty in the United States hits children harder than any other age group. While the poverty rate for the elderly has dropped from nearly 25 percent to about 13 percent since 1970, the rate for children has risen to about 22 percent. Overall, children younger than age 6 have the highest poverty rate in the nation, nearly 25 percent. (SOURCE: Social Policy Report, 1992.)

1992). Why? When financial stress is acute, poor parents cannot provide nutritional meals, comfortable housing, and the psychological support that young children need to thrive (Huston, 1992). The effects of persistent poverty (being poor for most of the child's early years) are far more devastating than the effects of transient poverty (being poor only for a short period of time) (Duncan, Brooks-Gunn, & Klebanov, 1993). And even beyond the effects of poverty in one's home are the effects of poverty in one's neighborhood: Children who grow up in communities with more affluent neighbors fare better than children from similar backgrounds who live in poorer neighborhoods (Duncan et al., 1993).

One of the most worrisome correlates of growing up in poverty is exposure to violence: Poor neighborhoods are often high-crime neighborhoods, especially in inner cities. Exposure to violence affects young children both directly—in that witnessing violent acts makes youngsters more aggressive and more emotionally distressed (for example, Cummings et al., 1985)—and indirectly, because violence in the neighborhood often compromises parents' child-rearing skills. Studies indicate, for example, that parents who are raising children under extremely stressful conditions are more likely to be depressed and irritable, which in turn adversely affects their parenting. Accordingly, young children growing up amidst poverty and violence are more likely to be treated inconsistently, harshly, or negligently by their parents (McLoyd, 1990). Excessively permissive or excessively authoritarian child rearing, as we noted earlier in this chapter, is associated with diminished competence in children. In Chapter 13, we'll look at violence and its effects on the lives of elementary school children.

● Homelessness

For some children, the consequences of poverty are even more severe. They have no homes. Families are the fastest growing segment of the homeless population, about 2.5 million people, one-third of whom are single mothers and young children (Bassuk & Rosenberg, 1990; U.S. Conference of Mayors, 1987). Homeless children have four times more health problems than average for their age; they are not properly immunized and are more likely to be both abused and neglected (Alperstein, Rapport, & Flanagan, 1988; Miller & Lin, 1988).

Compared to most poor children, the majority of homeless children living in emergency shelters are developmentally delayed and suffer from anxiety, depression, and learning difficulties. Young girls are the most affected (Bassuk & Rubin, 1987; Bassuk & Rosenberg, 1990; Rescorla, Parker, & Stolley, 1992).

While the large majority of poor children attend Head Start or other preschool education programs (see pages 226–227), only 15 percent of homeless children are enrolled (Rescorla et al., 1992). Many never get to such programs, and others are so disturbed that they are rejected even by Head Start.

DAY CARE AND EARLY CHILDHOOD PROGRAMS

Just 40 years ago, only 12 percent of women with preschool children worked outside the home. By 1975, the figure was nearly 40 percent; and by 1990, in the

FIGURE 10.7

The percentage of employed married women with children under 6 years old has been rising steadily since 1970. Between 1970 and 1990, the percentage of women working outside the home rose from 30 to 60 percent.
(Source: U.S. Dept. of Commerce, various years.)

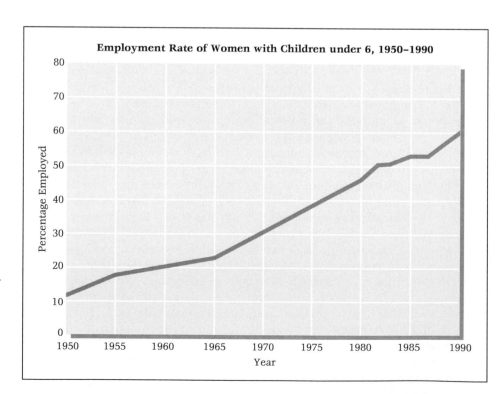

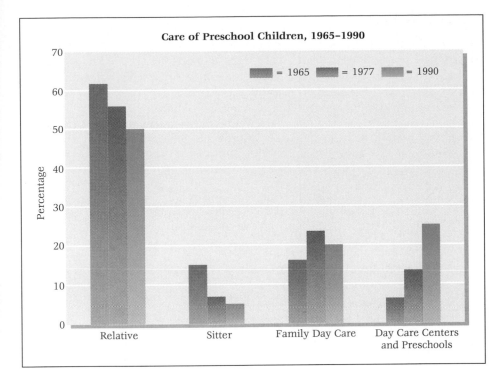

Care of Preschool Children, 1965–1990

= 1965   = 1977   = 1990

Percentage

Relative   Sitter   Family Day Care   Day Care Centers and Preschools

FIGURE 10.8
About half of preschoolers in day care stay with a family member. One-quarter attend day care centers or preschools, 20 percent are in family day care, and 5 percent spend the day with a sitter.
(Hofferth, 1992.)

wake of rising divorce rates, a growing need for two incomes, and women's desires for careers, approximately 60 percent of mothers with children under age 6 were employed (see Figure 10.7). Day care has become a necessity.

● Kinds of Programs

Any child care arrangement that parents use when they are away from their children is day care. In 1990, about one-half of those arrangements were with a preschooler's other parent or a relative. About one-fourth of preschoolers in day care attended a child care center, and about 20 percent stayed in a family day care home. All together, day care use has more than doubled since 1970 (Hofferth, 1992). (Figure 10.8 charts the changes in all types of day care used from 1965 to 1990.) Among other factors, such as convenience and cost, cultural preferences influence child care choices, with Asian and, especially, Anglo parents generally preferring more formal arrangements, and Hispanic parents preferring more informal care (Becerra & Chi, 1992).

Family day care is provided in a private home or apartment, usually by a woman who is also caring for her own young children. While offering flexible hours, the drawback is instability. Parents may have to make new arrangements on very short notice. In this country, most family day care homes are unlicensed and are staffed by people who may have no training in child development. In many unlicensed day care homes, children spend considerable time wandering around aimlessly, feeling unhappy and behaving aggressively (Carew, 1979). Of course, some family caregivers are very skilled, sensitive parents who enjoy young children and provide a stimulating, loving atmosphere.

● **family day care**
child care provided in a private home

MAKING A DIFFERENCE

HEAD START: PROGRESS, PROBLEMS, AND POSSIBILITIES

Launched in 1965, Head Start was a key strategy in President Lyndon Johnson's "War on Poverty." Its goal was simple: If, as countless studies had shown, the children of poverty were missing the early experiences that brought school success to middle-class children, then preschool programs would provide those experiences.

Head Start sought to help parents, too. Believing that education for parents would raise family incomes, Head Start planners encouraged parents to continue their educations and train for better-paying jobs. The program offers classes too, where parents not only gain family skills but grow to feel more in control of their own lives. Even participating in their children's Head Start programs can help: Mothers who attended parents' night or volunteered in the classroom reported fewer psychological problems, greater feelings of mastery, and greater satisfaction

with their lives at the end of a year's Head Start program than mothers who participated less (Parker, Piotrkowski, & Peay, 1987).

While supporting Head Start, child developmentalists have been concerned that society is expecting too much from a program that began by offering disadvantaged preschoolers a few weeks of special experience in the summer. Developmental researchers warned that even programs that were extended to an entire year should not be expected to work educational miracles. As one expert observed, "We cannot inoculate children in one year against the ravages of a life of deprivation" (Zigler, 1987, p. 258).

True enough, but even the gains that can be made in just one year have proved to be significant. In fact, the earliest experiments in compensatory preschool education for the economically disadvantaged have had the most long-lasting consequences. In particular, children who had been in these programs *with specially trained, reasonably paid, highly motivated teachers* were, when in public school, less likely to require

special education services, less likely to have to repeat a grade, and more likely as high school students to express pride in their accomplishments than age-mates who did not attend these early compensatory education programs (Lazar & Darlington, 1982). Furthermore, children in these pioneer programs were less likely to become delinquent teenagers (Schweinhart & Weikart, 1980; Zigler, 1992).

Troubling to developmentalists, though, is that children who have attended Head Start after the first wave of programs have shown only short-term intellectual gains that fall off over the long term (Brooks-Gunn & Schnur, 1988; Lee et al., 1990; McKey et al., 1985). But those children who benefited the most were those who were black, who were from the most disadvantaged homes, and who initially showed cognitive limitations (Lee et al., 1990).

Head Start's current critics, who focus on the "wash-out" effect, tend to ignore the differences between today's programs and the early models. Today's Head Start teach-

---

● **center-based day care**
child care licensed and regulated by a local authority and located in a central facility

Center-based day care programs—located in church basements, community centers, and school classrooms—are licensed and regulated by local governments. Two or more adults, some with child care training, care for 13 or more children. While not as flexible in hours as family day care homes and certainly not homelike, centers usually offer more stable care. Most centers offer a variety of stimulating activities for at least part of the day. Over the last 25 years, the number of children in day care centers has increased steadily, surpassing family day care (see Figure 10.8).

ers are trained less, paid less, and given fewer resources for their classrooms than teachers in the original program (Woodhead, 1988, 1992). Closing the gap in the cognitive development of economically advantaged and disadvantaged children requires much more than a year or two of educationally enriched preschool experience. Where Head Start excels is in supporting families, enabling parents to work, providing children with nutritious meals, and ensuring that children have periodic health checks. Benefits such as these suggest that Head Start should not be evaluated on the basis of intelligence scores alone. Particularly worrisome is that, because of budget limitations, the program reaches less than one-quarter of all eligible children. Since 1965 when the program started, 11 million low-income children have participated; but during the same period *50 million children who qualified were left out* (Zigler, 1992).

Even if we look only at the children who did participate, it is apparent that those who were most at

When properly funded and staffed with reasonably paid, highly motivated teachers, Head Start can enhance the development of economically disadvantaged children. But still, only about one-quarter of eligible children are enrolled.

risk for developmental problems still need the support of positive academic and social experiences throughout their years in public school. Even the best early intervention programs like Head Start cannot, by themselves, create enduring improvements in such children's chances for success—in school and in society (Lee et al.,

1990). One of the most important lessons we have learned in the last few decades is that what makes the biggest impact are parents: School intervention programs are most likely to have lasting benefits *when parents are involved in their children's early schooling* (Reynolds, 1989, 1992).

Preschools offer early social and cognitive experiences. Many preschools serve as day care centers as well, with some children staying all day. They are funded publicly and privately, routinely licensed, and staffed by professionals or by parent volunteers.

Compensatory education programs, often offered in church basements and community centers, are designed to serve the intellectual, emotional, and nutritional needs of children from poor families—children at high risk for failing in school. Best known among such programs is the federally mandated

● **preschools**
child care that offers planned social and cognitive experiences

● **compensatory education programs**
community-based programs designed to meet the needs of children at high risk of school failure

● **Head Start**
a federal program combining educational and social opportunities for 3- and 4-year-olds with social services for their low-income families

Head Start program, combining educational and social opportunities for 3- and 4-year-olds with social services for their low-income families. How well has Head Start served these families? See the accompanying Making a Difference box (pages 324–325).

● Day Care and Development

While Head Start children have been studied for almost two decades now, we are just beginning to explore the effects of other kinds of day care. How is non-parental child care affecting children?

Answering this question is difficult, for reasons similar to those relating to research on infant day care (see Chapter 7). Children are not randomly assigned by an experimenter to day care; they attend a family day care home, a day care center, or a nursery school because of their parents' decisions. And parents who use day care and those who do not differ in many ways, as do families choosing one kind of child care arrangement over another (Clarke-Stewart, 1992, Phillips & Howes, 1987). As we saw in Chapter 7, it is difficult to know whether differences in the behavioral development of day care children and those reared entirely at home result from their day care experiences or from the differences between their families. Nevertheless, based on the research so far, we can make some broad observations about the behavior patterns of children in day care (Clarke-Stewart, 1992; Clarke-Stewart & Fein, 1983).

● *Health.* Young children in day care run a high risk of contracting both minor and more serious illness because they are exposed to so many other children (Berg, Shapiro, & Capobianco, 1991; Wald, Guerra, & Byers, 1991). Over the years, though, day care children may get *fewer* respiratory infections than those who stay at home. Getting sick when they are young may immunize them against such illnesses later on (Hurwitz et al., 1991; Shannon, 1987).

● *Cognitive development.* Until age 5, children with and without day care experience show few cognitive differences (Belsky, Steinberg, & Walker, 1982; Clarke-Stewart, 1992). Cognitive gains appear when children have been directly stimulated by teachers and caregivers, through lessons and by "guided play." Children in such programs often have advanced language abilities and know more about the physical world and social roles (Clarke-Stewart, 1992).

These differences do not last, however. It seems, concludes noted researcher Alison Clarke-Stewart, that children in group care know certain kinds of information sooner, but their overall intellectual abilities do not seem to be affected (Clarke-Stewart, 1992). Generally, by the time children who have not experienced day care have completed the first grade, they have caught up with their peers who have.

● *Social development.* When quality of care is provided, early childhood programs seem to enhance social development. Children attending these programs are more self-confident, outgoing, independent, assertive, and knowledgeable about the social world than non-day care children (Clarke-Stewart, 1992). But regardless of the quality of the program, both boys and girls in day care also tend to be less polite, less agreeable, louder, more aggressive, and bossier (Belsky, Steinberg, & Walker, 1982). Poorer children seem more affected than children from higher-income homes (Clarke-Stewart, 1992).

● Quality Day Care

No matter what the type of care, we cannot really be confident about "the effects of day care" without considering its quality. And quality day care looks a lot like quality parenting: Adults treat children with sensitivity and offer adequate physical and mental stimulation. In group care, whether in a family home or a center, both group size and the ratio of children to caregivers are important. When groups exceed 15 to 18, and the child to caregiver ratio is more than 6 to 1 for very young children, or 10 to 1 for older preschoolers, caregivers may spend more time managing the children than instructing, nurturing, and stimulating them. For the children, this means more time spent in aimless activities and in waiting. The situation is even worse where caregivers lack training and caregiver turnover rates are high.

When caregivers are well trained, group sizes are small, and staffing is stable, children's development *does* tend to be positively influenced, because their day-to-day experiences are emotionally adequate and intellectually engaging (Belsky, 1984; Clarke-Stewart, 1992; Howes, Phillips, & Whitebook, 1990; Phillips, McCartney, & Scarr, 1988). For example, a California study of 122 publicly funded day care centers linked children's behavior to two factors: *adult to child ratio* and *caregiver behavior.* When the ratio of adults to children was low, so was the amount of aimless wandering and uninvolved activity. And the more the teachers positively engaged the children, the less the children cried, fought or seemed stressed or uninvolved. Conversely, where teachers were harsh, critical, and emotionally distant, children showed more signs of stress (Love, 1993).

Almost half of all preschoolers in day care attend group-care programs outside their homes. A low adult-to-child ratio and a variety of play materials can enhance both social and cognitive skills.

Quality care, then, is the main factor in enhancing and reinforcing cognitive and social development. It seems to matter less *where* children are cared for or what type of care they are in than *how* they are cared for day to day. And this applies to the home and to parenting styles as much as to any out-of-home day care situations.

What we know about quality day care and what most children actually experience, though, are far apart. A detailed study of 227 child care centers in five major U.S. metropolitan areas found low salaries for workers and "barely adequate" services for children (Whitebook et al., 1990, p. 4). At the other end of the spectrum are programs educators believed would give preschoolers a "superheadstart" on learning. As it turns out, though, early academic lessons may also bring early anxiety and other problems for children.

● Early Academics and the Hurried Child

During the 1960s and 1970s, the ideal American preschool was a lively, noisy, busy place. In these "child centered" programs, learning occurred through the activities children chose for themselves. Aside from daily story times, where teachers read aloud, rarely did all the children do the same thing at the same time.

The guiding theory behind such programs is that activities should be "developmentally appropriate," geared to children's cognitive, social, and emotional maturity. Paint, playdough, blocks, clothes, and props are a preschooler's best tools for learning and creating, argued developmentalists. Structured lessons and workbooks could wait until first grade.

Then came the 1980s, and parents of superbabies (Chapter 5) needed superkids. If an infant had swimming lessons at 6 months, then why not reading lessons at 4 years? Pressured by parents and by many educators as well, who worried about America's lagging test scores, preschools for middle-class and upper-middle-class children started changing. Many went from child-centered to teacher-centered, from developmentally appropriate to "academically focused." Workbooks and ditto sheets entered the preschool, and the focus shifted from *process* (the experience the child was having at the time) to *performance* (the result or achievement of an activity). Worksheets, workbooks, number and

Although some parents may think drawing on a computer gives their child an advantage, at age 4, every child can discover the joy of creativity with ordinary crayons, chalk, colored pencils, and paper.

alphabet drills, teacher direction and timed lessons entered the preschool. The "hurried child" was born (Elkind, 1982, 1987), and, say many developmentalists, the new emphasis on academics is not just inappropriate but harmful.

Developmentalists have predicted that starting teacher-controlled learning too soon stifles children's natural tendency to explore, to play, and to learn. They fear that emphasis on right and wrong answers at too young an age undermines children's confidence and their willingness to take academic risks. If adults make all the decisions about what to do and when to do it, and then judge how "right" it was done, children would become too dependent on adult authority and approval.

Apparently, these concerns were well-founded. Children in academically driven preschools may learn to read and to add a year or two earlier, but these gains are offset by adverse emotional and even cognitive consequences. Both during the preschool years and in kindergarten, more academically trained children are less creative, are more anxious about tests, and like school less than children who attended child-centered programs (Hirsh-Pasek, Hyson, & Rescorla, 1990).

This pattern is the same regardless of income or race. One study, for example, included 200 children, aged 4 to 6, who had attended either child-centered preschools and kindergartens or academic programs with formal instruction. The latter group scored higher on reading achievement tests but were not more advanced in arithmetic. They also rated their own abilities as *poorer* than they actually were. And compared with children who had had less formal academic training, they depended more on adults for instructions and approval, showed less pride in their accomplishments, and worried more about school. These effects were *the same* in poor and middle-class children, for minorities and for children from the majority culture (Stipek, Feiler, Daniels, & Milburn, 1993).

Furthermore, these effects continue in first and second grade. Kindergartners who spend their days in rote activities, drills, and group instruction become first and second graders who have trouble concentrating, get poorer conduct ratings, and are considered less helpful and willing to share than children who attended more developmentally appropriate kindergartens (Hart, Charlesworth, Burts, & DeWolf, 1993).

It seems fair to say, then, that pushing young children into rigid, academically oriented preschools and kindergartens harms them more than it helps them, perhaps for many years and in ways that we haven't fully discovered.

We turn now to a comparison of preschools in other cultures.

● Preschools and Culture

Some of the most profound ways in which preschool programs shape development stem from cultural values. Does a society want its adults to be primarily individualistic or group-oriented? How strongly does a culture value independent thought versus conformity? Answers to these questions can be found in every culture's preschools. How teachers treat children, daily activities, even lunch breaks and bathroom routines reflect some of the deepest values a society holds. Culture's influence on development becomes especially clear when we look at preschools in societies with sharply contrasting values. We examine preschools in four different cultures, three where values have been relatively stable and one undergoing dramatic change—Russia.

● *Preschool in Japan, China, the United States, and Russia.* In the United States, Japan, and China, researchers asked parents, teachers, and preschool directors, What is the most important reason for a society to have preschools?

Americans want their preschools "to make young children more independent and self-reliant." Indeed, in the preschool observed by Joseph Tobin and his colleagues, children do what appeals to them, using a variety of materials (Tobin, Wu, & Davidson, 1989). Here, freedom within structure is the norm. Group time, including teacher-led stories and songs, is brief. Teachers prefer variety and choice over regimentation. Children rarely do the same thing at the same time, and free play fills a good part of the day.

In short, American preschools reflect American values. Self-reliance and self-confidence are the traits Americans feel are most important for children to learn in preschool (Figure 10.9). Elsewhere, where the values are different, so are the preschools.

In Kyoto, Japan, 28 four-year-olds do a workbook project for about 30 minutes. "Throughout this session there is much laughing, talking, and even a bit of playful fighting among tablemates. [The teacher] makes no attempt to stop

FIGURE 10.9

This question was asked of 300 Japanese, 240 Chinese, and 210 American preschool teachers, administrators, parents, and child development specialists. Here are some of their first choices.
(SOURCE: Tobin, Wu, & Davidson, 1989.)

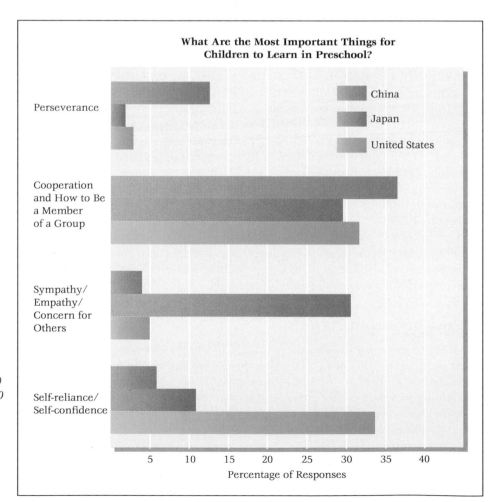

them but forges ahead with the task at hand" (Tobin, Wu, & Davidson, 1989). Later in the morning, after plenty of active, noisy free play, the children sit down for lunch. In unison, they sing a thank-you song to their mothers and then begin eating, as noisily as they please and at their own pace. During outdoor playtime, Midori complains to the teacher about Hiroki, who has been especially noisy and unruly for most of the day. With a pat on the back, the teacher encourages Midori to go back out and deal with the problem herself.

The teacher did not refrain from disciplining or quieting the children out of inexperience or timidity. Instead, her approach reflects how strongly the Japanese value group membership. Teachers prefer to remain in the background, refusing to single out or isolate a disruptive child from the group. Instead, they maintain order by encouraging children to deal with their classmates' misbehavior themselves.

The Chinese also value group membership, but obedience to authority comes first (see Figure 10.9). Children in the Dong-feng (East Wind) kindergarten in southwest China are eating lunch, silently. "Finish every bite," directs the teacher. "Concentrate on your eating as much as you do on you studying. That's the correct way to eat" (Tobin, Wu, & Davidson, 1989). Later, another teacher praises a child for her serious expression and for sitting with her hands behind her back. Instilling order, controlling, and regimenting are the essence of the Chinese preschool teacher's role, a role described by the word *guan,* meaning "to govern." Here, the teacher is a strong authority figure, and children are expected to obey.

Chinese parents and educators want their preschools to teach respect for the "values of self-control, discipline, social harmony, and responsibility." And indeed, teachers tell children to work silently, to play group games, and to cheer for their team. Encouraging creativity is a low priority. Handing out wooden parquetry blocks, a teacher commands, " . . . [P]ay attention to the picture of the building and build it. . . . Begin. Do your best. Build according to order."

Regimentation even governs physical needs. Explaining why preschoolers always go to the bathroom with their entire class of 26, one Chinese adult remarked, "Of course, if a child cannot wait, he is allowed to go to the bathroom when he needs to. But, as a matter of routine, it's good for children to learn to regulate their bodies and attune their rhythms to those of their classmates." Chinese preschoolers also learn to attune their rhythms to their teachers' plans. In a day that lasts from 8 A.M. until 6 P.M., the American observers noticed plenty of time for structured group activities and almost no time for free play and individuality. Despite these differences, though, preschools in each of these cultures teach children how to get along in a group and encourage them to identify with "something larger than themselves and their families."

What happens to preschools and to children after a culture changes radically? How, for example, has the drastic change from an autocratic to a democratic government in the former Soviet Union affected its day care centers? An American developmentalist who had visited preschools in Moscow during the 1970s returned in 1991 to find out. Visiting six day care centers in Moscow, Jean Ispa noted some sharp differences, especially concerning freedom and control.

No longer did the group come first. "Upbringers," as the teachers are called, remarked that the "'good' parts of collectivism (kindness, concern about one another) were still valued, but the 'bad' parts (conformity, inattention to individ-

In Chinese preschools, obedience to authority is valued and expected above all else. These children, on an outing, are all trying to follow their teacher's instructions.

ual differences) were not" (Ispa, 1992, p. 13). Accordingly, children who didn't want to join group activities could watch or choose something else to do.

Under communism, children were reprimanded when their drawings were not centered on the page, or when a pine tree was colored blue instead of green. "This time," reported Ispa, "I observed one young upbringer telling children that vases come in many shapes and colors, and that they should use their imaginations in sculpting their own" (1992, p. 13). Apparently, this teacher was an exception, as most preschoolers are still expected to copy the artwork of adults.

Children can now choose their own materials during free play, but teachers still direct the action of dramatic play, and they are still quick to solve conflicts rather than encouraging children to problem-solve on their own. So, while freedom and personal initiative have entered Russian preschools, they come with a distinctively Russian flavor.

TELEVISION AND DEVELOPMENT

A 5-year-old and his father were watching a television show about labor unrest. "He was absolutely fascinated," reported the father. "I said to him, 'Would you like me to explain this to you?' and he said, 'No, Daddy, I'm just watching'" (Winn, 1985, p. 43). "Just watching" is what American 2- to 5-year-olds do for an average of 2 to 3 hours every day (Condry, 1989). TV viewing increases dramatically over the first 5 years of life, to the point that American children spend more time watching television than in other activity except sleeping (Huston, Watkins, & Kunkel, 1989)! Television viewing levels off during the school-age years (Huston et al., 1992), but individual viewing patterns remain. Three-year-olds who watch lots of television tend to do the same during middle childhood (Huston et al., 1990).

What are preschoolers getting from their viewing time, and what are they not getting because of it? In this section, we consider the many claims made for and against television's influence on young children. Does television violence cause aggression in preschoolers? Can television teach positive social skills? Do *Sesame Street* and other educational programs enhance the cognitive skills of disadvantaged preschoolers, or do these shows promise more than they can deliver?

● Television and Social Experience

When television was introduced in the late 1940s, many thought it would bring families together. But the kinds of togetherness families share while watching television is not always the kind that enhances development.

When families watch, they talk less, play less, and argue more—about what to watch, when to eat, when to go to bed (Maccoby, 1951; Robinson, 1971). In short, television seems to reduce the potential for positive communication while it increases tension in family life.

A heated source of tension for many families comes from advertising. The average child sees over 30,000 commercials (Condry, Bence, & Scheibe, 1988), most of them for sugary foods and expensive toys (Huston, 1992). Until age 5, children don't really know the difference between the show and the commercial, and until 7 or 8 , they don't fully understand that advertising is designed to sell products (Kunkel, 1990; Wilson & Weiss, 1991).

Nevertheless, parents enjoy the free, convenient baby-sitting television provides (Steiner, 1963), and even most psychologists agree that a parent who has spent the day alone with a preschooler can get some needed relief by turning on *Mister Rogers' Neighborhood* or *Sesame Street*. The real issue is balance and judgment. No child is going to be harmed by watching these shows after a day of playing. The trouble is that many young children are parked in front of the television for hours at a time, day after day. To develop socially and emotionally, children need to participate with others instead of just watching them. Shy children may even use television to avoid playing with others.

As a group, heavy television watchers tend to be passive, bashful, and more distractible (Murray, 1971). But which came first? Most likely television did not cause these behaviors. Among the children in Murray's study, these traits appeared as early as age 3, suggesting that excessive television viewing is a symptom rather than a cause of poor social adjustment. Rather than watching television, such children can benefit from activities that will enhance their self-esteem and help to develop their social skills.

● Television and Cognitive Development

Researcher Aletha Huston asked a 4-year-old to explain what a commercial was. The child looked at her and said, "Huh?" "Did you ever see Tony the Tiger?" continued Huston. "Oh, yes, I like him. He wants me to eat Frosted Flakes." "Is Tony real?" asked Huston. "Yes," said the child (Huston, 1983). Because the line between fantasy and reality is still so blurred, preschoolers are apt to believe whatever they see, real or not. And even when what they see is real, most young children understand and remember very little, regardless of whether the show is informational or a fairy tale (Calvert & Watkins, 1979; Friedlander et al., 1974; Leiter et al., 1978).

As we saw in Chapter 8, young children's cognitive abilities are still relatively undeveloped. They can understand and remember simple sequences, but complex sequences are mentally taxing. Young children tend to see the actions in a TV show as a series of separate unrelated events, not as connected parts of a story (Collins & Duncan, 1984). Generally, children cannot really follow a story line until they reach 8 or 9 (Collins & Duncan, 1984).

● *The value of* **Sesame Street.** The picture changes with *Sesame Street,* a show specifically designed by educators and psychologists. Early research showed that girls and boys from a variety of social backgrounds learned a great deal from this show (Huston et al., 1992), and a more recent longitudinal study found that children's vocabularies improved when they watched *Sesame Street* regularly between ages 3 and 5 (Rice et al., 1990).

Children seem to benefit most from *Sesame Street* and other educational shows when adults watch with them, reinforcing the concepts presented (Huston, 1992; St. Peters et al., 1991). Discussing the show can extend the child's knowledge, reinforce what is learned, and enhance rapport between parent and child.

Probably the best way to use TV with young children is as a catalyst—for humor, for sharing, for learning. When *Sesame Street* is "brought to you by the letter B," children can be B-detectives, searching for B-things and -pictures. When Mr. Rogers discusses sensitive topics such as the birth of a sibling, starting school, or the death of a relative, parents can then continue the discussion. By watching together, parents can help children distinguish between "TV reality" and the real world: between cartoon violence and human cruelty, between TV stereotypes and real people, between the lure of commercials and the necessity for limits.

● Television and Aggression

Television and aggression go together like cigarettes and lung cancer—the link between the two has been so thoroughly tested that few outside the television industry dispute its strength (Huston et al., 1992; Parke & Slaby, 1983; Wood, Wong, & Chachere, 1991). And as with cigarettes, even a U.S. surgeon general has spoken out against televised violence, declaring, nearly two decades ago, that a causal link exists between television violence and aggressive behavior. The shows with the highest levels of violence of *any category* of television programming are cartoons and weekend programs for children (Gerbner & Signorelli, 1990; Huston et al., 1992).

When TV violence meets preschool viewers, the results can be both subtle and explosive. Not only do children who watch television violence become more aggressive, but they also show a passive acceptance of other people's aggression (Huston et al., 1992; Parke & Slaby, 1983). This is exactly opposite to the message that preschoolers need to receive as they struggle to control their own ag-

There's little doubt anymore that a steady diet of television violence increases childhood aggression—and aggressive children do watch more television violence. Even a nonviolent scene can elicit violent fantasies in preschoolers who identify with aggressive characters.

gression. Compounding this problem, boys watch more television violence than girls, and lower-class boys watch more than middle-class boys (Huston et al., 1990; Parke & Slaby, 1983). In short, children who may have the most trouble expressing their aggression nonviolently are watching the most television violence.

Even children *without* histories of highly aggressive behavior can become more aggressive after watching television violence. This was dramatically demonstrated by research that compared children's behavior before and after TV was introduced in some isolated Canadian towns (Williams, 1986). In fact, watching TV violence in childhood has been linked to aggressive behavior at age 18 and serious criminal behavior at age 30 (even when other explanations are taken into account) (Huston et al., 1992).

The relationship between aggression and television works two ways: viewing violence causes aggression, and aggressive children watch more television violence. Additionally, the more the child viewer believes that TV portrays life realistically, the more the child identifies with the aggressive characters in the show; and the more frequently the child has aggressive fantasies, the stronger is the link between television viewing and aggressive behavior (Huesmann et al., 1984).

Given the weight of this evidence, and the major campaign against television violence that was mounted in the mid-1970s by both parent and professional groups, it is discouraging to report that the amount of violence has not changed much since 1967. In part, this is because there has been no consensus on what exactly is to be regulated. Even commercials can spark aggression. Preschoolers behave more aggressively after watching highly charged commercials—with lots of action, quick pacing, and changing images—than after seeing slower-paced ads (Greer, Potts, Wright, & Huston, 1982). Children are also more likely to *watch* fast-paced commercials, and so there is no incentive for advertisers to slow them down. Many opponents of television violence argue, too, that restricting producers or advertisers by law raises serious questions about free speech and censorship.

Parents, however, have every right to turn off the television when their children choose to watch excessively violent shows. But despite the pleas of social scientists and others, most parents do little regulating (Huston et al., 1992). Parents can also regulate by watching with their children, counteracting the effects of antisocial behavior by disapproving of it and talking about nonviolent values (Huston et al., 1992). But, again, few do (Wright et al., 1990).

● Television and Prosocial Behavior

When children watch shows like *Mister Rogers' Neighborhood* or *Sesame Street,* do messages about respect for individual differences and other prosocial themes influence them? Can children learn cooperation, sensitivity, and persistence from television?

The answer is a qualified yes. One of the most prosocial shows for young children, *Mister Rogers' Neighborhood,* stresses helping, sharing, and respect for others. Nursery school children who viewed episodes of the show subsequently displayed greater cooperation, helpfulness, and willingness to work longer at a difficult task (Huston, Watkins, & Kunkel, 1989).

How lasting are these effects, and do they occur under some conditions more than others? The effects of watching prosocial programs are greatest in children from lower socioeconomic families, but they were not matched by a drop in aggressive behavior (Friedrich & Stein, 1973). Children in Head Start benefited the most when other aspects of the environment supported prosocial behaviors. The most prosocial interaction occurred when the class had play materials related to the show and when the children acted out the program's themes with a teacher. So even the context within which children watch prosocial shows makes a difference. As to the duration of positive effects, long-lasting effects have not been seen. Ultimately, quantity may count as much as quality. When respect and kindness outweigh rudeness and violence on television shows, perhaps children will be more likely to behave that way themselves.

SUMMARY

1. Developmentalists define parenting styles via two dimensions: responsive/nonresponsive and demanding/nondemanding. On the basis of these two dimensions, Baumrind has identified three main types of parenting styles: authoritative, authoritarian, and permissive. Authoritarian parents are demanding but nonresponsive; they value unquestioned obedience and rarely discuss the reasons for their demands. Permissive parents are nondemanding and nonthreatening, making few demands and imposing little discipline. Authoritative parents, both demanding and responsive, set clear standards and explain the reasons for their requests. (See page 503.)

2. Children of authoritarian parents tend to be moody, fearful, and withdrawn. As they grow older, they often have low self-esteem. Children of permissive parents are forced to make their own decisions with little guidance and may feel that their parents don't care what they do. Preschoolers usually do not do well with so much freedom and may become impulsive and aggressive. Preschoolers with authoritative parents approach new sit-

uations with curiosity. They are self-reliant and cheerful; as older children, they have high self-esteem. (See pages 304–307.)

3. Parenting styles are determined by a pattern of forces, including parents' personalities and their satisfaction with marriage and work, each child's own temperament and behavior, and the social forces of class and culture. (See pages 307–310.)

4. Child abuse, whether physical or emotional, compromises children's feelings about their own worth and their ability to trust others. Abused children are often overly aggressive and impulsive and have low self-esteem. Child abuse grows out of a web of factors: the parent's history and personality, the child's influence on the destructive relationship, and the impact of social and cultural forces on the parents. (See pages 310–313.)

5. Preschoolers often blame themselves when their parents divorce. Boys may act out their anger, becoming impulsive and demanding. Alternatively, they may become overly dependent and less masculine, especially if they are under 5 when their fathers leave. Girls seem to adjust more quickly but may develop problems during adolescence. After divorce, parenting is often diminished by anger, depression, guilt, and a sense of being overwhelmed. Financial security and emotional support from family and friends can help relieve the pressures divorced parents feel. (See pages 314–316.)

6. While divorce is the leading contributor to the high rate of single parenthood in contemporary America, single-parent families actually are a diverse group. Over the past decade the number of babies born to unmarried mothers has risen dramatically. Current estimates are that more than one-half of all children born in the United States today will spend part of their childhood in a single-parent household. (See pages 316–318.)

7. How siblings feel about each other has a lot to do with how the older child has been prepared for the younger one's birth and how she or he is treated afterward. If an older child feels ignored, misbehavior often follows. Older preschool siblings seem to do better with their younger siblings when the two children are more alike temperamentally, when the preschooler is able to talk about feelings, and when the older sibling gets along well with friends. Preschool girls seem to fit into the role of older sibling more easily than boys. (See pages 318–320.)

8. During the 1980s, the number of young children living in poverty rose so steadily that by 1989, in the United States, nearly one out of every four children under age 6 was poor. Poor children get sick more often, achieve less in school, and have more psychological problems than children who are not poor. (See pages 320–322.)

9. Day care for young children, whether in someone's home or in a more formal center or school, has become a necessity in contemporary society. Research on the effects of day care indicates that the quality of care a young child receives is related to his or her social and cognitive development. When caregivers are well trained, group sizes are small, and staffing is stable, children's development is positively influenced, because their day-to-day experiences are emotionally adequate and intellectually ongoing. Un-

fortunately, however, most day care in the contemporary United States is barely adequate. Preschools that emphasize academics over creativity and play can harm children both emotionally and cognitively. When formal instruction begins too early, children can become overly dependent on adults and anxious about learning. In every society, preschools both reflect and reinforce the dominant values of the culture. (See pages 322–329.)

10. Excessive television watching reduces the potential for positive communication while it increases tension in family life. Educational shows can stimulate cognitive development, if adults watch with children and reinforce the concepts presented. Children who watch television violence become more aggressive and show a passive acceptance of other people's aggression as well. The effects of watching prosocial behavior on television are greatest for children from low socioeconomic households, but these effects are not matched by a drop in aggression. (See pages 332–336.)

KEY TERMS

authoritarian parents	custody	permissive parents
authoritative parents	family day care	preschools
center-based day care	Head Start	
compensatory	induction	
education programs	joint custody	

SUGGESTED READINGS

Cicchetti, D., and Carlson, V. (Eds.). (1989). *Child maltreatment: Theory and research on the causes and consequences of child abuse and neglect.* New York: Cambridge University Press. This handbook of research and theory on child maltreatment provides a state-of-the-art evaluation of what is known about the causes and consequences of child abuse and neglect. It also provides reports on interventions designed to prevent maltreatment before it occurs and to remediate its disastrous consequences once they have emerged.

Emery, R. (1989). *Marriage, divorce, and children's adjustment.* Beverly Hills, CA: Sage. A clinical psychologist with expertise in research on family conflict and law related to child custody critically examines what we know about the effects of divorce and marital conflict on children's psychological and behavioral development.

Hamburg, D. (1992). *Today's children: Creating a future for a generation in crisis.* New York: Times Books. A prominent physician and public policy expert discusses how society has changed and what these changes have meant for children's well-being.

Phillips, D. (Ed.). (1987). *Quality in child care: What does research tell us?* Washington, DC: National Association for the Education of Young Children. State-of-the-art research on the conditions that foster positive child development during the preschool years.

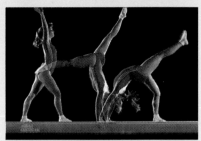

PART FOUR

MIDDLE
CHILDHOOD
AND THE
TRANSITION TO
ADOLESCENCE

CHAPTER 11

PHYSICAL AND
COGNITIVE
DEVELOPMENT
IN MIDDLE
CHILDHOOD

From ages 6 to 11, children hone the skills they'll use for the rest of their lives. Things as ordinary as driving a car, balancing a checkbook, or baking a cake are grounded in the physical and cognitive skills mastered during middle childhood. As strength and coordination rapidly mature, the 6-year-old who runs, skips, and throws can become a 10-year-old who swings a bat, shoots a basketball, kicks a soccer ball, or cuts a figure eight. Social skills and moral development are maturing as well on playing fields, streets, and in classrooms as children continue to learn how to compete, how to take turns, how to share, how to win, and how to lose.

Paralleling physical and social growth are major advances in thinking. The kindergartners who can recognize a few words, count to 30, and write their names will read novels and write stories by age 8; by age 11, some will even be solving for x. The pace of these developing skills is astounding. In this chapter we first consider some aspects of physical growth and then examine cognitive changes, schooling, intelligence tests, and social cognition.

PHYSICAL GROWTH AND DEVELOPMENT

From the quick, dramatic spurts of infancy and early childhood, growth becomes slower, gradual, and subtle. School-age children grow an average of 2 to 2½ inches and gain about 4½ to 6 pounds per *year* (Lowrey, 1978). Still, this steady change means that by the start of junior high school, children are about twice as heavy as they were in the preschool years. But because they are also about a foot taller, most are much slimmer than they were as preschoolers.

Girls and boys are physically equal during this period. Height and weight are about the same for both sexes, and most school-age girls can run as fast, jump as high, and hit a ball as well as most school-age boys. American society is slowly recognizing this equality, as both sexes now play together in sports such as soccer and Little League baseball, activities long reserved for boys only. Interestingly, there is some evidence for slight ethnic differences in motor skills at this age: One study found that African-American first graders were faster and more agile than their white counterparts, whereas the white youngsters had an advantage in hand-eye coordination (Plimpton & Regimbal, 1992).

As in infancy and early childhood, physical growth in middle childhood reflects both biological and environmental influences. Some children are genetically destined to be bigger and stronger than others and to develop faster, but environmental factors—such as diet, hygiene, medical care, and opportunities for physical exercise—strongly influence physical development as well. Typically, children living in advantaged environments who eat plenty of nourishing food, receive proper medical care, and are encouraged to exercise and participate in sports are likely to grow taller and stronger than children without these advantages.

● Exercise, Diet, and Health

One reason to be concerned about the eating and exercise patterns of school-children is that these patterns tend to persist into adulthood, sometimes with serious consequences (Williams et al., 1992). Sedentary adults with poor eating habits have much higher rates of obesity, heart disease, and related ailments than those who exercise and eat a healthy diet. And at least one study has found that childhood blood pressure and weight are strongly related to blood pressure and weight during adulthood (Lauer & Clarke, 1989).

New knowledge about the childhood antecedents of adult heart disease has sparked much medical research on how to intervene early. Concerned that their young patients were increasing their risk of heart disease in later life, a group of pediatricians tested 6,500 children between ages 3 and 18. Nearly 20 percent had too-high cholesterol levels, and among those who had the highest levels, nearly one-half had *no* family history of premature heart disease or high cholesterol counts. In other words, a genetic predisposition did not explain their high readings. The doctors concluded that all children should be routinely screened for blood cholesterol and that "high-risk coronary life-style behaviors"—eating too much fat and getting too little exercise—should be discouraged in children from 3 years old on (Garcia & Moodie, 1989).

Helping children to avoid future health problems takes firmness mixed with realism. While parents can't totally control what children eat, they can strongly influence their children's behavior. They can choose healthful snacks, serve nutritious meals, and exercise themselves. They can also turn off the TV. The more children watch, the less they move. Elementary school children report spending 16 hours a week watching television and only 5 hours a week on sports or other outdoor activities (Collins, 1984).

Besides influencing how much children exercise, television also affects what they eat. Commercials present a powerful message, and it isn't "eat your vegetables." Perhaps encouraged by commercials, many children eat diets high in fat, salt, and sugar (Shonkoff, 1984).

Children like these first- and fifth-graders who grow up eating healthful foods are likely to grow taller and stronger than those whose diets are inadequate.

MAKING A DIFFERENCE

CHOOSING UP SIDES IS OUT; FITNESS IS IN

Seeming to value competition above all else, traditional gym classes left less "naturally" athletic children feeling that there was no point in playing. Worse, emphasizing winning taught some children that they were born losers.

The well-documented links between childhood exercise habits and adult fitness have spurred new physical education programs that focus on a few basic principles:

1. *Shift the balance from competition to fun.* All children play on an equal basis; no one gets benched.

2. *Pay attention to physical differences.* Some children are naturally faster, taller, heavier, or stronger than others of the same age. Competing against others of roughly the same size—regardless of age—increases a child's chances of enjoying the game and continuing in the sport.

3. *Help each child find success in something.* While children should not participate only in sports which guarantee success, without some feeling of physical competence, they will drop out of athletic activities as soon as they can.

Across the country, schools are "replacing competitive sports with activities that prepare children for lifetime health rather than for varsity teams" (Henneberger, 1993). In new-style gym classes, students can climb a rope, swing on it, or just hold it. If they shoot baskets, they use a ball that is the right size for them, and they can keep the ball for long periods, shooting as often as they want. Most teams now have three or four players, so everyone has a chance to play, and those who dislike team sports can choose to do something else. While some complain that the athletically gifted are being penalized by the swing away from competitiveness, most see the benefits for the majority of children. (Henneberger, 1993).

Although schools may be deemphasizing competitive sports in their physical education classes, enrollment in out-of-school organized sports programs is at an all-time high in the United States. This has been both good and bad for children, according to experts. On the plus side, exercise certainly is good for children, many of whom would likely spend their Saturday mornings watching television if it were not for organized sports. On the minus side, however, many children are pushed into competitive sports before their skills are sufficiently developed; and as a consequence, many lose interest and drop out of the activity, never to return to it. Despite the growth of baseball, soccer, and football leagues for children as young as 5 or 6, many physicians believe that children "should not play regulation games on full-sized fields until they are at least 9 or 10" (Kolata, 1992, p. 15). In addition, pushing young children into competitive sports before they are physically ready for them increases the risk of injury. The message, then, is that children should be encouraged to be physically active, but in activities that they genuinely enjoy.

The current push toward fit-

In schools, only one out of every three school-age children participates in a daily program of physical exercise, and for adolescents, the number drops sharply. But in schools across the country, change has arrived. In classrooms, cafeterias, and gyms, schools are helping children learn to eat more healthfully and exercise more vigorously. In the Making a Difference box above, we look at a new physical education curriculum and other intervention programs designed to have a lifelong impact on health.

● Poverty and Nutrition

Milk, high-quality protein, fresh fruits, and vegetables can be expensive and are therefore scarce in poor children's diets. In contrast, sources of carbohydrates

ness is happening outside the gym and off the playing fields as well. In Washington, D.C., for example, the "Know Your Body" program seeks to reduce the risk of coronary heart disease among black children. At the start of the program, fourth, fifth, and sixth graders in nine schools were screened for coronary disease risk factors, including high blood pressure, excessive body fat, and elevated blood cholesterol levels. Children were randomly assigned to receive special instruction in nutrition, fitness, and the prevention of cigarette smoking. Two years later, they were tested again. The researchers concluded that the program "may have had a positive impact" on blood pressure, cholesterol levels, fitness, and smoking. Reduced blood pressure was also associated with weight loss, and overall, students knew more about health and had more negative attitudes toward smoking (Bush et al., 1989).

In Texas, one school district intervened in half of the third and fourth grades. Health education classes stressed the importance of good nutrition and exercise for

Having fun often gets lost amid the pressure to do well in organized sports. In new-style gym classes, choosing sides is out of style, as children are encouraged to enjoy exercising.

lifetime health; low fat and sodium meals replaced less healthful foods in school lunches; and vigorous activities rose from 10 to 40 percent of gym class time (Simons-Morton et al., 1991).

Perhaps the most sensitive campaign for fitness was waged by a middle school teacher in Iowa who got the school board to build indi-

vidual dressing and shower stalls in the locker rooms. "'When you ask kids whose bodies are changing to undress and shower in front of everyone, you've destroyed their self-esteem before they even get into the gym .... The only other place they make you do that is in prison.'" (Henneberger, 1993, p. 37).

(such as breads and rice) and fats (such as salt pork and other nonlean meat) are relatively inexpensive and are served frequently. The resulting diet—low in protein, vitamins, and minerals (particularly iron)—can have serious physical and mental consequences. Children who do not get enough milk are far more likely to have severe dental problems than those who get sufficient calcium.

Poor nutrition may also contribute to a variety of psychosocial and learning problems. Studies have found that severely malnourished children do not perform as well on intelligence tests as children with adequate nutrition (Levitsky, 1979). Poor nutrition also may mean less energy for learning. A child's brain needs two to three times more energy than an adult's brain (Smith, 1976). Recognizing this need, for many years U.S. schools have offered a nutritionally balanced hot lunch at minimal or no cost. Some schools also offer breakfast.

HIGHLIGHT ON DIVERSITY

CHILDREN IN KENYA: THE INFLUENCE OF NUTRITION, FAMILY, AND EDUCATION ON COGNITIVE PERFORMANCE

The links between malnutrition and cognitive performance are especially troubling if we think of the world as a whole. "More than 50 percent of the world's children live in developing countries . . . and estimates are that 48 percent of children in Africa are poorly nourished" (Werner, 1986, and Pollitt, 1988, cited in Sigman, Neumann, Jansen, & Bwibo, 1989).

The deadly consequences of severe malnutrition are well known, but the authors of this study were concerned about an even larger group of children: those whose malnutrition is not life threatening but may cause serious problems nevertheless. To study the effects of nutrition, family characteristics, and length of schooling on children's cognitive abilities, the researchers visited a group of families in rural Kenya. Families were scored for both socioeconomic status and parents' literacy level. Over the course of one year, researchers watched and recorded what the children ate and weighed them twice each month.

For all the children, those who were better nourished scored higher on cognitive tests. Among girls, those who were better nourished were also more attentive in school. As a group, cognitive scores were predicted by a group of factors including years in school, food intake, physical stature, and the family's socioeconomic status (Sigman, Neumann, Jansen, & Bwibo, 1989).

Children who have been severely malnourished for years usually score lower on both achievement and IQ tests than other children of the same age. Not surprisingly, these children may also have lower motivation for school tasks. Although some researchers have noted that it is difficult to separate the physiological effects of malnutrition on school achievement from other causes, such as social and genetic factors (Pollitt, Garza, & Leibel, 1984), there appears to be sufficient evidence, at least from studies of infants, that poor nutrition directly affects brain development. In the Highlight on Diversity box above, we look at a study that examines these factors from an international perspective.

● Childhood Obesity and Adult Health

Poor nutrition doesn't show itself only in calorie-starved bodies. In the United States, a malnourished child (that is, one whose nutrition is poor) actually is more likely to be *overweight*. In fact, at least 5 percent of all American schoolchildren are **obese:** They weigh at least 20 percent more than normal for their age, height, and sex. Because almost 50 percent of all obese adults were obese children—and because of the link between obesity and diabetes, hypertension, and heart disease in adulthood—childhood obesity is a serious health risk (Lauer & Clarke, 1989; Williams et al., 1992).

Obesity also leads to social rejection. Fat children are likely to be teased, passed over for team sports, and excluded from parties. Causes of childhood obesity include a hereditary predisposition to being overweight, lack of physical activity, and poor eating habits, including habits that may be especially valued within the child's culture. Members of some ethnic groups admire plumpness in children and promote excessive eating by constantly offering food.

● **obese**

refers to those individuals whose weight is at least 20 percent more than normal for their age, height, and sex

In the United States, malnourished children are more likely to be obese than underweight. Because of its direct connections to adult hypertension, diabetes, and heart disease, childhood obesity is a serious health problem.

Among Mexican-Americans, for example, mothers with little education encourage eating habits that lead to obesity in their children (Olvera-Ezzell et al., 1990). For all ethnic groups, the major causes of obesity in both children and adults are overeating—especially a diet laden with junk foods—and inactivity.

Except in very rare cases involving medical disorders, childhood obesity can be treated by a program of healthful eating and increased exercise. But equally important may be changing the way obese children feel about themselves. Parents and teachers need to help obese children feel competent (whether or not they lose weight), to praise weight-loss efforts, and to find substitutes for food as a reward.

COGNITIVE DEVELOPMENT: REVOLUTIONARY CHANGES

Around the world, children start school between ages 5 and 7. This is a time of tremendous growth in their abilities to think and learn. Indeed, the pace of change is so quick that some call it a "cognitive revolution."

What are the elements of this revolution? First, the ability to distinguish appearance from reality improves dramatically (see Chapter 8), so that by age 7,

conservation
the knowledge that basic physical dimensions remain the same despite superficial changes in appearance

causation
the relationship between a cause and its effect

classification
the cognitive ability to understand how things fit into categories and how these categories can be arranged relative to each other

manipulate symbols
to grasp the relationship between letters and sounds and to use this ability to learn to read and do arithmetic

children firmly understand enduring identities. They have grasped **conservation** (discussed in Chapter 8). Now they can judge number, amount, mass, and other physical dimensions based on actual quantitative changes in the objects. Superficial changes in the way things look no longer fool them. Whereas 5-year-olds have some understanding of the distinction between appearance and reality, they often need to be prompted to make this distinction (Flavell et al., 1989). They also tend to separate the two, thinking of appearance at one time and the contrasting reality at another. By age 7, children can think about the two simultaneously. Department store Santas no longer trigger tears, and if a row of cookies is spread out, children automatically know that the number hasn't changed.

Second, children reason better about **causation.** They realize that just because two things happen at about the same time, one does not necessarily cause the other. They can understand, for example, that rain does not cause thunder. But logical thinking is still limited. Children don't yet reason clearly about hypothetical situations, which is why Piaget called their thinking "concrete."

Third, **classification** skills improve. Preschoolers may not understand that dogs and people are both animals or that plants and animals are both part of the larger set of living things. By school age, however, children can classify objects based on several characteristics. They can understand how classes of things are related to each other in the phylogenetic scale, for example. Reasoning about arbitrary classes of shapes or different colors is also possible now.

Fourth, the intellectual revolution is characterized by children's increasing ability to **manipulate symbols.** Now children easily grasp the relation between letters and sounds, an ability that helps them learn to read. By ages 6 or 7, most children can add and subtract small numbers without using their fingers or counting the actual objects. Mental arithmetic and emerging abilities to read and write open the doors to academic learning.

We know much more about the "what" of the cognitive revolution than "why." Certainly, a lot of the "why" of cognitive development has to do with changes in the child's environment. As they spend more time at school and with peers, children are influenced by other people and challenged by new tasks to master. In school—in the classroom and on the playground—children learn to pay attention, to avoid distractions, to control their emotions, and to plan. When they tackle a math problem, they are more likely to *think* about it before trying a solution. They can list the materials they'll need before beginning an art project.

As they practice new skills, children begin to perform them automatically (Case, 1985). Where 5-year-olds sound out each letter of a word, 7-year-olds automatically recognize it. At 7, children can resist temptations and control their emotions without talking aloud to themselves, they can learn a short list of spelling words without too much repetition, and they can recall arithmetic facts without calculating each problem from scratch.

Social experiences promote cognitive changes as well. For example, 7-year-olds are more independent in many ways than 5-year-olds. They ride the bus, go to the store, stay over with friends, join teams and clubs, and meet new peers at school. As they share ideas and play together, they solve problems, and problem solving, in turn, fosters cognitive development (Flavell, 1985).

Along with these changes in experience, the continued maturation of the brain also contributes to more advanced thinking. As in earlier periods of development, intellectual growth in middle childhood is the product of a dy-

During the elementary school years, major cognitive advances enable children to learn computer programs and to succeed at games requiring principles of logic and strategy.

namic, ongoing interaction between biology and the environment. Experience stimulates brain growth; brain growth permits children to take advantage of their experiences.

Like the physical changes of the period, the cognitive changes occur gradually throughout middle childhood, and in each child they occur at a slightly different rate. Developmentalists use the term **5-to-7 transition** to refer to the age at which those changes usually *start,* even though many children do not complete this transition until the end of elementary school.

During the elementary school years, children improve old skills and develop new ones in many areas. By the age of 10 or so, most have the cognitive abilities to cope with many of the ordinary things of life—choosing clothes, repairing a leaky faucet, deciding how to spend free time. Underlying all these advances are the hallmarks of this cognitive stage: the major advances in logic and strategy. **Logic** refers to general principles about the relations among objects and people, and **strategy** is the ability to use those principles to solve problems. The first to identify and describe these milestones was Piaget.

● **5-to-7 transition**
a period in which children begin to develop a sense of logic and strategy as part of their cognitive skills

● **logic**
general principles about the relations among objects and people

● **strategy**
the ability to use logical principles to solve problems

● Piaget's Perspective: Concrete Operations

If you show a preschool child two balls of clay and then roll one into a long rope, she'll tell you that the rope has more clay than the ball. As Piaget observed, preschoolers pay attention to the way things *seem* rather than the way they *are* (Chapter 8). By 7, reality takes hold. Now, when you roll out a ball of clay and ask, "Are they the same amount now, or does one have more?" the concrete operational child (1) understands the trade-off between the length and thickness of the clay ball, (2) infers that the rope could be rolled back into a ball like the other piece of clay, and (3) is not fooled by the different appearances of the two pieces of clay. This new awareness, said Piaget, comes from a new cognitive ability.

Children can now perform mental operations: They can mentally represent or think about an action, and they know that it is reversible. Without rolling the clay back into a ball, children now grasp the principles involved: Physically rearranging things doesn't change their identity. What is arranged one way can be rearranged and then reversed. Moving beyond preoperational thinking (Chapter 8), now children know that lengthening a row of cookies won't yield more cookies. This operation conforms to the rule of arithmetic that states that if nothing has been added or subtracted, then identity (or numerosity) remains the same. Piaget called this period the stage of **concrete operations** because children's cognitive "actions" are applied to concrete objects or events. An operation is an action that is represented mentally, preserves an unchangeable relation, is reversible, and is part of a system of rules.

Now children begin to pay attention to and can remember several features of an object. They can infer changes in objects even if they don't see these changes; children can now use maps or other representations to guide them and are not easily fooled by physical appearances. School-age children can begin to reason quantitatively about number, distance, velocity, and time. They can reason about spatial relationships such as area and horizontality. Children think logically about observable, concrete objects or events but will have difficulty reasoning about hypothetical situations until they reach early adolescence and the stage of formal operations.

Piaget observed concrete operations in the rules children invent for playing games and in the judgments they make about moral issues. Foremost, though, he identified concrete operations in children's logical and mathematical thinking, as we'll see in the following three examples.

● *Classification.* Benjamin, age 5, has a set of baseball cards that he likes to sort by team (Yankees, Phillies, Cubs, and so on). If you ask him to sort them by playing position (catcher, pitcher, outfielder, and the like), he can do this too. But if you ask him to sort them by playing position *within* a team (Yankees' catchers, Phillies' pitchers, Cubs' outfielders), it is too taxing for him. He understands the instruction, but he seems able to focus on only one sort at a time. Piaget would not have been surprised. Until they reach the period of concrete operations, he claimed, children could not classify objects by two criteria simultaneously. Younger children are often confused by the idea that an object can be two "things" at once, that categories overlap.

Now, in middle childhood, children have developed a classification scheme. They can recognize relations between sets and subsets, between the whole and parts within the whole. For example, if you show children 10 flowers—3 roses and 7 daisies—and ask whether there are more daisies or more flowers, preoperational children say daisies, the larger subset, because they implicitly compare the roses and daisies. Children who have reached the concrete operational period can compare the whole set, flowers, to each of its subsets and correctly answer "more flowers." Because they understand hierarchical set relations, children at the operational stage delight in telling you that they live in Ottumwa,

● **concrete operations**
according to Piaget, the stage of development between ages 6 and 12 when children acquire the mental schemes of seriation, classification, and conservation that allow them to think logically about "concrete" objects

Team, position, league. In the period of concrete operations, children can easily classify baseball cards into several categories simultaneously, because now they understand the relationships between sets and subsets.

Iowa, U.S.A., in North America, on the planet Earth, in the Milky Way Galaxy.

Like many of Piaget's claims, his views about children's classification abilities have sparked controversy. Newer research shows that when the objects are part of a naturally occurring collection, such as a bunch of grapes or an army of toy soldiers, children are often able to compare the subsets with the total set (Markman, 1984). Nevertheless, Piaget correctly perceived that children progress during middle childhood in their ability to classify objects and to recognize relations between sets and subsets.

● *Seriation and transitivity.* **Seriation** is the ordering of objects according to a dimension, such as size. In one of his experiments, Piaget arranged a series of sticks from smallest to largest and asked children to do the same with their sticks. Preoperational children usually lined them up randomly or made groups of "big" and "little" sticks. By age 6, children can copy a seriated order, albeit with some difficulty. Even children who have not quite reached the concrete operational stage can order a series of coins and dolls from smallest to largest. But Piaget claimed that only children in the concrete operational stage could understand seriated orders. Part of the problem, he believed, is that children must first understand dimensions, such as size, and the rules of progressive change. Objects in the middle of the series are both smaller than some objects and larger than others. This *dual role* of each object confuses young children. Before they can create a seriated array, they need both decentration and reversibility. Because seriation preserves an invariant relation and is part of a system of rules, it is a good example of a concrete operation.

● **seriation**
the ability to rank objects in a meaningful order

CONSERVATION SKILL	BASIC PRINCIPLE	TEST FOR CONSERVATION SKILLS	
		Step 1	Step 2
Number (Ages 5 to 7)	The number of units in a collection remains unchanged even though the units are rearranged in space.	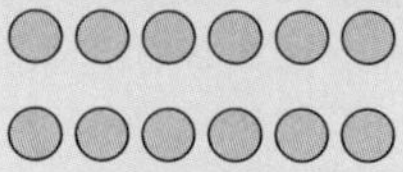 Two rows of pennies arranged in one-to-one correspondence	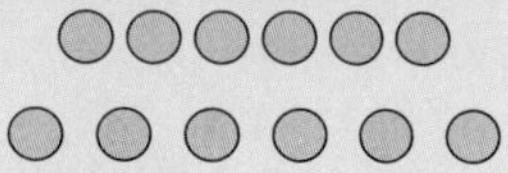 One of the rows elongated or contracted
Substances (Ages 7 to 8)	The amount of a malleable, plastic-like material remains unchanged regardless of the shape it assumes.	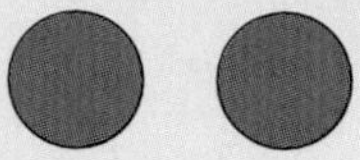 Modeling clay in two balls of the same size	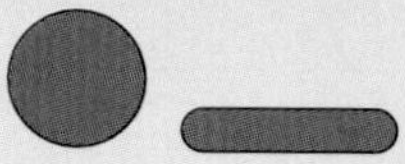 One of the balls rolled into a long, narrow shape
Length (Ages 7 to 8)	The length of a line or an object from one end to the other end remains unchanged regardless of how it is rearranged in space or changed in shape.	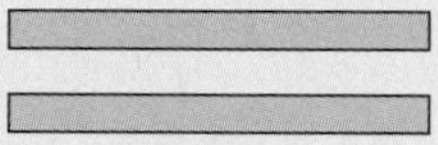 Strips of cloth placed in a straight line	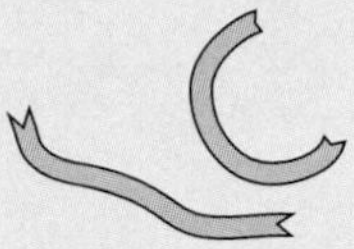 Strips of cloth placed in altered shapes
Area (Ages 8 to 9)	The total amount of surface covered by a set of plane figures remains unchanged regardless of the position of the figures.	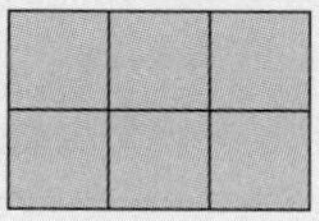 Square units arranged in a rectangle	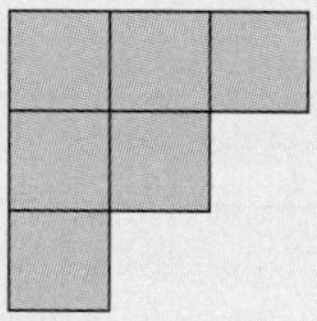 Square units rearranged
Weight (Ages 9 to 10)	The heaviness of an object remains unchanged regardless of the shape that it assumes.	 Units placed on top of each other	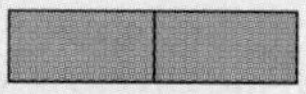 Units placed side by side
Volume (Ages 12 to 14)	The space occupied by an object remains unchanged regardless of a change in its shape.	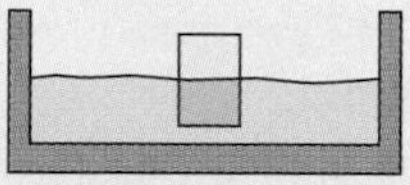 Displacement of water by object placed vertically in the water	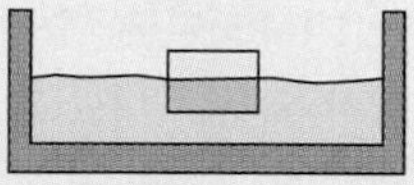 Displacement of water by object placed horizontally in the water

FIGURE 11.1

During the period of concrete operations, Piaget says, children develop conservation skills in a fixed sequence. They acquire the concept of conservation of number first, then that of substance, and so on. (SOURCE: Vander Zanden, 1993.)

Another concrete operation that children acquire between the ages of 7 and 11 is **transitivity.** Now they will know that if we ordered sticks A, B, and C from largest to smallest so that A is greater than B and B is greater than C, then A must be greater than C. This is a logical conclusion based on the transitive relation. When Piaget asked children questions such as, "If Lilly is fairer than Edith and Edith is fairer than Suzanne, then who is the fairest," concrete operational children knew it was Lilly.

● *Conservation.* Long after you have forgotten most of the information in this book, you will probably still remember *conservation,* the trademark of the concrete operational period. In his now classic experiment, Piaget showed children two identical glasses holding equal amounts of water (Figure 11.1). Then, with the children watching, he poured the water from one glass into a tall, skinny glass. "Now," he asked, "does one glass have more water, or do they both have the same amount?" Preoperational children, younger than 7, focus on the greater height in the tall, skinny glass and claim that it now has more water. Not until age 10 or 11, when they are well into the concrete operational stage, do children know that the amount of water remains constant. If you perform this experiment with children over age 10, they'll probably say, "It's the same. You could just pour it back, and it would have the same amount."

Children who fully understand conservation can reason about the weight, length, mass, or volume of objects without being fooled by changes in their external appearances as we saw earlier in the ball of clay experiment. Children learn conservation of number first, perhaps because they have more clues to help them reason about discrete quantities like coins (Siegler, 1981). Even young children can line up coins, count them, notice their correspondence, or move them around. These manipulations are not always possible for the other types of conservation, which may explain why conservation of liquid and mass usually follows conservation of number. Not until age 9 or 10 do children understand that weight can be conserved, and only by 10 or 11 do they understand conservation of volume.

Critics of Piaget's conservation studies claim that telling children to watch the experimenter may encourage them to think that something has been changed (Donaldson, 1979). Sometimes, too, the experimenter's words influence children's choices (Rose & Blank, 1974), and many experimenters believe that children know more about conservation than Piaget's experiments revealed (Siegler, 1986). But no one denies that children acquire a systematic set of rules or operations for reasoning from ages 7 to 11: (1) They pay attention to multiple characteristics of an object, (2) they can classify objects by several traits at the same time, (3) they understand that changing the way something looks doesn't change its amount, (4) they can reason about ordered series of objects, and (5) they can reverse actions mentally. These skills strengthen during middle childhood and underlie cognitive achievements during the school years.

● **The Information-Processing Perspective**

Recall Benjamin and his baseball cards. At age 5, he couldn't classify them into two categories at the same time. Piaget believed that preoperational children lacked a classification scheme that would permit double sorting, but informa-

● **transitivity**
the concrete operation acquired between ages 6 and 12 that rests on the understanding of relationships among objects

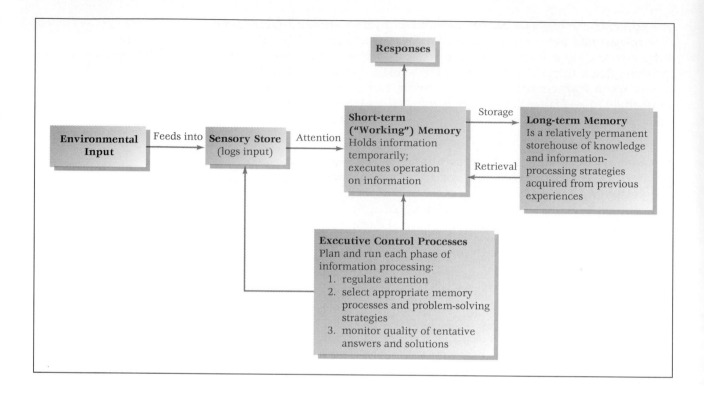

FIGURE 11.2
A schematic model of human information processing.
(Source: Atkinson & Shiffrin, 1968.)

tion-processing theorists offer a different reason. Whereas Piaget explained cognitive changes in terms of schemes and operations, information-processing theorists look to storage space and strategies, positing that new cognitive skills emerge from children's expanding memories. These theorists focus on the way we perceive, store, understand, and use information.

Generally, the theories suggest that information from the environment enters the brain's "sensory register," where it is first perceived; it is then transferred to short-term memory. Information stays in short-term or working memory for fewer than 30 seconds (see Figure 11.2). During this brief time, it is responded to, prepared for long-term memory (encoded), or discarded. The processes that act on information in short-term memory are critical for transferring information to and from long-term memory. Bottlenecks (or lapses of attention, perception, memory, and problem solving) occur because we cannot operate simultaneously on all incoming stimuli.

Information-processing theorists focus on four areas of cognition, which we will consider below: (1) attention, (2) memory, (3) metacognition, and (4) problem solving and reasoning.

● ***Attention.*** School-age children know what to pay attention *to*. They can focus on a central learning task while ignoring stimuli that distract younger children (Hagen, 1967; Maccoby & Hagen, 1965). They also become more strategic at focusing their attention. When 4- to 8-year-olds are asked to find similarities among groups of pictures, older children approach the task more systematically and efficiently than younger children (Vurpillot, 1968). One explanation for increased attention is that older children understand the *consequences* of paying attention. They begin to understand that if they want to comprehend something, they have to pay attention to it (Pillow, 1989). (See Figure 11.3.)

Now, too, holding children's attention begins to depend more on content than on visual stimulation. They pay more attention to television, but as children understand more of what they see, visual stimuli alone won't hold their interest; now attention depends on how involved they are with the show's content and how well they understand it (Anderson et al., 1981).

● *Memory.* Preschoolers have few strategies for recalling information, but between ages 5 and 11, memory improves dramatically. Two possible reasons for gains in recall involve (1) children's increased and better organized knowledge and (2) their growing use of strategies or methods for remembering.

Actually, when they are particularly knowledgeable about something, children can have better recall than adults, as a classic experiment demonstrated. When 10-year-olds and adults were given a list of digits to remember, the adults recalled more than the children. But when the children—all experienced chess players—were asked to remember chess positions, they were much more successful than the adults (Chi, 1978). Why the difference? Knowing the game enhanced the children's recall. Because organization strengthens memory, when information can be chunked and organized meaningfully, even young children can show considerable memory prowess. The psychologist who conducted the experiment described above concluded that the children performed better because of their organized knowledge about plausible chess positions (Chi, 1978).

In other words, the young chess players' memories were better because they could put the pieces into a familiar context (Rogoff, in Perlmutter, 1986). Although the adults and the children looked at the same board, the children saw it differently. The pieces formed an organized whole that appeared in a familiar context and so made sense. The non-chess players saw pieces scattered randomly across a board. Even for memory, then, context affects performance.

Curious about the effects of context on memory, researchers have tested children in Western and non-Western cultures on a variety of memory tasks. In a study involving Mayan (Guatemalan) and U.S. children, 9-year-olds were asked to recall a string of words or pictures (Kagan et al., 1978). In another test, they

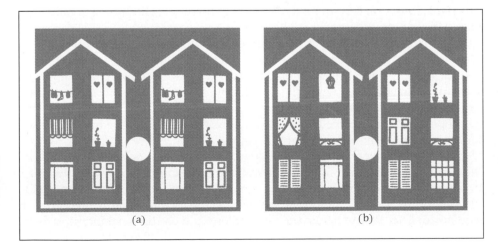

(a)   (b)

FIGURE 11.3

Children's ability to distinguish between houses that are the same (a) and different (b) increases with age. Not until age 6 do most children pay close enough attention to the information in the pictures to match the pairs correctly.
(SOURCE: Vurpillot, 1968.)

Memory improves dramatically in middle childhood. With enough practice, elementary school children can even learn the lines of Shakespeare.

studied a familiar scene created with figures appropriate to their own culture. After looking at the scene until they felt they knew it, the children had to re-create it using the same figures. As expected, inexperienced at memorizing lists of words, the Guatemalan children did more poorly than U.S. children on the list-memory tests. But their performance was much better on the second type of test, and they outscored the U.S. children when asked to re-create the scene. The U.S. children used their familiar strategy—repeating the names of the items—to memorize the scene. The Guatemalans, who lacked this strategy, focused on the way the scene *looked.* For both groups of children, memory was affected less by ability than by strategies they had learned—or not learned—in their cultures. A different team of researchers found similar results testing Australian Aboriginal youngsters and children of European backgrounds (Kearins, 1981). That is, memory on certain kinds of tests was better for children who had been reared in cultures where those skills were highly developed.

Learning information—lists of spelling words, math facts, poetry, a part in a play—is facilitated by specific methods or strategies. The most basic is *verbal rehearsal,* simply repeating information over and over (Flavell, 1985). When studying a list, children who rehearse the most recent word along with other words in a *cumulative* way tend to recall more words later than children who just repeat isolated words. Linking words creates a more active and larger set for memory (Ornstein, Baker-Ward, & Naus, 1975).

During the middle years, children develop many strategies that transform information, making it easier to remember. For example, they can organize information into categories such as animals, toys, and tools to facilitate recall. Although only a few 7- and 8-year-olds use categories to organize pictures or words, older children generate the associations and use them spontaneously as memory aids (Best & Ornstein, 1986; Salatas & Flavell, 1976).

Some strategies for retrieving information improve as we age. During the school years, children learn to use associations, inferences, and retrieval cues to recall information. To recall a former classmate's name, a child may try to visualize the seating arrangement in the old classroom and retrieve the name by associating the child with a specific location in the class. Children aged 10 to 12 remember what they read because they elaborate the information in the text, make it personally meaningful, summarize the main ideas, and use images and notes as memory cues. Some researchers claim that improvements in memory with age are more likely due to improvements in retrieval than to improvements in encoding.

● *Metacognition.* **Metacognition** is the awareness children develop about their own knowledge and abilities. It's a way of knowing what you know and what you don't know. Parents and teachers can help children improve their metacognitive skills by asking questions like "Where do you think you went wrong in doing this division problem?" Thinking about the answers helps students to examine the accuracy and efficiency of their own problem solving. When children say, "I think organizing pictures in groups will help me remember," "I have trouble remembering that 7 times 8 is 56," or "I'm good at adding but have trouble with subtracting," we know that they have developed at least some metacognition. We will discuss two aspects of metacognition: (1) metacognitive knowledge and (2) cognitive monitoring.

Metacognitive knowledge is knowledge that a child has about cognition. This is the cognitive skill that helps you decide *how* to remember something, because it enables you to think about the memory strategies that work best for you (Kail, 1984). For example, kindergartners and first, third, and fifth graders were asked, "Would it be easier to remember a phone number immediately after being told the number or after getting a drink of water?" Even young children knew that a delay would interfere with memory. Yet only half of the kindergarten and first-grade children understood that remembering a list of opposite word pairs would be easier than remembering pairs of arbitrary words (Kreutzer, Leonard, & Flavell, 1975).

Metamemory (thinking about the process of remembering) is important because what children believe about memory strategies influences whether they use them. If young children are unaware of various strategies or believe that they are not useful or necessary, then they are unlikely to apply them. For example, preschool children do not seem to realize that when listening to one message, they may not fully understand another simultaneous message. By kindergarten age, children do seem to understand that what they know and understand depends on what they pay attention to (Pillow, 1989).

The second aspect of metacognition is *cognitive monitoring,* which includes self-appraisal and self-management (Paris & Winograd, 1990). *Self-appraisal* means you can evaluate your own knowledge and then choose appropriate plans and strategies for increasing it. When writing a report, for example, self-appraisal helps you to see where you need more information. Self-appraisal also helps children to distinguish what they know from what they don't know. Before self-appraisal develops, children often miss stumbling blocks to comprehension when they listen and read. For example, when nonsense words appear in a reading passage, when words are scrambled, or when obvious contradictions occur in a reading passage, young children tend to miss these distortions

metacognition
the understanding and control of one's own thinking skills; the ability to think about thinking, including thinking about reasoning and thinking about memory

(Markman & Gorin, 1981; Paris & Meyers, 1981). Later in the chapter we'll see that metacognitive skills like self-appraisal are critical to children's independent learning.

Critical too is the second aspect of cognitive monitoring, *self-management,* the "executive management" of thinking. Self-management enables us to select appropriate strategies for solving a problem and to change those plans if they do not work. When children are able to shift gears in solving problems, they persist longer and are ultimately more successful (Brown, Bransford, Ferrara, & Campione, 1983). Self-management helps fourth graders to know that they've multiplied when they should have divided, for example.

● *Problem solving.* The fourth area of improvement involves problem solving. Children get better at explaining why things happen (causal reasoning) because they are now able to think about more than one dimension at the same time. As children's reasoning skills develop, they can use different types of information to determine what causes something to happen (Mendelson & Shultz, 1976).

When asked to explain what causes something to balance on a scale, for example, young children think only in terms of weight. A 4-year-old understands that two rocks weighing the same will balance a scale. Older children realize that two factors, weight and distance, must be considered together.

We turn now to children's emerging cognitive skills as they are applied in the classroom.

COGNITION IN ELEMENTARY SCHOOL

Psychologists devise experiments to test for cognitive developments, but one of the clearest settings in which to see the results of these improvements is in the classroom. Cognition in the classroom requires special strategies, metacognition, and motivation. And as the "three R's" become more sophisticated, these specific cognitive skills advance sharply as well.

● Reading

Five-year-old Sandra can't read a book yet, but she knows what a stop sign says, and she can spot her own name. And like many *Sesame Street* watchers who are read to often, she became comfortable with letters and sounds long before she began school. Like many other kindergartners, Sandra invents spellings and pretends to read. All these reading-related activities are signs of **emergent literacy** (Teale & Sulzby, 1986).

A key task for young readers is to "break the code"—to understand the relation of sounds and symbols. For example, beginning readers need to know how to break words into phonemes—or letter combinations such as *th, br,* and *st*—and how phonemes are related to sound combinations. Children whose phoneme skills are strong usually score high in word recognition at the end of first and second grade (Juel, Griffith, & Gough, 1986).

● **emergent literacy**
a focus on the creative use of reading and writing by young children before they learn the formal rules and conventions of print

When Chinese children learn to read, encoding written symbols solves only part of the puzzle. In the Chinese language, communicating meaning correctly also demands correct intonation.

Young readers also have to master print conventions. They have to perceive the difference between letters and numbers, train their eyes to read from left to right and from top to bottom (at least in many languages), and understand that the spaces between words and the periods between sentences are boundaries. These concepts about print and the nature of reading and writing are part of young children's metacognition. The concepts are usually mastered by third grade, but metacognition about reading—learning the strategies that enhance comprehension—continues to develop for many years (Garner, 1987; Lomax & McGee, 1987). By age 10 to 11, students can use the title, headings, and pictures as clues about a topic before they begin reading; they can infer information and create images as they read, helping them to consolidate the meaning. By this age, too, after they have read a selection, children can skim selectively to find information (Paris, Wasik, & Turner, in press). Spotting inconsistencies is now easier too. For example, 9- and 11-year-olds read a story in which koalas were first described as sleeping in trees and then, later, as sleeping on the ground. The 9-year-olds had trouble finding the contradiction, but the 11-year-olds found it easily (Baker, 1984).

Nevertheless, reading skills are still limited. Even seventh graders can't always distinguish important from unimportant ideas (Baker & Brown, 1984), and many college students have difficulty highlighting important information in a text and taking notes as they read. Cognitive strategies and concepts about reading continue to develop into adulthood, enhancing comprehension and memory.

● Writing

When most of us were in the fourth grade, writing a story or a composition meant that we stared at a blank piece of paper until, finally, we thought of something to say. We wrote it down and waited for another thought. When we'd filled the page, we made a "final copy" and handed it in.

Unless they are taught otherwise, elementary school children still typically use two strategies when writing an essay. One called *knowledge-telling,* is simply spilling everything they know in an unconnected series of sentences (Scardamalia & Bereiter, 1984). Instead of planning the composition, they focus on one aspect of the topic and simply tell what they know. Then they begin a new topic. The composition reads like a series of statements or observations instead of a coherent essay.

A second common but ineffective strategy is *copy-delete.* Young children use it most when they write reports from secondary sources. They read a passage in an encyclopedia and then selectively edit it by copying or paraphrasing some sentences and deleting others. The result is a series of disconnected sentences. Knowledge-telling and copy-delete are shortcuts that actually interfere with thoughtful writing.

Newer methods teach writing as a *process.* Children choose from a group of topics; they "brainstorm" or jot down all their ideas about it, write a first draft, edit it for the flow of ideas and for style, listen to a classmate's comments ("peer conferencing"), and then make final corrections. This approach recognizes that good writing involves metacognition and strategies such as brainstorming and outlining. It can be very effective in helping children get started and in overcoming the belief that, once written, an idea is forever fixed. Thus, process writing is an approach that fosters better strategies, metacognition, and motivation for learning.

● Mathematics

The way children first understand arithmetic is similar to their early attempts to read. Like the alphabet, the number string has to be memorized, and as with emergent literacy skills, math skills too exist well before first grade begins.

The stage of concrete operations makes it possible for elementary school children to learn increasingly complex mathematics. Now they can represent actions mentally, they know that the relationships between numbers are both fixed and reversible, and they can understand math as a system of rules.

Most kindergartners can easily add and subtract numbers below 10, and some 4- and 5-year-olds can automatically recall simple addition facts (Siegler & Shrager, 1984). Children of this age solve harder problems, such as 8 + 3, with backup strategies, such as counting on from the larger number or counting on their fingers. With these cognitive strategies, children can find an answer even when they can't immediately recall it. In one study, first graders who excelled at addition and subtraction used strategies more often and more effectively than other students (Siegler, 1988).

As children learn basic facts about arithmetic, they begin to induce rules about the relationships among numbers (Baroody, 1985). For example, children begin to understand that when zero is added to or subtracted from a number, the number doesn't change. They realize that adding 1 simply ups the number to the next number in the sequence. They learn that two numbers can be added by counting on from the higher number—5 + 2 yields the sequence 5-6-7—rather than starting at the number 1 and counting all the way to 7. Children also discover regularities for subtracting, multiplying, and dividing that reflect rules and strategies. These rules are based in part on a better conceptual understanding of number that involves operations such as seriation, transitivity, and reversibility. With the realization that addition and subtraction are complementary, just as multiplication and division are, comes deeper insight into mathematics.

But children do not always learn rules easily or smoothly. Sometimes they learn shortcuts or incorrect rules. For example, 7- to 9-year-olds often have difficulty borrowing from zero when subtracting, and so they devise shortcuts. Some children subtract zero from the other number, some subtract the number from 10 but forget to diminish the next column by 10, and others simply write zero whenever they see something subtracted from zero. Similarly, when subtracting 27 from 54, some children automatically subtract 4 from 7 to avoid borrowing. On the one hand, this is an extension of a successful rule in which smaller numbers are subtracted from larger ones. But on the other hand, this is the invention of an erroneous shortcut, similar to the copy-delete or knowledge-telling strategies that children devise for writing. Parents and teachers who are aware of these incorrect, or "buggy," strategies can help children overcome them.

Many children need special help with word problems. For example, "Nancy has 6 marbles. Eve has 3 marbles. How many marbles does Nancy need to give away to have as many as Eve?" Typically, third graders have trouble solving this problem. At age 8, they look for word clues, such as *more* and *less;* and when these signals don't appear, they get confused (Morales, Shute, & Pellegrino, 1985). By 10 or 11, children begin to interpret problems conceptually instead of looking for word cues. This change may reflect better reading skills, but part of the improvement comes from increased understanding of the conceptual relations among numbers, from grasping the concrete operations that Piaget identified.

To sum up, schoolwork and the cognitive skills of middle childhood reinforce each other. New skills enable children to do more sophisticated tasks, and the tasks exercise newly emerging skills. Many math problems are based on *conservation.* If you have five apples and give away three, you have only two, but there are still five apples. Science requires *classification* (is this leaf from a maple tree, an oak, a birch?), and social studies requires *seriation* (what country in the world has the biggest area? the next biggest? the next?). Similarly, learning spelling words and math facts improves memory skills.

School is particularly helpful in fostering *metacognitive abilities*. By the middle of elementary school, children begin to understand that considering how to attack a problem *before* starting it makes it easier to solve. For instance, when asked to compare distances when some figures are in miles and others are in kilometers, children learn that they must first convert both distances to one system or the other. And as their metacognitive skills develop, children are taught that memory aids can make remembering easier. Rhymes ("Thirty days has September, April, June, and November"), "chunking" (memorizing the names of the four New England colonies, the five Southern colonies, and so on), and rehearsal strategies (such as repeating information aloud) all help children remember.

Finally, elementary school promotes cognitive monitoring. In order to complete gradually more complex tests, children learn to pace themselves, judging when they've spent too much time on one problem and moving on to the next. In a problem with several steps, they learn to check their work; and as children read more independently, they learn to monitor their comprehension, to stop and read something over again when necessary.

INDIVIDUAL DIFFERENCES IN COGNITIVE DEVELOPMENT

If all normal children pass through the 5-to-7 transition by the middle of elementary school, then why are some in gifted classes while others work at grade level and still others fall behind? Any attempt to answer this question brings us back to the theme of individual differences. Differences in cognitive development include timing (at what age developmental changes occur), the speed with which the processes are used (how fast a child can retrieve information, for example), the size of a child's memory, and the amount of information to which a child has access. Some children have traveled around the country, for example, while others have never left their own neighborhood. How much environment influences intelligence is one of the most hotly debated topics in the field of child development.

● Intelligence and Intelligence Testing

We all know what intelligence is, or at least we think we do. Smarter people do better in school, can express themselves well in words, and know how to size up a situation quickly. But what about the child who gets A's in English but C's in math? Or the 7-year-old who can explain how an engine works but has trouble remembering that the word *engine* ends in the letter *e*? Clearly, intelligence is a complex ability, and most of us are smarter in some ways than in others. In many schools, particularly where children are grouped by ability, intelligence testing is done early in elementary school. But what are these tests actually measuring?

● Early Tests

One of the first to try measuring human intelligence was the English mathematician Francis Galton (1822–1911), who believed that most mental abilities are inherited. Galton tried to measure mental abilities with laboratory tests of hearing, vision, and reaction times (the time it takes a subject to press a key after hearing a buzzer, for example). But he found that people who did well on one kind of test often didn't do well on others, and that those who did well on all the tests didn't seem particularly gifted in school.

Another early investigator of intelligence was Alfred Binet (1857–1911), a French psychologist. In the early 1900s, Binet developed a test for the Paris school system aimed at identifying students who needed extra help with their schoolwork. Binet's test focused on mental skills that typically increase with age, such as verbal and reasoning ability. It was divided into a series of test items linked to chronological age. For example, a series aimed at 10-year-olds consisted of questions most children that age could answer, but most 9-year-olds could not. A 10-year-old who could not answer these questions would be deemed slow; a 9-year-old who could answer the 10-year-old questions would be considered gifted. Children who could answer most questions appropriate for their age, but not many beyond that series, would be considered average. These children were assigned a "mental age" equal to their chronological age.

In later tests, Binet used mental age to compute the number he called an **intelligence quotient**—the famous IQ score. In Binet's system, IQ is simply mental age divided by chronological age, multiplied by 100 to eliminate decimals. A child whose mental age is 10 and who is exactly 10 years old has an IQ of 100: $(10/10) \times 100 = 1 \times 100 = 100$. A child who is 8 but whose mental age is 10 has an IQ of 125: $(10/8) \times 100 = 1.25 \times 100 = 125$.

Binet believed that intelligence was complex, not a simple "thing" that people had more or less of throughout life, but many of his successors disagreed. One of them, Stanford psychologist Lewis Terman, thought that intelligence was a relatively stable quality determined mostly by inheritance. He revised Binet's test to produce the Stanford-Binet Test, which is still widely used today.

Some American psychologists, including David Wechsler, sided with Binet about the complex nature of intelligence. In the 1940s, Wechsler developed the Wechsler Intelligence Scale for Children (WISC), which was followed by the Wechsler Adult Intelligence Scale (WAIS). Because Wechsler saw intelligence as a broad concept involving many different abilities, not just scholastic aptitude, both the WISC and the WAIS include performance tasks, such as assembling puzzles, as well as verbal tasks. Within each of these two major categories are several subtests. The verbal category, for instance, includes subtests in general information ("What is steam made of?") and similarities ("In what way are a saw and a hammer alike?"). The Wechsler tests, instead of yielding a single IQ score, give several scores—one for each subtest, an overall verbal score, an overall performance score, and a summary IQ.

● How Useful Are Intelligence Tests?

One problem facing anyone seeking to test a child's intelligence is what to test. A child may be good at one kind of intellectual task and poor at another, and

● **intelligence quotient**
a measure of intelligence computed by dividing an individual's mental age by his or her chronological age. This number is multiplied by 100, with 100 being an average score and scores above and below 100 indicating greater or lesser intelligence, respectively

Testing for an IQ score is simple; using the test well is harder. Critics charge that tests are biased toward verbally skilled white middle-class children. Defenders argue that the tests measure abilities needed for success in school.

the kind of intelligence useful in one environment (a big city neighborhood) may be less vital in another (a farming village).

The tests typically given to U.S. schoolchildren measure the sort of intelligence that it takes to succeed in Western-style educational environments—what might be called "school smarts." Although the tests do measure problem-solving skills, they also rely heavily on verbal ability. The mathematically bright child who lags behind in English skills may not do well on a conventional intelligence test.

Another drawback of intelligence tests is that although they are useful for diagnosing learning problems and identifying students who need extra help, they are less reliable at predicting school achievement for the average child. This is because achievement is influenced by so many things besides intelligence, including motivation, opportunity, and the influence of parents and peers.

In recent years, intelligence testing has been both sharply attacked and staunchly defended. Critics have charged that most tests are biased against children from any but white, middle-class, English-speaking homes. Since many tests require extensive verbal ability and familiarity with middle-class culture, these charges cannot be easily dismissed. Defenders of the tests argue that they are basically sound and that, properly used, they do a good job of measuring mental ability—at least those aspects of mental ability needed to succeed in school.

● Intelligence and Inheritance

A persistent controversy involving intelligence concerns the extent to which it is inherited. Children's intelligence scores tend to resemble their parents' (Scarr & Weinberg, 1983), but heredity is only part of the reason. Another is environmental: Smart parents usually give their children the kinds of experiences that stimulate intellectual development.

Twenty years ago, the issue of intelligence *heritability* was hotly debated among psychologists and educators. Some scientists argued (on the basis of studies that have since been criticized) that intelligence was 80 percent genetic and only 20 percent environmental. They opposed compensatory education programs, arguing that it was a waste of money to try to stimulate intellectual development if intelligence were determined by inheritance. One proponent of this view, Arthur Jensen (1969), focused primarily on the differences in intelligence test scores between white and black children. On average, white youngsters score higher than blacks, and Jensen asserted that this difference resulted from genetic differences between the races. Jensen's position sparked a fierce debate about the heritability of intelligence, racial differences in test scores, and the nature and fairness of IQ tests in general.

Today, most psychologists disagree with Jensen's claims. Several studies have shown that intelligence is actually quite malleable and that efforts to stimulate children's intellectual development can succeed (Ramey & Haskins, 1981). Most agree, too, that trying to quantify genetic and environmental influences is pointless. Rather, we should ask how nature and nurture *interact* in shaping a child's intellect. As one psychologist put it, the question isn't "How much?" It's "How?" (Anastasi, 1958).

SOCIAL COGNITION IN MIDDLE CHILDHOOD

Most of children's thinking has nothing to do with logical problems or intelligence test questions. They are much more concerned with themselves and the other people in their lives. This kind of thinking—known as **social cognition**—focuses on interpersonal relations, social rules, and roles.

Researchers studying social cognition during middle childhood have focused on three main areas: the way children think about other people, how they view relationships between people, and how they think about morality. In all three areas a shift in thinking occurs between—you guessed it—ages 5 and 7, just as children's other cognitive skills are maturing too.

● **social cognition**
thinking about oneself and the other people in one's life, including awareness of interpersonal relations and social rules and roles

● New Conceptions about Other People

Five-year-old Lisa is working on a jigsaw puzzle when her little brother, Raymond, runs through the room and steps on it. The puzzle breaks apart, and Lisa tries to hit Raymond. Lisa has trouble distinguishing between accidental and deliberate behavior, because like most 5-year-olds, she judges actions mainly in terms of their consequences: good consequences, good intentions;

Unlike younger children who find it hard to see the value of something they wouldn't like for themselves, by age 7 to 10, most children can put themselves in the place of another. They don't have to want the gift but understand that the other person may.

bad consequences, bad intentions. So Lisa is as angry as if her brother had trampled her puzzle intentionally. While Piaget believed that children considered only consequences, newer research indicates that children can consider motives as well (Nelson-Le Gall, 1985). Certainly, within a few years, Lisa will understand that sometimes behavior is purposeful, sometimes it is accidental, and sometimes motivation is complicated.

Middle childhood is a time when children begin to think about motivation. Besides learning to distinguish between intentional and accidental behavior, children begin to recognize that other people have feelings, needs, and reasons for acting as they do. For example, in selecting a birthday present for his father, 4-year-old Peter chose a toy truck, assuming that since he wanted one, so would his father. By age 8, he knows that people have their own interests, and he buys a Toronto Blue Jays T-shirt for his baseball-loving father.

Being able to choose the right gift or to understand another's behavior rests on children's growing ability to take the perspective of another, to see things from others' points of view, and to see themselves through the eyes of others. According to a theory advanced by Robert Selman (1971), this ability unfolds in five stages (see Table 11.1).

In Selman's view, the most important shift occurs at the same time as the 5-to-7 cognitive transition, when children make the transition from level 1 to level 2 (see Table 11.1). Those who cannot see how their behavior looks to others will have difficulty making and keeping friends. Three-year-olds, for example, have trouble understanding that another person might have values, moral beliefs, or beliefs about social rules that are different from their own (Flavell et al., 1992). These results are consistent with Selman's ideas about level 0 perspective taking. (See Chapter 8.) In one study, level 1 children (4- to 9-year-olds) saw a picture. Then, all but a small part was covered, and the children were asked whether a puppet who "saw" only that small section would know what was in the picture. Children under 6 years old said that the puppet would know what was in the picture (Taylor, 1988).

Adults can help children to consider other perspectives when their own blinders interfere with healthy social experiences. If, for example, a 6-year-old, big for his age and overly aggressive, frequently pushes smaller children out of the way to get to the swings at playtime, he will have trouble making friends. When the other children refuse to play with him, he first calls them names and then forces his way into their games. Consequently, other children often leave the area when they see him coming.

Unable to see himself as others see him, this child has no idea why he is so unpopular. In fact, like many children with similar problems, he tends to misinterpret other people's reactions. He may even believe that the other children are afraid to play with him because he is bigger, stronger, and better at games than they are. Teachers and parents can help such children use role-playing

TABLE 11.1   SELMAN'S STAGES OF PERSPECTIVE TAKING

Level	Age	Characteristics	Example
0	Preschool	Blurred perspective; child attributes own point of view to others or refuses to understand another's viewpoint	"*Sesame Street* is my favorite show, and my mommy's too."
1	4–9 years	Understands that people can have different perspectives on the same situation	"I like to swim, but my brother doesn't."
2	6–12 years	Child can put self in others' shoes and see self through the eyes of others	"Danny doesn't like me because I'm always getting him in trouble."
3	9–15 years	Understands that a third person can have an opinion about a relationship between two others	"I think you think I'm crazy to go out with Mike, Dad, but Mom likes him."
4	12+ years	Thinks of social relations as part of larger networks; knows that society has viewpoints of its own	"'Jocks' just don't date 'Nerds.'"

SOURCE: After R. L. Selman (1971).

exercises, especially games in which the aggressor plays the victim of aggression and begins to see how that can feel. Simulation exercises such as "What if I didn't have any friends?" can also foster understanding of others' feelings.

● New Conceptions about Relationships

As children become more sensitive to other people's motives and feelings, they also begin to think about relationships in a new way. For toddlers and preschoolers, parents are both omniscient and omnipotent, but during the school years, children's views about relationships begin to change.

For some children, elementary school offers the first real exposure to an authority other than their parents. At first, they accept their teacher's authority as they do their parents'. Holding a kind of "might makes right" point of view, children often think that teachers and parents are right because they have the power to make them behave. Once they complete the 5-to-7 transition, though, children begin to place limits on adults' authority. A teacher can tell you to be quiet, but she can't tell you what to eat for lunch.

Children also begin to understand that authority can derive from knowledge and experience. Even they can know more than their parents about *some* things. But realizing that parents and teachers aren't omniscient seems to be a turning point: If grown-ups don't know everything, perhaps they don't know anything! Because most children are relatively obedient during the early elementary

Advances in cognition further social relationships as well. During middle childhood, friendship grows from sharing toys to sharing feelings.

school years, parents are often shocked when, around fourth grade, children begin to think of authority as something they can choose to disobey.

Children's conceptions about friendship change too as they spend less time with adults and more time with their peers. Specifically, they get better at understanding their friends' feelings. Whereas preschoolers base friendship on their own self-interest (someone to play with), the cognitive changes of the 5-to-7 transition lead children toward understanding that friendships are based on shared likes and dislikes and on caring. Relationships now tend to be more enduring than the friendships of preschoolers, partly because likes and dislikes last longer and partly because their increased understanding of how other people think and act helps children to act in friendly ways (sharing, helping, and so on) that maintain the relationship. By late elementary school, children perceive that friendship is based on understanding, intimacy, and mutuality and that it provides mutual intimacy and support. Relationships now become more permanent and much deeper, as we will discuss in more detail in the next chapter.

● Moral Development

"Where did you get that candy bar, Ricky?"

"From the store."

"Did you pay the man for it?"

"It's OK, Mommy. They have lots of candy bars."

Like every other child, 4-year-old Ricky was not born knowing right from wrong. He is slowly learning it, as now, when he must return the candy bar and apologize to the manager.

Psychologists who have studied children's ideas about ethical behavior believe that they change as their cognitive abilities develop. In fact, the most influential thinker in this field, Lawrence Kohlberg (1969), developed a theory that is related to Piaget's views about cognitive development. Kohlberg contended that children pass through distinct stages of **moral development;** that is, the way they reason about morality changes as they mature. To understand Kohlberg's theory, consider the following problem:

● **moral development**
the changes in the ability to reason about morality that occur as a child grows up

> In Europe, a woman was near death from a very serious disease, a special kind of cancer. A druggist in the woman's town had recently developed a new drug that the doctors said was her only hope. The drug was expensive to make, but the druggist was charging ten times its cost—$2000 for a small dose. The sick woman's husband, Heinz, went to everyone he knew to borrow money, but he could only raise about $1000. He told the druggist that his wife was dying, and asked him to sell the drug more cheaply or let him pay later. But the druggist refused. Desperate, Heinz broke into the store one night and stole some of the drug for his wife. Was it right or wrong for Heinz to do that? (Kohlberg & Gilligan, 1972)

In Kohlberg's model, whether a child thinks Heinz should steal the drug is less significant than the reasoning behind that decision. Kohlberg suggested that there are three levels of moral reasoning—preconventional, conventional, and principled (sometimes called postconventional)—which unfold in that or-

TABLE 11.2 KOHLBERG'S SIX STAGES OF MORAL REASONING

Level One: Preconventional	Child's Response to Theft of Drug
Stage 1 *Obedience-and-punishment orientation.* The child obeys rules to avoid punishment. There is as yet no internalization of moral standards.	*Pro:* Theft is justified because the drug did not cost much to produce *Con:* Theft is condemned because Heinz will be caught and go to jail.
Stage 2 *Naïve hedonistic and instrumental orientation.* The child's behavior is motivated by a selfish desire to obtain rewards and benefits. Although reciprocity occurs, it is self-serving, manipulative, and based on a marketplace outlook: "You can play with my blocks if I can play with your cars."	*Pro:* Theft is justified because his wife needs the drug and Heinz needs his wife's companionship and help in life. *Con:* Theft is condemned because his wife will probably die before Heinz gets out of jail, so it will not do him much good.

Level Two: Conventional	Child's Response to Theft of Drug
Stage 3 *"Good boy"—"nice girl" morality.* The child is concerned with winning the approval of others and avoiding their disapproval. In judging the goodness or badness of behavior, consideration is given to a person's intentions. The child has a concept of a morally good person as one who possesses a set of virtues, hence the child places much emphasis upon being "nice."	*Pro:* Theft is justified because Heinz is unselfish in looking after the needs of his wife. *Con:* Theft is condemned because Heinz will feel bad thinking of how he brought dishonor on his family; his family will be ashamed of his act.
Stage 4 *"Law-and-order" orientation.* The individual blindly accepts social conventions and rules. Emphasis is on "doing one's duty," showing respect for authority, and maintaining a given social order for its own sake.	*Pro:* Theft is justified because Heinz would otherwise have been responsible for his wife's death. *Con:* Theft is condemned because Heinz is a lawbreaker.

Level Three: Principled	Child's Response to Theft of Drug
Stage 5 *Social-contract orientation.* The individual believes that the purpose of the law is to preserve human rights and that unjust laws should be changed. Morality is seen as based on an agreement among individuals to conform to laws that are necessary for the community welfare. But since it is a social contract, it can be modified so long as basic rights like *life* and *liberty* are not impaired.	*Pro:* Theft is justified because the law was not fashioned for situations in which an individual would forfeit life by obeying the rules. *Con:* Theft is condemned because others may also have great need.
Stage 6 *Universal ethical principle orientation.* Conduct is controlled by an internalized set of ideas which, if violated, results in self-condemnation and guilt. The individual follows self-chosen ethical principles based upon abstract concepts (e.g., the equality of human rights, the Golden Rule, respect for the dignity of each human being) rather than concrete rules (e.g., the Ten Commandments). Unjust laws may be broken because they conflict with broad moral principles.	*Pro:* Theft is justified because Heinz would not have lived up to the standards of his conscience if he had allowed his wife to die. *Con:* Theft is condemned because Heinz did not live up to the standards of his conscience when he engaged in stealing.

der. Each level is composed of two stages (see Table 11.2). And as Piaget held for cognitive development, Kohlberg asserted that each level is qualitatively different from and more advanced and mature than previous ones.

During most of childhood, said Kohlberg, we reason at the preconventional level, but elementary school children are also capable of conventional moral reasoning. As Table 11.2 shows, **preconventional thinking** is not based on society's standards or conventions (hence the label *pre*conventional) but on external, physical events. When faced with a moral issue, children at this level do not ask themselves whether something is right or wrong. Instead, they focus on consequences: Will a decision bring rewards or punishment? One preconventional child might say that Heinz should not steal the drug because he could get caught and be sent to jail. Another might say that Heinz should steal the drug because people will treat him like a hero for saving his wife.

The parallel between overall cognitive development and moral development is clearly evident in children's transition to conventional thinking. While cognitive changes enable children to better understand society's rules and roles, **conventional thinking** enables them to consider how well people actually follow those rules and how well they play their social roles. A child at the conventional level might say that Heinz should not steal the drug because stealing is against the law. Another might counter that Heinz should steal the drug because that is what a good husband is supposed to do.

Researchers testing Kohlberg's theory have found that moral development generally proceeds in the sequence he described (Colby et al., 1983). Studies also support Kohlberg's idea that moral thinking is stimulated when children are exposed to ethical conflicts and to people who reason at a more advanced level. For example, children whose parents encourage them to participate in family discussions show more advanced levels of moral reasoning than children whose parents don't include them in family-related talks (Haan, Smith, & Block, 1968; Holstein, 1972).

But so far, research has not confirmed Kohlberg's contention that moral development proceeds in separate, distinct stages. Like cognitive development, reasoning about morality develops gradually. More advanced forms of reasoning do appear with age, but aspects of earlier kinds of reasoning are present in all ages, and different levels of reasoning are called into use at different times and in different situations. Although a preschooler's responses to moral dilemmas would probably be consistently preconventional, a schoolchild's responses would probably have a mixture of both preconventional and conventional responses. Like all of human development, moral development is not a perfectly regular, even process.

● **preconventional thinking** according to Kohlberg, the first level of moral development, in which children make decisions about what is right and wrong based not on society's standards or conventions but on external, physical events

● **conventional thinking** according to Kohlberg, the second level of moral development, in which children make decisions about what is right and wrong based on how well a person follows the rules and conventions of society and keeps within the roles people are expected to play

SUMMARY

1. In contrast to infancy and early childhood, physical growth during middle childhood is gradual, and many of the observable changes are subtle. Even though genes strongly influence size and strength, environmental factors—such as diet, hygiene, medical care, and opportunities for physical activity—play a role as well. (See pages 342–343.)

2. Patterns of eating and exercise in childhood tend to persist into adulthood, sometimes with serious consequences. Heavy television viewing, coupled with inactivity and a diet high in fats and sugars, can set the stage for obesity and, eventually, coronary disease. One reason for the high degree of physical inactivity among U.S. children may be the emphasis placed on competitive sports. Experts believe that if children's athletic programs downplayed the competitive aspect of sports, more children would benefit from the exercise and skills gained during athletics. (See pages 344–346.)

3. Obesity is the most common health problem among elementary school children. In addition to the health risks associated with obesity, children who are markedly overweight also often suffer social rejection. Except in very rare cases involving medical disorders, childhood obesity can be treated by a program of healthful eating and increased exercise. (See pages 346–347.)

4. Between ages 5 and 7 a cognitive revolution carries children into the stage of concrete operations. Gains are seen in the realms of conservation, causation, classification, and the manipulation of symbols. (See pages 347–349.)

5. According to Piaget, children's new cognitive attainments stem from their developing ability to perform mental operations. Operations are actions that are represented mentally, preserve an unchangeable relation, are reversible, and are part of a system of rules. Being able to perform operations expands children's logical thinking skills. Piaget called this stage the period of "concrete operations": Children think logically about observable, concrete objects or events but have difficulty reasoning about hypothetical situations. (See pages 349–353.)

6. Information-processing theorists have focused especially on four areas of cognition: attention, memory, metacognition (awareness of one's knowledge and abilities), and problem solving. According to these theorists, gains in overall cognitive abilities during middle childhood can be attributed to specific gains in each of these four areas. (See pages 353–358.)

7. Middle childhood is a time of tremendous growth in the basic skills that form the foundation for successful school achievement: reading, writing, and mathematics. Perhaps more important, schoolwork and the cognitive skills of middle childhood reinforce each other. The demands of school are especially important in fostering metacognitive growth. (See pages 358–362.)

8. Intelligence tests measure a range of intellectual abilities, focusing mainly on those that enable children to succeed in school. Many critics have charged that standardized intelligence tests such as the WISC are biased in favor of white middle-class children. Although scientists have long argued about nature and nurture as influences on intelligence, research has proved intelligence to be quite malleable, rather than fixed by inheritance. Instead of asking whether nature or nurture is more important, psychologists now ask how environment and heredity interact to shape a child's intellect. (See pages 362–365.)

9. Much of children's thinking concerns interpersonal relations and social rules and roles—what we call social cognition. As with other cognitive skills, the way children think in these areas changes between ages 5 and 7. One focus of research has been on changes in the way children think about other people and how they view relationships between people. (See pages 365–369.)

10. A second focus of research on social cognition concerns children's reasoning about moral issues. According to Kohlberg's theory of moral development, during the late elementary school years many children start employing conventional moral reasoning, judging right and wrong in terms of society's rules and standards. (See pages 369–371)

KEY TERMS

causation	5-to-7 transition	obese
classification	intelligence quotient	preconventional thinking
concrete operations	logic	seriation
conservation	manipulate symbols	social cognition
conventional thinking	metacognition	strategy
emergent literacy	moral development	transitivity

SUGGESTED READINGS

Bjorklund, D. (1989). *Children's thinking.* Pacific Grove, CA: Brooks-Cole. An overview of children's cognitive development with especially good coverage of research and theory on individual diffcrences in children's mental performance.

Elkind, D. (1981). *Children and adolescents: Interpretive essays on Jean Piaget* (3rd ed.). New York: Oxford University Press. A series of articles by a psychologist who demonstrates how children's behavior can be better understood through the application of Piaget's theory.

Schreiber, L. (1990). *The parent's guide to kid's sports.* Boston: Little, Brown. Practical advice for adults on helping children get the most out of sports and athletics.

Siegler, R. (1991). *Children's thinking.* (2nd ed.). Englewood Cliffs, NJ: Prentice-Hall. This overview of cognitive development during childhood emphasizes the information-processing approach to the study of cognition.

Turiel, E. (1983). *The development of social knowledge: Morality and convention.* New York: Cambridge University Press. This book examines numerous aspects of social cognition from a cognitive-developmental point of view.

CHAPTER 12

SOCIAL AND EMOTIONAL DEVELOPMENT IN MIDDLE CHILDHOOD

Interested in charting the changes in emotional and social development, a researcher asked different aged children if they would share some toys with a playmate:

Researcher: Suppose you and Sammy are playing together and you have these [five] toys? Would you give him any?

James (4 yrs., 8 mos.): I would give him these two.

Researcher: Why those two?

James: Because I got to keep three. These are the ones I like.

Researcher: Suppose Sammy said, "I want to have more"?

James: If he took one then I would take it back from him.

Researcher: Why is that?

James: Because I want three.

Researcher: What will Sammy do then?

James: He'll say that's O.K., because he likes these [the two toys originally given].

. . .

Researcher: Would you give Kevin any of these to play with?

Mike (6 yrs., 11 mos.): Yeah.

Researcher: You would?

Mike: I'd give these, so it'd be equal, so we can each have five.

Researcher: Well, where would you put that [extra] one?

Mike: Put it back.

Researcher: You wouldn't use it then?

Mike: Yeah.

Researcher: Why is that a good thing?

Mike: 'Cause like if I have six, that wouldn't be equal, like see—and if he has six, it wouldn't be equal.

Researcher: Why wouldn't that be a good thing?

Mike: Because then we would start fussin'. Like, say I have four and you have seven, then we start fighting. (Damon, 1977, pp. 78, 81)

Moving from early childhood's me-first, me-best style of interaction toward fairness signals the social growth that occurs during middle childhood. Mike, for example, is not yet 7, but he knows that sometimes equity serves his own interests best. By the end of middle childhood he will probably be more adept at settling disputes, more flexible when considering alternatives and judging what is fair.

During these years, social competence grows in many ways. Children's self-concept becomes more sophisticated, as does their ability to compare their own feelings and behavior to those of others. And as they gain control over their behavior, they need fewer curbs from adults.

School-age children begin forming true friendships based on mutual trust and shared interests. Many of these friendships form in school, where, for the first time, children's achievements are closely monitored. The 6-year-old enters a classroom very different from nursery school, a day care setting, or kindergarten. Now children have real "work" to do, work that will be judged and graded.

Outside of school, on teams and in clubs and organizations, children are evaluated, both by their peers and by adults. This is the age when the natural athletes and the less physically skilled are sorted out, when some are picked first and others are always chosen last.

Elementary school children increasingly judge each other's personal traits, and not measuring up to fairly strict codes of dress, speech, and behavior often means rejection. The social world of middle childhood, then, is not just broader than the preschool world; it is more demanding.

As we've seen in earlier stages of development, social and emotional advances are linked to cognitive changes. For example, in the opening excerpt, 4-year-old James is certain that Sammy *must* want the same distribution of toys that he does. In contrast, Mike's approach to sharing is more mature, partly because he has the cognitive ability to take another person's perspective. He grasps that shortchanging Kevin would annoy him.

And just as cognitive advances spur social development, social development spurs cognitive growth. The ability to form a close and lasting friendship, for example, creates an arena in which the intellectual challenge of taking another's perspective can be worked on and mastered. The interaction between cognitive and psychosocial development is especially clear when we look at the child's maturing sense of self.

In this chapter we will stress two basic themes: (1) Middle childhood is a time of developing psychological and social competence in a world that is both expanding and demanding; and (2) during middle childhood, psychosocial and cognitive development strongly interact. We turn first to the developing self.

WHO AM I? THE DEVELOPING SELF IN MIDDLE CHILDHOOD

The toddler who tries on a new hat and then looks at himself in the mirror has a rudimentary sense of himself. More advanced in her self-concept is the preschooler who proudly calls herself a "big girl" now. During the school years, a child's sense of self continues to develop into the highly personal mental image we call self-concept.

When studying the self, researchers consider three interrelated components: the cognitive, the affective, and the behavioral. The cognitive component is the way we *think* about ourselves. It is composed of the way people see and represent themselves—in short, their **self-conceptions.** A child may see herself as a redhead, a gymnast, a shy person.

● **self-conceptions**
the various attributes people see themselves possessing

The affective component of the self is the way that we *feel* about ourselves, how we *evaluate* the traits we associate with ourselves. A 10-year-old, for instance, might be proud of her musical and writing talents but ashamed of her clumsiness in sports. In sum, such feelings about the self form a person's **self-esteem.**

● **self-esteem**
one's feelings about oneself

How children feel about them-selves is influenced by how highly they regard their own traits and abilities. Succeeding in the school band or orchestra, for example, can boost the esteem of a child who does not do as well academically or in sports.

● **self-regulation**
the extent to which people can monitor and control their own behavior

The third component of the self is **self-regulation:** the extent to which we can monitor and control our own behavior. The growing ability of elementary school children to plan their own schedules, comply with social rules, tolerate frustration, and work toward goals illustrates their improving capacity for self-regulation. In the following sections we will look more closely at how each of these three components of the self develops in middle childhood. We begin with the development of self-conceptions.

● Changes in Self-Conception

Researcher: (addressing a girl, age 5½) Could you become Patches (child's dog) if you wanted to?

Girl: No.

Researcher: Why not?

Girl: 'Cause he's brown and black and white. And he has brown eyes. And 'cause he walks like a dog.

. . .

Researcher: (this time interviewing a girl who is almost 9) Could you become Tim (child's brother) if you wanted to?

Girl: No. Because I'm me and he's him. I can't change in any way 'cause I've got to stay this, like myself.

Researcher: Would you still stay the same even if your name were taken away?

Girl: I'd still be the same person.

Researcher: What stays the same?

Girl: (speaking slowly and carefully to get the pronunciation right) My per-son-al-i-ty? (Adapted from Guardo & Bohan, 1971)

When asked if anyone else could be exactly like himself, a 10-year-old replied: "I am one of a kind. There could be a person who looks like me or talks like me, but no one who has every single detail I have. Never a person who *thinks* exactly like me" (Broughton, 1978, p. 86). Notice how this change in self-conception parallels the change in children's understanding of others that occurs during the elementary school years. As we noted in Chapter 11, children this age are increasingly able to perceive the thoughts and feelings of other people and to grasp that others are unique individuals with their own personality traits. The shift to a less physically based view of the self is part of this same cognitive advance.

Although abstract conceptions of the self do not emerge until middle childhood, even young children understand that they have personalities: They know they have qualities that make them different from other children, and these qualities are not just physical (Eder, 1990; Marsh et al., 1991). In one study, researchers presented children with pairs of statements, each representing the high or low point of a psychological dimension. For example, "It's not fun to scare other people" and "It's fun to scare people" signal high and low levels of aggression. Even children as young as 3½ had conceptions of themselves that were psychologically accurate (Eder, 1990).

As elementary school children become increasingly able to "see inside themselves," they develop a much fuller, more mature understanding of what the self is feeling. For instance, when psychologist Susan Harter (1982) studied children's ability to understand ambivalent feelings in themselves, she found that preschoolers deny that someone can have opposite emotions at the same time (such as simultaneously feeling happy and sad). By about the age of 8, children begin to acknowledge that opposing feelings can coexist. At this stage, however, they tend to attribute the different emotions to different events or situations. An 8-year-old might say, for example: "I was happy when I saw my granddad in the hospital, but then I got sad when he said he couldn't come home with us." Finally, at about age 9 or 10, children grasp that a person can feel a positive emotion while also feeling a negative one. "I was happy to see my granddad," a 10-year-old might say, "but it also made me sad 'cause he was sick." And when children express such opposite feelings, they don't necessarily experience conflict (Whitesell & Harter, 1989).

Recognizing ambivalent feelings requires that the child integrate two pieces of information (the sense of happiness and the sense of sadness). Preschoolers have difficulty with cognitive tasks such as these, since they cannot yet focus on more than one thing at a time. Overcoming this cognitive limitation is an important step toward developing a more complex view of the self.

As children's cognitive abilities mature, so does their understanding that the self has many different traits, abilities, and roles (Craven et al., 1991; Harter, 1983). A 10-year-old, for instance, might point out that she plays the piano much better than she sings, that her spelling is better than her math, and that she is both a daughter to her mother and an aunt to her oldest sister's baby. The sense of self, in short, becomes more differentiated during middle childhood, partly because of a growing cognitive ability to integrate diverse pieces of information.

Other cognitive advances of the middle childhood years make possible other developmental changes in youngsters' self-conceptions. For example, the growing ability to adopt another person's perspective, discussed in Chapter 11, is closely related to the capacity to step back and critically view the self. A well-known developmental psychologist, Arnold Gesell, studied the emergence of self-criticism in children some 40 years ago (Gesell & Ilg, 1946). He found that at age 6 children criticize others, especially their peers, but they do not yet criticize themselves. At around age 7 youngsters start to become concerned about what *others* think of them (an indirect form of self-evaluation). And finally, at about age 8 or 9, they start to compare the self to their own internalized standards. This is the beginning of true self-criticism. When this new capacity emerges, it may be overworked for a while. "I'm so *clumsy*!" a 9-year-old might often remark, or "I'm so *stupid*!" Not surprisingly, 9-year-olds tend to be easily embarrassed by their mistakes, a sign that their view of the self is becoming more sophisticated and critical.

Middle childhood is also a time of continued development in the realm of sex-role identity (Serbin, Powlishta, & Gulko, 1993). During the elementary school years, children's knowledge of sex-role stereotypes increases, and their preferences for sex-typed activities, same-sex friendships, and sex-stereotyped occupations remain strong. At the same time, however, middle childhood is a time of increased *flexibility* regarding activity and occupation choices. In other words, although a sixth-grade boy is just as likely as a first-grade boy to personally *prefer* activities that are stereotypical for males, and more likely than the first grader to acknowledge the existence of sex-role stereotypes, the sixth grader is more apt to say that it would be acceptable for both girls and boys to engage in the traditionally male activity.

Of course, there are substantial differences among elementary school children in sex-typed behavior and beliefs (Serbin et al., 1993). In general, children's knowledge about sex roles—both their awareness of them and their flexibility in thinking about them—is linked to their overall cognitive maturity. Children's preferences for sex-typed activities, in contrast, are more tied to the degree of sex typing they are exposed to at home. Thus, "children whose mothers frequently modeled 'reversed' sex-role behaviors were less sex-typed in their own preferences" (Serbin et al., 1993, p. v.). Interestingly, the liberalizing effects of being exposed to nontraditional models at home are greatest for children whose cognitive maturity permits them to be more flexible in thinking about sex roles in general.

● Self-Esteem and Development

Self-esteem is not an all-or-nothing quality. People may feel very positively about some of their qualities and negatively about others. On the basis of many interviews with both children and adults, psychologists have concluded that we assess ourselves in four basic areas (Harter, 1983): (1) competence in meeting demands for achievement, especially on cognitive or physical tasks ("Am I good at schoolwork? At sports? At fixing things?"); (2) success at influencing other people, at getting others to go along with one's wishes and views ("Do others value my opinions? Do they follow my lead?"); (3) moral worth, or adherence to ethical standards ("Am I a good person? Do I usually do what is right?"); and (4) social acceptance, that is, receiving attention and affection from others ("Do other people like me? Do I have many friends?"). Self-assessment in each of these four areas adds up to a person's overall level of self-esteem. Children rate themselves in both absolute terms ("I got an 'A' so I must be smart") and in relative terms ("I got a 'B' but none of my friends did any better").

Studies of fifth and sixth graders show that self-esteem affects children's development in several important ways (Coopersmith, 1967). Children with high self-esteem have confidence in their abilities and judgments and expect to be successful. They are also more independent and less self-conscious than their peers with low self-esteem and are less likely to be preoccupied with personal problems.

You might think that this positive outlook would enable children high in self-esteem to achieve more than youngsters whose self-esteem is low, but research does not support this prediction. Increasing a child's self-esteem does not boost achievement. In fact, academic achievement seems to *precede* the self-perception of competence. Achievement, in other words, may boost self-esteem, but not usually vice versa (Connell, 1981; Harter, 1983; Harter & Connell, 1982).

Of course, academic achievement is not a child's only source of self-esteem. Psychologists believe that another important factor is how the significant people in a child's life, especially the parents, view that particular child. In Stanley Coopersmith's study of fifth and sixth graders, the parents of youngsters with high self-esteem tended to have several things in common. First, they were warm and accepting toward the child, both affectionate and involved. Second, they were strict in setting rules and limits, and firm and consistent in enforcing them. Third, they were willing to listen to the child's views and to take them into account when establishing rules and standards. And fourth, they used noncoercive discipline (withdrawal of privileges, for example, rather than physical punishment), and they took care to discuss with the child *why* certain behaviors are wrong. Recall that this parenting style matches what Diana Baumrind (1967) has called authoritative parenting (see Chapter 10).

It is easy to understand why love and acceptance from others would encourage a positive self-image. During childhood, how we see ourselves is shaped largely by how other people behave toward us. When parents show, through their words and actions, that they love their children just as they are, the children are likely to develop a favorable self-assessment. Similarly, when parents are willing to listen to their children's opinions and take the time to explain why certain behaviors are wrong, they are showing respect that is likely to encourage high self-esteem. Why parental strictness breeds positive self-regard is less clear. Perhaps parental rules help to make the social environment more manageable for children, thus helping them to feel more confident and in con-

High achievers, at sports and at school, often have high self-esteem as well, the quality that may spur their efforts to achieve.

trol. Children may also see their parents' rules as a sign that the parents consider the children worthy of adult concern.

When parents don't interact with their children in ways that lead to healthy self-esteem, children suffer. Those with depressed mothers, for example, show both higher anxiety and lower self-esteem than children with nondepressed mothers (Politano et al., 1992). Other adults in a child's life can help to counteract the consequences of inadequate parenting, however. For example, children with low esteem respond well to sports coaches who encourage and support them (Smith & Smoll, 1990), and other adults who are important to children can affect particular aspects of self-esteem (Cole, 1991).

Self-esteem can also be linked to group identity. When researchers studied children in different ethnic groups, they found that children with high esteem saw themselves as most similar to their group (Rotheram-Borus & Phinney, 1990). That is, African-American children who see themselves as similar to other African-American children have higher self-esteem than those who do not feel similar to other African-American children. All of these findings point to a recurrent theme: Like so many other aspects of development, self-esteem grows out of the context of a child's broad social environment.

● Growth in Self-Regulation

We expect very young children to have some trouble controlling their behavior, to act impulsively and to need frequent adult supervision, but by school age, most children can tolerate mild frustration. They can endure a brief delay without pushing and shoving, whining and complaining. Middle childhood's leap in self-regulation shows itself in other ways as well. Elementary school children can be counted on to act the "right" way in many situations. Visiting 3-year-olds need to keep hearing the rules against running in other people's houses and climbing on their furniture. By age 7, most children have internalized their parents' standards and don't need constant reminders.

School-age children are better, too, at balancing their own desires against social demands. Parents can reasonably expect children to catch the school bus, complete homework on time, and go to bed without a fight, even though they may not like it. Of course, same-aged children differ in their abilities to regulate themselves. Individual differences tend to be stable over time, so that children who can handle frustration when they are young are also better able to handle it when they are older (Pianta & Caldwell, 1991). Similarly, a cross-cultural study of boys from Finland and Canada found that patterns of aggression and hyperactivity were stable between the ages of 6 and 10 in both cultures (Pulkkinen & Tremblay, 1992).

● *Cognitive growth and self-control.* Many psychologists trace gains in self-control during childhood to the cognitive advances of the period. In particular, how children learn to "talk to themselves" is fundamental to their growing ability to manage their own behavior. The relationship between "inner speech" and self-regulation has been shown in many studies. In one, researchers observed through a one-way window as children tried to wait for a reward of two large marshmallows rather than taking an immediate reward of one small pretzel (Mischel & Underwood, 1974). The "waiters" distracted themselves in several ways (talking to themselves, singing little songs, making up games)

rather than just staring at the food. But even those 4- and 5-year-olds who could wait are generally unaware of the thoughts that helped them exert self-control. They might say, for example, that thinking about how sweet the marshmallows will taste will help them endure the delay (a thought that, in fact, makes waiting unbearable). In contrast, 7- to 9-year-olds are much more knowledgeable about using thoughts to control behavior.

The ability to use thoughts to exert self-control usually develops naturally as children mature cognitively. We saw in Chapter 11 that elementary school youngsters are increasingly able to plan and monitor their behavior and to think about their own thoughts, all of which are skills that aid them in controlling themselves. Newer research has also shown that self-regulation is a fairly stable trait that is linked to later academic and cognitive success. A longitudinal study found that preschoolers who had successfully delayed gratification were later judged by their parents to be highly competent adolescents, able to tolerate frustration and to cope well with stress (Shoda et al., 1990). The high rate of academic success among this group is probably influenced by their intelligence and attentional abilities, which are fairly stable over time. In fact, in a correlational study performed with seventh graders, self-regulation proved to be one of the best predictors of academic performance (Pintrich & De Groot, 1990),

Following the rules with relative ease is a mark of middle childhood, a time when self-regulation has become more consistent.

● ***Improving self-regulation.*** Given the importance of self-regulation for academic success, psychologists have developed several strategies that literally teach children how to control their impulses. For some children, identifying their specific problem is a first step toward control. ("I blurt out answers in class when it is not my turn.") Then they are encouraged to tell themselves things that will counteract the problem. ("Wait a minute. It's not my turn. Give someone else a chance.") Finally, they learn how to monitor their progress (Meichenbaum & Goodman, 1971).

Another program adds thinking about alternative behaviors that are incompatible with the problematic one. ("I will clench my teeth whenever I feel the urge to speak out of turn in class.") (Camp & Bash, 1981; Camp et al., 1977) Do these strategies work? In one study, such deployment strategies positively influenced children's ability to delay behavior (Rodriguez et al., 1989).

ACHIEVEMENT IN MIDDLE CHILDHOOD

> ● **achievement motivation**
> the desire to perform well

> ● **mastery motivation**
> the desire to master a challenge in order to acquire a new skill

> ● **industry versus inferiority**
> according to Erikson, the crisis over the sense of accomplishment, characteristic of middle childhood

With the middle years, children enter the achievement-oriented world of the classroom. From first grade (or even kindergarten) on, they are tested, evaluated, graded, and grouped. During this time, children develop and show differences in **achievement motivation,** the desire to perform well, especially on tasks involving intellectual skills and especially in settings where accomplishments are monitored and judged. Achievement motivation differs from **mastery motivation,** the desire to master a challenge in order to acquire a new skill. The 6-month-old who struggles to crawl across the room and the 3-year-old who works at perfecting a somersault are exhibiting mastery motivation. In contrast, the third grader who strives to learn the times tables in order to win a gold star and her parent's approval is spurred on largely by achievement motivation.

In Erikson's theory, the chief psychosocial crisis of middle childhood concerns the child's sense of accomplishment. Meeting the social and psychological challenges of this period gives children a sense of **industry,** a belief that they are competent and able to master things. Coupled with this belief is an eagerness to tackle new tasks and a willingness to persist in working toward their goals. In contrast, children who fail at, or withdraw from, the challenges of middle childhood develop a feeling of **inferiority.** Convinced that they are unable to master new skills, these children have little motivation to keep trying. Erikson contends that failing to resolve the challenges of middle childhood restricts a child's ability to meet the psychosocial challenges that lie ahead (Kowaz & Marcia, 1991).

● How Children Think about Ability

Underlying growth in achievement motivation is a change in the way children think about *ability* (Frieze, Francis, & Hanusa, 1981; Heckhausen, 1981; Stipek, 1981). For preschoolers, ability means mastering specific skills, especially physical ones: tying shoelaces, climbing a tree or monkey bars, catching a ball, jumping rope, or pumping on a swing. At this age, children are almost immune

Meeting challenges and mastering skills boost a child's confidence, essential for developing a sense of industry.

to failure: They keep on trying. But by age 6 or 7, children begin thinking about ability more as a global, psychological trait. "Ability is being smart and good at lots of stuff," an 8-year-old might say, implying that a person's degree of "smartness" is a relatively stable, general characteristic. Along with this changed perception comes a change in *judging* ability. Preschoolers say they "did good" just because they completed a task correctly, regardless of how their performance compares with that of their peers. By middle childhood, "doing good" turns to "doing better"—or worse—than someone else. Ability is now linked to comparison with others. ("I did better than most of the kids in my class.") Finally, preschoolers assess their own ability optimistically, foreseeing little difficulty in mastering a new skill. Older children perceive both challenges and their own abilities more accurately.

These developmental changes can work for or against achievement motivation. It is true that elementary school children value achievement more strongly than preschoolers and often strive to excel, but their more critical understanding of ability makes them very vulnerable to the effects of failure. Children who fail repeatedly think they are "dumb." They don't think that their teacher may not be very good or that other events in their lives may be keeping them from learning (for instance, school achievement often drops when a child's parents divorce or if a child is preoccupied for other reasons). And children who keep failing often just stop trying. A child's true ability, then, can be overwhelmed by self-defeating attitudes.

Differences in achievement motivation have intrigued generations of psychologists. Why, for example, are some children defeated by failure while others persevere? Why do some children expect to succeed while others imagine failure? And what can we do to change these attitudes and expectations about achievement?

● Differences in Achievement Motivation: Goals and Expectations

How can we explain and help to modify individual differences in achievement motivation? The answers are far from complete, but two are clear: (1) It is possible to change children's expectations and goals; and (2) for academic success, children's expectations for what they might achieve can be more important than their actual ability. We examine the evidence for each of these conclusions below.

● *The influence of goals.* How children respond to failure—whether they keep striving or give up—depends partly on the kinds of achievement goals they set for themselves. Educators distinguish between learning goals and performance goals.

learning goals
goals that place value on individual accomplishment for its own sake

Children for whom **learning goals** are the most important approach new tasks with the questions, How can I do this and what will I learn? These children stress the process of mastering things and the intrinsic value of gaining new skills: A difficult task becomes a challenge. Such children see their mistakes as a useful part of learning, providing feedback about how to do better.

performance goals
goals that place value on achieving in relation to others

In contrast, children for whom **performance goals** are the most important approach new tasks with the questions, Can I be successful and will I look smart? To these children, what matters most is whether effort will bring success and the esteem of others or failure and disparagement. For performance-oriented children, a difficult task is automatically threatening because it carries the risk of making them seem dumb. Mistakes are threatening too, because they suggest incompetence and might bring derision from others. Not surprisingly, performance-oriented children tend to avoid tasks at which they might fail (Dweck & Elliott, 1983).

While earlier research suggested that children had fairly fixed orientations toward achievement, newer studies have had more optimistic results. Children

Children motivated to do well in school typically set learning goals for themselves and are not afraid to make mistakes.

can become more oriented toward effort and learning and less fearful of failure, and no special coaching programs are needed. The key to change is in the assignments teachers make, even in the way directions are given for the same assignment (Stipek & Kowalski, 1989). A teacher who emphasizes the fun inherent in learning something new will affect children differently than one who stresses tests and other forms of evaluation.

The nature of the task also matters. For example, in a study of Chinese students, a group of fifth graders (10- to 11-year-olds) became tutors for a group of first graders. The researchers hypothesized that this activity would foster both high achievement goals and achievement itself among the *older* children. Results were positive: The young tutors' motives for achievement improved as did their scores on tests of verbal ability (Dewei, 1989). By strengthening mastery motivation, the task of helping others can improve feelings of competence and actual performance. In contrast, tasks that encourage competition with classmates can increase concerns with performance and interfere with learning (Butler, 1989a, 1989b, 1990; Skinner, 1990; Stipek & Mac Iver, 1990).

● *The influence of expectations.* For children, as well as adults, expectations about success or failure can be so powerful that they overshadow ability. In study after study, expectations for success are strongly related to actual achievement and achievement behaviors (Berndt & Miller, 1990). For example, in one study of black third and fifth graders from low-income families, how the children assessed their success at a task was more important in predicting whether they would ask for help than their actual performance (Nelson-Le Gall & Jones, 1990). Expectations can shape a student's course of study, regardless of his or her actual ability. If children "know" they will fail at something (such as scoring high on a math test), they are likely to give up trying as soon as they are stumped, or drop the subject as soon as they can. Conversely, believing in the possibility of success encourages persistence and higher achievement. Even within a single semester, when students begin to *think* they have ability in a subject, they try harder (Mac Iver et al., 1991).

A critical question for psychologists, therefore, is, How do children form their expectations about success and failure? And how can negative attitudes become more positive?

These questions are especially relevant to differences in achievement between the sexes. Far fewer girls than boys study advanced math and science in high school, even though girls do as well as boys in those subjects in the lower grades. Again, the differences appear to have more to do with attitudes than with abilities.

Girls *expect* to achieve less than boys, *even though their past performance is as good as or better than boys'* (Dweck & Elliott, 1983; Dweck, Goetz, & Strauss, 1980). If low expectations of achievement are not linked simply to having done poorly in the past, other factors must be involved. One powerful factor is the way students respond emotionally to success or failure. For boys and for girls, reactions are sharply different.

While a boy tends to shrug off occasional errors as not indicative of his "true" ability, a girl is likely to take her errors much more to heart. When he fails, a boy looks outside of himself: He wasn't "lucky"; the test was too hard. A girl, however, is likely to search within for the reasons for failure: She isn't smart enough. Conversely, when they succeed, girls, more than boys, find the reasons *outside* themselves ("I had a good day; the test was easy."). (Boggiano, 1991;

Weiner, 1986, in Stipek & Gralinski, 1991) Girls also tend to rate tasks as being harder than boys rate them. So even if a girl thinks that she has high ability, she may still expect lower achievement than a comparable boy because she sees the task as relatively more difficult.

These sex differences were nicely illustrated in a recent study of nearly 500 girls (approximately 200 third graders and 300 seventh graders). The children filled out questionnaires about their achievement beliefs before and after they took a regularly scheduled math test. "Girls rated their ability lower, expected to do less well, were less likely than boys to attribute success to high ability and failure to luck, and were more likely to attribute failure to low ability. Girls also reported less pride in their success and a stronger desire to hide their paper after failure and were less likely to believe that success could be achieved through effort" (Stipek & Gralinski, 1991). Interestingly, gender differences in beliefs about ability have been found in Taiwan and Japan, as well as in the United States (Lummis & Stevenson, 1990); in all three cultures, children and parents tend to believe that boys are better than girls at math, and girls better than boys at reading. Yet in all three cultures, there were few sex differences on curriculum-based tests of either math or reading.

● Parents, Teachers, and Children's Achievement Expectations

For both sexes, consistent achievers and underachievers do, in fact, show very different sets of beliefs about the value of personal effort in determining performance (Carr et al., 1991). In a German study, gifted children attributed high achievement to ability. More average students believed that success came from effort (Kurtz & Weinert, 1989). Whatever a child's attribution style, once formed, it tends to be stable over time unless attempts are made to change it (Fincham et al., 1989; Gottfried, 1990).

Children with seriously low achievement expectations usually suffer from evaluation anxiety, learned helplessness, or both. Children with **evaluation anxiety** feel so anxious in situations where they are being judged that they have trouble functioning and perform poorly most of the time. Evaluation anxiety is likely to develop when parents set high standards for performance and then react very critically when the child performs poorly. There may be an inborn

● **evaluation anxiety**
anxiety manifested in situations where a child is being judged

When parents believe that effort leads to success, children's expectations for achievement are strengthened.

HIGHLIGHT ON DIVERSITY

ETHNIC AND CROSS-CULTURAL DIFFERENCES IN ACHIEVEMENT

Psychologists and educators have discovered fairly consistent ethnic differences in school achievement among American students. Grades and standardized tests show that as a group, Asian-American children achieve higher than African-American and Hispanic-American children, with white youngsters falling somewhere between the two extremes.

Psychologists attribute the success of Asian youngsters—not only in the United States but in Asia as well—to cultural beliefs about the nature of achievement. In general, Asian cultures are more likely than others to attribute success to hard work (Holloway, 1988), which leads to better performance. This cultural difference appears in studies of both Asian-Americans and Asians (Hess, 1987). Asian-American youngsters' success, then, is strongly linked to motivation, attribution, and beliefs about achievement.

Harder to explain is the relatively poorer academic performance of African-American and Hispanic-American children. One of the most puzzling aspects of the poor academic performance of African-American and Hispanic-American youngsters is that in both groups, parents and children *do* value educational success (Mickelson, 1990). In the Chicago metropolitan area, for example, mothers of 1,000 first, third, and fifth graders were asked about their attitudes toward education. Black and Hispanic mothers were positive about education, and more than white mothers, they believed in the value of homework and a longer school day (Stevenson et al., 1990).

At the same time, however, researchers consistently have found that black students' high interest in academic achievement does not match their personal efforts to achieve (Coleman, 1966, cited in Mickelson, 1990). Why should this be? One answer has been suggested by the urban anthropologist John Ogbu, based on his extensive studies of African-Americans and Hispanic-Americans in Stockton, California (Ogbu, 1978).

According to Ogbu, youngsters from both minority groups are convinced that education leads to upward mobility. Oddly, students with poor academic records, even dropouts, believed this as strongly as successful students. Yet, as Ogbu points out, there is a world of difference between abstract beliefs about the value of education and concrete beliefs about whether your own life will be bettered by more schooling. Ogbu found that many of the youngsters in his study did not have faith that education would pay off *for them.* Two decades later, another psychologist explained the problem this way: Disadvantaged minority youngsters do believe in the importance of school as an ideal, but they don't think that education will make a difference *in their own lives.* And students who do not believe that schooling will have a real, concrete, personal payoff will not work as hard as they might (Mickelson, 1990). One solution to the problem of ethnic disparities in academic achievement, then, is making sure that *all* youngsters believe in the benefits of education and, of course, structuring education so that it does in fact benefit all youngsters.

Can culture influence achievement? Researchers have found that Asian societies attribute success to hard work. Many Asian children are expected to work hard and to be high achievers.

● **learned helplessness**
the belief or expectation that
one cannot control forces in
one's environment

component to evaluation anxiety, as some children may be more prone to anxiety than others.

Learned helplessness is the belief or expectation that you cannot control forces in your environment, that you cannot behave in ways that make a difference (Seligman, 1975). Regarding achievement, learned helplessness is reflected in the tendency to attribute failure to one's own lack of ability. ("I'm too dumb to solve these problems," such children think to themselves.) As a result, the youngsters simply give up trying as soon as they have difficulties. It is as if they believe they can't possibly succeed in such situations. Unlike evaluation anxiety, which *persistently* impairs performance, learned helplessness has different effects under different circumstances. The child who suffers from learned helplessness does as well as peers when achievement tasks are easy. As soon as the going gets tough, though, the child simply stops trying and performance plummets (Licht & Dweck, 1984). As with evaluation anxiety, theories about the causes of learned helplessness have to do with both nature and nurture. Temperament may make some children more prone to it. For some, it may come from having been too harshly criticized by parents or by teachers (Heyman et al., 1992). Learned helplessness and evaluation anxiety may also work together, but implicitly or explicitly, the message is that effort doesn't make a difference.

Studies indicate that girls are more prone to learned helplessness than boys. They also get very different messages about their ability from their teachers (Dweck, Davidson, Nelson, & Enna, 1978; Dweck, Goetz, & Strauss, 1980). Teachers criticize boys mainly for aspects of their work *not* related to ability. ("You did this sloppily." "You weren't trying very hard.") In contrast, they criticize girls mainly for things that *could* arise from low intelligence. ("You spelled that wrong." "You forgot to carry the two.") Consequently, girls may be more apt to conclude that they are just not smart enough.

Once they understand the effects of their messages, teachers can do a lot to help children overcome both evaluation anxiety and learned helplessness. Such children need to develop more positive expectations about themselves, so explaining that a failure is *not* due to lack of ability is crucial. In fact, when children with learned helplessness are taught to attribute failure to lack of *effort* rather than to lack of ability, they begin persisting when obstacles arise, and their performance improves markedly (Dweck, 1975). (Read the Highlight on Diversity box on page 390 to learn about ethnic differences in school achievement.)

SOCIAL RELATIONS IN MIDDLE CHILDHOOD

Researcher: Who's your best friend?

Matthew (5 yrs., 10 mos.): Larry.

Researcher: Why is Larry your best friend?

Matthew: 'Cause he plays with me a lot.

Researcher: Are you Larry's best friend?

Matthew: Yeah.

Researcher: How do you know that?

Matthew: 'Cause I'm friends with lots of people but Larry and me are best friends. . . .

Researcher: How did you get Larry to like you?

Matthew: He came to my house and I played with him and he liked me.

Researcher: Does everyone who goes to your house like you?

Matthew: Sometimes when I play with them, but when I don't play with them, they don't like me.

Researcher: How do you know who to play with?

Matthew: Like when I'm doing something and they're doing something else and I walk by, they grab me in. They just grab me by the hand and I fly in. (Damon, 1977, pp. 154–155)

Five-year-old Matthew's description of making friends is charmingly simplistic. By middle childhood, he will connect friendship to shared interests, mutual assistance, loyalty, and trust. Developmental psychologists believe that interactions with peers are critical to many of the social advances that occur in middle childhood. Striving to be accepted and liked by peers, youngsters gain new insights into the meaning of friendship. Through give-and-take with peers, children learn the importance of sharing, reciprocity, and cooperation. By trying to get peers to understand their thoughts and feelings, they learn to communicate more effectively. In fact, research shows that children are more relaxed, more "tuned in," and less stressed when interacting with friends than with acquaintances (Field et al., 1992).

Psychiatrist Harry Stack Sullivan rightly stressed the importance of childhood peers in his theory of interpersonal development (Sullivan, 1953a). According to Sullivan and many other psychoanalytic thinkers who came after Freud, biological drives and sexual conflicts are not the overriding factors in human development. Equally if not more important in shaping personality are the interpersonal relationships we form. Sullivan contended that we are all innately motivated to seek *security* by forming relationships with others who make us feel happy and safe. Such relationships are the "glue" holding together a healthy sense of self. Interacting with others who think well of us fosters a positive self-identity and strong self-esteem.

Sullivan proposed a developmental sequence of needs related to security, starting with the infant's need for physical contact and tenderness from adults. Next, children need adult participation in their learning experiences (the preschool years), followed by the need for peer acceptance (early middle childhood). Intimacy with a friend of the same sex is necessary in late middle childhood, followed by a need for love and sexual contact with an opposite-sex partner (early adolescence). Finally, during late adolescence, we feel the need for integration into adult society.

Like Erikson, Sullivan saw psychosocial development as cumulative. The experiences of past developmental periods affect current relationships and the developing sense of self. If, for example, a child's need for physical contact and tenderness is not met during infancy, she will be too insecure and distrustful to form cooperative relationships with adults during the preschool years.

Later on, if the need for peer acceptance is satisfied early in middle childhood, confidence to form very close friendships during the later elementary school years will grow.

Sullivan believed that through these friendships—or "chumships," as he called them—children learn how to share their thoughts and feelings and to build a mutually caring relationship based on loyalty and trust. He was convinced that chumships are a necessary prerequisite to forming intimate relationships in adolescence and adulthood. Chumships could even help overcome insecurities stemming from interpersonal problems in earlier developmental periods.

● Changing Conceptions of Friendship

As 5-year-old Matthew sees it, a friend is someone you play with, with whom you share toys. For most preschoolers and early elementary school children, friendships form quickly just by meeting and saying "Hi." As Matthew describes it, other children "grab me by the hand," they begin playing, and right away they are friends.

But around age 8 or 9, this simple view of friendship as a sharing of fun and toys starts maturing, first with the idea that friends help each other. As one 8-year-old girl explained when asked why Shelly was her best friend:

> Because she helps when I'm getting beaten up, she cheers me up when I'm sad, and she shares. . . . She's done the most for me. She never disagrees, she never eats in front of me, she never walks away when I'm crying, and she helps me on my schoolwork. (Damon, 1977, pp. 159–160)

Later, at about 11 or 12, children begin thinking of friends not only as those who help one another but also as those who share secrets, who understand each other's feelings, and who can be trusted not to betray the other person's confidences. Asked when he knew that Jimmy was his friend, one boy this age responded:

> After we found out that we didn't have to worry about the other guy blabbing and spreading stuff around. . . . You need someone you can tell anything to, all kinds of things that you don't want spread around. That's why you're someone's friend. (Damon, 1977, p. 63)

This increased capacity for intimacy in the late middle childhood years reflects both cognitive advances and emotional growth (Youniss, 1980). Cognitively, children are able to grasp not just the tangible basis of friendship (shared objects and activities) but the intangible, psychological basis as well. Emotionally, the growing capacity for intimacy means that children are secure enough to open up their innermost selves to another person. The close friendships of late middle childhood depend on both of these factors developing together.

● Middle Childhood Peer Groups

At a pizza parlor in Worcester, Massachusetts, seven boys in hockey uniforms have just been served a large pizza:

By about 11 or 12, friendships deepen into relationships based on trust, where two people can share their ideas and feelings. Both the cognitive and emotional advances of middle childhood make this new intimacy possible.

Child 1: Hey, there's eight pieces here. What about the extra piece?

Child 2: The guy who's the oldest should get it. How old are you?

Child 1: Nine.

Child 3: I'm nine and a quarter.

Child 1: My birthday's coming up this summer. I'm—I'll be ten in one, two months.

Child 2: How old are you?

Child 4: Eleven, and I'll be twelve next month.

Child 2: Well, I'm twelve so I'll get the extra piece.

Child 1: What about giving it to the one with the small piece?

Child 4: Well, who's got the smallest piece?

Child 1: I've got the smallest piece—look at it!

Child 2: C'mon, let's cut it. The oldest kid will get one piece and the kid with the smallest piece will get one piece. . . .

Child 5: Hey, can we get some water here? Who's gonna play hockey tomorrow?

Child 3: I am, I am! *[Jumps up and moves over to pizza tray with extra piece still on it. Begins picking cheese off the top. Children 1 and 2 gather around, and each takes pieces off the extra piece, with child 3 getting much more than the other two.]*

Child 6: Who's the biggest eater here—who's the piggiest?

Child 2: I can eat seven pieces of pizza, but I gotta give one to my mother.

Child 6: No, no. Who's the biggest eater of us all?

Child 4: Joey [child 3] is.

Child 1: Yeah, Joey is.

Child 3: Yeah, I can eat two whole pizzas myself.

Child 1: Two whole pizzas!

Child 6: Yeah, you're the biggest pig, all right. (Damon, 1977, pp. 59–60)

This dialogue suggests several things about middle childhood peer groups. First, and typically, members of the peer group are all the same sex (Hartup, 1983). While it may be common to see games of chase *between* the sexes on elementary school playgrounds, boys and girls in middle childhood rarely play *together*. Elementary schoolers prefer this gender segregation and actively strive to maintain it. Boys, especially, ostracize other boys who try to join the girls in their activities (Thorne, 1986). As physical separation increases, changes in the way boys and girls communicate also begin to appear, although they are still more alike than different (Leaper, 1991).

The scene above also suggests how important the norm of fairness is to children this age. No one simply snatches the whole slice of pizza, as a preschooler might do; they discuss who deserves it most. Granted, each boy proposes a criterion that biases the choice toward himself, but the criteria are at least defensible on rational grounds (the oldest boy is probably the biggest and therefore "needs" more food; the boy with the smallest piece has been shortchanged and therefore deserves extra). A preschooler would suggest some criterion that is totally irrelevant ("I get it because my dog eats pizza"), a kind of reasoning that declines sharply during middle childhood. Youngsters this age are also much less egocentric. They realize that fairness means you don't get all the best things for yourself.

Elementary school children learn other norms of conduct within their peer groups. In fact, children this age are extremely norm-conscious (Hartup, 1983). Bound, in part, by the "concreteness" of concrete operations, the stage of thought characteristic of this age, they expect each other to follow the rules, to dress, act, and talk in a certain manner. Those who do not are often ridiculed and rejected by their peers. Although elementary school children may seem too rigid in enforcing their ideas of correct behavior, the experiences they have while struggling to define proper and improper conduct will help to prepare them for the world of adolescence. Interestingly, norms for conduct may be similar even among children living in different countries. When shown the same videotaped sequences, English and Italian 8- to 11-year-olds could easily tell the difference between rough-and-tumble play and real fighting (Costabile, 1991).

● The Growth of Social Skills

The boys' conversation about distributing the extra pizza also shows advances in social communication. Compare this conversation with those between two preschoolers (Chapter 9), in which each child virtually ignores what the other is saying. Even if these children were strongly motivated to attend to one another (say, they wanted to build a play fort that required a cooperative effort), they probably would still have trouble really listening to each other and communicating their ideas.

This was illustrated in a study in which children sat on opposite sides of a screen with identical abstract drawings in front of them (Krauss & Glucksberg, 1969). One child was to try to explain to the other which picture he or she was holding. Preschool youngsters did very poorly on this task. One might say to the other "I've got the one with the funny shape" or, even less revealing, "I've got *this* one." They lacked the communication skills needed to help each other identify the drawings. Elementary school children did much better at describing the pictures, especially 10- to 12-year-olds. And if the meaning *was* still unclear, the listener quickly requested whatever additional information was needed.

Elementary school children communicate better than preschoolers in many other ways too. The young hockey players dividing their pizza are adept at directing visual attention to help make their points, as when child 1 points to his small slice and urges the others to "look at it!" They are also quite good at interpreting nonverbal messages, such as body posture, facial expressions, and tone of voice. Child 3, for example, knows that this is a lighthearted, playful discussion (otherwise he would never have simply jumped up and started picking at the extra piece). He knows this not so much through his friends' words as through their nonverbal signals. Elementary school children have also learned how to stick to a particular topic. Although they still introduce irrelevancies from time to time (as when child 5 abruptly changes the subject), they do so much less than preschoolers. They are also much better at inferring motives from the statements people make. For instance, all the boys realize that child 1 and child 2 are suggesting ways of distributing the extra piece that benefit themselves.

Psychologists believe that these communication advances stem from several factors, including improved role-taking abilities. Because elementary school children can imagine themselves in other people's situations, they can better interpret what others are thinking, feeling, and saying. At the same time, elementary schoolers may be forced to be better communicators because they are spending more time with their peers. Whereas adults sometimes speak *for* children and help them interpret others, conversations among peers don't provide these communication crutches. Peers must struggle to get ideas across and to understand each other. As a result, they learn techniques for communicating more effectively. Middle childhood also sees growth in other social skills: Sharing, cooperating, and helping others all increase (Radke-Yarrow, Zahn-Waxler, & Chapman, 1983). In turn, better social skills enhance children's social standing (Gnepp, 1989; Yeates et al., 1991).

Recall that we began this chapter by discussing the interplay of cognitive and social development: Social skills advance because cognitive skills have matured enough to allow children to reflect on the way their actions might affect others. And in fact, that seems to be a skill necessary for successful social relationships, a skill that stems from parenting. In turn, both of these social and cognitive advances will stimulate others. The accompanying Making a Difference box focuses on how children learn social skills at home.

MAKING A DIFFERENCE

HOW CHILDREN LEARN SOCIAL SKILLS AT HOME

If social skills influence acceptance by peers, then knowing how children learn those skills and why some are more socially skilled than others becomes important. Recently, a group of researchers sought some answers by studying differences in the way parents communicate with their children (Burleson et al., 1992). They focused on parenting practices known to influence children's social skills: basic patterns of discipline and nurturance (see Chapter 10) (Maccoby & Martin, 1983). Looking more closely at accepting and rejecting parents, these researchers focused on specific parenting techniques (Applegate et al., 1985): What are the qualities of nurturing and discipline that enhance children's social skills?

Burleson's research team hypothesized that children who were highly accepted by their peers had experienced quite a sophisticated

kind of parenting, an approach they call "reflection enhancing." When disciplined for doing something wrong, these children were asked to think about how their behavior might have affected others. When comforted, they were encouraged to talk about their own feelings and what had caused them. After observing children with their mothers and with their peers, the researchers concluded that their hypothesis was correct. Mothers who offered "reflection enhancing messages" did have children who were both less rejected by peers and more likely to be chosen as companions.

Some children, however, lag behind their peers in acquiring these social abilities. Earlier research suggested that their poor social skills may be related to growing up in harsh, autocratic households (Maccoby & Martin, 1983). And, concluded Burleson and his team, this seems to be correct. When parents disciplined with power tactics (by hitting, threatening, or forcing certain behaviors) rather than

Children who are accepted by their peers are also socially skilled. One of the things they've learned from their parents is to consider how their actions affect others as well as themselves.

with "reflective messages," their children were more often rejected by peers or isolated (Burleson et al., 1992). Other children may simply be inexperienced in social situations or lack the models for appropriate social behavior that many children have. Special programs that actively foster prosocial behavior, by modeling and rewarding it, are particularly helpful to those children.

COMMON PSYCHOSOCIAL PROBLEMS OF MIDDLE CHILDHOOD

Most preschoolers outgrow their fears or other problems by the time they reach middle childhood. But problems that arise during the middle years can signal trouble for several reasons. First, because behavior patterns tend to stabilize with age, problems in middle childhood may persist into later years, so adults become concerned about long-lasting effects. Second, the new settings children experience may highlight behaviors that may have been ignored or excused in younger children. Attention-deficit disorder, for example, is usually not noticed until formal schooling begins. Third, behaviors that would not have caused too much concern in younger children, when a lot of learning is still occurring, are more troubling now. We expect older children to accept more social rules now, so behaviors that once seemed like socialization deficiencies (being disruptive in a line, for example) now may signal more serious problems (trouble controlling impulses).

Earlier we discussed problems with achievement, evaluation anxiety, and learned helplessness. Now we turn to two other common psychosocial problems of school-age children: intense and irrational fears (often called *phobias*), and attention-deficit hyperactivity disorder.

● Childhood Phobias

The problem started when Julie became upset with a teacher who took her music book away from her in class. Rather than eating lunch at school that day, she went home at noontime, but her mother was nowhere to be found. Julie called her father and learned that her mother had a doctor's appointment to get an allergy shot. The next morning Julie complained that she did not feel well, but she was sent to school anyway. At school she seemed anxious and upset for no reason. This troubled behavior continued for several days until finally Julie became so panicky in the classroom that her mother had to come and take her home. Thereafter Julie refused to go to school. Each morning when her mother tried to rouse her from her bed, she complained of a terrible stomach ache and feelings of nausea. If her mother tried to coax her to get dressed she would cry so hard she could scarcely get her breath. Impatience and annoyance on her mother's part simply caused Julie to vomit. (Based on Sperling, 1961)

Fear is a normal emotional reaction to some perceived threat, and most school-age children can manage their fears without becoming overwhelmed by them. But for some, fears become intense and unreasonable—far out of proportion to the things that trigger them. Such intense, irrational fears directed toward specific objects or situations are **phobias.** Julie has developed a school phobia, a fear of attending school, and as is typical with phobias, her attacks of fear are accompanied by physical symptoms. Her stomach knots, she feels nauseated, and if pushed too far, she vomits.

● **phobias**
intense, irrational fears directed toward specific objects or situations

Childhood phobias typically fall into three major categories (Rutter & Garmezy, 1983). The first consists of phobias about *physical injury*, such as fear of germs, fear of choking, fear of having an operation, or fear of falling from a high place. The second consists of phobias about *natural events*, such as fear of the dark, fear of storms, fear of blood, or fear of animals (dog, snake, insect, and mice phobias are common). The third category consists of phobias about *social situations*, such as fear of crowds, fear of going to the doctor or dentist, fear of attending school, or fear of being separated from one's parents. Many experts believe that these last two social phobias are often related. Acute anxiety over being separated from one's parents often underlies a school phobia such as Julie's.

Psychologists disagree about the causes of childhood phobias. Psychoanalysts think they are symptoms of unconscious conflicts. The therapist who treated Julie, for example, suspected that the child really feared that something terrible would happen to her mother while she was away at school. This fear supposedly stemmed from the fact that Julie, in a moment of anger toward her mother, had wished that the mother were dead. Like many young children, Julie believed that "bad thoughts" can magically make things happen. When her mother suddenly had to go to the doctor, Julie was sure her horrible wish was coming true.

Psychoanalytic therapy involves helping children to understand the unconscious conflicts that are troubling them. Analysts believe that when conflicts are uncovered and discussed, they lose much of their power to control the child's behavior. In Julie's case, the therapist helped her to see that a recent fainting spell her mother had suffered had started the child's secret fear, which then quickly heightened with the unexpected visit to the doctor. The therapist reassured Julie that many children sometimes feel angry toward their mothers but that thoughts and wishes can't kill. After discovering these hidden conflicts and talking about them, Julie was able to go back to school.

A therapist who subscribes to social learning theory would have explored Julie's learned experiences rather than her unconscious conflicts. These therapists view phobias as learned responses. A child might learn to fear school, for example, after an incident in which she is embarrassed when her teacher criticizes her in front of peers. Thereafter the child associates school with humiliation and refuses to go. Staying home from school is reinforcing because it lowers anxiety.

But not all phobias begin with some incident in which the feared object is paired with real physical or psychological harm. A boy might learn to fear dogs, for example, even though he has never been bitten by one. Social learning theorists suspect that modeling may play a role in many of these cases. If the boys sees others acting fearfully toward dogs, he may begin to imitate them.

For social learning theorists, what is learned can be *un*learned. Phobic children relearn how *not* to fear. A cognitive-behavioral therapist looks for the stimuli that are controlling the fear response. A child with school phobia, for example, is asked which aspects of school make him feel most afraid (riding the school bus? being in the school yard? meeting a certain teacher?

For children with school phobia, an unreasonable fear of going to school, every school day may begin with a stomach ache or other physical symptoms.

answering questions in class?). Is the child also afraid of leaving his or her parents? Using this information, the therapist develops a program that gradually exposes the child to the school routine, starting with the least-feared aspects and working up to the most-feared ones. Throughout this process, called **desensitization,** the child is taught to remain calm, often using techniques of physical relaxation. Sometimes other children help by modeling how the behaviors can be performed without fear. When the phobic child's anxiety has lessened enough to make returning to school possible, rewards for school attendance are often offered while the inadvertent rewards for staying home (unlimited snacks and TV viewing, for instance) are withdrawn. All these methods have been successful, especially when used together.

● **desensitization**
gradual exposure to the feared aspect of the object of a phobia

● Attention-Deficit Hyperactivity Disorder

Seven-year-old Sammy tried the patience of everyone who knew him. He chattered constantly but never finished his sentences. His small, thin body was in perpetual motion—flitting around with jerky, bouncy movements, compulsively touching everything and everyone in sight. His mother could not remember a single meal or TV program that Sammy had managed to sit through from beginning to end. Sammy could never decide what he wanted to do. He would run outside to play, banging the door behind him, then a few minutes later he'd run back in, grab a piece of candy, and turn on the TV. After trying all the channels, he would abandon the set (leaving it on), and run to his closet, where he'd dig through the toys to find his baseball mitt. Simply unbuttoning a shirt could make him so impatient that he would tear it open, letting the buttons fly. Other children refused to play with Sammy because he would never share, wait his turn, or follow the rules of a game. At school Sammy exasperated his teacher. He didn't pay attention; he didn't concentrate; he didn't finish anything he started. After detailed instructions were given to the entire class, Sammy would inevitably shout out: "What are we supposed to do?" His parents asked the same question. (Based on Fine, 1980)

Most elementary school children show *some* of Sammy's behaviors once in a while. But those who display them all, day after day in a variety of settings, are usually diagnosed as having **attention-deficit hyperactivity disorder** (ADHD) (Shaywitz & Shaywitz, 1984). *Attention deficit* describes Sammy's inability to keep his mind on anything for very long. *Hyperactivity* refers to his constant and rapid motion. In short, Sammy can't pay attention and he can't sit still. This traditional way of thinking about ADHD stresses the cognitive aspect of the problem: Trouble paying attention is seen as an information-processing disorder. But we can also view it as a problem in motivation and in the ability to regulate oneself (Henker & Whalen, 1989). The best way to think about ADHD then is as a complicated condition, with cognitive, motivational, and behavioral features.

● **attention-deficit hyperactivity disorder**
a disorder in which children can neither pay attention nor remain still

● ***Effects of ADHD.*** Between 2 and 5 percent of elementary school children suffer from this disorder, and it affects three to four times more boys than girls (Lambert, Sandoval, & Sassone, 1978). Not all children with attention-deficit disorder are hyperactive, but many suffer from both problems. While academic success is difficult for ADHD children, school achievement is not their only problem. They are more likely to develop behavior problems, conduct disorders, and delinquency.

By adolescence, boys and girls who had been diagnosed as hyperactive as children continue having more conduct and learning problems and are more hyperactive, inattentive, and impulsive than nonhyperactive adolescents (Barkley et al., 1991). And in a longitudinal study of over 400 boys with and without this disorder, delinquent ADHD teenagers had shown antisocial behaviors even as preschoolers, and their delinquency persisted into the school years and adolescence. (But not all boys with ADHD are delinquent.) (Moffitt, 1990)

● *Causes of ADHD.* Growing evidence suggests that ADHD is biologically caused. Some very interesting research has linked the problem to reduced glucose metabolism in the brain, particularly in those areas involved with regulating attention and motor activity (*New England Journal of Medicine,* 1990, p. 1413). Mild head injury during early childhood does *not* cause ADHD (Bijur et al., 1990), but researchers have found links to prenatal or perinatal conditions and inherited factors (Goodman & Stevenson, 1989; Marshall, 1989; Shaywitz & Shaywitz, 1984). In fact, about 20 percent of hyperactive children have a parent who was also hyperactive (Cantwell, 1975; Morrison & Stewart, 1971).

But as we've seen throughout this text, biology does not negate the influence of environment. If, for example, a child with a biological predisposition to hyperactivity experiences prolonged excessive stress, symptoms may appear. Thereafter, stigmatizing the child with the label *hyperactive* may intensify the problem (Lambert & Hartsough, 1984). Over time, children with learning problems also suffer from lower self-esteem (Durrant et al., 1990; Kelly et al., 1989; Renick & Harter, 1989).

● *Treating ADHD.* No general link between food sensitivities and ADHD has been found, so in most cases, changing the child's diet, especially eliminating artificial food additives, does not reduce hyperactivity (Goyette &

Sitting still long enough to play a game of Monopoly is difficult for a hyperactive child. Treating this disorder with medication, such as Ritalin, coupled with behavior modification has shown long-term success.

Conners, 1977). During the 1970s, doctors often treated attention-deficit hyperactivity disorder with stimulant drugs, especially **Ritalin** (Whalen & Henker, 1976). Like all stimulants, Ritalin increases the ability to concentrate, and so children who take it usually perform better in school. These effects tend to last only 4 to 6 weeks though, so there seems to be little justification for keeping children on Ritalin year after year (Barkley & Cunningham, 1978).

More sensible is combining the short-term use of Ritalin with a program of behavior management that can effect a longer-lasting change. Such a program involves rewarding children with points, tokens, or stars whenever they behave appropriately (such as sitting still log enough to finish a meal or to do schoolwork). These "chips" can then be "cashed in" for a treat, toy, or privilege. Classroom behavior often improves with this type of treatment (O'Leary & Becker, 1967).

Since the early research, Ritalin has been found to work better in children who have attention-deficit disorder *and* hyperactivity rather than for those who are not hyperactive (Barkley et al., 1991). Ritalin also improves interactions between hyperactive children and their mothers: When their children completed tasks more easily, the mothers reduced their commands and became less controlling (Barkley, 1989).

● **Ritalin**
a stimulant drug used to treat attention-deficit hyperactivity disorder

SUMMARY

1. When studying the self, researchers consider three interrelated components: the cognitive, the affective, and the behavioral. The cognitive component is the way people see and represent themselves: their self-conceptions. As children's cognitive abilities mature, so does their understanding that the self has many different traits, abilities, and roles. During middle childhood, the child's self-concept becomes more stable as children recognize and organize the various attributes they possess. During the elementary school years, children's knowledge of sex-role stereotypes increases, and their preferences for sex-typed activities, same-sex friendships, and sex-stereotyped occupations remain strong. (See pages 376–380.)

2. The affective component of the self is the way that we feel about ourselves, or our self-esteem. Children with generally high self-esteem are generally more confident and independent than those with lower esteem. Children assess themselves in four basic areas: competence in meeting demands for achievement, success at influencing other people, adherence to ethical standards, and social acceptance. Parents of children with high self-esteem tend to be authoritative in their approach. (See pages 380–382.)

3. The behavioral component of the self is self-regulation: the extent to which we can monitor and control our own behavior. The capacity for self-regulation is markedly stronger than it was during early childhood. In middle childhood, children can now use their thoughts, or inner speech, to control their actions. Self-regulation is a fairly stable trait that is linked to later academic and cognitive success. (See pages 382–384.)

4. Achievement motivation, the desire to perform well, continues to develop and becomes especially important in settings where accomplishments are monitored and judged, such as school. Achievement motivation differs from mastery motivation, the desire to master a challenge in order to acquire a new skill. In Erikson's theory, the chief psychosocial crisis of middle childhood concerns the child's sense of accomplishment. Meeting the social and psychological challenges of this period gives children a sense of industry, a belief that they are competent and able to master things. Children who fail at or withdraw from the challenges of middle childhood develop a feeling of inferiority. (See page 384.)

5. Underlying growth in achievement motivation is a change in the way children think about ability. Rather than being tied to specific skills, as in early childhood, older children think of ability as a global, relatively stable psychological trait. Comparison with other children begins, and thinking about challenges becomes more realistic. But still, an immature understanding of ability makes children very vulnerable to the effects of failure. (See pages 384–385.)

6. Among the things that influence achievement motivation are children's attitudes and goals. Educators distinguish between learning goals and performance goals. Learning-oriented goals stress mastery, and mistakes are accepted as part of the process. In contrast, performance goals are more concerned with how one appears to others than with what one actually learns. Mistakes are particularly threatening since they carry the risk of appearing incompetent. Strong achievers believe that working hard will bring success. Children with chronically low achievement may suffer from evaluation anxiety or from learned helplessness. (See pages 386–389.)

7. The psychoanalytic theorist Harry Stack Sullivan believed that we are motivated to seek security by forming relationships with others who make us feel happy and safe. Interacting with others who think well of us fosters a positive self-identity and strong self-esteem. By age 11 or 12, children begin to appreciate the intimacy that friends can share, a capacity reflecting both cognitive and emotional growth. (See pages 391–392.)

8. Peer relationships are critical to many of the social advances of middle childhood. Give-and-take with friends teaches children the importance of sharing, reciprocity, and cooperation. By trying to get peers to understand their thoughts and feelings, children learn to communicate more effectively. Communication advances stem from several factors, including improved role-taking abilities. In addition, elementary schoolers may be forced to be better communicators because they are spending more time with their peers. (See pages 393–396.)

9. A common psychosocial problem of school-age children is phobia: an intense, irrational fear. Children's phobias typically fall into three major categories: physical injuries, natural events, and social situations. Treatment for phobias can include psychoanalytic therapy, which seeks to help children resolve inner conflicts that may cause their fears, and cognitive-behavioral therapy, which helps children "unlearn" fears that have been acquired. Through desensitization children are exposed gradually to the

things they fear and are rewarded for performing previously avoided behaviors. (See pages 396–399.)

10. Another common psychological problem of middle childhood is attention-deficit hyperactivity disorder—difficulty sitting still and paying attention. Growing evidence suggests that ADHD is biologically caused. Attention-deficit disorder is most successfully treated with both drugs and behavior modification techniques. (See pages 399–401.)

KEY TERMS

achievement motivation	industry versus inferiority	phobias
attention-deficit hyper-	learned helplessness	Ritalin
activity disorder	learning goals	self-conceptions
desensitization	mastery motivation	self-esteem
evaluation anxiety	performance goals	self-regulation

SUGGESTED READINGS

Colcs, R. (1990). *The spiritual life of children.* Boston: Houghton Mifflin. The noted child psychiatrist examines children's spiritual and religious beliefs, through interviews and case studies.

Damon, W., and Hart, D. (1988). *Self-understanding in childhood and adolescence.* New York: Cambridge University Press. An excellent discussion of the development of the self-system in middle childhood and adolescence.

Eisenberg, N., and Strayer, J. (Eds.) (1987). *Empathy and its development.* New York: Cambridge University Press. A collection of articles dealing with research and theory on this aspect of prosocial development.

Gottman, J., and Parker, J. (Eds.) (1987). *Conversations of friends.* New York: Cambridge University Press. An edited volume on how children establish and maintain friendships.

Kutner, L. (1991). *Parent & child: Getting through to each other.* New York: Morrow. A collection of advice-oriented essays on various aspects of child development and child rearing.

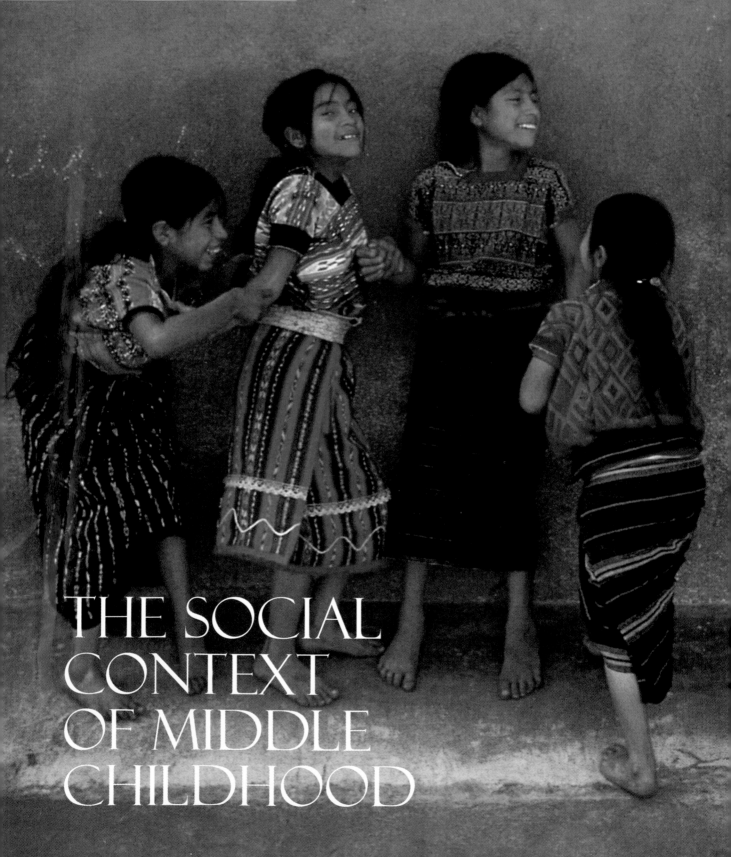

THE SOCIAL
CONTEXT
OF MIDDLE
CHILDHOOD

The preschool boys we discussed in Chapter 11 tested their strength, their daring, their cleverness through superhero scenarios. All foes could be vanquished; all fantasies, fulfilled. If the action got rough, a teacher was there to soothe hurt feelings or redirect the game. If girls' play was gentler and more domestic, imagination still reigned, and protective adults could still be counted on. And for many children, parents influenced whom they played with, when they played, and even what they played.

In middle childhood, psychological, physical, and cognitive advances lead boys and girls to a social world where they are both more independent and less protected. Children find their own friends, play their own games, learn their own rules—and going to a teacher or a parent for help is out. Boys generally stop pretending to be superheroes now; in sports and with peers they really have to *be* strong. Girls stop dressing in grown-up clothes, but they are often judged on how they look and act. For both sexes, the pressures to perform, to compete, to be popular all begin to grow.

Children also begin to make the choices that will shape their educations. Do you work hard or fool around, study for a math test or watch TV? These and many other decisions begin to have real consequences. Development is influenced too by the kind of school children attend. How well do teachers balance memorizing and creativity, rote learning and intellectual inquiry? How much do teachers' expectations influence students' performance? How does a child's ethnic group, and American culture as a whole, influence those expectations?

Within their own family, children become more active shapers of their lives. Many learn to negotiate effectively for what they want while they adapt to the personal styles of their parents and siblings. For too many children, survival itself is a challenge. War, terrorism, famine, and criminal violence threaten millions of children and their families worldwide. In this chapter we will examine the ordinary and the extraordinary contexts of middle childhood and their impact on the process of development.

CHILDREN IN FAMILIES

While middle-childhood boys and girls test and develop their social skills in peer groups and at school, considerable development is still going on within the family. Children at this age test their parents and other adult family members in many ways, a process that in turn strongly influences the way their parents or extended family members behave toward them.

In this section we'll look again at the give-and-take of family relations in the context of the larger social world. For example, how are changing trends in parental employment affecting children? What does the newest research on divorce and development in middle childhood show? Finally, we'll consider a question we asked about the Rivers brothers in Chapter 1: How can children within the same family be so different from one another?

● The Family Mosaic

You don't need a textbook to know that American family life is both diverse and changing. In the African-American community, extended families, often led by grandmothers, have been the norm for generations (Pearson et al., 1990; Wilson, 1989). Divorce rates for blacks and whites have made single-parent homes common, a growing number of women are choosing to give birth to and raise children without marrying at all, and gay and lesbian couples are forming families that include children. In the accompanying Highlight on Diversity box, we consider the variety of family structures in contemporary America.

● Parenting Styles: Effects on School Success and Behavior

The parenting styles we discussed in Chapter 11—authoritarian, authoritative, and permissive—continue to influence development across middle childhood. And the arenas for those effects broaden to peer groups, elementary and middle schools, and a variety of settings outside the family. Across the years, parents' styles tend to be the same. Those who were authoritative with young children are still that way when their children are older (McNally et al., 1991). As we revisit parenting styles, we will focus on the origins of those styles and the consequences for children. As you read, keep in mind that parenting is a two-way street, influenced both by children and by the larger context in which the family lives, including the child's own peer group. Overly harsh parenting can lead to aggressive behavior in children, leading children toward antisocial peer groups, enhancing their aggressiveness, and provoking harsh parenting. Rather than trying to solve the "which came first" puzzle, it is more useful to think of parenting as a process.

During middle childhood, the authoritarian style—with its perfectionism, rigidity, and harsh discipline—continues to affect children adversely, especially boys. Sons of authoritarian parents are lower than their peers in appropriate social assertiveness, cognitive ability, competence, and self-esteem; but they are more aggressive than other children (Coopersmith, 1967; Loeb et al., 1980;

HIGHLIGHT ON DIVERSITY

FAMILY STRUCTURES IN CONTEMPORARY AMERICA

The diversity of family forms in contemporary America was clearly illustrated in a classic study of first graders in Woodlawn, a poor neighborhood in Chicago (Kellam, Ensminger, & Turner, 1977). Of the nearly 1,100 families in the sample, approximately 1,000 children were either living with single mothers (517) or with their mother and father (483). But that left nearly *400* families who did not fall into one of these two groups. These families were distributed across a wide array of family structures, including children who were living with their mother and stepfather (52); mother and grandmother (38); grandmother alone (19); mother and aunt (16); mother, father, and aunt (15); mother, grandmother, and grandfather (13); mother, father, and an adult sister (13); and in various other arrangements.

By the way, here's something even more extraordinary: The data were collected nearly 30 years ago, before the "changing" American family was widely acknowledged.

SOURCE: Kellam, S., Ensminger, M., and Turner, R. (1977).

When we look at socially competent children we suspect that their families are warm and authoritative, but each child also brings with her qualities of temperment that may encourage or discourage warm or rejecting parenting styles.

Maccoby & Martin, 1983; Yarrow et al., 1968). Researchers found very similar results even in a culture where good parents are *expected* to punish children physically. In Saint Kitts, West Indies, where even children accept this norm, harsh, authoritarian parenting is still linked with poor psychological adjustment (Rohner et al., 1991).

Interestingly, overly permissive parents who set few limits and rarely punish have overly aggressive children as well. They may allow the child to behave aggressively for a variety of reasons: They may believe in letting a child "act out," they may be indifferent to the child, or they may be weary of dealing with chronically aggressive behavior (Olweus, 1980; Sears et al., 1957). Children of permissive parents also tend to be more impulsive, less self-reliant, and less responsible (Baumrind, 1967, 1971). They may also achieve less in school. In one study of about 150 boys, those whose parents showed little interest in their day-to-day schoolwork received lower grades than other children (Crouter et al., 1990).

In contrast, the children of authoritative parents are socially competent, are responsible, and show high self-esteem (Maccoby & Martin, 1983). Authoritative parents set clear standards and exert firm discipline, but they are warm, they listen to their children, and they respond to their children's reasonable demands. New research confirms that this kind of parenting is strongly linked to high achievement and children's ability to regulate their behavior in school (Grolnick & Ryan, 1989).

To what extent does parenting create a certain kind of child, and how much does the child elicit a certain kind of parenting? The problem with studies showing the "effects" of parents' behavior on children is that they ignore the influence of the child's inborn characteristics. How much of a parent's behavior stems from the parent's beliefs and personality, and how much stems from a child's innate self? Do responsible, competent children encourage warm, authoritative parenting, while aggressive children elicit harsh, controlling parenting behavior (Lewis, 1981)?

Researcher Gerald Patterson, who has studied the relationship between parents' disciplining techniques and highly aggressive children, contends that such children have characteristics that make them difficult to control in the first place. Typically, they seek instant gratification, ignoring the possible consequences of their actions. And though overly aggressive, they are *under*-responsive to many kinds of social stimulation, including both positive reinforcement for behaving properly and punishment for behaving badly. After observing families with overly aggressive and average boys, Patterson (1982) found that children with average amounts of aggressive behavior were less aggressive after being punished, but overly aggressive children were twice as likely to respond to punishment by maintaining or even *increasing* their aggressiveness. In fact, a cycle of aggression and punishment often develops in families with overly aggressive children, another instance of individual differences interacting with the environment. Breaking the cycle includes intervention: teaching parents to be more consistent in setting standards and guidelines and in providing rewards and punishments.

When the cycle is not broken—when parenting remains harsh and warm interactions are few—children continue to be aggressive and noncompliant, leading to failure in school and rejection by peers. In turn, these children are at greater risk for depression and for joining delinquent peer groups (Patterson, 1989).

Some relatively new research on the causes of parenting styles reveals that the way parents *think about* or *attribute* their children's behavior influences the way they discipline them. For example, authoritarian mothers attribute their children's misbehavior to the child's own negative qualities. Nonauthoritarian mothers more often thought the causes of the same misbehavior were outside of their child (for example, they were more likely to look for a "bad influence," such as the child's friends) (Dix & Reinhold, 1991). As children get older, however, even though their parents' basic style stays the same, parents consider whether children are old enough to have behaved properly. At that point, more authoritarian, "power-assertive" discipline may be favored (Dix et al., 1989).

Parents' attributions can even be influenced by how a child looks. If you've ever thought that baby-faced children got away with more than maturer-looking youngsters, you were right. Parents think older-looking kids misbehave intentionally, while they judge the same behaviors more leniently when done by baby-faced children of the same age. Older-looking children are also given more cognitively demanding tasks to do than baby-faced children (Zebrowitz et al., 1991).

She may be a professional at the office, but many working mothers still make the time to pack their children's lunch boxes, help them dress, write notes to their teachers, and attend school events. She has less time to spend with them, but a mother who works can be just as involved with her children's well-being and development as a nonemployed parent.

● Parents' Employment and Unemployment

In the 1980s, developmentalists studying the effects of parental employment on children focused on mothers. By 1986, 70 percent of women with children aged 6 to 17 were working; for all women with children under 18, the figure was 63 percent (U.S. Bureau of the Census, 1987). By 1995, an estimated 23.5 million children between 6 and 13 (about 2 out of 3) will have mothers in the labor force (Hofferth, in Booth, 1992).

During the 1980s, researchers looking at this trend focused on its impact on children (see Chapter 7), taking a broader look at employment trends and children. As the American economy soured in the late 1980s, researchers began wondering about the effects of parental *unemployment* on children, a topic we discuss below. The theme of this section is that family life is a *process*, influenced by many factors. Rather than comparing children from different "social addresses"—whether they have working or nonworking mothers, divorced, single, or married parents—researchers now look at processes of influence within families (Demo, 1992).

Consider maternal employment, for example. We now know that when working mothers share activities with their children, their youngsters are as competent in school as the children of nonworking mothers (Moorehouse, 1991). In other words, it is the process of mother-child interaction that makes a difference, not maternal employment per se.

Another part of the process that affects the child's development in homes of working mothers is the way the mother feels about working. What effect does a mother's *attitude* about working have on her children's development? In the past, when middle-class mothers routinely stayed at home, those who worked felt guilty, and society's disapproval only reinforced their fears. Today, working mothers are the norm, and the woman whose self-esteem benefits from her work may even become a better parent (Hoffman, 1983). In contrast, women who stay home when they would rather be working may be less effective mothers. Several studies have found that a mother's satisfaction with being a homemaker *or* an out-of-home worker matters more than whether she works. Simply put, children of parents who feel good about their lives tend to be better adjusted than children of more dissatisfied parents (Hoffman, 1974; Scarr, 1984).

From about age 11 on, children of working mothers are likely to have household responsibilities as well as specific rules structuring their activities (just one television show before homework, for example) (Hoffman, 1974). Wisely administered, such rules and responsibilities can enhance a child's development, but the effects of maternal employment on household labor seem to differ for girls and boys. Interestingly, in families where both parents work, sons spend only one-third as much time on chores as sons in families where mothers do not work. In contrast, daughters in dual-income homes spend 25 percent *more* time on chores. In the traditional families, though, chores tend to be sex-stereotyped: Boys garden or fix things; girls cook or clean (Benin & Edwards, 1990).

When girls are trained to be independent at home, they also tend to do well in school, both socially and academically (Hoffman, 1979). Daughters of employed mothers also are less likely to have sex-stereotyped attitudes about appropriate careers for men and women than girls whose mothers do not work (Hoffman, 1983). Many studies have found that girls with working mothers have higher self-esteem and career aspirations than those whose mothers don't work (Bronfenbrenner & Crouter, 1982; Hoffman, 1974).

The impact of a mother's employment on boys appears to vary with the family's social class, however. In general, middle-class boys are more affected—*positively and negatively*—by their mother's working than working-class boys (Hoffman, 1979; Lamb, 1982). Middle-class boys whose mothers work are less likely to develop sexist attitudes than the sons of full-time homemakers (Hoffman, 1979). But several studies also show that middle-class sons of working mothers don't do as well in school as boys whose mothers are not employed (Bogenschneider & Steinberg, in press; Bronfenbrenner & Crouter, 1982). For working-class boys, the differences between those whose mothers work and those whose mothers do not work are minimal. One reason for this pattern is that working-class families usually hold more traditional attitudes toward sex roles than middle-class households, regardless of the mother's work status. Relationships and ideas are therefore less likely to change as a result of a mother being in the labor force (Hoffman, 1979).

● *Unemployment and poverty.* As unemployment rose during the late 1980s and early 1990s, developmentalists began to study the effects on children of parents *not* working, particularly unemployment among fathers (McLoyd, 1989). Again, as a part of the process of family interactions, how fathers feel about their joblessness strongly affects how they react toward their children. Men who feel threatened and pessimistic tend to become more irritable, less nurturant, and more arbitrary with their children. Their children show greater risk for social and emotional problems, deviant behavior, and lowered expectations for their own futures. Again, some of the children's own qualities, including temperament and physical attractiveness, influence the way fathers respond to them. But when children have strong support from their mothers, when they are encouraged to be mature and autonomous, their resilience in times of economic hardship can be strong (McLloyd, 1989). This research is especially important to understanding the development of minority children, since their parents are disproportionately likely to experience unemployment.

As in infancy and early childhood, the impact of family poverty on children's development during the middle childhood years is substantial (McLoyd, 1989). Elementary school children from impoverished homes are more likely to show signs of depression, poor peer relations, antisocial behavior, low self-esteem, and school difficulties. These effects result both from the direct exposure of poor children to a wide range of stressors—including crime, inadequate housing (perhaps even homelessness), and poor nutrition—as well as from the harmful impact of poverty on the quality of parent-child relations, which, in turn, takes its toll on the psychological adjustment of the child. As we noted in earlier chapters, parents under economic stress are more likely to be inconsistent, punitive, and disengaged, and this sort of parenting has been shown to have negative effects on the children's psychological development.

● Latchkey Children

Relationships within a family also affect the way children react to being home alone after school. With an estimated 75 percent of mothers of school-age children working (Vandell & Ramanan, 1991), about one-fourth of elementary school children care for themselves for some time after school each day (Carnegie Corporation of New York, 1992). Whereas children in lower-income inner-city families are more likely to attend group-care after-school programs, middle- and upper-income white suburban or rural children are more likely to return home when no adult is present (Hofferth, 1989).

How are these so-called **latchkey children** doing? Better than many had predicted. A review of research done during the mid to late 1980s found "no evidence of increased problems in latchkey children" (Vandell & Ramanan, 1991).

But not all self-care situations are alike, and it can be misleading to group all latchkey children together (Steinberg, 1986). Self-care children who go straight home after school, report in by phone to their parents, and stay at home, for example, are far less likely to succumb to peer pressure and possibly get into trouble than children who stay unsupervised at a friend's house or just "hang out" after school (Galambos & Maggs, 1991). Among eighth graders as a whole, though, those who took care of themselves for at least 11 hours per week were at twice the risk for using alcohol, tobacco, and marijuana (Richardson et al., 1988). This risk held across a range of income levels, extracurricular activities, sources of social influence, and levels of stress.

Before we leave the subject of latchkey children, we consider one more factor: parenting. Children of authoritative parents are less susceptible to peer influence than those reared permissively, regardless of their after-school situations (Steinberg, 1986). In short, as we've seen earlier in this chapter, good parent-child relations probably influence a child's behavior more strongly than any type of child care arrangement. We should also note that most of the sub-

● **latchkey children**
children who stay home without an adult while their parents work

jects of these studies have been white middle-class children. Children in low-income families, inner cities, or minority populations have not often been included (Vandell & Ramanan, 1991). The accompanying Making a Difference box suggests a number of strategies that can make latchkey children feel more secure.

MAKING A DIFFERENCE

LATCHKEY CHILDREN: PRACTICAL SUGGESTIONS FOR PARENTS AND EDUCATORS

Generally, children at home without adults in urban neighborhoods tend to be more fearful than rural or suburban children, which is hardly surprising given the higher crime rates in city neighborhoods (Carnegie Corporation of New York, 1992). But regardless of where children live, parents who must leave them alone can do several things to help their children feel secure (Koblinsky & Todd, 1989).

By middle childhood, many children who are home without an adult after school can feel secure if they have guidelines to follow and a welcoming parent to talk to on the telephone.

1. Prepare the child for self-care before the arrangement begins. Have a regular place where the child is expected to be and a set of activities for the child to do. Give thorough instructions about how things work in the house, what to do in an emergency, what to do until parents come home, and when to expect a parent home. Make sure not to press the child into household responsibilities before he or she is ready for them.

2. Ask the child to "check in"—either in person or by telephone—with an adult as soon as he or she gets home. This can be a parent or a relative or neighbor.

3. Teach the child how to reach a nearby adult in case of problems. Children should be encouraged to call if they feel at all worried or concerned. Some neighborhoods identify an adult whom children on the block can call.

4. Give the child careful instructions about how to answer the phone and how to respond to visitors. Children should not tell strangers on the phone that they are home alone, nor should they let strangers into the house.

5. Parent in ways that facilitate healthy decision-making skills. Children raised authoritatively fare better on their own than others.

● The Effects of Divorce

Until recently, older elementary school children were thought to handle divorce better than younger children. By middle childhood, research suggested, most children whose parents divorced earlier had relatively few problems that were connected to their parents' separation. When problems did appear, they were generally seen in boys more than in girls (Hetherington & Camara, 1984). But later research offers some new insights.

On the basis of newer studies, these conclusions have been revised. We now know that there are consistent, although small, differences between elementary school children from divorced and nondivorced homes. Problems tend to show up in children's behavior and in poorer school performance. Fourth grade boys who have lived through *several* family transitions—with parents divorcing, remarrying, and divorcing again—show serious adjustment problems (Capaldi & Patterson, 1991). In general, though, boys do not have more problems than girls following divorce. (Girls may even be hurt more than boys.) While boys appear more affected at about age 6 to 7, this sex difference seems to be temporary (Allison & Furstenberg, 1989).

Nevertheless, for many children, there do seem to be "sleeper" effects that may not appear until adolescence (Hetherington et al., 1989). It is possible that researchers who study children only through middle childhood have missed the long-term consequences of an earlier divorce. At least one recent study indicates that some of the negative consequences of divorce often emerge years later (Wallerstein & Blakeslee, 1989). Wallerstein and Blakeslee studied a group of young adults whose adjustment, as children, to their parents' divorce had seemed smooth. But as young adults they reported feeling embittered and troubled. Because this study lacked a control group (young

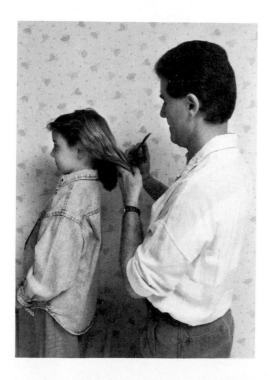

Adjusting to divorce is never easy, but harmful effects can be minimized if children live with a parent who remains loving and attentive to their needs.

adults whose parents did not divorce), the results should be considered inconclusive, although the study does remind us that in assessing any single life event, we need to look carefully at both long- and short-term consequences.

Perhaps the most conclusive thing research continues to show is that there is a great deal of variability among children whose parents divorce, and the variables associated with this diversity are more important for predicting adjustment than divorce per se. At the top of the list is family conflict, followed by the resources available to the family and the child, and the child's temperament (Hetherington, 1989). Generally, children adapt well after divorce if family conflict is low, that is, if former spouses stop fighting or can resolve their disputes (Amato & Keith, 1991; Cummings et al., 1991; Hetherington & Camara, 1984). Children are also buffered when they feel that they have enough emotional support (Cowen et al., 1990) and when the family's style of living does not decline sharply (Hetherington & Camara, 1984). Predictably, an adaptable temperament also helps children adjust to the loss they feel after divorce.

As we noted in Chapter 10, many of the behavior problems children exhibit thought to be caused by divorce may have existed long before the marriage ended. In a longitudinal study of British and American children, researchers identified the factors that caused children problems *before* their parents divorced (Cherlin et al., 1991). Many lived in dysfunctional families, where the parents' own psychological problems made normal development difficult for children. Typically, marital conflict was high as well, only adding to the child's emotional problems. The third source of problems for these children occurred *after* the divorce, when emotional upset, financial pressures, continued conflict between parents, and a breakdown in parenting were usually heightened.

● ***The effects of father absence.*** While more fathers may be gaining custody of their children, a large portion of fathers see their children rarely, if at all, after divorce (Dudley, 1991; Furstenberg et al., 1983). While earlier studies showed that children do better after divorce when their relationship with their father continues (Peterson & Zill, 1986), later studies offer some new insights.

In general, the effect of continued contact with a father after a divorce depends on the father's personality and the relationship between the father and the child's mother. If the father is well-adjusted, contributes to the child's financial support, and isn't embroiled in continuing conflict with his ex-spouse, his child will benefit from frequent contact. But if the father has psychological problems (problems which might have led to the divorce, such as substance abuse), refuses to pay child support, or is still in conflict with the child's mother, the child may be more harmed than helped by contact with him (Furstenberg, Morgan, & Allison, 1987).

● Differences among Siblings

They share the same parents, live in the same house, and even have some matching genes, but siblings' personalities may be as different as strangers'. The reasons lie in the innate differences of temperament and in the fact that, even within the same home, each child's experiences and feelings are unique (Daniels et al., 1985).

● ***Experiences within the family.*** One brother describes his family as close, while another feels it is distant. One sister finds her family life stressful, but her siblings do not. A girl recalls cooperation in her family; her brother says family members never cooperated. Such differences in experience and perception can have significant consequences for development. For example, children who say their parents are unaffectionate are far more likely to show signs of emotional or behavioral problems than siblings who do not perceive their families this way.

To understand how siblings can experience their families so differently, recall the theme of interaction that we've been discussing throughout this book: Within every family, each child's temperament and physical characteristics mesh differently with his or her parents' temperaments, characteristics, and life circumstances (Dunn et al., 1990; Hoffman, 1991; McHale & Pawletko, 1992). An athletic child may be favored by an athletic parent over a less active sibling. A disabled child may receive more attention than a physically normal child. Child 1 excels in school; child 2 is slower. In some families, child 1 is favored and child 2 is criticized; in others, child 2 gets extra help and support. One child may grow up during difficult financial times, while a later sibling is born in a more prosperous, less stressful period. A very sensitive child could have emotional difficulties in one set of circumstances but do much better in less stressful times.

● ***Birth order and family size.*** How many siblings you have and where you fall in the order strongly influence both your experiences and your development. New parents may lack confidence, but they may spend more time with their child. And while later-born children may feel shortchanged by their parents, they are usually more popular among their peers (Hartup, 1983). That may be because, as young children, firstborns spend more time with adults. Later-borns grow up with other children, learning social skills that help them get along with their peers.

A child's birth order doesn't automatically confer advantages or disadvantages, but last-born children do tend to enjoy special relationships with older siblings.

Generalizing about the effects of birth order is tricky, however, because these effects are themselves affected by spacing between siblings, gender, and family size. One of the most consistent findings in Western cultures, for example, is that only children do slightly better in school. But, again, pointing to culture's influence on development, researchers in China found that such differences applied only to children living in cities. Again, pointing to the role social context plays in development, in rural areas, firstborns do not have an academic edge—perhaps because they are expected to devote much of their time to family chores (Poston & Falbo, 1990).

Context again helps to explain why closely spaced children have different experiences from those of children born further apart, and why a firstborn girl will be treated differently from a third-born girl. But what if that same girl followed two boys? Similarly, being second of two is likely to be very different from being second of five.

● ***Sibling deidentification.*** Marie is the family athlete. Her younger sister Anna shuns sports and spends most of her free time drawing and reading. Are these differences inborn or cultivated? Would Anna be more athletic if Marie were less so? Perhaps. Some children deliberately carve out a unique identity. This phenomenon, **sibling deidentification** (Schachter, 1982), suggests again how children can actively shape their own development. By choosing to be unlike a sibling (that is, by *de*identifying with a brother or sister), children participate in determining their own personality. It is likely that the effects of sibling deidentification will persist into adulthood because many personality traits and interests are consolidated during adolescence.

More likely to change over time, though, is the relationship between siblings. In a study that surveyed children in grades 3, 6, 9, and 12, researchers concluded that as siblings get older, their relationships become more equal and less intense (Buhrmester & Furman, 1990). The reasons may have to do with older children spending more time with their friends than with their families.

● **sibling deidentification** one process through which children develop identities different from their siblings'

THE CHILD IN THE PEER GROUP

In William Golding's novel *Lord of the Flies,* a plane carrying a load of British schoolboys, aged 6 to 12, crashes on an uninhabited tropical island. All the adults are killed, and the boys must fend for themselves. Some try to impose organization; others resist, intent on acting out their own fantasies and running wild. Leaders emerge; cliques and rivalries form. Ultimately, the rational democratic group is overcome by the violent irrational group. Although we can argue over whether Golding's picture of these boys' social world is overly bleak, his novel accurately describes their peer group as a little society, with ingroups and outgroups, leaders and scapegoats, cliques and status hierarchies.

The development of a peer group is one of the most important transitions of middle childhood. Children have peer relations in early childhood, but they aren't organized around a social network with norms and standards that structure behavior. Here we will consider the structure of peer groups and how they function, why some children are more popular than others, and how peer relations affect psychological development.

● The Structure and Functioning of Children's Groups

● *Group characteristics.* Nothing distinguishes middle childhood peer groups so much as their sameness: same age, same sex, same race. In classrooms, clubs, and teams, children are grouped by age because their interests and developmental abilities are similar. But they tend to group themselves by race, from preschool through early adolescence (McCandless & Hoyt, 1961; Schofield & Sagar, 1977; Spencer, 1981). This is likely to be related to social class and residential patterns, but it is less prevalent among boys, for whom participation in sports tends to break down racial barriers.

An even stronger grouping factor than race is sex. By this age, boys and girls are becoming very sensitive to the way they think the sexes should behave. For the most part, boys and girls play separately because they play differently (Maccoby, 1990). Boys' play is rougher, more boisterous, more competitive, and it takes place in larger groups than girls' play (DiPietro, 1981; Feiring & Lewis, 1991; Lever, 1976). Girls tend to form more intimate, more exclusive groups than boys, and girls make a point of avoiding boys who play roughly (Haskett, 1971). Outside of school, though, at home and in their neighborhoods, boys

Having a group of close friends during middle childhood is one of the best predictors of later mental health. With their friends, children learn gender norms, how to negotiate, and how to be caring and supportive toward others.

and girls are more relaxed about joining in each other's games (Maccoby, 1988). But here, too, sex differences appear. Girls are more welcoming to newcomers who try to join their group, and girls and boys appear more comfortable when trying to join a group of their own sex (Borja-Alvarez et al., 1991).

Among boys particularly, middle childhood peer groups tend to be activity-oriented: Children who want to play the same game or sport come together whether they are friends or not. Among girls, whom you like usually counts more than what you do, as girls' groups center more on friendships than activities. Also, with age, peer groups become more coherently organized, and boys who appear more dominant are more stable in their organization (Pettit et al., 1990).

● *Group functioning.* In a now classic study known as the Robbers Cave experiment, social psychologists brought 22 fifth-grade boys to a summer camp and divided them into two groups with separate campsites (Sherif et al., 1961). Each group lived closely together, participating in both organized games and cooperative activities. Soon, strong feelings of cohesion developed among the boys in each group. When the two groups began to meet in friendly contests, such as baseball games and tugs-of-war, keen competitive feelings arose. At first, the losing group began turning against itself, with bickering and dissension accompanying each defeat, but things quickly changed. Intergroup competition *increased* the sense of cohesiveness and solidarity within each group, and all aggression was directed against the "others." Finally, the competition got out of hand. One side raided the other side's campsite, and armed with rocks, the boys whose camp was raided attempted a counterattack. Counselors intervened before any damage could be done.

Now, Sherif and his team tried to reduce the intergroup conflict. Joint activities, such as watching a film together, didn't work, but another strategy did. The boys were given a series of problems that could be solved only by *intergroup* cooperation. For instance, when the water supply broke down, the boys had to conduct a lengthy search of the pipes to find the source of the trouble. Another day a food supply truck developed engine trouble just when everyone was hungry. The boys worked together to get the engine started. A common goal, just as much as a common enemy, reduced group conflict and increased cohesiveness.

What Sherif and his colleagues discovered need not be confined to Robbers Cave. An after-school leader with a room full of squabbling children can encourage them to work toward a common goal, by designing a program logo or writing a skit. In classrooms, teachers have found that children perform better in situations where they must cooperate rather than compete. For example, cross-racial harmony can be aided by structuring cooperative interaction and activities.

While a group's goal affects its functioning, an adult's leadership style can be just as important. And as with parenting, authoritative adult leadership is more desirable than authoritarian or permissive leadership. The coach who screams at his players on the field ("You should have caught that") and reproaches them for losing ("You guys really blew this game") breeds only resentment and self-doubt in his players. But the coach who treats everyone with consideration, praises them for their successes, and works with them to improve their weaknesses engenders group contentment and cohesion.

● The Peer Group as a Context for Development

Peer groups foster development in several specific ways. Within the peer group, children learn sex-role norms; when, where, and whether to fight; how to cooperate and share with equals; how to nurture friendships. The peer group provides opportunities for sociability and for learning, and fosters a sense of belonging (Zarbatney et al., 1990). In a study of elementary school children, those who made friends easily did better academically and felt more positively toward school than children who were rejected by their peers (Ladd, 1990).

Children who have had poor relationships with their peers during middle childhood show a wide range of behavioral and psychological problems later on. In fact, one of the best childhood predictors of delinquency is not getting along with others (Hartup, 1983). Researchers studying male delinquents and nondelinquents used school records and self-evaluations to learn about their subjects' childhood peer relations. While similar in age, social class, IQ, and ethnicity, these two groups differed in one key way: The delinquents had poor relationships with their peers; they were both more aggressive and less well liked by other children (Conger & Miller, 1966). Often, children having trouble with peers are also having trouble at home. Both sets of problems—with family relationships and with friends—may lead a child to seek satisfaction outside of cultural norms.

Even during adulthood, psychological problems can be traced back to childhood peer relations. Eleven years after finishing third grade, subjects whose school records showed negative ratings by their peers were more than twice as likely to have been treated for mental health problems. Peer ratings, in fact, were the best predictors of later mental health—more accurate than IQ, school performance, school attendance, or even teacher ratings (Cowen et al., 1973; Hymel et al., 1990).

● Social Acceptance: The Effects of Personality and Culture

In Western cultures, popularity among school-age children comes to those who are socially skilled, have above-average intelligence and strong academic skills, and are physically attractive (Hartup, 1983). Strong self-esteem enhances popularity, and later-born children are often more popular than firstborns, perhaps because they have developed the social skills they needed to get along with their older siblings (Miller & Maruyama, 1976; Sells & Roff, 1964). One encouraging finding is that, at least during the early elementary school grades, a child's ethnicity is *not* related to his or her acceptance by peers (Howes & Wu, 1990).

Actually, the best predictor of healthy peer relations is a happy family life. Children who have good, supportive relationships with their parents are likely to get along with peers, and those with serious problems at home frequently have problems in the peer group (Maccoby & Martin, 1983). This is true even as early as kindergarten (Cassidy & Asher, 1992; Cohn, 1990; Keane et al., 1990).

Among third and fourth graders, children who were most rejected by their peers also reported the least supportive relationships with their fathers;

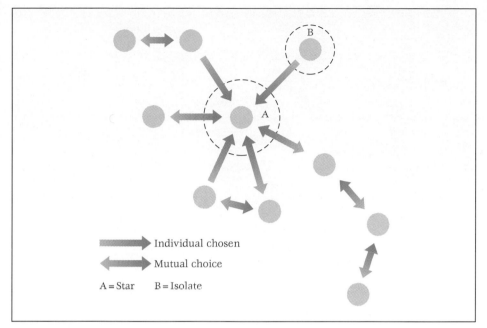

FIGURE 13.1
A Sociogram
To construct a sociogram, re-searchers ask people to name group members with whom they would like to participate in an activity. Responses are then diagrammed, and rela-tionships between individuals can be seen graphically. Here, "A" is a well-liked star, while "B" is an isolate.
(SOURCE: Vander Zanden, 1993.)

In the figure:
Individual chosen
Mutual choice
A = Star   B = Isolate

this was particularly true for rejected aggressive children (Patterson et al., 1990). Not surprisingly, the parenting techniques we've discussed in this chapter and in Chapter 10 are linked to children's popularity with their peers. Children whose mothers favored an authoritarian style were less accepted by their peers. The reason may be that these children, repeating their own treatment at home, strongly relied on their own aggressive tactics to resolve disputes (Hart et al., 1990). Again we see how family life and development outside the family are intimately connected.

One of the ways psychologists study popularity is by asking the students in a class to list the children with whom they would and wouldn't like to play. Using these techniques of **sociometry** (Figure 13.1) (measures of social rela-tionships within a group), researchers then categorize children into four groups, or levels of popularity (Asher & Gottman, 1981; Gottman, 1977; Peery, 1979).

● **sociometry**
measures of social relationships in a group

1. *Stars* are very well liked and have considerable status and influence in the peer group.

2. *Amiables* are liked by others, but they have less status and impact than the stars.

3. *Isolates* are neither liked nor disliked; these children are often simply ignored.

4. *Rejects* are actively disliked by others and have a negative impact on their peer group.

Both stars and amiables are smart and attractive, but the stars have better social skills and are more likely to act as leaders. They are the children who

Social isolates have trouble joining in. They hover and often don't know what to say.

organize a game at recess, who plan after-school games, who initiate parties and other social events.

Though unpopular in school, isolates and rejects have gotten a lot of attention from researchers, for two reasons. First, if we can identify the things these children do that cause others to stay away, intervention programs may help to modify those behaviors. Second, poor peer relationships may put children at risk for later problems, including delinquency and depression (Parker & Asher, 1987). So, early identification and treatment of children who have social adjustment problems may minimize their risk of problems later on. What then do we know about these children?

First, isolates and rejected children differ from one another. Isolates have poor social skills, but they don't behave in the bizarre, deviant, or dishonest ways that cause rejection. Researchers watching socially isolated children have discovered that these children do not know how to join in an activity or conversation of a group of peers. They hover on the fringes and then call attention to themselves in inappropriate ways—by disagreeing with group members, by asking irrelevant questions, by gratuitously stating their feelings or opinions, by telling stories involving themselves (Putallaz & Gottman, 1981; Putallaz & Wasserman, 1989). Usually, these awkward behaviors annoy the others, causing further isolation from the group. Recent research suggests that both isolated and rejected children may be suffering from depression. These children tend to hang back from the group and are generally more submissive than others (Kennedy et al., 1989).

In addition, rejected children, especially boys, are typically hostile and aggressive. Where isolates hover or stay away, rejects barge in and disrupt, a kind of behavior psychologists call "undercontrolled," "hyperactive," or "immature." This kind of behavior—disruptive, intentional, and provocative—disturbs other children, who then pull away (Coie et al., 1991; Dodge et al., 1990; Lancelotta & Vaughn, 1989; Pope et al., 1991). When group conflicts arise, rejected boys in particular respond in ways that only increase tensions (Rabiner & Lenhart, 1990). For rejected girls, the main problem is not aggression and overactivity but timidity (Rogosch & Newcomb, 1989). These girls often appear withdrawn and anxious, and their grades tend to be lower as well. Some rejected boys have the same problems, even though most tend to be aggressive (French, 1990).

What emerges, then, is a mix: Rejected children can be aggressive and bullying (especially, but not exclusively, boys) *or* depressed and timid (especially, but not exclusively, girls). And in both types of rejected children, researchers have noticed poor prosocial skills as well (Parkhurst & Asher, 1992). They are less skilled at things like sharing, cooperating, and empathizing with other children—some of the most important skills for developing and maintaining friends in school.

● ***Peer acceptance and culture.*** Generalizing about all children through a Western lens is risky. Suspecting that being accepted or rejected is not just a matter of personality, a team of researchers studied 8- and 10-year-olds in Ontario, Canada, and Shanghai, China (Chen, Rubin, & Sun, 1992). Specifically, they wondered whether overly aggressive and shy children would be treated similarly in these different cultures.

The results were "yes" and "no." In both countries, being too aggressive and intrusive causes rejection. In Ontario, the same is true for shyness, but in China, shyness and sensitivity are winning traits. Predictably, in Chinese culture, these traits are highly valued. "In Confucian philosophy," the authors explain, "inhibition and self-restraint are considered indices of accomplishment, mastery, and maturity; this is the highest stage of human development. Consistently shy, reticent, and quiet children are called 'Guai' in Mandarin, which means 'good' or 'well-behaved.' As well, children who are sensitive and reticent are believed to be 'Dong-Shi' (understanding), which is a commonly used term for praising a child in China" (Chen et al., 1992, p. 4). This study points again to the importance of looking at context in understanding children's development.

Even in a large group, such as a classroom, shy children tend to feel apart and remain quiet. In China, unlike in western cultures, however, the quiet child is considered refined and special.

MAKING A DIFFERENCE

TRAINING PROGRAMS FOR OVERLY AGGRESSIVE CHILDREN

When asked how he sees himself, a highly aggressive boy drew a picture of a fire-breathing dragon. Psychologists working with this child say the picture expresses the boy's wish to dominate others. Developmentalists are particularly concerned about such children because aggression during childhood is the *best predictor* of adjustment problems later in life, including drug abuse and criminality (Kupersmidt & Coie, 1990). When we intervene with such children, then, the gains affect us all.

In classrooms, the behavior of overly aggressive children looks very similar: When angry they strike out, and they get angry too often. Where other children know how to joke back when teased, these children flare up. Where others know an accidental bump from an intentional push, these children always feel pushed. They also feel differently about aggres-

sion itself, caring less than most children about the consequences of their aggression, such as hurting others or even being punished themselves or being rejected by others. What they valued more than any of these things was achieving a sense of control over the victim (Boldizar et al., 1989). Not surprisingly, they choose their victims carefully, selecting those children who don't fight back (Perry et al., 1990). Even so, they are disliked by others and become isolated, rejected, and alienated. And this pattern continues over time. In two separate studies, overly aggressive children followed from kindergarten through fourth grade and from fourth through tenth grades continued to fight more than other children (Cairns et al., 1989; Loeber et al., 1989).

As you would expect, both innate and environmental conditions are involved in excessive aggression (Patterson et al., 1989). (Also see Chapter 9.) Some children are, by temperament, more prone to outbursts and loss of

control than others; and for overly aggressive boys, an added factor may be that boys are, biologically, more prone to aggression than girls. But the families of these children give us some very specific clues. Aggressive children are more likely than others to live in hostile families where parents themselves are psychologically disturbed, antisocial, and overly punitive or aggressive toward their children (Capaldi & Patterson, in press; Walker et al., 1989). Social learning theory would explain that these children imitate or model that aggressive behavior with others. Psychodynamic theory adds that they are expressing the angry feelings induced by living with hostile parents. And, as well, the child's genetic predisposition toward angry outburst is evoking hostile reactions from his parents.

Intervention, or training, programs for aggressive children have two kinds of goals. One concerns gaining control over aggressive outbursts; the second involves expressing anger or frustration in

● *Emotional buffers for rejected children.* Regardless of one's culture, certain buffers can help children cope with peer rejection. (But keep in mind that in different cultures the buffers may differ as well.) In U.S. studies, for example, rejected children whose mothers are warm appear to have fewer problems overall, and a close relationship with a sibling can give some support to isolated children (Patterson et al., 1989). We also know that, in general, support and good problem-solving skills help children cope with stress of many kinds (Dubow & Tisak, 1989).

● *Intervention strategies.* Psychologists have developed specific strategies that help isolated and rejected children in several ways. One of the easiest is to encourage rejected children to *think* others will like them. Thinking positively about entering a group does, in fact, increase their acceptance (Rabiner

ways that will not harm others. During childhood, most aggression is spontaneous, so if we can help children delay their responses, they may act less aggressively. Meeting these goals means teaching children to check both their physical sensations (am I getting angry?) and their perceptions (*should* I be getting angry?). If a child is being teased, for example, spotting the physical cues to his own anger (feeling flushed or sensing his muscles tense up) can signal him to count to 10. By then, the impulse to lash out may be gone. Training children to appraise their own perceptions is often done in group sessions. After looking at drawings of social interactions, children explain what they think is happening. Psychologists working with them offer different interpretations, and what at first may have seemed threatening can become less so.

Many aggressive children don't know how to behave in ways that other children like. Through *social skills training* they learn new behaviors to use in situations that tend to make them angry. In one training program, "one kid said, for example, that he just stared at the kid who bumped him and told him not to do it again, then walked away. That put him in the position of exerting some control and keeping his self-esteem, without starting a fight" (John Lochman, in Goleman, 1988, p. B25). Teachers can show aggressive children how to ask for what they want ("You've been playing with that basketball for a long time; I'd like a turn"), how to behave prosocially in order to get what they want from someone ("Is it all right if I play, too?"), and how to respond when they feel aggressed against (saying "Watch where you're going" rather than hitting someone who bumped into you accidentally). Many social skills training programs are conducted in groups, so that aggressive children can learn appropriate strategies by brainstorming different situations along with their classmates. Other researchers (for example, Patterson et al., 1989) have been experiment-

When researchers showed this picture to overly aggressive children, interpretations differed. Some said the boy in the center was being picked on; some said the boy at left was bullying, while others said he was helping the middle child.

ing with family-based intervention, to help parents learn how to better discipline aggression-prone children.

& Coie, 1989). For isolates, learning to stop hovering and make an early bid to enter the group is a first step toward participation. An adult can tell a child to just say "Can I play?" Children can learn to fit into the group's frame of reference by asking relevant questions and sharing information, while avoiding inappropriate remarks. These are not easy tasks, and even popular children sometimes have trouble joining a new group.

Some children are helped by therapy that involves watching videotapes of themselves interacting with other children while a therapist points out better or more appropriate strategies. Rejected children need to learn how to join groups too, but for most, controlling their aversive or disruptive behavior is the main problem. Some theorists believe that very aggressive children have problems processing information when they meet with others (Dodge, 1986). As we noted in Chapter 9, highly aggressive children perceive hostile intentions where there are none. For example, if Barbara accidentally runs into Brian on the playground, instead of shrugging it off, as most children would, Brian responds as if the accident were deliberate. He punches Barbara, who then gets angry and upset. After a number of incidents like this, Brian gets labeled as a troublemaker and is rejected by the peer group. A psychologist working with Brian might try to help him develop more accurate perceptions of his own and others' behaviors. The child might also be taught how to exercise leadership skills in a nonaggressive way. One popular approach has focused on helping aggressive children learn to read social cues more accurately (Dodge, 1986; Slaby & Guerra, 1988). (See the Making a Difference box on training programs for overly aggressive children.)

SCHOOLS AND DEVELOPMENT

Nothing influences learning so much as attitudes and beliefs about what produces it. . . . Achievement can be torpedoed by the idea that it is mostly a matter of luck, wealth, or native ability—an idea altogether too prevalent in American education today. . . . When such hands-in-the-air resignation about achievement is reinforced by school administrators—who ought to know better—our national effort to provide equal intellectual opportunity to all our students is undermined.

Former Secretary of Education William Bennett wrote those words in a report called *American Education: Making It Work* (cited in Peterson, 1989, p. 174). Unfortunately, the consensus of experts is that American education is not "working" very well. Despite intensive efforts to reform U.S. schools, levels of achievement among students are lower than in other countries (Mullis et al., 1990). What do we need to do to raise student achievement?

This is a complex issue, but as you read the following pages, you will see that one of the keys to academic success is what happens between students and the significant adults in their life. As we saw earlier in the research on divorce, maternal employment, and day care, what goes on between a child and a significant adult is always more important than any "social address" or label.

We look now at the way schools and teachers affect children's emotional and cognitive development and their actual school achievement. Finally, we'll address the special needs of the physically, emotionally, or mentally handicapped child.

● Schools and Achievement: Expectations, Biases, and Culture

School is one of the most significant contexts in which students develop their attitudes about success and failure. Like the research on students and achievement we reviewed in Chapter 12, many of these studies are also about "expectancies." But now the focus is on *teachers:* How strongly do teachers' expectations and biases influence students' achievement?

"I never knew that." When teachers combine high expectations with personal warmth, children thrive.

● ***The power of expectations.*** That teachers have biases which can actually influence children's achievement is quite a powerful idea. No one had tried to test it until two psychologists devised a study that came to be called "Pygmalion in the Classroom."

In an ingenious experiment, Rosenthal and Jacobson manipulated teachers' expectations by changing the records of students' aptitude test scores. Children who were in fact low achievers were reranked as high achievers, and high achievers now had the scores of low achievers. What happened? By the end of the school year most of the children performed the way their *false* test scores—rather than their actual test scores—would have predicted.

The experimenters concluded two things: (1) Believing the test scores to be accurate, teachers expected certain children to be slow, average, bright; and (2) those *expectations* appeared to affect achievement more than ability itself (Rosenthal & Jacobson, 1968). Rosenthal and Jacobson believed they had identified a self-fulfilling prophecy at work in the classroom; that is, thinking that something is so can *make* it so. Although later researchers found that teacher expectations based on scores affected children's achievement less than Rosenthal and Jacobson had suggested (Brophy, 1983), the basic argument—that students achieve in part what teachers expect—is still, on balance, true.

● ***Race and class biases.*** Another self-fulfilling prophecy—based on race and class—is at work in the classroom too. When asked which children they liked and disliked, teachers tended to rate blacks lower than whites and low-income children below middle-class children, *even when the lower-rated children had high IQ scores* (Leacock, 1969). In addition, black children who misbehave are more likely than misbehaving white children to be punished physically and to be suspended from school (McFadden, Marsh, Price, & Hwang, 1992).

Teachers also sort children according to their work habits, a value so powerful that work habits predicted the way teachers judge students *even more than grades or actual skills* (Farkas et al., 1990). Poor minority children might not have the same work habits as white middle-class youngsters and may be at a disadvantage because of teacher bias.

Culture shapes all of our values and beliefs, including our strongest attitudes about achievement, as a recent series of studies by Harold Stevenson and his colleagues (Stevenson, 1992) makes clear. Americans and Asians, for example, think quite differently about the sources of school success. And when communicated to children, those beliefs can profoundly influence their achievement.

Generally, Asians believe that all children can learn and that how much they learn depends on how hard they work. This may be one of the reasons why Chinese and Japanese children consistently outscore American students on mathematics achievement tests. American children, though they claim to like the subject, do not appear to be as motivated to excel in math. The reason, say a team of American and Chinese researchers, is that American parents do not expect their children to do particularly well in math, and American teachers are less interested in teaching it than Chinese teachers (Stevenson et al., 1990).

Attitudes toward homework are also significantly different. Comparing these attitudes in the United States, China, and Japan, the authors of a cross-cultural study began a scholarly article this way:

> A common explanation of the poor performance of American children in cross-cultural comparisons of academic achievement is that American children spend little time in study. American children spend fewer hours in school and devote less time in school and after school to academic activities than do children in many other countries (e.g., Garden, 1987; Stevenson et al., 1986). *Among the after-school activities most relevant for academic achievement is homework.* [authors' italics] (Chen & Stevenson, 1989)

Even though American children get less homework, they dislike it more than Japanese and Chinese children. Japanese children dislike homework more than Chinese children do. Interestingly, these feelings coincide with the amount of help each group gets from family members. Chinese children get the most help with homework, followed by Japanese. American parents give their children the least amount of help (Chen & Stevenson, 1989). And despite the poorer performance of American students than their Asian counterparts, Stevenson's research found that American parents were more satisfied with their children's schoolwork and that American children had the most positive views of their academic competence (see Figure 13.2). Thus, one explanation for the relatively poorer achievement of American students may be that their parents may have lower performance standards and provide less support for excellence.

Stevenson's research shows also that there are important differences between the *teachers* in the three cultures. Unlike Asian teachers, American teachers tend to look at "ability" first. Even kindergartners are tested and grouped by *perceived* ability. Teachers may call them "bluebirds" and "robins," but perceptions about "fast" and "slow" learners are the unspoken labels that will influence the teachers' expectations for each group. So, although we believe in

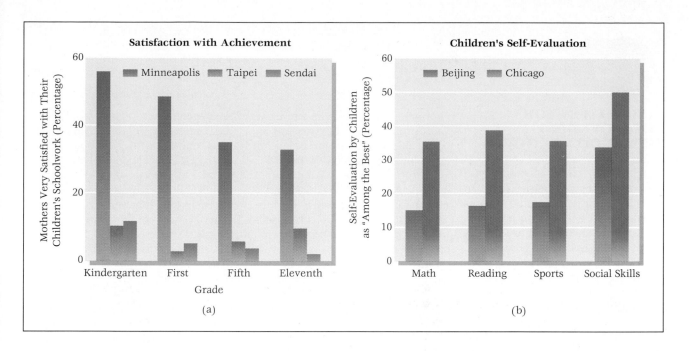

hard work, we also believe that innate ability sets limits on potential and that potential is set at an early age. Consequently, when children don't do well, American teachers are less likely than Asian teachers to encourage them to work harder. In fact, we tend to be so concerned about avoiding failure that we may lower standards so that every child can be "a success" (Finn, 1991, in Mac Iver, 1992). But discouraging a whole group of children from striving to learn hard material does them no favors. In the end, their true potential to learn and succeed goes untapped. Those students who are not expected to do well in difficult subjects can quickly lose confidence in their ability and gradually lose interest in school altogether (Minuchin & Shapiro, 1983, p. 228). Academic success, then, is shaped by the attitudes children absorb about themselves, even if they are sometimes dead wrong. In the Making a Difference box on page 430 we discuss an experimental program with an optimistic view of teaching and learning.

● **Different messages for different genders.** Not only minority and poor students are harmed by biased ideas about ability. Attitudes can even affect performance on a specific subject by a specific group. In the United States, China, and Japan, even first graders rate boys better at math and girls better at reading (Lummis & Stevenson, 1990). But, in fact, except for mathematically gifted students, where boys score higher, both sexes score *about the same* on math ability tests (Hanna, 1988, in Lummis & Stevenson, 1990). But by the time they are in high school, boys outnumber girls in math and science courses (Kavrell & Peterson, 1984).

Explanations point again to the power of perceptions. Right from the start, teachers treat boys and girls differently. Elementary school girls tend to do better than boys, and teachers criticize boys more than girls. But boys also get more positive attention, like being called on to answer a classroom question (Minuchin & Shapiro, 1983). By high school, boys are beginning to do better

FIGURE 13.2

Even though American children achieve less than Asian children, their mothers are more satisfied with their children's schoolwork (a). Reflecting their parents' attitudes, American students were far more likely to rate themselves "among the best" in academics, sports, and social skills than were children from Beijing, China (b).
(SOURCE: Stevenson, 1992.)

MAKING A DIFFERENCE

INCENTIVES FOR IMPROVEMENT IN INNER-CITY SCHOOLS

All children can learn. That belief drives a program being tested in the Baltimore City middle schools that is trying to change both attitudes and achievement among educationally disadvantaged students.

To achieve those goals, teachers are told to expect a lot from their students and to offer a lot to them. In traditional schools, when teachers follow that practice, educationally disadvantaged students are often doomed to fail because they are already behind in their learning (Mac Iver, 1992, p. 15). But the Incentives for Learning Program has been turning failure around with a relatively simple approach: Offer students challenging courses, give them specific goals, monitor their performance closely, and reward their achievement. How successful has the program been?

After one year, students were compared with similar groups of students at four other Baltimore City middle schools. Results showed that the grades of the students in the program were significantly better, and, writes Douglas Mac Iver, the leader of the research team, "there was also a small positive effect of the program on students' self-reported levels of effort" (1992, p. 2). Rather than lower standards to make students feel more accomplished, a better strategy is to take the steps necessary to promote genuine achievement.

Efforts to improve education in inner cities must also confront a dire situation unrelated to the curriculum: violence in children's schools and neighborhoods, which in some communities is so severe that many youngsters are simply afraid to go to school. According to a 1993 speech by President Clinton, each day, some 160,000 American schoolchildren stay home from school because they are afraid to go. Many youngsters must walk through some of the most dangerous areas of urban America in order to get from home to school and back each day. In some Philadelphia communities, schools and churches have banded together to create "safe corridors" through which children can pass unharmed on their way between home and school. These corridors are staffed by adult volunteers who monitor the intersections and crosswalks in dangerous neighborhoods during the hours in which children travel to their schools. In addition, many churches in these communities keep their doors open during the early morning and midafternoon hours, so that children can get assistance and protection from adults (Hinds, 1993).

When Timothy Atkins was on his way home from school in North Philadelphia, other children warned him to turn over his money, or "damage will be done." In response, adult volunteers formed a "safe corridor" for the 960 children there who walk to school.

than girls, particularly in science and math, and they maintain their confidence and persistence in academic work, despite more critical feedback from their teachers.

Apparently, however, how much feedback students get isn't what matters: It's what kind (Minuchin & Shapiro, 1983). Just as we saw earlier regarding achievement, messages about effort and success are crucial. They are also different for boys and for girls. For example, teachers tend to criticize the intellectual aspects of girls' work, while boys were more often criticized for not following rules *or not trying hard enough* (Henderson & Dweck, 1990). Girls get one message (don't bother to try harder; you just can't do the work), while boys learn another (try a little harder; you'll get it right next time). Not surprisingly, messages like these can reverberate in and out of the classroom, affecting both academic achievement and emotional development. Where boys learn to persevere through difficult tasks, girls often learn to feel helpless. We see again, then, that teachers' responses to students can have serious, enduring psychological consequences.

● *What makes good teachers?* In many ways, good teachers are like good parents. They make demands, but they are also highly responsive to their children. In elementary schools, effective teachers show warmth, set clear learning goals, and provide appropriate rewards and punishments. In short, good teachers are *authoritative,* not authoritarian or permissive (Minuchin & Shapiro, 1983; Rutter, 1983). Typically, they help students feel that they have control over their own success in school, feelings which, in fact, foster high achievement (Skinner et al., 1990). (See the discussion of achievement in Chapter 12.) Good teachers also respond differently to the needs of different children, offering less control to those capable of self-direction and more control to those who need more structure in learning. And as they move from elementary school to seventh grade, emotional support from teachers, especially in math, helps students to do well (Midgley et al., 1989).

We turn now to schoolchildren who have special educational needs: the physically, emotionally, and mentally handicapped.

● Educating Children with Special Needs

May is one of the most popular children in her first-grade class. Other children seek her out, show her their latest treasures, and banter happily with her. So many children want to eat lunch with May each day that the teacher has to keep an engagement calendar. May is a quadriplegic, propped up in a wheelchair, immobile below her neck. She is also one of about 10 percent of school-age children in the United States with special educational needs stemming from a physical, emotional, or mental handicap. Among this group are the mentally retarded, with an IQ under 70; children with severe speech impediments; the emotionally disturbed; children with learning disabilities; and children with visual and hearing impairments. Such a broad range of handicaps suggests an equally broad range of educational needs, and the debate persists among educators as to *where* these needs are best met: in special schools geared to special needs, or by **mainstreaming** these children in classrooms with the nonhandicapped.

Until 1950, few special programs existed; all children attended regular classrooms. Gradually, the idea of separate needs took hold, and the 1960s and 1970s saw a dramatic rise in the number of special education programs. But in the late 1970s, opinion turned *against* separate classes, and federal law mandated mainstreaming wherever possible.

● **mainstreaming**
the placement of handicapped children in classrooms with nonhandicapped children

Her wheelchair makes her less able in the school yard but not in science class. Because many physically disabled children are cognitively normal, mainstreaming offers many benefits, often to the rest of the class as well.

Mainstreaming has both benefits and costs. It allows handicapped children to interact and develop relationships with a wide range of peers and reduces the stigma associated with being segregated in a special class. Consequently, mainstreaming can aid a handicapped child's psychological development, particularly when the child develops close ties with classmates. Because differences often become more acceptable as they become more commonplace, mainstreaming can help to dispel prejudices toward the handicapped as it reduces other children's anxieties about them. It also prevents misdiagnosis (putting a normal child into a "slow" class by mistake, for example).

But despite its social and emotional benefits, mainstreaming may not be the best way to meet the cognitive needs of handicapped children. Teachers in regular classrooms gear their attention and lessons to a large group of students, most of whom are average. Those who fall below this range may not get the sort of instruction they need. Additionally, learning disabled children tend to be more rejected and generally less popular than normally achieving children, so mainstreaming may not serve them best (Kistner & Gatlin, 1989).

A compromise between mainstreaming and separate education may be the best solution. Handicapped children could stay in regular classrooms most of the time, spending part of each day in resource centers receiving individualized instruction. They might also attend additional programs after school to help them keep up. Nonhandicapped students could then gain a better understanding of their handicapped peers, while the handicapped could learn both the social skills needed to interact with others and the cognitive skills to progress in schoolwork.

● School and Family

We end our discussion of middle childhood where we began, with the family. How children behave with peers and how they learn at school often reflect the quality of their lives at home.

Good parent-child relations foster emotional and social maturity, which in turn contributes to achievement (Feldman & Wentzel, 1990; Steinberg et al., 1989). But encouraging achievement is more than just asking "What did you learn today?" or attending an occasional PTA meeting. Children do better in school when parents are actively interested in their homework, when they create an atmosphere conducive to studying, and when they provide sources of intellectual stimulation, whether on the bookshelf or at the dinner table.

What is learned at home reinforces what is learned at school. In one study of elementary school children, researchers examined achievement scores in September, June, and the next September (Heyns, 1982). Most children's achievement advanced at about the same rate during the school year, but some children showed improvements between June and September because they kept learning during the summer.

Family life can adversely affect school achievement as well. Children whose daily lives are stressful—during a divorce, for example—are generally less motivated, are more disruptive, and don't do as well in schoolwork as children from stable families (Hetherington, Featherman, & Camara, 1981). These effects are particularly true of boys and show up most often during the first year or two of the crisis at home. After that, children do adjust to new family circumstances and are more able to cope (Hetherington, 1989; Wallerstein & Kelley, 1980). Some parents, wanting to avoid labeling their child, try to conceal divorce from the school, but concealment does not help the child. Teachers need to be sensitive to the child's particular circumstances and to avoid labels that outlive the crisis. And schools need to keep *both* parents informed of the child's progress and of school activities. A nurturant school atmosphere that provides consistency, structure, warmth, and responsiveness can do a great deal to help children cope with changing life circumstances (Hetherington, Cox, & Cox, 1982).

The specific places on the globe this child learns are less important to his development than the respect for curiosity and learning his mother conveys.

We turn now to the challenges faced by children who live with the constant threat of danger. You will notice that even in extraordinary circumstances, it is still the ordinary routines of life that keep children feeling safe.

LIVING WITH DANGER

"An American child or teen-ager dies from gunshot wounds every two hours" (Herbert, *The New York Times,* January 26, 1994, p. A21; see also Children's Defense Fund, 1994). Many are victims of drug and gang wars. Others are shot for not showing "respect," or for wearing a jacket or sneakers that someone else with a gun wanted. Others just happened to be walking by the bullets.

Abroad, wars or other armed conflicts cause most violent deaths. Typically, more soldiers than civilians die in wars, but in recent years, the ratio of soldiers to civilians killed has shifted from 9:1 to *1:9.* In the Middle East, Africa, Northern Ireland, and lately, in the former Yugoslavia, many of the dead are children and mothers.

The other victims of violence are the survivors who see their families and friends murdered. In southside Chicago alone, 25 percent of children witness a homicide before age 17 (Bell, in press, in Garbarino, Kostelny, & Dubrow, 1991). What does daily exposure to violence do to children? Like Lafeyette Rivers, whom we introduced in Chapter 1, many children of the inner cities lose hope in their futures and worry, all too realistically, about the present. Many children cope by becoming overly aggressive themselves, which leads to problems in school and perhaps to criminal behavior. Others become emotionally withdrawn. Like adults exposed to violence or severe trauma through war, natural disasters, or serious crimes, children can develop posttraumatic stress disorder. Symptoms of this disorder may include reexperiencing the event through recollection or dreams, sleep disturbance, difficulties in concentration, and numbing detachment or estrangement from others.

This last effect, *numbing detachment,* interferes with the development of normal empathy for others and can have serious behavioral consequences. For example, a study looking at children's moral reasoning (see Chapter 11) found that advanced moral reasoning was far less common, indeed, almost nonexistent, among children growing up amidst conflict in Northern Ireland or Lebanon than among same-aged children growing up under more peaceful conditions (Fields, 1987, in Garbarino et al., 1991, p. 379). Since impaired moral development can itself lead to more violence and aggression, children who grow up with violence may become violent adults. Numbed to violence, they are incapable of seeing the immorality of it.

What can be done? We know moral thinking can be stimulated by engaging children in discussions that expose them to moral reasoning that is just beyond their own level (what Vygotsky called their "zone of proximal development"). At home or in school, adults can encourage children's higher-order thinking by discussing positions that are one stage above the child's characteristic way of thinking about the moral implications of social events (Garbarino et al., 1991). It is easy to imagine a warm, nurturant family sitting

(a)

When adults are brutal, the costs to children are overwhelming. In an inner-city neighborhood of the Bronx, New York City (a), and in an actual war zone, like Sarajevo, where children dodge sniper fire on their way home from school (b), children express fear and terror in their art work (c).

(b)

(c)

around the dinner table, with the adults suggesting an ethical, humane way to think about a moral issue, but can this approach work with children who grow up with constant danger and violence?

Garbarino's research suggests that it can, *as long as the adults in children's lives are coping well enough.* When adults can no longer absorb stress that is prolonged and extreme, he writes, "the development of young children deterio-

American children want the guns out of their neighborhoods and out of their schools. Here, a student in Washington, D.C. passionately asks Vice President Al Gore for her government's help.

rates rapidly and markedly. Reservoirs of resilience become depleted. Infant mortality rates soar. Day-to-day care breaks down, and rates of exploitation and victimization increase. Moral development itself may be compromised" (p. 380).

Garbarino observed these effects in refugee camps in the Sudan and in Ethiopia (1988a). In Brazil, "an anthropologist working in one village where parents are totally demoralized reported a mortality rate of 500 per 1,000 births (Scheper-Hughes, 1987, in Garbarino et al., 1991, p. 380). But as predictable as these effects seem to be, they are not inevitable. Even in times of crisis, children will be minimally affected if parents can (1) maintain a strong parent-child attachment; (2) retain their own self-esteem and identity; and (3) manage to establish routine and stable care-giving arrangements (Bronfenbrenner, 1986, in Garbarino et al., 1991).

In Sudanese villages suffering from severe drought, for example, when mothers had access to food and fuel, water, and basic medicines, their children seemed to be developing normally. For these children, their daily routines continued, and that, Garbarino believes is enough to maintain healthy development.

The implications of Garbarino's research pose challenges for society as a whole and for individual adults who live and work with children in America's inner cities. Social programs that help adults find jobs and safe affordable housing will also help their children. Adults who work with children can talk with them about the moral implications of the violence in their communities. Perhaps, too, adults need to listen to the children who are pleading with national leaders to get the guns out of their neighborhoods and schools.

SUMMARY

1. As in early childhood, authoritative parenting is linked with high self-esteem, social competence, and responsibility among elementary school children. Authoritarian parenting is associated with lower self-esteem and more aggressiveness, while children of permissive parents are less responsible and more impulsive. (See pages 407–410.)

2. Today, two-thirds of all U.S. children between ages 6 and 13 have mothers in the labor force. Research shows that it is the particulars of mother-child interaction that make a difference for the child's development, not maternal employment per se. For example, a mother's satisfaction with either working or not working affects children more than whether she works. All other factors being equal, however, girls whose mothers work tend to have higher career goals and self-esteem than girls whose mothers don't work. Middle-class sons of working mothers have more egalitarian attitudes about sex roles, but they may not do as well in school as boys whose mothers don't work. In working-class homes, where attitudes about sex roles are more fixed, boys are less affected by maternal employment. (See pages 410–411.)

3. Research on the effects of paternal unemployment indicates that how fathers feel about their joblessness strongly affects how they react toward their children. Men who feel threatened and pessimistic tend to become more irritable, less nurturant, and more arbitrary with their children. Their children show greater risk for social and emotional problems, deviant behavior, and lowered expectations for their own futures. In addition, elementary school children from impoverished homes are more likely to show signs of depression, poor peer relations, antisocial behavior, low self-esteem, and school difficulties. (See pages 411–412.)

4. Latchkey children, who stay home alone after school, are more affected by the relationship they have with their parents than by their after-school arrangements. Children raised by authoritative parents do best, especially when structure is provided for handling emergencies and for spending time alone. (See pages 412–413.)

5. There are consistent, although small, differences between elementary school children from divorced and nondivorced homes. Problems tend to show up in children's behavior and in poorer school performance. However, there is a great deal of variability among children whose parents divorce, and the variables associated with this diversity are more important for predicting adjustment than divorce per se. At the top of the list is family conflict, followed by the resources available to the family and the child and the child's temperament. (See pages 414–415.)

6. Despite their shared genes and family environment, siblings are often quite dissimilar in personality and behavior. The markedly different personalities of siblings result from differences in temperament, differential treatment by parents, and different circumstances outside the family. Birth order and the number of children in a family may also influence develop-

ment. Through sibling deidentification, too, children carve out identities sharply different from those of their brothers and sisters. (See pages 415–417.)

7. The peer groups that form during middle childhood, with their norms and structures, differ markedly from the friendships of early childhood. Now, groups include children of the same age, sex, and race. Working toward common goals increases cohesiveness and reduces conflict. Children who have had poor relationships with their peers during middle childhood show a wide range of behavioral and psychological problems later on. (See pages 417–420.)

8. Researchers differentiate among popular, amiable, isolated, and rejected children. The most popular children at this age are socially and academically skilled, intelligent, and physically attractive. Isolates have poor social skills, but they don't behave in the bizarre, deviant, or dishonest ways that cause rejection. Rejected children, especially boys, are typically hostile and aggressive, although some, especially girls, may be timid and withdrawn. Both social isolates and rejected children can learn the social skills they need to make friends. Training programs can help highly aggressive children to control aggressive impulses and to perceive other people's actions more accurately. (See pages 420–425.)

9. Teachers' expectations and biases, which are embedded in the broader context of schooling, influence students' achievement. Effective teachers, like good parents, are authoritative. They set clear learning goals, communicate warmth, and provide appropriate rewards and punishments. When teachers are prejudiced, children's expectations for themselves can decline. One account of the achievement differences between American and Asian students focuses on the different achievement expectations and beliefs held by adults in the different cultures. (See pages 425–429.)

10. Mainstreaming handicapped children has both benefits and costs. On the positive side, it allows handicapped children to interact and develop relationships with a wide range of peers and reduces the stigma associated with being segregated in a special class. On the negative side, mainstreaming may not be the best way to meet the cognitive needs of handicapped children. Teachers in regular classrooms gear their attention and lessons to a large group of students, most of whom are average. Those who fall below this range may not get the sort of instruction they need. A compromise between mainstreaming and separate education may be the best solution. (See pages 431–432.)

KEY TERMS

latchkey children   sibling deidentification   sociometry
mainstreaming

SUGGESTED READINGS

Coles, R. (1993). *The political life of children.* Boston: Houghton Mifflin. A leading child psychiatrist discusses how political conditions around the world—including Northern Ireland, Nicaragua, and South Africa—affect the lives of children.

Dunn, J. (1984). *Sisters and brothers.* London: Fondant. One of the leading researchers on sibling relations discusses the relationships children have with their brothers and sisters and the impact of siblings on development.

Fine, G. (1988). *With the boys.* Chicago: University of Chicago Press. An ethnographic study of a Little League season and the interactions of the preadolescent boys who play on the teams.

Hetherington, E. M., and Arasteh, J. (1988). *The effects of divorce, single parents, and stepparents on children.* Hillsdale, NJ: Erlbaum. An excellent collection of articles on family structure and its impact on child development.

Kidder, T. (1989). *Among schoolchildren.* Boston: Houghton Mifflin. A journalist's moving account of his year observing in an elementary school classroom.

THE TRANSITION INTO ADOLESCENCE

441

As the elementary school years draw to a close, the child begins to move into a new stage of the life cycle: adolescence. The word *adolescence* derives from the Latin verb *adolescere,* which means "to grow into adulthood." In all societies, adolescence is a time of growing up, of moving from the immaturity of childhood into the maturity of adulthood.

There is no single event or boundary line that denotes the end of childhood or the beginning of adolescence. Rather, the passage from childhood to adolescence is composed of a *set* of transitions that unfold gradually and that touch upon many aspects of the individual's behavior, development, and relationships.

In this final chapter, we explore the nature of the transition from childhood into adolescence. We have organized the material around four basic transitions: biological, cognitive, emotional, and social.

THE BIOLOGICAL TRANSITION INTO ADOLESCENCE

puberty
the physical transformation from child to adult

Not all adolescents experience identity crises, rebel against their parents, or fall madly in love, but virtually all undergo the biological changes associated with maturation into adult reproductive capability. Collectively, these biological changes are called **puberty.** The biological transition into adolescence is the strongest sign that childhood has ended.

● **The Physical Changes of Puberty**

Technically, puberty refers to the period during which an individual becomes capable of sexual reproduction. More broadly, puberty is used as a collective term to refer to all the physical changes that occur as a girl or boy passes from childhood into adulthood.

The five major changes during puberty are (Marshall, 1978):

1. *Rapid growth and weight gain.*

2. *Further development of the gonads, or sex glands.* In males, the testes become able to release sperm; in females, ovaries begin releasing ova, or egg cells.

3. *Development of secondary sex characteristics.* These characteristics include changes in the genitals and breasts; the growth of pubic, facial, and body hair; a deepening of the voice in males; and further development of the sex organs.

4. *Changes in body composition.* Specific changes in the quantity and distribution of fat and muscle.

5. *Changes in the circulatory and respiratory systems.* Strength and stamina increase.

Not a child, not a man. Between ages 9 and 14, hormonal changes during puberty spurred several inches of growth each year, as Jason's body changed from a child's to an adolescent's.

All these physical changes are triggered by **hormones,** chemical substances in the body that act on specific organs and tissues. Most students are surprised to learn that no new hormones are produced at puberty. Instead, there is an increase in the production of certain hormones that have been present since before birth. In boys a major change is the increased production of **testosterone,** a male sex hormone, while girls experience increased production of the female hormone **estrogen.** And in both sexes, a rise in growth hormone produces the adolescent growth spurt (Brooks-Gunn & Reiter, 1990).

● *The growth spurt.* In many homes, lines on a door mark the path of a child's growth. The lines move slowly upward, 1½ to 2 inches yearly. Then, soon after the eleventh line, the spaces between the lines widen—to 3, 4, even 5 inches in a single year—signaling the **adolescent growth spurt,** the pronounced increase in height and weight that marks the first half of puberty. At the peak of the adolescent growth spurt, teenagers grow at the same rate as toddlers: for boys, a little over 4 inches per year (10.5 centimeters); for girls, about 3½ inches (9.0 centimeters) (Tanner, 1972). As Figure 14.1 shows, the spurt for girls occurs about 2 years earlier than for boys, explaining why many seventh-grade girls tower over their male classmates.

● *Becoming a sexual being.* The most dramatic physical changes of puberty involve sexuality: Internally, through the development of **primary sex characteristics,** adolescents become capable of sexual reproduction. Externally, as **secondary sex characteristics** appear, girls and boys begin to look like mature women and men. In boys, primary and secondary sex characteristics usually emerge in a predictable order, with rapid growth of the testes and scrotum, accompanied by the appearance of pubic hair, coming first. About a year later, when the growth spurt begins, the penis also grows larger,

● **hormones**
chemical substances that act on specific organs and tissues

● **testosterone**
a male sex hormone

● **estrogen**
a female sex hormone

● **adolescent growth spurt**
the pronounced increase in height and weight during the first half of puberty

● **primary sex characteristics**
developments in the structure and function of the reproductive organs and systems

● **secondary sex characteristics**
the visible characteristics of sexual maturity not directly related to reproduction

● **menarche**
the first menstrual period

FIGURE 14.1

Left: Height (in centimeters) at different ages for the average male and female youngster. Right: Gain in height per year (in centimeters) for the average male and female youngster. Note the adolescent growth spurt.
(SOURCE: Marshall, 1978.)

and pubic hair becomes coarser, thicker, and darker. Later still comes the growth of facial and body hair, and a gradual lowering of the voice. Around midadolescence internal changes begin making a boy capable of producing and ejaculating sperm. The first ejaculation of semen usually occurs about a year after the beginning of accelerated penis growth (Tanner, 1972).

In girls, sex characteristics develop in a less regular sequence. Usually, the first sign of puberty is a slight elevation of the breasts, known as the breast buds, but sometimes this is preceded by the appearance of pubic hair. Pubic hair changes as it does in males—from sparse and downy to denser and coarser. Concurrent with these changes is further breast development. After the breast bud stage, the nipple and area around it (the areola) become distinct from the breast and project beyond it.

In teenage girls, internal sexual changes include maturation of the uterus, vagina, and other parts of the reproductive system. **Menarche,** the first menstrual period, happens relatively late, not at the start of puberty as many people believe. Regular ovulation and the ability to carry a baby to full term usually follow menarche by several years (Hafetz, 1976). It is possible, however, for a girl to become pregnant at any time after her first menstruation.

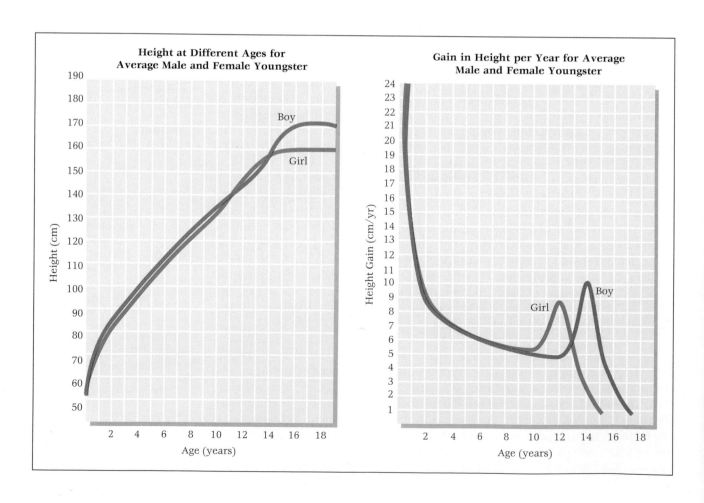

Though close in age, these teenagers are far apart in size. By the end of puberty, though, the shortest may become the tallest.

● *Variations in the timing of puberty.* The timing of physical maturation varies widely. Among the Lumi people of New Guinea, the average girl doesn't begin to menstruate until she is 18 (Eveleth & Tanner, 1976). In the United States, menarche typically occurs around age 12. And even within a single society, there are great differences. Some U.S. youngsters start puberty when they are only 8 or 9; others, when they are well into their teens. The duration of puberty also varies greatly: 1½ years to 6 years in girls and 2 years to 5 years in boys (Tanner, 1972). This means that someone who begins to mature early and does so quickly can have finished puberty by age 10 or 11—*7 years* before some other adolescents are winding up the process.

Why do some people mature early and others late? Both genetic and environmental factors play a part (Marshall, 1978). Identical twins are usually more similar in the timing and pace of puberty than other siblings, suggesting that each of us inherits a predisposition to begin the transition to adulthood at a certain age and to have that transition unfold at a certain rate. However, the extent to which this predisposition is actually realized depends on the environment, especially on nutrition and health. Puberty usually begins earlier among youngsters who have been well nourished and free of serious illness throughout life.

● Adjusting to Puberty

For many years, psychologists have studied whether puberty is stressful for young people. We now know that any difficulties associated with adjusting to puberty are minimized if adolescents know what changes to expect and have positive attitudes toward them.

Research does indicate, however, that adjusting to puberty may be difficult if the physical transformations are coupled with other major life changes.

The disagreements between teenagers and parents, generally most frequent at ages 12 and 13, may actually help adolescents to become autonomous.

For example, in one study, girls who started to menstruate, began dating, and entered junior high school all in the same year tended to suffer a decline in self-esteem not experienced by their later-maturing peers (Simmons & Blyth, 1987). Coping with all these changes at once seemed to take its toll, making these young adolescent girls less confident about themselves. Interestingly, boys in this study did not suffer a drop in self-esteem at puberty, perhaps because they physically matured *after* the transition to junior high school was over. This suggests that puberty, by itself, need not have negative effects on a youngster's self-image (Brooks-Gunn & Reiter, 1990).

Some researchers have focused on the impact of puberty on more transient emotional states, such as mood. One reason for this interest is that adolescents are thought to be moodier, on average, than adults. And, in fact, one study in which adolescents' moods were monitored repeatedly by electronic pagers showed that their moods do fluctuate during the course of the day more than the moods of adults (Csikszentmihalyi & Larson, 1984). But is adolescent moodiness directly related to the hormonal changes of puberty?

A number of studies have examined this question. One team of investigators has found that high levels of certain androgens (a category of hormones whose levels rise during puberty) may be related to sadness, aggression, and rebelliousness in adolescent boys (Susman et al., 1987), but that increases in levels of sex hormones, such as testosterone, may be related to better adjustment (Nottelmann, Susman, Inhoff-Germain, & Chrousos, 1987). Another team of scientists has found that rapid increases in estrogen may be related to depression among early adolescent girls (Brooks-Gunn & Warren, 1987). However, most researchers cautiously point out that the connection between hormones and mood is not strong and that we need to understand better how environmental and biological factors *interact* in influencing adolescents' mood and behavior. Indeed, although rapid increases in hormones early in puberty are associated with depressed mood in girls, stressful life events—such as problems in the family, in school, or with friends—play a far greater role in the development of depression than hormonal changes alone.

● Early versus Late Maturation

Although the immediate impact of puberty on the adolescent's self-image and mood may be hard to generalize about, the *timing* of physical maturation does affect social and emotional development in important ways, among both boys and girls. Early-maturing boys, for example, are more likely to experience problem behaviors, such as truancy, minor delinquency, and difficulties at school (Andersson & Magnusson, 1990; Duncan et al., 1985). For this group, physical maturity encourages them to make friends with older boys who lead them into "trouble." But early-maturing boys also tend to be more popular, to have more positive self-concept, and to be more self-assured than their later-maturing peers (Livson & Peskin, 1980).

For girls, early maturation leads to different—often opposite—experiences. This is partly because girls, on average, mature 2 years earlier than boys, so the early-maturing girl is far out of sync with her classmates, just as the late-maturing boy is. As a result, the early-maturing girl may feel awkward and self-conscious, even embarrassed about her body (Simmons & Blyth, 1987). This does not necessarily detract from her popularity, however. Frequently, she is just as popular as her later-maturing peers, sometimes even more so if the attitudes of boys are considered (Simmons, Blyth, & McKinney, 1983). But ironically, this attention from boys, particularly older ones, can cause an early-maturing girl anxiety and distress. Pressure to date or even to have sexual relations can be overwhelming when a girl is not psychologically ready. A sizable minority of early-maturing girls become drawn into deviant activities (drug use, truancy, delinquency) by older adolescents. This can have negative effects on their educational aspirations. In one study conducted in Sweden, early-maturing girls were much less likely to go beyond the compulsory level of high school than their late-maturing peers (Magnusson et al., 1986).

THE COGNITIVE TRANSITION INTO ADOLESCENCE

A second element of the transition into adolescence involves changes in the child's cognitive abilities.

● How Does Thinking Change in Early Adolescence?

Most people would agree that adolescents are "smarter" than children. Not only do teenagers know more than children but adolescents actually think in ways that are more advanced, more efficient, and generally more effective. This can be seen in five chief ways. First, adolescents become better able than children to think about what is *possible,* instead of limiting their thought to what is real. Second, they become better able to think about *abstract* things. Third, adolescents begin thinking more often about the *process of thinking* itself. Fourth, adolescents' thinking tends to become *multidimensional,* rather than limited to a single issue. Finally, adolescents are more likely than children to see things as *relative,* rather than absolute (Keating, 1990). Let's look at each of these changes.

● *Thinking about possibilities.* Children's thinking is oriented to concrete events, to things and events that they can observe directly. But adolescents are able to consider what they observe against a backdrop of what is possible. Put another way, for the child, what is possible is what is real; for the adolescent, what is real is but one subset of what is possible. Children, for example, do not wonder, the way adolescents often do, about the ways in which their personalities might change in the future or the ways in which their lives might be affected by different career choices. For the young child, you are who you are. But for the adolescent, who you are is just one possibility of who you could be.

Related to the adolescent's increased facility with thinking about possibilities is the development of **hypothetical thinking.** Hypothetical thinking is what is sometimes called "if-then" thinking. In order to think hypothetically, you need to see beyond what is directly observable and reason in terms of what might be possible. The ability to think through hypotheses is an enormously powerful tool. Being able to plan ahead, being able to see the future consequences of an action, and being able to provide alternative explanations of events are all dependent on being able to hypothesize effectively.

● *Thinking about abstract concepts.* The appearance of more systematic, abstract thinking is the second notable aspect of cognitive development during adolescence. For example, adolescents find it easier than children

● **hypothetical thinking**
what is sometimes called "if-then" thinking

What if. . . ? Adolescents think about what is and what might be. The ability to think abstractly—to imagine possibilities and to consider several sides of an issue—signals cognitive growth.

to comprehend the sorts of higher-order, abstract logic inherent in puns, proverbs, metaphors, and analogies. When presented with verbal analogies, children are more likely than adolescents to focus on concrete and familiar associations among the words than on the abstract, or conceptual, relations among them.

The adolescent's greater facility with abstract thinking also permits the application of advanced reasoning and logical processes to social and ideological matters. This is clearly seen in the adolescent's increased facility and interest in thinking about interpersonal relationships, politics, philosophy, religion, and morality—topics that involve such abstract concepts as friendship, faith, democracy, fairness, and honesty.

● *Thinking about thinking.* A third noteworthy gain in cognitive ability during adolescence involves thinking about thinking itself, or **metacognition.** Not only do adolescents "manage" their thinking more than children but they are also better able to explain to others the processes they are using.

● **metacognition**
the understanding and control of one's own thinking skills; the ability to think about thinking, including thinking about reasoning and thinking about memory

One interesting way in which thinking about thinking becomes more apparent during adolescence is in increased introspection, self-consciousness, and intellectualization. When we are introspective, after all, we are thinking about our own emotions. When we are self-conscious, we are thinking about how others think about us. And when we intellectualize, we are thinking about our own thoughts.

An interesting by-product of these metacognitive advances is the tendency for adolescents to develop a new kind of egocentrism. This is not the egocentrism of the preschooler who cannot see the perspectives of other people. Instead, it is an intense preoccupation with the self. Convinced that the self is unique, adolescents develop **personal fables**—erroneous beliefs that their thoughts, feelings, and experiences are totally different from those of other people (Elkind, 1978). A teenage boy, for example, might tell his mother that she couldn't possibly understand how he feels upon breaking up with his girlfriend, even though the mother, like most adults, has had the same experience. Many adolescents even develop the personal fable that they are so unique they are immune to ordinary dangers. Whether driving too fast or having sex without protection, "It can't happen to me" may be the thought behind these very serious risks. Although the creation of personal fables becomes more common in early adolescence, they by no means disappear in adulthood—as any cigarette smoker's behavior attests.

● **personal fables**
erroneous beliefs that one's thoughts, feelings, and experiences are unique

In the classic adolescent nightmare, everyone—on a bus, in a store, in a classroom, at a party—*everyone* stares at his ears, her tooth, his pimple. Acute adolescent egocentrism leads teenagers, even when awake, to believe that others are constantly watching and evaluating them, much as an audience glues its attention to an actor on a stage. Of course, this belief is again incorrect, which is why the effect is referred to as the **imaginary audience** (Elkind, 1978). This extreme self-consciousness declines with age, as young people come to realize that others are more concerned with their own thoughts.

● **imaginary audience**
the erroneous belief that one's appearance and behavior are the subject of public attention

● *Thinking in multiple dimensions.* A fourth way in which thinking changes during adolescence involves the ability to think about things in a multidimensional way. Whereas children tend to think about things one aspect at a time, adolescents can see things through more complicated lenses. For instance, when a certain hitter comes up to the plate in a baseball game, a preadolescent who knows that the hitter has a good home-run record might exclaim that the batter will hit the ball out of the park. An adolescent, however, would consider the hitter's record in relation to the specific pitcher on the mound and weigh both factors, or dimensions, before making a prediction (perhaps this player hits homers against left-handed pitchers but strikes out against righties).

But as is the case with other gains in cognitive ability, the increasing capability of individuals to think in multiple dimensions has consequences for their behavior and thinking outside of academic settings, too. Adolescents describe themselves and others in more differentiated and complicated terms ("I'm both shy and extroverted") and find it easier to look at problems from multiple perspectives ("I know that's the way you see it, but try to look at it from his point of view"). Being able to understand that people's personalities are not one-sided, or that social situations can have different interpretations depending on one's point of view, permits the adolescent to have far more sophisticated—and complicated—relationships with other people.

- *Adolescent relativism.* A final aspect of thinking during adolescence concerns the way in which adolescents look at things. Children tend to see things in absolute terms—things are right or wrong, good or bad. Adolescents see things as relative. They are more likely to questions others' assertions and less likely to accept "facts" as absolute truths.

This increase in relativism can be particularly exasperating to parents, who may feel as if their adolescent children question everything just for the sake of argument. Difficulties often arise, for example, when adolescents begin seeing their parents' values that they had previously considered absolutely correct ("A woman can't have a career and be a good mother") as completely relative ("Of course she can, Dad").

Adolescents' belief that everything is relative can become so overwhelming that they may begin to become extremely skeptical about many things (Chandler, 1987). In fact, once adolescents begin doubting the certainty of things that they had previously believed, they may come to feel as if everything is uncertain or that no knowledge is completely reliable. Some theorists have suggested that adolescents pass through such a period of extreme skepticism on the way toward reaching a more sophisticated understanding of the complexity of knowledge.

● Why Does Thinking Advance in Adolescence?

As in the study of cognitive development during childhood, theorists have suggested different explanations for the advances in thinking seen during adolescence. The two most important views are the Piagetian perspective and the information-processing perspective.

- *The Piagetian view of adolescent thinking.* In Piaget's cognitive scheme, from ages 6 to 12, children's thinking is at the concrete operational level (Chapter 11), the stage when the cognitive tools develop for handling most ordinary problems. Elementary school children can judge whether statements are true or false, solve many types of logical problems, and use evidence

Advanced work in science and math becomes possible as adolescents' cognitive abilities grow from concrete to the more abstract. Now, during the formal operational stage, thinking is based on theoretical, abstract principles of logic.

to make decisions. Even in adulthood most everyday problems can be answered quite adequately using concrete operational reasoning, but it has its limits.

As the term suggests, concrete operational thinking is tied to observable things; it is inadequate for possibilities and hypotheticals, for abstractions and alternatives. Concrete thinking can help you calculate the flying time to Chicago or Chattanooga, but it alone could never have gotten the Wright brothers off the ground.

Piaget believed that transitions to higher stages of reasoning are more likely to occur at times when biological readiness interacts with environmental demands, creating cognitive disequilibrium. Adolescence is one such time of life. At puberty, dramatic biological changes occur simultaneously with a new, much more demanding curriculum in the classroom. Old cognitive skills are often no longer enough, so youngsters are gradually stimulated to develop a higher level of reasoning, characteristic of the **formal operational stage.** In contrast with concrete thinking, formal thinking is based on abstract principles of logic.

The Piagetian perspective on cognitive development during adolescence has stimulated a great deal of research on how young people think. Generally, the concept of formal operations as defined by Piaget and his followers appears to account for many of the changes in thinking observed during the adolescent years. Specifically, the theory of formal operations helps to explain why adolescents are better able than children to think about possibilities, to think multidimensionally, and to think about thoughts. Where the Piagetian perspective on adolescent cognitive development appears to fall short is in its claim that cognitive development proceeds in a stagelike fashion and that the "stage" of formal operations is the stage of cognitive development characteristic of adolescence. Rather, research suggests that advanced reasoning capabilities

● **formal operational stage** according to Piaget, the stage at which one's thinking is based on theoretical, abstract principles of logic

CONTROVERSY

DO ADOLESCENTS MAKE "BAD" DECISIONS?

One new and fascinating practical application of research on adolescent thinking involves the study of adolescent decision making, and risky decision making in particular. The most common health problems of adolescents—injuries, sexually transmitted diseases, and drug addiction—result from behaviors that can be prevented. Some psychologists have suggested that we think of behaviors—including driving recklessly, drinking alcohol, and having intercourse without using contraception—as resulting from decisions that adolescents make. They argue that we need to better understand the cognitive processes behind such decision making. One line of research has attempted to examine whether adolescents make risky decisions because of deficiencies in their developing cognitive abilities (Furbey & Beyth-Marom, 1990).

A number of psychologists have studied adolescent risk taking from a perspective called *behavioral decision theory* (Fischoff, 1988; Kahneman, Slovic, & Tversky, 1982). According to this theory, all behaviors can be analyzed as the outcome of a process that involves (1) identifying alternative choices, (2) identifying the consequences that follow each choice, (3) evaluating the desir-

ability of each possible consequence, (4) assessing the likelihood of each possible consequence, and (5) combining all of this information according to some decision rule.

So, for example, a 16-year-old girl who is trying to decide whether to sleep with her boyfriend for the first time would (1) identify the choices (sleep with him or not sleep with him); (2) identify the consequences (sleeping with him may solidify our relationship but it exposes me to the possibility of getting pregnant or contracting AIDS, whereas not sleeping with him may risk the relationship but I won't feel guilty for doing something I don't really want to do); (3) evaluate the desirability of each consequence (getting pregnant would be a terrible thing, not respecting myself would be a terrible thing, losing my boyfriend would be a bad thing, but not a terrible one); (4) assess the likelihood of each consequence (I probably won't get pregnant because we'll be careful, I probably will feel guilty, he probably won't break up with me anyway); and (5) combine all the information according to some decision rule (all things considered, I think I'll wait).

According to most studies, adolescents make decisions using the same basic cognitive processes as adults (Furbey & Beyth-Marom, 1990). Indeed, the major gains in

decision-making abilities occur between childhood and adolescence, rather than between adolescence and adulthood (Keating, 1990). If this is the case, then, why do adolescents behave in ways that to adults appear excessively risky?

The answer may involve the different ways in which adolescents and adults evaluate the desirability of different consequences. For example, an individual's decision to try cocaine at a party may involve evaluating a number of different consequences, including the legal and health risks, the pleasure the drug will induce, and the way in which one will be judged by the other people present (positively and negatively). Whereas an adult and an adolescent may both consider all of these consequences, the adult may place relatively more weight on the health risks of trying the drug, while the adolescent may place relatively more weight on the social consequences of not trying. Although an adult may see an adolescent's decision to value peer acceptance more than health as "irrational," an adolescent may see the adult's decision as equally incomprehensible. Behavioral decision theory reminds us that all decisions—even risky ones—can be seen as "rational," once we understand the ways in which individuals estimate and evaluate the consequences of various courses of action.

(which may or may not be synonymous with what Piaget termed *formal operations*) develop gradually and continuously from childhood through adolescence and beyond, probably in more of a quantitative fashion than was proposed by Piaget (Keating, 1990).

● ***The information-processing view of adolescent thinking.*** Information-processing theorists take a different view of cognitive development. They believe that as children grow older, they acquire new capacities for inputting information, mentally storing and manipulating it, and arriving at answers and solutions. Information-processing researchers, as we've said in earlier chapters, study how these cognitive capacities change with age.

Studies of changes in specific components of information processing have focused on four sets of gains that appear to occur during adolescence. Taken together, these gains help to explain why adolescents are better than children at abstract, multidimensional, and hypothetical thinking. First, there are advances in individuals' ability to pay attention (Higgins & Turnure, 1984; Schiff & Knopf, 1985). Improvements in attention mean that adolescents are better able than children to concentrate and stay focused on complicated tasks.

Second, during adolescence our memory abilities improve. This is reflected in both short-term memory (being able to remember something for a brief period of time, such as 30 seconds) and long-term memory (being able to recall something from a long time ago) (Keating, 1990).

A third component of information processing that improves during adolescence involves improvements in individuals' organizational strategies (Siegler, 1988). Adolescents are more planful than children: They are more likely to approach a problem with an appropriate information-processing strategy in mind. For instance, think for a moment about how you approach learning the information in a new textbook chapter. After years of school, you are probably well aware of particular strategies that work well for you (underlining, highlighting, taking notes, writing in the margin of the textbook), and you automatically use these strategies. Because children are not as "planful" as adolescents, their learning is not as efficient.

Finally, individuals' knowledge about their own thinking processes improves during adolescence. We noted earlier that one of the most important gains to occur in adolescence is in the realm of thinking about thinking. Adolescents are more likely than children to think about their own thoughts—a tendency, as we saw, that helps to explain their greater self-consciousness. But from an information-processing perspective, adolescents' heightened self-consciousness results from advances in basic metacognitive abilities. Self-consciousness may be more a cognitive than emotional phenomenon: For the first time, the adolescent is capable of "thinking about thinking about thinking." (See the accompanying Controversy discussion about adolescent decision making and **behavioral decision theory**.)

● **behavioral decision theory**
a theory that all behaviors can be analyzed as the outcome of a process that involves identifying alternative choices and evaluating their consequences, their desirability, and their likelihood

THE EMOTIONAL TRANSITION INTO ADOLESCENCE

In addition to being a time of biological and cognitive change, early adolescence is also a time of emotional change and, in particular, changes in the way individuals view themselves and in their capacity to function independently.

● Changes in Self-Conceptions

During adolescence, important shifts occur in the way individuals think about and characterize themselves, that is, in their self-conceptions. As individuals mature intellectually and undergo the sorts of cognitive changes described earlier, they come to conceive of themselves in more sophisticated and differentiated ways. As you read earlier in this chapter, adolescents are much more capable than children of thinking about abstract concepts. This intellectual advantage affects the way in which individuals characterize themselves. Compared with children—who tend to describe themselves in relatively simple, concrete terms—adolescents are more likely to employ complex, abstract, and psychological self-characterizations (Harter, 1990).

As individuals' self-conceptions become more abstract and as they become more able to see themselves in psychological terms, they become more interested in understanding their own personalities and why they behave the way they do. You may recall having wondered as a teenager about your personality development, about the influences that shaped your character, about how your personality had changed over time. ("Am I more like my father or like my mother? Why do my sister and I seem so different? Will I always be so shy?") Although these sorts of questions may seem commonplace to you now, in all likelihood, you did not think about these things until adolescence, when your own self-conceptions become more abstract and sophisticated.

● Changes in Self-Esteem

Peering into the self, teenagers ask not only *what* they see but also how well they like it. Conventional wisdom holds that adolescents have low self-esteem—that they are more insecure and self-critical than children or adults. After all, the argument goes, the physical developments of adolescence are sometimes awkward and ungainly, while new cognitive abilities make teenagers more self-conscious and more worried about what others think of them.

But most research says otherwise. Although teenagers' feelings about themselves may fluctuate, especially during early adolescence, their self-esteem remains fairly stable from about age 13 on. If anything, self-esteem increases over the course of middle and late adolescence (McCarthy & Hoge, 1982).

These findings are generalizations, of course. Some adolescents do evaluate themselves more negatively than others. For instance, young adolescents (ages 12 to 14) tend to have lower self-esteem than either preadolescents (ages 8 to 11) or teenagers age 15 and older (Simmons, Rosenberg, & Rosenberg, 1973). Perhaps the dramatic physical changes of early adolescence—arriving too early or too late, growing too big or too small—are responsible. Interestingly, the young adolescents who feel *least* positive about themselves tend to be white females. Compared with young adolescent black girls and boys this age of either race, white girls ages 12 to 14 tend to say more negative things about themselves, feel insecure about their abilities, and worry about whether others like them. We don't know why so many adolescent white girls feel negatively about themselves; one suspicion is that, more than any other group, they feel a conflict between doing well in school and trying to be popular.

It is also not clear if a young adolescent's negative self-statements reflect temporary feelings about the self or more permanent ones. Some researchers think that self-esteem really has two aspects. One consists of moment-to-

Acutely self-conscious, adolescents can magnify even the smallest blemish to golf ball proportions.

moment shifts in self-assessment, as when a student who is normally self-confident becomes embarrassed because of a teacher's criticisms. This is called **barometric self-esteem** because, like a barometer, it fluctuates with changes in a person's situation or personal climate. In contrast, **baseline self-esteem** is a more stable, *general* feeling about oneself that endures despite temporary ups and downs. Apparently, the negative self-assessment sometimes seen in young adolescents is due to greater volatility in their barometric self-esteem, not to a more permanent drop in their baseline self-evaluation (Rosenberg, 1986). Because young adolescents are so conscious of others' reactions to them (recall our earlier discussion of the "imaginary audience"), they tend to be bothered more by the occasional blows to the ego that all of us experience. Young adolescents are also just beginning to realize that what people feel may be very different from what they do. If the boy who smiled at you on Monday ignores you on Tuesday, is it because he no longer likes you, or because he *does*? Adolescents worry about how others *really* see them, uncertainty that places their self-image on shaky ground.

Some researchers have argued that the question of whether self-esteem is stable during adolescence is a poor one. According to one recent study (Hirsch & DuBois, 1991), some adolescents show very high stability in self-esteem over time while others do not. These researchers identified four dramatically

● **barometric self-esteem**
moment-to-moment shifts in self-assessment

● **baseline self-esteem**
stable, general feelings about the self

different self-esteem trajectories followed by youngsters during the transition into junior high school. Approximately one-third of the adolescents were classified as consistently high in self-esteem, and approximately one-sixth were classified as chronically low. Half the sample showed impressive patterns of change over just a 2-year period; however, about one-fifth were categorized as steeply declining, and nearly one-third showed a small but significant increase in self-esteem.

Although most studies of adolescent self-esteem have focused on teenagers' overall feelings about themselves, most researchers today believe that self-esteem is multidimensional and that young people evaluate themselves along several different dimensions (Harter, 1990; Lau, 1990). As a consequence, it is possible for an adolescent to have high self-esteem when it comes to academic abilities, low self-esteem when it comes to athletics, and moderate self-esteem when it comes to physical appearance.

 ● *Self-esteem and social context.* The context in which adolescents develop has a substantial impact on the self-image. Some research indicates, for example, that high school aged youngsters who live in a social environment or go to a school in which their ethnic or socioeconomic group is in the minority are more likely to have self-image problems than those who are in the majority (Rosenberg, 1975). This seems to be true with regard to religion, socioeconomic status, race, and family structure (single-parent or two-parent home). African-American teenagers, for example, have a higher opinion of themselves when they go to schools in which African-American students are a majority than when they attend predominantly white schools, where they may feel out of place and pressured to play down their cultural heritage. Similarly, Jewish adolescents have higher self-esteem in schools in which there are many other Jewish students than in schools in which Jews constitute a small minority of the student body.

● The Adolescent Identity Crisis

If you were asked to talk about your own identity development, what sorts of things would you mention? Perhaps you would talk about a growing sense of purpose, or the clarification of your long-term plans and values, or the emerging feeling of knowing who you really are and where you are headed. If these are the sorts of things that come to mind when you think about identity development, you are thinking about an aspect of development that psychologists refer to as the sense of identity. The dominant view in the study of adolescent identity development emphasizes precisely these aspects of psychosocial development, and the theorist whose work has been the most influential in this area is Erik Erikson, whose theory of "psychosocial crises" we have discussed several times in previous chapters. Erikson theorized that the establishment of a coherent sense of identity is the chief psychosocial crisis of adolescence.

Before adolescence, the child's identity is like patches of fabric that have not yet been sewn together. But by the end of adolescence, these patches will be woven into a patchwork quilt that is unique to the individual. This process of

As their identities take shape, adolescents begin to concentrate on the interests, abilities, skills, and ideals that will shape their adult lives. At 13, Kenny turned a child's interest in taking pictures into a sophisticated interest in photography.

integration is at the center of the crisis of **identity versus identity diffusion.** The key to resolving the crisis of identity versus identity diffusion, argues Erikson, lies in the adolescent's interactions with others. Through responding to the reactions of people who matter, the adolescent selects and chooses from among the many elements that could conceivably become a part of his or her central identity. The other people with whom the young person interacts serve as a mirror that reflects back to the adolescent information about who he or she is and who he or she ought to be. As such, the responses of these important others shape and influence the adolescent's developing sense of identity. Through others' reactions, we learn where we are strong and weak, whether others find us attractive or plain, socially adept or clumsy. Perhaps more important, especially during periods when our sense of identity is still forming, we learn from others what it is we do that we ought to keep doing, and what it is we do that we ought not to do.

The social context in which the adolescent attempts to establish a sense of identity exerts a tremendous impact on the nature and outcome of the process. As a consequence, the course of identity development will vary in different cultures, among different subcultures within the same society, and over different historical eras. For example, the career options open to women in contemporary society have changed dramatically in the past 25 years and, consequently, so has the nature of adolescent girls' identity development. In the past, most young women assumed that their adult identity would be exclusively tied to marriage and family life. But today, far more alternative identities are open to women. As a result, the process of choosing among different alternatives has become more complicated than it once was.

● **identity versus identity diffusion**
according to Erikson, the psychosocial crisis of establishing one's identity, characteristic of adolescence

HIGHLIGHT ON DIVERSITY

THE DEVELOPMENT OF ETHNIC IDENTITY

For all individuals, but especially for those who are not part of the white majority, integrating a sense of ethnic identity into their overall sense of personal identity is likely to be an important task of adolescence, perhaps as important as establishing a coherent occupational, ideological, or interpersonal identity (Phinney & Alipuria, 1987). According to several writers (Cross, 1978; Kim, 1981, cited in Phinney & Alipuria, 1987), the process of ethnic-identity development follows in some respects the process of identity development in general, with an unquestioning view of oneself being displaced or upset by an identity crisis. Following the crisis, the individual may become immersed in his or her own ethnic group and turn against the white majority culture. Eventually, as the value and importance of having a strong ethnic identity become clear, the individual establishes a more coherent sense of personal identity

My people, myself. A strong sense of ethnic identity can enhance adolescents' feelings of self-esteem.

that includes this ethnic identity and, with growing confidence, attempts to help others deal with their own struggles with ethnic identity.

Do members of ethnic minorities have more difficulty than white adolescents in resolving the identity crisis, however? Researchers are just now beginning to examine this question, and the answer is still not known. The little research that has been done suggests more similarities than

---

● psychosocial moratorium
according to Erikson, a necessary "time out" from excessive obligations for adolescents

The complications inherent in identity development in modern society have created the need, Erikson argues, for a **psychosocial moratorium**—a time-out during adolescence from the sorts of excessive responsibilities and obligations that might restrict the young person's pursuit of self-discovery. Adolescents in contemporary America are given a moratorium of sorts by being encouraged to remain in school for a long time, where they can think seriously about their plans for the future without making irrevocable decisions.

During the psychosocial moratorium, the adolescent can experiment with different roles and identities, in a context that permits and encourages this sort of exploration. The experimentation involves trying on different postures, personalities, and ways of behaving. Sometimes, parents describe their teenage children as going through "phases." Much of this behavior is actually experimentation with roles and personalities.

differences in the process through which identity development occurs. One difference, though, appears to be quite important, if perhaps not very surprising: Having a strong ethnic identity is associated with higher self-esteem among minority youngsters, especially among African-American and Hispanic-American youth, but this is not the case among white youth (Phinney & Alipuria, 1987). It would seem, therefore, that establishing a sense of ethnic identity is more important to individuals who are part of an ethnic minority than for those who are part of a majority.

According to Phinney and her colleagues (Phinney et al., 1990), minority youth have four possibilities open to them for dealing with their ethnicity: assimilation (that is, trying to adopt the majority culture's norms and standards while rejecting those of one's own group), alienation (living within the majority culture but feeling estranged and outcast), separation (associating only with members of one's own culture and rejecting

majority culture), and biculturalism (maintaining ties to both the majority and the minority cultures). In the past, minority youth were encouraged by majority society to assimilate as much as possible. Assimilation, however, has not proved to be as simple as many nonminority individuals imagine. First, although minority youth are told to assimilate, they may be tacitly excluded from majority society on the basis of their physical appearance or language. This leads to a situation of marginality, in which the minority youth is on the edge of majority society but never really accepted as a full status member.

Second, minority youth who do attempt to assimilate are often scorned by their own communities for trying to "act white"—as captured in the array of pejorative terms minority youth have for their friends who have tried too hard to assimilate: Asian-Americans who act white are "bananas"; Hispanic-Americans are "coconuts"; African-Americans are "Oreos" (Spencer & Dornbusch,

1990, p. 132). Partly in reaction to this, many minority youth adopt a strategy of separation.

Some writers argue that a more viable alternative to assimilation or separation is biculturalism. Bicultural adolescents "shuttle successfully between their primary or familial culture and the dominant culture" (Spencer & Dornbusch, 1990, p. 133). One writer has proposed a flexibility model, in which minority youth have open to them the norms of both cultures and select between them depending on the situation. At a majority-controlled school, for example, it may be more adaptive to "act white" when being evaluated by white teachers, but more adaptive to conform with the minority group's own norms and standards when in one's neighborhood. Research that compares biculturalism with other strategies, such as assimilation or separation, is sorely needed.

Establishing a coherent sense of identity is a lengthy process. Most writers on adolescence and youth believe that identity exploration continues well into young adulthood. But rather than thinking of the adolescent as going through *an* identity crisis, it probably makes more sense to view the phenomenon as a series of crises that may concern different aspects of the young person's identity and that may surface—and resurface—at different points in time throughout the adolescent and young adult years. During adolescence, the feeling of well-being associated with establishing a sense of identity is somewhat fleeting. Ultimately, however, the identity crisis of adolescence, when successfully resolved, culminates in a series of basic life commitments: occupational, ideological, social, religious, ethical, and sexual. See the accompanying Highlight on Diversity box for a closer look at how adolescents cope with their growing sense of ethnic identity.

emotional autonomy
that aspect of independence related to changes in the individual's close relationships, especially with parents

behavioral autonomy
the capacity to make independent decisions and follow through with them

Psychologists have studied two different aspects of the development of autonomy in early adolescence. The first involves **emotional autonomy**—that aspect of independence related to changes in the individual's close relationships, especially with parents. The second corresponds to what is sometimes called **behavioral autonomy**—the capacity to make independent decisions and follow through with them.

● Feeling Independent

For most adolescents, establishing a sense of autonomy is as important a part of the emotional transition out of childhood as establishing a sense of identity. Becoming an autonomous person—a self-governing person—is one of the fundamental developmental tasks of the adolescent years. During adolescence, there is a movement away from the dependency typical of childhood toward the autonomy typical of adulthood.

One can see this in several ways. First, older adolescents do not generally rush to their parents whenever they are upset, worried, or in need of assistance. Second, they do not see their parents as all-knowing or all-powerful. Third, adolescents often have a great deal of emotional energy wrapped up in relationships outside the family; in fact, they may feel more attached to a boyfriend or a girlfriend than to their parents. And finally, older adolescents are able to see and interact with their parents as people—not just as their parents. Many parents find, for example, that they can confide in their adolescent children, something that was not possible when their children were younger, or that their adolescent children can easily sympathize with them when they have had a hard day at work. These sorts of changes in the adolescent-parent relationship all reflect the development of emotional autonomy (Steinberg, 1990).

Some theorists have suggested that the development of independence be looked at in terms of the adolescent's developing sense of "emotional autonomy,"

The cognitive and emotional advances of adolescence helped Jamel Oeser-Sweat (left) to make a series of decisions that will shape his adult identity. With the help of several adults, Jamel avoided the drugs and violence that plagued his neighborhood and focused on becoming a serious student. A finalist in the Westinghouse Science Talent Search, he spends time each week tutoring children in a local elementary school in New York City.

or **individuation.** One such theorist is the noted psychoanalyst Peter Blos. According to him, "individuation implies that the growing person takes increasing responsibility for what he does and what he is, rather than depositing this responsibility on the shoulders of those under whose influence and tutelage he has grown up" (1967, p. 168). The process of individuation, which begins during infancy and continues well into late adolescence, involves a gradual, progressive sharpening of one's sense of self as autonomous, as competent, and as separate from one's parents. Individuation, therefore, has a great deal to do with the development of a sense of identity, in that it involves changes in how we come to see and feel about ourselves.

The process of individuation does not necessarily involve stress and turmoil. Rather, individuation entails relinquishing childish dependencies on parents in favor of more mature, more responsible, and less dependent relationships. Adolescents who have been successful in establishing a sense of individuation can accept responsibility for their choices and actions instead of looking to their parents to do it for them (Josselson, 1980). For example, rather than rebelling against her parents' midnight curfew by deliberately staying out later, a 16-year-old girl who has a healthy sense of individuation might say to her parents before going out, "This party tonight may last longer than midnight. If it does, I'd like to stay a bit longer. Suppose I call you at eleven o'clock and let you know when I'll be home."

Research indicates that the development of emotional autonomy is a long process, beginning early in adolescence and continuing well into young adulthood. In one study (Steinberg & Silverberg, 1986), a questionnaire measuring several aspects of emotional autonomy was administered to a sample of 10- to 15-year-olds. Three of the components studied were (1) the extent to which adolescents de-idealized their parents ("My parents sometimes make mistakes"); (2) the extent to which adolescents were able to see their parents as people ("My parents act differently with their own friends than they do with me"); and (3) the degree to which adolescents depended on themselves, rather than their parents, for assistance. Scores on all three of the scales increased over the age period studied.

● **Acting Independently**

Being independent means more than merely *feeling* independent, of course. It also means being able to make your own decisions and to select a sensible course of action by yourself. This is an especially important capability in contemporary society, where many adolescents are forced to become independent decision makers at an early age (Elkind, 1981). For instance, young teenagers must often make choices about drinking, drug use, and sex, choices that many are very reluctant to discuss with their parents. Many adolescents are also expected to function without adult supervision each day until their parents get home from work. This independence requires better decision-making skills, including what to do in an emergency, whether to allow some friends to come over, how to make dinner.

Adolescents' more sophisticated reasoning processes enable them to consider several viewpoints simultaneously, an ability that is crucial for weighing the opinions and advice of others. In addition, because adolescents are better able to think in hypothetical terms, they are more likely to consider

● **individuation**
the process of becoming a separate person who can both act independently and accept responsibility for choices

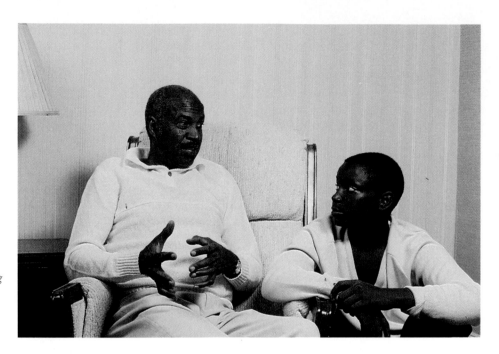

While adolescents are becoming more intimate with their own friends, they may be surprised to find their parents beginning to confide in them.

the possible long-term consequences of choosing one course of action over another. And the enhanced role-taking capabilities of adolescence permit the teenager to consider another person's opinion while taking into account that persons' perspective. This is important in determining whether someone who gives advice has special areas of expertise, particular biases, or vested interests that one should keep in mind. Taken together, these cognitive changes result in improved decision-making skills and, consequently, in the individual's greater ability to behave independently.

Decision-making abilities improve over the course of the adolescent years, with gains continuing well into the later years of high school. These developments provide the cognitive tools for behavioral autonomy: being able to look ahead and assess risks and likely outcomes of alternative choices, being able to recognize the value of turning to an independent "expert," and being able to see that someone's advice may be tainted by his or her own interests. Whether these changes in decision-making abilities translate into changes in actual behavior, however, is a different matter. Older adolescents may be more intellectually skilled when it comes to decision making, but are they actually more able to resist pressures to conform? This is the question asked by researchers who study adolescent conformity and susceptibility to peer pressure.

Researchers have studied conformity and peer pressure during adolescence by putting adolescents in situations in which they must choose between the pressures of their parents and the pressures of their peers, or between their own wishes and those of others—typically, parents or friends. For example, an adolescent might be told to imagine that he and his friends discover something on the way home from school that looks suspicious. His friends tell him that they should keep it a secret. But the adolescent tells his mother about it, and she advises him to report it to the police. He then would be asked by the researchers to say what he would do.

In general, studies that contrast parents' and peers' influences indicate that in some situations, peers' opinions are more influential, while in others, parents' are more influential. Specifically, adolescents are more likely to conform to their peers' opinions when it comes to short-term, day-to-day, and social matters—styles of dress, tastes in music, choices among leisure activities, and so on. This is particularly true during junior high school and the early years of senior high. When it comes to long-term questions concerning educational or occupational plans, however—or questions of values, religious beliefs, or ethics—teenagers are primarily influenced by their parents (Young & Ferguson, 1979).

Studies that contrast the influence of peers and adults do not really get to the heart of peer pressure, however, because most peer pressure operates when adults are absent from the scene—at a party, on the way home from school, on a date. In order to get closer to this issue, researchers have studied how adolescents respond when placed between the pressure of their friends and their own opinions of what to do. For example, an adolescent might be asked whether he would go along with his friends' pressure to vandalize some property even though he did not want to do so (Berndt, 1979).

In general, most studies using this approach show that during childhood, boys and girls are highly oriented toward their parents and far less so toward their peers; peer pressure during the early elementary school years is not especially strong. As they approach adolescence, however, children become somewhat less oriented toward their parents and more oriented toward their peers; peer pressure begins to escalate. During early adolescence, conformity to parents continues to decline and both conformity to peers and peer pressure continue to rise. It is not until middle adolescence, then, that genuine behavioral independence emerges, when conformity to parents as well as peers declines.

THE SOCIAL TRANSITION INTO ADOLESCENCE

Accompanying the biological, cognitive, and emotional transitions from childhood into adolescence are important changes in the adolescent's social relationships. Developmentalists have spent considerable energy charting the changes that occur in the family and in the peer group as the individual enters the adolescent years. During early adolescence, important transformations take place in each of these contexts.

● The Generation Gap: Fact or Fiction?

Whenever the topic of family relations in adolescence is raised, people invariably think of parent-adolescent conflict. Indeed, one of the most long-standing stereotypes of adolescence is that it is a period of family "storm and stress."

Is there a gap between adolescents and their parents, and if so, how wide is it? In order to answer these questions, researchers have found it necessary to distinguish among family relationships, values and attitudes, and personal tastes. In some of these respects, there is indeed a schism between the generations. But in others, there is not.

If we consider the quality of adolescents' relationships with their parents, we find that there is very little gap between young people and their elders. Study after study on this issue has shown that although some adolescents and their parents have serious interpersonal problems, the overwhelming majority of adolescents feel close to their parents, respect their parents' judgment, feel that their parents love and care about them, and have a lot of respect for their parents as individuals (Steinberg, 1990). If intergenerational conflict exists, it is not of the sort that seriously affects the quality or closeness of most adolescents' family relationships. Most systematic studies indicate that among the 25 percent of teenagers and parents who report having problems, about 80 percent had problematic relations during childhood (Rutter et al., 1976). Thus, only about 5 percent of families who enjoy positive relations during childhood can expect to develop serious problems during adolescence.

When we look at intergenerational differences in values and attitudes, we also find little evidence in support of a generation gap—or, at least, of a schism as large as many people have been led to believe exists. Adolescents and their parents have similar beliefs about the importance of hard work, about educational and occupational ambitions, and about the personal characteristics and attributes they feel are important and desirable (Conger, 1977). Indeed, when it comes to more basic values—concerning religion, work, education, and

Dressing like their friends helps adolescents feel that they belong to a group that is different from their parents' generation.

the like—diversity within the adolescent population is much more striking than differences between the generations.

In matters of personal taste there *is* often a gap between the generations, however. It is most clearly seen in styles of dress, preferences in music, and patterns of leisure activity. Adolescents are more likely to be influenced by their friends than by their parents in these matters, and as a consequence, disagreements and differences in opinion between old and young often result. And it is over these matters that much of the bickering that occurs in families takes place (Montmayor, 1983). A mother and her daughter may argue about such things as the daughter's curfew, how the daughter spends her spare time, whether the daughter keeps her room clean enough, or what sorts of clothes the daughter wears. Unlike values, which develop gradually over time and are shaped from an early age, preferences and tastes are far more transitory and subject to the immediate influences of the social environment. Because adolescents spend a great deal of time with their friends (and because a good deal of that time is spent in social activities in which taste in clothes, music, and the like, is especially important), teenagers' tastes are likely to be shaped to a large measure by forces outside the family.

● Changes in Family Relationships

Although adolescence does not lead to intense conflict in most families, early adolescence does bring significant change and reorganization in family relationships.

Think for a moment about the relationship between parents and a 12-year-old and that between parents and an 18-year-old. In most families, there is a movement during adolescence from patterns of influence and interaction that are asymmetrical and unequal to ones in which parents and their adolescent children are on a more equal footing. And there is some evidence that early adolescence—when this shift toward more egalitarian relationships first begins—may be a time of temporary disruption in the family system.

Studies of family interaction suggest that early adolescence may be a time during which young people begin to try to play a more forceful role in the family, but when parents may not yet acknowledge the adolescents' input. As a result, young adolescents may interrupt their parents more often but have little impact. By middle adolescence, however, teenagers act and are treated much more like adults. They have more influence over family decisions, but they do not need to assert their opinions through interruptions and similarly immature behavior (Steinberg, 1990).

The adolescent's biological and cognitive maturation may play a role in unbalancing the family system during early adolescence. Several researchers have demonstrated that family relationships change during puberty, with conflict between adolescents and their parents increasing—especially between adolescents and their mothers—and closeness between adolescents and their parents diminishing somewhat (Paikoff, Brooks-Gunn, & Warren, 1991, Steinberg, 1988; Susman et al., 1987). Although puberty seems to distance adolescents from their parents, it is not associated with familial "storm and stress," however. The conflict is more likely to take the form of bickering over day-to-day issues such as household chores rather than outright fighting. Similarly, the diminished closeness is more likely to be manifested in increased privacy on the part of the adolescent and diminished physical affection between teenagers and parents, rather than any serious loss of love or respect between parents and children (Montmayor, 1983). Research suggests that the distancing effect of puberty is temporary, though, and that relationships may become less conflicted and more intimate during late adolescence. In any event, it does appear that early adolescence may be a somewhat more strained time for the family than childhood or later in adolescence.

Several researchers also have emphasized changes in the adolescent's cognitive abilities and how these changes may reverberate throughout the family. Changes in the ways adolescents view family rules and regulations may contribute to increased conflict between them and their parents (Smetana, 1989). Research also indicates that early adolescence is a time of changes in youngsters' views of family relationships and in family members' expectations of each other. For example, one study asked adolescents of different ages to characterize their actual and "ideal" families in terms of how close and dominant different family members were (Feldman & Gehring, 1988). With age, the gap between adolescents' actual and "ideal" portraits widened, indicating that as they become older, adolescents became more aware of their families' shortcomings—at least in comparison to what they believed a perfect family was like.

● Changes in the Peer Group

One of the most noteworthy aspects of the social transition into adolescence is the increase in the amount of time individuals spend with their peers. In fact, American teenagers spend more time talking to their friends each day than in any other activity (Csikszentmihalyi & Larson, 1984). High school students spend twice as much of their time each week with peers than with parents or other adults—even discounting time in class (B. Brown, 1990). Virtually all adolescents spend most of each weekday with their peers while at school, and the vast majority also see or talk to their friends in the afternoon, in the evening, and over the weekend (Medrich et al., 1982).

Visit any elementary school playground and you will readily see that peer groups are an important feature of the social world of childhood, as you read in Chapter 13. But even though peer groups exist well before adolescence, during the teenage years they change in significance and structure. Four specific developments stand out (B. Brown, 1990).

First, as we noted earlier, there is a sharp increase during adolescence in the sheer amount of time individuals spend with their peers and in the relative time they spend in the company of peers versus adults. If we count school as being a setting in which adolescents are mainly with age-mates, well over half of the typical adolescent's waking hours are spent with peers, as opposed to only 15 percent with adults—including parents (a good deal of the remaining time is spent alone or with a combination of adults and age-mates). When asked to list the people in their life who are most important to them—what psychologists call their *significant others*—nearly half of the people adolescents mention are their peers. By sixth grade, adults other than parents account for less than 25 percent of the typical adolescent's social network—the people he or she interacts with most regularly. And among early-maturing teenagers, this figure is only about 10 percent (B. Brown, 1990).

Second, during adolescence, peer groups function much more often without adult supervision than they do during childhood (B. Brown, 1990). Groups of children typically play where adults are present, or in activities that are organized or supervised by adults (for example, Little League, Brownies), whereas adolescents are granted far more independence. A group of teenagers may go off to the mall on their own or to the movies, or they will deliberately congregate at the home of someone whose parents are out.

Third, during adolescence increasingly more contact with peers is with opposite-sex friends. During childhood, peer groups are highly sex-segregated, a phenomenon known as *sex cleavage*. This is especially true of children's peer activities in school and other settings organized by adults, although somewhat less so of their more informal activities, such as neighborhood play (Maccoby, 1988). During adolescence, however, an increasingly larger proportion of an individual's "significant others" are opposite-sex peers, even in public settings (B. Brown, 1990).

Finally, whereas children's peer relationships are limited mainly to pairs of friends and relatively small groups—three or four children at a time, for example—adolescence marks the emergence of larger collectives of peers, or "crowds." In junior high school cafeterias, for example, the "popular" crowd sits in one section of the room, the "brains" in another, and the "druggies" in yet a third (see Eder, 1985). These crowds typically develop their own minicultures, which include particular styles of dressing, talking, and behaving. Studies show that it is not until early adolescence that individuals can confidently list the different crowds that characterize their schools and reliably describe the stereotypes that distinguish one group from another (B. Brown, 1990).

● *Cliques and crowds.* It is helpful to think of adolescents' peer groups as organized around two related, but different, structures (B. Brown, 1990). **Cliques** are small groups of between two and twelve individuals generally of the same sex and age. Cliques can be defined by common activities (the "drama" group, or a group of students who study together regularly, for example) or simply by friendship (a group of girls who have lunch together every day, or a group of boys who have known each other for a long time). The importance of the clique, whatever its basis, is that it provides the main social context in which adolescents interact with each other. The clique is the social setting in which adolescents "hang out," talk to each other, and form close friendships (B. Brown, 1990).

Cliques differ in structure and purpose from crowds. **Crowds** are "large, reputation-based collectives of similarly stereotyped individuals who may or may not spend much time together" (B. Brown, 1990, p. 177). In contemporary American high schools, typical crowds are "jocks," "brains," "nerds," "populars," "druggies," and so on. In contrast to cliques, crowds are not settings for adolescents' intimate interactions or friendships but, instead, serve to locate the adolescent (to himself and to others) within the social structure of the school. As well, the crowds themselves tend to form a sort of social hierarchy or map of the school (see Figure 14.2), and different crowds are seen as having different degrees of status or importance.

● **cliques**
exclusive social circles of friends

● **crowds**
loosely formed groups organized on the basis of shared activities rather than close friendship

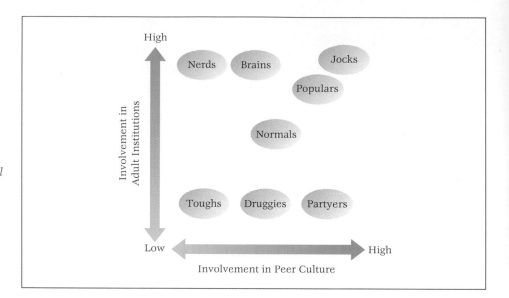

FIGURE 14.2

A model for mapping the social world of adolescent peer groups. Note that "nerds," "brains," and "jocks" are all highly involved with adult institutions. "Toughs" are uninvolved with both peer and adult institutions.
(SOURCE: Brown, 1990.)

Membership in a crowd is based mainly on reputation and stereotype, rather than on actual friendship or social interaction. In concrete terms—and perhaps ironically—an adolescent does not have to actually have "brains" as friends, or to hang around with "brainy" students, to be a member of the "brain" crowd. If he dresses like a "brain," acts like a "brain," and takes honors courses, then he is a "brain" as far as his crowd membership goes. Knowing where an adolescent fits into the social system of the school can often tell us a fair amount about the individual's behavior and values. This is because crowds contribute to the definition of norms and standards for such things as clothing, leisure, and tastes in music. Being a jock, for example, means more than simply being involved in athletics. Jocks wear certain types of clothes, listen to certain types of music, spend Saturday nights in certain hangouts, and use a particular slang when they talk. They accept many of the values of the adults around them but also value many elements of the contemporary peer culture.

● **Intimacy and Friendship**

The emergence of cliques during early adolescence coincides with changes in individuals' needs for intimacy. A need for intimacy with friends emerges at age 11 or 12. As children begin to share secrets with their friends, a new sense of loyalty and commitment grows, a belief that friends can trust each other. After interviewing children between the ages of 6 and 12, one researcher identified several different bases of friendship they have (Berndt, 1981). These included *play or association* ("He calls me all the time"), *prosocial behavior* ("She helps me do things"), *intimacy and trust* ("I can tell her secrets"), and *loyal support* ("He'll stick up for me when I'm in a fight"). Children of all the ages studied mentioned association and prosocial behavior as bases of their friendships, but the youngest ones never talked about intimacy, trust, and loyal support. These more sophisticated ideas about friendship didn't appear until the later elementary school years.

During adolescence, the search for intimacy intensifies, and self-disclosure between best friends becomes an important pastime. Teenagers, especially girls, spend hours discussing their innermost thoughts and feelings, trying to understand one another. The discovery that they tend to think and feel the same as someone else becomes another important basis of friendship (Diaz & Berndt, 1982; Sharabany, Gershoni, & Hofman, 1981).

Why does this increased intimacy with friends occur during adolescence? Partly because adolescents need it and partly because they can now achieve it. In short, the biological, social, and cognitive changes of adolescence combine to make intimacy not only desirable but possible. Along with their awakening sexuality come questions and concerns that almost demand baring one's soul: How do you act on a date? When do you kiss? How much?

In addition, intimacy grows because it *can* grow. Children have a narrow ability to see things from another person's perspective, which limits their capacity for intimacy (Selman, 1980). The cognitive changes of adolescence, though, include a growing capacity for empathy, for understanding another's feelings and needs. With such understanding comes the ability to form more mature friendships. Furthermore, since many teenagers feel awkward discussing sex and other boy-girl matters with their parents, they naturally turn to their friends. But at the same time, many parents now view their children as near-adults, and who confides in whom sometimes takes a new twist (Youniss & Smollar, 1985).

So while adolescents are becoming closer to their friends, they aren't necessarily distancing themselves from their parents. In one study, adolescents from the age of about 12 on reported that they were closer to their best friends than to their parents. This didn't mean that their feelings toward their parents had grown cooler. It was simply that relationships between friends were becoming so much stronger (Hunter & Youniss, 1982).

As the search for intimacy grows, adolescents share secrets and experiences with best friends.

● Dating and Sex

One of the most important social transitions that takes place in adolescence concerns the emergence of sexual and romantic relationships. In contemporary society, most young people begin dating sometime during early adolescence.

"Dating" during adolescence can mean a variety of different things, from group activities that bring males and females together (without much actual contact between the sexes); to group dates, in which a group of boys and girls go out jointly (and spend part of the time in couples and part of the time in large groups); to casual dating in couples; to serious involvement with a steady boyfriend or girlfriend. More adolescents have experience in mixed-sex group activities like parties or dances than in dating, and more have experience in dating than in having a serious boyfriend or girlfriend (Tobin-Richards, 1985).

We do not know very much about the impact of dating on adolescent development. One reason for this absence is that researchers have not paid enough attention to differences among various types of dating activities. There is some evidence, for example, that especially for girls, it may be important to differentiate between group versus couple activities in examining the impact of dating on psychological development. Participating in mixed-sex activity in group situations—going to parties or dances, for example—may have a positive impact on the psychological well-being of young adolescent girls, while serious dating in couples may have a more negative effect (Tobin-Richards, 1985). The reasons for this are not entirely clear, but researchers believe that pressures on girls to engage in sexual activity when they are out alone on dates or involved with a steady boyfriend may have a negative impact on their mental health (Simmons & Blyth, 1987). Although boys may feel peer pressure to become sexually active, this may be a very different sort of pressure—with very different consequences—from what girls feel. Because boys generally begin dating at a later age than girls—and date people who are younger rather than older—beginning to date in couples may be less anxiety-provoking for the adolescent boy, who has the advantage of a few additional years of "maturity," than for the adolescent girl.

Although most teenagers begin dating by age 16, the sharing of intimate thoughts and feelings between the sexes tends to come later.

Most adolescents' first experience with sex falls into the category of "auto-erotic behavior"—sexual behavior that is experienced alone (Katchadourian, 1990). The most common autoerotic activities reported by adolescents are having erotic fantasies (about three-quarters of all teenagers report having sexual fantasies, mainly about television personalities or movie stars) and masturbation (reported by about half of all adolescent boys and one-fourth of all adolescent girls). According to one study (Sorensen, 1973), most girls who masturbated began at around age 12, whereas most boys began at around age 14. This sex difference parallels differences in the age of puberty, with girls maturing, on average, about 2 years earlier than boys.

By the time most adolescents have reached high school, they have had some experience with sex in the context of a relationship (Katchadourian, 1990). Most studies indicate that the developmental progression of sexual behaviors, from less intimate to more intimate, has not changed very much over the past 30 years, and that the sequence in which males and females engage in various sexual activities is remarkably similar. Necking and petting are more common activities and occur earlier than genital contact or intercourse, which in turn occur earlier than oral sex. Although boys engage in these activities at a somewhat earlier age than girls, the similarities in age of first experience and in prevalence are far more striking than the differences.

● ***Adolescent intercourse.*** Estimates of the prevalence of sexual intercourse among American adolescents vary considerably from study to study, depending on the nature of the sample surveyed and the year and region in which the study was undertaken. Only a few studies have examined sexual intercourse among adolescents younger than age 15. These indicate that, overall, about 12 percent of boys and 6 percent of girls report having intercourse by age 13 (Katchadourian, 1990). There are vast regional and ethnic differences in the prevalence of sexual activity during the junior high school years, however (Dreyer, 1982). Thus, while only 12 percent of white males are sexually active by this age, 19 percent of Hispanic males and 42 percent of African-American males are (Hayes, 1987). The comparable figures for girls are 5 percent, 4 percent, and 10 percent, respectively.

There are also large regional differences in the prevalence of early sexual intercourse, with sexual activity occurring earlier in rural and inner-city communities than in the suburbs. One recent study, for example, found that more than half of all eighth graders living in a rural area reported having had sexual intercourse—about twice the rate found in studies of nationwide samples of adolescents from this age group (Alexander et al., 1989). In this study of rural youth, and in studies of inner-city teenagers (for example, Zabin et al., 1986), about 85 percent of the African-American male 14-year-olds surveyed report having had sexual intercourse. As noted earlier, the prevalence of early sexual activity varies widely among cultures, and such variability is apparent even within American society. Although these regional and ethnic variations make it difficult—if not misleading—to generalize about the "average" age at which American adolescents initiate sexual intercourse, national surveys of young people indicate that more adolescents are sexually active at an earlier age today than in the recent past.

For many years, researchers studied the psychological and social characteristics of adolescents who engaged in premarital sex, assuming that sexually active teenagers were more troubled than their peers. This view has been replaced as sexual activity has become more prevalent. Indeed, several recent studies show that sexual activity during adolescence is decidedly not associated with psychological disturbance. Two studies, for example, showed that adolescents who became sexually active earlier than their peers had levels of self-esteem and life satisfaction similar to that of other adolescents (Billy et al., 1988; Jessor et al., 1983).

● *Homosexuality.* It is not uncommon for young adolescents to engage in sex play with members of the same sex or to have questions about the nature of their feelings for same-sex peers. By age 16, over 20 percent of adolescent boys have engaged in homosexual activity to the point of orgasm (Kinsey, Pomeroy, & Martin, 1948). But even though many adolescents have such homosexual experiences, nearly all young people—over 90 percent, in fact—develop an exclusive preference for heterosexual relationships by the end of adolescence. And contrary to myths about the increasing prevalence of homosexuality in contemporary American society, the proportion has remained at or near this level since the mid-1940s, when researchers began studying the phenomenon (Hunt, 1974).

Studies of the antecedents of homosexuality generally have focused on two sets of factors: biological influences, such as hormones, and social influences, including the parent-child relationship and early patterns of play. More is known about the development of homosexuality among men than women—the prevalence of homosexuality is much greater among males—but the weight of the evidence thus far suggests that an adolescent's sexual preference is likely to be shaped by a complex interaction of social and biological influences (Green, 1980, 1987; Savin-Williams, 1988).

Support for the contention that homosexuality is at least partly biologically determined comes from several sources. First, there is suggestive, albeit indirect, evidence that gay and lesbian adults may have been exposed prenatally to certain hormones that in theory could affect sexual orientation through their effect on early brain organization (Savin-Williams, 1988). Second, there is some evidence that homosexuality has a strong genetic component, since sexual orientation is more likely to be shared among close than distant relatives and between identical than fraternal twins (Savin-Williams, 1988). Although environmental explanations for this similarity cannot be ruled out, chances are that at least some of the predisposition to develop a homosexual orientation is inherited.

Homosexuality is not considered by mental health experts to be a form of psychopathology, an indicator of an underlying psychological disturbance, or a condition warranting psychological treatment. Perhaps as we begin to understand more about the interplay among biological and social factors that contribute to the development of a homosexual orientation, our attitudes toward homosexuality will change for the better. Indeed, as one expert noted, "society tends to treat . . . homosexuals as if they had a choice about their sexual orientation, when in fact they have no more choice about how they develop than heterosexuals do" (Marmor, quoted in Brody, 1986, p. 17).

● *Contraceptive use.* One of the reasons for the great concern of adults over the sexual activity of adolescents is the failure of many sexually active young people to use birth control measures regularly, an increasingly worrisome phenomenon given the fast spread of *acquired immunity deficiency syndrome* (**AIDS**) within the adolescent population (see the Making A Difference box on page 474). Yet, despite the high awareness among teenagers of the need for sexual protection, only one-third of sexually active adolescents always use birth control. Only half of all young women report having used some method of birth control the first time they had intercourse, and nearly one-sixth of all 15- to 19-year-old sexually active women report never having used any contraception. In general, older adolescents are more likely to use contraception than younger ones, and adolescents are more likely to use contraception when they plan in advance to have sex than when intercourse is unplanned (Hayes, 1987).

Why do so few adolescents use contraception regularly? Social scientists point to several factors. First, for a sizable minority of adolescents, contraceptives are not readily available—or if they are, young people may not know where to get them. Approximately 15 percent of adolescent girls and 25 percent of adolescent boys report that they did not use contraceptives when they had sex for the first time because they could not get them (Hayes, 1987; Katchadourian, 1990). This is likely to be an especially important barrier among younger adolescents, who may feel uncomfortable discussing their sexual activity with parents or other adults whose help or consent may be necessary in order to obtain birth control. Having ready access to a free, confidential family planning service that does not require parents' consent is a strong predictor of whether adolescents will use contraceptives at all or use them consistently (Brooks-Gunn & Furstenberg, 1989).

Second, many young people are insufficiently educated about sex, contraception, and pregnancy (Trussell, 1989). Many young people do not fully understand that the likelihood of pregnancy varies over the course of a woman's menstrual cycle, and more than half mistakenly believe that it is during menstruation that the risk of pregnancy is greatest (Zelnick & Kantner, 1973). At the time of first intercourse, about one-third of all teenagers who do not use contraception fail to do so because they don't know about contraception or didn't think about using contraceptives (Hayes, 1987).

Psychological factors also play a role in adolescents' failure to use contraception. Although it certainly is a misconception that many young women unconsciously want to become pregnant, many young people nevertheless do not recognize the seriousness of pregnancy and take the possibility lightly (Hayes, 1987). More than 25 percent of nonusers report that they or their partners simply did not want to use birth control. From a cognitive perspective, the limited ability of young adolescents to engage in long-term hypothetical thinking, and their occasionally egocentric tendency to believe that they are immune from the forces that affect others (the personal fable), may impede their consideration of pregnancy as a likely outcome of sexual activity.

Perhaps most important, many adolescents fail to use birth control because doing so would be tantamount to admitting that they are planfully and willingly sexually active (Cvetkovich et al., 1975). Going on the pill or purchasing a condom requires an adolescent to acknowledge that he or she is having sexual relations. For many young people, this is an extremely difficult admis-

● **acquired immune deficiency syndrome (AIDS)** a deadly viral disease, transmitted through body fluids, that attacks the immune system

MAKING A DIFFERENCE

AIDS AND ADOLESCENTS: A PREVENTABLE PLAGUE

During the 1980s, a new and deadly sexually transmitted disease began appearing in the U.S. population: *acquired immune deficiency syndrome (AIDS)*. As yet incurable and always fatal, AIDS is transmitted only through intimate contact with infected semen, vaginal secretions, and blood. AIDS is caused by a virus that attacks the immune system, destroying the body's ability to defend itself against disease. The Centers for Disease Control in Atlanta estimates that 1 million to 1.5 million Americans have the AIDS virus. About 25 percent of all infected people develop symptoms within 5 years, and about half of all individuals in the United States known to have AIDS have died as a result. Most researchers think that the others will eventually die as well. Of particular concern to doctors is the growing spread of AIDS among adolescents.

Each year, 2.5 million teenagers are infected with a sexually transmitted disease, indicating that condoms are not being used (Gans, 1990). Additionally, "one of every six sexually active high school girls has had at least four different partners" (Kolata, 1989a). In an AIDS epidemic, too few condoms and too many partners spell disaster.

Although the incidence of AIDS in the United States was initially concentrated within two groups, gay men and drug users who use needles, recent surveys indicate that the transmission of AIDS through heterosexual activity is a clear danger within the adolescent community, particularly among inner-city minority youngsters. In one inner-city clinic, for example, between 2 and 3 percent of adolescents from ages 15 to 19 tested positive for the presence of HIV (DiClemente, 1990). Because there is a long period of time between HIV infection and the actual manifestation of illness, however— sometimes, as long as 10 years— many more adolescents are likely to be asymptomatic carriers of the HIV virus who may develop AIDS in young adulthood (Hein, 1988).

The chances of contracting HIV are greatest among individuals who use intravenous drugs, have unprotected sex, have many sexual partners, and already have another sexually transmitted disease (such as gonorrhea). Because

sion to make. This may be especially true for young women who feel ambivalent and guilty about sleeping with someone for the first time. And many teenagers do not anticipate having intercourse (Trussell, 1989).

Taken together, this evidence suggests that there is a great deal that adults can do to improve the contraceptive behavior of adolescents. First, adults can see that contraceptives are made accessible to the young people who feel they need them. In many large cities, for example, condoms are now distributed to teenagers at school. Second, adults can provide sex education at an early enough age to instruct young people in the fundamentals of pregnancy and birth control before, rather than after, the adolescents have become sexually active. Third, parents and teachers can make adolescents feel more free to talk about their sexual interests and concerns, so that young people will be more apt to look at their own behavior seriously and thoughtfully. Finally, the mass media need to portray sex in a more responsible fashion, showing contraception use along with sexual activity. When, for instance, was the last time you saw a couple in a film or on television interrupt sex in order to discuss birth control?

these risk factors are more common among young people than adults, the risk of HIV infection among adolescents is substantial. Accordingly, in recent years numerous efforts have been made to develop AIDS education programs specifically aimed at teenagers (Shayne & Kaplan, 1988).

Unfortunately, despite numerous attempts at programs designed to reduce the prevalence of HIV infection among adolescents, many young people, especially minority youth, remain confused and misinformed about AIDS (DiClemente et al., 1988). Educating young people about the risk factors associated with AIDS is important, because adolescents who believe that they are at risk are more likely to take precautions during intercourse (Brooks-Gunn et al., 1988). Unfortunately, public education

about AIDS has been least successful in reaching those adolescents at greatest risk.

Most experts believe that, short of abstinence, the best way for teenagers to protect themselves against contracting HIV is by using condoms during sexual intercourse. Unfortunately, while most adolescents now recognize this—largely through public health education efforts—it has been difficult to convince teenagers to translate this knowledge into safer behavior (Kegeles et al., 1988). As one team of authors concluded, "dissemination of information, in and of itself, is unlikely to deter the spread of AIDS significantly" (Shayne & Kaplan, 1988, p. 199). For this reason, sex education programs that combine AIDS information with the distribution of condoms hold the most promise.

Contrary to widespread public opinion, such programs do not increase the likelihood of adolescents becoming sexually active (Furstenberg et al., 1985; Hanson et al., 1987).

"When I found out I had HIV at age 17, I learned that anyone can get it."

One in 250 Americans is infected with HIV.
1-800-342-AIDS

SUMMARY

1. In all societies, adolescence is a time of growing up, of moving from the immaturity of childhood into the maturity of adulthood. There is no single event or boundary line that denotes the end of childhood or the beginning of adolescence. Rather, experts think of the passage from childhood to adolescence as composed of a set of transitions that unfold gradually and that touch upon many aspects of the individual's behavior, development, and relationships. (See page 442.)

2. Puberty refers to all the physical changes that occur in the growing girl or boy as the individual passes from childhood into adulthood. The most important physical changes during puberty are a rapid gain in height and weight, known as the growth spurt; the development of reproductive capability; and the appearance of secondary sex characteristics. (See pages 442–444.)

3. Puberty, by itself, need not have negative effects on a youngster's self-image or mood. However, the timing of physical maturation does affect social and emotional development in important ways. In general, early maturers enjoy more popularity with their peers but are more likely to get involved in problem behavior. Early maturation also may take a particular psychological toll on the mental health of girls. (See pages 445–447.)

4. Adolescents think in ways that are more advanced, more efficient, and generally more effective than children. First, adolescents are better able than children to think about what is possible, instead of limiting their thought to what is real. Second, they are better able to think about abstract things. Third, adolescents think more often about the process of thinking itself. Fourth, in adolescence, thinking tends to become multidimensional, rather than limited to a single issue. Finally, adolescents are more likely than children to see things as relative, rather than absolute. (See pages 447–450.)

5. The two most important theoretical perspectives on adolescent thinking are the Piagetian perspective and the information-processing perspective. Piaget focused on the development of advanced logical reasoning abilities as individuals entered the stage of formal operations. Information-processing theorists have emphasized gains in basic cognitive processes, such as attention, memory, and metacognition. (See pages 450–453.)

6. Early adolescence is a time of changes in the way individuals view themselves. Compared with children—who tend to describe themselves in relatively simple, concrete terms—adolescents are more likely to employ complex, abstract, and psychological self-characterizations. Although teenagers' feelings about themselves may fluctuate, especially during early adolescence, their self-esteem remains fairly stable from about age 13 on. If anything, self-esteem increases over the course of middle and late adolescence. (See pages 454–456.)

7. Erik Erikson theorized that the establishment of a coherent sense of identity is the chief psychosocial crisis of adolescence. Most writers on adolescence and youth believe that identity exploration continues well into young adulthood. Rather than thinking of the adolescent as going through a single identity crisis, it probably makes more sense to view the phenomenon as a series of crises that may concern different aspects of the young person's identity and that may surface—and resurface—at different points in time throughout the adolescent and young adult years. (See pages 456–460.)

8. Becoming an autonomous person is also a fundamental developmental task of the adolescent years. The process of individuation, which begins during infancy and continues well into late adolescence, involves a gradual, progressive sharpening of one's sense of self as autonomous, as competent, and as separate from one's parents. Adolescence is also a time of improvement in decision-making abilities, although early adolescence seems to be a time of heightened conformity to peers. (See pages 460–463.)

9. Although it is incorrect to characterize adolescence as a time of conflict in most families, early adolescence is nevertheless a period of significant change and reorganization in family relationships. It is also a time of significant change in the structure and significance of peer groups. Adolescents' social relations tend to be organized around cliques and crowds. (See pages 463–468.)

10. The emergence of cliques during early adolescence coincides with changes in individuals' needs for intimacy, and friendships become more intense during early adolescence. Early adolescence also marks the beginning of romantic relationships, as youngsters begin to experiment with dating and sex. Although few adolescents have had sexual intercourse before reaching high school, the majority have experimented with sex by that time. (See pages 468–472.)

KEY TERMS

acquired immune deficiency syndrome (AIDS)
adolescent growth spurt
barometric self-esteem
baseline self-esteem
behavioral autonomy
behavioral decision theory
cliques

crowds
emotional autonomy
estrogen
formal operational stage
hormones
hypothetical thinking
identity versus identity diffusion
imaginary audience
individuation

menarche
metacognition
personal fable
primary sex characteristics
psychosocial moratorium
puberty
secondary sex characteristics
testosterone

SUGGESTED READINGS

Feldman, S., and Elliott, G. (Eds.) (1990). *At the threshold: The developing adolescent.* Cambridge: Harvard University Press. An up-to-date collection of summaries of what is known about various aspects of adolescent development.

Kett, J. (1977). *Rites of passage: Adolescence in America, 1790 to the present.* New York: Basic Books. The history of adolescence in America, with an emphasis on how people's conception of this stage in the life cycle has changed.

Spacks, P. (1981). *The adolescent idea.* New York: Basic Book. A thorough examination of how writers, philosophers, and scientists have looked at adolescence over the years.

Steinberg, L., and Levine, A. (1990). *You and your adolescent: A parent's guide for ages 10 to 20.* A comprehensive practical guidebook to growth and development during the adolescent years.

GLOSSARY

accommodation According to Piaget, the process by which people alter their existing schemes to adapt to new information that doesn't "fit" an existing scheme.

achievement motivation The desire to perform well.

acquired immune deficiency syndrome (AIDS) A deadly viral disease, transmitted through body fluids, that attacks the immune system.

activity A dimension of temperament; highly active babies are always on the go, while those with lower activity levels look and listen more than they move.

adolescent growth spurt The pronounced increase in height and weight during the first half of puberty.

agency Active, assertive, and self-confident behavior.

alleles Alternative genes for the same trait.

amniocentesis A medical technique for diagnosing genetic abnormalities *in utero* by analysis of the amniotic fluid.

amniotic sac The protective, fluid-filled membrane surrounding the embryo and fetus.

androgens The class of hormones, including testosterone, that occur in higher levels in males.

animism Crediting nonliving things with human qualities.

anoxia Lack of oxygen in the fetus.

anxious-avoidant attachment An insecure attachment in which an infant shows indifference to its mother or father and avoids interaction with her or him.

anxious-resistant attachment An insecure attachment in which an infant shows much distress at separation from and anger at reunion with its mother or father.

Apgar test A test that measures a baby's heart rate, breathing, muscle tone, reflexes, and color immediately after birth.

arborization The proliferation of connections among neurons by branching.

assimilation According to Piaget, the process by which people incorporate new information into their existing schemes.

attachment The close, significant emotional bond between the mother (or father) and the infant.

attention-deficit hyperactivity disorder A disorder in which children can neither pay attention nor remain still.

authoritarian parents Parents who have an absolute set of standards and expect unquestioning obedience.

authoritative parents Parents who set clear standards but legitimate their authority through warmth and explanation.

autonomy and initiative The ability to be independent, resourceful, and self-motivated.

autonomy versus shame and doubt According to Erikson, the toddler's major "crisis"—the conflict between the desire for independence and the desire for security—as the sense of self emerges.

babbling An infant's repetitive sound combinations, before first words are spoken.

barometric self-esteem Moment-to-moment shifts in self-assessment.

baseline self-esteem Stable, general feelings about the self.

basic trust An infant's strong sense that its needs will be met and the world is not a threatening place; according to Erikson, the establishment of trust is the major task of infancy.

Bayley Scales Tests for assessing an infant's mental and motor skills by comparison with age-related norms.

behavioral autonomy The capacity to make independent decisions and follow through with them.

behavioral decision theory A theory that all behaviors can be analyzed as the outcome of a process that involves identifying alternative choices and evaluating their consequences, their desirability, and their likelihood.

behaviorism A learning theory that looks at how concrete stimuli can, through reinforcement and punishment, produce observable changes in people's behavior.

binocular convergence The ability to focus both eyes on the same object.

blastula The hollow-ball form the new organism takes from about 4 days to 2 weeks following conception.

bloody show The blood-tinged mucus in a pregnant woman's urine or discharge, which is a sign of impending labor.

breech birth A birth in which the baby emerges feet or buttocks first.

canalization The extent to which a trait is susceptible to modification by the environment or by experience.

case study A study that amasses detailed information about one person or, at most, a few people.

castration anxiety Freud's label for a little boy's fear that he will be punished for being his father's rival.

causation The relationship between a cause and its effect.

center-based day care Child care licensed and regulated by a local authority and located in a central facility.

centration Focusing on only one aspect of a stimulus.

cephalocaudal development The pattern of growth proceeding from the head downward.

cerebral cortex The wrinkled outer layer of the brain, which is the most highly evolved part of the brain, responsible for perception, muscle control, thought, and memory.

cerebral lateralization The process by which certain brain functions are located in one hemisphere.

cesarean section Surgery in which the uterus is opened and the baby is lifted out.

chlamydia A bacterial sexually transmitted disease that can harm the fetus during birth.

chorionic villus biopsy (CVB) A prenatal diagnostic technique that analyzes cells taken from hairlike villi on the embryonic sac for genetic problems.

chromosomes Twisted strands of DNA that carry genetic instructions from generation to generation.

classical conditioning Learning through the repeated pairing of a stimulus and a response.

classification The cognitive ability to understand how things fit into categories and how these categories can be arranged relative to each other.

cliques Exclusive social circles of friends.

colic A condition in newborns involving acute abdominal pains, high-pitched crying, and facial grimacing; at the same time, the babies will flex their elbows, clench their fists, and either pull up their knees or keep them stiffly extended.

communion Supportive, helpful, and empathic behavior.

compensatory education programs Community-based programs designed to meet the needs of children at high risk of school failure.

complementary and reciprocal play Active, turn-taking play.

complex social pretend play Play in which children get more involved in who plays what role and in how they are supposed to behave.

complexity The number and intricacy of traits like color or pattern in a stimulus.

compressed sentences Phrases made up of several words slurred into one long sound.

concrete operations According to Piaget, the stage of development between ages 6 and 12 when children acquire the mental schemes of seriation, classification, and conservation that allow them to think logically about "concrete" objects.

conservation The knowledge that basic physical dimensions remain the same despite superficial changes in appearance.

contractions Movements of the muscular walls of the uterus that push the baby out of the mother's body.

conventional thinking According to Kohlberg, the second level of moral development, in which children make decisions about what is right and wrong based on how well a person follows the rules and conventions of society and keeps within the roles people are expected to play.

cooperative social pretend play Play in which two children act out complementary roles in a make-believe scenario.

correlational studies An assessment of the extent to which two or more factors tend to be related.

critical periods Periods during gestation during which particular developing organs and structures are most vulnerable to environmental influences.

cross-modal abilities Abilities that cut across sensory modes; abilities to transfer data from one sensory system to another.

cross-sectional study A study using subjects of different ages and assessing them simultaneously.

cross-sequential study A study using subjects of different ages studied over a period of time.

crowd A loosely formed group organized chiefly on the basis of shared activities rather than close friendship.

custody The legal care or guardianship of children.

decentration Focusing on more than the self; the extension of activity and awareness beyond one's own physical boundaries.

defense mechanisms Mechanisms used by the ego to repress the id.

deferred imitation Duplication of behavior seen or experienced earlier.

deoxyribonucleic acid (DNA) A chemical substance that is the carrier of genetic information in chromosomes.

desensitization Gradual exposure to the feared aspects of the object of a phobia.

developmental gradualness The principle stating that specific motor skills appear initially in rudimentary forms and specific contexts; over time, these skills become more complex and wide-ranging.

developmental quotient (DQ) A score on the Bayley Scales based on age-mates' scores.

differentiation (1) The process by which groups of cells descended from the same zygote become specialized for the various tissues and organs. (2) The ability to make specific, goal-directed movements.

difficult child A baby with high negative emotionality and an undependable schedule.

dishabituation The reaction to (recovery of interest in) a novel stimulus.

dominant gene A gene that is expressed whether paired with an identical or a recessive allele.

Down syndrome A hereditary disorder caused by an extra twenty-first chromosome.

easy child An adaptable, calm baby with a predictable schedule.

ectoderm The outer layer of the embryo, which will eventually become the skin and nervous system.

ego According to Freud, the part of the personality that regulates emotion, thought, and behavior.

egocentrism The inability to consider others' perspectives.

Electra complex According to Freud, a psychological conflict for girls, arising from their sexual feelings toward their fathers.

embryonic disk The cells on the outer edge of the blastula, which will develop into the embryo.

embryonic period The second stage of prenatal development, from 2 to 8 weeks after conception.

emergent literacy A focus on the creative uses of reading and writing by young children before they learn the formal rules and conventions of print.

emotional autonomy That aspect of independence related to changes in the individual's close relationships, especially with parents.

empathize To know what another person is feeling.

endoderm The innermost layer of the embryo, which will become the internal organs.

engagement (lightening) The movement of the fetus into position for birth.

engrossment Parental absorption, preoccupation, and interest in the infant.

episiotomy An incision made below the vaginal opening during childbirth.

equilibration The process through which balance is restored to the cognitive structure.

equivalence The recognition that similar stimuli, or the same stimuli under changed conditions, belong to the same basic category.

estrogen A female sex hormone.

ethological theory An analysis of human and animal behavior patterns in evolutionary terms.

evaluation anxiety Anxiety manifested in situations where a child is being judged.

experiment A scientific tool designed to investigate causes.

extended families Relatives in addition to the child's parents.

family day care Child care provided in a private home.

fast-mapping A strategy used by children to fill gaps in their vocabulary; a child relates a word to a general domain of meaning immediately after hearing it for the first time.

fetal alcohol syndrome (FAS) A group of symptoms, including cognitive, motor, and growth retardation, suffered by some children of alcoholic mothers.

fetal monitor An electronic device that keeps track of the fetal heartbeat and uterine pressure during childbirth.

fetal period The third and final stage of prenatal development, from 8 weeks to birth.

fine motor skills Physical abilities involving the small-muscle groups.

5-to-7 transition A period in which children begin to develop a sense of logic and strategy as part of their cognitive skills.

forceps delivery A method of delivery using an instrument shaped like two large interlocking spoons, which the doctor fits around the baby's head.

formal operational stage According to Piaget, the stage at which one's thinking is based on theoretical, abstract principles of logic.

fraternal twins Twins born from two different ova fertilized at the same time by two different sperm.

gender constancy The understanding that one's sex will never change.

gender identity The knowledge that one is female or male.

gender labeling Differentiating between males and females.

genes The basic units of heredity, each gene consisting of a segment of a chromosome that controls some aspect of development.

genital herpes A sexually transmitted viral disease that can cause damage to the fetus during pregnancy and delivery.

genotype An individual's genetic makeup, consisting of all inherited genes.

germinal period The first 2 weeks of prenatal development.

Gesell Developmental Schedules One of the first sets of tests for assessing children 1 month to 6 years old on physical, cognitive, language, and social skills according to average developmental rates.

gestation The period of prenatal development.

gonorrhea A sexually transmitted disease caused by a bacterium.

goodness of fit The way the personalities and expectations of the parents mesh with their child's temperament.

gross motor skills Physical abilities involving the large-muscle groups.

growth hormone deficiency An endocrine disorder causing short stature.

habituation The adaptation to (loss of interest in) an unchanging stimulus.

hand dominance A strong preference for using the left or right hand.

haptic perception The ability to acquire information about objects by handling them, rather than simply by looking at them.

Head Start A federal program combining educational and social opportunities for 3- and 4-year-olds with social services for their low-income families.

heterozygous Inheriting different alleles for a given trait from each parent.

high-risk infants Infants whose physical and psychological well-being may be in jeopardy due to premature birth and/or low birth weight.

holophrases Single words that stand for whole thoughts.

homozygous Inheriting the same alleles for a given trait from both parents.

hormones Chemical substances that act on specific organs and tissues.

hostile aggression Physical and/or verbal aggression that is deliberately harmful.

hypothesis An educated proposition about how factors being studied relate to each other.

hypothetical thinking What is sometimes called "if-then" thinking.

id According to Freud, the part of the personality that includes all inborn human drives.

identical twins Twins born from a single fertilized ovum that divides in two.

identification A process in which children adopt the same-sex parent's attitudes, behaviors, and values.

identity versus identity diffusion According to Erikson, the psychosocial crisis of establishing one's identity, characteristic of adolescence.

imaginary audience The erroneous belief that one's appearance and behavior are the subject of public attention.

implantation The process by which the blastula attaches to the uterus.

individuation The process of becoming a separate person who can both act independently and accept responsibility for choices.

individuation and separation According to Mahler, the striving toward independence and a sense of separate self during infancy and toddlerhood.

induction Discipline involving the use of reasoning to explain the expectations of the parent.

industrial pollutant Environmental hazards resulting from the emission of contaminants in the atmosphere.

industry versus inferiority According to Erikson, the crisis over the sense of accomplishment, characteristic of middle childhood.

information processing One of the theories concerning the development of thinking; it emphasizes the growth of basic cognitive processes over time.

initiative versus guilt In Erikson's theory, the conflict for preschoolers between the wish to do and prohibitions against doing.

inner speech Verbal self-communication.

insecure attachment A relation of an infant to its mother (or father) based on lack of trust.

instrumental aggression Aggression arising out of conflicts over ownership, territory, and perceived rights.

intelligence quotient (IQ) A measure of intelligence computed by dividing an individual's mental age by his or her chronological age. This number is multiplied by 100, with 100 being an average score and scores above and below 100 indicating greater or lesser intelligence, respectively.

intentional behavior Goal-directed activity, which begins to appear from 8 to 12 months.

intentionality The purposeful coordination of activity toward a goal.

interactive imagery (elaboration) A strategy for recall.

interview A research technique in which researchers personally question people.

joint custody Custody in which both parents share legal guardianship of their children equally.

karyotype A profile of an individual's

chromosomes created from a tissue sample.

kwashiorkor A disease affecting children ages 2 to 3, caused by a severe protein deficiency, usually after weaning.

Lamaze method Natural or prepared childbirth.

latchkey children Children who stay home without an adult while their parents work.

lead An environmental hazard that damages fetuses as well as children and adults.

lead poisoning An illness that can severely affect brain maturation in early childhood; caused by exposure to high levels of lead.

learned helplessness The belief or expectation that one cannot control forces in one's environment.

learning A more or less permanent change in behavior that occurs as a consequence of experience.

learning goals Goals that place value on individual accomplishment for its own sake.

logic General principles about the relations among objects and people.

longitudinal study A study following the same group of people over an extended period of time.

low birth weight A weight of less than 5½ pounds at birth.

mainstreaming The placement of handicapped children in classrooms with nonhandicapped children.

manipulate symbols To grasp the relationship between letters and sounds and to use this ability to learn to read and do arithmetic.

marasmus A disease affecting infants under 1 year, caused by an insufficient and often contaminated food supply.

mass-to-specific development The pattern of growth from large to small muscles.

mastery motivation The desire to master a challenge in order to acquire a new skill.

memory strategies Plans that aid recall.

menarche The first menstrual period.

mental combinations Mental coordinations of several actions in sequence.

mesoderm The middle layer of the embryo, which will become the skeleton and muscles.

metacognition The understanding and control of one's own thinking skills; the ability to think about thinking, including thinking about reasoning and thinking about memory.

modeling A component of social learning that involves imitation.

moral development The changes in the ability to reason about morality that occur as a child grows up.

motherese A form of slow, high-pitched, simplified, well-enunciated language used by mothers and others in speaking to infants.

motor development The increasing ability to control the body in purposeful motion.

mutual exclusivity A principle in acquiring new words whereby children assume that a word can only refer to one object.

myelin An insulating fatty sheath on nerve fibers.

myelinization The process by which nerves become insulated with myelin, which forms a fatty sheath.

natural experiment An experiment that takes advantage of a naturally occurring event.

natural selection The process by which physical traits that enhance a species' chances for surviving in its particular environment are passed on from generation to generation.

naturalistic observations Observations of people in their own environments.

negative emotionality A dimension of temperament; negative emotional qualities in an infant include such things as a high degree of irritability (crying often, strongly, and for long periods of time).

negative reinforcement Reinforcement through the removal of unpleasant stimuli.

neonatology The branch of medicine focusing on newborns.

neurons Nerve cells; the primary functional units of the nervous system.

New York Longitudinal Study (NYLS) A pioneering study of infant temperament.

Newborn Behavioral Assessment Scale Brazelton's test evaluating a newborn's state of control, sensory capacities, reflexes, and motor abilities.

obese Refers to those individuals whose weight is at least 20 percent more than normal for their age, height, and sex.

object permanence The slowly developing understanding that objects exist separate from one's perception of them.

observational learning Learning through observation and imitation of others' behavior.

Oedipus complex According to Freud, a psychological conflict for boys, arising from their sexual feelings toward their mothers.

overextension Using words too broadly; using the same word to stand for a number of similar things.

overregularization Applying grammatical rules too stringently.

parallel aware Play in which children begin to acknowledge each other by making eye contact.

parallel play Play in which children are apparently playing together but are actually focused on their own activities.

PCBs Polychlorinated biphenyls; a common industrial pollutant.

perceive To interpret sensations.

performance goals Goals that place value on achieving in relation to others.

permissive parents Parents who are generally noncontrolling and non-threatening, allowing children to regulate their own behavior.

personal fables Erroneous beliefs that one's thoughts, feelings, and experiences are unique.

personality Behaviors and response patterns developed through experience.

phenotype An individual's observable physical and behavioral traits, the result of the interaction of genetic potential and environment.

phenylketonuria (PKU) A hereditary metabolic disorder caused by a double dose of a recessive gene that blocks amino acid breakdown.

phobias Intense, irrational fears directed toward specific objects or situations.

pitocin A synthetic form of the natural labor-inducing hormone oxytocin.

placenta The organ along the uterine wall where nutrients and oxygen from the mother and wastes from the baby are exchanged.

plasticity Flexibility.

polygenic Caused by the interaction of a number of genes.

positive emotionality A dimension of temperament; positive emotional qualities in an infant include such things as the expression of joy.

positive reinforcement Reinforcement through the addition of pleasant stimuli.

preconventional thinking According to Kohlberg, the first level of moral development, in which children make decisions about what is right and wrong based not on society's standards or conventions but on external, physical events.

prelinguistic communication Literally, before-language communication; communication between parents and infants through games, gestures, sounds, facial expressions, and imitation.

premature (preterm) baby A baby born before 35 weeks of gestation.

prenatal development Development during the period before birth.

preoperational period According to Piaget, the period of transition from sensorimotor intelligence to rule-governed thought.

prepared (natural) childbirth Childbirth without medication or anesthetics, based on relaxation techniques and psychological and physical preparation.

preschools Child care that offers planned social and cognitive experiences.

primary circular reaction An infant's repetition of a chance action involving a part of the infant's body.

primary sex characteristics Developments in the structure and function of the reproductive organs and systems.

proportional phenomenon The characteristic of an infant's growth in which different parts of the infant's body grow at different rates, resulting in alterations in their relative proportions.

prosocial behavior Positive, helping acts.

proximodistal development The pattern of growth from the center of the body outward.

psychosocial moratorium According to Erikson, a necessary "time out" from excessive obligations for adolescents.

puberty The physical transformation from child to adult.

pulmonary surfactant An essential lubricating substance in the lungs.

punishment An aversive consequence that decreases the frequency of a behavior.

questionnaire A written set of carefully prepared questions given to subjects to answer.

radiation An environmental hazard resulting from the emission of radiant energy, such as from an atomic bomb.

reaction range The genetically established upper and lower limits to development of a given trait; a trait's potential for expression.

recall memory Memory based on information retrieved without strong clues.

recessive gene A gene that is not expressed if paired with its dominant allele.

reciprocal feedback A pattern of mutual, interdependent influences in which each member of a system affects and is affected by the others.

recognition memory Memory based on recognition of a previously seen object.

referential communication Communication that refers to something specific.

reflex A motor behavior not under conscious control.

rehearsal The labeling and repeating of names or other information to aid memory.

reinforcement A consequence that produces repetition of behavior.

representational thinking Thinking that involves manipulation of mental images (symbols).

respiratory distress syndrome (RDS) A breathing disorder in premature babies, caused by immaturity of the lungs and lack of pulmonary surfactant.

reversibility The concept representing that an action can be done and undone.

Rh factor A protein found on red blood cells.

rhythmical stereotypies Apparently reflexive, repeated rhythmic movements that serve as transition from random to controlled movement.

Ritalin A stimulant drug used to treat attention-deficit hyperactivity disorder.

rubella German measles.

schemes According to Piaget, mental representations and patterns of action that structure a person's knowledge.

scientific method A procedure to collect reliable, objective information that can be used to support or refute a theory.

scripts Sequences of day-to-day activities.

secondary circular reactions Repetitions of actions that trigger responses in the external environment (for example, squeeze a toy—it squeaks).

secondary reinforcer Anything (or anyone) associated with the satisfaction of a need, so chances of a given response recurring are increased by the presence of the reinforcer.

secondary sex characteristics The visible characteristics of sexual maturity not directly related to reproduction.

secure attachment A positive, healthy relationship of an infant to its mother (or father), based on the infant's trust in the parent's love and availability.

secure base An attachment object (usually the mother) who provides a foundation for curious exploration.

self-conceptions The various attributes people see themselves possessing.

self-esteem One's feelings about oneself.

self-regulation The extent to which people can monitor and control their own behavior.

sensorimotor Describes Piaget's first stage of cognitive development, in which infants explore their world with their senses and motor actions.

separation protest An infant's reaction, based on fear, to separation from its mother or other caregiver.

seriation The ability to rank objects in a meaningful order.

sex chromosomes The twenty-third pair of chromosomes, which determine the sex of the child; there are two types, X-shaped and Y-shaped.

sex-role development How children learn to behave in the ways we call feminine and masculine.

sex roles The tasks and traits that society assigns to females and males.

sex stereotypes Social expectations about how males and females behave.

sibling deidentification One process through which children develop identities different from their siblings'.

simple-social play Play in which contact grows as children play near each other and begin talking, smiling, and exchanging toys.

slow-to-warm-up child A child characterized by mild emotions and an initial fear of new experiences.

sociability A dimension of temperament concerning a child's reaction to new people and new situations.

social cognition Thinking about oneself and the other people in one's life, including awareness of interpersonal relations and social rules and roles.

social context The total environment in which we live.

social learning theorists Psychologists who study how people learn from one another.

social learning theory A learning theory that looks at the way social rewards and punishments influence behavior and expectations.

social networks People who provide parents with emotional support, instrumental assistance (help with routine tasks), and social expectations (guidelines for child rearing).

social referencing Looking to someone else for guidance in emotional response to new stimuli or situations.

social smile An infant's smile for pleasure in response to familiar people.

sociobiologists Psychologists who study social organization in humans, particularly concerning genetics and evolution.

sociobiology The comparative study of social organization in animals and humans, particularly concerning genetics and evolution.

sociometry Measures of social relationships in a group.

sound localization The ability to locate the source of a sound.

standardized test A carefully developed test that allows individual scores to be compared with previously established norms.

state control The ability of newborns to shift from one state of arousal to another in response to either internal or external stimulation.

states and transformations The concepts involved in understanding that objects and states can be transformed and rearranged.

states of arousal Varying levels of energy, attention, and activity.

strange situation An experimental procedure for observing attachment patterns.

stranger wariness The fear of unfamiliar people, which sets in at about the age of 6 to 8 months.

strategy The ability to use logical principles to solve problems.

structured observations Observations of people in controlled environments.

sudden infant death syndrome (SIDS) Death in early infancy for no apparent reason.

superego According to Freud, the part of the personality that serves as a conscience.

symbiosis The merging of self with another, as an infant with its mother.

symbolic system A system, like language, that represents and labels elements of the world and their interrelations.

symbolic thought Mental representation of the world.

syphilis A bacterial sexually transmitted disease that can cross the placenta.

system An organized, interacting, interdependent group, functioning as a whole.

Tay-Sachs disease A hereditary disorder that destroys nerve cells, leading to mental retardation, loss of muscle control, and death.

temperament The unique, inborn pattern of responsiveness and mood.

teratogen Any substance, influence, or agent that causes birth defects.

testosterone A male sex hormone.

thyroxine deficiency A thyroid disorder that may cause short stature, stunted growth, and mental retardation.

transition The end of the first stage of labor, with the cervix fully dilated.

transitional object An object, like a blanket or teddy, to which an infant transfers attachment feeling as he or she moves toward independence.

transitivity The concrete operation acquired between ages 6 and 12 that rests on the understanding of relationships among objects.

transverse presentation A condition in which the fetus lies horizontally in the uterus.

turn-taking Conversational give-and-take.

ultrasonography A technique that produces a picture from sound waves bounced off the fetus; used for diagnosing developmental problems *in utero.*

umbilical cord The lifeline attaching the embryo (and fetus) to the placenta; it transports maternal nutrients from, and wastes to, the placenta.

underextension Using words too restrictively.

vacuum extraction A method of delivery using a tube that pulls or "sucks" the baby out.

vernix A slippery substance that coats the newborn.

very low birth weight (VLBW) A weight of less than 1,500 grams at birth.

villi Hairlike projections from the blastula that burrow into the uterine lining.

visual acuity Clarity of vision.

visual recognition memory Memory for stimuli seen before.

zone of proximal development Vygotsky's theory that children's intellectual development is stimulated through interactions with people more capable than they; children advance when adults encourage them to reach a little further intellectually, to try activities a bit more difficult than those they can do on their own.

zygote The fertilized cell resulting from the fusion of the ovum and sperm.

BIBLIOGRAPHY

Abell, T. (1992). Low birth weight, intrauterine growth-retarded, and preterm infants. *Human Nature, 3,* 335–378.

Abell, T., Baker, L., Clover, R., & Ramsey, C. (1991). The effects of family functioning on intra-uterine growth retardation. *Journal of Family Practice, 32,* 37–44.

Aber, J. L., & Allen, J. P. (1987). Effects of maltreatment on young children's socioemotional development: An attachment theory perspective. *Development Psychology, 23*(3), 406–414.

Abramovitch, R., Freedman, J. L., Thoden, K., & Nikolich, C. (1991). Children's capacity to consent to participation in psychological research: Empirical findings. *Child Development, 62,* 1100–1109.

Achenbach, T., Phares, V., Howell, C., Rauh, V., & Nurcombe, B. (1990). Seven-year outcome of the Vermont Intervention Program for low-birthweight infants. *Child Development, 61*(6), 1672–1681.

Acheson, R. M. (1960). Effects of nutrition and disease on human growth. In J. M. Tanner (Ed.), *Human growth* (pp. 73–92). New York: Pergamon.

Acredolo, L., & Goodwyn, S. (1988). Symbolic gesturing in normal infants. *Child Development, 59,* 450–466.

Adams, G., & Crane, P. (1980). An assessment of parents' and teachers' expectations of preschool children's social preference for attractive or unattractive children and adults. *Child Development, 51,* 224–231.

Adams, L., & Davidson, M. (1987). Present concepts of infant colic. *Pediatric Annals, 16,* 817–820.

Adams, R. (1987). An evaluation of color preference in early infancy. *Infancy Behavior and Development, 10,* 143–150.

Ainsworth, M. D. S. (1973). The development of infant-mother attachment. In B. M. Caldwell & H. N. Ricciuti (Eds.), *Review of child development research* (Vol. 3, pp. 1–94). Chicago: University of Chicago Press.

Ainsworth, M. D. S. (1979). Attachment as related to mother-infant interaction. *Advances in the Study of Behavior, 9,* 2–49.

Ainsworth, M. D. S., & Wittig, B. (1969). Attachment and exploratory behavior of one-year-olds in a strange situation. In B. M. Foss (Ed.), *Determinants of infant behavior* (Vol. 4). New York: Wiley.

Akhtar, N., Dunham, F., & Dunham, P. (1991). Directive interactions and early vocabulary development: The role of joint attentional focus. *Journal of Child Language, 18,* 41–49.

Alessandri, S. (1991). Play and social behavior in maltreated preschoolers. *Development and Psychopathology, 3,* 191–205.

Alexander, C., Ensminger, M., Kim, Y., Smith, B. J., Johnson, K., & Dolan, L. (1989). Early sexual activity among adolescents in small towns and rural areas: Race and gender patterns. *Family Planning Perspectives, 21,* 261–266.

Allen, L., & Majida-Ahi, S. (1990). Black-American children. In J. Gibbs & L. Huang (Eds.), *Children of color* (pp. 148–178). San Francisco: Jossey-Bass.

Allhusen, V. (1992, May). Caregiving quality and infant attachment in day care contexts of varying quality. Poster presented at the Eighth International Conference on Infant Studies, Miami, FL.

Allison, P., & Furstenberg, F., Jr. (1989). How marital dissolution affects children: Variations by age and sex. *Developmental Psychology, 25,* 540–549.

Almli, R., & Finger, S. (1987). Neural insult and critical period concepts. In M. Borstein (Ed.), *Sensitive periods in development* (pp. 123–139). Hillsdale, NJ: Erlbaum.

Alperstein, G., Rapport, C., & Flanagan, J. (1988). Health problems of homeless children in New York City. *American Journal of Public Health, 78,* 1232–1233.

Amato, P. (1993). Children's adjustment to divorce: Theory, hypotheses and empirical support. *Journal of Marriage and the Family, 55,* 23–38.

Amato, P., & Keith, B. (1991). Parental divorce and the well-being of children: A meta-analysis. *Psychological Bulletin, 110*(1), 26–46.

Ambrose, J. (1961). The development of the smiling response in early infancy. In B. M. Foss (Ed.), *Determinants of infant behavior* (Vol. 1). London: Methuen.

American Academy of Pediatrics (1985). *Pediatrics nutrition handbook* (2nd ed.). Elk Grove, IL: Author.

Anastasi, A. (1958). Heredity, environment, and the question "How?" *Psychological Review, 65,* 197–208.

Anderson, D. R., Lorch, E. P., Field, D. E., Collins, P. A., & Nathan, J. G. (1986). Television viewing at home: Age trends in visual attention and time with TV. *Child Development, 57,* 1024–1033.

Anderson, D. R., Lorch, E. P., Field, D. E., & Sanders, J. (1981). The effects of TV program comprehensibility on preschool children's visual attention to television. *Child Development, 52,* 151–157.

Andersson, B. (1989). Effects of public day-care. *Child Development, 60,* 857–866.

Andersson, B. (1992). Effects of day-care on cognitive and socioemotional competence of thirteen-year-old Swedish schoolchildren. *Child Development, 63,* 20–36.

Andersson, T., & Magnusson, D. (1990). Biological maturation in adolescence and the development of drinking habits and alcohol abuse among young males: A prospective longitudinal study. *Journal of Youth and Adolescence, 19,* 33–42.

Anisfeld, M. (1991). Neonatal imitation. *Developmental Review, 11,* 60–97.

Antonov, A. (1947). Children born during the siege of Leningrad in 1942. *Journal of Pediatrics, 30,* 250–259.

Antonucci, T., & Mikus, K. (1988). The power of parenthood: Personality and attitudinal changes during the transition to parenthood. In G. Michals & W. Goldberg (Eds.), *The transition to parenthood* (pp. 62–84). New York: Cambridge University Press.

Apgar, V., & Beck, J. (1973). *Is my baby all right?* New York: Trident Books.

Aronfreed, J. (1968). *Conduct and conscience: The socialization of internal controls over behavior.* New York: Academic.

Asher, S. R., & Gottman, J. M. (1981). *The development of children's friendships.* New York: Cambridge University Press.

Aslin, R. (1981). The development of smooth pursuit in human infants. In D. Fisher, R. Monty, & J. Senders (Eds.), *Eye movements: Cognition and visual perception* (pp. 31–52). Hillsdale, NJ: Erlbaum.

Aslin, R., Pisoni, D., & Jusczyk, P. (1983). Auditory development and speech perception in infancy. In J. Campos & M. Haith (Eds.), *Handbook of child psychobiology: Vol. 2. Infancy and developmental psychobiology* (pp. 573–688). New York: Wiley.

Assor, A. (1988). *Representation of mother and dependency in kindergarten children.* Unpublished manuscript. Ben-Gurion University, Israel.

Bahrick, L. E. (1983). Infants' perception of substance and temporal synchrony. *Infant Behavior & Development, 6,* 429–450.

Bahrick, L. E. (1988). Intermodal learning in infancy: Learning on the basis of two kinds of invariant relations in audible and visible events. *Child Development, 59,* 197–209.

Bakeman, L. B., & Adamson, L. B. (1984). Coordinating attention to people and objects in mother-infant and peer-infant interaction. *Child Development, 55,* 1278–1289.

Bakeman, R., & Brown, J. (1980). Analyzing behavioral sequences: Differences between preterm and full-term infant-mother dyads during the first months of life. In D. Sawin, R. C. Hawkins, II, L. O. Walker, & J. H. Pentieuff (Eds.), *Exceptional infant: Vol. 4. Psychosocial risks in infant-environment transactions.* New York: Brunner/Mazel.

Baker, L. (1984). Spontaneous versus instructed use of multiple standards for evaluating comprehension: Effects of age, reading proficiency, and type of standard. *Journal of Experimental Child Psychology, 38,* 289–311.

Baker, L., & Brown, A. L. (1984). Metacognitive skills and reading. In P. D. Pearson, M. Kamil, R. Barr, & P. Mosenthal (Eds.), *Handbook of reading research* (pp. 353–394). New York: Longman.

Baldwin, D. A., & Markham, E. M. (1989). Establishing word-object re-

lations: A first step. *Child Development, 60,* 1291–1306.

Bandura, A. (1965). Influence of models' reinforcement contingencies on the acquisition of imitative responses. *Journal of Personality and Social Psychology, 1,* 589–595.

Bandura, A. (1977). *Social learning theory.* Englewood Cliffs, NJ: Prentice-Hall.

Bandura, A., Ross, D., & Ross, S. (1961). Transmission of aggression through imitation of aggressive models. *Journal of Abnormal and Social Psychology, 63,* 575–582.

Bar-Tal, D., Raviv, A., & Goldberg, M. (1982). Helping behavior among preschool children: An observational study. *Child Development, 53,* 396–402.

Barber, B. (1987). Marital quality, parental behavior and adolescent self-esteem. *Family Perspective, 21,* 244–368.

Barglow, P., Vaughn, B., & Molitor, N. (1987). Effects of maternal absence due to employment on the quality of infant-mother attachment in a low-risk sample. *Child Development, 58,* 945–954.

Barkley, R. A., (1989). Hyperactive girls and boys: Stimulant drug effects on mother-child interactions. *Journal of Child Psychology and Psychiatry, 30*(3), 379–390.

Barkley, R. A., & Cunningham, C. (1978). Do stimulant drugs improve the academic performance of hyperkinetic children? A review of outcome research. *Clinical Pediatrics, 17,* 85–93.

Barkley, R. A., DuPaul, G. J., & McMurray, M. B. (1991). Attention deficit disorder with and without hyperactivity: Clinical response to three dose levels of methylphenidate. *Pediatrics, 87,* 519–531.

Barkley, R. A., Fischer, M., Edelbrock, C., & Smallish, L. (1991). The adolescent outcome of hyperactive children diagnosed by research criteria: III. Mother-child interactions, family conflicts and maternal psychopathology. *Journal of Child Psychology and Psychiatry, 32*(2), 233–255.

Barnard, K., & Bee, H. (1983). The impact of temporally patterned stimulation on the development of preterm infants. *Child Development, 54,* 1156–1167.

Barnes, K. E. (1971). Preschool play norms: A replication. *Developmental Psychology, 5,* 99–103.

Baroody, A. J. (1985). Mastery of basic number combinations. *Journal for Research in Mathematics Education, 16,* 83–98.

Barr, H., Streissguth, A., Darby, B., & Sampson, P. (1990). Prenatal exposure to alcohol, caffeine, tobacco, and aspirin: Effects on fine and gross motor performance in four-year-old children. *Developmental Psychology, 26,* 339–348.

Barr, R. (1990a). The early crying paradox: A modest proposal. *Human Nature, 1,* 355–389.

Barr, R. (1990b). The normal crying curve: What do we really know? *Developmental Medicine and Child Neurology, 32,* 356–362.

Barr, R. (1992, May). *Crying and colic.* Paper presented at the Eighth International Conference on Infant Studies, Miami, FL.

Barr, R., McMullan, S., Spiess, H., Leduc, D., Yaremko, J., Barfield, R., Francoeur, T., & Hunziker, U. (1991). Carrying as colic "therapy": A randomized controlled trial. *Pediatrics, 87,* 623–630.

Barrett, D. E., Radke-Yarrow, M., & Klein, R. E. (1982). Chronic malnutrition and child behavior: Effects of early caloric supplementation on social and emotional functioning at school age. *Developmental Psychology, 18,* 541–556.

Baruk, A., Feldman, S., & Noy, A. (1991). Traditionality of children's interests as related to their parents' gender stereotypes and traditionality of occupations. *Sex Roles, 23,* 511–517.

Bassuk, E., & Rosenberg, L. (1990). Psychosocial characteristics of homeless children and children with homes. *Pediatrics, 85,* 257–261.

Bassuk, E., & Rubin, L. (1987). Homeless children. *American Journal of Orthopsychiatry, 57,* 279–286.

Bates, E., Bretherton, I., & Snyder, L. (1988). *From first words to grammar.* New York: Cambridge University Press.

Bates, E., Camaioni, L., & Volterra, V. (1975). The acquisition of performatives prior to speech. *Merrill-Palmer Quarterly, 21,* 205–226.

Bauer, P. (1993). Memory for gender-consistent and gender-inconsistent event sequences by twenty-five-month-old children. *Child Development, 64,* 285–297.

Bauer, P., & Mandler, J. (1989). One thing follows another: Effects of temporal structure on 1- to 2-year-olds' recall of events. *Developmental Psychology, 25,* 197–206.

Bauer, P., & Mandler, J. (1992). Putting the horse before the cart: The use of temporal order in recall of events by one-year-old children. *Developmental Psychology, 28,* 441–452.

Baumrind, D. (1967). Child care practices anteceding three patterns of preschool behavior. *Genetic Psychology Monographs, 75,* 43–88.

Baumrind, D. (1971). Current patterns of parental authority. *Developmental Psychology Monograph, 4*(1, Pt. 2.).

Baumrind, D. (1972). An exploratory study of socialization effects on black children: Some black-white comparisons. *Child Development, 43,* 261–267.

Baumrind, D. (1980). New directions in socialization research. *Psychological Bulletin, 35,* 639–652.

Baumrind, D. (1989a). Rearing competent children. In W. Damon (Ed.), *Child development today and tomorrow* (pp. 349–378). San Francisco: Jossey-Bass.

Baumrind, D. (1989b, April). *Sex-differentiated socialization effects in childhood and adolescence in divorced and intact families.* Paper presented at the meeting of the Society for Research in Child Development, Kansas City, MO.

Baumrind, D., & Black, A. E. (1967). Socialization practices associated with dimensions of competence in preschool boys and girls. *Child Development, 38,* 291–327.

Baydar, N., & Brooks-Gunn, J. (1991). Effects of maternal employment and child care arrangements on preschoolers' cognitive and behavioral outcomes. *Developmental Psychology, 27,* 932–945.

Beal, C., & Lockhart, M. (1989). The effect of proper name and appearance changes on children's reasoning about gender constancy. *International Journal of Behavioral Development, 12,* 195–205.

Becerra, R., & Chi, I. (1992). Child care preferences among low-income minority families. *International Social Work, 35,* 35–47.

Beckwith, L. (1971). Relationships between attributes of mothers and their infants' IQ scores. *Child Development, 42,* 1083–1097.

Beere, C. A. (1979). *Women and women's issues: A handbook of tests and measures.* San Francisco: Jossey-Bass.

Bell, D., Gleiber, D. W., Mercer, A. A., Phifer, R., Guinter, R. H., Cohen, A., Epstein, E., & Narajanan, M. (1989). Illness associated with child day care. *Amercian Journal of Public Health, 79,* 479–484.

Bellinger, D., Leviton, A., Waternaux, C., Needleman, H., & Rabinowitz, M. (1987). Longitudinal analyses of prenatal and postnatal lead exposure and early cognitive development. *New England Journal of Medicine, 316,* 1037–1043.

Belsky, J. (1984). The determinants of parenting: A process model. *Child Development, 55,* 83–96.

Belsky, J. (1988). The "effects" of infant day care reconsidered. *Early Childhood Research Quarterly, 3,* 235–272.

Belsky, J. (1990a). Children and marriage. In F. Fincham & T. Bradbury (Eds.), *The psychology of marriage* (pp. 172–200). New York: Guilford.

Belsky, J. (1990b). Parental and nonparental child care and children's socioemotional development: A decade in review. *Journal of Marriage and the Family, 52,* 885–903.

Belsky, J. (1992). *The etiology of child maltreatment.* Paper commissioned by the National Academy of Sciences, National Research Council, Panel on Research on Child Abuse and Neglect. Washington, DC: National Academy of Sciences.

Belsky, J. (1993). Etiology of child maltreatment: A develomental-ecological analysis. *Psychological Bulletin, 114,* 413–434.

Belsky, J., & Benn, J. (1982). Beyond bonding: A family-centered approach to enhancing parent-infant relations in the newborn period. In L. Bond & J. Joffee (Eds.), *Facilitating infant and early childhood development: Sixth Vermont Conference on the Primary Prevention of Psychopathology* (pp. 281–308). Hanover, NH: University Press of New England.

Belsky, J., & Braungart, J. (1991). Are insecure-avoidant infants with extensive day care experience less stressed by and more independent in the strange situation? *Child Development, 62,* 567–571.

Belsky, J., & Cassidy, J. (1993). Attachment: Theory and evidence. In M. Ritter, D. Hay, & S. Baron-Cohn (Eds.), *Developmental principles and clinical issues in psychology and psychiatry.* Oxford, England: Blackwell.

Belsky, J., & Eggebeen, D. (1991). Early and extensive maternal employment and young children's socioemotional development. *Journal of Marriage and the Family, 53,* 1083–1110.

Belsky, J., Fish, M., & Isabella, R. (1991). Continuity and discontinuity in infant negative and positive emotionality. *Developmental Psychology, 27,* 421–431.

Belsky, J., Garduque, L., & Hrncir, E. (1984). Assessing performance, competence, and executive capacity in infant play: Relations to home environment and security of attachment. *Developmental Psychology, 20,* 406–417.

Belsky, J., Lang, M., & Huston, T. (1986). Sex typing and division of labor as determinants of marital change across the transition to parenthood. *Journal of Personality and Social Psychology, 50,* 517–522.

Belsky, J., & Nezworski, T. (1988). Clinical implications of attachment: An introduction. In J. Belsky & T. Nezworski (Eds.), *Clinical implications of attachment* (pp. 3–17). Hillsdale, NJ: Erlbaum.

Belsky, J., & Pensky, E. (1988). Marital change across the transition to parenthood. *Marriage and Family Review, 12,* 133–156.

Belsky, J., Pensky, E., & Youngblade, L. (1990). Childrearing history, marital quality and maternal affect: Intergenerational transmission in a low-risk sample. *Development and Psychopathology, 1,* 294–304.

Belsky, J., & Rovine, M. (1984). Social network contact, family support, and the transition to parenthood. *Journal of Marriage and the Family, 46,* 455–462.

Belsky, J., & Rovine, M. (1988). Nonmaternal care in the first year of life and the security of infant-parent attachment. *Child Development, 59,* 157–167.

Belsky, J., & Rovine, M. (1990). Patterns of marital change across the transition to parenthood. *Journal of Marriage and the Family, 52,* 5–19.

Belsky, J., Rovine, M., & Fish, M. (1989). The developing family system. In M. Gunnar & E. Thelen (Eds.), *Minnesota Symposia on Child Psychology: Vol. 22. Systems and development* (pp. 119–158). Hillsdale, NJ: Erlbaum.

Belsky, J., Rovine, M., & Taylor, D. G. (1984). The Pennsylvania Infant and Family Development Project: 3. The origins of individual differences in infant-mother attachment: Maternal and infant contributions. *Child Development, 55,* 706–717.

Belsky, J., & Steinberg, L. (1978). The effects of day care: A critical review. *Child Development, 49,* 929–949.

Belsky, J., Steinberg, L., & Walker, A. (1982). The ecology of day care. In M. E. Lamb (Ed.), *Nontraditional families* (pp. 71–116). Hillsdale, NJ: Erlbaum.

Belsky, J., & Tolan, W. (1981). Infants as producers of their own development: An ecological analysis. In R. Lerner and N. Busch-Rossnagle (Eds.), *Individuals as producers of their own development: A lifespan perspective* (pp. 87–116). New York: Academic Press.

Belsky, J., & Volling, B. (1989). Mothering, fathering, and marital interaction in the family triad during infancy: Exploring family system's processes. In P. Berman & F. Pedersen (Eds.), *Men's transition to parenthood: Longitudinal studies of early family experience* (pp. 37–63). Hillsdale, NJ: Erlbaum.

Belsky, J., & Vondra, J. (1989). Lessons from child abuse: The determinants of parenting. In D. Cicchetti & V. Carlson (Eds.), *Child maltreatment. Theory and research on the causes and consequences of child abuse and neglect* (pp. 153–202). New York: Cambridge University Press.

Belsky, J., Ward, M., & Rovine, M. (1986). Prenatal expectations, postnatal experiences, and the transition to parenthood. In R. Ashmore & D. Brodzinsky (Eds.), *Thinking about the family.* Hillsdale, NJ: Erlbaum.

Belsky, J., Youngblade, L., Rovine, M., & Volling, B. (1991). Patterns of marital change and parent-child interaction. *Journal of Marriage and the Family, 53,* 487–498.

Benin, M. H., & Edwards, D. A. (1990). Adolescents' chores: The difference between dual- and single-earner families. *Journal of Marriage and the Family, 52,* 361–373.

Berenbaum, S. (1990). Congenital adrenal hyperplasia: Intellectual and psychosexual functioning. In C. Holmes (Ed.), *Psychoneuroendocrinology: Brain, behavior and hormonal interactions* (pp. 227–260). New York: Springer-Verlag.

Berenbaum, S., & Hines, M. (1992). Early androgens are related to childhood sex-typed toy preferences. *Psychological Science, 3,* 203–206.

Berg, A., Shapiro, E. & Capobianco, C. (1991). Group day care and the risk of serious infectious illness. *American Journal of Epidemiology, 133,* 154–163.

Berk, L. E., & Garvin, R. A. (1984). Development of private speech among low-income Appalachian children. *Developmental Psychology, 20,* 271–286.

Berndt, T. (1979). Developmental changes in conformity to peers and parents. *Developmental Psychology, 15,* 608–616.

Berndt, T. (1981). Relations between social cognition, nonsocial cognition, and social behavior: The case of friendship. In J. Flavell & L. Ross (Eds.), *Social cognitive development: Frontiers and possible futures* (pp. 179–199). Cambridge, England, Cambridge University Press.

Berndt, T., & Miller, K. E. (1990). Expectancies, values, and achievement in junior high school. *Journal of Educational Psychology, 82*(2), 319–326.

Bertenthal, B. I., Campos, J. J., & Barnett, K. C. (1984). Self-produced locomotion: An organizer of emotional, cognitive, and social development in infancy. In R. N. Emde & R. J. Harman (Eds.), *Continuities and discontinuities in development* (pp. 175–210). New York: Plenum.

Best, D. L., & Ornstein, P. A. (1986). Children's generation and communication of mnemonic organizational strategies. *Developmental Psychology, 22,* 845–853.

Best, D. L., Williams, J. E., Cloud, J. M., Davis, S. W., Robertson, L. S., Edwards, J. R., Giles, H., & Fowles, J. (1977). Development of sex-trait stereotypes among young children in the United States, England, and Ireland. *Child Development, 48,* 1375–1384.

Bettes, B. (1988). Maternal depression and motherese: Temporal and intonational features. *Child Development, 59,* 1089–1096.

Bever, T. G. (1970). The cognitive basis for linguistic structures. In J. R. Hayes (Ed.), *Cognition and the development of language* (p. 424). New York: Wiley.

Bierman, K. (1986). The relationship between social aggression and peer rejection in middle childhood. In R. Prinz (Ed.), *Advances in behavioral assessment of children and families* (Vol. 2, pp. 151–178). Greenwich, CT: JAI Press.

Bierman, K., Miller, C., & Stabb, S. (1987). Improving the social behavior and peer acceptance of rejected boys. *Journal of Consulting and Clinical Psychology, 55,* 194–200.

Bigler, R., & Liben, L. (1990). The role of attitudes and intentions in gender-schematic processing. *Child Development 61,* 440–452.

Bijur, P. E., Haslum, M., & Golding, J. (1990). Cognitive and behavioral sequelae of mild head injury in children. *Pediatrics, 86,* 337–344.

Biller, H. B. (1970). Father absence and the personality development of the male child. *Developmental Psychology, 2,* 181–201.

Biller, H. B., & Borstelmann, L. J. (1967). Masculine development: An integrative review. *Merrill-Palmer Quarterly, 13,* 253–294.

Billy, J., Landale, N., Grady, W., & Zimmerle, D. (1988). Effects of sexual activity on adolescent social and psychological development. *Social Psychology Quarterly, 51,* 190–212.

Birch, L., Marlin, D., & Rotter, T. (1984). Eating as the "means" activity in a contingency: Effects on young children's food preference. *Child Development, 55,* 431–439.

Birch, L., Zimmerman, S., & Hind, H. (1984). The influence of social-affective context on preschool children's food preference. *Child Development, 51,* 856–861.

Biringen, Z., Emde, R., & Campos, J. (1991, April). *Infant walking onset: Home observations of affectivity and autonomy.* Paper presented at the biennial meeting of the Society for Research in Child Development, Seattle, WA.

Bisnaire, L. M. C., Firestone, P., & Rynard, D. (1990, January). Factors associated with academic achievement in children following parental separation. *American Journal of Orthopsychiatry, 60*(1), 67–76.

Black, B., & Hazan, N. (1990). Social status of communication in acquainted and unacquainted preschool children. *Developmental Psychology, 3,* 379–387.

Black, J., & Greenough, W. (1986). Induction of pattern in neural structure by experience. In M. Lamb, A. Brown, & B. Rogoff (Eds.), *Advances in developmental psychology* (Vol. 4, pp. 1–41). Hillsdale, NJ: Erlbaum.

Blakemore, J. (1990). Children's nurturant interactions with their infant siblings. *Sex Roles, 22,* 43–49.

Blass, E. (1992). The ontogeny of motivation. *Current Directions in Psychological Science, 1,* 116–120.

Blass, E., Ganchrow, J., & Steiner, J. (1984). Classical conditioning in newborn humans 2–48 hours of age. *Infant Behavior and Development, 7,* 223–235.

Bloch, H. (1989). On early coordinations and their future. In A. de Ribaupierre (Ed.), *Transitions in child development* (pp. 259–282). New York: Cambridge University Press.

Block, J. H. (1983). Differential premises arising from differential socialization of the sexes: Some conjectures. *Child Development, 54,* 1335–1354.

Block, J. H., & Gjerde, P. F. (1988). Parental functioning and the home environment of families of divorce: Prospective and current analyses. *Journal of the American Academy of Child and Adolescent Psychiatry, 27,* 207–213.

Bloom, L., Beckwith, R., & Capatides, J. B. (1988). Developments in the expression of affect. *Infant Behavior and Development, 11,* 169–186.

Bloom, L., Merkin, S., & Wootten, J. (1982). Wh-questions: Linguistic factors that contribute to the sequence of acquisition. *Child Development, 53,* 1084–1092.

Blos, P. (1967). The second individuation process of adolescence. In R. S. Eissler et al. (Eds.), *Psychoanalytic study of the child* (Vol. 15). New York: International Universities Press.

Boccia, M., & Campos, J. (1983, April). *Maternal emotional signaling: Its effect on infants' reaction to strangers.* Paper presented at the meeting of the Society for Research in Child Development, Detroit, MI.

Boggiano, A. K., Main, D. S., & Katz, P. (1991). Mastery motivation in boys and girls: The role of intrinsic versus extrinsic motivation. *Sex Roles, 25*(9, 10), 511–520.

Bohannon, J., & Stanowicz, L. (1988). The issue of negative evidence: Adult responses to children's language errors. *Developmental Psychology, 24,* 684–689.

Boivin, M., & Bégin, G. (1989). Peer status and self-perception among early elementary school children: The case of the rejected children. *Child Development, 60,* 591–596.

Boldizar, J. P., Perry, D. G., & Perry, L. C. (1989). Outcome values and aggression. *Child Development, 60,* 571–579.

Borja-Alvarez, T., Zarbatany, L., & Pepper, S. (1991). Contributions of male and female guests and hosts to peer group entry. *Child Development, 62,* 1079–1090.

Borke, H. (1975). Piaget's mountains revisted: Changes in the egocentric landscape. *Developmental Psychology, 11,* 240–243.

Bornstein, M. (1981). Two kinds of perceptual organization near the beginning of life. In W. A. Collins (Ed.), *Aspects of the development of competence.* Hillsdale, NJ: Erlbaum.

Bornstein, M. (1989a). Cross-cultural development comparisons: The case of Japanese-American infant and mother activities and interactions. *Developmental Review, 9,* 171–204.

Bornstein, M. (1989b). Stability in early mental development: From attention and information processing in infancy to language and cognition in childhood. In M. Bornstein & N. A. Krasnegor (Eds.), *Stability and continuity in mental development: Behavioral and biological perspectives* (pp. 147–170). Hillsdale, NJ: Erlbaum.

Bornstein, M., & Lamb, M. (1992). *Development in infancy: An introduction.* New York: McGraw-Hill.

Bornstein, M., Pêchaux, M.-G., & Leguyer, R. (1988). Visual habituation in human infants: Development and rearing circumstances. *Psychological Research, 50,* 130–133.

Bornstein, M., & Sigman, M. (1986). Continuity in mental development from infancy. *Child Development, 57,* 251–274.

Bornstein, M., Tal, J., Rahn, C., Galperin, C., Pêchaux, M., Lamour, M., Toda, S., Azuma, H., Ogino, M., & Tamis-LeMonda, C. S. (1992a). Functional analysis of the contents of maternal speech to infants of 5 and 13 months in four cultures: Argentina, France, Japan, and the United States. *Development Psychology, 28,* 593–603.

Bornstein, M., Tal, J., & Tamis-LeMonda, C. S. (1991). Parenting in cross-cultural perspective: The United States, France, and Japan. In M. Bornstein (Ed.), *Cultural approaches to parenting* (pp. 69–90). Hillsdale, NJ: Erlbaum.

Bornstein, M., & Tamis-LeMonda, C. S. (1990). Activities and interactions of mothers and their firstborn infants in the first six months of life: Covariation, stability, continuity, correspondence, and prediction. *Child Development, 61,* 1206–1217.

Bornstein, M., & Tamis-LeMonda, C. S. (1991). *Origins of cognitive skills in infants.* Paper presented at the International Conference on Infant Studies, Los Angeles.

Bornstein, M., Tamis-LeMonda, C. S., Tal, J., Ludemann, P., Toda, S., Rahn, C., Pêchaux, M., Azuma, H., & Vardi, D. (1992b). Maternal responsiveness to infants in three societies: The United States, France, and Japan. *Child Development, 63,* 808–821.

Bornstein, M., Toda, S., Azuma, H., Tamis-LeMonda, C. S., & Ogino, M. (1990). Mother and infant activity and interaction in Japan and in the United States: II. A comparative microanalysis of naturalistic exchanges focused on the organization of infant attention. *International Journal of Behavioral Development, 13,* 289–308.

Bowerman, M. (1976). Semantic factors in the acquisition of rules for word use and sentence construction. In D. M. Morehead & A. E. Morehead (Eds.), *Normal and deficient child language.* Baltimore, MD: University Park Press.

Bowlby, J. (1969–1980). *Attachment and loss* (Vols. 1–3). London: Hogarth.

Boysson-Bardies, B., Sagart, L., & Durand, C. (1984). Discernible differences in the babbling of infants according to target language. *Journal of Child Language, 11,* 1–15.

Brackbill, Y. (1958). Extinction of the smiling response in infants as a function of reinforcement. *Child Development, 29,* 115–124.

Brackbill, Y. (1979). Obstetrical medication and infant behavior. In J. Osofsky (Ed.), *Handbook of infant development* (pp. 76–125). New York: Wiley.

Bradley, R. H., Caldwell, B. M., & Rock, S. L. (1988). Home environment and school performance: A ten-year follow-up and examination of three models of environmental action. *Child Development, 59,* 852–867.

Brand, E., Clingempeel, W. G., & Bowen-Woodward, K. (1988). Family relationships and children's psychological adjustment in stepmother and stepfather families: Findings and conclusions from the Philadelphia Stepfamily Research Project. In E. M. Hetherington & J. D. Arasteh (Eds.), *Impact of divorce, single parenting and stepparenting on children* (pp. 299–324). Hillsdale, NJ: Erlbaum.

Braungart, J., & Plomin, R. (1992, May). *Genetic influence on change in temperament.* Paper presented at the Eighth International Conference on Infant Studies, Miami, FL.

Braungart, J., Plomin, R., DeFries, J., & Fulker, D. (1992). Genetic influence on tester-rated infant temperament as assessed by Bayley's infant behavior record. *Developmental Psychology, 28,* 40–47.

Bray, J. H. (1988). Children's development during early remarriage. In E. M. Hetherington & J. D. Arasteh (Eds.), *Impact of divorce, single parenting and stepparenting on children* (pp. 279–298). Hillsdale, NJ: Erlbaum.

Bray, J. H. (1990). *Developmental issues in stepfamilies: Research project final report.* Unpublished manuscript.

Brazelton, T. (1978). Introduction. In A. Sameroff (Ed.), *Organization and stability of newborn behavior. Monographs of the Society for Research in Child Development, 43*(Serial No. 77).

Brazelton, T., Tronick, E., Lechtig, A., Lasky, R. E., & Klein, R. E. (1977). The behavior of nutritionally deprived Guatemalan infants. *Developmental Medicine and Child Neurology, 19,* 364–372.

Brodekamp, S. (1987). *Developmentally appropriate practice in early childhood programs serving children from birth through age 8.* Washington, DC: National Association for the Education of Young Children.

Bretherton, I. (1978). Making friends with one-year-olds: An experimental study of infant-stranger interaction. *Merrill-Palmer Quarterly, 24,* 29–51.

Bretherton, I., Stolberg, U., & Kreye, M. (1981). Engaging strangers in proximal interaction: Infants' social initiative. *Developmental Psychology, 17,* 746–755.

Brice-Heath, S. (1988). Language socialization. *New Directions for Child Development* (42) 29–41.

Bristol, M. (1987). Mothers of children with autism or communication disorders: Successful adaptations and the double ABCX model. *Journal of Autism and Developmental Disabilities, 17,* 469–486.

Bristol, M., Gallagher, J., & Schopler, E. (1988). Mothers and fathers of young developmentally disabled and nondisabled boys: Adaptation and spousal support. *Developmental Psychology, 24,* 441–451.

Broberg, A., Lamb, M., & Hwang, P. (1990). Inhibition: Its stability and correlates in sixteen- to forty-month-old children. *Child Development, 61,* 1153–1163.

Brody, J. (1988, December 16). Effeminacy and homosexuality. *The New York Times,* pp. 17 ff.

Brodzinsky, D. (1990). A stress and coping model of adoption and adjustment. In D. Brodzinsky & M. Schnecter (Eds.), *The psychology of adoption* (pp. 3–24). Oxford, England: Oxford University Press.

Brodzinsky, D., & Huffman, L. (1988). Transition to adoptive parenthood. *Marriage and Family Review, 12,* 267–286.

Bronfenbrenner, U. (1979). *The ecology of human development: Experiments by nature and design.* Cambridge, MA: Harvard University Press.

Bronfenbrenner, U., & Crouter, A. (1982). Work and family through time and space. In S. Kammerman & C. Hayes (Eds.), *Families that work: Children in a changing world.* Washington, DC: National Academy Press.

Brooks, J., & Lewis, M. (1976). Infants' responses to strangers: Midget, adult, and child. *Child Development, 47,* 323–332.

Brooks-Gunn, J., Boyer, C., & Hein, K. (1988). Preventing HIV infection and AIDS in children and adolescents. *American Psychologist, 43,* 958–964.

Brooks-Gunn, J., & Furstenberg, F., Jr. (1989). Adolescent sexual behavior. *American Psychologist, 44,* 249–257.

Brooks-Gunn, J., & Lewis, M. (1982). Affective exchanges between normal and handicapped infants and their mothers. In T. Field & A. Fogel (Eds.), *Emotion and early interaction.* Hillsdale, NJ: Erlbaum.

Brooks-Gunn, J., & Lewis, M. (1984). The development of visual self-recognition. *Developmental Review, 4,* 215–239.

Brooks-Gunn, J., & Reiter, E. (1990). The role of pubertal processes. In S. Feldman & G. Elliott (Eds.), *At the threshold: The developing adolescent* (pp. 16–53). Cambridge, MA: Harvard University Press.

Brooks-Gunn, J., & Warren, M. (1987, March). *Biological contributions to affective expression in young adolescent girls.* Paper presented at the biennial meeting of the Society for Research in Child Development, Baltimore, MD.

Brophy, J. E. (1983). Research on the self-fulfilling prophecy and teacher expectations. *Journal of Educational Psychology, 75,* 631–661.

Broughton, J. (1978). Development of concepts of self, mind, reality, and knowledge. *New Directions for Child Development, 1,* 75–100.

Brown, A. L., Bransford, J. D., Ferrara, R. A., & Campione, J. C. (1983). Learning, remembering, and understanding. In J. H. Flavell & E. M. Markman (Eds.), *Handbook of child psychology: Vol. 3. Cognitive development* (pp. 77–166). New York: Wiley.

Brown, A. L., & Campione, J. C. (1972). Recognition memory for perceptually similar pictures in preschool children. *Journal of Experimental Psychology, 95,* 55–62.

Brown, B. (1990). Peer groups. In S. Feldman & G. Elliott (Eds.), *At the threshold: The developing adolescent* (pp. 171–196). Cambridge, MA: Harvard University Press.

Brown, J. V., Bakeman, R., Snyder, P. A., Frederickson, W. T., Morgan, S. T., & Hepler, R. (1975). Interactions of black inner-city mothers with their newborn infants. *Child Development, 46,* 677–686.

Brown, P., & Elliott, R. (1965). Control of aggression in a nursery school class. *Journal of Experimental Child Psychology, 2,* 103–107.

Brown, R. (1966). Organ weight in malnutrition with special reference to brain weight. *Developmental Medicine and Child Neurology, 8,* 512–522.

Brown, R. (1968). The development of *wh* questions in child speech. *Journal of Verbal Learning and Verbal Behavior, 7,* 279–290.

Brown, R. (1977). An examination of visual and verbal coding processors in preschool children. *Child Development, 48,* 38–45.

Brownell, C. (1986). Covergent developments: Cognitive-developmental correlates of growth in infant/toddler peer skills. *Child Development, 57,* 275–286.

Brownell, C. (1990). Peer social skills in toddlers: Competencies and constraints illustrated by same-age and mixed-age interaction. *Child Development, 61,* 838–848.

Bruner, J. S. (1973). *Beyond the information given: Studies in the psychology of knowing.* New York: Norton.

Buchanan, C. M., Maccoby, E., & Dornbusch, S. M. (1992). Adolescents and their families after divorce: Three residential arrangements compared. *Journal of Research on Adolescence, 2*(3), 261–291.

Buck, G., Michalek, A., Kramer, A., & Batt, R. (1991). Labor and delivery events and risk of sudden infant death syndrome. *American Journal of Epidemiology, 133,* 900–906.

Bugental, D., Blue, J., & Lewis, J. (1990). Caregiver beliefs and dysphoric affect directed to difficult children. *Developmental Psychology, 26,* 631–638.

Buhrmester, D., & Furman, W. (1990). Perceptions of sibling relationships during middle childhood and adolescence. *Child Development, 61,* 1387–1398.

Bullock, M., Gelman, R., & Baillargeon, R. (1982). The development of causal reasoning. In W. Friedman (Ed.), *The developmental psychology of time* (pp. 209–254). New York: Academic.

Burleson, B. R., Delia, J. D., & Applegate, J. L. (1992). Effects of maternal communication and children's social-cognitive and communication skills on children's acceptance by the peer group. *Family Relations, 41,* 264–272.

Burns, A. (1992, spring). Mother-headed families: An international perspective and the case of Australia. *SRCD Social Policy Report, 6,* 1–22.

Bush, P. J., Zuckerman, A. E., Theiss, P. K., Taggart, V. S., Horowitz, C., Sheridan, M. J., & Walter, H. J. (1989). Cardiovascular risk factor prevention in black schoolchildren: Two-year results of the "know your body" program. *American Journal of Epidemiology, 129*(3), 466–482.

Bushnell, E., & Boudreau, J. (1993). Motor development and the mind: The potential role of motor abilities as a determinant of aspects of perceptual development. *Child Development, 64,* 1005–1021.

Buss, A. H., & Plomin, R. (1984). *Temperament: Early developing personality traits.* Hillsdale, NJ: Erlbaum.

Butler, J. A., Starfield, V., & Stenmark, S. (1984). Child health policy. In H. W. Stevenson & A. W. Siegel (Eds.), *Child development research in social policy* (Vol. 1, pp. 110–188). Chicago: University of Chicago Press.

Butler, N. R., & Goldstein, H. (1973). Smoking in pregnancy and subsequent child development. *British Medical Journal, 4,* 573–575.

Butler, R. (1989a). Interest in the task and interest in peers' work in competitive and noncompetitive conditions: A developmental study. *Child Development, 60,* 562–570.

Butler, R. (1989b). Mastery versus ability appraisal: A developmental study of children's observations of peers' work. *Child Development, 60,* 1350–1361.

Butler, R. (1990). The effects of mastery and competitive conditions on self-assessment at different ages. *Child Development, 61,* 201–210.

Cain, V. S., & Hofferth, S. L. (1989, February). Parental choice of self-care for school-age children. *Journal of Marriage and the Family, 51,* 65–77.

Cairns, R. B., Cairns, B. D., Neckerman, H. J., Ferguson, L. L., & Gariépy, J.-L. (1989). Growth and aggression: 1. Childhood to early adolescence. *Developmental Psychology, 25*(2), 320–330.

Calvert, S. L., & Huston, A. (1987). Television and children's gender schema. In L. Liben & M. Signorella (Eds.), *Children's gender schemata: New directions for child development* (No. 38). San Francisco: Jossey-Bass.

Calvert, S. L., & Watkins, B. A. (1979, April). *Recall of television content as a function of content type and level of production feature use.* Paper presented at the biennial meeting of the Society for Research in Child Development, San Francisco.

Camara, K., & Resnick, G. (1988). Interparental conflict and cooperation. In E. M. Hetherington & J. D. Arasteh (Eds.), *Impact of divorce, single parenting, and stepparenting on children* (pp. 169–195). Hillsdale, NJ: Erlbaum.

Camp, B. W., & Bash, M. A. (1981). *Think aloud: Increasing social and cognitive skills—A problem-solving program for children.* Champaign, IL: Research Press.

Camp, B. W., Blom, G. E., Herbert, F., & van Doorninck, W. J. (1977). "Think aloud": A program for developing self-control in young aggressive boys. *Journal of Abnormal Child Psychology, 5*(2), 157–169.

Campbell, S. (1979). Mother-infant interactions as a function of maternal ratings of temperament. *Child Psychiatry and Human Development, 10,* 67–76.

Campos, J., Barrett, K., Lamb, M., Goldsmith, H., & Stenberg, C. (1983). Socioemotional development. In J. Campos & M. Haith (Eds.), *Handbook of child psychobiology: Vol. 2. Infancy and psychobiology* (pp. 783–916). New York: Wiley.

Campos, J., Bertenthal, B., & Kermoian, R. (1992). Early experience and emotional development: The emergence of wariness of heights. *Psychological Science, 1,* 61–64.

Campos, J., & Stenberg, C. (1981). Perception, appraisal and emotion: The onset of social referencing. In M. Lamb & L. R. Sherrod (Eds.), *Infant social cognition.* Hillsdale, NJ: Erlbaum.

Camras, L. (1992). A dynamical systems perspective on expressive development. In K. Strongman (Ed.), *International review of studies on emotion.* New York: Wiley.

Camras, L., Oster, H., Campos, J., Miyake, K., & Bradshaw, D. (1992). Japanese and American infants' responses to arm restraint. *Developmental Psychology, 28,* 578–583.

Camras, L., & Sachs, V. (1991). Social referencing and caretaker expressive behavior in a day care setting. *Infant Behavior and Development, 14,* 27–36.

Cantor, D. S., Fischel, J. E., & Kaye, H. (1983). Neonatal conditionability: A new paradigm for exploring the use of interceptive cues. *Infant Behavior and Development, 6,* 403–413.

Cantwell, D. P. (1975). Genetic studies of hyperactive children. In R. Fieve, D. Rosenthal, & H. Brill (Eds.), *Genetic research in psychiatry*. Baltimore, MD: Johns Hopkins University Press.

Capaldi, D. M., & Patterson, G. R. (1991). Relation of parental transitions to boys' adjustment problems: I. A linear hypothesis. II. Mothers at risk for transitions and unskilled parenting. *Developmental Psychology, 27,* 489–504.

Caplan, G. (1974). *Support systems and community mental health: Lectures on concept development.* New York: Behavioral Publications.

Capron, C., & Duyme, M. (1989). Assessment of effects of socioeconomic status on IQ in a full crossfostering study. *Nature, 340,* 552–554.

Carew, J. V. (1979, April). *Observation study of caregivers and children in daycare homes: Preliminary results from home observations.* Paper presented at the biennial meeting of the Society for Research in Child Development, San Francisco.

Carey, S. (1977). The child as word learner. In M. Halle, J. Bresnan, & G. A. Miller (Eds.), *Linguistic theory and psychological reality.* Cambridge: Massachusetts Institute of Technology Press.

Carlson, D., & Labarba, R. (1979). Maternal emotionality during pregnancy and reproductive outcome: A review of the literature. *International Journal of Behavioral Development, 2,* 343–376.

Carr, M., Borkowski, J. G., & Maxwell, S. E. (1991). Motivational components of underachievement. *Developmental Psychology, 27*(1), 108–118.

Carson J., & Parke, R. (1993, March). *Sociometric status differences in affect sequences in preschool children's play with parents.* Paper presented at the biennial meeting of the Society for Research in Child Development, New Orleans, LA.

Carver, J., Pimentael, B., Cox, W., & Barness, L. (1991). Dietary nucleotide effects upon immune function in infants. *Pediatrics, 88,* 359–363.

Case, R. (1985). *Intellectual development: Birth to adulthood.* New York: Academic.

Cassano, P., Koepsell, T., & Farwell, J. (1990). Risk of febrile seizures in childhood in relation to prenatal cigarette smoking and alcohol intake. *American Journal of Epidemiology, 132,* 462–473.

Cassidy, J., Parke, R., Butkowsky, L., & Braungart, J. (1992). Family-peer connections: The role of emotional expressiveness within the family and children's understanding of emotions. *Child Development, 63,* 603–618.

Cazden, C. (1968). The acquisition of noun and verb inflections. *Child Development, 39,* 433–448.

Ceci, S., Ross, D., & Toglia, M. (1987). Suggestibility of children's memory: Psychological implications. *Journal of Experimental Psychology: General, 116,* 38–49.

Cernoch, J., & Porter, R. (1985). Recognition of maternal axillary odors by infants. *Child Development, 56,* 1593–1599.

Chance, N. (1984). Growing up in a Chinese village. *Natural History, 93,* 72–81.

Chandler, M. (1987). The Othello effect: Essay on the emergence and eclipse of skeptical doubt. *Human Development, 30,* 137–159.

Chapman, M. (1977). Father absence, stepfathers, and the cognitive performance of college students. *Child Development, 48,* 1152–1154.

Chase-Lansdale, P. L., & Owen, M. (1987). Maternal employment in a family context: Effect on infant-mother and infant-father attachment. *Child Development, 58,* 1505–1512.

Chavez, A., & Martinez, C. (1984). Behavioral measurements of activity in children and their relation to food intake in a poor community. In E. Pollitt & P. Amante (Eds.), *Energy intake and activity* (pp. 303–321). New York: Liss.

Chen, C., & Stevenson, H. W. (1989). Homework: A cross-cultural examination. *Child Development, 60,* 551–561.

Chen, X., & Rubin, K. H. (1992). Correlates of peer acceptance in a Chinese sample of six-year-olds. *International Journal of Behavioral Development 15* (2), 259–273.

Chen, X., Rubin, K. H., & Sun, Y. (1992). Social reputation and peer relationships in Chinese and Canadian children: A cross-cultural study. *Child Development 63*(6), 1336–1343.

Cherlin, A. J. (1981). *Marriage, divorce, remarriage: Changing patterns in the postwar United States.* Cambridge, MA: Harvard University Press.

Cherlin, A. J., Chase-Lansdale, P. L., Furstenberg, F., Jr., Kiernan, K., Robins, P. K., Morrison, D. R., & Teitler, J. O. (1991, April). *How much of the effects of divorce on children occurs before the separation? Longitudinal evidence from Great Britain and the United States.* Paper presented at the meeting of the Society for Research in Child Development, Seattle, WA.

Cherlin, A. J., Furstenberg, F., Jr., Chase-Lansdale, P. L., Kiernan, K. E., Robins, P. K., Morrison, D. R., & Teitler, J. O. (1991). Longitudinal studies of effects of divorce on children in Great Britain and the United States. *Science, 252,* 1386–1389.

Chess, S., & Thames, A. (1984). *Origins and evolution of behavior disorders from infancy to early adult life.* New York: Brunner/Mazel.

Chi, M. T. H. (1978). Knowledge structure and memory development. In R. Siegler (Ed.), *Children's thinking: What develops?* (pp. 73–96). Hillsdale, NJ: Erlbaum.

Children's Defense Fund (1987). *A children's defense budget, FY 1988: An analysis of our nation's investment in children.* Washington, DC: Author.

Chilmonczyk, B., Knight, G., Palomaki, G., Pulkkinen, A., Williams, J., & Haddow, J. (1990). Environmental tobacco smoke exposure during infancy. *American Journal of Public Health, 80,* 1205–1208.

Chodorow, N. (1974). Family structure and feminine personality. In M. Z. Rosaldo & L. Lamphere (Eds.), *Women, culture and society.* Stanford, CA: Stanford University Press.

Chodorow, N. (1978). *The reproduction of mothering: Psychoanalysis and the sociology of gender.* Berkeley: University of California Press.

Chu, S., Buehler, J., Oxtoby, M., & Kilbourne, B. (1991). Impact of human immunodeficiency virus epidemic on mortality in children in the United States. *Pediatrics, 87,* 806–810.

Chun, R., Pawsat, R., & Forster, F. (1960). Social localization in infancy. *Journal of Nervous and Mental Diseases, 130,* 472–476.

Cicchetti, D. (1990). The organization and coherence of socioemotional, cognitive and representational development: Illustrations through a developmental psychopathology perspective on Down syndrome and child maltreatment. In R. Thompson (Ed.), *Nebraska Symposium on Motivation: Vol. 36. Socioemotional development* (pp. 259–366). Lincoln, NE: University of Nebraska Press.

Cicchetti, D., & Barnett, D. (1991). Attachment organization in maltreated preschoolers. *Development and Psychopathology, 3,* 397–411.

Cicchetti, D., & Beeghly, M. (Eds.). (1990). *Children with Down syndrome: A developmental perspective.* New York: Cambridge University Press.

Cicchetti, D., & Sroufe, L. (1976). The relationship between affective and cognitive development in Down's syndrome infants. *Child Development, 46,* 920–929.

Clark, E. (1983). Meanings and concepts. In J. Flavell and E. Markman (Eds.), *Handbook of child psychology: Vol. III. Cognitive development* (pp. 789–837). New York: Wiley.

Clark, E., Gellman, S. A., & Lane, N. M. (1985). Compound nouns and category structure in young children. *Child Development, 56,* 84–94.

Clarke-Stewart, A. (1992). Consequences of child care for children's development. In A. Booth (Ed.), *Child care in the 1990s* (pp. 63–82). Hillsdale, NJ: Erlbaum.

Clarke-Stewart, K. A. (1973). Interactions between mothers and their young children: Characteristics and consequences. *Monographs of the Society for Research in Child Development, 38* (6–7, Serial No. 153).

Clarke-Stewart, K.A. (1973). *A review of research and some propositions for policy: Child care in the family.* New York: Academic.

Clarke-Stewart, K. A. (1980). Observation and experiment: Complementary strategies for studying day care and social development. In S. Kilmer (Ed.), *Advances in early education and day care.* Greenwich, CT: JAI Press.

Clarke-Stewart, K. A. (1989). Infant day care: Maligned or malignant? *American Psychologist, 44,* 266–273.

Clarke-Stewart, K. A., & Fein, G. G. (1983). Early childhood programs. In J. Campos & M. Haith (Eds.), *Handbook of child psychology: Vol. 2. Infancy and developmental psychobiology* (pp. 917–999). New York: Wiley.

Cochran, M. M., & Brassard, J. A. (1979). Child development and personal social networks. *Child Development, 50,* 601–616.

Cohen, D. (1991). Finding meaning in one's self and others: Clinical studies of children with autism and Tourette's syndrome. In F. S. Kessel, M. Bornstein, and A. J. Sameroff (Eds.), *Contemporary constructions of the child* (pp. 159–175). Hillsdale, NJ: Erlbaum.

Cohen, D., Stern, V., & Balaban, N. (1983). *Observing and recording the behavior of young children* (3rd ed.). New York: Teachers College Press.

Cohen, L. B. (1972). Attention-getting and attention-holding processes of infant visual preferences. *Child Development, 43,* 869–879.

Cohen, L. B., DeLoache, J. S., & Strauss, M. S. (1979). Infant perceptual development. In J. D. Osofsky (Ed.), *Handbook of infant development.* New York: Wiley.

Cohen, R., Stevenson, D., et al. (1982). Favorable results of neonatal intensive care for very low birthweight infants. *Pediatrics, 69,* 621–625.

Cohn, D. A. (1990). Child-mother attachment of six-year-olds and social competence at school. *Child Development, 61,* 152–162.

Cohn, J., Campbell, S., Matias, R., & Hopkins, J. (1990). Face-to-face interactions of postpartum depressed and nondepressed mother-infant pairs at 2 months. *Developmental Psychology, 26,* 15–24.

Cohn, J., Campbell, S., & Ross, S. (1991). Infant response in the still-face paradigm at 6 months predicts avoidant and secure attachment at 12 months. *Development and Psychopathology, 3,* 367–376.

Coie, J., Dodge, K., & Kupersmidt, J. (1990). Peer group behavior and social status. In S. Asher & J. Coie (Eds.), *Peer rejection in childhood: Origins, consequences and intervention* (pp. 17–59). New York: Cambridge University Press.

Coie, J., Dodge, K., Terry, R., & Wright, V. (1991). The role of aggression in peer relations: An analysis of aggression episodes in boys' play groups. *Child Development, 62,* 812–826.

Colby, A., Kohlberg, L., Gibbs, J., & Lieberman, M. (1993). A longitudinal study of moral judgment. *Monographs of the Society for Research in Child Development, 48*(Serial No. 200).

Cole, D. A. (1991). Change in self-perceived competence as a function of peer and teacher evaluation. *Developmental Psychology, 27*(4), 682–688.

Coll, C., Halpern, L., Vohr, B., Seifer, R., & Oh, W. (1992). Stability and correlates of change of early temperament in preterm and full-term infants. *Infant Behavior and Development, 15,* 137–153.

Colletta, N. D. (1983). At risk for depression: A study of young mothers. *Journal of Genetic Psychology.*

Collin, M., Halsey, C., & Anderson, C. (1991). Emerging developmental sequelae in the "normal" extremely low birthweight infant. *Pediatrics, 88,* 115–120.

Collins, W. (1984). Introduction. In W. Collins (Ed.), *Development during middle childhood* (pp. 1–23). Washington, DC: National Academy Press.

Condon, J., & Watson, T. (1987). The maternity blues: Exploration of a psychological hypothesis. *Acta Psychiatrica Scandavia, 76,* 164–171.

Condry, J. (1989). *The psychology of television.* Hillsdale, NJ: Erlbaum.

Condry, J., Bence, P., & Scheibe, C. (1988). Nonprogram content of children's television. *Journal of Broadcasting and Electronic Media, 32,* 255–270.

Conger, J. J. (1977). *Adolescence and youth* (2nd ed.). New York: Harper & Row.

Conger, J. J., & Miller, W. C. (1966). *Personality, social class and delinquency.* New York: Wiley.

Conger, R., Conger, K., Elder, G., Lorenz, F., Simons, R., & Whitbeck, L. (1992). A family process model of economic hardship and adjustment of early adolescent boys. *Child Development, 63*(3), 526–541.

Connell, J. (1981). *A model of the relationships among children's self-related cognitions, affects, and academic achievement.* Unpublished doctoral dissertation, University of Denver, Denver, CO.

Connor, J. M., & Serbin, L. A. (1977). Behaviorally based masculine- and feminine-activity-preference scales for preschoolers: Correlates with other classroom behaviors and cognitive tests. *Child Development, 48,* 1411–1416.

Connor, J. M., & Serbin, L. A. (1978). Children's responses to stories with male and female characters. *Sex Roles, 4,* 637–646.

Conway, E., & Brackbill, Y. (1970). Delivery medication and infant outcome: An empirical study. In W. A. Bowes, Jr., Y. Brackbill, E. Conway, & A. Steinschneider (Eds.), The effects of obstetrical medication on fetus and in-fant. *Monographs of the Society for Research in Child Development, 35*(Serial No. 137, pp. 24–34).

Cooper, R., & Aslin, R. (1990). Preference for infant-directed speech in the first month after birth. *Child Development, 61,* 1584–1595.

Coopersmith, S. (1967). *The antecedents of self-esteem.* San Francisco: Freeman.

Corby, D. G. (1978). Aspirin in pregnancy: Maternal and fetal effects. *Pediatrics, 62*(Suppl.), 930–937.

Costabile, A. (1991). Cross-national comparison of how children distinguish serious and playful fighting. *Developmental Psychology, 27*(5), 881–887.

Coste, J., Job-Spira, N., & Fernandez, H. (1991). Increased risk of ectopic pregnancy with maternal cigarette smoking. *American Journal of Public Health, 81,* 199–201.

Coster, W., Gersten, M., Beeghly, M., & Cicchetti, D. (1989). Communicative functioning in maltreated toddlers. *Developmental Psychology, 25,* 1020–1029.

Cotterell, J. (1986). Work and community influence on the quality of childrearing. *Child Development, 57,* 362–374.

Cowan, C., & Cowan, P. (1992). *When parents become partners.* New York: Basic Books.

Cowen, E. L., Pederson, A., Babijian, H., Izzo, L. D., & Trost, M. A. (1973). Long-term follow-up of early detected vulnerable children. *Journal of Consulting and Clinical Psychology, 41,* 438–446.

Cowen, E. L., Pedro-Carroll, J. L., & Alpert-Gillis, L. J. (1990). Relationships between support and adjustment among children of divorce. *Journal of Child Psychology and Psychiatry, 31*(5), 727–735.

Cox, M., Owen, M., Henderson, V., & Margand, N. (1992). Prediction of infant-father and infant-mother attachment. *Developmental Psychology, 28*(3), 474–483.

Cox, M., Owen, M., Lewis, J., & Henderson, V. (1989). Marriage, adult adjustment and early parenting. *Child Development, 60,* 1015–1024.

Craven, R. G., Marsh, H. W., & Debus, R. L. (1991). Effects of internally focused feedback and attributional feedback on enhancement of academic self-concept. *Journal of Educational Psychology, 83*(1), 17–27.

Cravioto, J., & DeLicardie, E. (1970). Mental performance in school aged children. *American Journal of Diseases of Children, 120,* 404.

Cravioto, J., & DeLicardie, E. (1976). Microenvironmental factors in severe protein-energy malnutrition. In N. Scrimshaw & M. Behar (Eds.), *Nutrition and agricultural development: Significance and potential for the tropics* (pp. 25–35). New York: Plenum.

Crawley, S., & Spiker, D. (1983). Mother-child interactions involving 2-year-olds with Downs syndrome: A look at individual differences. *Child Development, 54,* 1312–1323.

Crittenden, P. M. (1988). Relationships at risk. In J. Belsky & T. Nezworski (Eds.), *Clinical implications of attachment* (pp. 136–174). Hillsdale, NJ: Erlbaum.

Crockenberg, S. (1987). Predictors and correlates of anger toward and punitive control of toddlers by adolescent mothers. *Child Development, 58,* 964–975.

Crockenberg, S. (1992, April). How children learn to resolve conflicts in families. *Zero to Three.*

Crockenberg, S., & Litman, C. (1990). Autonomy as competence in 2-year-olds: Maternal correlates of child defiance, compliance, and self-assertion. *Developmental Psychology, 26*(6), 961–971.

Crook, C. (1987). Taste and olfaction. In P. Salapatek & L. Cohen (Eds.), *Handbook of infant perception* (Vol. 1, pp. 237–260). New York: Academic.

Cross, W. (1978). The Thomas and Cook models of psychological nigrescence: A literature review. *Journal of Black Psychology, 4,* 13–31.

Crouter, A. C., MacDermid, S. M., McHale, S. M., & Perry-Jenkins, M. (1990). Parental monitoring and perceptions of children's school performance and conduct in dual- and single-earner families. *Developmental Psychology, 26*(4), 649–657.

Crowell, J., & Feldman, S. (1988). Mothers' internal working models of relationships and children's behavioral and developmental status: A study of mother-child interaction. *Child Development, 59,* 1273–1285.

Crowell, J., & Feldman, S. (1991). Mothers' working models of attachment relationships and mother and child behavior during separation and reunion. *Developmental Psychology, 27,* 597–605.

Csikszentmihalyi, M., & Larson, R. (1984). *Being adolescent.* New York: Basic Books.

Cummings, E. M., Ballard, M., El-Sheikh, M., & Lake, M. (1991). Resolution and children's responses to interadult anger. *Developmental Psychology, 27*(3), 462–470.

Cummings, E. M., Iannotti, R., & Zahn-Waxler, C. (1985). Influence of conflict between adults on the emotions and aggression of young children. *Developmental Psychology, 21,* 495–507.

Cvetkovich, G., Grote B., Bjorseth, A., & Sarkissian, J. (1975). On the psychology of adolescents' use of contraceptives. *Journal of Sex Research, 11,* 256–270.

Dahl, R., et al. (1989). The effects of prenatal marijuana exposure: Evidence of EEG sleep disturbances continuing through 3 years of age. *Journal of Developmental and Behavioral Pediatrics, 10,* 264.

Damon, W. (1977). *The social world of the child.* San Francisco: Jossey-Bass.

Daniels, D., Dunn, J., Furstenberg, F., Jr., & Plomin, R. (1985). Environmental differences within the family and adjustment differences within pairs of adolescent siblings. *Child Development, 56,* 764–774.

Das, R., & Berndt, T. (1992). Relations of preschoolers' social acceptance to peer ratings and self-perceptions. *Early Education and Development, 3,* 221–231.

Davidson, R. (1992). Emotion and affective style: Hemispheric substrates. *Psychological Science, 3,* 39–43.

Davie, R., Butler, N., & Goldstein, H. (1972). *From birth to seven: The second report of the child development study (1958 cohort)*. London: Longman & National Children's Bureau.

Davis, D. (1991, March 1). Fathers and fetuses. *The New York Times*.

Davison, A., & Dobbing, J. (1966). Myelination as a vulnerable period in brain development. *British Medical Bulletin, 22,* 40–44.

Dawson, D., & Cain, V. (1990). Child care arrangements. In *Advance data: Vital and health statistics of the National Center for Health Statistics* (p. 187). Hyattsville, MD: National Center for Health Statistics.

Dawson, D. A. (1991). Family structure and children's health and well-being: Data from the 1988 National Health Interview Survey on Child Health. *Journal of Marriage and the Family, 53.*

Day, N., Richardson, G., Robles, N., Sambamoorthi, U., Taylor, P., Scher, M., Stoffer, D., Jasperse, D., & Cornelius, M. (1990). Effect of prenatal alcohol exposure on growth and morphology of offspring at 8 months of age. *Pediatrics, 85,* 748–752.

Day, N., Robles, N., Richardson, G., Geva, D., Taylor, P., Scher, M., Stoffer, D., Cornelius, M., & Goldschmidt, L. (1991a). Effect of prenatal alcohol use on the growth of children at three years of age. *Alcoholism: Clinical and Experimental Research, 15,* 67–71.

Day, N., Sambamoorthi, U., Taylor, P., Richardson, G., Robles, N., Jhon, Y., Scher, M., Stoffer, D., Cornelius, M., & Jasperse, D. (1991b). Prenatal marijuana use and neonatal outcome. *Neurotoxicology and Teratology, 13,* 329–334.

DeCasper, A., & Fifer, W. (1980). Of human bonding: Newborns prefer their mothers' voices. *Science, 208,* 1174–1176.

DeCasper, A., & Spence, M. (1986). Prenatal maternal speech influences newborns' perception of speech sounds. *Infant Behavior and Development, 9,* 133–150.

DeLisi, R., & Gallagher, A. (1991). Understanding of gender stability and constancy in Argentinian children. *Merrill-Palmer Quarterly, 37,* 483–502.

DeLoache, J. (1991). Symbolic functioning in very young children: Understanding of pictures and models. *Child Development, 62,* 736–752.

Demo, D. H. (1992). Parent-child relations: Assessing recent changes. *Journal of Marriage and the Family, 54.*

Denham, S., & McKinley, M. (1993). Sociometric nominations of preschoolers: A psychometric analysis. *Early Education and Development, 4,* 108–122.

Denham, S., McKinley, M., Couchoud, E., & Holt, R. (1990). Emotional and behavioral predictors of preschool peer ratings. *Child Development, 61,* 1145–1152.

Denham, S., Renwick, S., & Holt, R. (1991). Working and playing together: Prediction of preschool social-emotional competence from mother-child interaction. *Child Development, 62,* 242–249.

Dennis, W. (1940). Infant reactions to restraint. *Transactions of the New York Academy of Science, 2,* 202–217.

Dennis, W. (1960). Causes of retardation among institutional children: Iran. *Journal of Genetic Psychology, 96,* 46–60.

DePaulo, B. M., Tang, J., Webb, W., Hoover, C., Marsh, K., & Litowitz, C. (1989). Age differences in reactions to help in a peer tutoring context. *Child Development, 60,* 423–439.

Desor, J. A., Maller, O., & Greene, L. S. (1977). Preferences for sweet in humans: Infants, children and adults. In J. M. Weiffenbach (Ed.), *Task and development: The genesis of sweet preference.* Bethesda, MD: National Institute of Dental Research.

De Villier, P., & Forsyth, C. (1988). The downward mobility of divorced women and dependent children. *Sociological Spectrum, 8,* 295–302.

DeVries, R. (1969). Constancy of gender identity in the years three to six. *Society for Research in Child Development Monographs, 34*(3, Serial No. 127).

Dewei, L. (1989). The effect of role change on intellectual ability and on the ability self-concept in Chinese children. *American Journal of Community Psychology, 17,* 73–81.

Diamond, J. (1992). *The third chimpanzee: The evolution and future of the human animal.* New York: Harper-Collins.

Diaz, R. (1985). Bilingual cognitive development. *Child Development, 56,* 1376–1388.

Diaz, R., & Berndt, T. (1982). Children's knowledge of a best friend: Fact or fancy? *Developmental Psychology, 18,* 787–794.

Dickstein, S., & Parke, R. D. (1988). Social referencing in infancy: A glance at fathers and marriage. *Child Development, 59,* 506–511.

DiClemente, R. (1990). The emergence of adolescents as a risk group for human immunodeficiency virus infection. *Journal of Adolescent Research, 5,* 7–17.

DiClemente, R., Boyer, C., & Morales, E. (1988). Minorites and AIDS: Knowledge, attitudes, and misconceptions among black and Latino adolescents. *American Journal of Public Health, 78,* 55–57.

DiLalla, L. F., Thompson, L. A., Plomin, R., Phillips, K., Fagan, J. F., Haith, M. M., Cyphers, L. H., & Fulker, D. W. (1990). Infant predictors of preschool and adult IQ: A study of in-fant twins and their parents. *Developmental Psychology, 17,* 50–58.

DiPietro, J. A. (1981). Rough and tumble play: A function of gender. *Developmental Psychology, 17,* 50–58.

Dittrichova, J. (1969). Development of sleep in infancy. In R. J. Robinson (Ed.), *Brain and Early Behavior.* New York: Academic.

Dix, T., & Grusec, J. (1983). Parent attribution processes in child socialization. In I. Siegal (Ed.), *Parental belief systems* (pp. 201–233). Hillsdale, NJ: Erlbaum.

Dix, T., & Reinhold, D. P. (1991). Chronic and temporary influences on mothers' attributions for children's disobedience. *Merrill-Palmer Quarterly, 37,* 251–271.

Dix, T., Ruble, D. N., & Zambarano, R. J. (1989). Mothers' implicit theories of discipline: Child effects, parent effects, and the attribution process. *Child Development, 60,* 1373–1391.

Dobbing, J. (1964). The influence of early malnutrition on the development of myelination of the brain. *Proceedings of the Royal Society of London, 159*(Series B), 503–509.

Dodge, K. (1982). Social information processing variables in the development of aggression and altruism in children. In C. Zahn-Waxler, M. Cummings, & M. Radke-Yarrow (Eds.), *The development of altruism and aggression: Social and sociobiological origins.* New York: Cambridge University Press.

Dodge, K. (1986). A social information-processing model of social competence in children. In M. Perlmutter (Ed.), *Minnesota Symposia on Child Psychology* (Vol. 18, pp. 77–125). Hillsdale, NJ: Erlbaum.

Dodge, K., Bates, J., & Petit, G. (1990). Mechanisms in the cycle of violence. *Science, 250,* 1678–1683.

Dodge, K., Coie, J., Pettit, G., & Price, J. M. (1990). Peer status and aggression in boys' groups: Developmental and contextual analyses. *Child Development, 61,* 1289–1309.

Dodge, K., Price, J. M., Coie, J., & Christopoulos, C. (1990). On the development of aggressive dyadic relationships in boys' peer groups. *Human Development, 33,* 260–270.

Doescher, S., & Suganara, A. (1992). Impact of prosocial home- and school-based interventions on preschool children's cooperative behavior. *Family Relations, 41,* 200–204.

Dollaghan, C. (1985). Child meets word: "Fast mapping" in preschool children. *Journal of Speech and Hearing Research, 28,* 449–454.

Dornbusch, S., Ritter, P., Liederman, P., Roberts, D., & Fraleigh, M. (1987). The relation of parenting style to adolescent school performance. *Child Development, 58,* 1244–1257.

Downey, G., & Coyne, J. (1990). Children of depressed parents: An integrative review. *Psychological Bulletin, 108,* 50–76.

Drake, C. T., & McDougall, D. (1977). Effects of the absence of a father and other male models on the development of boys' sex roles. *Developmental Psychology, 13,* 537–538.

Dreyer, P. (1982). Sexuality during adolescence. In B. Wolman (Ed.), *Handbook of developmental psychology* (pp. 559–601). Englewood Cliffs, NJ: Prentice-Hall.

Dromi, E. (1987). *Early lexical development.* Cambridge, England: Cambridge University Press.

Dubow, E. F., & Tisak, J. (1989). The relation between stressful life events and adjustment in elementary school children: The role of social support and social problem-solving skills. *Child Development, 60,* 1412–1423.

Dubowitz, H. (1989). Prevention of child maltreatment. *Pediatrics, 83,* 570–577.

Dudley, J. R. (1991). Increasing our understanding of divorced fathers who have infrequent contact with their children. *Family Relations, 40,* 279–285.

Duncan, P., Ritter, P., Dornbusch, S., Gross, R., & Carlsmith, J. (1985). The effects of pubertal timing on body image, school behavior, and deviance. *Journal of Youth and Adolescence, 14,* 227–236.

Duncan, S., & Markman, H. (1988). Intervention programs for the transition to parenthood. In G. Michals & W. Goldberg (Eds.), *The transition to parenthood* (pp. 270–310). New York: Cambridge University Press.

Dunham, P., & Dunham, F. (1992). Lexical development during middle infancy: A mutually-driven infant-caregiver process. *Developmental Psychology, 28,* 414–420.

Dunn, J. (1983). Sibling relationships in early childhood. *Child Development, 54,* 787–811.

Dunn, J. (1985). *Sisters and brothers.* Cambridge, MA: Harvard University Press.

Dunn, J., Brown, J., & Beardsall, L. (1991). Family talk about feeling states and children's later understanding of others' emotions. *Developmental Psychology, 27,* 448–455.

Dunn, J., & Kendrick, C. (1982). *Siblings: Love, envy, and understanding.* Cambridge, MA: Harvard University Press.

Dunn, J., Stocker, C., & Plomin, R. (1990). Nonshared experiences within the family: Correlates of behavioral problems in middle childhood. *Development and Psychopathology, 2,* 113–126.

Durrant, J. E., Cunningham, C. E., & Voelker, S. (1990). *Journal of Educational Psychology, 82*(4), 657–663.

Dweck, C. S. (1975). The role of expectations and attributions in the alleviation of learned helplessness. *Journal of Personality and Social Psychology, 31,* 674–685.

Dweck, C. S., Davidson, W., Nelson, S., & Enna, B. (1978). Sex differences in learned helplessness: II. The contingencies of evaluative feedback in the classroom. III. An experimental analysis. *Developmental Psychology, 14,* 268–276.

Dweck, C. S., & Elliot, E. S. (1983). Achievement motivation. In F. M. Hetherington (Ed.), *Handbook of child psychology: Vol. 4. Socialization, personality, and social development* (pp. 643–692). New York: Wiley.

Dweck, C. S., Goetz, T. E., & Strauss, N. (1980). Sex differences in learned helplessness: IV. An experimental

and naturalistic study of failure generalization and its mediators. *Journal of Personality and Social Psychology, 38,* 441–452.

Dyer, E. (1963). Parenthood as crisis: A restudy. *Marriage and Family Living, 25,* 488–496.

Dyson, S. E., & Jones, D. G. (1976). Undernutrition and the developing nervous system. *Progress in Neurobiology, 7,* 171–196.

East, P. L., & Rook, K. S. (1992). Compensatory patterns of support among children's peer relationships: A test using school friends, nonschool friends, and siblings. *Developmental Psychology, 28,* 163–172.

Easterbrooks, M. A. (1988). Effects of infant risk status on the transition to parenthood. In G. Michals & W. Goldberg (Eds.), *The transition to parenthood* (pp. 176–208). New York: Cambridge University Press.

Eckerman, C. O., Davis, C. C., & Didow, S. M. (1989). Toddlers' emerging ways of achieving social coordination with a peer. *Child Development, 60,* 440–453.

Eckerman, C. O., & Whatley, J. L. (1975). Infants' reactions to unfamiliar adults varying in novelty. *Developmental Psychology, 11,* 562–567.

Edelman, B., & Maller, O. (1982). Facts and fictions about infantile obesity. *International Journal of Obesity, 6,* 69–81.

Eder, D. (1985). The cycle of popularity: Interpersonal relations among female adolescents. *Sociology of Education, 58,* 154–165.

Eder, R. A. (1990). Uncovering young children's psychological selves: Individual and developmental differences. *Child Development, 61,* 849–863.

Edwards, C., & Whiting, B. (1988). *Children of different worlds.* Cambridge, MA: Harvard University Press.

Egeland, B., Jacobvitz, D., & Papatola, K. (1987). Intergenerational continuity of abuse. In R. Gelles & J. Lancaster (Eds.), *Child abuse and neglect: Biosocial dimensions* (pp. 255–276). New York: Aldine.

Eggebeen, D., & Lichter, D. (1991). Race, family structure and changing poverty among American children, 1960–1988. *American Sociological Review, 56,* 801–817.

Eisenberg, N. (1992). *The caring child.* Cambridge, MA: Harvard University Press.

Eisenberg, R. (1970). The organization of auditory behavior. *Journal of Speech and Hearing, 13,* 454–471.

Eisenberg-Berg, N., & Neal, C. (1979). Children's moral reasoning about their own spontaneous presocial behavior. *Developmental Psychology, 15,* 228–229.

Ekman, P. (1971). Universals in cultural differences in facial expressions of emotion. In J. K. Cole (Ed.), *Nebraska Symposium on Motivation* (Vol. 19, pp. 1–32). Lincoln: University of Nebraska Press.

Elkind, D. (1978). Understanding the young adolescent. *Adolescence, 13,* 127–134.

Elkind, D. (1981). *The hurried child.* New York: Addison-Wesley.

Elkind, D. (1986). *Miseducation: Preschoolers at risk.* New York: Knopf.

Ellis, G., & Petersen, L. (1992). Socialization values and parental control techniques: A cross-cultural analysis of child-rearing. *Journal of Comparative Family Studies, 23,* 39–54.

Elmen, J., DeFrain, J., & Fricke, J. (1987, March). *A nationwide comparison of divorced parents with sole vs. joint custody.* Paper presented at the biennial meeting of the Society for Research in Child Development, Baltimore, MD.

Emde, R., Gaensbauer, T., & Harmon, R. (1976). Emotional expression in infancy: A biobehavioral study. *Psychological Issues, 10*(37).

Emde, R., Plomin, R., Robinson, J., Corley, R., DeFries, J., Fulker, D., Reznick, J. S., Campos, J., Kagan, J., & Zahn-Waxler, C. (1992). Temperament, emotion, and cognition at 14 months. *Child Development, 63*(6), 1437–1455.

Engel, M., & Keane, W. (1975, April). *Black mothers and their infant sons: Antecedents, correlates, and predictors of cognitive development in the second and sixth year of life.* Paper presented at the biennial meeting of the Society for Research in Child Development, Denver, CO.

Engfer, A. (1988). The interrelatedness of marriage and the mother-child relationship. In R. Hinde and J. Stevenson-Hinde (Eds.), *Relationships within families* (pp. 104–118). Oxford, England: Oxford University Press.

Engle, P. (1991). Maternal work and child-care strategies in peri-urban Guatemala: Nutritional effects. *Child Development, 62,* 954–965.

Enns, J. T. (Ed.). (1990). *The development of attention: Research and theory.* New York: North Holland.

Erickson, M., Egeland, B., & Sroufe, L. (1985). The relationship between quality of attachment and behavior problems in a high-risk sample. In I. Bretherton & E. Waters (Eds.), Growing point in attachment theory and research. *Monographs of the Society for Research in Child Development, 50* (1–2, Serial No. 209).

Erikson, E. (1963). *Childhood and society* (2nd ed.). New York: Norton.

Erikson, E. (1980). *Identity and the life cycle.* New York: Norton. (Original work published 1959)

Ervin-Tripp, S. (1970). Discourse agreement: How children answer questions. In J. R. Hayes (Ed.), *Cognition and the development of language.* New York: Wiley.

Etaugh, C., Grinell, K., & Etaugh, A. (1989). Development of gender labelling. *Sex Roles, 21,* 769–775.

Eveleth, P. (1986). Population differences in growth. In F. Falkner & J. Tanner (Eds.), *Human growth* (pp. 221–239). New York: Plenum.

Eveleth, P., & Tanner, J. (1976). *Worldwide variation in human growth.* New York: Cambridge University Press.

Eyer, D. (1993). *Mother-infant bonding: A scientific fiction.* New Haven, CT: Yale University Press.

Fabes, R., Fultz, J., Eisenberg, N., May-Plumlee, T., & Christopher, F. S. (1989). Effects of rewards on children's prosocial motivation. *Developmental Psychology, 25,* 509–515.

Fagan, J., III (1992). Intelligence: A theoretical viewpoint. *Current Directions in Psychological Science, 1,* 82–86.

Fagan, J., III, & Knevel, C. (1989, April). *The prediction of above-average intelligence from infancy.* Paper presented at the biennial meeting of the Society for Research in Child Development, Kansas City, MO.

Fagan, J. F. (1976). Infants' recognition of invariant features of faces. *Child Development, 47,* 627–638.

Fagot, B. (1977). Consequences of moderate cross-gender behavior in preschool children. *Child Development, 48,* 902–907.

Fagot, B., Leinbach, M., & O'Boyle, C. (1992). Gender labelling, gender stereotyping, and parenting behaviors. *Developmental Psychology, 28,* 225–230.

Fajardo, B., Browning, M., Fisher, D., & Paton, J. (1990). Effect of nursery environment on state regulation in very-low-birth-weight premature infants. *Infant Behavior and Development, 13,* 287–303.

Fantz, R. L. (1963). Pattern vision in newborn infants. *Science, 140,* 296–297.

Fantz, R. L. (1965). Visual perception from birth as shown by pattern selectivity. *Annals of the New York Academy of Sciences, 118,* 793–814.

Farkas, G., Grobe, R. P., Sheehan, D., & Shuan, Y. (1990). Cultural resources and school success: Gender, ethnicity, and poverty groups within an urban school district. *American Sociological Review, 55,* 127–142.

Feagans, L., & Haskins, R. (1986). Neighborhood dialogues of black and white 5-year-olds. *Journal of Applied Developmental Psychology, 7,* 181–200.

Fein, G. G. (1979). Play and the acquisition of symbols. In L. Katz (Ed.), *Current topics in early childhood education.* Norwood, NJ: Ablex.

Fein, G. G. (1991). Bloodsuckers, blisters, cooked babies, and other curiosities: Affective themes in pretense. In F. S. Kessel, M. H. Bornstein, & A. J. Sameroff (Eds.), *Contemporary constructions of the child* (pp. 143–157). Hillsdale, NJ: Erlbaum.

Feiring, C., Fox, N., Jaskir, J., & Lewis, M. (1987). The relation between social support, infant risk status and mother-infant interaction. *Developmental Psychology, 23,* 400–405.

Feiring, C., & Lewis, M. (1991). The development of social networks from early to middle childhood: Gender differences and the relation to school competence. *Sex Roles, 25,* 237–253.

Feldman, S., & Gehring, T. (1988). Changing perceptions of family cohesion and power across adolescence. *Child Development, 59,* 1034–1045.

Feldman, S., & Wentzel, K. R. (1990). Relations among family interaction patterns, classroom self-restraint, and academic achievement in preadolescent boys. *Journal of Educational Psychology, 82,* 813–819.

Fenster, L., Eskenazi, B., Windham, G., & Swan, S. (1991). Caffeine consumption during pregnancy and fetal growth. *American Journal of Public Health, 81,* 458-461.

Fernald, A. (1993). Approval and disapproval: Infant responsiveness to vocal affect in familiar and unfamiliar languages. *Child Development, 64,* 657-674.

Fernald, A., & Mazzie, C. (1991). Prosody and focus in speech to infants and adults. *Developmental Psychology, 27,* 209-221.

Fernald, A., & Morikawa, H. (1993). Common themes and cultural variations in Japanese and American mothers' speech to infants. *Child Development, 64,* 637-656.

Fernald, A., Taeschner, T., Dunn, J., Papousek, M., deBoysson-Bardies, B., & Fukui, I. (1989). A cross-language study of prosodic modifications in mothers' and fathers' speech to preverbal infants. *Journal of Child Language, 16,* 477-501.

Field, D. (1987). A review of preschool conservation training: An analysis of analyses. *Developmental Review, 7,* 210-251.

Field, T. (1982). Affective displays of high-risk infants during early interactions. In T. Field & A. Fogel (Eds.), *Emotion and interactions.* Hillsdale, NJ: Erlbaum.

Field, T. (1984). Separation stress of young children transferring to new schools. *Developmental Psychology, 20,* 786-792.

Field, T. (1991). Quality infant day-care and grade school behavior and performance. *Child Development, 62,* 863-870.

Field, T., Greenwald, P., Morrow, C., Healy, B., Foster, T., Guthertz, M., & Frost, P. (1992). Behavior state matching during interactions of preadolescent friends versus acquaintances. *Developmental Psychology, 28,* 242-250.

Field, T., Healy, B., Goldstein, S., & Guthertz, M. (1990). Behavior-state matching and synchrony in mother-infant interactions of nondepressed versus depressed dyads. *Developmental Psychology, 26,* 7-14.

Field, T., Healy, B., Goldstein, S., Perry, S., Bendell, D., Schanberg, S., Zimmerman, E. A., & Kuhn, C. (1988). Infants of depressed mothers show "depressed" behavior even with nondepressed adults. *Child Development, 59,* 1569-1579.

Field, T., Masi, W., Goldstein, S., & Parl, S. (1988). Infant day care facilitates preschool social behavior. *Early Childhood Research Quarterly, 3,* 341-359.

Field, T., Schanberg, S., Scafidi, F., Bauer, C., Vega-Lahr, N., Garcia, R., Nystrom, J., & Kuhn, C. (1986). Tactile/kinesthetic stimulation effects on preterm infants. *Pediatrics, 77,* 654-658.

Field, T., Widmayer, S. M., Stringer, S., & Ignatoff, E. (1980). Teenage, lower-class, black mothers and their preterm infants: An intervention and developmental follow-up. *Child Development, 51,* 426-436.

Field, T., Woodson, R., Greenberg, R., & Cohen, D. (1982). Discrimination and imitation of facial expressions by neonates. *Science, 218,* 179-181.

Fincham, F. D., Hododa, A., & Sanders, R., Jr. (1989). Learned helplessness, text anxiety, and academic achievement: A longitudinal analysis. *Child Development, 60,* 138-145.

Fine, M. (Ed.). (1980). *Intervention with hyperactive children.* New York: SP Medical and Scientific Books.

Fischer, K. (1983). Illuminating the processes of moral development. In A. Colby, L. Kohlberg, J. Gibbs, & M. Lieberman (Eds.), A longitudinal study of moral judgment. *Monographs of the Society for Research in Child Development, 48*(Serial No. 200).

Fischer, K. (1987). Relations between brain and cognitive development. *Child Development, 58,* 623-632.

Fischer, K., & Bidell, T. (1992, Winter). Even younger ages: Constructive use of nativist findings about early development. *SRCD Newsletter,* 1 ff.

Fischer, K., & Silvern, L. (1985). Stages and individual differences in cognitive development. *Annual Review of Psychology, 36,* 613-648.

Fischoff, B. (1988). Judgment and decision making. In R. Sternberg and E. Smith (Eds.), *The psychology of human thought* (pp. 153-187). New York: Cambridge Univeristy Press.

Fivush, R., Kuebli, J., & Clubb, P. (1992). The structure of events and event representation: A developmental analysis. *Child Development, 63,* 188-201.

Flavell, J. H. (1985). *Cognitive development* (2nd ed.). Englewood Cliffs, NJ: Prentice-Hall.

Flavell, J. H. (1988). The development of children's knowledge about the mind: From cognitive connections to mental representations. In J. W. Astington, P. L. Harris, & D. R. Olson (Eds.), *Developing theories of mind* (pp. 244-267). New York: Cambridge University Press.

Flavell, J. H., Flavell, E. R., & Green, F. L. (1989). A transitional period in the development of the appearance-reality distinction. *International Journal of Behavioral Development, 12,* 509-526.

Flavell, J. H., Green, F. L., & Flavell, E. (1986). Development of knowledge about the appearance-reality distinction. *Monographs of the Society for Research in Child Development, 51*(1, Serial No. 212).

Flavell, J. H., Mumme, D. L., Green, F. L., & Flavell, E. R. (1992). Young children's understanding of different types of beliefs. *Child Development, 63,* 960-977.

Floyd, F., & Zmich, D. (1991). Marriage and the parenting partnership. *Child Development, 62,* 1434-1448.

Fogel, A. (1979). Peer versus mother-directed behavior in one- to three-month-old infants. *Infant Behavior and Development, 2,* 215-226.

Fox, N., Kimmerly, N., & Schafer, W. (1991). Attachment to mother/attachment to father: A meta-analysis. *Child Development, 62,* 210-225.

Fraiberg, S. (1959). *The magic years.* New York: Scribner.

Fraiberg, S. (1977). *Every child's birthright.* New York: Basic Books.

Frankel, K., & Bates, J. (1990). Mother-toddler problem solving: Antecedents in attachment, home behavior and temperament. *Child Development, 61,* 810-819.

Frauenglass, M., & Diaz, R. (1985). Self-regulatory functions of children's private speech. *Developmental Psychology, 21,* 357-364.

Freedman, D. J. (1979). Ethnic differences in babies. *Human Nature,* 15-20.

French, D. C. (1990). Heterogeneity of peer-rejected girls. *Child Development, 61,* 2028-2031.

French, L. A. (1989). Young children's responses to "when" questions: Issues of directionality. *Child Development, 60,* 225-236.

Freud, S. (1938). *An outline of psychoanalysis.* London: Hogarth Press.

Fricker, H., & Segal, S. (1978). Narcotic addiction, pregnancy and the newborn. *American Journal of the Diseases of Children, 132,* 360–366.

Fried, P., & Watkinson, B. (1990). 36- and 48-month neurobehavioral follow-up of children prenatally exposed to marijuana, cigarettes and alcohol. *Developmental and Behavioral Pediatrics, 11,* 49–58.

Fried-Patti, S., & Finitzo, T. (1990). Language learning in a prospective study of otitis media with effusion in the first two years of life. *Journal of Speech and Hearing Research, 33,* 188–194.

Friedlander, B. Z., Wetstone, H. S., & Scott, C. S. (1974). Suburban preschool children's comprehension of an age-appropriate informational television program. *Child Development, 45,* 561–565.

Friedman, S., Zahn-Waxler, C., & Radke-Yarrow, M. (1982). Perceptions of cries of full-term and preterm infants. *Infant Behavior and Development, 5,* 161–173.

Friedrich, L. K., & Stein, A. H. (1973). Aggressive and prosocial television programs and the natural behavior of preschool children. *Monographs of the Society for Research in Child Development, 38*(Serial No. 151).

Frieze, I., Francis, W., & Hanusa, B. (1981). Defining success in classroom settings. In J. Levine & M. Wang (Eds.), *Teacher and student perceptions: Implications for learning* (pp. 3–28). Hillsdale, NJ: Erlbaum.

Frisch, H. L. (1977). Sex stereotypes in adult-infant play. *Child Development, 48,* 1671–1675.

Frodi, A., Lamb, M., Leavitt, L., Donovan, W., Neff, C., & Sherry, D. (1978). Fathers' and mothers' responses to the faces and cries of normal and premature infants. *Developmental Psychology, 14,* 490–498.

Furbey, L., & Beyth-Marom, R. (1990). *Risk taking in adolescence: A decision-making perspective.* Washington, DC: Carnegie Council on Adolescent Development.

Furstenberg, F., Jr. (1988). Child care after divorce and remarriage, In E. M. Hetherington & J. D. Arasteh (Eds.), *Impact of divorce, single parenting and stepparenting on children* (pp. 245–261). Hillsdale, NJ: Erlbaum.

Furstenberg, F., Jr., Moore, K., & Peterson, J. (1985). Sex education and sexual experience among adolescents. *American Journal of Public Health, 75,* 1331–1332.

Furstenberg, F., Jr., Morgan, S., & Allison, P. (1987). Paternal participation and children's well-being after marital dissolution. *American Sociological Review, 52,* 695–701.

Furth, H. G. (1971). Linguistic deficiency and thinking: Research with deaf subjects 1964–1969. *Psychological Bulletin, 76,* 58–72.

Galambos, N. L., & Maggs, J. L. (1991). Out-of-school care of young adolescents and self-reported behavior. *Developmental Psychology, 27*(4), 644–655.

Galler, J. (1984). Behavioral consequences of malnutrition in early life. In J. Galler (Ed.), *Nutrition and behavior* (pp. 63–117). New York: Plenum.

Galler, J., Ramsey, F., & Solimanon, G. (1984). The influence of early malnutrition on subsequent behavioral development: 3. Learning disabilities as a sequel to malnutrition. *Pediatric Research.*

Gandour, M. J. (1989). Activity level as a dimension of temperament in toddlers: Its relevance for the organismic specificity hypothesis. *Child Development, 60,* 1092–1098.

Garai, J. E., & Scheinfeld, A. (1968). Sex differences in mental and behavioral traits. *Genetic Psychology Monographs, 77,* 169–299.

Garbarino, J., Kostelny, K., & Dubrow, N. (1991). What children can tell us about living in danger. *American Psychologist, 46,* 376–383.

Garbarino, J., & Sherman, D. (1980). High-risk neighborhoods and high-risk families. *Child Development, 51,* 188–198.

Garcia, E. (1983). Becoming bilingual during early childhood. *International Journal of Behavioral Development, 6,* 375–404.

Garcia, E., Maez, L., & Gonzalez, G. (1981). *A national study of Spanish/English bilingualism in young Hispanic children of the United States* (Bilingual Education Paper Series 4, No. 12). Los Angeles: National Dissertation and Assessment Center, California State University.

Garcia, R. E., & Moodie, D. S. (1989). Routine cholesterol surveillance in childhood. *Pediatrics, 84,* 751–755.

Garcia Coll, C. (1990). Developmental outcome of minority infants: A process-oriented look into our begin-

nings. *Child Development, 61,* 270–289.

Gardner, H. (1980). *Artful scribbles: The significance of children's drawings.* New York: Basic Books.

Garfinkel, I., & McLanahan, S. (1989). *Single mothers and their children.* Washington, DC: Urban Institute Press.

Garn, S., & Clark, D. (1975). Nutrition, growth, development and motivation. *Pediatrics, 56,* 306–319.

Garner, R. (1987). *Metacognition and reading comprehension.* Norwood, NJ: Ablex.

Garrett, E. (1983, August). *Women's experiences of early parenthood: Expectations versus reality.* Paper presented at the annual meeting of the American Psychological Association, Anaheim, CA.

Garvey, C., & Hogan, R. (1973). Social speech and social interaction: Egocentrism revisted. *Child Development, 44,* 562–568.

Gath, A. (1978). *Down's syndrome and the family.* London: Academic.

Gelles, R. (1989). Child abuse and violence in single-parent families. *American Journal of Orthopsychiatry, 59,* 492–501.

Gelman, R. (1979). Preschool thought. *American Psychologist, 34,* 900–905.

Gelman, R. (1982). Accessing one-to-one correspondence: Still another paper on conservation. *British Journal of Psychology, 73,* 209–220.

Gelman, R., & Baillargeon, R. (1983). A review of some Piagetian concepts. In J. Flavell & E. M. Markman (Eds.), *Handbook of child psychology: Vol. 3. Cognitive development* (pp. 167–230). New York: Wiley.

Gelman, R., Bullock, M., & Meck, E. (1980). Preschoolers' understanding of simple object transformations. *Child Development, 51,* 691–699.

Gelman, R., & Gallistel, C. R. (1978). *The child's understanding of number.* Cambridge, MA: Harvard University Press.

Gelman, S. (1988). The development of induction within natural kind and artifact categories. *Cognitive Psychology, 20,* 65–95.

Gelsand, D., & Teti, D. (1993, March). *Helping housebound mothers fight depression: Evaluation of a home intervention program for mothers and infants.* Paper presented at the biennial meeting of the Society for Research in Child Development, New Orleans, LA.

General Accounting Office (1984). *WIC evaluations provide some favorable but no conclusive evidence on the effects expected for the special supplemental program for women, infants, and children* (PEMD-84-4). Washington, DC: U.S. Government Printing Office.

Gerbner, G., & Signorelli, N. (1990). *Violence profile, 1967 through 1988-89: Enduring patterns.* Unpublished manuscript, University of Pennsylvania, Annenberg School of Communications, Philadelphia.

Gesell, A., & Ames, L. B. (1937). Early evidence of individuality in the human infant. *Scientific Monthly, 45,* 217-255.

Gesell, A., & Ilg, F. (1946). *The child from five to ten.* New York: Harper & Row.

Gewirtz, J. (1979, April). *Maternal "attachment" outcomes.* Paper presented at the meeting of the Society for Research in Child Development, San Francisco.

Gewirtz, J., & Gewirtz, H. (1965). Caretaking settings, background events, and behavior differences in four Israeli child rearing environments: Some preliminary trends. In B. M. Foss (Ed.), *Determinants of infant behavior* (Vol. 4). London: Methuen.

Gibson, E. J. (1969). *Principles of perceptual learning and development.* New York: Appleton-Century-Crofts.

Gibson, E. J., & Walker, A. S. (1984). Development of knowledge of visual-tactual affordances of substance. *Child Development, 55,* 453-460.

Gilligan, C. (1982). *In a different voice: Psychological theory and women's development.* Cambridge, MA: Harvard University Press.

Glenn, N. D., & McLanahan, S. (1981). Children and marital happiness: A further specification of the relationship. *Journal of Marriage and the Family, 44,* 63-72.

Glick, P. (1989). The family life cycle and social change. *Family Relations, 38,* 123-129.

Glick, P., & Lin, S. (1986). Recent changes in divorce and remarriage. *Journal of Marriage and the Family, 48,* 737-747.

Globus, M., Loushman, W., Epstein, C., Halbasch, G., Stephens, J., & Hall, B. (1979). Prenatal genetic diagnosis in 3000 amniocenteses. *New England Journal of Medicine, 300,* 157-163.

Gnepp, J. (1989). Personalized inferences of emotions and appraisals: Component processes and correlates. *Developmental Psychology, 25,* 277-288.

Gnepp, J., & Gould, M. (1985). The development of personalized inferences: Understanding other people's emotional reactions in light of their experiences. *Child Development, 56,* 1455-1464.

Goduka, I. N., Poole, D. A., & Aotaki-Phenice, L. (1992). A comparative study of black South African children from three different contexts. *Child Development, 63,* 509-525.

Goldberg, S. (1978). Prematurity: Effects on parent-infant interaction. *Journal of Pediatric Psychology, 3,* 137-144.

Goldfield, B., & Reznick, J. (1990). Early lexical acquisition. *Journal of Child Language, 17,* 171-183.

Goldfield, B., & Snow, C. E. (1989). Individual differences in language acquisition. In J. B. Gleason (Ed.), *The development of language* (pp. 303-322). Columbus, OH: Merrill.

Goldman-Rakic, P. (1987). Development of cortical circuitry and cognitive function. *Child Development, 58,* 601-622.

Goldsmith, H. (1978). *Behavior-genetic analyses of early personality (temperament): Developmental perspectives from the longitudinal study of twins during infancy and early childhood.* Unpublished doctoral dissertation, University of Minnesota.

Goldsmith, H., Buss, A., Plomin, R., Rothbart, M., Thomas, A., Chess, S., Hinde, R., & McCall, R. (1987). Roundtable: What is temperament? Four approaches. *Child Development, 58,* 505-529.

Goldsmith, H., & Campos, J. (1990). The structure of temperamental fear and pleasure in infants. *Child Development, 61,* 1944-1964.

Goldsmith, H., & Gottesman, I. I. (1981). Origins of variation in behavioral style: A longitudinal study of temperament in young twins. *Child Development, 52,* 91-103.

Goodall, M. M. (1980). Left-handedness as an educational handicap. In R. S. Laura (Ed.), *Problems of handicap.* Melbourne: Macmillan.

Goodman, R., & Stevenson, J. (1989). A twin study of hyperactivity: II. The aetiological role of genes, family relationships and perinatal adversity. *Journal of Child Psychology and Psychiatry, 30,* 691-709.

Goosens, F., & van IJzendoorn, M. (1990). Quality of infants' attachment to professional caregivers. *Child Development, 61,* 832-837.

Gopnik, A., & Meltzoff, A. (1987). The development of categorization in the second year and its relation to other cognitive and linguistic developments. *Child Development, 58,* 1511-1523.

Gottfried, A. E. (1990). Academic intrinsic motivation in young elementary school children. *Journal of Educational Psychology, 82*(3), 525-538.

Gottfried, A. W. (Ed.) (1984). *Home environment and early cognitive development.* New York: Academic.

Gottfried, A. W., & Bathhurst, K. (1983). Hand preference across time is related to intelligence in young girls, not boys. *Science, 22,* 1074-1076.

Gottfried, A. W., Rose, S. A., & Bridger, W. H. (1977). Cross-model transfer in human infants. *Child Development, 48,* 118-123.

Gottlieb, B., & Pancer, S. (1988). Social networks and the transition to parenthood. In G. Michals & W. Goldberg (Eds.), *The transition to parenthood* (pp. 235-269). New York: Cambridge University Press.

Gottlieb, L. N., & Mendelson, M. J. (1990). Parental support and firstborn girls' adaption to the birth of a sibling. *Journal of Applied Developmental Psychology, 11,* 29-48.

Gottman, J. M. (1977). Toward a definition of social isolation in children. *Child Development, 48,* 513-517.

Gould, S. J. (1976). Human babies as embryos. *Natural History, 85,* 22-26.

Goyette, C. H., & Conners, C. K. (1977). *Food additives and hyperkinesis.* Paper presented at the annual meeting of the American Psychological Association.

Graham, S., & Barker, G. P. (1990). The down side of help: An attributional-developmental analysis of helping behavior as a low-ability cue. *Journal of Educational Psychology, 82,* 7-14.

Green, R. (1980). Homosexuality. In H. Kaplan, A. Freedman, & B. Sadock (Eds.), *Comprehensive textbook of psychiatry* (Vol. 2., 3rd ed.). Baltimore, MD: Williams & Wilkins

Green, R. (1987). *The "sissy boy" syndrome and the development of homosexuality.* New Haven, CT: Yale University Press.

Greenbaum, C. W., & Landau, R. (1982). The infant's exposure to talk by familiar people: Mothers, fathers, and siblings in different environments. In M. Lewis & L. Rosenblum (Eds.), *The social network of the developing child.* New York: Plenum.

Greenberg, D. (1971). Accelerating visual complexity levels in the human infant. *Child Development, 42,* 905–918.

Greenberg, M., & Morris, N. (1974). Engrossment: The newborn's impact upon the father. *American Journal of Orthopsychiatry, 44,* 520–531.

Greenberg, R., Bauman, K. E., Strecher, V. J., Keyes, L. L., Glover, L. H., Haley, N. J., Stedman, H. C., & Loda, F. A. (1991). Passive smoking during the first year of life. *American Journal of Public Health, 81,* 850–853.

Greenough, W., Black, J., & Wallace, C. (1987). Experience and brain development. *Child Development, 58,* 539–559.

Greer, D., Potts, R., Wright, J., & Huston, A. (1982). The effects of television commercial form and commercial placement on children's social behavior and attention. *Child Development, 53,* 611–619.

Grieser, T., & Kuhl, P. (1988). Maternal speech to infants in atonal language: Support for universal prosodic features in motherese. *Developmental Psychology, 24,* 14–20.

Griffen, H. (1984). The coordination of meaning in the creation of shared make believe reality. In I. Bretherton (Ed.), *Symbolic play* (pp. 73–100). New York: Academic.

Griffiths, P. (1987). Early vocabulary. In P. Fletcher & M. Garman (Eds.), *Language acquisition* (pp. 279–306). New York: Cambridge University Press.

Grolnick, W. S., & Ryan, R. M. (1989). Parent styles associated with children's self-regulation and competence in school. *Journal of Educational Psychology, 81,* 143–154.

Grolnick, W. S., Ryan, R. M., & Deci, E. L. (1991). Inner resources for school achievement: Motivational mediators of children's perceptions of their parents. *Journal of Educational Psychology, 83,* 508–517.

Grossman, K., & Grossman, K. E. (1982, March). *Maternal sensitivity to infants' signals during the first year as related to the year olds' behavior in Ainsworth's strange situation in a sample of Northern German families.* Paper presented at the meeting of the Inter-

national Conference on Infant Studies, Austin, TX.

Grossman, K., Grossman, K. E., Huber, F., & Wartner, U. (1981). German children's behavior towards their mothers at 12 months and their fathers at 18 months in Ainsworth's strange situation. *International Journal of Behavioral Development, 4,* 157–182.

Grossman, K., Scheurer-Englisch, H., & Stephen, C. (1989). *Attachment research: Lasting effects and domains of validity.* Paper presented at the tenth biennial meeting of the International Society for the Study of Behavioral Development, Jyväskylä, Finland.

Grusec, J., & Kuczynski, L. (1980). Direction of effect in socialization: A comparison of the parent's vs. the child's behavior as determinants of disciplinary techniques. *Developmental Psychology, 16,* 1–9.

Grusec, J., & Lytton, H. (1988). *Social development.* New York: Springer-Verlag.

Guardo, C. J., & Bohan, J. B. (1971). Development of a sense of self in children. *Child Development, 42,* 1909–1921.

Gunnar, M., Larson, M., Hertsgaard, L., Harris M., & Brodersen, L. (1992). The stressfulness of separation among nine-month-old infants. *Child Development, 63,* 290–303.

Gunnar, M., Mangelsdorf, S., Larson, M., & Hertsgaard, L. (1989). Attachment, temperament and adrenocortical activity in infancy. *Developmental Psychology, 25,* 355–363.

Guralnick, M. J., & Paul-Brown, D. (1977). The nature of verbal interactions among handicapped and non-handicapped preschool children. *Child Development, 48,* 254–260.

Gutmann, D. (1975). Parenthood: A key to the comparative study of the life cycle. In N. Datan & L. Ginsberg (Eds.), *Life-span developmental psychology: Normative life crisis.* New York: Academic.

Hann, N., Smith, M., & Block, J. (1968). Moral reasoning of young adults: Political-social behavior, family background, and personality correlates. *Journal of Personality of Social Psychology, 10,* 183–201.

Habicht, J., Yarbrough, C., Lectis, A., & Klein, R. (1974). Relation of maternal

supplementary feeding during pregnancy to birth weight and other sociobiological factors. In M. Winick (Ed.), *Nutrition and fetal development* (pp. 127–145). New York: Wiley.

Hack, M., Breslau, N., Weissman, B., Aram, D., Klein, N., & Borawski, E. (1991). Effect of very low birth weight and subnormal headsize on cognitive abilities at school age. *New England Journal of Medicine, 325,* 231–237.

Hackel, L., & Ruble, D. (1992). Changes in the marital relationship after the first baby is born: Predicting the impact of expectancy disconfirmation. *Journal of Personality and Social Psychology, 62,* 944–957.

Hadeed, A., & Siegel, S. (1989). Maternal cocaine use during pregnancy: Effect on the newborn infant. *Pediatrics, 84,* 205–210.

Hafetz, E. (1976). Parameters of sexual maturity in man. In E. Hafetz (Ed.), *Perspectives in human reproduction: Vol. 3. Sexual maturity: Physiological and clinical parameters.* Ann Arbor, MI: Ann Arbor Science Publishers.

Hagekull, B., & Bohlin, G. (1990). Early infant temperament and maternal expectations related to maternal adaptation. *International Journal of Behavioral Development, 13,* 199–214.

Hagen, J. W. (1967). The effect of distraction on selective attention. *Child Development, 38,* 685–694.

Haglund, B., & Cnattingius, S. (1990). Cigarette smoking as a risk factor for sudden infant death syndrome. *American Journal of Public Health, 80,* 29–32.

Haith, M. (1978). Visual competence in early infancy. In R. Held, H. Leibowitz, & H. Teuber (Eds.), *Handbook of sensory physiology* (Vol. 8, pp. 311–356). New York: Springer-Verlag.

Haith, M. (1980). *Rules that babies look by.* Hillsdale, NJ: Erlbaum.

Haith, M. (1981). Gratuity, perception-action integration and future orientation in infant vision. F. Kessel, A. Sameroff, & M. Bornstein (Eds.), *Contemporary constructions of the child: Essays in honor of William Kessen* (pp. 23–43). Hillsdale, NJ: Erlbaum.

Haith, M., Bergman, T., & Moore, M. (1977). Eye contact and face scanning in early infancy. *Science, 198,* 853–855.

Hakita, K., & Garcia, E. (1989). Bilingualism and education. *American Psychologist, 44,* 374–379.

Halford, G. (1989). Reflections on 25 years of Piagetian cognitive developmental psychology, 1963–1988. *Human Development, 32,* 325–387.

Hall, J. A., & Halberstadt, A. G. (1980). Masculinity and femininity in children: Development of the Children's Personal Attitude Questionnaire. *Developmental Psychology, 16,* 270–280.

Hall, W., Bartlet, E., & Hughes, A. (1988, winter). Patterns of information requests. *New Directions for Child Development, 42,* 43–58.

Halliday, M. A. K. (1975). *Learning how to mean–Explorations in the development of language.* London: Edward Arnold.

Halpern, E., Corrigan, R., & Aviezer, O. (1983). In, on, and under: Examining the relationship between cognitive and language skills. *International Journal of Behavioral Development, 6,* 153–166.

Hamilton, V. L., Blumenfeld, P. C., Akoh, H., & Miura, K. (1989a). Citizenship and scholarship in Japanese and American fifth grades. *American Educational Research Journal, 26,* 42–72.

Hamilton, V. L., Blumenfeld, P. C., Akoh, H., & Miura, K. (1989b). Japanese and American children's reasons for the things they do in school. *American Educational Research Journal, 26,* 545–571.

Handler, A., Kistin, N., Davis, F., & Ferre, C. (1991). Cocaine use during pregnancy: Perinatal outcomes. *American Journal of Epidemiology, 133,* 818–825.

Hann, D. (1989). A systems conceptualization of the quality of mother-infant interaction. *Infant Behavior and Development, 12,* 251–263.

Hanna, E., & Meltzoff, A. N. (1989, April). *Peer imitation in the second year of life.* Paper presented at the biennial meeting of the Society for Research in Child Development, Kansas City, MO.

Hanson, S., Myers, D., & Ginsberg, A. (1987). The role of responsibility and knowledge in reducing teenage out-of-wedlock childbearing. *Journal of Marriage and the Family, 49,* 241–256.

Hapgood, C., Elkind, G., & Wright, J. (1988). Maternity blues. *Australian and New Zealand Journal of Psychiatry, 22,* 299–306.

Hardy-Brown, K., Plomin, R., & DeFries, J. (1981). Genetic and environmental influences on the rate of communicative development in the first year of life. *Developmental Psychology, 17,* 704–717.

Harkness, S., & Super, C. M. (1992). Childcare in Kenya. In M. Lamb, K. J. Sternberg, C. P. Hwang, & A. G. Broberg (Eds.), *Childcare in context: Cross-cultural perspectives* (pp. 419–476). Hillsdale, NJ: Erlbaum.

Harlap, S., Shiono, P. H., & Ramcharan, S. (1979). Alcohol and spontaneous abortions. *American Journal of Epidemiology, 110,* 372.

Harlow, H. F., & Zimmermann, R. (1959). Affectional responses in the infant monkey. *Science, 130,* 421–432.

Harris, P. (1983). Infant cognition. In M. Harth & J. Campos (Eds.), *Handbook of child psychology: Vol. 2. Infancy and developmental psychology* (pp. 689–782). New York: Wiley.

Hart, C., Charlesworth, R., Burts, D., & DeWolf, M. (1993, March). *The relationship of attendance in developmentally appropriate or inappropriate kindergarten classrooms to first and second grade behavior.* Paper presented at the biennial meeting of the Society for Research in Child Development, New Orleans, LA.

Hart, C., DeWolf, D., Wozniak, P., & Burts, D. (1992). Maternal and paternal disciplinary styles: Relations with preschoolers' playground behavioral orientations and peer status. *Child Development, 63,* 879–892.

Hart, C., Ladd, G., & Burleson, B. (1990). Children's expectations of the outcomes of social strategies: Relations with sociometric status and maternal disciplinary styles. *Child Development, 61,* 127–137.

Harter, S. (1982). Children's understanding of multiple emotions: A cognitive-developmental approach. In W. Overton (Ed.), *The relationship between social and cognitive development.* Hillsdale, NJ: Erlbaum.

Harter, S. (1983). Developmental perspectives on the self system. In E. M. Hetherington (Ed.), *Handbook of child psychology: Vol. 4. Socialization, personality, and social development* (pp. 275–386). New York: Wiley.

Harter, S. (1990). Identity and self development. In S. Feldman & G. Elliott (Eds.), *At the threshold: The developing adolescent* (pp. 352–387). Cambridge, MA: Harvard University Press.

Harter, S., & Connell, J. (1982). A comparison of alternative models of the relationships between academic achievement and children's perceptions of competence, control, and motivational orientation. In J. Nicholls (Ed.), *The development of achievement-related cognitions and behaviors.* Greenwich, CT: JAI Press.

Harter, S., Waters, P., Pettit, L., & Jordan, J. (1993, March). *Autonomy and connectedness as dimensions of relationship styles in adult women and men.* Paper presented at the biennial meeting of the Society for Research in Child Development, New Orleans, LA.

Hartup, W. (1983). Peer relations. In E. M. Hetherington (Ed.), *Handbook of child psychology: Vol. 4. Socialization, personality, and social development* (pp. 103–196). New York: Wiley.

Hartup, W., Moore, S. G., & Sager, G. (1963). Avoidance of inappropriate sex-typing by young children. *Journal of Consulting Psychology, 27,* 467–473.

Harwood, R. (1992). The influence of culturally derived values on Anglo and Puerto Rican mothers' perceptions of attachment behavior. *Child Development, 63,* 822–839.

Haskett, G. J. (1971). Modifications of peer preferences of first-grade children. *Developmental Psychology, 4,* 429–433.

Haskett, M., & Kistner, J. (1991). Social interactions and peer perceptions of young physically abused children. *Child Development, 62,* 979–990.

Hawley, T., & Disney, E. (1992). Crack's children: The consequences of maternal cocaine abuse. *SRCD Social Policy Report, 6,* 1 ff.

Hay, D. F., Nash, A., & Pederson, J. (1983). Interaction between six-month-old peers. *Child Development, 54,* 557–562.

Hay, D. F., & Rheingold, H. L. (1979). *The early appearance of some valued social behaviors.* Unpublished manuscript, State University of New York at Stony Brook.

Hayes, C. (Ed.). (1987). *Risking the future: Adolescent sexuality, pregnancy, and childbearing.* Washington, DC: National Academy Press.

Hayes, D. S. (1978). Cognitive bases for liking and disliking among preschool children. *Child Development, 49,* 906–909.

Healy, J. M., Jr., Malley, J. E., & Stewart, A. J. (1990, October). Children and their fathers after parental separation. *American Journal of Orthopsychiatry, 60*(4), 531–543.

Heckhausen, H. (1981). The development of achievement motivation. In W. Hartup (Ed.), *Review of child development research* (Vol. 6, pp. 600–668). Chicago: University of Chicago Press.

Hein, K. (1988). *AIDS in adolescence: A rationale for concern.* Washington, DC: Carnegie Council on Adolescent Development.

Henker, B., & Whalen, C. K. (1989). Hyperactivity and attention deficits. *American Psychologist, 44*(2), 216–223.

Henneberger (1993, May 16). *The New York Times,* p. A1.

Hess, R., Chih-Mei, C., & McDevitt, T. (1987). Cultural variations in family beliefs about children's performance in mathematics: Comparisons among People's Republic of China, Chinese-American, and Caucasian-American families. *Journal of Educational Psychology, 79,* 179–188.

Hetherington, E. M. (1979). Divorce: A child's perspective. *American Psychologist, 34,* 851.

Hetherington, E. M. (1988). Parents, children and siblings six years after divorce. In R. Hinde and J. Stevenson-Hinde (Eds.), *Relationships within families* (pp. 311–331). Cambridge, MA: Cambridge University Press.

Hetherington, E. M. (1989). Coping with family transitions: Winners, losers, and survivors. *Child Development, 60,* 1–14.

Hetherington, E. M., et al. (1992). Coping with family transitions: A family systems perspective. *Monographs of the Society for Research in Child Development, 57*(Serial No. 227).

Hetherington, E. M., & Camara, K. (1984). Families in transition: The processes of dissolution and reconstitution. In R. Parke (Ed.), *Review of child development research* (Vol. 7, pp. 398–440). Chicago: University of Chicago Press.

Hetherington, E. M., Cox, M., & Cox, R. (1978a). The aftermath of divorce. In J. H. Stevens, Jr., & M. Matthew (Eds.), *Mother-child, father-child relations* (pp. 149–176). Washington, DC: National Association for the Education of Young Children.

Hetherington, E. M., Cox, M., & Cox, R. (1978b, May). Family interaction and social, emotional and cognitive development of children following divorce. In *The Family: Setting Priorities.* Symposium sponsored by the Institute for Pediatric Service of the Johnson & Johnson Baby Company, Washington, DC.

Hetherington, E. M., Cox, M., & Cox, R. (1982). Effects of divorce on parents and children. In M. Lamb (Ed.), *Nontraditional families* (pp. 233–288). Hillsdale, NJ: Erlbaum.

Hetherington, E. M., Cox, M., & Cox, R. (1985). Long-term effects of divorce and remarriage on the adjustment of children. *Journal of the American Academy of Psychiatry, 24,* 518–530.

Hetherington, E. M., Stanley-Hagan, M., & Anderson, E. R. (1989). Marital transitions: A child's perspective. *American Psychologist, 44,* 303–312.

Heyman, G. D., Dweck, C. S., & Cain, K. M. (1992). Young children's vulnerability to self-blame and helplessness: Relationship to beliefs about goodness. *Child Development, 63,* 401–415.

Heyns, B. (1982). *Summer learning and the effects of schooling.* New York: Academic.

Higgins, A., & Turnure, J. (1984). Distractibility and concentration of attention in children's development. *Child Development, 44,* 1799–1810.

Hinds, M. (1993, November 27). Volunteers line "safe corridor" for schoolchildren. *The New York Times.*

Hines, M. (1982). Prenatal gonadal hormones and sex differences in human behavior. *Psychological Bulletin, 92,* 56–80.

Hinshaw, S. P. (1992). Externalizing behavior problems and academic underachievement in childhood and adolescence: Casual relationships and underlying mechanisms. *Psychological Bulletin, 111,* 127–155.

Hirsch, H., & Spinelli, D. (1970). Visual experience modifies distribution of horizontally and vertically oriented receptive field in cats. *Science, 168,* 869–871.

Hirsch-Pasek, K., Hyson, M., & Rescorla, L. (1990). Academic environments in preschool. *Early Education and Development, 1,* 401–424.

Hirschberg, L. M., & Svejda, M. (1990). When infants look to their parents: I. Infants' social referencing of mothers compared to fathers. *Child Development, 61,* 1175–1186.

Ho, H. Z. (1987). Interaction of early caregiving environment and infant developmental status in predicting subsequent cognitive performance. *British Journal of Developmental Psychology, 5,* 183–191.

Hobbs, D., & Wimbish, J. (1977). Transition to parenthood by black couples. *Journal of Marriage and the Family, 39,* 677–689.

Hofer, M. (1981). *The roots of human behavior.* San Francisco: Freeman.

Hoff-Ginsberg, E. (1991, April). *Mother-child conversations in different social classes and communicative settings.* Paper presented at the biennial meeting of the Society for Research in Child Development, Seattle, WA.

Hofferth, S. L. (1992). The demand for and supply of child care in the 1990s. In A. Booth (Ed.), *Child care in the 1990s: Trends and consequences* (pp. 3–25). Hillsdale, NJ: Erlbaum.

Hoffman, H., Damus, K., Hillman, L., & Krongrad, E. (1988). Risk factors for SIDS. In P. Schwartz, D. Southall, & M. Valdes-Dapena (Eds.), Sudden infant death syndrome: Cardiac and respiratory mechanisms and interventions (pp. 13–31). *Annals of the New York Academy of Science, 533.*

Hoffman, L. W. (1963). Mother's enjoyment of work and effects on the child. In F. I. Nye & L. W. Hoffman (Eds.), *The employed mother in America.* Chicago: Rand McNally.

Hoffman, L. W. (1974). Effects of maternal employment on the child: A review of the research. *Developmental Psychology, 10,* 204–228.

Hoffman, L. W. (1979). Maternal employment. *American Psychologist, 34,* 859–865.

Hoffman, L. W. (1983). Work, family, and the socialization of the child. In R. Parke (Ed.), *Review of child development research: Vol. 7. The family* (pp. 223–282). Chicago: University of Chicago Press.

Hoffman, L. W. (1991). The influence of the family environment on personality: Accounting for sibling differences. *Psychological Bulletin, 110,* 187–203.

Hoffman, M. L. (1970). Moral development. In P. H. Mussen (Ed.), *Carmichael's manual of child psychology* (Vol. 2). New York: Wiley.

Hoffman-Plotkin, D., & Twentyman, C. T. (1984). A multimodal assessment of behavioral and cognitive deficits in abused and neglected preschoolers. *Child Development, 55,* 794–802.

Holden, G., & Ritchie, K. (1991). Linking extreme marital discord, child rearing and child behavior problems. *Child Development, 62,* 311–327.

Holloway, S. (1988). Concepts of ability and effort in Japan and the United States. *Review of Educational Research, 58,* 327–345.

Holstein, C. (1972). The relation of children's moral judgment level to that of their parents and to communication patterns in the family. In R. Smart & M. Smart (Eds.), *Readings in child development and relationships.* New York: Macmillan.

Hong, G., & Hong, L. (1991). Comparative perspectives on child abuse and neglect: Chinese versus Hispanics and whites. *Child Welfare, 70,* 463–475.

Hong, K., & Townes, B. (1976). Infants' attachment to inanimate objects. *Journal of the American Academy of Child Psychiatry, 15,* 49–61.

Honig, A., & Pollock, B. (1990). Effects of a brief intervention program to promote prosocial behavior in young children. *Early Education and Development, 1,* 438–444.

Hook, E. (1980). Genetic counseling dilemmas: Down syndrome, paternal age, and recurrence risk after remarriage. *American Journal of Medical Genetics, 5,* 145.

Hoopes, J. (1982). *Prediction in child development: A longitudinal study of adoptive and nonadoptive families.* New York: Child Welfare League of America.

Hopkins, B., & Westra, T. (1988a). Maternal expectations of their infants' development: Some specific cultural differences. *Developmental Medicine and Child Neurology, 31,* 384–390.

Hopkins, B., & Westra, T. (1988b). Maternal handling and motor development: An intracultural study. *Genetic, Social and General Psychology, 31,* 377–408.

Hopkins, B., & Westra, T. (1990). Motor development, maternal expectation, and the role of handling. *Infant Behavior and Development, 13,* 117–122.

Hopkins, J., Marcus, M., & Campbell, S. (1984). Postpartum depression: A critical review. *Psychological Bulletin, 95,* 498–515.

Hossain, A., & Roopnarine, J. (1993). African-American fathers' involvement with infants. *Infant Behavior and Development, 16.*

Howard, J. (1978). The influence of children's developmental dysfunctions on marital quality and family interaction. In R. Lerner & G. Spanier (Eds.), *Child influence on marital and family interaction.* New York: Academic.

Howe, N. (1991). Sibling-directed internal state language, perspective taking, and affective behavior. *Child Development, 62,* 1503–1512.

Howes, C. (1987). Social competence with peers in young children: Developmental sequences. *Developmental Review, 7,* 252–272.

Howes, C. (1988). Peer interaction in young children. *Monographs of the Society for Research in Child Development, 53*(1, Serial No. 217).

Howes, C. (1990). Can the age of entry into child care and the quality of child care predict adjustment in kindergarten? *Developmental Psychology, 26,* 292–303.

Howes, C. (1991). A comparison of preschool behaviors with peers when children enroll in child care as infants or older children. *Journal of Reproductive and Infant Psychology, 9,* 105–116.

Howes, C., & Hamilton, C. (1992). Children's relationships with caregivers. *Child Development, 63,* 859–866.

Howes, C., & Matheson, C. (1992). Sequences in the development of competent play with peers: Social and social pretend play. *Developmental Psychology, 28,* 961–974.

Howes, C., Phillips, D., & Whitebook, N. (1990). Thresholds of quality. *Child Development, 63,* 449–460.

Howes, C., Rodning, C., Galluzzo, D., & Myers, L. (1988). Attachment and child care: Relationships with mother and caregiver. *Early Childhood Research Quarterly, 3,* 403–416.

Howes, C., Unger, O., & Matheson, C. (1990). *The collaborative construction of pretend.* Paper presented at the International Conference on Infant Studies, Toronto.

Howes, C., Unger, O., & Seidner, L. B. (1989). Social pretend play in toddlers: Parallels with social play and with solitary pretend. *Child Development, 60,* 77–84.

Howes, C., & Wu, F. (1990). Peer interactions and friendships in an ethnically diverse school setting. *Child Development, 61,* 537–541.

Howes, P., & Markman, H. (1989). Marital quality and child functioning. *Child Development, 60,* 1044–1051.

Howes, P., & Markman, H. (1991, April). *Longitudinal relations between premarital and prebirth adult interaction and subsequent parent-child attachment.* Paper presented at the biennial meeting of the Society for Research in Child Development, Seattle, WA.

Hubbard, F., & van IJzendoorn, M. (1991). Maternal unresponsiveness and infant crying across the first 9 months: A naturalistic longitudinal study. *Infant Behavior and Development, 14,* 299–312.

Huesmann, L. R., Lagerspetz, K., & Eron, L. D. (1984). Intervening variables in the TV violence-aggression relation: Evidence from two countries. *Developmental Psychology, 20,* 746–775.

Humphrey, M., & Kirkwood, R. (1982). Marital relationship among adopters. *Adoption and Fostering, 6,* 44–48.

Hunt, J. M. (1970). Attention preference and experience: I. Introduction. *Journal of Genetic Psychology, 117,* 99–107.

Hunt, M. (1974). *Sexual behavior in the 1970s.* Chicago: Playboy Press.

Hunter, F., & Youniss, J. (1982). Changes in functions of three relations during adolescence. *Developmental Psychology, 18,* 806–811.

Hunter, R. S., Kilstrom, N., Kraybill, E. N., & Loda, F. (1978). Antecedents of child abuse and neglect in premature infants. *Pediatrics, 61,* 624–635.

Hurwitz, E. S., Gunn, W. J., Pinsky, P. F., & Schonberger, L. B. (1991). Risk of respiratory illness associated with day care attendance. *Pediatrics, 87,* 62–69.

Huston, A. (1983). Sex typing. In E. M. Hetherington (Ed.), *Handbook of child psychology: Vol. 4. Socialization, personality, and social development* (pp. 387–467). New York: Wiley.

Huston, A. (1992). Antecedents, consequences and possible solutions. In A. Huston (Ed.), *Children in poverty.* Cambridge, NY: Cambridge University Press.

Huston, A., Donnerstein, E., Fairchild, H., Feshbach, N., Katz, P., Murray, J., Rubinstein, E., & Wilcox, B. (1992). *Big world, small screen.* Lincoln: University of Nebraska Press.

Huston, A., Watkins, B., & Kunkel, D. (1989). Public policy and children's television. *American Psychologist, 44,* 424–433.

Huston, A., Wright, J. C., Rice, M. L., Kerkman, D., & St. Peters, M. (1990). The development of television viewing patterns in early childhood: A longitudinal investigation. *Developmental Psychology, 26,* 409–420.

Huttenlocher, J., Haight, W., Bryk, A., Seltzer, M., & Lyons, T. (1991). Early vocabulary growth. *Developmental Psychology, 27,* 236–248.

Hymel, S., Rubin, K. H., Rowden, L., & LeMare, L. (1990). Children's peer relationships: Longitudinal prediction of internalizing and externalizing problems from middle to late childhood. *Child Development, 61,* 2004–2021.

Iannotti, R. (1985). Naturalistic and structural assessments of prosocial behavior in preschool children. *Developmental Psychology, 21,* 46–55.

Infant Health and Development Program (1990). Enhancing the outcomes of low-birth-weight, premature infants. *Journal of American Medical Association, 263,* 3035–3042.

Irwin, O. (1947). Infant speech: Consonant sounds according to the manner of articulation. *Journal of Speech Disorders, 12,* 397–401.

Isabella, R., & Belsky, J. (1991). Interactional synchrony and the origins of infant-mother attachment: A replication study. *Child Development, 62,* 373–384.

Isabella, C., Belsky, J., & von Eye, A. (1989). The origins of infant-mother attachment: An examination of interactional synchrony during the infant's first year. *Developmental Psychology, 25,* 12–21.

Ispa, J. (1992). Some thoughts on freedom and control in Russian day care. *SRCD Newsletter, 9,* 14.

Izard, C. E. (1971). *The face of emotion.* New York: Appleton-Century-Crofts.

Izard, C. E., Hembree, E. A., & Huebner, R. R. (1987). Infants' emotional expressions to acute pain: Developmental change and stability of individual differences. *Developmental Psychology, 23,* 105–113.

Jackson, J. (1993). Multiple caregiving among African Americans and infant attachment: The need for an emic approach. *Human Development, 36,* 87–102.

Jacobson, J., & Willie, D. (1984). Influence of attachment and separation experience on separation distress at 18 months. *Developmental Psychology, 20,* 477–484.

Jacobson, J., Jacobson, S., Fein, G. G., & Schwartz, P. M. (1984). Factors and clusters for the Brazelton Scale: An investigation of the dimensions of neonatal behavior. *Developmental Psychology, 20,* 339–353.

Jacobson, J., Jacobson, S., & Humphrey, H. (1990). Effects of exposure to PCBs and related compounds on growth and activity in children. *Neurotoxicology and Teratology, 12,* 319–326.

Jacobson, J., Jacobson, S., Padgett, R., Brumitt, G., & Billings, R. (1992). Effects of prenatal PCB exposure on cognitive processing efficiency and sustained attention. *Developmental Psychology, 28,* 297–306.

Jarvis, P., Myers, B., & Creasy, G. (1989). The effects of infants' illness on others' intentions with prematures at 4 and 8 months. *Infant Behavior and Development, 12,* 25–35.

Jennings, K., & Connors, R. (1989). Mothers' interactional style and children's competence at 3 years. *International Journal of Behavioral Development, 12,* 155–175.

Jennings, K., Stagg, V., & Connors, R. (1991). Social networks and mothers' interactions with their preschool children. *Child Development, 62,* 966–978.

Jensen, A. R. (1969). How much can we boost IQ and scholastic achievement? *Harvard Educational Review, 39,* 1–123.

Jessor, R., Costa, F., Jessor, L., & Donovan, J. (1983). Time of first intercourse: A prospective study. *Journal of Personality and Social Psychology, 44,* 608–626.

John, E., Savitz, D., & Sandler, D. (1991). Prenatal exposure to parents' smoking and childhood cancer. *American Journal of Epidemiology, 133,* 123–132.

Johnson, D., & Breckenridge, J. N. (1982). The Houston Parent-Child Development Center and the primary prevention of behavior problems in young children. *American Journal of Community Psychology, 10,* 305–316.

Johnson, D., & Walker, T. (1987). Primary prevention of behavior problems in Mexican-American children. *American Journal of Community Psychology, 15,* 375–385.

Johnson, D., Walker, T., & Rodriguez, G. (1993, March). *Teaching low-income mothers to teach their children.* Paper presented at the biennial meeting of the Society for Research in Child Development, New Orleans, LA.

Johnson, J. (1989, July 19). Bush administration seeks policy that will reduce infant deaths. *The New York Times,* p. D24.

Johnson, J., & Newport, E. (1989). Critical period effects in second language learning: The influence of maturational state on the acquisition of English as a second language. *Cognitive Psychology, 21,* 60–99.

Johnson, M., Dziurawiec, Z., Bartrip, J., & Morton, J. (1992). The effects of movement of internal features on infants' preferences for face like stimuli. *Infant Behavior and Development, 15,* 129–136.

Johnston, J., Gonzalez, R., & Campbell, L. (1987). Ongoing postdivorce conflict and child disturbance. *Journal of Abnormal Child Psychology, 15,* 493–509.

Jones, D., Liggon, C., & Biringen, Z. (1991, April). *Elation after walking onset.* Paper presented at the biennial meeting of the Society for Research in Child Development, Seattle, WA.

Jordan, B. (1980). *Birth in four cultures.* Montreal: Eden.

Josselson, R. (1980). Ego development in adolescence. In J. Adelson (Ed.), *Handbook of adolescent psychology.* New York: Wiley.

Jouriles, E., Murphy, C., Farris, A., Smith, D., Richters, J., & Waters, E. (1991). Marital adjustment, parental disagreements about childrearing, and behavior problems in boys. *Child Development, 62,* 1424–1433.

Juel, C., Griffith, P., & Gough, P. (1986). The acquisition of literacy: A longitudinal study of children in first and second grades. *Journal of Educational Psychology, 78,* 243–255.

Jussim, L. (1989). Teacher expectations: Self-fulfilling prophecies, perceptual biases, and accuracy. *Journal of Personality and Social Psychology, 57,* 469–480.

Kach, J., & McGhee, P. (1982). Adjustment to early parenthood: The role of accuracy of preparenthood expectations. *Journal of Family Issues, 3,* 361–374.

Kagan, J. (1967). The growth of the "face" schema: Theoretical significance and methodological issues. In J. Hellmuth (Ed.), *The exceptional infant: Vol. 1. The normal infant.* New York: Brunner/Mazel.

Kagan, J. (1989). Tempermental contributions to social behavior. *American Psychologist, 44,* 668–674.

Kagan, J., Kearsley, R., & Zelazo, P. R. (1978). *Infancy: Its place in human development.* Cambridge, MA: Harvard University Press.

Kagan, J., & Snidman, N. (1991). Infant predictors of inhibited and uninhibited profiles. *Psychological Science, 2,* 40–44.

Kagan, S., & Zigler, E. (Eds.). (1986). *Early schooling: The national debate.* New Haven, CT: Yale University Press.

Kahneman, D., Slovic, P., & Tversky, A. (Eds.). (1982). *Judgment under uncertainty: Heuristics and biases.* New York: Cambridge University Press.

Kail, R. V., Jr. (1984). *The development of memory in children* (2nd ed.). San Francisco: Freeman.

Kaler, S., & Kopp, C. (1990). Compliance and comprehension in very young toddlers. *Child Development, 61,* 1997–2003.

Kaminski, M., Rumeau, C., & Schwartz, D. (1978). Alcohol consumption in pregnant women and the outcome of pregnancy. *Alcoholism: Clinical and Experimental Research, 2,* 155–163.

Karzon, R. (1985). Discrimination of polysyllabic sequences by 1- to 4-month-old infants. *Journal of Experimental Child Psychology, 39,* 326–342.

Katchadourian, H. (1990). Sexuality. In S. Feldman & G. Elliott (Eds.), *At the threshold: The developing adolescent* (pp. 330–351). Cambridge, MA: Harvard University Press.

Katz, P. (1987). Variations in family constellation: Effects of gender schemata. In L. Liben & M. Signorella (Eds.), *Children's gender schemata: New directions for child development research* (No. 38). San Francisco: Jossey-Bass.

Katz, P., & Walsh, P. (1991). Modification of children's gender-stereotypical behavior. *Child Development, 62,* 338–351.

Katz, V. (1971). Auditory stimulation and developmental behavior of the premature infant. *Nursing Research, 20,* 196–201.

Kaufman, J., & Cicchetti, D. (1989). The effects of maltreatment on school-age children's socioemotional development. *Developmental Psychology.*

Kaufman, J., & Zigler, E. (1989). The intergenerational transmission of child abuse. In D. Cicchetti & V. Carlson (Eds.), *Child maltreatment* (pp. 129–150). New York: Cambridge University Press.

Keane, S. P., Brown, K. P., & Crenshaw, T. M. (1990). Children's intention-cue detection as a function of maternal social behavior: Pathways to social rejection. *Developmental Psychology, 26,* 1004–1009.

Kearins, J. M. (1981). Visual spatial memory in Australian aboriginal children of desert regions. *Cognitive Psychology, 13,* 434–460.

Keating, D. (1990). Adolescent thinking. In S. Feldman & G. Elliott (Eds.), *At the threshold: The developing adolescent* (pp. 54–89). Cambridge, MA: Harvard University Press.

Kegeles, S., Adler, N., & Irwin, C., Jr. (1988). Sexually active adolescents and condoms: Changes over one year in knowledge, attitudes and use. *American Journal of Public Health, 78,* 460–461.

Kellam, S., Ensminger, M., & Turner, R. (1977). Family structure and the mental health of children. *Archives of General Psychiatry, 34,* 1012–1022.

Kelley, M., Power, T., & Wimbush, D. (1992). Determinants of disciplinary practices in low-income black mothers. *Child Development, 63,* 573–582.

Kelley, M., & Tseng, H. (1992). Cultural differences in child rearing: A comparison of immigrant Chinese and Caucasian American mothers. *Journal of Cross-Cultural Psychology, 23,* 444–455.

Kellogg, R. (1970). *Analyzing children's art.* Mountain View, CA: Mayfield.

Kelly, J. (1990). Treating the child abuser. In R. Ammerman & M. Hersen (Eds.), *Children at risk* (pp. 269–287). New York: Plenum.

Kelly, P. C., Cohen, M. L., Walker, W. O., Caskey, O. L., & Atkinson, A. W. (1989). Self-esteem in children medically managed for attention deficit disorder. *Pediatrics, 83,* 211–217.

Kemp, J., & Thach, B. (1991). Sudden death in infants sleeping on polystyrene-filled cushions. *New England Journal of Medicine, 324,* 1858–1864.

Kemple, K., Speranza, H., & Hazen, N. (1992). Cohesive discourse and peer acceptance. *Merrill-Palmer Quarterly, 38,* 364–381.

Kennedy, E., Spence, S. H., & Hensley, R. (1989). An examination of the relationship between childhood depression and social competence amongst primary school children. *Journal of Child Psychology and Psychiatry, 30*(4), 561–573.

Kennell, J., Jerauld, L., Wolf, P., Chesler, R., Kreger, N., McAlpine, W., Steffa, M., & Kennell, J. (1974). Maternal behavior one year after early and extended post-partum contact. *Developmental Medicine and Child Neurology, 16,* 172.

Kennell, J., & Klaus, M. H. (1976). Caring for parents of a premature or sick infant. In M. H. Klaus & J. H. Kennell (Ed.), *Maternal-infant bonding.* St. Louis, MO: Mosby.

Kerr, M., Begues, J., & Kerr, D. (1978). Psychosocial functioning of mothers of malnourished children. *Pediatrics, 62,* 778–784.

Kessen, W. (1979). The American child and other cultural inventions. *American Psychologist, 34,* 815–820.

Kestenbaum, R., Farber, E., & Sroufe, L. A. (1989). Individual differences in empathy among preschoolers: Relation to attachment history. In N. Ersenkes (Ed.), *New directions for child development: Vol. 44. Empathy and related emotional responses* (pp. 51–64). San Francisco: Jossey-Bass.

Kilbride, J. E. (1977). Mother-infant interaction and infant sensorimotor development among the Baganda of Uganda. *Dissertation Abstracts International, 37*(10-B), 5326–5327.

Kilbride, J. E., & Kilbride, P. L. (1975). Sitting and smiling behavior of Baganda infants. *Journal of Cross-Cultural Psychology, 6,* 88–107.

Kinsey, A., Pomeroy, W., & Martin, C. (1948). *Sexual behavior in the human male.* Philadelphia, PA: Saunders.

Kistin, N., Benton, D., Rao, S., & Sullivan, M. (1990) Breast-feeding rates among black urban low-income women: Effects of prenatal education. *Pediatrics, 86,* 741–746.

Kistner, J. A., & Gatlin, D. F. (1989). Sociometric differences between learning-disabled and nonhandicapped students: Effects of sex and race. *Journal of Educational Psychology, 81,* 118–120.

Kitzinger, S. (1985). *The complete book of pregnancy and childbirth.* New York: Knopf.

Klaus, M., Jerauld, R., Kreger, N., McAlpine, W., Steffa, M., & Kennell, J. (1972). Maternal attachment: Importance of the first post-partum days. *New England Journal of Medicine, 286,* 460–463.

Klimes-Dougan, B., & Kistner, J. (1990). Physically abused preschoolers' responses to peers' distress. *Developmental Psychology, 26,* 599–602.

Kline, M., Johnston, J., & Tschann, J. (1991). The long shadow of marital conflict: A model of children's post-divorce adjustment. *Journal of Marriage and the Family, 53,* 297–309.

Knight, G. P., Tein, J. Y., Shell, R., & Roosa, M. (1992). The cross-ethnic equivalence of parenting and family interaction measures among Hispanic and Anglo-American families. *Child Development, 63,* 1392–1403.

Knox, V. (1993). *The effects of child support payments on developmental outcomes for children in single mother families* (Working Paper No. H-93-6). Cambridge, MA: Malcolm Wiener Center for Social Policy, Harvard University.

Koblinsky, S. A., & Todd, C. M. (1989). Teaching self-care skills to latchkey children: A review of research. *Family Relations, 38,* 431–435.

Kochanska, G. (1991). Socialization and temperament in the development of guilt and conscience. *Child Development, 62,* 1379–1392.

Kochanska, G. (1992). Children's interpersonal influence with mothers and peers. *Developmental Psychology, 28,* 491–499.

Kochanska, G., & Radke-Yarrow, M. (1992). Inhibiton in toddlerhood and the dynamics of the child"s interaction with an unfamilar peer at age five. *Child Development, 63,* 325–335.

Kohlberg, L. (1966). A cognitive-developmental analysis of children's sex-role concepts and attitudes. In E. Maccoby (Ed.), *The development of sex differences* (pp. 82–172). Stanford, CA: Stanford University Press.

Kohlberg, L. (1969). Stage and sequence: The cognitive-developmental approach to socialization. In D. Goslin (Ed.), *Handbook of socialization the-*

ory and research. Chicago: Rand McNally.

Kohlberg, L., & Gilligan, C. (1972). The adolescent as philosopher: The discovery of the self in a postconventional world. In J. Kagan & R. Coles (Eds.), *Twelve to sixteen: Early adolescence* (pp. 144–179). New York: Norton.

Kohn, M. L. (1987). Cross national research as an analytic strategy. *American Sociological Review, 52,* 713–731.

Kolata, G. (1989a, October 8). AIDS is spreading in teen-agers, a new trend alarming to experts. *The New York Times,* pp. 1, 30.

Kolata, G. (1989b, August 11). In cities, poor families are dying of crack. *The New York Times,* pp. A1, A13.

Kolata, G. (1992, April 26). A parent's guide to kids' sports. *The New York Times Magazine* (Part 2), pp. 12 ff.

Kolb, B. (1989). Brain development, plasticity and behavior. *American Psychologist, 44,* 1203–1212.

Korbin, J. (1991). Cross-cultural perspectives and research directions for the 21st century. *Child Abuse and Neglect, 15,* 67–77.

Korner, A., & Grobstein, R. (1967). Individual differences at birth: Implications for mother-infant relationship and development. *Journal of the American Academy of Child Psychiatry, 6,* 676–690.

Korner, A., & Thoman, E. (1972). The relative efficacy of contact and vestibular-proprioceptive stimulation in soothing neonates. *Child Development, 43,* 443–453.

Korner, A., Zeanah, C., Lindin, J., Berkowitz, R., Krapmen, H., & Agras, W. (1985). The relation between neonatal and later activity and temperament. *Child Development, 56,* 38–42.

Kotelchuck, M., Schwartz, J., Anderka, M., & Finison, K. (1984). WIC participation and pregnancy outcomes: Massachusetts Statewide Evaluation Project. *American Journal of Public Health, 74,* 10–14.

Kowaz, A. M., & Marcia, J. E. (1991). Development and validation of a measure of Eriksonian industry. *Journal of Personality and Social Psychology, 60,* 390–397.

Kramer, L., & Gottman, J. (1992). Becoming a sibling: "With a little help from my friends." *Developmental Psychology, 28,* 685–699.

Kramer, M., Barr, R., Leduc, M., Boisjoly, C., McVey-White, L., & Pless, I. (1985). Determinants of weight and adiposity in the first year of life. *Journal of Pediatrics, 106,* 10–14.

Krauss, R., & Glucksberg, S. (1969). The development of communication: Competence as a function of age. *Child Development, 40,* 255–266.

Krauss, R., & Glucksberg, S. (1977). Social and nonsocial speech. *Scientific American, 236,* 100–105.

Kreutzer, M. A., Leonard, C., & Flavell, J. H. (1975). An interview study of children's knowledge about memory. *Monographs of the Society for Research in Child Development, 40* (Serial No. 159).

Krugman, R., Lenherr, M., Betz, L., & Fryer, G. (1986). The relationship between unemployment and physical abuse of children. *Child Abuse and Neglect, 10,* 415–418.

Kuczja, S. A. (1978). Children's judgments of grammatical and ungrammatical irregular past-time verbs. *Child Development, 49,* 319–326.

Kuczynski, L. (1984). Socialization goals and mother-child interaction: Strategies for long-term and short-term compliance. *Developmental Psychology, 20,* 1061–1073.

Kuhn, D. (1992). Cognitive development. In M. Bornstein & M. Lamb (Eds), *Developmental psychology: An advanced textbook* (3rd ed., pp. 133–177). Hillsdale, NJ: Erlbaum.

Kumanyika, S., Huffman, S., Bradshaw, M., Waller, H., Ross, A., Serdula, M., & Paige, D. (1990). Stature and weight status of children in an urban kindergarten population. *Pediatrics, 85,* 783–790.

Kunkel, D. (1990). *Children and television advertising.* Paper presented at the meeting of the International Communication Association, Dublin, Ireland.

Kupersmidt, J., & Coie, J. (1990). Preadolescent peer status, aggression, and school adjustment as predictors of externalizing problems in adolescence. *Child Development, 61,* 1350–1362.

Kurinij, N., Shiono, P. H., & Rhoads, G. G. (1988). Breast-feeding incidence and duration in black and white women. *Pediatrics, 81,* 365–371.

Kurtz, B. E., & Weinert, F. E. (1989). Metamemory, memory performance, and causal attributions in gifted and average children. *Journal of Experimental Child Psychology, 48,* 45–61.

Ladd, G. (1990). Having friends, keeping friends, making friends, and being liked by peers in the classroom: Predictors of children's early school adjustment? *Child Development, 61,* 1081–1100.

Ladd, G., & Asher, S. (1985). Social skill training and children's peer relations. In L. L'Abate & M. Milan (Eds.), *Handbook of social skills training and research* (pp. 219–244). New York: Wiley.

LaFreniere, P., Strayer, F., & Gauthier, R. (1984). The emergence of same-sex preferences among preschool peers. *Child Development, 55,* 1958–1965.

Lamb, M. (1976). The role of the father: An overview. In M. E. Lamb (Ed.), *The role of the father in child development.* New York: Wiley.

Lamb, M. (1981). The development of father-infant relationships. In M. Lamb (Ed.), *The role of the father in child development.* New York: Wiley.

Lamb, M. (1991, March). *Successful parenting in the 1990s.* Invited public lecture, Center for Effective Living, Singapore.

Lamb, M., & Bornstein, M. (1987). *Development in infancy: An introduction* (2nd ed.). New York: Random House.

Lamb, M., & Hwang, C. (1982). Maternal attachment and mother neonate bonding: A critical review. In M. E. Lamb & A. Brown (Eds.), *Advances in developmental psychology* (Vol. 2, pp. 1–33). Hillsdale, NJ: Erlbaum.

Lamb, M., & Oppenheim, D. (1989). Fatherhood and father-child relationships. In S. Cath, A. Gurwitt, & L. Gunsberg (Eds.), *Fathers and their families* (pp. 1–26). Hillsdale, NJ: Erlbaum.

Lamb, M., & Sternberg, K. (1989). Daycare. In H. Keller (Ed.), *Handbuch der Kleinkind forschung.* Heidelberg, Germany: Springer-Verlag.

Lambert, N., & Hartsough, C. (1984). Contribution of predispositional factors to the diagnosis of hyperactivity. *American Journal of Orthopsychiatry, 54,* 97–109.

Lambert, N., Sandoval, J., & Sassone, D. (1978). Prevalence of hyperactivity in elementary school children as a func-

tion of social system definers. *American Journal of Orthopsychiatry, 48,* 446–463.

Lampl, M., Veldhuis, J., & Johnson, M. (1992). Saltation and stasis: A model of human growth. *Science, 258,* 801–803.

Lancelotta, G. X., & Vaughn, S. (1989). Relation between types of aggression and sociometric status: Peer and teacher perceptions. *Journal of Educational Psychology, 81,* 86–90.

Landberg, L., & Lundberg, L. (1990). Phonetic development in early infancy. *Journal of Child Language, 16,* 19–40.

Landesman-Dwyer, S. (1981). Drinking during pregnancy: Effects on human development [Monograph]. *Alcohol and Health, 4.*

Landesman-Dwyer, S., & Emmanuel, I. (1979). Smoking during pregnancy. *Teratology, 119–126.*

Landesman-Dwyer, S., Keller, L. S., & Streissguth, A. P. (1978). Naturalistic observations of newborns: Effects of maternal alcohol intake. *Alcoholism: Clinical and Experimental Research, 2,* 171–177.

Landesman-Dwyer, S., Ragozin, A. S., & Little, R. E. (1982). Behavioral correlates of prenatal alcohol exposure: A four-year follow-up study. *Neurobehavioral Toxicology and Teratology, 46,* 24–38.

Langlois, J., & Downs, A. (1980). Mothers, fathers, and peers as socialization agents of sex-typed play behaviors in young children. *Child Development, 51,* 1237–1247.

Langlois, J., Ritter, J., Roggman, L., & Vaughn, L. (1991). Facial diversity and infant preferences for attractive faces. *Developmental Psychology, 27,* 153–159.

Langlois, J., Roggman, L., & Rieser-Danner, L. (1990). Infants' differential social responses to attractive and unattractive faces. *Developmental Psychology, 26,* 153–159.

Lau, S. (1990). Crisis and vulnerability in adolescent development. *Journal of Youth and Adolescence, 19,* 111–132.

Lauer, R. M., & Clarke, W. R. (1989). Childhood risk factors for high adult blood pressure: The Muscatine study. *Pediatrics, 84,* 633–641.

Launer, L., Habicht, J., & Kardjati, S. (1990). Breast feeding protects infants in Indonesia against illness and

weight loss due to illness. *American Journal of Epidemiology, 131,* 322–331.

Lawton, T. (1992). *Maternal cocaine addiction: Correlates and consequences.* Unpublished doctoral dissertation, University of Michigan, Ann Arbor.

Lazar, I., & Darlington, R. (1982). Lasting effects of early education: A report from the Consortium of Longitudinal Studies. *Monographs of the Society for Research in Child Development, 47* (2–3, Serial No. 195).

Leacock, E. B. (1969). *Teaching and learning in city schools.* New York: Basic Books.

Leaper, C. (1991). Influence and involvement in children's discourse: Age, gender, and partner effects. *Child Development, 62,* 797–811.

Lebra, T. S. (1976). *Japanese patterns of behaviour.* Honolulu: University of Hawaii Press.

Lee, K., Paneth, N., Gartner, L., Pearlman, M., & Gruss, L. (1980). Neonatal mortality: An analysis of recent improvements in the United States. *American Journal of Public Health, 70,* 15–21.

Lee, V., Brooks-Gunn, J., Schnur, E., & Liaw, F. (1990). Are Head Start effects sustained? *Child Development, 61,* 495–507.

Legerstee, M. (1991). The role of person and object in eliciting early imitation. *Journal of Experimental Child Psychology, 51,* 423–433.

Lempers, J., & Elrod, M. (1983). Children's appraisal of different sources of referential communicative inadequacies. *Child Development, 54,* 509–515.

Lenneberg, E. H. (1967). *Biological foundations of language.* New York: Wiley.

Lenssen, B. G. (1973). Infants' reactions to peer strangers. *Dissertation Abstracts International, 33,* 60–62.

Lester, B. (1975). Cardiac habituation of the orienting response in infants of varying nutritional status. *Developmental Psychology, 11,* 432–442.

Lester, B. (1979). A synergistic process approach to the study of prenatal malnutrition. *International Journal of Behavioral Development, 2,* 377–394.

Lester, B., Corwin, M. J., Sepkoski, C., Peucker, M., McLaughlin, S., & Golub, H. L. (1991). Neurobehavioral syndromes in cocaine-exposed newborn infants. *Child Development, 62,* 694–705.

Lester, B., & Dreher, M. (1989). Effects of marijuana use during pregnancy on newborn cry. *Child Development, 60,* 765–771.

Lester, B., Zachariah Boukydis, C. F., Garcia-Coll, C., Hole, W., & Peucker, M. (1992). Infantile colic: Acoustic cry characteristics, maternal perception of cry, and temperament. *Infant Behavior and Development, 15,* 15–26.

Lester, B., & Zeskind, P. (1982). A biobehavioral perspective on crying in early infancy. In H. Fitzgerald, B. Lester, & M. Yogman (Eds.), *Theory and research in behavioral pediatrics* (Vol. 1). New York: Plenum.

Lever, J. (1976). Sex differences in the games children play. *Social Problems, 23,* 479–487.

Levitsky, D. A. (1979). *Malnutrition, environment, and behavior.* Ithaca, NY: Cornell University Press.

Levy, G. (1989). Relations among aspects of children's social environments, gender schematization, gender role knowledge and flexibility. *Sex Roles, 21,* 803–810.

Levy-Shiff, R., Bar, O., & Har-Even, D. (1990). Psychological profile of adoptive parents-to-be. *American Journal of Orthopsychiatry, 60,* 258–267.

Levy-Shiff, R., Goldschmidt, I., & Har-Even, D. (1991). Transition to parenthood in adoptive families. *Developmental Psychology, 27,* 131–140.

Levy-Shiff, R., & Israelashvili, R. (1988). Antecedents of fathering. *Developmental Psychology, 24,* 434–440.

Lewis, C. C. (1981). The effects of parental firm control: A reinterpretation of findings. *Psychological Bulletin, 90,* 547–563.

Lewis, M., Alessandri, S. M., & Sullivan, M. W. (1990). Violation of expectancy, loss of control, and anger expressions in young infants. *Developmental Psychology, 26,* 745–751.

Lewis, M., & Brooks, J. (1974). Self, other, and fear: Infants' reactions to people. In M. Lewis & L. A. Rosenblum (Eds.), *The origins of fear.* New York: Wiley.

Lewis, M., Feiring, C., McGuffog, C., & Jaskir, J. (1984). Predicting psychopathology in six-year-olds from early social relations. *Child Development, 55,* 123–136.

Lewis, M., & Goldberg, W. (1969). Perceptual-cognitive development in infancy: A generalized expectancy model as a function of the mother-infant relationship. *Merrill-Palmer Quarterly, 15,* 81–100.

Liben, L., & Bigler, R. (1987). Reformulating children's gender schemata. In L. Liben & M. Signorella (Eds.), *Children's gender schemata: New directions for child development* (No. 38). San Francisco: Jossey-Bass.

Liben, L., & Signorella, M. (1993). Gender-schematic processing in children. *Developmental Psychology, 29,* 141–149.

Licht, B. G., & Dweck, C. S. (1984). Determinants of academic achievement: The interaction of children's achievement orientations with skill area. *Developmental Psychology, 20,* 628–636.

Lifter, K., & Bloom, L. (1989). Object knowledge and the emergence of language. *Infant Behavior and Development, 12,* 395–423.

Light, H., & Fenster, C. (1974). Maternal concerns during pregnancy. *American Journal of Obstetrics and Gynecology, 118,* 46–50.

Lin, C.-Y. C., & Fu, V. R. (1990). A comparison of child-rearing practices among Chinese, immigrant Chinese, and Caucasian-American parents. *Child Development, 61,* 429–433.

Lindell, S. G. (1988). Education for childbirth: A time for change. *Journal of Obstetrics, Gynecology, and Neonatal Nursing, 17,* 108–112.

Littenberg, R., Tulkin, S., & Kagan, J. (1971). Cognitive components of separation anxiety. *Developmental Psychology, 4,* 387–388.

Little, R., Anderson, K., Ervin, C., Worthington-Roberts, R., & Clarren, S. (1989). Maternal alcohol use during breast-feeding and infant mental and motor development at one year. *New England Journal of Medicine, 321,* 425–430.

Livson, N., & Peskin, H. (1980). Perspectives on adolescence from longitudinal research. In J. Adelson (Ed.), *Handbook of adolescent psychology* (pp. 47–98). New York: Wiley.

Lobel, T., & Menashin, J. (1993). Relations of conceptions of gender-role transgressions and gender constancy to gender-typed toy preferences. *Developmental Psychology, 29,* 150–155.

Locke, J., & Pearson, D. (1990). Linguistic significance of babbling. *Journal of Child Language, 17,* 1–16.

Loeb, R. C., Horst, L., & Horton, P. J. (1980). Family interaction patterns associated with self-esteem in preadolescent girls and boys. *Merrill-Palmer Quarterly, 26,* 203–217.

Loeber, R., Tremblay, R. E., Gagnon, C., & Charlebois, P. (1989). Continuity and desistance in disruptive boys' early fighting at school. *Development and Psychopathology, 1,* 39–50.

Lomax, R. G., & McGee, L. M. (1987). Young children's concept about print and reading: Toward a model of word reading acquisition. *Reading Research Quarterly, 22,* 237–256.

Long, N., & Forehand, R. (1987). The effects of parental divorce and parental conflict on children: An overview. *Developmental and Behavioral Pediatrics, 8,* 292–297.

Lowry, G. H. (1978). *Growth and development of children* (7th ed.). Chicago: Medical Year Book.

Lozoff, B. (1989). Nutrition and behavior. *American Psychologist, 44,* 231–235.

Lummis, M., & Stevenson, H. (1990). Gender differences in beliefs and achievements: A cross-cultural study. *Developmental Psychology, 26,* 254–263.

Luria, A. R. (1961). *The role of speech in the regulation of normal and abnormal behaviour.* New York: Pergamon.

Luster, T., Rhoades, K., & Haas, B. (1989). The relation between parental values and parenting behavior. *Journal of Marriage and the Family, 51,* 139–147.

Lyons-Ruth, K., Connell, D. B., Zoll, D., & Stahl, J. (1987). Infants at social risk: Relations among infant maltreatment, maternal behavior, and infant attachment behavior. *Developmental Psychology, 23,* 223–232.

Lytton, H., & Romney, D. (1991). Parents' differential socialization of boys and girls: A meta-analysis. *Psychological Bulletin, 2,* 267–296.

Maccoby, E. (1951). Television: Its impact on school children. *Public Opinion Quarterly, 15,* 421–444.

Maccoby, E. (1988). Gender as a social category. *Developmental Psychology, 24,* 755–775.

Maccoby, E. (1990). Gender and relationships: A developmental account. *American Psychologist, 45,* 513–520.

Maccoby, E., Doering, C. H., Jacklin, C., & Kraemer, H. (1979). Concentrations of sex hormones in umbilical-cord blood: Their relation to sex and birth order of infants. *Child Development, 50,* 632–642.

Maccoby, E., & Hagen, J. W. (1965). Effects of distraction upon central versus incidental recall: Developmental trends. *Journal of Experimental Child Psychology, 2,* 280–289.

Maccoby, E., & Jacklin, C. (1987). Gender segregation in childhood. In H. Reese (Ed.), *Advances in child development and behavior* (Vol. 20, pp. 239–287). New York: Academic.

Maccoby, E., & Martin, J. (1983). Socialization in the context of the family: Parent-child interaction. In E. M. Hetherington (Ed.), *Handbook of child psychology: Vol. 4. Socialization, personality, and social development* (pp. 1–102). New York: Wiley.

Maccoby, E., Snow, M., & Jacklin, C. (1984). Children's dispositions and mother-child interaction at 12 and 18 months: A short-term longitudinal study. *Developmental Psychology, 20,* 459–472.

MacDermid, S., Huston, T., & McHale, S. (1990). Changes in marriage associated with the transition to parenthood. *Journal of Marriage and the Family, 52,* 475–486.

MacDonald, K. (1987). Parent-child physical play with rejected, neglected and popular boys. *Developmental Psychology, 23,* 705–711.

MacDonald, K. (Ed.). (1988). *Sociobiological perspectives on human development.* New York: Springer-Verlag.

MacDonald, K., & Parke, R. (1984). Bridging the gap: Parent-child play interaction and peer interactive competence. *Child Development, 55,* 1265–1277.

MacFarlane, J. A. (1975). Olfaction in the development of social preferences in the human neonate. In *Parent-infant interaction: CIBA Foundation Symposium, 33,* 103–117 (New Series). Amsterdam: Elsevier.

MacGowan, R. J., MacGowan, C. A., Serdula, M. K., Lane, J. M., Jocsoef, R. M., & Cook, F. H. (1991). Breast-feeding among women attending women, infants, and children clinics in Georgia, 1987. *Pediatrics, 87,* 361–366.

Mac Iver, D. J. (1992, April 7). *Motivating disadvantaged early adolescents to reach new heights: Effective evaluation, reward, and recognition structures.* Paper presented at the Center for Research on Effective Schooling for Disadvantaged Students (CDS), The Johns Hopkins University, Baltimore, MD.

Mac Iver, D. J., Stipek, D. J., & Daniels, D. H. (1991). Explaining within-semester changes in student effort in junior high school and senior high school courses. *Journal of Educational Psychology, 83,* 201–211.

MacKinnon, C. E. (1989). An observational investigation of sibling interactions in married and divorced families. *Developmental Psychology, 25,* 36–44.

Magnusson, D., Stattin, H., & Allen, V. (1986). Differential maturation among girls and its relation to social adjustment in a longitudinal perspective,. In P. Baltes, D. Featherman, & R. Lerner (Eds.), *Life span development and behavior* (Vol. 7). Hillsdale, NJ: Erlbaum.

Mahaffey, K. (1992). Exposure to lead in childhood: The importance of prevention. *New England Journal of Medicine, 327,* 1308–1309.

Mahler, M. S., Pine, F., & Bergman, A. (1970). The mother's reaction to her toddler's drive for individuation. In E. J. Anthony & T. Benedek (Eds.), *Parenthood: Its psychology and psychopathology.* Boston: Little, Brown.

Mahler, M. S., Pine, F., & Bergman, A. (1975). *The psychological birth of the human infant.* New York: Basic Books.

Main, M., & Weston, D. R. (1981). The quality of the toddler's relationship to mother and to father: Related to conflict behavior and the readiness to establish new relationships. *Child Development, 52,* 932–940.

Malatesta, C. Z., Culver, C., Tesman, J. R., & Shepard, B. (1989). The development of emotion expression during the first two years of life. *Monographs of the Society for Research in Child Development, 54*(1–2, Serial No. 219).

Malhotra, S. (1989). Varying risk factors and outcomes: An Indian perspective. In W. Carey & S. McDevitt (Eds.), *Clinical and educational applications of temperament research* (pp. 91–95). Amsterdam: Swets & Zeitlinger.

Mangelsdorf, S. (1992). Developmental changes in infant-stranger interaction. *Infant Behavior and Development, 15,* 191–208.

Mangelsdorf, S., Gunnar, M., Kestenbaum, R., Lang, S., & Andreas, D. (1990). Infant proneness-to-distress temperament, maternal personality, and mother-infant attachment. *Child Development, 61,* 820–831.

Mangelsdorf, S., & McHale, J. (1992, May). *A new look at the associations between temperament and attachment.* Paper presented at the Eighth International Conference on Infant Studies, Miami, FL.

Marcus, D. E., & Overton, W. F. (1978). The development of cognitive gender constancy and sex role preferences. *Child Development, 49,* 434–444.

Marcus, R. F., Telleen, S., & Roke, E. J. (1979). Relation between cooperation and empathy in young children. *Developmental Psychology, 15,* 346–347.

Markman, E. (1984). The acquisition and hierarchical organization of categories by children. In C. Sophian (Ed.), *Origins of cognitive skills.* Hillsdale, NJ: Erlbaum.

Markman, E., & Gorin, L. (1981). Children's ability to adjust their standards for evaluation comprehension. *Journal of Educational Psychology, 73,* 320–325.

Markman, E., & Wachtel, G. (1988). Children's use of mutual exclusivity to constrain the meanings of words. *Cognitive Psychology, 20,* 121–157.

Markman, H., & Kadushin, F. (1986). Preventive effects of Lamaze training for first time parents. *Journal of Consulting and Clinical Psychology, 54,* 872–874.

Marsh, H. W., Craven, R. G., & Debus, R. (1991). Self-concepts of young children 5 to 8 years of age: Measurement and multidimensional structure. *Journal of Educational Psychology, 83,* 377–392.

Marshall, P. (1989). Attention deficit disorder and allergy: A neurochemical model of the relation between the illnesses. *Psychological Bulletin, 106,* 434–446.

Marshall, W., & Tanner, J. (1978). Puberty. In F. Falkner & J. Tanner (Eds.), *Human growth* (Vol. 2, pp. 171–203). New York: Plenum.

Martin, C. (1989). Children's use of gender-related information in making social judgments. *Developmental Psychology, 25,* 80–88.

Martin, C., & Halverson, C. F., Jr. (1981). A schematic processing model of sex typing and stereotyping in children. *Child Development, 52,* 1119–1134.

Martin, P. (1989, October 24–25). Kids in the '90s. *Asbury Park Press,* pp. B5–B13.

Martinez, G. (1984). Trends in breast feeding in the United States. In *Report of the Surgeon-General's Workshop on Breastfeeding and Human Lactation* (pp. 19–23). Washington, DC: U.S. Department of Health and Human Services.

Marzollo, J. (1976). *9 months, 1 day, 1 year: A guide to pregnancy, birth, and baby care.* New York: Harper & Row.

Masataka, N. (1992). Early ontogeny of vocal behavior of Japanese infants in response to maternal speech. *Child Development, 63,* 1177–1185.

Matheny, A. (1992, June). *Neonatal temperament predicts children's unintentional injuries during 1–3 years.* Paper presented at the annual meeting of the American Psychological Society, San Diego, CA.

Matthews, W. S. (1978, March). *Interruptions of fantasy play: A matter of breaking frame.* Paper presented at the meeting of the Eastern Psychological Association, Washington, DC.

Maurer, D., Lewis, T., Cavanaugh, P., & Anstis, S. (1989). A new test of luminous efficiency for babies. *Investigative Ophthalmology and Visual Science, 30,* 297–303.

Maurer, D., & Maurer, C. (1988). *The world of the newborn.* New York: Basic Books.

Maurer, D., & Salapatek, P. (1976). Developmental changes in the scanning of faces by young infants. *Child Development, 47,* 523–527.

Mayes, L., Granger, R., Bornstein, M., & Zuckerman, B. (1992). The problem of prenatal cocaine exposure: A rush to judgment. *Journal of the American Medical Association, 267,* 406–408.

McBride, B. (1990). The effects of a parent education/play group program on father involvement in child rearing. *Family Relations, 39,* 250–256.

McBride, B. (1991). Parent education and support programs for fathers. *Early Childhood Development and Care, 67,* 73–85.

McCall, R. B. (1974). Exploratory manipulation and play in the human infant. *Monographs of the Society for Research in Child Development, 39* (2, Serial No. 155).

McCandless, B. R., & Hoyt, J. M. (1961). Sex, ethnicity and play preferences of preschool children. *Journal of Abnormal and Social Psychology, 62,* 683–685.

McCarthy, J., & Hoge, D. (1982). Analysis of age effects in longitudinal studies of adolescent self-esteem. *Developmental Psychology, 18,* 372–379.

McColl, R., & Carriger, M. (1993). A meta-analysis of infant habituation and recognition memory performances as predictors of later IQ. *Child Development, 64,* 57–79.

McFadden, A., Marsh, G., Price, B., & Hwang, Y. (1992). A study of race and gender bias in the punishment of school children. *Education and Treatment of Children, 15,* 140–146.

McGauhey, P., Starfield, B., Alexander, C., & Ensminger, M. (1991). Social environment and vulnerability of low birthweight children. *Pediatrics, 88,* 943–951.

McHale, S. M., & Pawletko, T. M. (1992). Differential treatment of siblings in two family contexts. *Child Development, 63,* 68–81.

McHenry, P., & Fine, M. (1993). Parenting following divorce: A comparison of black and white single mothers. *Journal of Comparative Family Studies, 24,* 99–111.

McKenna, J. (1990a). Evolution and sudden infant death syndrome: I. Infant responsivity to parental contact. *Human Nature, 1,* 145–177.

McKenna, J. (1990b). Evolution and sudden infant death syndrome: II. Why human infants? *Human Nature, 1,* 179–206.

McKenna, J. (1990c). Evolution and sudden infant death syndrome: III. Infant arousal and parent-infant cosleeping. *Human Nature, 1,* 291–330.

McKey, R., Condelli, L., Granson, H., Barrett, B., McConkey, C., & Plantz, M. (1985). The impact of Head Start on children, families and communities. *Final report of the Head Start evaluation, synthesis and utilization project.* Washington, DC: CSR, Inc.

McLaughlin, B. (1984). *Second language acquisition in children: Preschool children.* Hillsdale, NJ: Erlbaum.

McLoyd, V. (1989). Socialization and development in a changing economy: The effects of paternal job and income loss on children. *American Psychologist, 44,* 293–302.

McLoyd, V. (1990). The impact of economic hardship on black families and children: Psychological distress, parenting and socioemotional development. *Child Development, 61,* 311–346.

McNally, S., Eisenberg, N., & Harris, J. D. (1991). Consistency and change in maternal child-rearing practices and values: A longitudinal study. *Child Development, 62,* 190–198.

Mead, M., & Newton, N. (1967). Cultural patterning of perinatal behavior. In S. Richardson & A. Guttmacher (Eds.), *Childbearing: Its social and psychological aspects* (pp. 142–244). Baltimore, MD: Williams & Wilkins.

Medrich, E., Roizen, J., Rubin, V., & Buckley, S. (1982). *The serious business of growing up.* Berkeley: University of California Press.

Meichenbaum, D., & Goodman, J. (1971). Training impulsive children to talk to themselves: A means of developing self-control. *Journal of Abnormal Psychology, 77,* 115–126.

Melhuish, E. C., & Moss, P. (1991). Introduction. In E. C. Melhuish & P. Moss (Eds.), *Day care for young children* (pp. 1–9). London: Routledge & Kegan Paul.

Meltzoff, A., & Moore, M. (1977). Imitation of facial and manual gestures by human neonates. *Science, 198,* 75–78.

Meltzoff, A., & Moore, M. (1983). Newborn infants imitate adult facial gestures. *Child Development, 54,* 702–709.

Meltzoff, A., & Moore, M. (1989). Imitation in newborn infants: Exploring the range of gestures imitated and the underlying mechanisms. *Developmental Psychology, 25,* 954–962.

Menaghan, E., & Parcel, T. (1991). Determining children's home environment. *Journal of Marriage and the Family, 51,* 417–431.

Mendelson, R., & Shultz, T. R. (1976). Covariation and temporal contiguity as principles of causal inference in young children. *Journal of Experimental Child Psychology, 22,* 408–412.

Mennella, J., & Beauchamp, G. (1991). The transfer of alcohol to human milk. *New England Journal of Medicine, 325,* 981–985.

Menyuk, P. (1977). *Language and maturation.* Cambridge: Massachusetts Institute of Technology Press.

Menyuk, P. (1985). Early communication and language behavior. In J. Rosenblith & J. Simms-Knight (Eds.), *In the beginning: Development in the first two years of life.* Monterey, CA: Brooks/Cole.

Menyuk, P. (1993). Relationship of otitis media to speech processing and language development. In J. Katz (Ed.), *Central auditory processing: A transdisciplinary view.* Cambridge: Massachusetts Institute of Technology Press.

Meredith, H. V. (1984). Body size of infants and children around the world in relation to socio-economic status. In H. W. Reese (Ed.), *Advances in child development and behavior* (Vol. 18, pp. 81–145). Orlando, FL: Academic.

Merritt, T. A., et al. (1986). Prophylactic treatment of very premature infants with human surfactant. *New England Journal of Medicine, 315,* 785–790.

Messinger, D., & Freedman, D. (1992). Autonomy and interdependence in Japanese and American mother-toddler dyads. *Early Development and Parenting, 1,* 33–38.

Mickelson, R. A. (1990). The attitude-achievement paradox among black adolescents. *Sociology of Education, 63,* 44–61.

Midgley, C., Feldlaufer, H., & Eccles, J. S. (1989). Student/teacher relations and attitudes toward mathematics before and after the transition to junior high school. *Child Development, 60,* 981–992.

Milewski, A. (1976). Infants' discrimination of internal and external pattern elements. *Journal of Experimental Child Psychology, 22,* 229–246.

Miller, B., & Sollie, P. (1980). Normal stresses during the transition to parenthood. *Family Relations, 29,* 459–465.

Miller, D., & Lin, E. (1988). Children in sheltered homeless families. *Pediatrics, 81,* 668–673.

Miller, N., & Maruyama, G. (1976). Ordinal position and peer popularity. *Journal of Personality and Social Psychology, 33,* 123–131.

Minturn, L., & Hitchcock, J. (1963). The Kajputs of Khalapur, India. In B. Whiting (Ed.), *Six cultures studies of child rearing.* New York: Wiley.

Minuchin, P., & Shapiro, E. (1983). The school as a context for social development. In E. M. Hetherington (Ed.), *Handbook of child psychology: Vol. 4. Socialization, personality, and social development* (pp. 197–274). New York: Wiley.

Mischel, W., & Underwood, B. (1974). Instrumental ideation in delay of gratification. *Child Development, 45,* 1083–1088.

Mittendorf, R., Williams, M. A., Berkey, C. S., & Cotter, P. F. (1990). The length of uncomplicated human gestation. *Obstetrics and Gynecology, 75,* 929–932.

Miyake, K., Chen, S., & Campos, J. J. (1985). Infant temperament, mother's mode of interaction, and attachment in Japan: An interim report. *Monographs of the Society for Research in Child Development, 50,* 276–297.

Mize, J., & Ladd, G. (1990). A cognitive-social learning approach to social skill training with low-status preschool children. *Developmental Psychology, 26,* 388–397.

Mizukami, K., Kobayashi, N., Ishii, T., & Iwata, H. (1990). First selective attachment begins in early infancy. *Infant Behavior and Development, 13,* 257–271.

Moffitt, T. E. (1990). Juvenile delinquency and attention deficit disorder: Boys' developmental trajectories from age 3 to age 15. *Child Development, 61,* 893–910.

Molnar, J., & Klein, T. (1991, April). *The developmental status of homeless preschoolers living in emergency shelters in New York City.* Paper presented at the biennial meeting of the Society for Research in Child Development, Seattle, WA.

Money, J., & Ehrhardt, A. A. (1972). *Man & woman: Boy & girl.* Baltimore, MD: Johns Hopkins University Press.

Montmayor, R. (1983). Parents and adolescents in conflict: All families some of the time and some families most of the time. *Journal of Early Adolescence, 3,* 83–103.

Moore, C., Bryant, D., & Furrow, D. (1989). Mental terms and the development of certainty. *Child Development, 60,* 167–171.

Moore, M. L. (1992). The family as portrayed on prime-time television, 1947–1990: Structure and characteristics. *Sex Roles, 26,* 41–61.

Moorehouse, M. J. (1991). Linking maternal employment patterns to mother-child activities and children's school competence. *Developmental Psychology, 27,* 295–303.

Mora, J. O., et al. (1979). Nutritional supplementation, early stimulation, and child development. In J. Brozek (Ed.), *Behavioral effects of energy and protein deficits.* Bethesda, MD: U.S. Department of Health, Education, and Welfare.

Morales, R. V., Shute, V. J., & Pellegrino, J. W. (1985). Developmental differences in understanding and solving simple word problems. *Cognition and Instruction, 2,* 41–57.

Morelli, G. A., & Tronick, E. Z. (1991). Parenting and child development in the Efe foragers and Lese farmers of Zaire. In M. H. Bornstein (Ed.), *Cultural approaches to parenting* (pp. 91–113). Hillsdale, NJ: Erlbaum.

Morgan, G. A., & Ricciuti, H. N. (1969). Infants' responses to strangers during the first year. In B. M. Foss (Ed.), *Determinants of infant behavior* (Vol. 4). New York: Wiley.

Morisset, C., Bernard, K., Greenberg, M., Booth, C., & Spieker, S. (1990). Environmental influences on early language development. *Development and Psychopathology, 2,* 127–149.

Morrell, P., & Norton, W. (1980). Mylew. *Scientific American, 242,* 99–119.

Morrison, J. R., & Stewart, M. A. (1971). A family study of the hyperactive child syndrome. *Biological Psychiatry, 3,* 189–195.

Muir, D., Abraham, W., Forbes, B., & Harris, L. (1979). The ontogenesis of an auditory localization response from birth to four months of age. *Canadian Journal of Psychology, 33,* 320–334.

Munn, P., & Dunn, J. (1989). Temperament and the developing relationship between siblings. *International Journal of Behavioral Development, 12,* 433–451.

Murphy, L. (1992). Sympathetic behavior in very young children. *Zero to Three, 12,* 1–5.

Murphy, L. B. (1937). *Social behavior and child personality.* New York: Columbia University Press.

Murray, A., & Morrison, B. (1989). Passive smoking by asthmatics. *Pediatrics, 84,* 451–459.

Murray, J. P. (1971). Television in inner-city homes: Viewing behavior of young boys. In E. Rubinstein, G. Comstock, & J. Murray (Eds.), *Tele-*

vision and social behavior (Vol. 4). Washington, DC: U.S. Government Printing Office.

Murray, L. (1992). The impact of postnatal depression on infant development. *Journal of Child Psychology and Psychiatry, 33,* 543–561.

Mussen, P. H. (1969). Early sex-role development. In D. A. Goslin (Ed.), *Handbook of socialization theory and research* (pp. 707–732). Chicago: Rand McNally.

Mussen, P. H., & Eisenberg-Berg, N. (1977). *Caring, sharing and helping.* San Francisco: Freeman.

Myers, B., Jarvis, P., Creasey, G., Kerkering, K., Markowitz, P., & Best, A. (1992). Prematurity and respiratory illness. *Infant Behavior and Development, 15,* 27–41.

Myers, N. A., & Perlmutter, M. (1978). Memory in the years from two to five. In P. A. Ornstein (Ed.), *Memory development in children* (pp. 191–218). Hillsdale, NJ: Erlbaum.

Nadel, L., & Zola-Morgan, S. (1984). Infantile amnesia: A neurobiological perspective. In M. Moscovitch (Ed.), *Advances in the study of communication and affect: Infant memory* (Vol. 9, pp. 145–172). New York: Plenum.

Naerye, R., Diener, M., & Dellinger, W. (1969). Urban poverty: Effects of prenatal nutrition. *Science, 166,* 1206–1209.

Nahmias, A., et al. (1975). Herpes simplex virus infection of the fetus and newborn. In A. Gershan & S. Krugman (Eds.), *Infection of the fetus and newborn.* New York: Ciss.

Nakagawa, M., Teti, D., & Lamb, M. (1992). An ecological study of child-mother attachments among Japanese sojourners in the United States. *Developmental Psychology, 28,* 584–592.

Nash, A. (1988). Ontogeny, phylogeny and relationships. In S. W. Duck (Ed.), *Handbook of personal relationships* (pp. 121–141). New York: Wiley.

National Center for Children in Poverty (1991). *Five million children: 1991 update.* New York: Columbia University Press.

National Center for Clinical Infant Programs (1987). *Infants can't wait: The numbers.* Washington, DC: Author.

National Public Radio (1989). *Health of America's children* (Cassette Recording). Washington, DC: National Public Radio Cassettes.

Neal, J. (1983, March). Children's understanding of their parents' divorce. In L. Kurdek (Ed.), *Children and divorce: New directions for child development* (No. 19). San Francisco: Jossey-Bass.

Neale, M., & Stevenson, J. (1989). Rater bias in EASI temperament scales. *Journal of Personality and Social Psychology, 56,* 446–455.

Nelson, K. (1971). Accommodation of visual tracking patterns in human infants to object movement patterns. *Journal of Experimental Child Psychology, 12,* 182–196.

Nelson, K. (1973). Structure and strategy in learning to talk. *Monographs of the Society for Research in Child Development, 38.*

Nelson, K. (1974). Concept, word and sentence: Interrelations in acquisition and development, *Psychological Bulletin, 81,* 267–285.

Nelson, K. (1977). First steps in language acquisition. *Journal of the American Academy of Child Psychiatry, 16,* 563–583.

Nelson, K. (1981a). Individual differences in language development: Implications for development and language. *Developmental Psychology, 2,* 170–187.

Nelson, K. (1981b). Social cognition in a script framework. In H. H. Flavell & L. Ross (Eds.), *Social cognitive development: Frontiers and possible futures* (pp. 97–118). New York: Cambridge University Press.

Nelson, K., Carskaddon, G., & Bonvillian, J. (1973). Syntax acquisition: Impact of experimental variation in adult verbal interaction with the child. *Child Development, 44,* 497–504.

Nelson, K., & Gruendel, J. (1981). Generalized event representations: Basic building blocks of cognitive development. In M. Lamb & A. L. Brown (Eds.), *Advances in developmental psychology* (Vol. 1, pp. 131–158). Hillsdale, NJ: Erlbaum.

Nelson, K., & Hudson, J. (1988). Scripts and memory: Functional relationships in development. In F. Weinert & M. Perlmutter (Eds.), *Memory development: Universal changes and individual differences* (pp. 147–168). Hillsdale, NJ: Erlbaum.

Nelson-Le Gall, S. (1985). Motive-outcome matching and outcome foreseeability: Effects on attribution of intentionality and moral judgments. *Developmental Psychology, 21,* 332–337.

Nelson-Le Gall, S., & Jones, E. (1990). Cognitive-motivational influences on the task-related help-seeking behavior of black children. *Child Development, 61,* 581–589.

Nelson-Le Gall, S., Kratzer, L., Jones, E., & DeCooke, P. (1990). Children's self-assessment of performance and task-related help seeking. *Journal of Experimental Child Psychology, 49,* 245–263.

Neuspiel, D., Rush, D., Butler, N., Golding, J., Bijur, P., & Kurzon, M. (1989). Parental smoking and post-infancy wheezing in children. *American Journal of Public Health, 79,* 168–171.

Newman, R. S. (1990). Children's help-seeking in the classroom: The role of motivational factors and attitudes. *Journal of Educational Psychology, 82,* 71–80.

Newman, R. S., & Goldin, L. (1990). Children's reluctance to seek help with schoolwork. *Journal of Educational Psychology, 82,* 92–100.

Newport, E. (1990). Maturational constraints on language learning. *Cognitive Science, 14,* 11–28.

Nichols, P. L. (1977, March). *Minimal brain dysfunction: Associations with perinatal complications.* Paper presented at the biennial meeting of the Society for Research in Child Development, New Orleans, LA.

Ninio, A. (1980). Picture-book reading in mother-infant dyads belonging to two subgroups in Israel. *Child Development, 51,* 587–590.

Norbeck, J., & Tilden, V. (1983). Life stress, social support, and emotional disequilibrium in complications of pregnancy. *Journal of Health and Social Behavior, 24,* 30–46.

Nottelman, E., Susman, E., Inhoff-Germain, G., & Chrousos, G. (1987, March). *Concurrent and predictive relations between hormone levels and social-emotional functioning in early adolescence.* Paper presented at the biennial meeting of the Society for Research in Child Development, Baltimore, MD.

Nsamenang, A. B. (1992). Childcare in Cameroon. In M. Lamb, K. J. Sternberg, C. P. Hwang, & A. G. Broberg (Eds.), *Child care in context: Cross-cultural perspectives* (pp. 419–476). Hillsdale, NJ: Erlbaum.

Nugent, J. (1991). Cultural and psychological influences on the father's role in infant development. *Journal of Marriage and the Family, 53,* 475–485.

O'Connor, M., Cohen, S., & Parmelee, A. (1984). Infant auditory discrimination in preterm and full-term infants as a predictor of five-year intelligence. *Developmental Psychology, 20,* 159–165.

O'Connor, M., Sigman, M., & Brill, N. (1987). Disorganization of attachment in relation to maternal alcohol consumption. *Journal of Consulting and Clinical Psychology, 55,* 831–836.

Okagaki, L., & Sternberg, R. (1993). Parental beliefs and children's school performance. *Child Development, 64,* 36–56.

Olds, D., & Henderson, C. (1989). The prevention of child maltreatment. In D. Cicchetti & V. Carlson (Eds.), *Child maltreatment* (pp. 722–763). New York: Cambridge University Press.

O'Leary, K. D., & Becker, W. (1967). Behavior modification of an adjustment class: A token reinforcement program. *Exceptional Children, 33,* 637–642.

Olshan, A., Baird, P., & Teschke, K. (1989). Paternal occupational exposures and the risk of Down syndrome. *American Journal of Human Genetics, 44,* 646–651.

Olson, H., Sampson, P., Barr, H., & Streissguth, A. (1992). Prenatal exposure to alcohol and school problems in late childhood. *Development and Psychopathology, 4,* 341–359.

Olvera-Ezzell, N., Power, T. G., & Cousins, J. H. (1990). Maternal socialization of children's eating habits: Strategies used by obese Mexican-American mothers. *Child Development, 61,* 395–400.

Olweus, D. (1979). Stability and aggressive reaction patterns in males. A review. *Psychological Bulletin, 86,* 852–875.

Olweus, D. (1980). Familial and temperamental determinants of aggressive behavior in adolescent boys: A causal analysis. *Developmental Psychology, 16,* 644–660.

Olweus, D. (1982a). Continuity in aggressive and inhibited, withdrawn behavior patterns. *Psychiatry and Social Science.*

Olweus, D. (1982b). Development of stable aggressive reaction patterns in males. In R. Blanchard & C. Blanchard (Eds.), *Advances in the study of aggression* (Vol. 1). New York: Academic.

Omer, H., & Everly, G. (1988). Psychological factors in preterm labor *American Journal of Psychiatry, 145,* 1507–1513.

Ornstein, P. A., Baker-Ward, L., & Naus, M. J. (1988) The development of mnemonic skill. In F. Weinert & M. Perlmutter (Eds.), *Memory development: Universal changes and individual differences* (pp. 31–50). Hillsdale, NJ: Erlbaum.

Osofsky, J. D. (1987). *Handbook of infant development.* New York: Wiley.

Osterwell, Z., & Nagano-Nakamura, K. (1992). Maternal views on aggression: Japan and Israel. *Aggressive Behavior, 18,* 263–270.

Ostrea, E., & Chavez, C. (1979). Perinatal problems in maternal drug addiction: A study of 830 cases. *Journal of Pediatrics, 94,* 292–295.

Otake, M., & Schull, W. (1984). In vitro exposure to A-bomb radiation and mental retardation: A reassessment. *British Journal of Radiology, 57,* 409–414.

Ottenbacher, K., Muller, L., Brandt, D., Heintzelman, A., Hojem, P., & Sharpe, P. (1987). The effectiveness of tactile stimulation as a form of early intervention. *Journal of Developmental and Behavioral Pediatrics, 8,* 68–76.

Oyellette, E. M., Rosett, H. L., Rosman, N. P., & Weiner, L. (1977). Adverse effects on offspring of maternal alcohol abuse during pregnancy. *New England Journal of Medicine, 297,* 528–530.

Paden, E., Matthies, M., & Novak, M. (1989). Recovery from OME-related phonologic delay following tube placement. *Journal of Speech and Hearing Disorders, 54,* 94–100.

Paikoff, R., Brooks-Gunn, J., & Warren, M. (1991). Effects of girls' hormonal status on depressive and aggressive symptoms over the course of one year. *Journal of Youth and Adolescence, 20,* 191–216.

Paley, V. G. (1984). *Boys and girls: Superheroes in the doll corner.* Chicago: University of Chicago Press.

Paley, V. G. (1986). *Mollie is three: Growing up in school.* Chicago: University of Chicago Press.

Paris, S. G., & Myers, M. (1981). Comprehension monitoring, memory, and study strategies of good and poor readers. *Journal of Reading Behavior, 13,* 5–22.

Paris, S. G., & Winograd, P. (1990). How metacognition can promote children's academic learning. In B. Jones & L. Idol (Eds.), *Dimensions of thinking* (pp. 15–51). Hillsdale, NJ: Erlbaum.

Park, K., & Waters, E. (1989). Security of attachment and preschool friendships. *Child Development, 60,* 1076–1081.

Parke, R. (1977a). Punishment in children: Effects, side effects, and alternative strategies. In H. L. Horn & P. L. Robinson (Eds.), *Psychological processes in early childhood* (pp. 71–97). New York: Academic.

Parke, R. (1977b). Some effects of punishment on children's behavior—Revisited. In P. Cantor (Ed.), *Understanding a child's world.* New York: McGraw-Hill.

Parke, R. (1978). Perspectives in father-infant interaction. In J. Osofsky (Ed.), *Handbook of infancy.* New York: Wiley.

Parke, R., & Beitel, A. (1988). Disappointment: When things go wrong in the transition to parenthood. *Marriage and Family Review, 12,* 221–265.

Parke, R., MacDonald, K., Beitel, A., & Bhavnagri, N. (1988). The role of the family in the development of peer relationships. In R. Peters & R. McMahan (Eds.), *Marriages and families: Behavioral treatments and processes* (pp. 17–44). New York: Brunner/Mazel.

Parke, R., O'Leary, S. E., & West, W. (1972). Mother-father-newborn interaction: Effects of maternal medication, labor, and sex of infant. *Proceedings of the American Psychological Association, 7,* 85–86.

Parke, R., & Slaby, R. (1983). The development of aggression. In E. M. Hetherington (Ed.), *Handbook of child psychology: Vol. 4. Socialization, personality, and social development* (pp. 547–642). New York: Wiley.

Parker, F., Piotrkowski, D., & Peay, L. (1987). Head Start as a social support for mothers: The psychological benefits of involvement. *American Journal of Orthopsychiatry, 57,* 220–233.

Parker, J. G., & Asher, S. R. (1987). Peer relations and later personal adjustment: Are low-accepted children at risk? *Psychological Bulletin, 102,* 357–389.

Parkhurst, J. T., & Asher, S. R. (1992). Peer rejection in middle school: Subgroup differences in behavior, loneliness, and interpersonal concerns. *Developmental Psychology, 28,* 231–241.

Parmalee, A. H., & Sigman, M. D. (1983). Perinatal brain development and behavior. In J. Campos & M. Haith (Eds.), *Handbook of child psychology: Vol. 2. Infancy and child psychobiology* (pp. 96–155). New York: Wiley.

Parten, M. (1932). Social participation among preschool children. *Journal of Abnormal Psychology, 27,* 243–269.

Pascoe, J. M., Loda, F. A., Jeffries, V., & Earp, J. A. (1981). The association between mother's social support and provision of stimulation to their children. *Developmental and Behavioral Pediatrics, 2,* 15–19.

Patterson, C. J. (1992). Children of lesbian and gay parents. *Child Development, 63,* 1025–1042.

Patterson, C. J., Cohn, D. A., & Kao, B. T. (1989). Maternal warmth as a protective factor against risks associated with peer rejection among children. *Development and Psychopathology, 1,* 21–38.

Patterson, C. J., Kupersmidt, J., & Griesler, P. C. (1990). Children's perceptions of self and of relationships with others as a function of sociometric status. *Child Development, 61,* 1335–1349.

Patterson, C. J., Kupersmidt, J., & Vaden, N. A. (1990). Income level, gender, ethnicity, and household composition as predictors of children's school-based competence. *Child Development, 61,* 485–494.

Patterson, G. R. (1982). *Coercive family process.* Eugene, OR: Castalia.

Peacock, J., & Sorubbi, R. (1983). Disseminated herpes simplex virus infection during pregnancy. *Obstetrics and Gynecology, 61,* 135–168.

Pearson, J. L., Hunter, A. G., Ensminger, M. E., & Kellam, S. G. (1990). Black grandmothers in multigenerational households: Diversity in family structure and parenting involvement in the Woodlawn community. *Child Development, 61,* 434–442.

Pease, D., & Gleason, J. B. (1985). Gaining meaning: Semantic development. In J. B. Gleason (Ed.), *The development of language.* Columbus, OH: Merrill.

Pederson, D., Moran, G., Sitko, C., Campbell, K., Ghesquire, K., & Acton, H. (1990). Maternal sensitivity and the security of infant-mother attachment. *Child Development, 61,* 1974–1983.

Peery, J. C. (1979). Popular, amiable, isolated, rejected: A reconceptualization of sociometric status in preschool children. *Child Development, 50,* 1231–1234.

Perlmutter, M., Behrend, S. D., Kuo, F., & Muller, A. (1989). Social influences on children's problem solving. *Developmental Psychology, 25,* 744–754.

Perris, E., Myers, N., & Clifton, R. (1990). Long-term memory for a single infancy experience. *Child Development, 61,* 1796–1807.

Perry, D. G., Williard, J. C., & Perry, L. C. (1990). Peers' perceptions of the consequences that victimized children provide aggressors. *Child Development, 61,* 1310–1325.

Peterson, J., & Zill, N. (1986). Marital disruption, parent-child relationships, and behavior problems in children. *Journal of Marriage and the Family, 48,* 295–307.

Peterson, P. L. (1989). Alternatives to student retention: New images of the learner, the teacher and classroom learning. In L. Shepard & M. Smith (Eds.), *Flunking grades* (pp. 174–201). New York: Falmer.

Pettit, G., Bakshi, A., Dodge, K., & Coie, J. (1990). The emergence of social dominance in young boys' play groups: Developmental differences and behavioral correlates. *Developmental Psychology, 26,* 1017–1025.

Pettit, G., Dodge, K., & Brown, M. (1988). Early family experience, social problem solving patterns, and children's social competence. *Child Development, 59,* 107–120.

Petitti, D., & Coleman, C. (1990). Cocaine and the risk of low birth weight. *American Journal of Public Health, 80,* 25–28.

Petitto, L., & Marentette, P. (1991). Babbling in the manual mode. *Science, 251,* 1493–1494.

Phelps, E., & Damon, W. (1989). Problem solving with equals: Peer collaboration as a context for learning mathematics and spatial concepts. *Journal of Educational Psychology, 81,* 639–646.

Phillips, D. (1991). Day care for young children in the United States. In E. C. Melhuish & P. Moss (Eds.), *Day care for young children* (pp. 161–184). London: Routledge & Kegan Paul.

Phillips, D., & Howes, C. (1987). Indicators of quality child care: Review of research. In D. Phillips (Ed.), *Quality in child care.* Washington, DC: National Association for the Education of Young Children.

Phinney, J., & Alipuria, L. (1987, March). *Ethnic identity in older adolescents from four ethnic groups.* Paper presented at the biennial meeting of the Society for Research in Child Development, Baltimore, MD.

Phinney, J., Lochner, B., & Murphy, R. (1990). Ethnic identity development and psychological adjustment in adolescence. In A. Stiffman & L. Davis (Eds.), *Ethnic issues in adolescent mental health* (pp. 53–72). Newbury Park, CA: Sage.

Piaget, J. (1952). *The origins of intelligence in children.* New York: International Universities Press.

Piaget, J. (1959). *The language and thought of the child* (3rd ed.). London: Routledge & Kegan Paul.

Piaget, J., & Inhelder, B. (1956). *The child's conception of space.* London: Routledge & Kegan Paul.

Picariello, M., Greenberg, D., & Pillemer, D. (1990). Children's sex-related stereotyping of colors. *Child Development, 61,* 1453–1460.

Pierrehumbert, B., Frascarolo, F., Bettschart, W., & Plancherel, B. (1991). A longitudinal study of infants' social-emotional development and the implications of extra-parental care. *Journal of Reproduction and Infant Psychology, 9,* 91–104.

Pillow, B. H. (1989). The development of beliefs about selective attention. *Merrill-Palmer Quarterly, 35,* 421–443.

Pintrich, P. R., & De Groot, E. V. (1990). Motivational and self-regulated learning components of classroom academic performance. *Journal of Educational Psychology, 82,* 33–40.

Pinyerd, B., & Zipf, W. (1989). Colic: Ideopathic, excessive infant crying. *Journal of Pediatric Nursing, 4,* 147–161.

Plimpton, C., & Regimbal, C. (1992). Differences in motor proficiency according to gender and race. *Perceptual and Motor Skills, 74,* 399–402.

Plomin, R. (1987). Developmental behavior genetics and infancy. In J. Osofsky (Ed.), *Handbook of infant development* (2nd ed., pp. 363–417). New York: Wiley.

Plomin, R. (1989). Environment and genes: Determinants of behavior. *American Psychologist, 44,* 105–111.

Plomin, R., & DeFries, J. C. (1983). The Colorado Adoption Project. *Child Development, 54,* 276–289.

Plomin, R., & DeFries, J. C. (1985). *The origins of individual differences in infancy: The Colorado Adoption Project.* New York: Academic.

Plomin, R., DeFries, J. C., & Loehlin, J. C. (1977). Genotype-phenotype interaction and correlation in the analysis of human behavior. *Psychological Bulletin, 84,* 309–322.

Plomin, R., DeFries, J. C., & McClearn, G. (1990). *Behavioral genetics: A primer* (2nd ed.). New York: Freeman.

Politano, P. M., Stapleton, L. A., & Correll, J. A. (1992). Differences between children of depressed and nondepressed mothers: Locus of control, anxiety and self-esteem: A research note. *Journal of Child Psychology and Psychiatry, 32,* 451–455.

Pollitt, E., Garza, C., & Leibel, R. L. (1984). Nutrition and public policy. In H. W. Stevenson & A. E. Siegel (Eds.), *Child Development Research and Social Policy* (Vol. 1, pp. 421–470.). Chicago: University of Chicago Press.

Pollitt, E., & Martorell, R. (1992, February). *Early supplementary feeding and cognition in adolescence.* Paper presented at Conference on School Readiness: Scientific Perspectives, Columbia, MD.

Pomerleau, A., Boduc, D., Malcuit, G., & Cossette, L. (1990). Pink or blue: Environmental gender stereotypes in the first two years of life. *Sex Roles, 22,* 359–365.

Pope, A. W., Bierman, K. L., & Mumma, G. H. (1991). Aggression, hyperactivity, and inattention-immaturity: Behavior dimensions associated with peer rejection in elementary school

boys. *Developmental Psychology, 27* (4), 663–671.

Porter, R., Cernoch, J., & McLaughlin, F. (1983). Maternal recognition of neonates through olfactory cues. *Physiology and Behavior, 30,* 151–154.

Porter, R., Makin, J., Davis, L., & Christensen, K. (1992). Breast-fed infants respond to olfactory cues from their own mother and unfamiliar lactating females. *Infant Behavior and Development, 15,* 85–93.

Power, T. G., & Parke, R. D. (1983). Patterns of mother and father play with their 8-month-old infant: A multiple analyses approach. *Infant Behavior and Development, 6,* 453–459.

Pressley, M. (1982). Elaboration and memory development. *Child Development, 53,* 296–309.

Pulkkinen, L., & Tremblay, R. (1992). Patterns of boys' social adjustment in two cultures and at different ages: A longitudinal perspective. *International Journal of Behavioral Development, 15,* 527–553.

Putallaz, M. (1983). Predicting children's sociometric status from their behavior. *Child Development, 52,* 986–994.

Putallaz, M. (1987). Maternal behavior and children's sociometric status. *Child Development, 59,* 324–340.

Putallaz, M., & Gottman, J. (1981). Social skills and group acceptance. In S. Asher & J. Gottman (Eds.), *The development of children's friendships.* New York: Cambridge University Press.

Putallaz, M., & Sheppard, B. H. (1990). Social status and children's orientations to limited resources. *Child Development, 61,* 2022–2027.

Putallaz, M., & Wasserman, A. (1989). Children's naturalistic entry behavior and sociometric status: A developmental perspective. *Developmental Psychology, 25,* 297–305.

Rabiner, D., & Coie, J. (1989). Effect of expectancy inductions on rejected children's acceptance by unfamiliar peers. *Developmental Psychology, 25,* 450–457.

Rabiner, D., & Lenhart, L. (1990). Automatic versus reflective social problem solving in relation to children's sociometric status. *Developmental Psychology, 26,* 1010–1016.

Radke-Yarrow, M., Zahn-Waxler, C., &

Chapman, M. (1983). Children's prosocial dispositions and behavior. In E. M. Hetherington (Ed.), *Handbook of child psychology: Vol. 4. Socialization, personality, and social development* (pp. 469–545). New York: Wiley.

Ramey, C., & Haskins, R. (1981). The modification of intelligence through early experience. *Intelligence, 5,* 5–19.

Read, M., Habich, J. P. Lechtis, A., & Klein, R. (1973, May). *Maternal malnutrition, birth-weight and child development.* Paper presented at the International Symposium on Nutrition, Growth, and Development, Valencia, Spain.

Reich, P. (1986). *Language development.* Englewood Cliffs, NJ: Prentice-Hall.

Reinisch, J. M. (1981). Prenatal exposure to synthetic progestins increases potential for aggression in humans. *Science, 211,* 1171–1173.

Rende, R. D., Slomkowski, C. L., Stocker, C., Fulker, D. W., & Plomin, R. (1992). Genetic and environmental influences on maternal and sibling interaction in middle childhood: A sibling adoption study. *Developmental Psychology, 28,* 484–490.

Renick, M. J., & Harter, S. (1989). Impact of social comparisons on the developing self-perceptions of learning disabled students. *Journal of Educational Psychology, 81,* 631–638.

Renkin, B., Egeland, B., Marvinney, D., Stroufe, L. A., & Mangelsdorf, S. (1989). Early childhood antecedents of aggression and passive-withdrawal in early elementary school. *Journal of Personality, 57,* 257–281.

Rescorla, L., Parker, R., & Stolley, P. (1992). Ability, achievement and adjustment in homeless children. *American Journal of Orthopsychiatry, 61,* 210–220.

Rescorla, L., Provence, S., & Naylor, A. (1982). The Yale Child Welfare Research Program description and results. In E. Zigler & E. Gordon (Eds.), *Day care: Scientific and social policy issues* (pp. 163–199). Boston: Auburn House.

Reynolds, A. (1989). A structural model of first-grade outcomes of an urban, low socioeconomic status, minority population. *Journal of Educational Psychology, 81,* 594–603.

Reynolds, A. (1992). Mediated effects of preschool interventions. *Early Edu-*

cation and Development, 3, 139–164.

Reznick, J., & Goldfield, B. (1992). Rapid change in lexical development in comprehension and production. *Developmental Psychology, 28,* 406–413.

Rheingold, H. L. (1982). Little children's participation in the work of adults, a nascent prosocial behavior. *Child Development, 53,* 114–125.

Rhoads, G., Jackson, L., Schlesselman, S., de la Cruz, F., Desnick, R., Golbus, M., Ledbetter, D., Lubs, H., Mahoney, M., & Pergament, E. (1989). The safety and efficacy of chorionic villus sampling for early prenatal diagnoses of cytogenetic abnormalities. *New England Journal of Medicine, 320,* 609–617.

Rice, M. (1989). Children's language acquisition. *American Psychologist, 44,* 149–156.

Rice, M., Huston, A., Truglio, R., & Wright, J. C. (1990). Words from Sesame Street: Learning vocabulary while viewing. *Developmental Psychology, 26,* 421–428.

Richards, M. P. M., & Bernal, J. F. (1972). An observational study of mother-infant interaction. In N. B. Jones (Ed.), *Ethological studies of child behaviour* (pp. 175–197). Cambridge, England: Cambridge University Press.

Richardson, J. L., Dwyer, K., McGuigan, K., Handen, W. B., Dent, C., Johnson, C. A., Sussman, S. Y., Brannon, B., & Flay, B. (1989). Substance use among eigth-grade students who take care of themselves after school. *Pediatrics, 84,* 556–566.

Richman, A., Miller, P., & Levine, R. (1992). Cultural and educational variations in maternal responsiveness. *Developmental Psychology, 28,* 614–621.

Roberts, R. J., Jr., & Patterson, C. (1993). Perspective taking and referential communication: The question of correspondence reconsidered. *Child Development, 54,* 1005–1014.

Robertson, E., Elder, G., Skinner, M., & Conger, R. (1991). The costs and benefits of social support in families. *Journal of Marriage and the Family, 53,* 403–416.

Robinson, J. P. (1971). Television's impact on everyday life: Some cross-national evidence. In *Television and social behavior* (Vol. 4, pp. 410–432). Washington, DC: U.S. Government Printing Office.

Rodning, C., Beckwith, L., & Howard, J. (1989). Characteristics of attachment organization and play organization in prenatally drug-exposed toddlers. *Development and Psychopathology, 1,* 277–289.

Rodning, C., Beckwith, L., & Howard, J. (1992). Quality of attachment and home environments in children prenatally exposed to PCP and cocaine. *Development and Psychopathology, 3,* 351–366.

Rodriguez, M. L., Mischel, W., & Shoda, Y. (1989). Cognitive person variables in the delay of gratification of older children at risk. *Journal of Personality and Social Psychology, 57,* 358–367.

Rogoff, B. (1986). The development of strategic use of context in spatial memory. In M. Perlmutter (Ed.), *Perspectives on intellectual development: Vol. 19. Minnesota Symposia on Child Psychology* (pp. 107–123). Hillsdale, NJ: Erlbaum.

Rogoff, B., Mistry, J., Göncü, A., & Mosier, C. (1991). Cultural variation in the role relations of toddlers and their families. In M. Bornstein (Ed.), *Cultural approaches to parenting* (pp. 173–183). Hillsdale, NJ: Erlbaum.

Rogosch, F. A., & Newcomb, A. F. (1989). Children's perceptions of peer reputations and their social reputations among peers. *Child Development, 60,* 597–610.

Rohner, R. P., Kean, K. J., & Cournoyer, D. E. (1991). Effects of corporal punishment, perceived caretaker warmth, and cultural beliefs on psychological adjustment of children in St. Kitts, West Indies. *Journal of Marriage and the Family, 53,* 681–693.

Romero-Gwynn, E., & Carias, L. (1989). Breast-feeding intentions and practice among Hispanic mothers in southern California. *Pediatrics, 84,* 626–631.

Roopnarine, J. (1984). Sex-typed socialization in mixed-age preschool classrooms. *Child Development, 55,* 1078–1084.

Roopnarine, J., et al. (1992). Personal well being, kinship tie and mother-infant and father-infant interactions in single-wage and dual-wage families in New Delhi, India. *Journal of Marriage and the Family, 54,* 293–301.

Rose, S. A. (1989). Measuring infant intelligence: New perspectives. In M. Bornstein & N. A. Krasnegor (Eds.), *Stability and continuity in mental development: Behavioral and biological perspectives* (pp. 171–188). Hillsdale, NJ: Erlbaum.

Rose, S. A., & Blank, M. (1974). The potency of context in children's cognition. *Child Development, 45,* 499–502.

Rose, S. A., Feldman, J., Wallace, I., & Cohen, P. (1991). Language: A partial link between infant attention and later intelligence. *Developmental Psychology, 27,* 798–805.

Rose, S. A., Feldman, J., Wallace, I., & McCarton, C. (1991). Information processing at 1 year. *Developmental Psychology, 27,* 723–737.

Rose, S. A., Gottfried, A., & Bridger, W. (1981a). Cross-modal transfer and information processing by the sense of touch in infancy. *Developmental Psychology, 17,* 90–98.

Rose, S. A., Gottfried, A., & Bridger, W. (1981b). Cross-modal transfer in 6-month-old infants. *Developmental Psychology, 17,* 661–669.

Rose, S. A., & Ruff, H. (1987). Cross-modal abilities in human infants. In J. Osofsky (Ed.), *Handbook of infant development* (pp. 318–362). New York: Wiley.

Rose, S. A., Rose, S. L., & Feldman, J. (1989). Stability of behavior problems in very young children. *Development and Psychopathology, 1,* 5–9.

Rosenberg, M. (1975). The dissonant context and the adolescent self-concept. In S. Dragastin & G. Elder, Jr. (Eds.), *Adolescence in the life cycle.* Washington, DC: Hemisphere.

Rosenberg, M. (1986). Self-concept from middle childhood through adolescence. In J. Suls & A. Greenwald (Eds.), *Psychological perspectives on the self* (Vol. 3). Hillsdale, NJ: Erlbaum.

Rosenblith, J. F., & Sims-Knight, J. E. (1985). *In the beginning: Development in the first two years.* Monterey, CA: Brooks/Cole.

Rosenthal, R., & Jacobson, L. (1968). *Pygmalion in the classroom: Teacher expectation and pupils' intellectual development.* New York: Holt, Rinehart, & Winston.

Ross, G., Lipper, E., & Auld, P. (1990). Social competence and behavior problems in premature children at school age. *Pediatrics, 86,* 391–397.

Rossetti-Ferreira, M. C. (1978). Malnutrition and mother-infant asynchrony: Slow mental development. *International Journal of Behavioral Development, 1,* 207–219.

Rotheram-Borus, M. J., & Phinney, J. S. (1990). Patterns of social expectations among black and Mexican-American children. *Child Development, 61,* 542–556.

Rovee, C., Cohen, R., & Schlapack, W. (1975). Life-span stability in olfactory sensitivity. *Developmental Psychology, 11,* 311–318.

Rovee-Collier, C. (1987). Learning and memory in infancy. In J. Osofsky (Ed.), *Handbook of infant development* (2nd ed., pp. 98–148). New York: Wiley.

Rovee-Collier, C., & Hayne, H. (1987). Reactivation of infant memory. In H. Reese (Ed.), *Advances in child development and behavior* (Vol. 20, pp. 185–238). New York: Academic.

Rubin, D., Krasilnikoff, P., Leventhal, J., Weile, B., & Berget, A. (1986, August 23). Effects of passive smoking on birth weight. *Lancet,* 415–417.

Rubin, J. Z., Provenzano, F. J., & Luria, Z. (1974). The eye of the beholder: Parents' view on sex of newborns. *American Journal of Orthopsychiatry, 44,* 512–519.

Rubin, K. H., Fein, G., & Vandenberg, B. (1983). Play. In E. M. Hetherington (Ed.), *Handbook of child psychology: Vol. 4. Socialization, personality and social development* (pp. 693–774). New York: Wiley.

Rubin, Z. (1980). *Children's friendships.* Cambridge, MA: Harvard University Press.

Ruble, D., Fleming, A., Hackel, L., & Stangor, C. (1988). Changes in the marital relationship during the transition to first-time parenthood: Effects of violated expectations concerning division of household labor. *Journal of Personality and Social Psychology, 55,* 78–87.

Rudy, L., & Goodman, G. (1991). Effects of participation on children's reports: Implications for children's testimony. *Developmental Psychology, 27,* 527–538.

Rush, D., Sloan, N., Leighton, J., Alvir, J., Horvitz, D., Seaver, W., Garbowski, G., Johnson, S., Kulka, R., & Holt, M. (1988). Longitudinal study of pregnant women. *American Journal of Clinical Nutrition, 48,* 439–483.

Russell, C. (1974). Transition to parenthood: Problems and gratifications. *Journal of Marriage and the Family, 36,* 294–301.

Russell, M., Mendelson, T., & Peeke, H. (1983). Mothers' identification of their infants' odors. *Ethology and Sociobiology, 4,* 29–31.

Rutter, M. (1983). School effects on pupil progress: Research findings and policy implications. *Child Development, 54,* 1–29.

Rutter, M. (1989). Intergenerational continuities and discontinuities in serious parenting difficulty. In D. Cicchetti and V. Carlson (Eds.), *Child maltreatment* (pp. 317–348). New York: Cambridge University Press.

Rutter, M. (1990). Commentary: Some focus and process considerations regarding effects of parental depression on children. *Developmental Psychology, 26,* 60–67.

Rutter, M., & Garmezy, N. (1983). Developmental psychopathology. In E. M. Hetherington (Ed.), *Handbook of child psychology: Vol. 4. Socialization, personality, and social development* (pp. 775–912). New York: Wiley.

Rutter, M., Graham, P., Chadwick, F., & Yule, W. (1976). Adolescent turmoil: Fact or fiction? *Journal of Child Psychology and Psychiatry, 17,* 35–56.

Sagi, A., & Hoffman, M. L. (1976). Empathic distress in the newborn. *Developmental Psychology, 12,* 175–176.

Sagi, A., van IJzendoorn, M., & Koren-Karie, N. (1991). Primary appraisal of the strange situation: A cross-cultural analysis of preseparation episodes. *Developmental Psychology, 27,* 587–596.

Salatas, H., & Flavell, J. H. (1976). Behavioral and metamnemonic indicators of strategic behavior under remember instructions in first grade. *Child Development, 47,* 81–89.

Salt, P., Galler, J., & Ramsey, F. (1988). The influence of early malnutrition on subsequent behavioral development: VII. The effects of maternal depressive symptoms. *Journal of Developmental and Behavioral Pediatrics, 9,* 1–5.

Sameroff, A., & Cavanaugh, P. (1979). Learning in infancy: A developmental perspective. In J. Osofsky (Ed.), *Handbook of infant development.* New York: Wiley.

Sameroff, A., & Chandler, M. (1975). Reproductive risk and the continuum of caretaking casualty. In F. D. Horowitz (Ed.), *Review of child development research, 4,* 187–244. Chicago: University of Chicago Press.

Sancilio, M. F. M., Plumert, J. M., & Hartup, W. W. (1989). Friendship and aggressiveness as determinants of conflict outcomes in middle childhood. *Developmental Psychology, 25,* 812–819.

Sandler, D., Everson, R., Wilcox, B., & Browder, J. (1985). Cancer risk in adulthood from early life exposure to parents' smoking. *American Journal of Public Health, 75,* 487–492.

Santrock, J. W., & Sitterlee, K. A. (1987). Parent-child relationships in stepmother families. In K. Pasley & M. Ihinger-Tallman (Eds.), *Remarriage and stepparenting today: Current theory and research* (pp. 273–299). New York: Guilford.

Saudino, K., & Eaton, W. (1991). Infant temperament and genetics. *Child Development, 62,* 1167–1174.

Savin-Williams, R. (1976). An ethological study of dominance formation and maintenance in a group of human adolescents. *Child Development, 47,* 972–979.

Savin-Williams, R. (1988). Theoretical perspectives accounting for adolescent homosexuality. *Journal of Adolescent Health Care, 9,* 95–104.

Scafidi, F., Field, T., Schanberg, S., Bauer, C., Tucci, K., Roberts, J., Morrow, C., & Kuhn, C. (1990). Massage stimulates growth in preterm infants: A replication. *Infant Behavior and Development, 13,* 167–188.

Scafidi, F., Field, T., Schanberg, S., Bauer, C., Vega-Lahr, N., Garcia, R., Poirier, J., Nystrom, G., & Kuhn, C. (1986). Effects of tactile/kinesthetic stimulation on the clinical course and sleep/wake behavior of preterm neonates. *Infant Beahvior and Development, 9,* 91–105.

Scardamalia, M., & Bereiter, C. (1984). Written composition. In M. Wittrock (Ed.), *Handbook of research on teaching* (pp. 778–803). New York: Macmillan.

Scarr, S. (1984). *Mother care, other care.* New York: Basic Books.

Scarr, S., & McCartney, K. (1983). How people make their own environments: A theory of genotype-environment effects. *Child Development, 54,* 424–435.

Scarr, S., & Weinberg, R. (1976). IQ performance of black children adopted by white families. *American Psychologist, 31,* 726–739.

Scarr, S., & Weinberg, R. (1983). The Minnesota adoption studies: Malleability and genetic differences. *Child Development, 34,* 260–267.

Schachter, F. (1982). Sibling deidentification and split-parent identification: A family tetrad. In M. Lamb & B. Sutton-Smith (Eds.), *Sibling relationships: Their nature and significance across the lifespan* (pp. 123–197). Hillsdale, NJ: Erlbaum.

Schaffer, H. R. (1979). Acquiring the concept of dialogue. In M. Bornstein & W. Kessen (Eds.), *Psychological development from infancy.* Hillsdale, NJ: Erlbaum.

Schaffer, H. R., & Emerson, P. E. (1964a). The development of social attachments in infancy. *Monographs of the Society for Research in Child Development, 29*(Whole No. 94).

Schaffer, H. R., & Emerson, P. E. (1964b). Patterns of response to physical comfort in early human development. *Journal of Child Psychology and Psychiatry, 5,* 1–13.

Schardein, J. (1976). *Drugs as teratogens.* Cleveland, OH: CRC Press.

Scheibel, A., Paul, L., Fried, I., Forsythe, A., Tomiyasu, U., Wechsler, A., Kao, A., & Slotnick, J. (1985). Dendritic organization of the anterior speech area. *Experimental Neurology, 87,* 109–117.

Schiff, A., & Knopf, I. (1985). The effects of task demands on attention allocation in children of different ages. *Child Development, 56,* 621–630.

Schmidt, C. R., & Paris, S. G. (1984). The development of verbal communicative skills in children. In H. W. Reese (Ed.), *Advances in child development and behavior* (Vol. 18, pp. 1–47). New York: Academic.

Schneider-Rosen, K., & Cicchetti, D. (1991). Early self-knowledge and emotional development. *Developmental Psychology, 27,* 471–478.

Schofield, J. W., & Sagar, H. A. (1977). Peer interaction patterns in an integrated middle school. *Sociometry, 40,* 130–138.

Schuster, C. S., & Ashburn, S. S. (1986). *The process of human development* (2nd. ed.). Boston: Little, Brown.

Schwartz, P. (1983). Length of day-care attendance and attachment behavior in eighteen-month-old infants. *Child Development, 54,* 1073–1078.

Schweinhart, L. J., & Weikart, D. P. (1980). Young children grow up: The effects of the Perry Preschool Program on youths through age 15. *Monographs of the High/Scope Educational Research Foundation* (No. 7).

Sears, R. R., Maccoby, E., & Levin, H. (1957). *Patterns of child rearing.* New York: Harper & Row.

Sedlack, A. (1989, April). *National incidence of child abuse and neglect.* Paper presented at the biennial meeting of the Society for Research in Child Development, Kansas City, MO.

Seegmiller, B., & King, W. (1975). Relations between behavioral characteristics of infants, their mothers' behaviors, and performance on the Bayley mental and motor scales. *Journal of Psychology, 90,* 99–111.

Segall, M. (1972). Cardiac responsivity to auditory stimulation in premature infants. *Nursing Research, 21,* 15–19.

Seifer, R. (1992). Mother-infant interaction during the first year. *Infant Behavior and Development, 15,* 405–426.

Seitz, V. Rosenbaum, L., & Apfel, N. (1985). Effects of family support intervention: A ten-year follow-up. *Child Development, 56,* 376–391.

Self, P. A., Horowitz, F. D., & Paden, L. Y. (1972). Olfaction in newborn infants. *Developmental Psychology, 7,* 249–363.

Seligman, M. (1975). *Helplessness.* San Francisco: Freeman.

Sells, B., & Roff, M. (1964). Peer acceptance—Rejection and birth order. *Psychology in the Schools, 1,* 156–162.

Selman, R. (1971). Taking another's perspective: Role-taking development in early childhood. *Child Development, 42,* 1721–1734.

Selman, R. (1980). *The growth of interpersonal understanding: Developmental and clinical analyses.* New York: Academic.

Serbin, L., Powlishta, K., & Gulko, J. (1993). The development of sex typing in middle childhood. *Monographs of the Society for Research in Child Development, 58*(Serial No. 232).

Sexton, M., Fox, N., & Hebel, J. (1990). Prenatal exposure to tobacco: II. Effects on cognitive functioning at age three. *International Journal of Epidemiology, 19,* 72–77.

Shannon, J. (1987, October). Crisis in health care. *Health.*

Shannon, S. (1990). English in the barrio: The quality of contact among immigrant children. *Hispanic Journal of Behavioral Sciences, 12,* 235–276.

Shantz, C. (1983). Social cognition. In J. H. Flavell & E. M. Markman (Eds.), *Handbook of child psychology: Vol. 3. Cognitive development* (pp. 495–555). New York: Wiley.

Sharabany, R., Gershoni, R., & Hofman, J. (1981). Girlfriend, boyfriend: Age and sex differences in intimate friendship. *Developmental Psychology, 17,* 800–808.

Shatz, M. (1983). Communication. In J. H. Flavell & E. M. Markman (Eds.), *Handbook of child psychology: Vol. 3. Cognitive development* (pp. 841–889). New York: Wiley.

Shatz, M., & Gelman, R. (1973). The development of communication skills: Modifications in the speech of young children as a function of listener. *Monographs of the Society for Research in Child Development, 38*(2, Serial No. 152).

Shayne, V., & Kaplan, B. (1988). AIDS education for adolescents. *Youth and Society, 20,* 180–208.

Shaywitz, S., & Shaywitz, B. (1984). Evaluation and treatment of children with attention deficit disorders. *Pediatrics in Review, 6,* 99–109.

Shedler, J., & Block, J. (1990). Adolescent drug use and psychological health: A longitudinal inquiry. *American Psychologist, 45,* 612–630.

Shell, R., & Eisenberg, N. (1990). The role of peers' gender in children's naturally occurring interest in toys. *Developmental Journal of Behavioral Development, 13,* 373–388.

Sherif, M., Harvey, O. J., White, B. J., Hood, W. R., & Sherif, C. W. (1961). *Inter-group conflict and cooperation: The Robbers Cave experiment.* Norman: University of Oklahoma Press.

Sherrod, L. (1990). How do babies know their friends and foes? *Human Nature, 1,* 331–353.

Shinn, M. (1978). Father absence and children's cognitive development. *Psychological Bulletin, 85,* 295–324.

Shoda, Y., Mischel, W., & Peake, P. K. (1990). Predicting adolescent cognitive and self-regulatory competencies from preschool delay of gratification: Identifying diagnostic conditions. *Developmental Psychology, 26,* 978–986.

Shonkoff, J. (1984). The biological substrate and physical health in middle childhood. In W. A. Collins (Ed.), *Development during middle childhood* (pp. 24–69). Washington, DC: National Academy Press.

Shotwell, J. M., Wolf, D., & Gardner, H. (1979). Exploring early symbolization: Styles of achievement. In B. Sutton-Smith (Ed.), *Play and learning* (pp. 127–156). New York: Gardner.

Siegel, L. S. (1989). A reconceptualization of prediction from infant test scores. In M. Bornstein & N. A. Krasnegor (Eds.), *Stability and continuity in mental development: Behavioral and biological perspectives* (pp. 89–103). Hillsdale, NJ: Erlbaum.

Siegler, R. S. (1981). Developmental sequences within and between concepts. *Monographs of the Society for Research in Child Development, 46* (Serial No. 189).

Siegler, R. S. (1986). *Children's thinking.* Englewood Cliffs, NJ: Prentice-Hall.

Siegler, R. S. (1988). Individual differences in strategy choices: Good students, not-so-good students, and perfectionists. *Child Development, 59,* 833–851.

Siegler, R. S., & Shrager, J. (1984). Strategy choices in addition and subtraction: How do children know what to do? In C. Sophian (Ed.), *Origins of cognitive skills.* Hillsdale, NJ: Erlbaum.

Sigman, M., Beckwith, L., Cohen, S. E., & Parmelee, A. H. (1989). Stability in the biosocial development of the child born preterm. In M. Bornstein & N. A. Krasnegor (Eds.), *Stability and continuity in mental development: Behavioral and biological perspectives* (pp. 29–42). Hillsdale, NJ: Erlbaum.

Sigman, M., Neumann, C., Jansen, A. A. J., & Bwibo, N. (1989). Cognitive abilities of Kenyan children in relation to nutrition, family characteristics, and education. *Child Development, 60,* 1463–1474.

Simmons, R., & Blyth, D. (1987). *Moving into adolescence.* New York: Aldine de Gruyter.

Simmons, R., Blyth, D., & McKinney, K. (1983). The social and psychological effects of puberty on white females. In J. Brooks-Gunn & A. Petersen (Eds.), *Girls at puberty* (pp. 229–272). New York: Plenum.

Simmons, R., Rosenberg, F., & Rosenberg, M. (1973). Disturbance in the self-image at adolescence. *American Sociological Review, 38,* 553–568.

Simner, M. L. (1971). Newborn's re-sponse to the cry of another infant. *Developmental Psychology, 5,* 136–150.

Simons, R., Whitbeck, L., Conger, R., & Wu, C. (1991). Intergenerational transmission of harsh parenting. *Developmental Psychology, 27,* 159–171.

Simons-Morton, B. G., Parcel, G. S., Baranowski, T., Forthofer, R., & O'Hara, N. M. (1991). Promoting physical activity and a healthful diet among children: Results of a school-based intervention study. *American Journal of Public Health, 81,* 986–991.

Sinclair, D. (1913). *Human growth after birth* London: Oxford University Press.

Singer, J. L., & Singer, D. G. (1976). Imaginative play and pretending in early childhood. In A. Davids (Ed.), *Child personality and psychopathology.* New York: Wiley.

Singer, J. L., Singer, D. G., & Sherrod, L. R. (1980). A factor analytic study of preschooler's play behavior. *American Psychology Bulletin, 2,* 143–156.

Singer, L., Brodzinsky, D., Ramsay, D., Steir, M., & Waters, E. (1985). Mother-infant attachment in adoptive families. *Child Development, 56,* 1543–1551.

Siqueland, E. R. (1968). Reinforcement patterns and extinction in human newborns. *Journal of Experimental Child Psychology, 6,* 431–442.

Skinner, B. F. (1938). *The behavior of organisms: An experimental approach.* New York: Appleton-Century.

Skinner, E. A. (1990). Age differences in the dimensions of perceived control during middle childhood: Implications for developmental conceptualizations and research. *Child Development, 61,* 1882–1890.

Skinner, E. A., Wellborn, J. G., & Connell, J. P. (1990). What it takes to do well in school and whether I've got it: A process model of perceived control and children's engagement and achievement in school. *Journal of Educational Psychology, 82,* 22–32.

Slaby, R., & Frey, K. S. (1975). Development of gender constancy and selective attention to same-sex models. *Child Development, 46,* 849–856.

Slaby, R., & Guerra, N. (1988). Cognitive mediators of aggression in adolescent offenders: 1. Assessment. *Developmental Psychology, 24,* 580–588.

Slater, A. M. (1989). Visual memory and perception in early infancy. In A.

Slater & G. Bremner (Eds.), *Infant development* (pp. 43–69). Hillsdale, NJ: Erlbaum.

Slater, A. M. (1990). Infant development: The origins of competence. *The Psychologist, 3,* 109–113.

Slaughter-Defoe, D. T., Nakagawa, K., Takanishi, R., & Johnson, D. J. (1990). Toward cultural/ecological perspectives on schooling and achievement in African- and Asian-American children. *Child Development, 61,* 363–383.

Slobin, D. (1971). Universals of grammatical development in children. In G. Flores D'Arcais & W. Levelt (Eds.), *Advances in psycholinguistics* (pp. 174–184). New York: American Elsevier.

Smetana, J. (1989). Adolescents' and parents' reasoning about actual family conflict. *Child Development, 60,* 1052–1067.

Smith, C., & Lloyd, B. (1978). Maternal behavior and perceived sex of infant: Revisited. *Child Development, 49,* 1263–1266.

Smith, L. H. (1976). *Improving your child's behavior chemistry.* Englewood Cliffs, NJ: Prentice-Hall.

Smith, R. E., & Smoll, F. L. (1990). Self-esteem and children's reactions to youth sport coaching behaviors: A field study of self-enhancement processes. *Developmental Psychology, 26,* 987–993.

Snow, C. E. (1977a). The development of conversation between mothers and babies. *Journal of Child Language, 4,* 1–22.

Snow, C. E. (1977b). Mother's speech research: From input to interaction. In C. E. Snow & C. A. Ferguson (Eds.), *Talking to children. Language input and acquisition.* London: Cambridge University Press.

Sodian, B. (1988). Children's attributions of knowledge to the listener in a referential communication task. *Child Development, 59,* 378–385.

Sollie, D., & Miller, B. (1980). The transition to parenthood as a critical time for building family strengths. In N. Stinnet & P. Knaub (Eds.), *Family strengths: Positive models of family life.* Lincoln: University of Nebraska Press.

Sophian, D. (1988). Early developments in children's understanding of number: Inferences about numerosity and one-to-one correspondence. *Child Development, 59,* 1397–1414.

Sorensen, R. (1973). *Adolescent sexuality in contemporary society.* New York: World Book.

Southern Regional Project on Infant Mortality (1993). Black infant mortality alarming. *Special Delivery, II,* 1 ff.

Spencer, M. (1981). *Personal-social adjustment of minority children: Final report* (Project No. 5-R01-MH 31106). Atlanta, GA: Emory University.

Spencer, M., & Dornbusch, S. (1990). Challenges in studying minority youth. In S. Feldman & G. Elliott (Eds.), *At the threshold: The developing adolescent* (pp. 123–146). Cambridge, MA: Harvard University Press.

Sperling, M. (1961). Analytic first aid in school phobias. *Psychoanalytic Quarterly, 30,* 504–518.

Spiker, D., Ferguson, J., & Brooks-Gunn, J. (1993). Enhancing maternal interactive behavior and child social competence in low birth weight, premature infants. *Child Development, 64,* 754–768.

Spock, B. M., & Rothenberg, M. B. *Dr. Spock's baby and child care* (rev. ed.). New York: Pocket Books.

Sroufe, L. A. (1977). Wariness of strangers and the study of infant development. *Child Development, 48,* 1184–1199.

Sroufe, L. A. (1983). Infant-caregiver attachment and patterns of adaption and competence. In M. Perlmutter (Ed.), *Minnesota Symposia on Child Psychology* (Vol. 16, pp. 41–83). Hillsdale, NJ: Erlbaum.

Sroufe, L. A., Egeland, B., & Kreutzer, T. (1990). The fate of early experience following developmental change. *Child Development, 61,* 1363–1373.

Sroufe, L. A., Fox, N., & Pancake, V. (1983). Attachment and dependency in developmental perspective. *Child Development, 54,* 1615–1627.

Sroufe, L. A., Waters, E., & Matas, L. (1974). Contextual determinants of infant affective response. In M. Lewis & L. Rosenblum (Eds.), *The origins of behavior.* New York: Wiley.

Standley, K., Soule, A. B., III, Copans, S. A., & Duchowny, M. S. (1974). Local-regional anesthesia during childbirth: Effect on newborn behaviors. *Science, 186,* 534–535.

Stangor, C., & Ruble, D. (1987). Development of gender role knowledge and gender constancy. In L. Liben & M. Signorella (Eds.), *Children's gender schemata: New directions for child development* (No. 38). San Francisco: Jossey-Bass.

Stanjek, K. (1978). Das Überreichen von Gaben: Funktion und Entwicklung in den ersten Lebensjahren. *Zeitschrift für Entwicklungspsychologie und Pedagogische Psychologie, 10,* 103–113.

Steinberg, L. (1986). Latchkey children and susceptibility to peer pressure: An ecological analysis. *Developmental Psychology, 22,* 433–439.

Steinberg, L. (1988). Reciprocal relation between parent-child distance and pubertal maturation. *Developmental Psychology, 24,* 122–128.

Steinberg, L. (1990). Autonomy, conflict, and harmony in the family relationship. In S. Feldman & G. Elliott (Eds.), *At the threshold: The developing adolescent* (pp. 255–276). Cambridge, MA: Harvard University Press.

Steinberg, L., Catalano, R., & Dooley, D. (1981). Economic antecedents of child abuse. *Child Development, 52,* 975–985.

Steinberg, L., & Silverberg, S. (1986). The vicissitudes of autonomy in early adolescence. *Child Development, 57,* 841–851.

Steiner, G. (1963). *The people look at television.* New York: Knopf.

Steiner, J. (1977). Facial expressions of the neonate infant in indicating the hedonics of food-related chemical stimuli. In J. Werffenbach (Ed.), *Taste and development.* Washington, DC: U.S. Department of Health, Education, and Welfare.

Stenberg, C. R., & Campos, J. J. (1990). The development of anger expressions in infancy. In N. L. Stein, B. Leventhal, & T. Trabasso (Eds.), *Psychological and biological approaches to emotion* (pp. 247–282). Hillsdale, NJ: Erlbaum.

Stergachis, A., Scholes, D., Daling, J., Weiss, N., & Chu, J. (1991). Maternal cigarette smoking and the risk of tubal pregnancy. *American Journal of Epidemiology, 133,* 332–337.

Stern, D. (1974). Mother and infant at play: The dyadic interaction involving facial, vocal, and gaze behaviors. In M. Lewis & L. Rosenblum (Eds.), *The effect of the infant on its caregiver.* New York: Wiley.

Stern, M., & Karraker, K. (1989). Sex stereotyping of infants. *Sex roles, 20,* 501–515.

Stevens, J. (1988). Social support, locus of control and parenting in three low-income groups of mothers. *Child Development, 59,* 635–642.

Stevenson, H. (1992). Learning from Asian schools. *Scientific American, 267,* 70–76.

Stevenson, H. W., Chen, C., & Uttal, D. H. (1990). Beliefs and achievement: A study of black, white, and Hispanic children. *Child Development, 61,* 508–523.

Stewart, R. (1983). Sibling attachment relationships: Child-infant interactions in the strange situation. *Developmental Psychology, 19,* 192–199.

Stewart, R. (1990). *The second child.* Newbury Park, CA: Sage.

Stewart, R., Mobley, L., Van-Tuyl, S., & Salvador, M. (1987). The first-born's adjustment to the birth of a sibling. *Child Development, 58,* 341–355.

Stifter, C., & Fox, N. (1990). Infant reactivity. *Developmental Psychology, 26,* 582–588.

Stilwell, R. (1983). *Social relationships in primary school children as seen by children, mothers, and teachers.* Unpublished doctoral thesis, University of Cambridge, England.

Stipek, D. (1981). Adolescents—Too young to earn, too old to learn? Compulsory school attendance and intellectual development. *Journal of Youth and Adolescence, 10,* 113–139.

Stipek, D., Feiler, R., Daniels, D., & Milburn, S. (1993, March). *Effects of different instructional approaches on young children's achievement and motivation.* Paper presented at the biennial meeting of the Society for Research in Child Development, New Orleans, LA.

Stipek, D., & Gralinski, J. H. (1991). Gender differences in children's achievement-related beliefs and emotional responses to success and failure in mathematics. *Journal of Educational Psychology, 83,* 361–371.

Stipek, D., & Kowalski, P. S. (1989). Learned helplessness in task-orienting versus performance-orienting testing conditions. *Journal of Educational Psychology, 81,* 384–391.

Stipek, D., & Mac Iver, D. (1989). Developmental change in children's assessment of intellectual competence. *Child Development, 60,* 521–538.

St. James-Roberts, I., & Halil, T. (1991). Infant crying patterns in the first year. *Journal of Child Psychology and Psychiatry, 32,* 951–968.

Stockbauer, J. (1986). Evaluation of the Missouri WIC program: Prenatal components. *Journal of the American Dietetic Association, 1,* 61–67.

Stone, L. J., Smith, H., & Murphy, L. (Eds.). (1973). *The competent infant.* New York: Basic Books.

Storr, R., Dubowitz, H., & Bush, B. (1990). The epidemiology of child maltreatment. In R. Ammerman & M. Hersen (Eds.), *Children of risk* (pp. 23–53). New York: Plenum.

St. Peters, M., Fitch, M., Huston, A., Wright, J., & Eakins, D. (1991). Television and families: What do young children watch with their parents? *Child Development, 62,* 1409–1423.

Strauss, M., Lessen-Firestone, J., Starr, R., & Ostrea, E. (1975). Behavior of narcotics-addicted newborns. *Child Development, 46,* 887–897.

Streissguth, A. P., Barr, H. M., Sampson, P. D., Darby, B., & Martin, D. C. (1989). IQ at age 4 in relation to maternal alcohol use and smoking during pregnancy. *Developmental Psychology, 25,* 3–11.

Streissguth, A. P., Barr, H. M., Sampson, P. D., Parrish-Johnson, J., Kirchner, G., & Martin, D. C. (1986). Attention, distraction, and reaction time at age 7 years and prenatal alcohol exposure. *Neurobehavioral Toxicology and Teratology, 8,* 717–725.

Streissguth, A. P., Landesman-Dwyer, S., Martin, D. C., & Smith, D. W. (1980). Teratogenic effects of alcohol in humans and laboratory animals. *Science, 209,* 353–361.

Streissguth, A. P., Martin, D. C., Barr, H. M., Sandman, B., Kirchner, G., & Darby, B. (1984). Intrauterine alcohol and nicotine exposure: Attention and reaction time in 4-year-old children. *Developmental Psychology, 20,* 533–541.

Streissguth, A. P., Treder, R. P., Barr, H. M., Shepard, T. H., Bleyer, W. A., Sampson, P. D., & Martin, D. C. (1987). Aspirin and acetaminophen use by pregnant women and subsequent child IQ and attention decrements. *Teratology, 35,* 211–219.

Stuckey, M., McGhee, P., & Bell, N. (1982). Parent-child interaction: The influence of maternal employment.

Developmental Psychology, 18, 635–644.

Stucki, M., Kaufmann-Hayoz, R., & Kaufmann, F. (1987). Infants' recognition of a face revealed through motion. *Journal of Experimental Child Psychology, 44,* 80–91.

Stunkard, A., Harris, J., Pedersen, N., & McClearn, G. (1990). The body mass index of twins who have been reared apart. *New England Journal of Medicine, 322,* 1483–1487.

Suess, G., Grossmann, K., & Sroufe, L. (1992). Effects of infant attachment to mother and father on quality of adaptation in preschool. *International Journal of Behavioral Development, 15,* 43–65.

Suitor, J. (1991). Marital quality and satisfaction with the division of household labor across the family life cycle. *Journal of Marriage and the Family, 53,* 221–230.

Sullivan, H. S. (1953a). *The interpersonal theory of psychiatry.* New York: Norton.

Sullivan, H. S. (1953b). *Conceptions of modern psychiatry.* New York: Norton.

Super, C. (1981). Cross-cultural studies of infancy. In *Handbook of cross-cultural psychology.* New York: Wiley.

Super, C., Herrera, M., & Mora, J. (1990). Long-term effects of food supplementation and psychosocial intervention on the physical growth of Colombian infants at risk of malnutrition. *Child Development, 61,* 29–49.

Susman, E., Nottelmann, E., Loriaux, D., Cutler, G., Jr., & Chrousos, G. (1987). Hormones, emotional dispositions, and aggressive attributes in young adolescents. *Child Development, 58,* 1114–1134.

Susman, E., Inoff-Germain, G. E., Loriaux, D., Cutler, G., & Chrouses, G. (1987). Hormones, emotional dispositions and aggressive attitudes in young adolescents. *Child Development, 58,* 1114–1134.

Svejda, M., Campos, J., & Emde, R. N. (1980). Mother-infant "bonding": Failure to generalize. *Child Development, 51,* 775–779.

Taffel, S. (1989). *Trends in low birth weight: United States, 1975–85: Vital and health statistics* (DHHS Publication No. PHS 89-1926). Hyattsville, MD: U.S. Department of Health and Human Services.

Takahashi, K. (1990). Age of female adult strangers as determinants of affective behaviors of Japanese toddlers. *Merrill-Palmer Quarterly, 36,* 315–328.

Tamis-LeMonda, C. S., & Bornstein, M. (1989). Habituation and maternal encouragement of attention in infancy as predictors of toddler language, play, and representational competence. *Child Development, 60,* 738–751.

Tamis-LeMonda, C. S., & Bornstein, M. (1990). Language, play, and attention at one year. *Infant Behavior and Development, 13,* 85–98.

Tamis-LeMonda, C. S., & Bornstein, M. (1991). Individual variation, correspondence, stability, and change in mother and toddler play. *Infant Behavior and Development, 14,* 143–162.

Tamis-LeMonda, C. S., Bornstein, M., Cyphers, L., Toda, S., & Ogino, M. (1992). Language and play at one year: A comparison of toddlers and mothers in the United States and Japan. *International Journal of Behavioral Development, 15,* 19–42.

Tan, L. E. (1985). Laterality and motor skills in 4-year-olds. *Child Development, 56,* 119–124.

Tanner, D. (1972). *Secondary education.* New York: Macmillan.

Tanner, J. (1970). Physical growth. In P. H. Mussen (Ed.), *Carmichael's manual of child psychology* (Vol. 1). New York: Wiley.

Tanner, J. (1978). *Foetus into man: Physical growth from conception to maturity.* London: Open Books.

Taylor, A. R., & Trickett, P. K. (1989). Teacher preference and children's sociometric status in the classroom. *Merrill-Palmer Quarterly, 35,* 343–361.

Taylor, E., & Emery, J. (1988). Trends in unexpected infant deaths in Sheffield. *The Lancet, 13,* 1121–1122.

Teale, W. H., & Sulzby, E. (1986). *Emergent literacy: Writing and reading.* Norwood, NJ: Ablex.

Teller, D. Y., & Bornstein, M. (1986). Infant color vision and color perception. In P. Salapatek & L. B. Cohen (Eds.), *Handbook of infant perception* (pp. 185–232). New York: Academic.

Teller, D. Y., & Lindsey, D. T. (1989). Motion nulls for white versus isochromatic gratings in infants and adults. *Journal of the Optical Society of America, 6,* 1945–1954.

Teti, D., & Abelard, K. (1989). Security of attachment and infant-sibling relationships. *Child Development, 60,* 1519–1528.

Teti, D., & Gelfand, D. (1991). Behavioral competence among mothers of infants in the first year. *Child Development, 62,* 918–929.

Teti, D., et al. (1991, April). *Transition to siblinghood among preschool-aged children.* Paper presented at the biennial meeting of the Society for Research in Child Development, Seattle, WA.

Thelen, E. (1979). Rhythmical stereotypes in normal human infants. *Animal Behavior, 27,* 699–715.

Thelen, E. (1981). Rhythmical behaviors in infancy: An ethological perspective. *Developmental Psychology, 17,* 237–257.

Thelen, E. (1984). Learning to walk: Ecological demands and phylogenetic constraints. *Advances in Infancy Research, 3,* 213–250.

Thelen, E., Skala, K. D., & Kelso, J. S. (1987). The dynamic nature of early coordination: Evidence from bilateral leg movements in young infants. *Developmental Psychology, 23,* 179–186.

Thoman, E. (1990). Sleeping and waking states in infants. *Neuroscience and Biobehavioral Review, 14,* 93–107.

Thoman, E., Davis, D., & Denenberg, V. (1987). The sleeping and waking states of infants: Correlations across time and person. *Psychology and Behavior, 41,* 531–537.

Thoman, E., & Graham, S. (1986) Self-regulation of stimulation by premature infants. *Pediatrics, 78,* 855–860.

Thoman, E., & Whitney, M. (1990). Behavioral states in infants: Individual differences and individual analyses. In J. Colombo & J. Fagen (Eds.), *Individual differences in infancy* (pp. 113–136). Hillsdale, NJ: Erlbaum.

Thomas, A., & Chess, S. (1977). *Temperament and development.* New York: Brunner/Mazel.

Thomas, A., & Chess, S. (1980). *The dynamics of psychological development.* New York: Brunner/Mazel.

Thomas, A., Chess, S., & Birch, H. (1968). *Temperament and behavior disorders in children.* New York: New York University Press.

Thomas, H. (1973). Unfolding the baby's mind: The infant's selection of visual stimuli. *Psychological Review, 80,* 468–488.

Thompson, L., Fagan, J., & Fulker, D. (1991). Longitudinal prediction of specific cognitive abilities from infant novelty preference. *Child Development, 62,* 530–538.

Thompson, R. A. (1990). Emotion and self-regulation. In R. A. Thompson (Ed.), *Nebraska Symposium on Motivation: Vol. 36. Socioemotional development* (pp. 367–467). Lincoln: University of Nebraska Press.

Thompson, R. A. (1991). Infant day care: Concerns, controversies and choices. In J. Lerner & N. Galambos (Eds.), *Employed mothers and their children* (pp. 9–36). New York: Garland.

Thompson, R. A., & Limber, S. (1991). "Social anxiety" in infancy: Stranger wariness and separation distress. In H. Leitenberg (Ed.), *Handbook of social and evaluation anxiety* (pp. 85–137). New York: Plenum.

Thorne, B. (1986). Girls and boys together . . . but mostly apart: Gender arrangements in elementary schools. In W. Hartup & Z. Rubin (Eds.), *Relationships and development* (p. 468). Hillsdale, NJ: Erlbaum.

Thorpe, K., Dragonas, T., & Golding, J. (1992). The effects of psychosocial factors on the mother's emotional well-being during early parenthood: A cross-cultural study of Britain and Greece. *Journal of Reproductive and Infant Psychology, 10,* 205–217.

Tobin, J. J., Wu, D. Y. H., & Davidson, D. H. (1989, April). How three key countries shape their children. *World Monitor,* pp. 36–45.

Tobin-Richards, M. (1985). *Sex differences and similarities in heterosexual activity in early adolescence.* Paper presented at the biennial meeting of the Society for Research in Child Development, Toronto.

Toda, S., Fogel, A., & Kawai, M. (1990). Maternal speech to three-month-old infants in the United States and Japan. *Journal of Child Language, 17,* 279–294.

Tolson, T. F. J., & Wilson, M. N. (1990). The impact of two- and three-generational black family structure on perceived family climate. *Child Development, 61,* 416–428.

Too many cesareans (1991, February). *Consumer Reports,* 120–126.

Tooke, S. (1974). *Adjustment to parenthood among a select group of disadvantaged parents.* Unpublished master's thesis, Montana State University.

Trevarthan, W. (1987). *Human birth: An evolutionary perspective.* New York: Aldine de Gruyter.

Trickett, P., Aber, J. L., Carlson, V., & Cicchetti, D. (1991). Relationship of socioeconomic status to the etiology and developmental sequelae of physical child abuse. *Developmental Psychology, 27,* 148–158.

Trickett, P., & Kuczynski, L. (1986). Children's misbehaviors and parental discipline strategies in abusive and nonabusive families. *Developmental Psychology, 22,* 115–123.

Tronick, E. (1989). Emotions and emotional communication in infants. *American Psychologist, 44,* 112–119.

Tronick, E. Z., Cohn, J., & Shea, E. (1986). The transfer of affect between mothers and infants. In T. B. Brazelton & M. W. Yogman (Eds.), *Affective development in infancy* (pp. 11–25). Norwood, NJ: Ablex.

Tronick, E., Morelli, G., & Ivey, P. (1992). The Efe forager infant and toddler's pattern of social relationships: Multiple and simultaneous. *Developmental Psychology, 28,* 568–577.

Trussell, J. (1989). Teenage pregnancy in the United States. *Family Planning Perspectives, 21,* 262–269.

Tschann, J., Johnston, J., Kline, M., & Wallerstein, J. (1989). Family process and children's functioning during divorce. *Journal of Marriage and the Family, 51,* 431–444.

Tudge, J., & Rogoff, B. (1989). Peer influences on cognitive development: Piagetian and Vygotskian perspectives. In M. Bornstein and J. S. Bruner (Eds.), *Interaction in human development* (pp. 17–40). Hillsdale, NJ: Erlbaum.

Tulkin, S., & Covitz, F. (1975, April). *Mother-infant interaction and intellectual functioning at age six.* Paper presented at the biennial meeting of the Society for Research in Child Development, Denver, CO.

Tulkin, S., & Kagan, J. (1972). Mother-child interaction in the first year of life. *Child Development, 43,* 31–41.

Turner, G., & Collins, E. (1975). Fetal effects of regular salicylate ingestion in pregnancy. *Lancet, 2,* 338–339.

U.S. Bureau of the Census (1987). Who's minding the kids? Childcare arrangements: Winter 1984–85. *Current population reports* (Series P-70, No. 9, p. 5).

Washington, DC: U.S. Government Printing Office.

U.S. Conference of Mayors (1987). *Status report on homeless families.* Washington, DC: Author.

U.S. Department of Commerce (1992, February). *Current population reports* (Special Studies, Series P-23, No. 177). Washington, DC: Author.

Umbel, V., Pearson, P., Fernandez, M., & Oller, D. (1992). Measuring bilingual children's receptive vocabularies. *Child Development, 63,* 1012–1020.

Urban, J., Carlson, E., Egeland, B., & Sroufe, L. A. (1992). Patterns of individual adaptation across childhood. *Development and Psychopathology, 3,* 445–460.

Uttal, D., & Wellman, H. (1989). Young children's representation of spatial information acquired from maps. *Developmental Psychology, 25,* 128–138.

Užgiris, I. C. (1989). Transformations and continuities: Intellectual functioning in infancy and beyond. In M. Bornstein & N. A. Krasnegor (Eds.), *Stability and continuity in mental development* (pp. 123–143). Hillsdale, NJ: Erlbaum.

Valenzuela, M. (1990). Attachment in chronically underweight young children. *Child Development, 61,* 1984–1996.

van Baar, A. (1990). Development of infants of drug dependent mothers. *Journal of Child Psychology and Psychiatry, 31,* 911–920.

van de Bor, M., Walther, F., & Ebrahimi, M. (1990). Decreased cardiac output in infants of mothers who abused cocaine. *Pediatrics, 85,* 733–736.

van de Bor, M., Walther, F., & Sims, M. (1990). Increased cerebral blood flow velocity in infants of mothers who abuse cocaine. *Pediatrics, 85,* 30–32.

Vandell, D., & Corasaniti, M. (1990). Child care and the family. *New Directions for Child Development: Child Care and Maternal Employment, 49,* 23–38.

Vandell, D., Henderson, V. K., & Wilson, K. (1988). A longitudinal study of children with day-care experiences of varying quality. *Child Development, 59,* 1286–1292.

Vandell, D., & Powers, C. (1983). Day care quality and children's free play activities. *American Journal of Orthopsychiatry, 53,* 493–500.

Vandell, D., & Ramanan, J. (1991). Children of the National Longitudinal Survey of Youth: Choices in after-school care and child development. *Developmental Psychology, 27,* 637–643.

Vandell, D., & Ramanan, J. (1992). Effects of early and current maternal employment on children from high risk families. *Child Development, 63,* 938–949.

van den Boom, D. (1990), Preventive intervention and the quality of mother-infant interaction and infant exploration in irritable infants. In W. Koops et al. (Eds.), *Developmental psychology behind the dikes* (pp. 249–270). Amsterdam: Eburon.

van den Boom, D. (1992, May). *Social competence with peers in irritable children: A longitudinal perspective.* Paper presented at the Eighth International Conference on Infant Studies, Miami, FL.

van den Boom, D., & Hoeksma, J. (1993). *The interaction of mothers and their irritable and nonirritable infants.* University of Leiden, The Netherlands. Manuscript submitted for publication.

Van de Perre, P., Simonon, A., Msellati, P., Hitimana, D., Vaira, D., Bazubagira, A., Van Goethem, C., Stevens, A., Karita, E., Sondag-Thull, D., Dabis, F., & Lepage, P. (1991). Postnatal transmission of human immunodeficiency virus type I from mother to infant. *New England Journal of Medicine, 325,* 593–598.

van IJzendoorn, M. (1992). Intergenerational transmission of parenting. *Developmental Review, 12,* 76–99.

van IJzendoorn, M., Goldberg, S., Kroonenberg, P., & Frenkel, O. (1992). The relative effects of maternal and child problems on the quality of attachment. *Child Development, 63,* 840–858.

van IJzendoorn, M., & Kroonenberg, P. M. (1988). Cross-cultural patterns of attachments: A meta-analysis of the strange situation. *Child Development, 59,* 147–156.

Vaughan, V. C., McKay, R. J., & Behrman, R. (1979). *Nelson textbook of pediatrics* (11th ed.). Philadelphia, PA: Saunders.

Vaughn, B., Gove, F. L., & Egeland, B. (1980). The relationship between out-of-home care and the quality of infant-mother attachment in an economically disadvantaged population. *Child Development, 51,* 971–975.

Vaughn, B., & Langlois, J. H. (1983). Physical attractiveness as a correlate of peer status and social competence in preschool children. *Developmental Psychology, 19,* 561–567.

Vibbert, M., & Bornstein, M. (1989). Specific associations between domains of mother-child interaction and toddler referential language and pretense play. *Infant Behavior and Development, 12,* 163–184.

Victora, C., Smith, P., Vaughn, J., Nobre, L., Lombardi, L., Teixeira, A., Fuchs, S., Moreira, L., Gigante, L., & Barros, F. (1989). Infant feeding and deaths due to diarrhea. *American Journal of Epidemiology, 129,* 1032–1041.

Vogel, E. (1963). *Japan's new middle class.* Berkeley: University of California Press.

Volling, B., & Belsky, J. (1992). The contribution of mother-child and father-child relationships to the quality of the sibling relationship. *Child Development, 63,* 1209–1222.

Vondra, J., Barnett, D., & Cicchetti, D. (1990). Self-concept, motivation and competence among preschoolers from maltreating and comparison families. *Child Abuse and Neglect, 14,* 525–540.

Vuori, L., Christiansen, N., Clement, J., Mora, J., Wagner, M., & Herrera, M. (1979). Nutritional supplementation and the outcome of pregnancy. II. Visual habituation at 15 days. *Journal of Clinical Nutrition, 32,* 463–469.

Vurpillot, E. (1968). The development of scanning strategies and their relation to visual differentiation. *Journal of Experimental Child Psychology, 6,* 632–650.

Vygotsky, L. S. (1962). *Thought and language.* Boston: Massachusetts Institute of Technology Press.

Vygotsky, L. S. (1978). *Mind in society.* Cambridge, MA: Harvard University Press.

Wachs, T. (1992). *The nature of nurture.* Beverly Hills, CA: Sage.

Wachs, T., Bishry, Z., Sobhy, A., McCabe, G., Galal, O., & Shaheen, F. (1993). Relation of rearing environment to adaptive behavior of Egyptian toddlers. *Child Development, 64,* 586–604.

Wachs, T., Sigman, M., Bishry, Z., Moussa, W., Jerome, M., Neumann, C., Bwibo, N., & McDonald, M. (1992). Caregiver child interaction patterns in two cultures in relation to nutritional intake. *International Journal of Behavioral Development, 15,* 1–18.

Waddington, C. H. (1966). *Principles of development and differentiation.* New York: Macmillan.

Waite, L., & Lillard, L. (1991). Children and marital disruption. *American Journal of Sociology, 96,* 930–953.

Wakschlag, L., Chase-Lansdale, P., & Brooks-Gunn, J. (1993, March). *Intergenerational continuities: The influence of the mother-grandmother relationship on parenting of young African-American mothers.* Paper presented at the biennial meeting of the Society for Research in Child Development, New Orleans, LA.

Wald, E., Guerra, N., & Byers, C. (1991). Upper respiratory tract infections in young children. *Pediatrics, 87,* 129–133.

Walden, T. A., & Baxter, A. (1989). The effect of context and age on social referencing. *Child Development, 60,* 1511–1518.

Walker, E., Downey, G., & Bergman, A. (1989). The effects of parental psychopathology and maltreatment on child behavior: A text of the diathesis-stress model. *Child Development, 60,* 15–24.

Walker-Andrews, A. S., & Gibson, E. J. (1987). What develops in bimodal perception? In L. P. Lipsitt & C. K. Rovee-Collier (Eds.), *Advances in infancy research* (Vol. 4). Norwood, NJ: Ablex.

Walker-Andrews, A. S., & Lennon, E. M. (1985). Auditory-visual perception of changing distance by human infants. *Child Development, 56,* 544–548.

Wallace, P., & Gotlib, I. (1990). Marital adjustment during the transition to parenthood. *Journal of Marriage and the Family, 52,* 21–29.

Wallach, L., & Sprott, R. L. (1964). Inducing number conservation in children. *Child Development, 35,* 1057–1071.

Wallerstein, J., & Kelley, J. (1980). *Surviving the breakup: How children and parents cope with divorce.* New York: Basic Books.

Wallis, C. (1985, February 4). Chlamydia: The silent epidemic. *Time,* p. 67.

Wang, T. H., & Creedon, C. F. (1989). Sex role orientations, attributions for achievement, and personal goals of Chinese youth. *Sex Roles, 20,* 473–486.

Wasik, B., Ramey, C., Bryant, D., & Sparling, J. (1990). A longitudinal study of two early intervention strategies: Project CARE. *Child Development, 61,* 1682–1696.

Wasserman, R., DiBlasio, C., Bond, L., Young, P., & Colletti, R. (1990). Infant temperament and school-age behavior. *Pediatrics, 85,* 801–807.

Waters, E., Wippman, J., & Sroufe, L. A. (1979). Attachment, positive affects, and competence in the peer group: Two studies in construct validation. *Child Development, 50,* 821–829.

Webster, R., Steinhardt, M., & Senter, M. (1972). Changes in infants' vocalizations as a function of differential acoustic stimulation. *Developmental Psychology, 7,* 39–43.

Wegman, M. E. (1991). Annual summary of vital statistics—1990. *Pediatrics, 88,* 1081–1092.

Weikart, D., & Schweinhart, L. (1991). Disadvantaged children and curriculum effects. *Academic Instruction in Early Childhood: Challenge or Pressure?: New Directions for Child Development, 53,* 57–64.

Weinraub, M., & Jaeger, E. (1990). The timing of mothers' return to the workplace. In J. Hyde & M. Essex (Eds.), *Parental leave and child care.* Philadelphia, PA: Temple University Press.

Weinraub, M., & Lewis, M. (1977). The determinants of children's responses to separation. *Monographs of the Society for Research in Child Development, 48,* 1240–1249.

Weisman, S. R. (1988, July 20). No more guarantees of a son's birth. *The New York Times,* pp. A1, A9.

Weiss, G. (1990). Hyperactivity in childhood. *New England Journal of Medicine, 323,* 1413–1415.

Weissberg, J. A., & Paris, S. G. (1986). Young children's remembering in different contexts. *Child Development, 57,* 1123–1129.

Weitzman, M., Gortmaker, S., Walker, D., & Sobol, A. (1990). Maternal smoking and childhood asthma. *Pediatrics, 85,* 505–511.

Weizmann, F., Cohen, L. B., & Pratt, R. J. (1971). Novelty, familiarity, and the development of infant attention. *Developmental Psychology, 4,* 149–154.

Wellman, H. (1988). First steps in the child's theorizing about the mind. In J. W. Astington, P. L. Harris, & D. R. Olson (Eds.), *Developing theories of mind* (pp. 64–92). Cambridge, England: Cambridge University Press.

Wellman, H. M., & Estes, D. (1986). Early understanding of mental entities: A reexamination of childhood realism. *Child Development, 57,* 910–923.

Wellman, H. M., & Johnson, C. (1979). Understanding mental processes: A developmental study of "remember" and "forget." *Child Development, 50,* 79–88.

Wellman, H. M., Ritter, K., & Flavell, J. H. (1975). Deliberate memory behavior in the delayed reactions of very young children. *Developmental Psychology, 11,* 780–787.

Wellman, H. M., & Somerville, S. C. (1980). The development of human search ability. In M. Lamb & A. L. Brown (Eds.), *Advances in developmental psychology* (Vol. 2). Hillsdale, NJ: Erlbaum.

Werker, J. F. (1989). Becoming a native listener. *American Scientist, 77,* 54–59.

Werker, J. F., & McLeod, P. J. (1989). Infant preference for both male and female infant-directed talk: A developmental study of attentional and affective responsiveness. *Canadian Journal of Psychology, 43,* 230–246.

Werner, E., & Smith, R. (1982). *Vulnerable but invincible: A study of resilient children.* New York: McGraw-Hill.

Werner, L., & Gillenwater, J. (1990). Pure-tone sensitivity of 2- to 5-week old infants. *Infant Behavior and Development, 13,* 355–375.

Whalen, C., & Henker, B. (1976). Psychostimulants and children: A review and analysis. *Psychological Bulletin, 83,* 1113–1130.

Whipple, E., & Webster-Stratton, C. (1991). The role of parental stress in physically abusive families. *Child Abuse and Neglect, 15,* 279–291.

Whitebook, M., Howes, C., & Phillips, D. (1990). *Who cares? Child care teachers and the quality of care in America: The National Child Care Staffing Study.* Oakland, CA: Child Care Employer Project.

Whitesell, N. R., & Harter, S. (1989). Children's reports of conflict between simultaneous opposite-valence emotions. *Child Development, 60,* 673–682.

Widom, C. (1989). The cycle of violence. *Science, 244,* 160–166.

Wilkerson, I. (1987, June 26). Infant mortality: Frightful odds in the inner cities. *The New York Times,* pp. A1, A20.

Will, J., Self, P., & Datan, N. (1976). Maternal behavior and perceived sex of infant. *American Journal of Orthopsychiatry, 46,* 135–139.

Williams, D. P., Going, S. B., Lohman, T. G., Harsha, D. W., Srinivasan, S. R., Webber, L. S., & Berenson, G. S. (1992). Body fatness and risk for elevated blood pressure, total cholesterol, and serum lipoprotein ratios in children and adolescents. *American Journal of Public Health, 82,* 358–363.

Williams, T. M. (Ed.). (1986). *The impact of television: A natural experiment in three communities.* New York: Academic.

Williamson, W., Wilson, G., Lifschitz, M., & Thurber, S. (1990). Nonhandicapped very-low-birth-weight infants at one year of age. *Pediatrics, 85,* 405–510.

Wilson, B., & Weiss, A. (1991, April). *Developmental differences in children's reactions to a program-related advertisement.* Paper presented at the biennial meeting of the Society for Research in Child Development, Seattle, WA.

Wilson, M. N. (1986). The black extended family: An analytical consideration. *Developmental Psychology, 22,* 246–258.

Wilson, M. N. (1989). Child development in the context of the black extended family. *American Psychologist, 44,* 380–385.

Wilson, M. N., & Tolson, T. F. J. (1985). *An analysis of adult-child interaction patterns in three-generational black families.* Unpublished manuscript, University of Virginia, Charlottesville.

Wimmer, H., & Perner, J. (1983). Beliefs about beliefs: Representation and constraining function of wrong beliefs in young children's understanding of deception. *Cognition, 13,* 103–128.

Winick, M. (1970). Nutrition and nerve cell growth. *Federation Proceedings, 29,* 1510–1515.

Winick, M., Meyers, K., & Harris, R. (1975). Malnutrition and environmental enrichment by early adoption. *Science, 190,* 1173–1175.

Winick, M., & Rosso, P. (1969). Head circumference and cellular growth of the brain in normal and marasmic children. *Journal of Pediatrics, 74,* 774–778.

Winn, M. (1985). *The plug-in drug.* New York: Penguin.

Winnicott, D. (1971). *Playing and reality.* New York: Basic Books.

Wolf, D., & Grollman, S. H. (1982). Ways of playing: Individual differences in imaginative style. In D. J. Pepler & K. H. Rubin (Eds.), *The play of children: Current theory and research.* Basel, Switzerland: Karger AG.

Wolf, D., Rygh, J., & Altshuler, J. (1984). Agency and experience: Actions and states in play narratives. In I. Bretherton (Ed.), *Symbolic play* (pp. 195–217). New York: Academic.

Wolfe, D. (1989). Child-abusive parents. *Psychological Bulletin, 97,* 462–482.

Wolff, P. (1966). The causes, controls, and organization of behavior in the neonate [Monograph]. *Psychological Issues, 5*(1, Whole No. 17). New York: International University Press.

Wolff, P. (1969). The natural history of crying and other vocalizations in early infancy. In B. M. Foss (Ed.), *Determinants of infant behavior* (Vol. 4). London: Methuen.

Wolman, P. (1984). Feeding practices in infancy and prevalence of obesity in preschool children. *Journal of the American Dietetic Association, 84,* 436–438.

Wood, D., Valdez, R., Hayashi, T., & Shen, A. (1990). Health of homeless children and housed, poor children. *Pediatrics, 86,* 858–866.

Wood, W., Wong, F., & Chachere, J. (1991). Effects of media violence on viewers' aggression in unconstrained social interaction. *Psychological Bulletin, 109,* 371–383.

Woodhead, M. (1988). When psychology informs public policy: The case of early childhood intervention. *American Psychologist, 43,* 443–455.

Wright, J. C., St. Peters, M., & Huston, A. (1990). Family television use and its relation to children's cognitive skills and social behavior. In J. Bryant (Ed.), *Television and the American family* (pp. 227–252). Hillsdale, NJ: Erlbaum.

Wright, P. J., Henggeler, S., & Craig, L. (1986). Problems in paradise: A lon-

gitudinal examination of the transition to parenthood. *Journal of Applied Developmental Psychology, 7,* 277–291.

Yarrow, L. (1961). Maternal deprivation: Toward an empirical and conceptual re-evaluation. *Psychological Bulletin, 58,* 459–490.

Yarrow, L. (1984). *Parents' book of pregnancy and birth.* New York: Ballantine.

Yarrow, L., Goodwin, M., Manheimer, H., & Milowe, I. (1973). Infancy experiences and cognitive and personality development at 10 years. In L. Stone, H. Smith, & L. Murphy (Eds.), *The competent infant* (pp. 1274–1281). New York: Basic Books.

Yarrow, M. R., Campbell, J. D., & Burton, R. (1968). *Child rearing: An inquiry into research and methods.* San Francisco: Jossey-Bass.

Yeates, K. O., Schultz, L. H., & Selman, R. L. (1991). The development of interpersonal negotiation strategies in thought and action: A social-cognitive link to behavioral adjustment and social status. *Merrill-Palmer Quarterly, 37,* 369–406.

Young, H., & Ferguson, L. (1979). Developmental changes through adolescence in the spontaneous nomination of reference groups as a function of decision context. *Journal of Youth and Adolescence, 8,* 239–252.

Young, K. T. (1991). What parents and experts think about infants. In F. S. Kessel, M. Bornstein, & A. J. Sameroff (Eds.), *Contemporary constructions of the child* (pp. 79–90). Hillsdale, NJ: Erlbaum.

Youngblade, L., & Belsky, J. (1992). Parent-child antecedents of five-year-olds' close relationships. *Developmental Psychology, 28,* 700–713.

Youniss, J. (1980). *Parents and peers in social development: A Sullivan-Piaget perspective.* Chicago: University of Chicago Press.

Youniss, J., & Smollar, J. (1985). *Adolescent relations with mothers, fathers, and friends.* Chicago: University of Chicago Press.

Yussen, S., & Berman, L. (1981). Memory predictions for recall and recognition in first-, third-, and fifth-grade children. *Developmental Psychology, 17,* 224–229.

Zabin, L., et al. (1986). Ages of physical maturation and first intercourse. *Demography, 23,* 595–605.

Zahn-Waxler, C., & Kochanska, G. (1988). The origins of guilt. In R. A. Thompson (Ed.), *Nebraska Symposium on Motivation: Vol. 36. Socioemotional development* (pp. 183–258). Lincoln, NE: University of Nebraska Press.

Zahn-Waxler, C., & Radke-Yarrow, M. (1982). The development of altruism: Alternative research strategies. In N. Eisenberg-Berg (Ed.), *The development of prosocial behavior.* New York: Academic.

Zajonc, R. B., & Markus, G. B. (1975). Birth order and intellectual development. *Psychological Review, 82,* 74–88.

Zarbatney, L., Hartmann, D. P., & Rankin, D. B. (1990). The psychological functions of preadolescent peer activities. *Child Development, 61,* 1067–1080.

Zaslow, M. (1989). Sex differences in children's response to parental divorce. *American Journal of Orthopsychiatry, 59,* 118–141.

Zebrowitz, L. A., Kendall-Tackett, K., & Fafel, J. (1991). The influence of children's facial maturity on parental expectations and punishments. *Journal of Experimental Child Psychology, 52,* 221–238.

Zelazo, P. (1983). The development of walking: New findings and old assumptions. *Journal of Motor Behavior, 15,* 99–137.

Zelnick, M., & Kantner, J. (1973). Sex and contraception among unmarried teenagers. In C. Westoff et al. (Eds.), *Toward the end of growth: Population in America.* Englewood Cliffs, NJ: Prentice-Hall.

Zeskind, P. (1983). Cross-cultural differences in maternal perceptions of cries of low- and high-risk infants. *Child Development, 54,* 1119–1128.

Zeskind, P., & Lester, B. (1978). Acoustic features and auditory perceptions of the cries of newborns with parental and perinatal complications. *Child Development, 49,* 580–589.

Zigler, E. (1987). Formal schooling for four-year olds? No. *American Psychologist, 42,* 254–260.

Zigler, E. (1992, June 6). Head Start falls behind. *The New York Times.*

Zigler, E., & Hall, N. (1989). Physical abuse in America. In D. Cicchetti & V. Carlson (Eds.), *Child maltreatment* (pp. 38–75). New York: Cambridge University Press.

Zill, N. (1988). Behavior, achievement, and health problems among children in stepfamilies: Findings from a national survey of child health. In E. M. Hetherington & J. D. Arasteh (Eds.), *Impact of divorce, single parenting and stepparenting on children* (pp. 325–368). Hillsdale, NJ: Erlbaum.

Zimiles, H., & Lee, V. E. (1991). Adolescent family structure and educational progress. *Developmental Psychology, 27,* 314–320.

Zuckerman, B., & Frank, D. (1992, February). "Crack kids": Not broken. *Pediatrics, 89,* 337–339.

Zuckerman, B., Frank, D., Hingson, R., Amaro, H., Levenson, S., Kayne, H., Parker, S., Vinci, R., Aboagye, K., Fried, L., Cabral, H., Timperi, R., & Bouchner, H. (1989). Effects of maternal marijuana and cocaine use on fetal growth. *New England Journal of Medicine, 320,* 762–768.

Zuravin, S. (1989). The ecology of child abuse and neglect. *Violence and Victims, 4,* 101–120.

Zuravin, S., & Grief, G. (1989). Normative and child maltreating AFDC mothers. *Social Casework, 42,* 76–84.

CREDITS

TEXT

Chapter 1

Pages 4 & 5: From THERE ARE NO CHILDREN HERE: THE STORY OF TWO BOYS GROWING UP IN URBAN AMERICA by Alex Kotlowitz. Copyright © 1991 by Alex Kotlowitz. Used by permission of Doubleday, a division of Bantam Doubleday Dell Publishing Group, Inc.

Table 1.1: From Elizabeth Hall, *Growing and Changing.* Copyright © 1987. Used by permission of Random House, Inc.

Chapter 2

Figure 2.1: Adapted from Allegier & Allegier: *Sexual Interactions* 3/e, p. 101. Copyright © 1991. Used by permission of D.C. Heath.

Figure 2.3: John Karapelou/© 1992 The Walt Disney Co. Reprinted with permission of Discover Magazine.

Table 2.1: From "Down Syndrome in live births by single-year maternal age in a Swedish study," by E. Hook and A. Lindsjo, *American Journal of Human Genetics,* 30, No. 19, 1978. Used by permission of The University of Chicago Press.

Figure 2.6: Adapted with permission of the publisher, McGraw-Hill, Inc. from *The Nature of Life* by J. Postlethwait and J.L. Hopson, 1989.

Figure 2.7: Adapted from *The Developing Human,* 5/e by K.L. Moore, copyright © 1993. Used by permission of W.B. Saunders.

Chapter 3

Page 88: "Cesarean Spiral." Copyright 1991 by Consumers Union of U.S., Inc., Yonkers, NY 10703-1057. Adapted with permission from CONSUMER REPORTS, February 1991. Although this material originally appeared in CONSUMER REPORTS, the selective adaptation and resulting conclusions presented are those of the author(s) and are not sanctioned or endorsed in any way by Consumers Union, the publisher of CONSUMER REPORTS.

Table 3.1: Apgar, V. & Beck, J. Is My Baby All Right? New York: Trident Books, 1973.

Figure 3.2: From "Infant Crying Patterns in the First Year," by L. St. James-Roberts and T. Holit, *International Journal of Child Psychiatry and Psychology,* 32, 1991 pp. 951-968. Copyright © 1991. Used by permission.

Table 3.3: From "The Causes, Controls, and Organization of Behavior in the Neonate," by P. Wolff, *Psychological Issues,* 5, 1966, (1, Whole No. 17). Used by permission of International Universities Press, Inc.

Figure 3.3: Reproduced by permission of *PEDIATRICS,* Vol. 88, Page 1081. Copyright 1991.

Chapter 4

Figure 4.1: From Rugh & Shettles, *From Conception to Birth: The Drama of Life's Beginnings.* Copyright © 1971. Used by permission of HarperCollins Publishers Inc.

Figure 4.2: From M.M. Shirley, *The First Two Years: A Study of Twenty-Five Babies,* Vol. 2. Copyright 1933 by The University of Minnesota. Published by the University of Minnesota Press.

Figure 4.3: Reprinted by permission of the publishers from THE POSTNATAL DEVELOPMENT OF THE HUMAN CEREBRAL CORTEX by J.L. Conel, Cambridge, Mass: Harvard University Press, Copyright © 1959 by the President and Fellows of Harvard College.

Figure 4.4: Source: *Five Million Children—1993 Update.* Nation Center for Children in Poverty, Columbia University School of Public Health, 154 Haven Avenue, New York, NY 10032, (212) 927-8793; FAX (212) 927-9162. Used with permission.

Figure 4.5: Source: *Five Million Children—1993 Update.* National Center for Children in Poverty, Columbia University School of Public Health, 154 Haven Avenue, New York, NY 10032, (212) 927-8793; FAX (212) 927-9162. Used with permission.

Figure 4.6: Source: *Five Million Children—1993 Update.* National Center for Children in Poverty, Columbia University

School of Public Health, 154 Haven Avenue, New York, NY 10032, (212) 927-8793; FAX (212) 927-9162. Used with permission.

Chapter 6

Figure 6.1: Reprinted by permission of the publishers from INFANCY: ITS PLACE IN HUMAN DEVELOPMENT by Jerome Kagan, Richard B. Kearsley, and Philip R. Zelazo, Cambridge, Mass.: Harvard University Press, Copyright © 1978 by the President and Fellows of Harvard College.

Figure 6.2: Adapted from M. van IJzendoorn & P. M. Kroonenberg. "Cross-cultural patterns of attachments: A meta-analysis of the strange situation." *Child Development, 59* 147-156. © 1988 The Society for Research in Child Development, Inc. Used with permission.

Chapter 7

Figure 7.1: From "Patterns of Marital Change and Parent-Child Interaction: by Jay Belsky, Lise Youngblade, Michael Rovine, and Brenda Volling, *Journal of Marriage and the Family,* 53:2, 1991, pp. 487-498. Copyrighted 1991 by the National Council on Family Relations, 3989 Central Ave. NE, Suite 550, Minneapolis, MN 55421. Reprinted by permission.

Figure 7.2: From "Early Human Experience: A Family Perspective," by J. Belsky, *Developmental Psychology, 17,* 1981, pp. 3-23. Copyright 1981 by the American Psychological Association. Adapted by permission of the publisher.

Table 7.1: From S. B. Kanterman, "Child Care, Women, Work and the Family: An International Overview of Child Care Services and Related Policies," in J. S. Lande and N. Gunzenhauser (eds.), *Caring for Children: Challenge to America.* Copyright © 1989. Used by permission of Lawrence Erlbaum Associates, Inc.

Chapter 8

Table 8.1: Compiled from L. Skinner, *Motor Development in the Preschool Years,*

1979. Courtesy of Charles C. Thomas, Publisher, Springfield, Illinois.
Figure 8.1: From *Analyzing Children's Art* by Rhoda Kellogg. Copyright © 1970. Used by permission of Mayfield Publishing Company.
Pages 268, 289, & 290: From *Mollie Is Three: Growing Up in School* by V.G. Paley. Reprinted by permission of the publisher, The University of Chicago Press.

Chapter 9

Figure 9.1: From "Exploring Early Symbolism: Style of Achievement," by J.M. Shotwell, D. Wolf, & H. Gardner in *Play and Learning* by B. Sutton-Smith. Copyright © 1979. Used by permission of Johnson & Johnson.

Chapter 10

Figure 10.2: From J. Belsky, (1984). The determinants of parenting: A process model. *Child Development, 55,* 83–96. © The Society for Research in Child Development, Inc.

Figure 10.4: From A. Burns, "Mother-headed families: An international perspective and the case of Australia," *SRCD Social Policy Report, 6,* Spring 1992, pp. 1–22.

Figure 10.5: From A. Burns, "Mother-headed families: An international perspective and the case of Australia," *SRCD Social Policy Report, 6,* Spring 1992, pp. 1–22.

Figure 10.8: From S.L. Hofferth, "The demand for and supply of child care in the 1990s," in A. Booth (ed.), *Child Care in the 1990s: Trends and Consequences,* pp. 3–25. Copyright © 1992. Used by permission.

Figure 10.9: Adapted from Joseph J. Tobin, David Y.H. Wu, and Dana H. Davidson, *Preschool in Three Cultures.* Copyright © 1989. Used by permission of the publisher, Yale University Press.

Chapter 11

Figure 11.1: From W. VanderZanden, HUMAN DEVELOPMENT, 5/e. Copyright © 1993. Reproduced by permis-

sion of the publisher, McGraw-Hill, Inc.

Figure 11.2: From R.C. Atkinson and R.M. Shiffrin, "Human memory: A proposed system and its control processes," in K.W. Spence and J.T. Spence (eds.), *The Psychology of Learning and Motivation: Advances in Research and Theory, Vol. 2.* Copyright © 1968. Used by permission of Academic Press.

Figure 11.3: From E. Vurpillot, "The development of scanning strategies and their relation to visual differentiation," *Journal of Experimental Psychology, 6,* pp. 632–650. Copyright © 1968. Used by permission of the American Psychological Association.

Table 11.1: Adapted from "Taking Another's Perspective: Role-Taking Development in Early Childhood," by R.L. Selman, *Child Development,* 42, pp. 1721–1732. Copyright © 1971. Used with permission.

Chapter 13

Figure 13.1: Adapted from J. Vander Zanden, *Human Development, 5/e.* Copyright © 1993. Reproduced with permission of the publisher, McGraw-Hill, Inc.
Figure 13.2: From "Learning from Asian Schools" Harold W. Stevenson. Copyright © 1992 by Scientific American, Inc. All rights reserved.

Chapter 14

Figure 14.1: From Marshall, W. (1978), *Puberty* in F. Faulkner and J. Tanner, (eds), *Human Growth,* Vol 2. Copyright © 1978. Used by permission of Plenum Publishing Corporation.
Figure 14.2: Brown, B. (1990). Peer groups. In S. Feldman & G. Elliott (Eds.), *At the threshold: The developing adolescent* (pp. 171-196). Cambridge, MA: Harvard University Press.

PHOTOS

Chapter 1

Pages 2 & 3: Will & Deni McIntyre/Photo Researchers

Page 5: Kevin Horan
Page 7: Bob Daemmrich/Stock, Boston
Page 9: Lewis Hine
Page 10: Robert Brenner/PhotoEdit
Page 11: James H. Simon/The Picture Cube
Page 14: Erika Stone
Page 16: Bob Daemmrich/Stock, Boston
Page 19: Courtesy of Albert Bandura
Page 21: Mary Kate Denny/PhotoEdit
Page 24: Terry E. Eiler/Stock, Boston
Page 26: David Sanders/Arizona Daily Star
Page 31: Hank Morgan/Rainbow

Chapter 2

Pages 38 & 39: Petit Format/Nestle/Science Source/Photo Researchers
Page 42: Sundstrum/Gamma-Liaison
Page 43: (*top*) The Bettmann Archive; (*bottom*) CNRI/Science Photo Library/Photo Researchers
Page 44: W. Rosin Malecki/PhotoEdit
Page 48: Eastcott/Momatiuk/The Image Works
Page 51: Mario Ruiz
Page 52: Omikron/Photo Researchers
Page 57: Petit Format/Nestle/Photo Researchers
Page 60: Petit Format/Nestle/Photo Researchers
Page 61: J. Stevenson/Photo Researchers
Page 65: CARE Photo
Page 69: James W. Hanson, M.D., Professor of Pediatrics, Division of Medical Genetics, University of Iowa
Page 71: American Heart Association
Page 74: Spencer Grant/Stock, Boston

Chapter 3

Pages 78 & 79: Felicia Martinez/PhotoEdit
Page 81: Lawrence Migdale/Stock, Boston
Page 83: Mimi Forsyth/Monkmeyer
Page 86: David Schaefer/The Picture Cube
Page 90: Milton Feinberg/The Picture Cube
Page 91: Margaret Miller/Photo Researchers
Page 95: (*left*) Petit Format/J. da Cunha/Photo Researchers; (*center*) Spencer Grant; (*right*) Elizabeth Crews/The Image Works
Page 96: Safra Nimrod
Page 101: David Schaefer
Page 105: Joseph Nettis/Stock, Boston

NAME INDEX

Frailberg, S., 154
Fraleigh, M., 27
Framenglass, M., 260
Francis, W., 384
Frank, D., 67–68
Frederickson, W. T., 82
Freedman, D., 226, 228
Freedman, D. J., 41–42, 97
Freedman, J. L., 32
French, D. C., 423
French, L. A., 255
Freud, S., 11–13, 22, 34, 187, 276–277
Frey, K. S., 271
Fricke, J., 318
Fricker, H., 67
Fried, I., 127
Fried, L., 67
Fried, P., 67, 70
Friedlander, B. Z., 334
Friedman, S., 105, 205
Fried-Patti, S., 165
Friedrich, L. K., 336
Frieze, I., 384
Frisch, H. L., 279
Frodi, A., 105
Frost, P., 391
Fryer, G., 313
Fulker, D., 176
Fulker, D. W., 167
Furbey, L., 452
Furman, W., 417
Furrow, D., 250
Furstenberg, F., Jr., 314–315, 318, 414–
    415, 473, 475
Furth, H. G., 253

Gaensbauer, T., 181
Gagnon, C., 424
Galambos, N. L., 412
Gallagher, A., 278
Gallagher, J., 212–213
Galler, J., 132–133, 135
Galluzzo, D., 221
Galperin, C., 164
Galton, F., 363
Ganchrow, J., 103
Gandour, 180
Gans, 474
Garai, J. E., 239
Garbarino, J., 313, 434–436
Garcia, E., 261–262
Garcia, R., 109
Garcia, R. E., 343
Garcia Coll, C., 66, 73, 94, 106, 116, 184,
    224
Garden, 428
Gardner, H., 263, 296
Garduque, L., 195
Garfinkel, I., 316
Gariépy, J.-L., 424

Garmezy, N., 397
Garn, S., 235
Garrett, E., 211
Gartner, L., 104
Garvey, C., 258
Garvin, R. A., 260
Garza, C., 346
Gath, A., 213
Gatlin, D. F., 432
Gauthier, R., 289
Gelfand, D., 217
Gelles, R., 313
Gellman, S. A., 255
Gelman, R., 245–247, 259
Gelman, S., 245
Gelsand, D., 225
General Accounting Office, 134
Gerbner, G., 334
Gerner, R., 359
Gershoni, R., 469
Gersten, M., 311
Gesell, A., 121, 166
Gessell, A., 380
Geva, D., 67, 69
Gewirtz, H., 182
Gewirtz, J., 91, 182
Ghesquire, K., 191
Gibbs, J., 371
Gibson, E. J., 144–146
Giles, H., 273–274
Gilligan, C., 270, 277, 369
Ginsberg, A., 475
Ginsburg, H., 171
Gjerde, P. F., 315
Gleason, J. B., 254
Glenn, N. D., 210
Glick, D., 318
Glick, P., 316
Globus, M., 56
Glucksberg, S., 258, 395
Gnepp, J., 250, 395
Goduka, I. N., 8
Goetz, T. E., 387, 389
Going, S. B., 343
Golbus, M., 56
Goldberg, M., 283
Goldberg, S., 106
Goldberg, W., 142–143, 230
Goldfield, B., 159–160, 163
Golding, J., 217, 400
Golding, W., 417
Goldman-Rakic, P., 161
Goldschmidt, L., 67, 69
Goldshmidt, I., 212
Goldsmith, H., 175, 178
Goldstein, H., 70
Goldstein, S., 99, 221
Goldwyn, 308
Goleman, 286, 425
Golman-Rakic, P., 128

Golub, H. L., 67
Göncü, A., 227
Gonzalez, G., 261
Goodall, M. M., 239
Goodman, G., 253
Goodman, J., 384
Goodman, R., 400
Goodwin, M., 212, 285
Goosens, F., 221
Gore, A., 436
Gorin, L., 358
Gossman, 308
Gottesman, I. I., 178
Gottfried, A., 171
Gottfried, A. E., 388
Gottfried, A. W., 146, 224, 239
Gottlieb, B., 216
Gottlieb, I., 210
Gottlieb, L. N., 215
Gottman, J., 320, 403, 422
Gottman, J. M., 421
Gough, P., 358
Gould, M., 250
Gould, S. J., 57
Goyette, C. H., 400
Grady, W., 472
Graham, P., 464
Graham, S., 110
Gralinski, J. H., 388
Granger, R., 68
Granson, H., 324
Green, F. L., 245, 348, 367
Green, R., 472
Greenbaum, C. W., 196
Greenberg, D., 141, 272
Greenberg, M., 92, 163
Greenberg, R., 103
Greene, L. S., 102
Greenough, W., 127–128
Greenspan, N., 205
Greenspan, S., 205
Greenwald, P., 391
Greer, D., 335
Grief, G., 313
Griffith, P., 358
Griffiths, P., 160
Grinnell, K., 272
Grobe, R. P., 428
Grobstein, R., 102
Grollman, S. H., 296
Grolnick, W. S., 409
Gross, R., 447
Grossman, K., 92, 191
Grossman, K. E., 92, 191
Grossmann, K., 194–195
Grote, B., 473
Grove, F. L., 219
Gruendel, J., 251
Grusec, J., 306, 308–309
Gruss, L., 104

SUBJECT INDEX